PrincetonReview.com

GUIDE TO

COLLEGE MAJORS

EVERYTHING YOU NEED TO KNOW
TO CHOOSE THE RIGHT MAJOR

2008 EDITION

The Staff of The Princeton Review

Random House, Inc.

New York

The Princeton Review, Inc.
2315 Broadway
New York, NY 10024
E-mail: bookeditor@review.com

ISBN 978-0-375-76637-4

Publisher: Robert Franek
Editor: Laura Braswell
Designer and Director of Print Production: Scott Harris
Senior Production Editor: M. Tighe Wall

Printed in the United States of America.

9 8 7 6 5 4 3 2 1

2008 Edition

CONTENTS

ACKNOWLEDGMENTS

My first major was industrial engineering. My strengths in high school had been math and science, and I figured I could get a good job right out of college. But as I got further into the curriculum heavy with calculus and physics, I realized that I didn't particularly enjoy those classes as much as I did my English and lit classes. I found myself putting all of my energy into writing a play (that was assigned as a persuasive essay) for a final paper and dreading the 25 calc problems that were due the next morning. After numerous comments from professors, friends, and my dad about my being an "English person," I realized I was in the wrong major.

But aren't writers part of that starving-artist crowd?

If this book had been around, I would have learned that I could afford a dinner or two working in a creative industry that offers opportunity after opportunity to expand in so many artistic directions. After some researching and soul searching, I decided on a journalism major focusing on magazine editing with a creative writing minor. After years of learning and putting into practice various aspects of the publishing business, I honestly love my job and the directions in which my career has taken me.

In this 2008 edition of *Guide to College Majors*, you'll find profiles of more than 400 major programs. In addition to the biggies, such as business administration and management, English, chemistry, and education (which are also broken down into specialties), we also have the unexpected ones, such as forestry, turfgrass science, and museum studies. We also added nine new majors and a section of fast-track majors that can get you in a new career in less than two years.

Of course, something so comprehensive and detailed as this guide is the collaborative effort of many talented people.

Writers Andrew Baker, Emily Curtin, Spencer Foxworth, Maureen Johnson, Andrea Kornstein, Margo Orlando, Eric Owens, Chris Maier, Dinaw Mengestu, and Lorna Lindquist all spent hours collecting enormous amounts of information and shaping that information into an informative and representative profile of each major. Special thanks to Andrea Kornstein for her help with editing and Melissa Lopez for her assistance in finding those funky fun facts.

Our data team, which consists of Ben Zelevansky, David Soto, and Perry Medina, never ceases to amaze me with its ability to compile, comprehend, and explain the massive amounts of data that form the intricate framework of a project like this—and all with a sense of humor.

The ever-talented production team—Scott Harris, Tighe Wall, and Meave Shelton—keeps the books looking good and on time, no matter what kind of curve balls we throw them.

Adrinda Kelly—who does so much—for her unfailing patience and guidance.

The one and only Robert Franek, our publisher, somehow manages to make everything look effortless and exciting and enthusiastically supports our staff's creativity.

Tom Russell and Jeane Krier at Random House make the business of publishing books a pleasure.

Finally, the men upstairs: John Katzman, Michael Perik, Mark Chernis, and Young Shin continue to encourage and value our publishing department's ideas and efforts. Their commitment to providing our readers with the most useful information inspires us.

With this book in your hands, I hope you start your journey through the college experience with knowledge and insight that will help you map out an exciting career path.

Laura Braswell

Editor

August 2007

INTRODUCTION

College. It's what you're working for, right? After all those AP classes, extracurricular activities (the soccer practices, the community service, the music lessons), plus your sparkling personality—you know you've got what it takes to get in whether the college admissions process is in five years or five months. You might even know how you'll decorate your dorm room. We know better than to ask where you want to go because it's tough choosing a college—so tough that it warrants a book of its own (such as *Best 366 Colleges*). But we'll ask a different question instead: What are you going to do when you get there?

Choosing a college major might seem like a life-and-death decision to you right now. After all, what you major in determines to a large degree how you'll spend four years of your life. And doesn't your major determine how you'll spend the rest of your life, too? If we said yes to that, you'd have reason to stress. But in almost all cases, your major doesn't carve your future in stone. You have options; and that's great, since you have a million different plans. Your life will take you down paths you might not even know about yet. The world is your oyster. Really. So why does choosing a major seem so scary?

Well, it's one of Life's Big Decisions. Decisions of that magnitude often make a lot of us sick to our stomachs. Fortunately, this book will arm you with the information you need to make that decision with confidence.

Academic Program Prestige and Availability

We all want the best, and we hope you're considering schools that offer the best of *everything*. It's not always easy to discern what the best really is, since "best" means different things to different people. When choosing a college, you primarily want to consider what each school emphasizes for its students. Is it financial success? Scientific research? Religious values? Different colleges may emphasize different aspects of the undergraduate experience, leading and shaping their students in different ways. The ethical and philosophical missions of a school will affect how it views itself as well as how it is viewed by others. So as you scope out different schools, it's worth reading each one's mission statement. These can generally be found on colleges' websites and sometimes in college brochures.

If a school keeps popping up in various publications and is consistently highly ranked, you can reasonably believe that its reputation has been earned. But don't completely rely on outside sources; investigate and form your own opinions. Studies and rankings are only one part of the very complicated and personal process of selecting a college. You should visit every college you're seriously considering attending and speak with current students and professors.

Something you definitely shouldn't do is choose a college based on the perceived prestige of a particular academic program, especially if you haven't experienced it in person. If you're in high school and are *pretty* sure you want to major in English, well, you might major in English just as you planned, but there's a good chance you'll change your mind by the time you actually have to declare a major. (Some colleges give you until the end of your sophomore year to make up your mind.) It doesn't mean you're immature—it means you're human. College is going to change you in many ways and open your eyes to new and exciting possibilities. Committing to a program (and by committing we mean selecting a school based solely on the prestige of that program) before you even know what else is out there would limit you in many ways.

One more thing about prestige: Of course you should always aim for the best, but we want you to find the school and the program that's the best for *you*. There's a lot of pressure to choose prestige above all else, but prestige doesn't always translate into student success, either within the classroom or after graduation. There are many, many more students who graduate from "unprestigious" schools and become equally successful. Don't let a ranking make your decision for you. Famous professors, cutting-edge research, and a stellar reputation do make for an enticing package in an academic program, and certainly some programs are better than others, but for now we recommend keeping all your options open.

Choosing a school because of program availability, however, is a different story. If you have a strong feeling that you'd like to do something in engineering, it wouldn't be a good idea to choose a small liberal arts college without an engineering program. Likewise, if you have a keen interest in teaching the deaf, you'll want to make sure your prospective schools have education of the deaf as a major program. Of course, you won't be bound to these programs if you change your mind, but if you have a passion for a specific field, try to find a school that has a corresponding program so if you eventually decide to pursue it as a major, you can.

Liberal Arts College or Research University?

A liberal arts college is generally a small school with broad academic offerings within the humanities, social sciences, natural sciences, and fine arts. Many liberal arts colleges require all students to take general education courses in a variety of disciplines; these classes are often referred to as the core curriculum or general education requirements. Faculty members usually focus more on their teaching than on their research, and often have opportunities for undergraduates to assist them in their research. Liberal arts colleges are generally committed to high-quality undergraduate education—that is, education leading to baccalaureate (or bachelor's) degrees.

In contrast, research universities are usually larger and offer a wider range of pre-professional disciplines such as engineering, business, and education, as well as humanities, fine arts, and natural science programs. Research is a top priority for many faculty members, and working with graduate students is often their focus, as research universities usually have several doctoral programs. This means that some faculty view teaching undergraduates as a step down, and many of your classes could be taught by teaching assistants who are themselves graduate students. Research universities sometimes—at least more often than liberal arts colleges—don't require students to complete a core curriculum, since many programs require a greater degree of specialization, and they figure you should cut to the chase.

Of course these characteristics aren't universal. Not all research universities are focused solely on research. Some pride themselves on being teaching institutions, where research is less emphasized than instruction. Even at true research schools, not all professors will be working on research all of the time, and not all professors divide their time between graduate and undergraduate students.

Which sort of school should you choose? It depends on what your goals are. You might have more flexibility in your curriculum at a liberal arts college, but you might thrive in the bustling atmosphere of a larger school. If you want to do research as an undergrad, chances are you won't be able to if grad students are assisting the professors. At a larger research university, your lecture classes could be huge (we're talking hundreds of students), while at a liberal arts college you will likely have more direct and personal contact with faculty. Like we said though, every school is different. There are plenty of research universities where you'll find intimate, collegial communities as well as liberal arts colleges where there is a heavy emphasis on graduate-level work.

You'll likely have some idea of the kind of environment you'll like best by the time you begin to look at schools. You might be best suited for a college experience that is highly intellectual; you might blossom in an environment where what goes on outside the classroom is just as important as the academics. You might gravitate toward programs that prepare you for specific career tracks or toward programs with goals that aren't as specific. And our *Best 366 Colleges* and *Complete Book of Colleges* can be helpful tools in figuring out where you might fit best. And our free website, PrincetonReview.com, is home to vast databases of information on specific colleges.

General Education Requirements

Okay, so you're an engineer. You like math and science. You're a numbers girl or a computer guy. So what's up with required courses like English, philosophy, and history? How does stuff like that relate to *you*? Well, they're part of your general education requirements.

General education requirements appear in most undergraduate curricula. Regardless of your major (or lack thereof) you'll have to take gen-ed classes. Most likely, you'll take most of them within your first two years of college. Why do you take them at all? Well, for a lot of reasons.

First of all, education is a process. You can't learn everything at once. And you can't build something from nothing. In other words, you can't become a truly knowledgeable person without having a strong foundation of a broad array of subject areas. Philosophers need math and science, just as mathematicians need to read and write. Academic disciplines aren't firmly divided with a ruler. More and more—and you'll discover this once you begin your program of study—academic fields overlap, blur into one another, exchange secrets. Gen-ed classes introduce you to the common ideas and vocabulary that exist between disciplines, and how different disciplines affect and inform each other. This might not be spelled out in the courses themselves, but by taking them, chances are you'll get the picture on your own. "Interdisciplinary" is probably a buzzword you'll hear describing many courses of study. So listen up: gen-ed classes aren't a chance just to nap and doodle. This is college! You need to take them seriously to keep up in an increasingly interdisciplinary world.

Gen-ed courses are also important for students pursuing career-oriented degrees such as engineering, education, or business. These sorts of majors have demanding course requirements of their own with little room for outside electives. Gen-ed courses ensure that these students will still be exposed to the basics of history, English, philosophy, math, natural science, social science, and (if the school has a religious affiliation) religion, just like their liberal arts peers.

Gen-ed classes also have a lot to do with the reason you bought this book. If you're not sure what you want to major in, what better way to decide than to sample, sample, sample? You'll get a taste of many different subjects, and along the way you'll get a better idea of what sparks your interest and kindles your passion. A certain area of study might catch your eye, and it may be something you never even thought about before. (Hey, who knew entomology would be so cool?) Keep in mind that most gen-ed classes serve as prerequisites for upper-level courses. If you want to take Abnormal Psych, for example, you'll have to test the Psych 101 waters first.

Eliminating majors one by one isn't the most effective or realistic way to make your decision. Not all gen-ed courses satisfy prerequisites for all majors either, so you truly can't select gen-eds willy-nilly. They are a good way to explore, but try to explore in a focused way with an eye on subject areas that truly interest you. Your academic advisor (more on him or her later) can help in wisely selecting gen-ed courses.

Finally, gen-ed classes are a way for you to make some headway in becoming a more complete student. Sound daunting? Sure it is. But we can't expect to move forward in the arts, sciences, and technology without studying the great achievements made before we were around. Identity, progress, religion, history, invention, innovation—these themes and many others will likely crop up in many of your early college courses, even if you doubt that you'll take much away from a required Biology 101 course. Most colleges feel that all students should be on the same page intellectually before moving into more specific disciplines. And no one can succeed without learning basic skills like critical and ethical thinking, effective oral and written communication, and teamwork—fundamentals of any field of study.

Still not convinced you need these courses that "don't have anything to do with you"? Well, no offense, but we think you might change your tune after a semester or two of college. Once you start school your ideas about what is and isn't relevant to your life will surely go through some adjustments, so try to resist making judgments before you've even begun.

If all this isn't enough to sway you into viewing gen-ed classes as anything more than drudgery, then make sure you investigate colleges' gen-ed philosophies before you apply. While most colleges—especially liberal arts colleges—emphasize core classes, there are some that don't and some that fall in between. Be sure you understand exactly what will be required of you both in and out of your major.

The College Application: To Declare or Not To Declare?

You've got the college application in front of you, completed and ready to go . . . except for the one glaring blank space meant for your intended major. Your stomach sinks. Your hands turn clammy. You have no idea what your major will be. Are you going to have to *lie*?

Relax. In most cases, you won't be required to declare a major on your application. In fact, most colleges won't require you to declare a major until the end of your sophomore year, giving you plenty of time to explore some possibilities. Seem simple? Well, sort of. Problems arise when you are thinking about majoring in a program that limits its enrollment—meaning that if you don't declare that major now, you might not get into that program later on.

What we mean is that many programs—especially career-oriented programs like engineering—restrict the number of students they accept. So if you think you want to be an engineering major but you put "undecided" on your application, someone else may take your spot. This isn't to say it's impossible to major in engineering later on if you're accepted into the college as an undecided student, but in this case you might have been better off declaring engineering. If you enroll as an engineering major and then change your mind, however, you can easily transfer into another, less-selective program.

There's another tricky situation you should be aware of that's sort of the flip side of what we just described. Sometimes students declare a major on their application that they believe will boost their chances of getting into a college. For example, they might declare a major in a university's school of arts and sciences when their real goal is to attend the school of business. Since there are more slots in the school of arts and sciences, they think they have a greater chance of being admitted to the university in general. Once enrolled in the school of arts and sciences, these students run into trouble because they don't really want to be there. Why can't they just switch to the school of business you ask? Well, it's not always that easy. If you were trying to switch majors *within* the same school—say, from English to philosophy—you wouldn't have much of a problem. The trouble comes when you try to switch from one school to another—from the school of arts and sciences to the school of business. Switching *between* schools isn't always easy, or sometimes even possible, because of enrollment restrictions, funding, and other tricky admissions problems. These are good issues to bring up with admissions counselors at the colleges to which you plan on applying.

Another thing to consider is whether the school you're applying to offers scholarships to incoming students with certain majors. Some departments have money set aside for this reason. If you're leaning toward a major, and your financial situation dictates it, this might be reason enough to declare it.

Finally, don't feel anxious about declaring yourself undeclared. Jay Leno once joked, "Undeclared is the one area you can concentrate on in college when you want to throw your parents' money away," but that's simply not true. Being undeclared means you're exploring your options so you find the right major.

One more thing: Because so many students tend to want to say undecided or undeclared at first, some schools offer undeclared engineering or undeclared arts so students can narrow it down a little bit. (Undeclared engineering students, for example, will take more math and science courses so that if they choose engineering, they won't be too far behind their classmates in their coursework.) If you're leaning toward putting undecided on your application, be sure to check out whether your prospective colleges offer an undeclared option within your broader area of interest.

Although you probably won't have to declare a major until your sophomore year, this doesn't mean you can rest easy until then. You need to be actively thinking about your decision from day one. Keep in mind some majors have a strictly regimented order of courses you must take, and if you get behind, you may extend your college stay for a semester (or two or three or four). Career-oriented degrees like engineering, education, and business usually have these rigid structures. You generally have more wiggle room in the liberal arts.

Majors, Minors, and Double Majors

What the heck is a major, anyway? A *major* is simply a cluster of classes related in subject matter that will comprise the bulk of your college coursework. Do you have to declare a major before getting to college? Not always. Do you have to declare one eventually? Yes. (We'll get to this a little later.) What you should know right now is that majors can be career-oriented or not, and they encompass a huge variety of professional fields and academic subjects. As you can see from the sheer heft of this book, there are a lot to choose from, and we haven't even included some of the more obscure ones. If you have a passion—and we know you do—you can usually count on finding a major to match it.

Majors are important because they indicate you've gained some authority in a certain field. Needless to say, college education comprised only of introductory-level courses won't be of much value. The beauty of a major is that each course builds on the ones before it, so besides enhancing your body of knowledge, you learn how to integrate ideas and exercise higher levels of thinking with that wider range of knowledge. In the best-organized majors, you'll gain an understanding of how each of your courses relates to the field. You'll learn why certain courses are required, how the field has grown and changed, and what you have in common with people within your field and outside it.

A minor is similar to a major in that it is an area of academic concentration. A minor consists of fewer courses, the completion of which shows strong knowledge in the field. For instance, you probably can't get a minor in French if you've only taken Introductory French I, II, and III. A French minor would probably require courses in conversation, composition, French art and literature. . . you get the picture. Some minors have more requirements than others, too.

While a major is mandatory, a minor is optional, and you might wonder why anyone would choose to do one. There are a lot of reasons. For one, a minor gives you the chance to study something outside your major. This doesn't mean your minor has to be in something vastly different from your major; in fact, a divergent minor might not even be possible, since many upper-level courses have prerequisite classes that you may not be able to fit into your schedule. (It can often be done; it just takes some careful planning.) More commonly, a minor will be related in some way to your major—for instance, English and philosophy, history and anthropology, psychology and sociology. The pairings are up to you, but a minor should be something you feel might give your education a little something extra. A minor gives you the chance to pursue an interest that might not be directly covered in your major's required classes, or explore something you feel will inform your major in some productive way. A minor makes your education more specific, since a baccalaureate degree usually indicates that you're a generalist in your field. If you know you want to focus on a certain facet in your field of study, getting a minor in a closely related field will help focus your education on what interests you most. For example, if you major in political science, in which you'll do a lot of statistical analysis, statistics would be a perfect minor to enhance your knowledge of your major subject.

You don't have to complete a minor, so does it matter if you do? Will it mean the difference between a so-so grad school and a great one, or an okay job and your dream career? How exactly do prospective employers and graduate school admissions committees view them? Generally, a minor demonstrates to the world that you've obtained knowledge in a field of study outside of your major—that is, you've dedicated yourself to exploring a field that complements your major. You'll be seen as someone with a wider range of knowledge, someone willing to explore another subject in-depth. The right combination of a major and minor can make a difference in augmenting your portfolio of skills, and that will give your college education more applicability to the real world.

A minor is a great chance to pursue an interest in a focused, structured way. So relax, take your time, and if you find you've taken three Spanish courses and only need one more for a minor, why not go for it?

Or, if you really, really love Spanish, why not double major? A *double major* is—you guessed it—two clusters of courses you'll complete during your time in college. There are a lot of reasons to complete a double major, many of them similar to the reasons you might choose to pursue a minor. A bachelor's degree usually means that you are an authority in your major subject. A minor makes your knowledge a bit more applicable to the real world. A double major does that too—but to a greater degree. It indicates that you've pursued a second field of study at a more intensive level than you would pursue a minor. Think back for a moment to what we've said about general education courses. By taking these courses, you'll discover that many fields of study are fundamentally related to one another and that different fields affect and inform each other. A double major is a chance to put those relationships into practice. Say you want to work with mechanical systems. You might consider double majoring in mechanical and electrical engineering. Or, if you're interested in becoming a manager, you might pair an English major (a subject that will enhance your communication skills) with a business major (a subject that demands excellent communication skills). Being well-versed in a cross-discipline is a valuable and marketable educational experience.

Is it marketable? Absolutely. A double major proves especially advantageous when facing prospective employers and grad school admissions committees. Your double major means you have an intimate knowledge of two academic fields; you're familiar with two sets of values, views, and vocabularies; and you're able to communicate—and do business with—a wider variety of peers and colleagues. You'll also be more likely to see connections between other fields of knowledge, and you'll be better able to draw from each as you embark on a job or advanced degree. You'll simply have a greater breadth and depth of knowledge, and others will see you as someone who made the most of your college experience—a "self starter," in hackneyed business parlance. However, a double major doesn't guarantee a higher income. As one professor friend of ours advises, "Think of the second major as a minor on steroids." That's how employers and grad school admissions committees will see it, anyway.

The main problem with double majors is time. You may be able to complete a double major in the standard four years—it's definitely doable, if you plan your courses carefully. Some pairs of majors lend themselves to doubling, as many of the required courses overlap. In other cases, you may need to stay on for an extra semester, or even another year, to finish the required course work. You shouldn't feel pressure to double major. But if you feel that a double major will be valuable to you and your future plans, you should try your best to obtain one.

Believe it or not, there is such a thing as a *triple major*, not offered at every college, but available at some. Does anyone actually do one? Sure. You'll find there are students doing just about everything in college these days. Should you do one? Well, consider your motivations. If your life goals necessitate you having vast knowledge of physics, mathematics, and engineering and you absolutely must study all three *now*, then a triple major might be an option. In this case, your voracious appetite for knowledge should give you the drive and motivation to plow ahead, however long it takes (a triple major is almost guaranteed to extend your college stay). If, on the other hand, you don't really feel that burning desire but think a triple will look good on your resume, think again. Sure, it's impressive. But wouldn't a master's degree be more impressive? If you're willing to extend your stay in college to get another undergraduate degree, why not just go for the master's? Two undergraduate majors and a master's definitely pack more of a punch with a potential employer. Actually, this is something to think about when considering a double major, too.

And remember that multiple majors only hold weight if they demonstrate your passion and dedication. Racking up degrees without real reasons for doing so isn't the most valuable use of your time—or your money.

Pre-professional Degrees

Pre-professional degrees are designed to provide a specific base of knowledge for the professional degree you want to pursue after graduation. In this book and on PrincetonReview.com, we detail six pre-professional degrees you might consider: pre-veterinary medicine, pre-seminary, pre-optometry, pre-medicine, pre-law, and pre-dentistry. In all cases, these majors will prepare you for the rigors and curriculum of the corresponding graduate program. Majoring in a pre-professional field, however, neither guarantees you acceptance into graduate or professional school, nor prohibits you from pursuing other options. With these majors you'll simply focus your attention on a particular field, gaining all (well, almost all) of the valuable knowledge you'll need to succeed. Generally, majors like premedicine, pre-dentistry, pre-optometry, and pre-veterinary medicine will be heavy on math and science courses, while pre-law and pre-seminary will focus on subjects like philosophy, religion, English, and logic. Also, keep in mind that not all colleges will offer these particular pre-professional degrees—some schools may instead offer them as concentrations, or not at all.

One of the most attractive qualities of pre-professional majors is that they are usually designed to prepare you well for the standardized tests you'll be required to take for entrance into professional schools: MCAT (medical school) and LSAT (law school) are the big two. These exams are intense. But don't fret, plenty of students take these tests without having majored in a pre-professional field and score very well. (Just as plenty of students major in a pre-professional field and bomb the test, too.)

If you're absolutely certain you're going to attend medical school, law school, or another pre-professional school, then obtaining a pre-professional degree will give you a head start. If you're sure you're going to medical school though, does that mean you *must* major in premedicine? No. As with all of these professional fields, you can come at it from a variety of angles—there are English majors who go to medical school, math majors who go into law. What could be more appealing to an admissions committee than an applicant with critical reading, writing, and thinking skills? There isn't just one narrow path you must follow to your goal. So if you think you want to go on to professional school but you're not sure, consider majoring in a field in which your options will still be open in case you change your mind. For example, a biology degree might serve you better than a pre-medicine degree if you don't go to medical school, and an English degree will give you excellent preparation for a range of careers besides law. Actually, graduate or professional schools generally don't favor applicants whose majors are pre-professional. What matters to them are your grades, your college achievements, and your standardized test scores.

Keep in mind that in order to gain admittance to medical school with a non-science undergraduate degree, you may need to investigate post-baccalaureate programs that are designed to give you the prerequisite courses you'll need to enroll (because face it, your Chaucer seminar won't be much help with organic chemistry). But don't let this scare you off. The hard work you put into these extra studies will pay off.

Designing Your Own Major

Once you get to college and get involved in your studies, you may come to realize that the sort of major that would best serve you simply isn't offered. In some cases, you can design your own major. Some—not all—colleges will allow you to do this by consulting and collaborating with advisors, department chairs, and individual faculty members. Designing your own major means you can study what you want to study within the focused structure of a major, and join disciplines in a way that might not have yet been formally considered.

Creating your own major is discouraged at some colleges because the process is ardouous for faculty and administration—they're the ones, after all, who must oversee your course selections and make sure those selections are shaping into a valuable field of study. Another problem is that since college majors are structured with painstakingly selected courses, a self-created major may be considered by some as lacking in rigor. Sometimes students design a major with the notion that they can major in something they already know about so that they won't have to waste time with classes that supposedly don't pertain to their goals. But remember, one of the major points of college is to learn brand-new things, things you've never thought about before, so it's worth it to stop and think before you decide what is and isn't relevant to you.

An alternative route is to major in something closely related to this field you already know something about and use it as a minor or double major. This is the sort of planning your academic advisor or department head can help you with.

Some schools offer majors in general studies, which is another possibility if you feel the school you love doesn't offer the specific major you love. General studies requirements differ from school to school. Some programs have a specifically designed set of courses covering a wide range of subjects; others allow you to choose several areas to focus on. General studies might be a good idea if your goals truly require a broad base of knowledge but remember, being a "jack of all trades, master of none" won't always win you many points when you're looking for a job or applying to graduate school.

Switching Majors

You may be worried that once you choose a major, there's no going back. You've made a commitment, signed your life away, sold your soul. Take heart. Many, if not most, college students change majors at least once, and some do it over and over again. If you choose a major and realize later that you're miserable, that this wasn't what you planned, that it's nothing like what you thought it'd be, then you should change majors. Spending your college years studying something you hate or feel is completely useless to what you want to do with your life is a waste of time—yours and the university's. If you don't like your major, chances are you won't excel in it, nor will you make any extra effort that will expand the success and reputation of your department. College isn't about finding the perfect major; it's about finding a major that's *right for you*.

Generally, if you're in one of the liberal arts and switch to another liberal arts major in the first year or two, you'll have no problem graduating in four years—those gen-ed courses are required of almost all liberal arts majors and you probably will have yet taken many major-specific courses. On the other hand, if you change majors after those first two years, or if you change to a degree program like engineering where you'll be behind in your requirements, you might be looking at an additional semester or two, which in the grand scheme of things might not be so bad if you're moving to a major you enjoy.

One last point to consider when contemplating changing majors: In many cases, scholarships you could be receiving may be major-specific. In other words, you may lose some funding if you leave your original major. Again, don't go into the process of switching majors with your eyes closed, but be sure to keep your perspective and have the courage to pursue what you enjoy.

Internships and Cooperative Education Programs

As you page through this book and read about the different majors, you'll often see internships or co-operatives mentioned. Both offer the opportunity to apply theoretical knowledge to the real world, in a real work environment—very important since the gap between the college world and the real world can often seem insuperable. Ever wonder how you can get a job without experience, and how you can get experience without a job? It's a catch-22 that you can overcome by getting at least one internship or co-op. These experiences also offer you the chance to test out a career path and decide if you truly like it. And if you don't, you'll still have time to change your mind.

An internship is a position held within an actual company that will offer you hands-on experience with the type of work you may eventually choose to do. Internships are most often offered during summer break, but they also can be available during the academic year. They can be as short as a few weeks or as long as a few months or more. Some are even part-time positions. They are a fantastic way to experience first-hand what goes on in a business that interests you. The bad part: They're often (but not always) unpaid. As a college student, though, you should value experience over monetary profit. You can research several hundred of the most selective and best paying internships at PrincetonReview.com.

Co-ops—cooperative education programs—are similar to internships, though these usually pay better. Co-ops are generally held by engineering majors and take place during both the summer and the school year. If you choose to co-op during the school year, you'll probably extend your college stay by a semester to a year. Like internships, co-ops offer hands-on experience within your field of study, and in most cases you'll be treated as a real employee—working full days on actual projects. It's worth repeating: Co-oping offers a fantastic opportunity to get experience in your field, and many companies hire their co-ops for full-time positions after graduation. In fact, some companies hire *only* former co-ops.

While co-ops are usually major-specific, internships are often not. In fact, it's sometimes possible to have internships in fields unrelated to your major. A warning, though: As with any job, you should investigate the duties an internship requires. The term internship is sometimes used too liberally, and a month-long stint spent stuffing envelopes or making photocopies isn't going to get you very far. Be sure the internships you consider offer work experience that will be worth talking about in interviews when you're looking for your first real job.

Other opportunities for learning outside the classroom include capstone courses, which are industry-sponsored projects that require students to collaborate and work in teams to solve specific real-world problems. Your college might offer additional opportunities with different names, and you should investigate these.

The bottom line is that prospective employers and grad school admissions committees give high regard to internship and co-op experiences. A Chinese proverb explains what an internship or a co-op on your resume communicates to a potential employer or a graduate/professional school admissions committee: "Tell me and I will forget; show me and I will remember; involve me and I will understand." Co-ops and internships give you the opportunity to practice what you've learned—to see first-hand how all those textbook chapters play out in real life. They demonstrate that you're committed to learning about your profession and that you took the initiative to gain real-world experience. Prospective employers and grad school admissions committees will definitely notice these experiences—and will notice them even more if you can clearly articulate what you took away from them. So pay attention.

Advanced Study: Higher Income or a Truckload of Debt?

Hold on, you may be thinking. *Graduate school? How can I think about graduate school when I can't even decide what I want to do in college?* Don't worry. You don't have to map out your post-college life just yet. But it's never too early to consider your options. Your plans may change, but at least you'll have thought about them. And you can always come back to this guide or PrincetonReview.com when you're considering your next step. Chances are, you've got a question about higher ed, and we've got the answer.

People pursue a master's degree for all sorts of reasons. Some students just want to keep being students and avoid the real world for a few more years. But pursuing a master's in a field you don't really dig or you're unsure you want to stay in just postpones the inevitable. There are plenty of other reasons to take the leap, such as the way a master's degree will increase your income in almost all cases. You'll be regarded as a more knowledgeable and qualified candidate, especially if you've gotten some real-world experience, too. Determining exactly how much your income will increase, however, will be almost impossible. There are countless ways of using (and not using) your degrees once you're out in the real world, and income is affected by geographical area, size, and type of company, and in what capacity you use your skills. Let's be realistic—a Master of Business Administration (MBA) carries a lot more financial weight than a master's degree in, say, history. When considering a master's, however, you can rest assured that it will add value to your total package as a potential employee—your drive, knowledge, skill set, dedication, and responsibility will undoubtedly set you apart from the crowd.

You may be wary of pursuing an advanced degree. You may think that advanced study means you'll be a penniless student forever. This isn't always the case—there's plenty of money out there if you take the time to look around. Many master's programs help out their students financially through scholarships, fellowships, and assistantships. This usually entails the grad student teaching intro courses to undergrads to qualify for a stipend. Another option is to pursue a master's after you've established yourself in a career. Many companies will pay for their employees to earn a master's degree—an ideal situation, since you can work to pay off student loans while not accruing any more. There are many other ways to juggle the money worries; these are just a couple ideas to get you thinking.

You may also be worried that advanced study will *limit* your options. Believe it or not, there is such a thing as being overqualified for a job. A master's probably won't make you so specialized that your job possibilities are narrowed to just one or two. A PhD is what makes your field of knowledge incredibly specific—hence the reason why so many PhDs go into academia. While a master's can be useful in most careers, a PhD is hardly ever required unless you plan to teach at the college level, or launch rockets into space.

A master's is a great opportunity to deepen and to broaden your chosen field of study. However, it's definitely possible to pursue an advanced degree in something outside the realm of your college major. Lots of students do it. Why? Because it's easy (and natural) to change your mind. Also, once you've graduated you may realize you need an entirely new field of knowledge to succeed and to excel at what you're doing. In most cases, like we said, your undergraduate major won't limit your options for advanced study.

To get into graduate and professional schools, you'll need to take the appropriate entrance exam, like the GRE (for graduate school in the arts and sciences), LSAT (for law school), MCAT (for medical school), or GMAT (for business school). Almost all students study hard for these exams, regardless of their background. Certainly, ten chemistry courses in college will help out with the MCAT, but if you have drive and dedication, you can take any exam and score well. (We can help. Our test-prep books and courses have helped countless students get the scores they want and need. You may have used our *Cracking the SAT* already, and there's a *Cracking* book for each of the tests mentioned above, plus others for exams like the Test of English as a Foreign Language.)

Advising

Feeling overwhelmed? Don't worry, you're not on your own here. When you get to college, in most cases you'll be assigned an academic advisor. Sometimes this advisor will be a professor in the department of your major, or, if you're undeclared, a professor assigned to you based on other criteria. (We won't romanticize; most of the time it's completely dependent on the first letter of your last name. Other times it will be a person whose only duty is advising students.) Our advice: Use these people. They are there to help you make sense of all the options open to you. With the best advisors, you can talk about your academic strengths and weaknesses, discuss the ins and outs of different majors, and use them as a source of information for internships, co-ops, and other opportunities. They'll help you build your schedule each semester—especially helpful if you're undecided on a program.

Not all advisors, however, are so involved. Different colleges view advising differently, and some advisors have responsibilities no more complex than signing your registration form or making sure you're not flunking out. So take a stand if you feel your advisor isn't involved enough. Make appointments. Ask questions.

Talk to your dean about getting some guidance. Or find other resources on campus that will help. The campus counseling center and career services center are good places to start. You may find a faculty member—one of your first-semester professors, perhaps—who's willing to talk things over with you. In all cases, be prepared with questions. Be prepared to take an active part in the advisor-advisee relationship.

Once you declare a major, your advisor may play a different role, becoming more of a guide for career and course counseling. This person can act as your liaison to the entire department of your major, someone to go to with questions or concerns. In graduate school (and some undergraduate programs), you'll probably have a thesis advisor. This person will guide you as you complete your thesis and should work with you closely. This is more of a mentoring relationship and a valuable part of any advanced study.

In all cases, remember that advisors are there for *you* and should always have your best interests at heart. If you feel that yours doesn't, find another who does.

Make no mistake: Advisors aren't there to take the decision-making burden off your shoulders. A lousy advisor doesn't mean you can shrug off all hope for success with an "Oh, well." Even if you have the greatest advisor in the world, you still should take an active role in the shaping of your college experience. Your education should be proactive. You should be in charge of deciding what you want and how to get it, and in charge of going ahead and doing what needs to be done. This is how you'll make great things happen during college and more importantly, after college. Ask yourself questions: What do I want for my major, my career, my life? What steps do I need to take to achieve those goals? Your advisor can be a valuable resource for letting you know what's out there, but you should take just as active a role—a more active role, actually—in pursuing opportunities yourself. There's a lot to be learned outside the classroom, and it's just as important to your college experience as what you learn inside.

And the Point of College Is...?

As you deliberate on your major, you might take a minute or two and think about why you're going to college in the first place. You might be heading off to college without giving much thought to what you want to accomplish once you're there. Figuring out why you're in college is a good first step in figuring out what your major should be.

Be honest—do you want your college education to prepare you for a specific job? Career preparation is a popular and valid reason for heading to college. If you recognize this as *your* reason, then you should consider a career-focused major like engineering, business, education, nursing, or a similar option. Your education will be geared toward a vocation and in most cases you'll take a job in that specific field when you graduate.

Another reason to attend college is to expand your general knowledge without a specific career in mind. In this case you should consider the liberal arts since these fields emphasize critical thinking, creativity, integration of information, and other skills. Majoring in a field such as history won't often lead you to a specific type of job (how many actual historians do you know?), but you'll graduate with a whole slew of marketable and legitimate job skills, and you'll most likely be ready to test the waters in a variety of positions and industries.

Remember, your major does not determine your life. You do. Your values, personal ambitions, and dreams will ultimately be what propel you into the kind of life you desire.

So think it through. Objectively, no one major is better than any other, and different people are cut out for very different things. You don't have to know what career you want right away, either. But you might have more of an idea of the sort of life you want to build for yourself than you realize.

So, Oh Yeah, How to Choose a Major

We've profiled more than 375 majors in this book. Although students eventually find their majors in their own ways, we thought we'd give you some ideas here on how to start your search.

First, forget high school. You know what we mean. College is a whole new ball game. Subjects you hated senior year might turn out to be completely different in a brand-new time and place. Mind-numbingly boring civics might suddenly come alive; tear-your-hair-out calculus might become crystal clear and beautifully illustrated by the physical world around you. In other words, don't automatically rule anything out, even if right now you're sure it's not for you. Give everything a chance. You never know.

Keep an open mind and take advantage of those gen-ed courses we told you about. Don't just pick whatever's easiest. If your college offers several courses that will fit the requirements, try to choose ones that seem genuinely interesting. Football Physics might get you an easy A, but it probably won't make your pulse race or leave you with a real sense of achievement. And once you're in your classes, be aware of what strikes you. Did the lecture in calculus on Enlightenment philosophers have you on the edge of your seat? Did your ears perk up when your bio professor discussed the origins of life? Have your radar on for clues that might be pointing you in interesting directions.

Do bear in mind that testing a major by taking a course in that field sometimes isn't the best way of investigating a major. Courses within a major often focus on a specific topic, and if you find that one topic uninspiring, you might rule out the entire field prematurely. Some courses truly are broad enough, however, to get a clear picture of what the major is like. Aim for these if you want to go this route. Some colleges offer survey courses for just this reason. Or talk to your advisor or the head of the department for reasonable options.

Third, make good use of your college bulletin. Take an afternoon and go through it page by page. Highlight any class that even remotely interests you. You might see a pattern—if you've marked two engineering classes and twenty English classes, well, your interests might be clearer than you think.

Some other suggestions:

- Talk to your advisor about possibilities and doubts. That's why your advisor is there.

- Look online to find class syllabi. See what the assignments are like, what books are required, what sorts of essays must be written. Do the requirements for the courses in one major seem more palatable (i.e., interesting, not easy) than another? Try to pinpoint why. If you're drawn to math problem sets but not essay assignments, that's a clue to where you might be headed.

- Discuss majors with upperclassmen, like your resident advisor. Are they happy with what they're studying? Are they inspired by the work they do? Do they look forward to class or dread it? Is the major what they'd thought it'd be? Why or why not? Try to find out what their interests are and how they channel them through their major.

- Keep checking out PrincetonReview.com. We're continually adding new profiles of majors to our easy-to-search site, and you'll also find other information that might be of use to you during your college and major search.

- Make a list of some careers you might eventually like to pursue. Read about them on PrincetonReview.com. We list the majors that often lead to those careers.

- Don't forget about minors and double majors. Sometimes *not* choosing is okay, too.

- Talk to professionals in fields you find interesting. Ask them exactly what their jobs entail, how the jobs do (or don't) relate to their college majors, and what those college majors were. Learning about the paths others took to get where they are is often valuable and enlightening, and even more often, surprising.

- Pay attention to your passions. If you love playing video games, that might mean that you'd love making them. Majoring in something that can lead to a career as a software engineer could make sense for you.

Remember, you should take a proactive role in exploring possible majors. Treat your search as another class and devote as much time to this homework as to any other.

Continuing Education

You might be worried that choosing a major essentially means you're choosing a career. This simply isn't so, as we hope the variety of career possibilities in this guide and profiled on PrincetonReview.com demonstrate. In certain fields, yes, the degree essentially dictates the career. Engineering students, in most cases, aren't going to pursue jobs as psychologists (at least not right out of college). But many students use their majors as stepping-stones into other fields. As you've probably noticed, our world is changing fast; the jobs of today might not be around tomorrow, and some of the jobs of tomorrow aren't even on our radar yet. After all, you can't major in a field that hasn't even developed. Does this disqualify you from all the exciting opportunities ahead? Are you obsolete and outdated before you've even begun? Just the opposite. The best college experience prepares you for a changing job market and new opportunities. Employers seek out students who demonstrate creative thinking, innovation, computer knowledge, motivation, great communication and interpersonal skills, flexibility, and a solid academic background. Having a college degree means you've accomplished something important—you've shown that you know how to think, write, discuss, analyze, solve problems, organize your time, and learn about a field in-depth. These are all qualities of a good employee.

A broad-based, liberal arts education will give you the flexibility you need to adapt to the changing job world—but no matter what your degree, be prepared for a lifetime of learning. To be successful in any field you'll need to stay on top of new developments, to be aware of progress, and to keep up with changing value systems, ideas, and debates. Graduating from college doesn't mean the learning stops. In fact, that's usually when the real learning begins.

Final Thoughts

Okay. So now you know the difference between liberal arts colleges and research universities. You know the benefits and drawbacks of advanced study. You have got an idea of how academic advising works and whether a pre-professional degree is worth it. You even know a few tricks for finding the major that just might turn out to be yours. What don't you have? Yup. A major.

We can't tell you what to do. And you know what? We're not sorry. Our job would be a lot less fun if we could, and your college years would be a lot less fun, too. College is the first point in your life where you're free to really make decisions on your own, where you're free to explore the world and to find your place in it. Choosing a major is just one of the many important decisions to come. There'll be options; there'll be choices. Sometimes you'll think there are too many. But it's up to you to sift through the information, figure out what to listen to and what to ignore, and decide what's right for you. Let this book be your starting point. Good luck. We know you're going to have a blast.

TOP TEN MOST POPULAR
COLLEGE MAJORS

1. Business Administration and Management/Commerce

2. Psychology

3. Nursing—Registered Nurse Training (RN, ASN, BSN, MSN)

4. Biology/Biological Sciences

5. Education

6. English Language and Literature

7. Economics

8. Communications Studies/Speech, Communication, and Rhetoric

9. Political Science and Government

10. Computer and Information Sciences

Each year we collect data from colleges on the subject of—among many other things—undergraduate academic offerings. We not only ask colleges to report which undergraduate majors they offer, but we also ask them to identify which three of their majors have the highest undergraduate enrollment. The list above reflects which majors were reported as one of those three most popular majors by the greatest number of colleges responding to our survey.

HOW TO USE THIS BOOK

1) **The name of the major/program.** The name we use for a major or program isn't necessarily the only name it goes by. For example, agricultural economics will be found under the name "agribusiness" at some colleges. When a program sometimes goes by a different name like this, we've tried to point out the possibilities in the Basics section of the profile. Also, in response to the overwhelming demand by the student users of PrincetonReview.com, we've included profiles of certain non-undergraduate programs of study. Chiropractic, something you don't major in as an undergraduate, is an example. You'll discover which programs aren't specifically undergraduate majors by reading the profiles.

2) **The grouping to which the major belongs.** We placed each major in one of fourteen broad categories to make it easier to research majors that match your general academic interests. You can find an index of the majors in each group on page 832.

3) **The Basics.** In layman's terms, what the major is all about. What (and how) you can expect to learn, what kind of work you might encounter in college, and (sometimes) whether or not graduate school should be in your future.

4) **If You Like _____, You May Also Like . . . .** Having extensively researched and written about more than 400 majors, we've noticed connections between the major you're reading about and others we've profiled. These majors might be connected by a number of similarities, such as the subject material you'll study, the skills you're supposed to develop by majoring in these subjects, or the careers to which they often lead. This section is qualitative—it's our advice to you based on what we know—and you shouldn't look at the majors in this section as your only other options. You absolutely can study both film and astrophysics even if we didn't draw connections between them in this book.

5) **Suggested High School Prep for _____.** We base our suggestions on how to prepare for a particular major on the course work you'll actually do in college for that major. For example, if your major entails taking a lot of classes that require skills in complex math, like physics will, we suggest that you get a firm grounding in mathematics, taking the most advanced and complex math available at your high school. For certain majors, we suggest some extracurricular activities and independent research that will help you form a better idea of what a major requires inside and outside of the classroom.

6) **Sample College Curriculum for _____.** Having pored over the course catalogues of numerous colleges and the degree requirements for specific majors at those colleges, we've developed a list of examples to show you the types of courses you'll likely have to take and to pass to complete each major. As with the names of majors, the name we use for a certain course isn't necessarily the name used by all schools. (For instance, schools often have razzle-dazzle names like Dynamic Matrices—or something equally goofy—for a class on developing spreadsheets.) Some sample curricula are longer than others; this usually means that there just wasn't as much overlap in degree requirements as there was for majors with shorter samples.

7) **Fun Facts.** These are interesting factoids we came across during our research that are in some way related to the field. And for the sticklers, yes, you'll find some related jokes as well. Hopefully you'll also find a laugh.

8) **Availability Meter.** This reveals roughly what percentage of colleges filling out our survey offer this major. There are fifteen possible different readings for the meter.

9) **Careers and Salary.**

   a) The first part of this section tells you how much you could reasonably expect to make with a degree in this major if you graduated from college this year. If you're just starting college, or are a few years away from starting, keep in mind that these figures will probably change by the time you graduate. For some majors you'll find averages, for others ranges, and for many, both. We used a variety of online resources when determining starting salaries. There is more information out there on salaries for some majors than there are for others. The more thorough the information available, the more specific we are with figures. Salaries were updated in 2006 or 2007 for the 2008 edition of this book.

   b) The second part of this section tells you the careers to which the major often leads. The career options we've associated with the major are usually those we profile in our book, *Guide to Your Career*, and on our website, PrincetonReview.com. You can read about specific careers' average salaries, a typical day in the life, and much, much more for free on our site. As with the If You Like_____, You Might Also Like . . . section, these are careers our own research has led us to suggest, and the list is therefore not exhaustive. In other words, just because you major in chemistry doesn't mean you can't be a writer.

So What Schools Offer This Major?

We deliberated long and hard about whether we should list the schools that offer specific majors in this book, and we decided not to. Such a list would be so long that it would not only add considerably to the heft of an already sizeable book, but it also would make it more costly to you, the reader. You can, however, find out for free which schools offer specific majors at PrincetonReview.com.

THE MAJORS

ACCOUNTING

Basics

If you like free enterprise, thank an accountant. No, really. While accounting isn't exactly glamorous, it's absolutely central to any properly functioning free market system.

In a nutshell, if you major in accounting you'll learn how to keep financial records of business transactions and how to prepare statements concerning assets, liabilities, and operating results. It's a fairly technical and very numbers- and detail-oriented field that involves economics, the interpretation of financial data, and management skills. It's also a rapidly growing profession, and that's not likely to change any time soon because monolithic corporations, governments, charities, labor unions, individuals, and pretty much all other kinds of entities need accountants.

While it's possible to be a general accountant, specialization is a big aspect of being in this field. Many accountants specialize in auditing, taxes, or consulting. There are also several professional designations within the field of accounting. There's your garden-variety CPA (certified public accountant) as well as your CMA (certified management accountant) and your CIA (certified internal auditor). Keep in mind that you have to pass an extremely challenging exam after graduation to earn any one of these titles.

If You Like Accounting, You May Also Like . . .

Actuarial science, advertising, applied mathematics, business administration and management, business communications, entrepreneurship, finance, human resources management, industrial management, international business, logistics management, managerial economics, public administration, public policy analysis, risk management, statistics

> ### Sample College Curriculum for Accounting
>
> Accounting Information Systems
>
> Business Ethics
>
> Calculus
>
> Cost Accounting
>
> Finance
>
> Financial Accounting
>
> Introduction to Accounting
>
> Macroeconomics
>
> Marketing
>
> Microeconomics
>
> Not-for-Profit Organizational Accounting
>
> Statistics
>
> Taxation
>
> Workplace Communication

Suggested High School Prep for Accounting

No surprises here. If you want to major in accounting, you need a strong background in math. Ideally, you will have completed four or five years of college-prep math by the time you are a first-year student, as accounting majors generally take calculus in their first year of college. Experience with computers and business-related software programs will also prove extremely beneficial.

Fun Facts

CPAs' Trial by Fire

If you want to become a certified public accountant, you have to jump through a lot of hoops. Requirements differ by state. Nearly every state obligates would-be CPAs to obtain a bachelor's degree plus thirty additional credit hours. Some states require you to be a United States citizen. Some require you to work for a few years before you can get officially licensed. Some require that you pass an ethics test. One thing you can count on, though, is that you'll have to take a ridiculously difficult test (so difficult that you are allowed to take it several times and pass it in parts), and the exam fee will be pretty steep.

Accountant Joke

A man takes a balloon ride at a local county fair. A ferocious wind unexpectedly carries the balloon and its occupant far out into a rural area. The balloon eventually lands in a farmer's field, but the man has no clue how far he has flown or where he is. Seeing another man walking nearby, the man in the balloon cries out, "Excuse me, sir, can you tell me where I am?"

Eyeing the man in the balloon, the passerby says, "You are in a downed balloon in a farmer's field."

"You must be an accountant, sir," replied the balloon's unhappy resident.

"How could you possibly know that?" asked the passerby.

"Because what you have told me is absolutely correct but of absolutely no use to me now," answered the accidental balloonist.

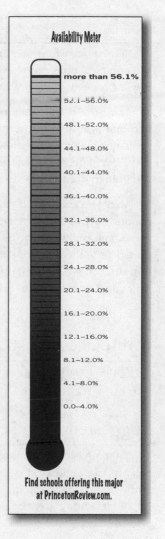

Availability Meter

more than 56.1%

52.1–56.0%

48.1–52.0%

44.1–48.0%

40.1–44.0%

36.1–40.0%

32.1–36.0%

28.1–32.0%

24.1–28.0%

20.1–24.0%

16.1–20.0%

12.1–16.0%

8.1–12.0%

4.1–8.0%

0.0–4.0%

Find schools offering this major at PrincetonReview.com.

Careers and Salary

Salaries for newly minted accountants with bachelor's degrees tend to vary pretty widely depending on the companies at which they work. Starting salaries range anywhere from $35,000 to a whopping $75,000 per year. The average starting salary is a little more than $35,000, and the median is $39,000. The average CPA with several years of experience makes about $74,000 annually.

CAREER OPTIONS

Accountant/Auditor	Financial Aid Officer	Management Consultant
Actuary	Financial Analyst	Small Business Owner
Bank Officer	Financial Planner	Statistician
Benefits Administrator	Insurance Agent/Broker	Trader
Bookkeeper	Investment Banker	Venture Capitalist/Investor
Entrepreneur		

ACOUSTICS

Basics

Remember when you first heard the echo of your own voice? As a kid, you probably weren't aware of the complex physics involved in that echo—but as an acoustics major, you will learn to understand every single property of each wave.

Acoustics is the study of sound. It reveals the science behind the art, such as the subtle nuances of a Baroque symphony in terms of its constituent acoustic waves, but it's much more than just that. As an acoustics major, you'll study the physical makeup of sound and its production: wave theory, the acoustic wave equation, vibration, reflection, singularity expansion theory, and a host of other intricate—and inter-disciplinary—concepts.

After you graduate, if you opt not to continue your studies in graduate school (although many acoustics majors do pursue advanced degrees), you'll be well-equipped to launch a career alongside architects (designing buildings) or biologists (studying the use of sound by animals, such as echolocation with dol-phins), or in the fields of health diagnostics, aeronautics, underwater acoustics, engineering, and many other options. You'll need a sharp, inquisitive mind that is flexibly creative as well as a math- and physics-savvy. And you'll never hear an echo quite the same way again.

If You Like Acoustics, You May Also Like . . .

Applied mathematics, architectural engineering, atmospheric science, music, physics

Suggested High School Prep for Acoustics

Make physics your number-one priority—take any AP physics courses you can—and don't neglect your algebra, trig, and calculus coursework. To keep yourself focused on the phenomenal world, it won't hurt to study music either; singing in a chorus will remind you that the wave mechanics you're studying are capa-ble of facilitating great beauty.

SAMPLE COLLEGE CURRICULUM FOR ACOUSTICS

Calculus-Based Physics I

Engineering Acoustics

Fluid Mechanics

Noise Control Design

Principles of Engineering

Thermodynamics I

Vibrations I

Fun Facts

Did You Know?

The Doppler effect—what happens when the sound produced by a moving source drops in pitch as it moves away from a stationary listener—can be likened to the "red shift" observed in light emitted from distant galaxies.

Killer Sperm

Some marine biologists posit that the sperm whale uses powerful ultrasound to stun or kill its prey.

Careers and Salary

Your career path options are multiple and varied. You could continue on in academia as a researcher and professor, work with the military to improve sonar technology, or advise architects as they design concert halls. Bioengineers who manufacture hearing aids and automobile designers who work to build quieter cars will rely on your expertise. Salaries increase with experience and education but start at about $43,000 to $51,000.

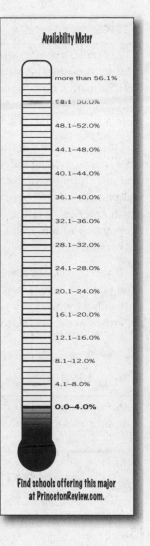

Availability Meter

more than 56.1%

52.1–56.0%

48.1–52.0%

44.1–48.0%

40.1–44.0%

36.1–40.0%

32.1–36.0%

28.1–32.0%

24.1–28.0%

20.1–24.0%

16.1–20.0%

12.1–16.0%

8.1–12.0%

4.1–8.0%

0.0–4.0%

Find schools offering this major at PrincetonReview.com.

CAREER OPTIONS

Architectural Consultant	Aerospace Engineer	Civil Engineer

ACTUARIAL SCIENCE

Basics

As Frank Drebin so wisely reminds us in *The Naked Gun*, "You take a chance getting up in the morning, crossing the street, or sticking your face in a fan." Exactly how risky is it to stick your face in a fan, though? For that matter, how can a corporation determine the financial risks of manufacturing shoes in China? How does an insurance company know how much to charge automobile owners for collision insurance? Do people really keep tabs on such things?

Of course they do. These risk evaluators are called actuaries, and they spend their days calculating the costs of assuming all different kinds of risks. More precisely, actuarial science is the mathematical and statistical underpinning of every kind of insurance on earth: health insurance, life insurance, property insurance, and pension plans. There really aren't that many people in the actuarial profession—fewer than 20,000 in North America—but they make good money their entire careers (most end up in upper management and executive positions), and they like what they do. Actuaries consistently give their line of work stellar job satisfaction ratings.

If you major in actuarial science you'll become something of a Zen master in statistics, and upon graduation you will likely take a job in the insurance industry. You should note that actuaries achieve professional status only by passing a series of hairy examinations prescribed by the Casualty Actuarial Society (CAS) or Society of Actuaries (SOA). Examinations are held twice each year, in the spring and fall.

If You Like Actuarial Science, You May Also Like . . .

Accounting, applied mathematics, business administration and management, business communications, computer and information science, computer systems analysis, data processing, entrepreneurship, finance, industrial management, international business, logistics management, managerial economics, mathematics, risk management, statistics

> **SAMPLE COLLEGE CURRICULUM FOR ACTUARIAL SCIENCE**
>
> Actuarial Mathematics
>
> Calculus I–IV
>
> Cost Accounting
>
> Finance
>
> Financial Accounting
>
> Insurance and Risk
>
> Linear Algebra
>
> Macroeconomics
>
> Microeconomics
>
> Probability and Statistics I–IV
>
> Theory of Interest

Suggested High School Prep for Actuarial Science

Actuarial work involves lots of math. Take every available math course in your high school, particularly the ones that are intended to prepare you for the rigors of college math. Actuaries must also be abreast of business issues and trends in social science and economics, so plan accordingly.

BUSINESS, MARKETING, AND RELATED FIELDS

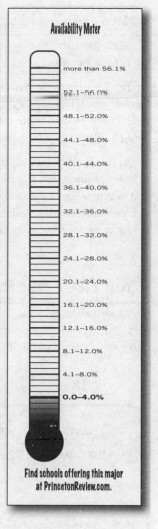

Fun Facts

Did You Know?

Hartford, Connecticut, is the undisputed insurance capital of the United States.

Things That Have Been Insured by Lloyd's of London

- Exhibitors insured a 2,000-year-old Chinese wine jar complete with contents, which had turned blue over the years.
- Cutty Sark Whisky offered very large cash rewards to anyone who could capture the Loch Ness monster alive or produce an authentic extraterrestrial gadget. Cutty Sark wisely guarded against any loss by purchasing a Lloyd's policy.
- A car dealership in Omaha, Nebraska, offered $10,000 to anyone who bought a car during December, provided four inches of snow fell locally on Christmas Day. More than 65 customers would have qualified for the offer in the city of Omaha. The dealership took out a $1.5 million insurance policy at Lloyd's, just in case.
- Movie bombshell Betty Grable insured her million-dollar legs with Lloyd's.

Actually Actuarial

The increased demand for long-term insurance coverage turned actuarial science into a formal mathematical discipline in the late 17th century.

(Source: http://en.wikipedia.org/wiki/Actuarial_science)

The Ins of Insurance

The insurance industry provides some 2.3 million jobs in the United States that encompass a wide variety of careers, from human resource administration to public relations management to financial analysis.

(Source: http://www.iii.org/media/facts/statsbyissue/careersandemployment)

Availability Meter

more than 56.1%
52.1–56.0%
48.1–52.0%
44.1–48.0%
40.1–44.0%
36.1–40.0%
32.1–36.0%
28.1–32.0%
24.1–28.0%
20.1–24.0%
16.1–20.0%
12.1–16.0%
8.1–12.0%
4.1–8.0%
0.0–4.0%

Find schools offering this major at PrincetonReview.com.

Careers and Salary

Beginning salaries for actuaries range from about $42,000 to $53,000 annually. Of course, that doesn't include your fat signing bonus. One big factor in determining your salary will be your progress on the professional actuarial examinations while in college. The average salary for experienced actuaries is about $100,000 a year. If you make it all the way to senior management, the sky's the limit; you can make hundreds of thousands of dollars annually.

CAREER OPTIONS

Accountant/Auditor	Economist	Statistician
Actuary	Financial Planner	Venture Capitalist/Investor
Bank Officer	Investment Banker	

ADULT DEVELOPMENT AND AGING

Basics

With the baby boomer population of the United States getting older, guess who's going to be responsible for the health of their aging family and friends? You've got it—your generation.

Health care organizations need professionals to inform their strategies, to lobby politicians, and to allocate necessary resources. Government groups need people to help guide lawmaking and public policy. Institutions need people trained in the biological and psychological phases of aging to improve the lives of aging adults.

In this major, you'll study all of these subjects and prepare for what will essentially be a career of service to elder generations. Courses of study in this major at most colleges are interdisciplinary; they bridge social and health sciences with biology and often business management. If you already spend as many evenings as you can catching up with your grandparents, or if you found your calling when you cared for a sick older family member, you have the essential tools—and the heart—required for this major.

If You Like Adult Development and Aging, You May Also Like . . .

American studies, clinical psychology, counseling, developmental psychology, gerontology, health administration, human development, mental health services, nursing, physical assistant, physical therapy, premedicine, psychology, public health, rehabilitation services, social worker, sociology

SAMPLE COLLEGE CURRICULUM FOR ADULT DEVELOPMENT AND AGING

Administration

Aging, the Individual, and Society

General Psychology

Health and Aging

Health Care Law

Human Anatomy and Physiology

Organization and Structure of Health Care Services Industry

Philosophy of Death and Dying

Principles of Nursing Home Administration

Proposal Writing

Psychology of Aging

Suggested High School Prep for Adult Development and Aging

Social sciences will best prepare you for this major, as will biological sciences and math. While what you study isn't medicine per se, much of what you will learn crosses over into the realm of "harder" science, so keep up with that as well as your English studies. Concentrating on your foreign language studies and volunteering at a nursing home or assisted living residence could certainly help as well.

Fun Facts

"Old" Is Only Relative

In 1900, the average adult's life expectancy was only 47 years old. Today, it's 78 years old—and the elderly are the nation's fastest-growing demographic.

The Science of Aging

Senescence refers to the state or process of aging.

From Wikipedia.org: "Lately the role of telomeres in cellular senescence has aroused general interest, especially with a view to the possible genetically adverse effects of cloning. The successive shortening of the chromosomal telomeres with each cell cycle is also believed to limit the number of divisions of the cell, thus contributing to aging. There have, on the other hand, also been reports that cloning could alter the shortening of telomeres. Some cells do not age and are therefore described as being 'biologically immortal.' It is theorized by some that when it is discovered exactly what allows these cells, whether it be the result of telomere shortening or not, to divide without limit that it will be possible to genetically alter other cells to have the same capability. It is further theorized that it will eventually be possible to genetically engineer all cells in the human body to have this capability by employing gene therapy and thereby to stop or to reverse ageing, effectively making the entire organism potentially immortal" [emphasis ours].

Akin to Aging?

NIA (National Institute on Aging), one of the 27 Institutes and Centers of the National Institute of Health, leads a broad scientific effort to understand the nature of aging and to extend the healthy, active years of life. In 1974, Congress granted authority to form NIA to provide leadership in aging research, training, health information dissemination, and other programs relevant to aging and older people. Subsequent amendments to this legislation designated the NIA as the primary Federal agency on Alzheimer's disease research.

(Source: http://www.nia.nih.gov/AboutNIA)

Living Longer and Longer

The United States is on the brink of a longevity revolution. By 2030, the number of older Americans will have more than doubled to 70 million, or one in every five Americans. The growing number and proportion of older adults places increasing demands on the public health system and on medical and social services.

(Source: http://www.cdc.gov/aging)

Availability Meter

more than 56.1%

52.1–56.0%

48.1–52.0%

44.1–48.0%

40.1–44.0%

36.1–40.0%

32.1–36.0%

28.1–32.0%

24.1–28.0%

20.1–24.0%

16.1–20.0%

12.1–16.0%

8.1–12.0%

4.1–8.0%

0.0–4.0%

Find schools offering this major at PrincetonReview.com.

Careers and Salary

Since people are living longer and the population at large is growing older, job opportunities in this field are plentiful. Expect long, emotionally demanding hours for relatively low pay—at least at first. Starting salaries ring in about $22,000 to $30,000.

CAREER OPTIONS

Long-term Care Administrator	Senior Center Director	Social Worker

ADVERTISING

Basics

What, with the gazillions of television channels, radio stations, Internet sites, and periodicals out there, there's certainly no lack of media in the world. And as everybody knows, the driving force behind nearly all media is ads. If you major in advertising, you'll become something of an expert in advertising principles, copywriting and layout, media campaigns, and media economics. You'll also hone your writing, presentation, and problem-solving skills.

You'll become a pretty good psychologist, too. You'll learn how and why people make decisions and how to influence those decisions. Behind all the glitz and the cool slogans, advertising is really about understanding what motivates people to buy a product, to use a service, or to support a cause.

Advertising is an overwhelmingly project-oriented major. You'll spend enormous chunks of time looking at ads, talking about them, and criticizing them. (By the way—and this stands to reason—if you don't like to talk about ads already, you probably shouldn't make them your life.) However, you'll mostly learn about advertising by doing advertising. You'll develop concepts and portfolios. You'll swamp yourself in market research (maybe even for real firms). You'll create sales presentations and come up with irresistible jingles designed to motivate your target audience. Most important, you'll have internships. They are utterly indispensable. When recruiters come to campus or employers eyeball you for that big first job, they'll be a lot more interested in you if you have a few internships under your belt.

After graduation, most advertising majors go to work for traditional advertising agencies, media conglomerates, or marketing firms.

SAMPLE COLLEGE CURRICULUM FOR ADVERTISING

Advertising and Culture

Advertising and Public Relations
  Campaigns

Advertising Copywriting

Advertising History

Advertising Media Sales and
  Management

Advertising Portfolio Practicum

Advertising Principles

Advertising Research Methods

Audience Analysis

Graphic Design

Marketing Strategy

Psychology

Radio and TV Writing

Statistics

If You Like Advertising, You May Also Like . . .

American studies, art, economics, English, film, journalism, marketing, mass communication, political science, psychology, radio and television, theater, visual communication

Suggested High School Prep for Advertising

Take lots of English courses. Any other writing-intensive courses are good as well. If your high school offers courses that will teach you how to create computer-based graphic art, take them. You'll probably be required to take a foreign language in college if you choose to major in advertising. Plan accordingly. Last, and perhaps most important, advertising programs almost universally involve some fairly challenging statistics courses. Consequently, if you ignore math in high school, you'll be in for a rude awakening.

Fun Facts

Bet You Can Name Them All

Think you are immune to advertising? Check out some of these classic advertising slogans and note just how lodged in your subconscious they are.

"Think different." Apple Macintosh, Chiat/Day, 1998

"Don't leave home without it." American Express, Ogilvy & Mather, 1975

"A diamond is forever." De Beers Consolidated, J. Walter Thompson, 1950

"Snap! Crackle! Pop!" Kellogg's Rice Krispies, J. Walter Thompson, 1932

"Just do it." Nike, Wieden & Kennedy, 1988

The Big Names

Here's a list of the most successful advertising agencies on the planet. Most of them are based in New York City, but many of these mammoth firms have offices in other major cities too.

- Ammirati Puris Lintas, New York
- Bates Worldwide, New York
- BBDO Worldwide, New York
- Bozell Worldwide, New York
- Brann Worldwide; Deerfield, Illinois, and Cirencester, United Kingdom
- D'Arcy Masius Benton & Bowles, New York
- DDB Needham Worldwide, New York
- Euro RSCG Worldwide, New York
- Foote, Cone & Belding, New York
- Grey Advertising, New York
- J. Walter Thompson Co., New York
- Leo Burnett Co., Chicago
- Lowe & Partners Worldwide, New York
- McCann-Erickson Worldwide, New York
- Ogilvy & Mather Worldwide, New York
- Publicis Worldwide, New York
- Saatchi & Saatchi, New York
- TBWA Worldwide, New York
- TMP Worldwide, New York
- Young & Rubicam, New York

Famous People Who Majored in Advertising

Garth Brooks (country music superstar, Oklahoma State University)

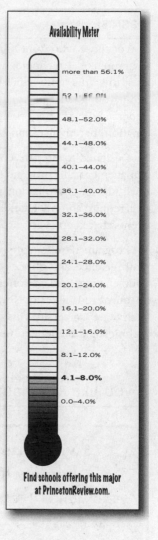

Availability Meter

more than 56.1%

52.1–56.0%

48.1–52.0%

44.1–48.0%

40.1–44.0%

36.1–40.0%

32.1–36.0%

28.1–32.0%

24.1–28.0%

20.1–24.0%

16.1–20.0%

12.1–16.0%

8.1–12.0%

4.1–8.0%

0.0–4.0%

Find schools offering this major at PrincetonReview.com.

Careers and Salary

Entry-level salaries in advertising average about $30,000. You can expect to make about $50,000 after a few years of experience and more than $100,000 at the top level. If you stick it out, advertising can be a very lucrative field.

CAREER OPTIONS

Advertising Executive	Graphic Designer	Promoter
Agent	Market Researcher	Public Relations Professional
Art Dealer	Marketing Executive	Publicist
Consultant	Media Planner	Researcher
Editor	Media Specialist	Website Designer

AERONAUTICAL TECHNOLOGY

Basics

For those who want to fly the friendly skies from behind the scenes, several colleges now offer degrees in aeronautical technology. This specialization within the engineering programs at several colleges gears itself toward a more hands-on approach than some of its predecessors with students often jumping into— and if you like out of—planes within their first two semesters of course work. Once students have a basic understanding of the principals of air travel, they move into training that will lead to higher levels of coordination that involves much more than a single flight's specific logistics.

Designed to prepare college students for any number of jobs ranging from ground technician to fleet management, this program focuses on several of the "behind the scenes" aspects of airport management and quality. Fleet coordination, maintenance, scheduling and management are all highly professional positions that require an understanding of both the day-to-day work that must be done as well as the overall web of events that keep every airport compliant with federal regulations.

Program requirements will vary from school to school, but most classes will rely heavily on in-depth math, science, and physics classes with the option to specialize in mechanics or management and business courses. Some colleges offering this degree include Andres University, Embry Riddle Aeronautical University, LeTourneau University, New York Institute of Technology, Purdue University, Tennessee State University and Utah State University. This type of degree would prepare a student for a career as an inspector, mechanic, technician, designer and fleet management.

If you like Aeronautical Technology, you may also like...

Aviation, aviation mechanic, aviation inspector, professional pilot programs, flight instructor, commercial or charter pilot, corporate aviator or pipeline patrol pilot

Suggested High School Prep for Aeronautical Technology

While most high schools don't have air strips or private fleets to practice on, every high school has classes that will help you learn the building blocks on which aeronautical technology relies. Such classes include advanced math, physics, computer design and drafting, auto shop, economics and pre-business classes.

SAMPLE COLLEGE CURRICULUM FOR AERONAUTICAL TECHNOLOGY

Aircraft Structure

Aircraft Assembly Rigging and Inspections

Aircraft Electrical Systems

Aircraft Fuels and Fuel Systems

Aircraft Systems for Pilots

Airframe

Aviation, FAA-Approved Instrument Ground Training

Commercial Flight Planning

Federal Regulations

Techniques of Mission Flying

Fun Facts

There are roughly 5,100 airports in the United States with paved runways (2006 World Records) and another 8,000 to 9,000 regional airports (2003 CIA Factbook) each of which send hundreds and thousands of flights over the American skies every day. The only time in modern air travel that all flights have been ordered to land was on September 11, 2001 when nearly 5,000 domestic flights carrying 350,000 people were safely rerouted in a matter of hours ("Grounded on 9/11") thanks to the highly skilled air traffic controllers and fleet managers across the nation.

Careers and Salary

Starting salaries will vary greatly depending on the sector of specialization each student chooses, as well as how large the market in which you get your first job is. Most average starting salaries range from $30,000 to $55,000.

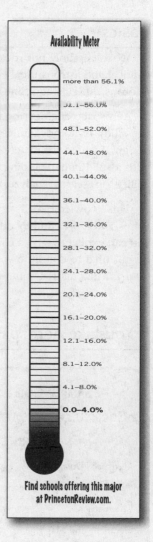

Availability Meter

more than 56.1%

52.1–56.0%

48.1–52.0%

44.1–48.0%

40.1–44.0%

36.1–40.0%

32.1–36.0%

28.1–32.0%

24.1–28.0%

20.1–24.0%

16.1–20.0%

12.1–16.0%

8.1–12.0%

4.1–8.0%

0.0–4.0%

Find schools offering this major at PrincetonReview.com.

CAREER OPTIONS

Aerospace Engineer	Aviation Inspector	Flight Instructor
Air Force National Guard	Fleet Manager	Pilot
Aircraft Technician		

AEROSPACE ENGINEERING

Basics

We're certainly not rocket scientists, but you can be one by choosing aerospace engineering (or aeronautical and astronautical engineering, as it's often called) as your major. Be forewarned, though: It will be rigorous, difficult, and time-consuming.

Aerospace engineering is all about flight—airplanes, spacecraft, hovercraft, and helicopters. It includes the study of aerodynamics, aerospace structures, propulsion, flight mechanics and systems, and vehicle design. If you major in aerospace engineering you'll endure four seriously intense years, but you'll graduate with a solid understanding of the physical fundamentals underlying atmospheric and space flight and the ability to research, analyze, and design the flying machines of the future.

This knowledge will serve you well. The aerospace industry is the second largest industry in the United States, and it is definitely one of the largest employers of engineers. With a major in aerospace engineering, you can expect to land a fairly lucrative job with a large aircraft manufacturer, an airline, or NASA. You'll also be qualified to continue your education at the graduate level or to work in any number of nonaerospace (and, for that matter, nonengineering) fields.

If You Like Aerospace Engineering, You May Also Like . . .

Agricultural and biological engineering, applied mathematics, applied physics, architectural engineering, astronomy, astrophysics, atmospheric science, biochemistry, chemical engineering, chemistry, civil engineering, computer and information science, computer engineering, electrical engineering, engineering design, environmental and environmental health engineering, genetics, industrial engineering, mathematics, mechanical engineering, microbiology, molecular genetics, naval architecture, neurobiology, neuroscience, nuclear engineering, petroleum engineering, physics, statistics

SAMPLE COLLEGE CURRICULUM FOR AEROSPACE ENGINEERING

Aerospace Design

Calculus and Analytic Geometry

Chemistry

Electricity and Magnetism

Flight Mechanics

Flight Vehicle Dynamics

Fluid Mechanics

Jet Propulsion

Linear Algebra

Linear Systems Engineering

Physics

Solid Mechanics

Space Vehicle Components

Thermodynamics

Viscous Flow and Heat Transfer

Suggested High School Prep for Aerospace Engineering

A strong background in mathematics and physics is absolutely vital if you want to pursue aerospace engineering, as is extensive knowledge of computers and computer programming skills. Take AP physics and chemistry, as well as calculus or the highest-level math class that your high school offers.

Fun Facts

Georgia Tech's Yellow Jacket Flying Club

The Yellow Jacket Flying Club at the Georgia Institute of Technology in Atlanta is made up of current and former students who want to learn how to fly. The club owns four airplanes, which are available solely to YJFC members, 24 hours a day, 7 days a week. For about $2,800 (compared with the $4,000 you could expect to pay for flight training in the real world), you can begin instruction virtually immediately once you join the club. If you want, you can even work toward your commercial aviation license through the club.

The good news is that the Yellow Jacket Flying Club is the cheapest way you'll ever find to learn to fly, short of Uncle Bob letting you use his Cessna free of charge. The bad news is that no matter how cheap flying is, you always want to do more than you can afford! The cost of flight training can vary widely depending on individual abilities and scheduling. You'll see all sorts of numbers quoted by flight schools, but most include only the bare minimum number of hours, which is not a realistic expectation. Overall, an average cost for someone in the YJFC, including all fees and supplies, ranges from $2,500 to $3,200. The corresponding package in the outside world will run you $3,500 to $4,500.

What Is the Temperature in Space?

It depends. Near Earth and our moon, objects exposed to direct sunlight can heat up to temperatures of about 250 degrees Fahrenheit. In the shade, it gets a little chillier—down to around –250 degrees Fahrenheit. This is why it is so important to keep your space suit on at all times while in space.

The Final Frontier

The term "rocket scientist" is sometimes used to describe a person of remarkable or higher than average intelligence. Aerospace engineering has also been represented as the more "glittery pinnacle of engineering". The movie Apollo 13 depicts the ground team as a group of heroes in a Hollywood fashion glorifying the intelligence and competence of aerospace professionals.

(Source: http://en.wikipedia.org/wiki/Aerospace_engineering)

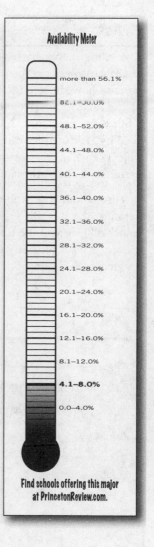

Availability Meter

more than 56.1%

52.1–56.0%

48.1–52.0%

44.1–48.0%

40.1–44.0%

36.1–40.0%

32.1–36.0%

28.1–32.0%

24.1–28.0%

20.1–24.0%

16.1–20.0%

12.1–16.0%

8.1–12.0%

4.1–8.0%

0.0–4.0%

Find schools offering this major at PrincetonReview.com.

Careers and Salary

With a bachelor's degree in aerospace engineering, you can expect to make about $51,000 during your first year at your first job. With a master's degree, your starting salary should be approximately $63,000 annually.

CAREER OPTIONS

Aerospace Engineer	Astronaut	Pilot
Air Force National Guard	Avionics Technician	Professor
Air Force (Officer)		

AFRICAN AMERICAN STUDIES

Basics

A multidisciplinary major, African American studies will offer you an understanding of what it means to be African American. You'll learn how African Americans have affected and been affected by American culture and how those effects have been perceived by society throughout history. You'll study the problems African Americans have encountered in the past and the problems they face today, such as economic and political discrimination. You'll study the roles of African American women throughout history, the problems faced by African American children and teenagers, and the issue of race in the media. You might encounter subjects such as the portrayal of African Americans in the news; the problems and benefits of government programs, such as affirmative action; and the influence of African Americans on pop culture.

Throughout your studies you'll gain exposure to African art, language, music, politics, psychologies, and literature. You'll begin to form ideas of how the relationship between identity and race has evolved. This major will give you the opportunity to become knowledgeable in many different fields, including political science, English, women's studies, psychology, sociology, history, and many others. African American studies is a great major for anyone interested in the black experience.

SAMPLE COLLEGE CURRICULUM FOR AFRICAN AMERICAN STUDIES

African American Film

African American History

African American Voices in U.S. Literature

African American Youth Cultures

African Americans and the Law

African Civilization

Caribbean Literature

Contemporary Black Drama

Introduction to African Politics

Philosophy in Contemporary African Literature

The Politics of Gender and Race

Politics and Society

Race and Art

Themes in African American Literature

If You Like African American Studies, You May Also Like . . .

African studies, American history, American literature, American studies, art history, Asian American studies, comparative literature, East Asian studies, East European studies, history, Islamic studies, Jewish studies, Medieval and Renaissance studies, Middle Eastern studies, peace studies, philosophy, South Asian studies, Southeast Asian studies

Suggested High School Prep for African American Studies

You'll be best prepared for a major in African American studies by taking courses in English, history, philosophy, and religion. Foreign language, art, and music courses might be useful as well. Your best preparation for the multidisciplinary nature of this major is a diverse background of knowledge.

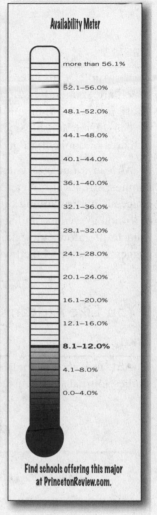

Availability Meter

more than 56.1%

52.1–56.0%

48.1–52.0%

44.1–48.0%

40.1–44.0%

36.1–40.0%

32.1–36.0%

28.1–32.0%

24.1–28.0%

20.1–24.0%

16.1–20.0%

12.1–16.0%

8.1–12.0%

4.1–8.0%

0.0–4.0%

Find schools offering this major
at PrincetonReview.com.

Fun Facts

Recommended Reading

If you're interested in the African American perspective, consider spending some time with one of the following books:

- *Their Eyes Were Watching God* by Zora Neale Hurston
- *Native Son* and *Black Boy* by Richard Wright
- *Poems on Various Subjects* by Phillis Wheatley
- *Incidents in the Life of a Slave Girl* by Harriet Jacobs
- *The Famished Road* by Ben Okri
- *The Cattle Killing* by John Edgar Wideman

Important Dates in the American Civil Rights Movement

1954—Brown v. Board of Education

1955—Montgomery bus boycott

1957—Desegregation of Little Rock, Arkansas

1960—Sit-in campaign (launched by Joseph McNeill in Greensboro, North Carolina, after he was refused service at a lunch counter)

1961—Freedom rides (attempt to end segregation of bus terminals)

1962—Mississippi riot (caused by the arrival of James Meredith, the first black student at the University of Mississippi)

1963—Birmingham, Alabama (protest march led by Dr. Martin Luther King Jr., Reverend Abernathy, and Reverend Shuttlesworth)

1965—Selma, Alabama (On "Bloody Sunday" police attacked African Americans who were marching in protest)

(Source: Western Michigan University)

Careers and Salary

As with most humanities majors, African American studies majors will have a vast selection of careers from which to choose. Most liberal arts majors can expect a starting salary in the mid twenties, but that can vary widely depending on the field.

CAREER OPTIONS

Anthropologist	Journalist	Translator
Archaeologist	Sociologist	Writer
Diplomat/Attaché/Foreign Service Officer	Teacher	

AFRICAN LANGUAGES, LITERATURES, AND LINGUISTICS

Basics

Do you have an interest in Africa and a gift for languages? Africa has 800-plus spoken languages, 50 of which are spoken by half a million people or more, and some of which are spoken only by small tribes. Those interested in linguistics—the study of the units, structure, nature, and development of languages, as well as the relationships between different languages and language branches—will find Africa an especially rich area of concentration.

African Languages, Literatures, and Linguistics majors learn one or more languages from the following families: Afro-Asiatic, Niger-Kordofanian, Nilo-Saharan, and Khoisan. More important than memorizing languages is understanding the nature and history of African languages, with special attention to phonology, morphology, syntax, and semantics. Students study philology, the study of language, as it relates to and is used in literature, and take classes in African literature. Because few African languages have written languages, literature studied will often be in the form of transcribed oral tradition.

If You Like African Languages, Literatures, and Linguistics, You May Also Like . . .

African American studies, African studies, anthropology, archaeology, English, film, French, history, Islamic studies, journalism, linguistics, sociology

---

SAMPLE COLLEGE CURRICULUM FOR AFRICAN LANGUAGES, LITERATURES, AND LINGUISTICS

Africa in the Twentieth Century

African Film

African Folktales

Beginning Swahili

Comparative Linguistics

Introduction to African Languages and Literature

Language in African Society

Yoruba Diaspora in the New World

Suggested High School Prep for African Languages, Literatures, and Linguistics

Immerse yourself in the humanities, concentrating on history and English classes. Take four years of French, plus any additional language your school offers to get your brain ready for some headier linguistic challenges.

Fun Facts

Speaking in Click

The Khoisan, or Click languages, makes up a unique linguistic family whose speakers communicate with clicking sounds. The clicking sounds, which serve as consonants, are made by sucking air with the tongue, and are varied by the position of the tongue and the way air is released into the mouth. These clicks sound like a horse's hooves clipping on pavement.

(Source: www.bartleby.com/65/af/AfricanIng.html)

Liquids: In a Class of Their Own

While Indo-European tongues feature only three noun classifications (masculine, feminine, and neuter), some Niger-Kordofanian languages have as many as 20 noun classes, including one for human beings, another for animals, and another used exclusively for liquids. Each class has its own pair of affixes, which indicates singular and plural.

(Source: www.infoplease.com/ce6/society/A0856502.html)

Ample Languages in Africa

By most estimates, Africa contains well more than a thousand languages—more than two thousand by some estimates. Most of them are of African origin and a few of them are European in origin. Africa is considered the most polyglot continent in the world, and it is not rare to find those who can fluently speak several African languages as well as one or two European ones.

(Source: http://en.wikipedia.org/wiki/Africa)

Careers and Salary

Starting salaries vary depending on career path, but liberal arts graduates can expect to make from $20,000 to $30,000 a year.

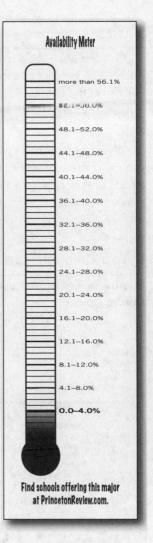

Availability Meter

more than 56.1%

52.1–56.0%

48.1–52.0%

44.1–48.0%

40.1–44.0%

36.1–40.0%

32.1–36.0%

28.1–32.0%

24.1–28.0%

20.1–24.0%

16.1–20.0%

12.1–16.0%

8.1–12.0%

4.1–8.0%

0.0–4.0%

Find schools offering this major at PrincetonReview.com.

CAREER OPTIONS

Anthropologist	Documentary Filmmaker	Professor
Archivist	Fundraiser/Institutional Solicitor	Sociologist
Curator	Journalist	Translator
Diplomat/Attaché/Foreign Service Officer	Lobbyist	Writer

AFRICAN STUDIES

Basics

Colleges often list a major in African studies within a broader major of African American/Afro-American studies. This broader context will provide you the opportunity to look not only at African culture and history, but also at the relationship between that and the African American experience in the United States. Areas of focus within the African studies major include history, religion, cultural and social issues, literature, and the arts.

Given the breadth of African history and African American culture, there are plenty of areas from which you may choose. Whether it's women's issues in contemporary Africa or the political, economic, and social effects of slavery within the United States, the African studies major is a wonderful opportunity to explore the connections between Africa and the rest of the world.

If You Like African Studies, You May Also Like . . .

African American studies, anthropology, Arabic, French, international studies, Islamic studies, Middle Eastern studies

---

SAMPLE COLLEGE CURRICULUM FOR AFRICAN STUDIES

African American History

African American Voices in U.S. Literature

Caribbean, African American, and African Literature

Contemporary Black Drama

Introduction to African American and African Studies

Introduction to African Civilization

Introduction to African Literature

Introduction to African Politics

Philosophy in Contemporary African Literature

Themes in African American Literature

Suggested High School Prep for African Studies

The best preparation for a major in African studies is a strong interest in and commitment to the humanities. English courses, especially those in which discussion of texts is the normal way class is conducted, get you ready for a major that often involves polemic issues. A knowledge of geography is essential as there are more than 40 countries in Africa, and learning them all has been compared with learning the periodic table of elements.

Fun Facts

You Knew This

Africa is the second largest of the world's continents, covering about one-fifth of the total land surface of Earth.

The name Africa originally applied only to the northern coast of the continent, which was, in effect, regarded as a southern extension of Europe. The Romans, who for a time ruled the North African coast, are also said to have called the area south of their settlements Afriga, or the Land of the Afrigs—the name of a Berber community south of Carthage.

Divvying up a Diamond

The world's largest diamond was found in South Africa in 1905. It was called the Cullinan, and it weighed 3,106.75 carats uncut. It was cut into the Great Star of Africa (weighing 530.2 carats), the Lesser Star of Africa, (317.40 carats), and 104 other diamonds of nearly flawless color and clarity. They now form part of the British crown jewels.

(Source: http://www.africaguide.com/facts.htm)

A Nobel Address

The only street in the world to be the residence of two Nobel Peace Prize winners is Vilakazi Street, Orlando West in Soweto, southwest of Johannesburg. Nelson Mandela and Archbishop Desmond Tutu both have houses there.

(Source: http://www.southafrica.info/ess_info/sa_glance/sustainable/sustdevfacts.htm)

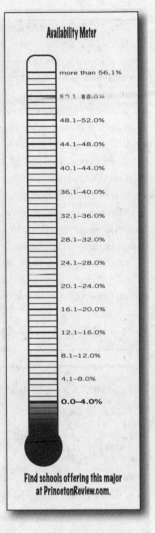

Availability Meter

more than 56.1%

52.1–56.0%

48.1–52.0%

44.1–48.0%

40.1–44.0%

36.1–40.0%

32.1–36.0%

28.1–32.0%

24.1–28.0%

20.1–24.0%

16.1–20.0%

12.1–16.0%

8.1–12.0%

4.1–8.0%

0.0–4.0%

Find schools offering this major at PrincetonReview.com.

Careers and Salary

Starting salaries for African studies majors range from $24,000 to $30,000.

CAREER OPTIONS

Anthropologist	Art Dealer	Diplomat/Attaché/Foreign Service Officer
Antiques Dealer	Consultant	
Archaeologist	Curator	

AGRICULTURAL AND BIOLOGICAL ENGINEERING

Basics

The 1978 low-budget film *Attack of the Killer Tomatoes* opens with a fresh tomato coming to life and rolling toward the lady of the house as she does housework. In subsequent scenes, overgrown tomatoes gurgle, grunt, fly, and fling themselves at moving cars. A bioengineer's dream come true . . . or worst nightmare? Hard to say. But if you pursue a career in agricultural and biological engineering, you may well be involved in developing tools that make it easier—and safer—to produce and distribute food of the highest quality. Agricultural and biological engineering are swiftly evolving fields that integrate the principles of biological and physical sciences and use them to solve agricultural and environmental problems. Engineers in these fields design systems and equipment that increase agricultural productivity and food safety. They also work to manage and conserve soil, water, air, energy, and other agricultural resources.

As an agricultural and biological engineering major, you'll learn the skills of engineering as they relate to agriculture, food production, and resource conservation. For example, as a bioengineer, your interests might lie in working to create a breed of fatter, tastier tomatoes (nonattacking variety) or to speed up the fermentation of grape juice.

These majors are not for the fainthearted; you'll take advanced and difficult courses in many different subjects, including math, physics, chemistry, biology, and engineering. Laboratory work and computer science will also be big components of your studies.

Students who graduate in these highly specialized fields often choose to continue their studies in graduate or medical school. Others who go on to immediately pursue careers also find that they are highly prized by government agencies, consulting firms, and monolithic corporations such as International Paper, Tyson Foods, Archer Daniels Midland, and Haliburton.

If You Like Agricultural and Biological Engineering, You May Also Like . . .

Agricultural economics, agricultural technology management, agriculture, agronomy and crop science, animal science, applied mathematics, applied physics, architectural engineering, biochemistry, biology, botany and plant biology, cell biology, chemical engineering, chemistry, civil engineering, computer engineering, ecology, electrical engineering, engineering design, environmental and environmental health engineering, environmental science, feed science, genetics, grain science, horticulture, industrial engineering, industrial management, mechanical engineering, microbiology, molecular genetics, nuclear engineering, petroleum engineering

Suggested High School Prep for Agricultural and Biological Engineering

You don't need to be a whiz in engineering, agriculture, or biology to pursue these majors, but having an enduring love of math and the physical sciences will help immensely. Take all the math, physics, biology, and chemistry courses that your high school offers. Experience with computers and computer programming will also prove valuable. If your high school offers agriculture courses, you'll obviously want to take those too. If you know where you want to apply, consider contacting the university for information on their agricultural and biological engineering programs; this way, you can choose high school courses that will satisfy admission requirements and prepare you for the workload ahead.

SAMPLE COLLEGE CURRICULUM FOR AGRICULTURAL AND BIOLOGICAL ENGINEERING

- Animal Nutrition
- Biology
- Bioprocess and Biological Systems
- Calculus and Analytic Geometry
- Computer Science
- Construction Technology
- Differential Equations
- Genetics
- Grain Drying, Handling, and Storage
- Hydraulics
- Landscape Irrigation
- Mechanics of Solids
- Microbiology
- Organic Chemistry
- Physics
- Statics and Dynamics

Fun Facts

We're Number One

In 1905, J. B. Davidson, the father of agricultural and biological engineering, devised the first professional agricultural curriculum at—where else?—Iowa State University.

A Bug's Life

Can bugs drive cars? Bioengineering student Steven Bathiche and neurophysiologist Jeff Bloomquist say yes. The two scientists began to train bugs to drive as part of their quest to design a wheelchair that could be controlled by the very smallest of movements, such as the twitch of a facial muscle. They secured cockroaches and hawkmoths in toy cars and harnessed the electrical signals emitted by the insects' wings to power them. They envisioned that the bugs in their cars would serve as a small-scale model of the technology needed for the wheelchair.

(Source: "The Mothmobile," *Discover*, July 1998)

Academic and Agricultural

A large percentage of agricultural engineers work in academia or for government agencies such as the U.S. Department of Agriculture.

(Source: http://en.wikipedia.org/wiki/Agricultural_engineering)

The Doings of Deere

In 1836, John Deere, a blacksmith from Vermont, set up shop in the small town of Grand Detour, Illinois. Deere found many discouraged farmers who were having trouble cultivating the sticky Midwestern soil. Convinced that the soil would shed itself from a plow that was highly polished and properly shaped, he forged such a plow using a discarded saw blade a year later. His "self-polishing" plow became popular and helped forge the successful company that bears his name.

(Source: http://www.deere.com/en_US/attractions/historicsite/index.html)

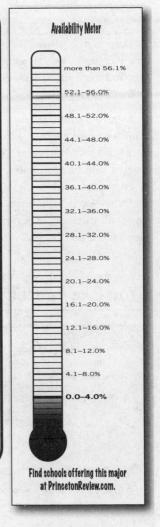

Availability Meter

more than 56.1%
52.1–56.0%
48.1–52.0%
44.1–48.0%
40.1–44.0%
36.1–40.0%
32.1–36.0%
28.1–32.0%
24.1–28.0%
20.1–24.0%
16.1–20.0%
12.1–16.0%
8.1–12.0%
4.1–8.0%
0.0–4.0%

Find schools offering this major at PrincetonReview.com.

Careers and Salary

The starting salary for most engineering fields is in the $40,000 to $50,000 range. Your salary will depend on your area of employment, location, and previous experience. Those who go into farming are more likely to earn about $26,000 to $32,000.

CAREER OPTIONS

Agricultural/Biological Engineer	Biologist	Farmer
Biochemist	Ecologist	Geneticist
Bioengineer	Environmentalist/Environmental Scientist	Production Manager

AGRICULTURAL BUSINESS AND MANAGEMENT

Basics

Do you have a head for business and an interest in agriculture? Then a major in agricultural business management might be for you. Agriculture in the twenty-first century is a complex, multifaceted, and cutting-edge industry, and to ensure that the farm products Americans need are grown, manufactured, and distributed effectively, all agricultural businesses need managers to take charge.

As an agricultural business management major, you'll be studying all the fundamentals of business—economics, management, marketing, finance, and others—while learning exactly how these fields apply to the world of agriculture. You'll apply your business skills to areas such as natural resources management, food systems, and biotechnology. You'll investigate ways to maintain the delicate balance between environmental protection and profitable business. You'll explore the processing and distribution of agricultural commodities. You'll also learn about the newest advances in technology and computer science that have improved the field of agriculture and made agricultural practices more efficient and convenient. With this major, you'll get the skills and knowledge you need to be successful in this lively industry.

If You Like Agricultural Business and Management, You May Also Like . . .

Agricultural economics, agricultural education, agricultural and biological engineering, agricultural journalism, agricultural mechanization, agricultural technology management, agriculture, agronomy and crop science, business administration and management, business communications, economics, horticulture, international business, logistics management, managerial economics, marketing, natural resources conservation, operations management, sustainable resource management, wildlife management

SAMPLE COLLEGE CURRICULUM FOR AGRICULTURAL BUSINESS AND MANAGEMENT
Agricultural Marketing
Agricultural Mathematics
Analyzing Alternative Enterprises
Applied Macroeconomics
Applied Microeconomics
Business Law
Crop Production Practices
Employment Communication
Farm Management
Food and Agricultural Sales
Land Measurement and Surveying
Markets, Marketing, and Prices
Pesticide Use and Safety
Plant Propagation
Soils and Fertilizers

Suggested High School Prep for Agricultural Business and Management

If you're considering a major in agricultural business management, your best bets for building a good academic foundation are math, biology, chemistry, business, and computer courses. Business classes your high school offers would be perfect. You may also want to get involved in agricultural clubs to see what the agriculture world is all about.

Fun Facts

Why Do We Need Agricultural Business Managers?

Because the journey of farm products from farm to kitchen is long and complicated. Penn State University gives the following example:

Consider the typical route of a common product, milk, before it arrives at our breakfast tables. The Pennsylvania dairy herd may be fed with corn from Iowa, wheat from the Dakotas, and alfalfa from Idaho. The cows may be from purebred stock developed through Penn State research. After the raw milk is produced on the farm, it is picked up by a tanker truck for delivery to the plant for processing. The milk must be then processed and transported to wholesalers and stores for retail marketing. The milk may end up on your table as milk for drinking or as another product such as butter, cheese, yogurt, ice cream, baked goods, snack foods, or any of hundreds of other products.

Careers and Salary

The starting salary for agricultural business managers is usually in the $27,000 to $35,000 range and can go higher or lower depending on where they live and how much experience they've had.

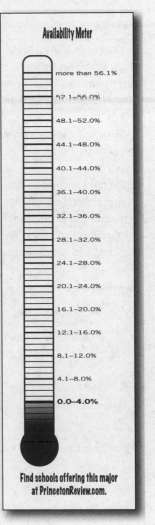

Availability Meter

more than 56.1%

52.1–56.0%

48.1–52.0%

44.1–48.0%

40.1–44.0%

36.1–40.0%

32.1–36.0%

28.1–32.0%

24.1–28.0%

20.1–24.0%

16.1–20.0%

12.1–16.0%

8.1–12.0%

4.1–8.0%

0.0–4.0%

Find schools offering this major at PrincetonReview.com.

CAREER OPTIONS

Accountant/Auditor	Farmer	Marketing Executive
Ecologist	Lobbyist	Production Manager
Economist	Manufacturing Executive	Property Manager
Environmentalist/Environmental Scientist	Market Researcher	

AGRICULTURAL ECONOMICS

Basics

Consider the Twinkie. Its primary ingredient is flour, which typically comes from wheat. Let's say the wheat is grown in Iowa, then shipped to factories in places such as San Francisco, mixed with mysterious ingredients like dextrin, sleekly packaged, and finally shipped to your favorite convenience store. The crazy thing is, after all that work everybody involved in this process makes a profit and you can enjoy a tasty Twinkie for not much more than the cost of a postage stamp.

Your enjoyment of that Twinkie is possible thanks in large part to the brilliance of those in the agribusiness industry, which accounts for almost one-fifth of the United States gross national product. To be a part of this huge national and international food industry (which has more jobs than applicants), you need a strong background in agriculture and business.

Agricultural economics—also called agribusiness—prepares you for just such a future. Agricultural economics majors put economic theory into practice. They develop management and financial strategies for the food and farming industries. They focus on understanding and correcting problems in the manufacturing, selling, financing, and distribution of food products. They also work to preserve natural resources and the environment.

If you major in agricultural economics you'll forecast market prices, develop marketing strategies for new products, and participate in case studies of the successes and failures of real products and real farms. You'll also participate in internships with agribusiness companies and government agencies.

SAMPLE COLLEGE CURRICULUM FOR AGRICULTURAL ECONOMICS
Agricultural Commodities Marketing
Agricultural Markets and Prices
Calculus
Economic Development in Developing Countries
Environmental Economics
Farm Business Management
Finance
International Business
Managerial Economics
Money and Banking
Nutritional Science
Principles of Farm and Ranch Management
Principles of Macroeconomics
Principles of Microeconomics
Statistics
Wage and Price Theory

If You Like Agricultural Economics, You May Also Like . . .

Accounting, agricultural business and management, agricultural education, agricultural and biological engineering, agricultural journalism, agricultural technology management, agriculture, agronomy and crop science, animal science, bakery science, business administration and management, computer and information science, economics, entomology, entrepreneurship, feed science, grain science, horticulture, industrial management, international business, international relations, public policy analysis, rural sociology, soil science, statistics, surveying

Suggested High School Prep for Agricultural Economics

Agricultural economics involves lots of critical thinking and heavy doses of math and science. If you think you might major in agricultural economics, try to get as many advanced math courses under your belt as possible while you are still in high school. Experience with computers is good too, as is any introduction you can get to formal logic. Obviously, if your high school offers economics or agriculture courses as electives, you should take them. Biology and chemistry are pretty vital as well.

Fun Facts

Pure Science

According to the T.W.I.N.K.I.E.S. Project conducted during an especially stressful finals week by Rice University students, dehydrated Twinkies burn rather well and are even suitable as firewood in a pinch. However, Twinkies react poorly to microwave cooking, and they pretty much dissolve when immersed in water. Check out the rest of these crucial findings at TwinkiesProject.com.

Start to Finish

Montana State University offers a three-credit course titled Follow the Grain. In the course, students literally follow grain from the laboratories where new strains of wheat are developed, to the fields where wheat is grown, to the silos where it's stored, to the places where it's shipped around the world, and to bakeries the world over where the grain becomes bread. It's an interactive course in which students get to meet geneticists, farmers, grain handlers, grain shippers, and bakers.

Careers and Salary

Annual salaries for freshly minted agricultural economics and agribusiness majors range from $30,000 to $40,000. The average is just less than $30,000. Graduates go to work for global conglomerates such as Purina Mills, John Deere, Nestlé, Dole, and Monsanto.

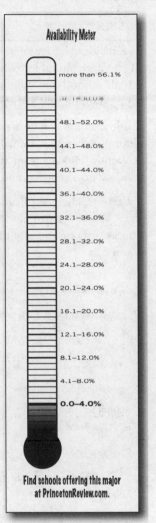

Availability Meter

more than 56.1%

48.1–52.0%

44.1–48.0%

40.1–44.0%

36.1–40.0%

32.1–36.0%

28.1–32.0%

24.1–28.0%

20.1–24.0%

16.1–20.0%

12.1–16.0%

8.1–12.0%

4.1–8.0%

0.0–4.0%

Find schools offering this major at PrincetonReview.com.

CAREER OPTIONS

Bank Officer	Farmer	Researcher
Buyer	Lobbyist	Stockbroker
Economist		

AGRICULTURAL EDUCATION

Basics

A major in agricultural education provides the communication skills, leadership training, and the technical and agricultural knowledge necessary to be certified as a teacher of agricultural education, particularly in high schools and community colleges. You can also find employment in agricultural development, personnel training, and sales positions in various agricultural-related industries.

Agricultural teachers need a broad background in agriculture. As such, expect to take courses in agricultural economics, animal science, entomology, veterinary science, and crop and weed sciences. You can frequently choose from among several certification areas, including horticulture, agribusiness, natural resource management, and agricultural production.

State teacher certification is based on the guidelines from the departments of education of individual states. Wherever you are though, it's a virtual certainty that you'll participate in student teaching at high schools near campus. By the way, keep in mind that you should make your student teaching plans as early as you can.

SAMPLE COLLEGE CURRICULUM FOR AGRICULTURAL EDUCATION

Agricultural Economics

Animal Science

Biology

Chemistry

Dairy Science

Educational Psychology

Feeds and Feeding

History and Philosophy of Extension Education

Instructional Planning, Methods, and Assessment

Leadership and Presentation Techniques

Methods of Teaching Agriculture

Principles of Crop Production

Soil Science

Statistics

Student Teaching

World Food Crops

If You Like Agricultural Education, You May Also Like . . .

Agricultural economics, agricultural and biological engineering, agricultural journalism, agricultural technology management, agriculture, agronomy and crop science, animal science, bakery science, education, education administration, educational psychology, feed science, grain science, horticulture, physical education, rural sociology, technology education

Suggested High School Prep for Agricultural Education

English and history courses are a very good idea, as are agriculture courses (of course) if your high school offers them. In addition, courses in biology, chemistry, math, and earth science will serve you well. Courses in speech (and anything else involving public speaking) are also recommended.

Fun Facts

Did You Know?

According to the folks at Northwest Missouri State University, there is a critical shortage of agriculture teachers across the fruited plain. Consequently, most agricultural education majors have no problem finding jobs, and starting salaries are fairly spectacular.

Careers and Salary

Beginning salaries for agricultural education majors range from $25,000 to about $34,000 annually.

Average Starting Salaries of Agricultural Education Majors by State

- California: $32,000

- Georgia: $26,000

- Ohio: $31,000

- Oklahoma: $31,000

- Virginia: $30,000

- Washington: $32,000

- Wisconsin: $32,000

(Source: www.naae.org)

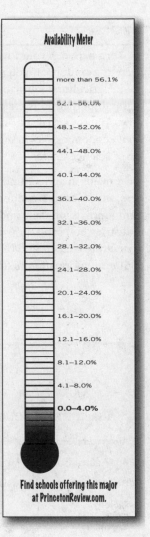

Availability Meter

more than 56.1%

52.1–56.0%

48.1–52.0%

44.1–48.0%

40.1–44.0%

36.1–40.0%

32.1–36.0%

28.1–32.0%

24.1–28.0%

20.1–24.0%

16.1–20.0%

12.1–16.0%

8.1–12.0%

4.1–8.0%

0.0–4.0%

Find schools offering this major at PrincetonReview.com.

CAREER OPTIONS

Biologist	Farmer	Teacher
Environmentalist/Environmental Scientist	Park Ranger	

AGRICULTURAL JOURNALISM

Basics

Torn between your love for broadcast media and your passion for farming? We know the feeling. Luckily, there is a solution. If you're interested in communicating about science, agriculture, health, or the environment, agricultural journalism (also known as agricultural communication) is just the thing. A major in agricultural journalism is exactly what it sounds like. You take courses in newswriting, advertising, broadcast news, photojournalism, and editing and design. You also take courses in animal and plant science, agricultural economics, biochemistry, and forestry. Upon completion of the major program, you'll receive a bachelor of science degree.

A major in agricultural journalism prepares you for a variety of career opportunities in agriculture, business, and science. Depending on the journalism courses you take, you can apply for editorial positions with farm journals, on daily and weekly newspapers, or in the radio, television, advertising, and public relations industries. You can also work for nonspecialized newspapers and nonfarm radio and television stations. The agriculture background of agricultural journalism majors helps them to organize and transmit scientific and technical information in a way that regular folks can understand.

SAMPLE COLLEGE CURRICULUM FOR AGRICULTURAL JOURNALISM

Agricultural Economics

Agricultural Journalism Internship

Basic Reporting and Newswriting

Biology

Chemistry

Computer Applications in Agriculture

Editing

Entomology

Feeds and Feeding

Horticulture

Investigative Reporting

Photojournalism

Principles of Public Relations

Soil and Crop Science

Writing for Agricultural Media

Writing for Television

If You Like Agricultural Journalism, You May Also Like . . .

Agricultural economics, agricultural education, agricultural and biological engineering, agricultural technology management, agriculture, agronomy and crop science, animal science, feed science, grain science, horticulture, journalism, radio and television, rural sociology

Suggested High School Prep for Agricultural Journalism

If possible, get on your high school newspaper or yearbook staff. If your high school has any broadcast media, join that as well. English and history courses are also a very good idea. As for the agriculture angle, take courses in biology, chemistry, and earth science, and obviously, if your high school offers agriculture courses you should take a few.

Fun Facts

National Agricultural Communicators of Tomorrow (ACT)

The National Agricultural Communicators of Tomorrow (ACT is the organization's acronym) is the dominant student organization in the field of agricultural journalism. It's designed for college students who have a professional interest in the fields of communications and agriculture. If you join ACT—and you should if you major in agricultural journalism—you'll meet students with similar career interests and, more important, be able to schmooze with professionals who can help you land a job out of school. And all this time you thought the ACT was a college admissions exam.

Important Dates in the History of Agricultural Journalism

1810—Agricultural Museum, the first American agricultural periodical, begins publication

1822—First issue of the New England Farmer

1828—First issue of the Southern Agriculturist

1840—Agricultural journalism is permanently established, with about 30 farm journals and a total circulation of more than 100,000

Careers and Salary

The starting salary for agricultural journalism majors ranges from $24,000 to $34,000 annually, depending on location, experience, and area of specialization.

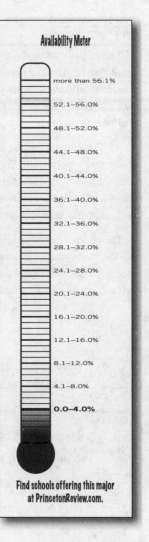

Availability Meter

more than 56.1%

52.1–56.0%

48.1–52.0%

44.1–48.0%

40.1–44.0%

36.1–40.0%

32.1–36.0%

28.1–32.0%

24.1–28.0%

20.1–24.0%

16.1–20.0%

12.1–16.0%

8.1–12.0%

4.1–8.0%

0.0–4.0%

Find schools offering this major at PrincetonReview.com.

CAREER OPTIONS

Biologist	Farmer	Park Ranger
Book Publishing Professional	Journalist	Photographer
Ecologist	Lobbyist	Public Relations Professional
Editor	Media Specialist	Writer

AGRICULTURAL MECHANIZATION

Basics

The history of agricultural mechanization is filled with exciting technological advances and complicated social issues. Agriculture, once a harrowing and back-breaking endeavor, has been vastly improved in the past few centuries thanks to inventions such as the tractor, thresher, and baler. These inventions—and the sweeping changes in the agricultural field that resulted thanks to them—are generally referred to as agricultural mechanization.

As a major, agricultural mechanization aims to expose you to the technological and mechanical aspects of farming equipment. You'll study areas such as electric power and processing, construction and maintenance, and water management. You'll learn the ins and outs of engines, combines, tractors, balers, and other machines. You'll study building construction and learn mechanical skills such as welding and drafting. Ultimately, you'll gain the knowledge you need to design, build, repair, sell, manage, and operate farm equipment.

There are many career options open to you as an agricultural mechanization major. Many students choose to begin their own business; others embark on careers in service management, product service or testing, or agricultural management. Whatever the case, know that you're advancing a field that has allowed agriculture to come amazingly far.

If You Like Agricultural Mechanization, You May Also Like . . .

Agricultural business and management, agricultural economics, agricultural education, agricultural and biological engineering, agricultural journalism, agricultural technology management, agriculture, agronomy and crop science, mechanical engineering

Suggested High School Prep for Agricultural Mechanization

Your best preparation for a major in agricultural mechanization is to take as many advanced-level math and science courses as possible. You'll be using mathematics in many areas of this field and the broader your foundation when you get to college, the better. You may also try to investigate agricultural clubs at your school to gain some knowledge about the farming world.

SAMPLE COLLEGE CURRICULUM FOR AGRICULTURAL MECHANIZATION

Agricultural Electrification

Agricultural Engines and Tractors

Agricultural Machinery

Agricultural Power Units and Control Systems

Agricultural Structures

Environmental Control Systems

Hydraulics in Agriculture

Irrigation Engineering

Mechanization in Agriculture

Soil and Water Conservation Engineering

Fun Facts

Important Dates in Agricultural Mechanization

1904—Benjamin Holt develops the gas-powered tractor.

1907—Henry Ford built his first experimental tractor.

1915—Fenno-Ronning invents the corn silage harvester.

1935—Harry Ferguson develops the hydraulic draft control system for agricultural tractors, greatly improving the operator's ability to control implements, a system that is adopted worldwide.

1940—Self-tying hay baler is invented.

1943—E. W. Rowland-Hill develops the rotary threshing concept.

1947— Frank Zybach invents the center-pivot irrigation machine, revolutionizing irrigation technology.

1948—John and Mack Rust develop the mechanical cotton picker.

1950s—Walter Sohne develops the theoretical basis for soil traction mechanics, important in the design of tractors and tillage implements.

1976—Rotary and tine separator combines are developed.

(Source: National Academy of Engineering)

How Important Could Agricultural Mechanization Really Be?

You may be amazed to know exactly how much agricultural mechanization has helped us. According to *In the Service of Abundance* by John K. Schueller, a farmer could feed only 2.5 people at the beginning of the twentieth century. But thanks to agricultural mechanization, that same farmer can now feed 97 Americans and 32 people abroad!

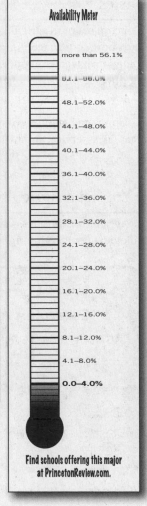

Availability Meter

more than 56.1%

52.1—56.0%

48.1—52.0%

44.1—48.0%

40.1—44.0%

36.1—40.0%

32.1—36.0%

28.1—32.0%

24.1—28.0%

20.1—24.0%

16.1—20.0%

12.1—16.0%

8.1—12.0%

4.1—8.0%

0.0—4.0%

Find schools offering this major
at PrincetonReview.com.

Careers and Salary

The starting salary for agricultural mechanization majors ranges from $25,000 to $35,000, although it is difficult to estimate because their major can take them in so many different directions from manufacturing, to government agencies, to farms. Their salaries will be determined by where they live, what experience they've had, and in what capacity they choose to use their degrees.

CAREER OPTIONS

Auto Mechanic	Machinist	Product Designer
Farmer		

AGRICULTURAL TECHNOLOGY MANAGEMENT

Basics

If you major in agricultural technology management, you'll study agricultural and biological sciences and learn how to manage the production and processing of food and agricultural products. Agricultural technology management courses are mostly practical in nature. You'll spend a large chunk of your time applying physical science concepts to problems in agricultural systems and food production. You'll also spend a good deal of time studying math, chemistry, business, agricultural economics, and computer science.

Upon graduation, agricultural technology management majors frequently find employment in the technical sales, service, and management side of agribusiness and agricultural production.

If You Like Agricultural Technology Management, You May Also Like . . .

Agricultural business and management, agricultural economics, agricultural education, agricultural and biological engineering, agricultural journalism, agricultural mechanization, agriculture, agronomy and crop science, animal science, botany and plant biology, business administration and management, environmental and environmental health engineering, environmental science, feed science, food science, grain science, horticulture, industrial management, international agriculture, landscape horticulture, natural resources conservation, operations management, plant pathology, soil science, sustainable resource management

SAMPLE COLLEGE CURRICULUM FOR AGRICULTURAL TECHNOLOGY MANAGEMENT

Agricultural and Biological Systems

Agricultural Building Systems

Agricultural Chemical Application Systems

Agricultural Economics

Computer Applications in Agriculture

Functional Components of Machines

Global Agriculture and International Relations

Internship in Agricultural Technology Management

Introduction to Agricultural Systems Technology

Irrigation Systems

Production Machinery Systems

Soil Erosion Control

Technology Management

Water Resources and Hydrology

Suggested High School Prep for Agricultural Technology Management

Agricultural technology management involves physical sciences, agriculture, and some math. If you think you might major in agricultural technology management, try to get as many advanced math courses under your belt as possible while you are still in high school. Experience with computers is good too, and courses in chemistry and biology are essential. Obviously, if your high school offers agriculture courses, you should take them.

Fun Facts

Did You Know?

The first state agricultural college in the United States was the Agricultural College of Michigan in Lansing. On May 14, 1857, the six-member faculty began teaching classes to 63 students. By the way, the school was later renamed the Michigan State College of Agriculture and Applied Science.

Did You Know?

Scientists at the Agricultural Research Service in Beltsville, Maryland, have developed a process that allows the fiber from chicken feathers to be used in disposable diapers.

Careers and Salary

The starting salary for agricultural technology management majors fresh out of college is about $24,000. If they are able to take some engineering classes, they can expect to start out at $26,000 or so annually.

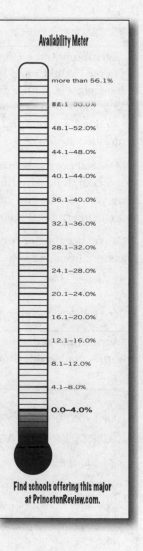

Availability Meter

more than 56.1%

52.1–56.0%

48.1–52.0%

44.1–48.0%

40.1–44.0%

36.1–40.0%

32.1–36.0%

28.1–32.0%

24.1–28.0%

20.1–24.0%

16.1–20.0%

12.1–16.0%

8.1–12.0%

4.1–8.0%

0.0–4.0%

Find schools offering this major at PrincetonReview.com.

CAREER OPTIONS

Construction Manager

Environmentalist/Environmental Scientist

Farmer

Machinist

Service Sales Representative

AGRICULTURE

Basics

Agriculture is the largest and most diverse industry on the planet. It employs no fewer than 20 percent of people in the United States—from traders waving frantically on the floor of the Chicago Board of Trade to bioengineers at huge state universities to farmers in the boondocks of Southeast Missouri. It strikes us as strange that enrollment in most colleges of agriculture has declined lately despite the fact that the demand for food in the world and for qualified employees in the agriculture and food production industry have not diminished at all.

General programs in agriculture are broad in scope. In fact, at many schools, the colleges of agriculture are so comprehensive that you must decide on a much narrower area of study by the end of your sophomore year so that you can complete the particular requirements in that area within four years. Specialty areas include animal science, horticulture, agronomy and crop science, and agricultural economics.

If you decide (and are allowed) to major in agriculture generally, you'll have an endless array of courses to choose from and you can pursue a wealth of well-paying career options in agriculture and agribusiness.

If You Like Agriculture, You May Also Like . . .

Agricultural economics, agricultural education, agricultural and biological engineering, agricultural journalism, agricultural technology management, agronomy and crop science, animal science, entomology, feed science, grain science, horticulture

SAMPLE COLLEGE CURRICULUM FOR AGRICULTURE

Agricultural Economics

Agricultural Mechanics

Agricultural Pollution Control

Agricultural Systems Management

Animal Husbandry

Biology

Chemistry

Computer Applications in Agriculture

Entomology

Farm Management

Feeds and Feeding

Genetics of Livestock and Plant Improvement

Horticulture

Soil and Crop Science

Suggested High School Prep for Agriculture

If you think you might major in agriculture, try to get as many physical sciences courses as you can while you are in high school. Courses in chemistry and biology are essential. Obviously, if your high school offers agriculture courses, you should take them.

Fun Facts

Farming Abroad

Purdue University in West Lafayette, Indiana, offers an array of study abroad programs through its School of Agriculture. The program in Ireland, for example, allows you to live and work on a farm for about seven weeks in exchange for room, board, and spending money. Oh, and you take classes through University College Dublin too.

Purdue's School of Agriculture offers study abroad programs in other far-flung places as well, including France, Honduras, Japan, Mexico, New Zealand, Poland, and Sweden.

Interested? Contact:

International Programs in Agriculture

Purdue University

1168 Ag Admin Building, Room 26

West Lafayette, IN 47907-1168

The World's Largest Cow

The World's Largest Holstein Cow is Sue, a towering work of art in New Salem, North Dakota, that is nearly 40 feet tall, 50 feet long, and visible from more than 4 miles away. It weighs 12,000 pounds and is, not surprisingly, a source of great pride for local dairy farmers. For the record, Sue is not the world's largest talking cow. That honor belongs to a cow in nearby Wisconsin.

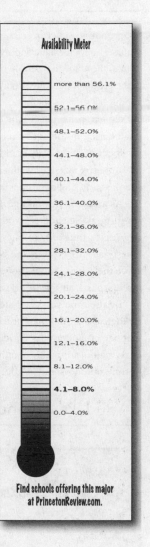

Availability Meter

more than 56.1%

52.1–56.0%

48.1–52.0%

44.1–48.0%

40.1–44.0%

36.1–40.0%

32.1–36.0%

28.1–32.0%

24.1–28.0%

20.1–24.0%

16.1–20.0%

12.1–16.0%

8.1–12.0%

4.1–8.0%

0.0–4.0%

Find schools offering this major at PrincetonReview.com.

Careers and Salary

The average starting salary for an agriculture major just out of college is about $30,000, but it varies widely.

CAREER OPTIONS

Biochemist

Biologist

Botanist

Ecologist

Environmentalist/Environmental Scientist

Farmer

Lobbyist

Park Ranger Teacher

Veterinarian

AGRONOMY AND CROP SCIENCE

Basics

Now here's a down-to-earth major—studying what the soil produces and what we do with it to survive. The study of agronomy and crop science will take you all over the map of crop production, soil management, and food-producing plants. The focus of agronomy and crop science, historically and presently, has been on growing crops and providing safe, edible chow for the people of the planet—from a shiny red apple to a spongy yellow Twinkie. To that end, crop science is the study of the fairly complicated process plants go through to become food for humans, feed for animals, and other products (such as shampoo and pajamas). Crop science also involves the application of biological, chemical, and physical science principles to the cultivation of these plants. The application of biotechnology and agricultural and biological engineering in the agriculture industry is becoming increasingly important as the global economy takes shape and the prospect of genetically engineered foods becomes a reality. What does all this mean for you and your major in agronomy and crop science? Well—in addition to tastier, juicier strawberries, for example—you can expect to see more math-, physics-, and engineering-related course matter.

As an agronomy and crop science major, you'll be immersed in biotechnology, cell biology, plant physiology, genetics, turfgrass science, crop quality, chemistry, computer science, animal sciences, botany, agricultural economics, entomology (that's the study of bugs), plant pathology, and the conservation and improvement of natural resources. Get set to investigate the growth and behavior of crops, the development of new plant varieties, and the soils and nutrients that serve them best. You'll also learn about the production of quality seed, different soil environments, and control of weeds, insects/pests, and plant diseases.

By the time you graduate, you should have a solid understanding of the interrelationships among the physical and biological factors inherent to crop production. Armed with this knowledge, you'll be ready to innovate solutions to all manner of modern-day agricultural problems. This major offers a wide variety of career paths—agronomy and crop science majors are highly sought after in today's economy. Another plus is that agronomists are able to spend a great deal of time outdoors and in cool laboratories (i.e., not behind desks).

If You Like Agronomy and Crop Science, You May Also Like . . .

Agricultural economics, agricultural and biological engineering, agricultural technology management, agriculture, animal science, atmospheric science, biochemistry, biology, botany and plant biology, cell biology, chemistry, ecology, entomology, environmental science, feed science, forestry, genetics, geology, grain science, horticulture, microbiology, natural resources conservation, plant pathology, soil science, sustainable resource management

Suggested High School Prep for Agronomy and Crop Science

You don't need to know anything about agronomy and crop science to major in it, but having an enduring love of biology and the physical sciences will help you immensely. Take all the biology and chemistry courses that your high school offers—as well as agriculture courses, should those be offered. Learn everything you can learn about climate, soil, water, and plants both in and out of the classroom. Also, get used to working outdoors and in laboratories. Familiarity with computers won't hurt either. Seek out volunteer opportunities that offer hands-on experience in the field.

SAMPLE COLLEGE CURRICULUM FOR AGRONOMY AND CROP SCIENCE

Biochemistry

Chemistry

Crop Plant Development

Entomology

Genetics

Grain Crops

Grassland Management

Pest Control and Management

Plant Biology

Plant Breeding

Plant Physiology

Seed Science

Soil Management

Weed Science

Fun Facts

Did You Know?

One bushel of wheat will produce 73 one-pound loaves of bread. In case you were wondering, that's enough of the stuff of life to provide an ordinary human with two slices for each meal for 195 days

Top of the Crop

Top Five Cotton-Producing States

Texas

California

Mississippi

Arkansas

Georgia

Top Five Potato-Producing States

Idaho

Washington

Colorado

North Dakota

Wisconsin

Top Five Oat-Producing States

North Dakota

South Dakota

Wisconsin

Minnesota

Iowa

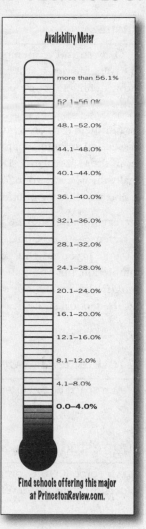

Availability Meter

more than 56.1%

52.1–56.0%

48.1–52.0%

44.1–48.0%

40.1–44.0%

36.1–40.0%

32.1–36.0%

28.1–32.0%

24.1–28.0%

20.1–24.0%

16.1–20.0%

12.1–16.0%

8.1–12.0%

4.1–8.0%

0.0–4.0%

Find schools offering this major at PrincetonReview.com.

Careers and Salary

The average starting salary for an agronomy and crop science major is about $26,000 to $30,000.

CAREER OPTIONS		
Biologist	Environmentalist/Environmental Scientist	Geneticist
Botanist		Lobbyist
Ecologist	Farmer	

AIR FORCE R.O.T.C.

Basics

Okay, so you've memorized every line from *Top Gun* and you know the difference between an F14 and an F16 fighter jet. It still can't compare with knowing how to do a double barrel roll while going mach two, and it definitely won't compare with the skills training that only an Air Force R.O.T.C. program can offer you.

Although Air Force R.O.T.C. is technically not a major, it is still an intense two- or four-year program of classes and activities that will take you through all of the necessary steps to becoming a commissioned officer in the U.S. Air Force. Does this mean you'll get to fly? Yes, if you're good enough. Does this mean you can finally throw away your *Top Gun* poster and live the real thing? Definitely. Does this mean you can still major in fine arts, history, political science, physics, or whatever else interests you? Of course.

As with other R.O.T.C. programs, enrolling does not mean you've signed your life over to the Department of Defense—that is, unless you're taking one of those R.O.T.C. college scholarships that can go as high as $60,000. If you do choose to see it through the long haul, you will not only be a second lieutenant upon completion, but you will also get rigorous physical and academic training that will prepare you for everything from jumping out of helicopters to flying reconnaissance missions over Eastern Europe to mapping out the tactical strategies of war.

If You Like Air Force R.O.T.C., You May Also Like . . .

Aerospace engineering, Army R.O.T.C., aviation, Marine Corps R.O.T.C., military science, Navy R.O.T.C.

Suggested High School Prep for Air Force R.O.T.C.

Air Force R.O.T.C. programs are looking for strong, intelligent leaders with a wide array of skills. Strong leadership skills are developed and demonstrated through your extracurricular activities, whether they're volunteering, playing sports, or student government.

SAMPLE COLLEGE CURRICULUM FOR AIR FORCE R.O.T.C.

Air Force Leadership and Management

The Air Force Today

The Development of Air Power

Leadership Laboratory

National Security Forces in Contemporary America

Courses in your chosen field of concentration

Fun Facts

Did You Know?

The Wright brothers, after inventing the airplane, built the U.S. Army's first plane, in 1909. It cost $30,000 (the F16 costs $200 million), flew at a speed of 42.5 miles per hour, and was airborne for 1 hour, 12 minutes, and 40 seconds. The F16 fighter jet can fly at an altitude of 40,000 feet and at a speed of 1,320 miles per hour.

Careers and Salary

The starting salary for an officer in the air force is $25,000 plus housing and health insurance.

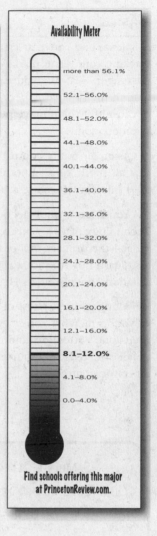

Availability Meter

more than 56.1%

52.1–56.0%

48.1–52.0%

44.1–48.0%

40.1–44.0%

36.1–40.0%

32.1–36.0%

28.1–32.0%

24.1–28.0%

20.1–24.0%

16.1–20.0%

12.1–16.0%

8.1–12.0%

4.1–8.0%

0.0–4.0%

Find schools offering this major at PrincetonReview.com.

CAREER OPTIONS

Air Force National Guard	FBI Agent	Military Officer
Air Force (Officer)	Human Resources Manager	Pilot

AIR TRAFFIC CONTROL

Basics

Next time you're at cruising altitude, say thanks to the air traffic controllers below—they're the ones tracking your plane, marking its progress, and clearing a flight path to assure the safe travel of thousands of passengers just like you each hour. Sound like a stressful job? It is. It's an occupation with tremendous responsibilities, partly because air traffic controllers have life and death in their hands every day and partly because they help move people all over creation, which has exponential effects on the health and growth of an economy.

As an air traffic control major, you'll learn exactly how to keep planes flying safely and how to ensure that air traffic runs smoothly and without delay. Most controllers monitor traffic in and out of airports and alert pilots to changing weather conditions.

You'll study all aspects of flight and how to communicate with pilots and ground crew members. Technology plays a vital role in today's aviation industry, and your curriculum will have you working with radar—the primary tool of the air traffic controller—radio, and other electronic scanning equipment. You'll also learn how to plot a flight path, and your studies will likely include a cooperative stint at the Federal Aviation Administration Flight Control Center.

Along with the stress of the job, however, comes the satisfaction of controlling a 747 with the mere wave of your arm. What you say goes. And they better listen. Air traffic control requires a Zen master's ability to focus one's attention, and it doesn't hurt to possess nerves of steel. If you work well under pressure, are detail oriented, can multitask effectively, and are well organized, you've got the right stuff to succeed as an air traffic controller.

SAMPLE COLLEGE CURRICULUM FOR AIR TRAFFIC CONTROL

Advanced Radar

Aeronautical Science

Air Transportation Analysis

Airport Management

Aviation Communications

Aviation Human Factors

Aviation Law

Geography of Transportation

Meteorology

The National Aviation System

Principles of Air Traffic Control

If You Like Air Traffic Control, You May Also Like . . .

Aerospace engineering, Air Force R.O.T.C., astrophysics, atmospheric science, aviation

Suggested High School Prep for Air Traffic Control

Since careful attention to detail and supreme organization are key to this field, almost all of your high school courses can serve as useful preparation for this major. Consider also the importance of computer classes—the more you know, the easier it will be to learn the advanced technology knowledge required of an air traffic controller. Upper-level math courses, as well as English, languages, and business courses, could prove valuable in college and beyond.

Fun Facts

Pushing Tin

"Pushing tin" is a phrase used to describe what air traffic controllers do for a living. It's also the name of a fun fictional account of the pressures of their profession, starring John Cusack and Billy Bob Thornton as rival air traffic controllers. The movie, directed by Mike Newell, is based on an article from the *New York Times Sunday Magazine* by Darcy Frey titled "Something's Got to Give."

The Real Deal

Want to learn more about what being an air traffic controller is really like? *Vectors to Spare: The Life of an Air Traffic Controller* by Milovan S. Brenlove may give you some insights. Brenlove was an air traffic controller for 12 years, so his story is worth a read.

Window of Opportunity

In addition to meeting a stringent set of requirements, applicants for air traffic control positions in airport towers or en route centers must be younger than 31 years old; retirement is mandatory at age 56.

Careers and Salary

Salaries for air traffic controllers vary, but a good estimate is about $57,000; maximum salaries can exceed $140,000.

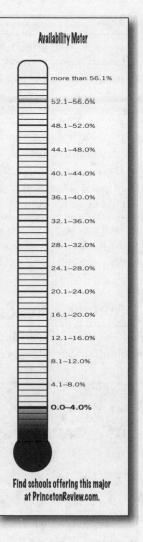

Availability Meter

more than 56.1%

52.1–56.0%

48.1–52.0%

44.1–48.0%

40.1–44.0%

36.1–40.0%

32.1–36.0%

28.1–32.0%

24.1–28.0%

20.1–24.0%

16.1–20.0%

12.1–16.0%

8.1–12.0%

4.1–8.0%

0.0–4.0%

Find schools offering this major at PrincetonReview.com.

CAREER OPTIONS

Air Traffic Controller	**Airplane Dispatcher**	**Transportation Specialist**
Airfield Operations Specialist	**Flight Control Officer**	

AMERICAN HISTORY

Basics

An American history major is really just a specialized version of a regular history major. In practice, if you decide to major in American history, you'll take several American history courses, but you'll also be required to take a wide variety of other kinds of history courses within the larger department.

No matter how thrilling (or dull) your high school American history and civics classes have been, we can pretty much guarantee that American history courses in college will be a lot more exciting. You won't have to memorize a bunch of names and dates. There will be few—if any—matching quizzes in college-level history courses. Instead, you'll pursue major developments in American foreign policy from colonial times to the present, analyze the unique and fascinating contributions of the American West to the evolution of the United States, and discuss Jacksonian Democracy, Reconstruction, Progressivism, American Imperialism, and many other -isms.

But can you get a job if you major in American history? Absolutely. If you major in American history, you'll learn how to think clearly and critically, write clearly and convincingly, and read intelligently. These are exactly the things all employers want.

If You Like American History, You May Also Like . . .

American studies, anthropology, archaeology, architectural history, art history, Asian American studies, biblical studies, classics, East Asian studies, East European studies, economics, English, geography, great books, historic preservation, history, international studies, peace studies, philosophy, political science, public policy analysis, religious studies, rhetoric, sociology, theology, urban studies, women's studies

SAMPLE COLLEGE CURRICULUM FOR AMERICAN HISTORY

African American History 1550–1880

American Democracy

American Economic History

The American Revolution

The American West

Asian American History

Civil War and Reconstruction

The New Deal

Religion in American History

The Sixties

The United States Constitution

United States History 1880 to Present

United States History to 1860

Women in Early and Victorian America

Suggested High School Prep for American History

History in general involves lots of critical thinking and a great deal of reading and writing. If you want to major in American history, you obviously want to take as many courses in American history, civics, world history, and geography as you can. You should also take English composition so you can get good at writing essays. Finally, take foreign language classes because you are almost certainly going to be required to take several foreign language classes as a liberal arts major.

Fun Facts

Did You Know?

The mouths of the president's faces on Mount Rushmore are 18 feet wide.

Did You Know?

Abraham Lincoln's favorite Shakespearean play was *Macbeth*.

A Note About Printing Notes

Currency and stamps are designed, engraved, and printed 24 hours a day on 30 high speed presses. Since October 1, 1877, all U.S. currency has been printed by the Bureau of Engraving and Printing, which started out as a six person operation using steam powered presses in the basement of the Department of Treasury, which now employs 2,300 employees and occupies 25 acres of floor space in two buildings in Washington, D.C. There is also a satellite printing plant in Ft. Worth, Texas. At any one time, $200 million in notes may be in production--95 percent will replace unfit notes, and 5 percent will support economic growth.

(Source: http://www.frbsf.org/federalreserve/money/funfacts.html)

In 1981, President Ronald Reagan appointed Sandra Day O'Connor to the U.S. Supreme Court. O'Connor--a former Assistant Attorney General, State Senator, and Appeals Court Judge in Arizona. She became the first woman to ever serve on the Supreme Court, and she served from 1981 until 2006. The second woman on the Supreme Court was Ruth Bader Ginsburg. She was appointed by President Bill Clinton in 1993.

(Source: http://myweb.uiowa.edu/bdisarro/Fun%20Facts.htm)

President Lincoln kept important papers tucked inside his top hat.
(Source: http://americanhistory.si.edu/kids/funfacts.cfm)

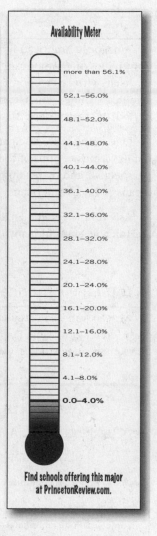

Availability Meter

- more than 56.1%
- 52.1–56.0%
- 48.1–52.0%
- 44.1–48.0%
- 40.1–44.0%
- 36.1–40.0%
- 32.1–36.0%
- 28.1–32.0%
- 24.1–28.0%
- 20.1–24.0%
- 16.1–20.0%
- 12.1–16.0%
- 8.1–12.0%
- 4.1–8.0%
- 0.0–4.0%

Find schools offering this major at PrincetonReview.com.

Careers and Salary

American history majors who look for jobs directly out of college earn an average salary of $30,000.

CAREER OPTIONS

Advertising Executive	Corporate Lawyer	Mediator
Anthropologist	Curator	Politician
Antiques Dealer	Diplomat/Attaché/Foreign Service	Trial Lawyer
Archaeologist	Officer	Writer
Attorney	Editor	
Clergy—Priest, Rabbi, Minister	Film Director	

AMERICAN LITERATURE

Basics

A major in American literature is a specialization of a more general major in English, and as such, many universities offer American literature as a concentration. American literature is as varied and rich as the country itself, with layer upon layer of historical, social, and cultural interpretations of texts. Some of the more significant things you'll learn about are the three significant movements of American writing: the naturalist period, the realist period, and the romantic period.

One of the more fascinating characteristics of American literature is the vast difference in literature written in various regions of the country: literature from the South, West, Midwest, and so on. Each has a unique perspective, and by reading widely you will begin to form a deeper and more personal vision about what it means to be an American.

As with the general English major, you will learn to be a critical reader and a skilled writer, both of which are valuable skills in many lines of work.

If You Like American Literature, You May Also Like . . .

African American studies, American history, American studies, Asian American studies, comparative literature, creative writing, English, English composition, English literature, film, great books, history, Medieval and Renaissance studies, women's studies

SAMPLE COLLEGE CURRICULUM FOR AMERICAN LITERATURE

African American Literature

Colonial Literature

Crime and Punishment in American Novels

Ernest Hemingway

Identity in Literature

Literature of the American West

Literature of the South

Native American Literature

The Poetry of Emily Dickinson

Race and Racism

Survey of American Literature

Travel Writing in American Language

William Faulkner

Suggested High School Prep for American Literature

You should try to take as many English courses as possible, focusing on both reading and writing. Because you'll be looking at American literature through the ages, history courses will give you valuable background and perspective. Spanish courses will be useful if you plan to study literature of Hispanic Americans. Read the newspaper. Remember that you live in the America of today. Knowing what goes on in your nation will give you a deeper perspective of what "being American" really means.

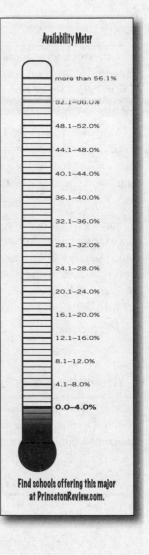

Availability Meter

more than 56.1%

52.1–56.0%

48.1–52.0%

44.1–48.0%

40.1–44.0%

36.1–40.0%

32.1–36.0%

28.1–32.0%

24.1–28.0%

20.1–24.0%

16.1–20.0%

12.1–16.0%

8.1–12.0%

4.1–8.0%

0.0–4.0%

**Find schools offering this major
at PrincetonReview.com.**

Fun Facts

National Book Award

The National Book Award is an annual award given to the best book written in America by an American citizen. Instituted in 1950 by the American Book Publishers Council, the Book Manufacturers Institute, and the American Booksellers Association, the prize is given to the best book in fiction, poetry, nonfiction, and young people's literature. In addition to the prestige that accompanies the award, each winner receives $10,000.

Some of the Pros of Prose

Vladimir Nabokov, J.D. Salinger, Joseph Heller, Thomas Pynchon, Kurt Vonnegut, Jr., Norman Mailer, and Don DeLillo represent a group of writers whose experimentation in style and form during the 1950s has continued to impact American Literature. Nabokov, although Russian-born, is considered to be one of the greatest masters of English prose. Lolita (1955) and Pale Fire (1962), novels with American settings, revolutionized the standard categories for prose and became foremost examples of tragicomedy. Salinger's The Catcher in the Rye, written in 1951, is humorous and horrifying in its portrayal of rebellious adolescence. Catch-22 (1961), a darkly comic and wildly inventive novel by Joseph Heller, uses satire to highlight the insanity of war and the absurdity of military authority.

(Source: http://ca.encarta.msn.com/encyclopedia_761564847_9/American_Literature_Prose.html)

A Poem by a Legendary American Poet, Emily Dickinson

My life closed twice before its close;
It yet remains to see
If Immortality unveil
A third event to me,
So huge, so helpless to conceive
As these that twice befel.
Parting is all we know of heaven,
And all we need of hell.

Careers and Salary

Salaries for literature majors depend mainly on the career courses they choose to follow, but they can expect salaries of about $30,000.

CAREER OPTIONS

Anthropologist	Professor	Translator
Editor	Public Relations Professional	Writer
Journalist	Teacher	

AMERICAN SIGN LANGUAGE

Basics

A theater background couldn't hurt when you enter the study of American Sign Language because often you'll find all eyes on you. This language is not about theatrics, of course, although it can be rather dramatic to watch. The set of hand motions that make up ASL is as varied and intricate as any spoken language, and the study of ASL is, in many respects, similar to studying French, Spanish, or German.

As an American Sign Language major, you'll not only study the signs themselves but also the accompanying facial expressions and body language that are crucial pieces of this unique communication system. Like any other language, it will take time, patience, and dedication to become fluent. Courses will cover translation and transcription as well as the culture of the deaf—their challenges, communities, and perspectives and interpretations of the world.

Some programs employ deaf instructors for the language courses, giving students an enhanced opportunity to truly communicate with the deaf and ask questions about the experiences of the deaf community. If your program offers a concentration in interpreting, you'll gain the skills necessary to become a competent, professional interpreter—a job that could take you around the world. Other programs may ask students to combine their studies in ASL with another academic field such as psychology or education. However you put it to use, ASL is a challenging major that offers abundant rewards for both you and those with whom you interact.

If You Like American Sign Language, You May Also Like . . .

Anthropology, child development, chinese, communication disorders, education, education of the deaf, French, German, Hebrew, Italian, Japanese, linguistics, mass communication, Modern Greek, psychology, Russian, social work, Spanish, special education, speech communication, speech pathology, teaching English as a second language, theater

---

SAMPLE COLLEGE CURRICULUM FOR AMERICAN SIGN LANGUAGE

Beginning American Sign Language

Communication Disorders

Deaf Culture and Community

Interpretation

Introduction to American Sign Language

Sign Language Studies

Transliteration

Internships within the deaf community

Suggested High School Prep for American Sign Language

Like any other language, ASL requires knowledge of more than just "vocabulary." Studying another foreign language in high school would be useful, as would any studies in culture, history, English, psychology, and philosophy. If possible, try to get involved in the deaf community in your area through volunteer work—you may even get a head start on learning ASL.

Fun Facts

Foreign (Sign) Languages

Did you know that sign languages differ between countries and regions just as spoken languages do? Although many of the signs remain somewhat constant, there are differences. British Sign Language is one example that differs markedly from American Sign Language.

French Roots

French Sign Language is thought to be one possible foundation for ASL. FSL was brought to the United States in 1817 by Laurent Clerc, who settled in Hartford, Connecticut, and began the first school for the deaf. Deaf people, however, had already developed a form of sign language on their own, and many of these "natural" signs are still part of the language. The ASL we know today is most likely drawn from both local sign language and FSL.

(Source: http://deafness.about.com)

Move It

Want to see some signs in action? Check out an online Animated American Sign Language Dictionary to see the alphabet "acted out" right on your own computer.

Learning Language Early

Research shows that deaf children who are exposed to a language when they are six months old can and do develop written language skills as early as well as their hearing peers.

(Source: http://www.coloroflanguage.com/quickfacts.htm)

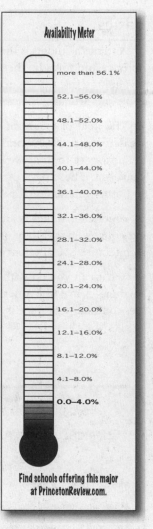

Availability Meter

more than 56.1%

52.1–56.0%

48.1–52.0%

44.1–48.0%

40.1–44.0%

36.1–40.0%

32.1–36.0%

28.1–32.0%

24.1–28.0%

20.1–24.0%

16.1–20.0%

12.1–16.0%

8.1–12.0%

4.1–8.0%

0.0–4.0%

Find schools offering this major at PrincetonReview.com.

Careers and Salary

The starting salary for ASL majors ranges from $25,000 to $40,000, but this varies widely depending on your chosen area of employment. Interpreters generally begin earning about $20,000 for federal jobs. Many interpreters work on a freelance basis and can make anywhere from $35 to $300 a day.

CAREER OPTIONS

Diplomat	Social Worker	Teacher
Interpreter	Speech Therapist	Translator
Psychologist		

AMERICAN STUDIES

Basics

American studies is the academic analysis of the various movements, cultures, and subcultures of North America and (mostly) the United States, both past and present. It is the exploration of all things Americana: revolutions, institutions, transformations, religion, race, gender, sexuality, fine arts, popular culture, baseball, apple pie, artifacts, values, customs, ideals, and everyday experience.

The field of American studies really emerged toward the end of the Great Depression and to an even greater degree after World War II. At first it focused on national identity, national character, and exploring the history of thoroughly American cultural concepts like the frontier, the American dream, and rugged individualism. These days, American studies departments tend to focus more on race, class, gender, ethnicity, and other multicultural issues.

American studies is an interdisciplinary field. Therefore, if it's your major, you are likely to end up taking courses in a variety of disciplines, including (but certainly not limited to) history, English, art history, architecture, social sciences, and geography.

What can you do with a major in American studies? As with any liberal arts major, you can do virtually anything. A major in American studies will mold you into a skilled cultural critic and will enhance your abilities to think, write, speak, and do research—all of which will take you far.

> ### SAMPLE COLLEGE CURRICULUM FOR AMERICAN STUDIES
>
> African American History
>
> American Domestic Architecture
>
> American Literature Survey
>
> American Popular Culture
>
> Cultural Criticism
>
> Fundamentals of Urban Planning and Design
>
> Geography of North America
>
> History of Women in America
>
> Indians of the American Southwest
>
> Race and Ethnicity
>
> Religion in American Culture
>
> United States Constitutional History
>
> United States Social History

If You Like American Studies, You May Also Like . . .

African American studies, anthropology, architectural history, architecture, art history, Asian American studies, economics, English, geography, historic preservation, history, Jewish studies, landscape architecture, philosophy, political science, public policy analysis, religious studies, sociology, theology, urban planning, urban studies, women's studies

Suggested High School Prep for American Studies

American studies involves lots of writing, reading, analysis, and criticism. American history and English composition courses are important. In addition, you'll probably want (or be required) to take a college-level statistics course, so some math isn't a bad idea. Here is part of what the American studies department at Bowling Green State University has to say regarding high school preparation: "An open mind, active imagination, and willingness to engage in serious study of the culture that shapes our lives are the strongest prerequisites."

Fun Facts

Some Examples

The following are a few projects by students in the American studies program at the University of Virginia:

- "*The Simpsons* in Myth and Reality"
- "Coffee Today: Manifestations of the Caffeination Fascination"
- "The Confederate Flag: Controversy and Culture"
- "*Star Wars*: The Toy"
- "The Inventor's Finest Creation: Thomas Edison and the Making of a Myth"
- "*The Dukes of Hazzard*"
- "Barbie: The Image of Us All"

The Things That Count

"Four of the best things in America are Walt Whitman's leaves, Herman Melville's whales, the sonnets of Barnstone, and my daily corn flakes."

— Jorge Luis Borges

Famous People Who Majored in American Studies

Tom Wolfe (author and social critic, Yale University, PhD)

Switching the Soup for Salad

The United States has traditionally been known as a melting pot, but recent academic opinion is leaning toward the image of a salad bowl rather than a melting pot. Due to the diversity in the American culture, there are many integrated but unique subcultures within the United States. An individual in the United States can be associated with cultural affiliations that depend on social class, political orientation, and a multitude of demographic characteristics such as ancestral traditions, gender, and sexual orientation.

(Source: http://en.wikipedia.org/wiki/Culture_of_the_United_States)

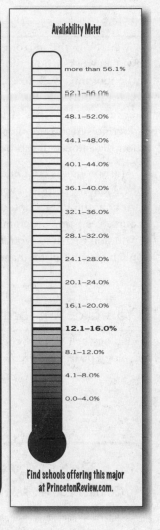

Availability Meter

more than 56.1%

52.1–56.0%

48.1–52.0%

44.1–48.0%

40.1–44.0%

36.1–40.0%

32.1–36.0%

28.1–32.0%

24.1–28.0%

20.1–24.0%

16.1–20.0%

12.1–16.0%

8.1–12.0%

4.1–8.0%

0.0–4.0%

Find schools offering this major at PrincetonReview.com.

Careers and Salary

It varies, but the average starting salary for an American studies major ranges from $24,000 to $30,000.

CAREER OPTIONS

Advertising Executive	Clergy—Priest, Rabbi, Minister	Mediator
Anthropologist	Editor	Philosopher
Antiques Dealer	Journalist	Political Campaign Worker
Archaeologist	Librarian	Social Worker
Art Dealer	Lobbyist	Writer
Attorney	Management Consultant	

ANATOMY

Basics

We look in the mirror every day, but rarely do we stop to think about what's underneath our skin and how it all works—how thousands of parts (some microscopic) rely on one another just to get us out of bed in the morning, walk to class, eat lunch, read a book, or do yoga. As an anatomy major, you'll study all the nitty-gritty intricacies of the structures and functions of the human body. Cells, tissues, muscles, and bones? They're your new best friends. You'll study the major systems of the body too—the nervous system, endocrine system, and musculoskeletal system. Eventually, you'll fancy yourself a bit of an expert on respiration, digestion, and reproduction, among other life processes. In short, you'll just know how bodies work.

Most programs combine anatomy with some studies in physiology, so besides these basics, you'll gain an understanding of how evolution has shaped—and continues to shape—the bodies of vertebrates. You'll learn how the interaction of anatomy, evolutionary biology, and behavior affected our views of nature and of ourselves. Some programs encourage you to participate in research projects or initiate your own. And just so you don't have to wonder if all those pictures in your textbook really add up, you'll head to the dissection lab for a bit of firsthand interaction with your subject: the body.

If You Like Anatomy, You May Also Like . . .

Biology, cell biology, chemistry, genetics, medicine, molecular genetics, neurobiology, neuroscience, pharmacology, pharmacy, premedicine, public health

Suggested High School Prep for Anatomy

If your high school offers anatomy, that's your best bet to get a head start on your anatomical knowledge. Science courses such as chemistry, biology, and physics are also a great chance for building a strong foundation. Most science majors require math components, so advanced courses such as calculus will be invaluable.

SAMPLE COLLEGE CURRICULUM FOR ANATOMY

Cellular and Molecular Foundations
  of Biomedical Science

Developmental Biology

Embryology

Evolutionary Biology

Functional Morphology

Gross Anatomy

Histology

Human Anatomy

Mammalian Evolution

Neuroscience

Physiology

Fun Facts

For Joiners

Anatomy majors are welcome to join the American Association of Anatomists, which is a professional organization supporting anatomical researchers, students, and teachers. The AAA even reserves two seats on its Board of Directors for student representatives.

The Seven Chakras

You'll learn all about bones and muscles as an anatomy major, but your textbooks might not teach you about the seven chakras—the seven points of physical and spiritual energy in the body. The chakras are, according to about.com, the "inner organs of our esoteric anatomy," and consist of

- Root—located at the base of the spine and holds our need for survival, security, and safety.
- Belly—located below the navel and holds our need for sexuality, creativity, intuition, and self-worth.
- Solar Plexus—located below the breastbone and behind the stomach and is our center for personal power, ego, passions, impulses, anger, and strength.
- Heart—located behind the breastbone and between the shoulder blades and is our center for love, compassion, and spirituality.
- Throat—located at the V of the collarbone and is our center for communication, sound, and creative expression.
- Third Eye—located in the middle of the forehead and is our center for psychic ability, intuition, and the energies of spirit and light.
- Crown—located behind the top of the skull and is our center for spirituality, enlightenment, dynamic thought, and energy.

It is important for chakras to be balanced. If they're not, you may feel listless or depressed, and the body may experience disease. A cure for unbalanced chakras? Crystals and gemstones.

(Source: http://healing.about.com)

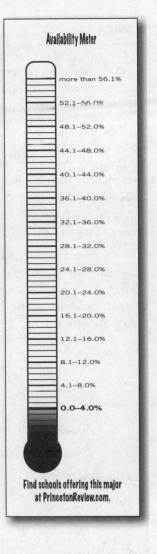

Availability Meter

more than 56.1%

52.1–56.0%

48.1–52.0%

44.1–48.0%

40.1–44.0%

36.1–40.0%

32.1–36.0%

28.1–32.0%

24.1–28.0%

20.1–24.0%

16.1–20.0%

12.1–16.0%

8.1–12.0%

4.1–8.0%

0.0–4.0%

Find schools offering this major
at PrincetonReview.com.

Careers and Salary

The starting salary for anatomy majors is difficult to determine, as how you apply your skills and how much education you pursue will have a major impact. Generally, science majors receive about $27,000 to $32,000 to start.

CAREER OPTIONS

Biochemist	Nurse	Physician Assistant
Biologist	Paramedic	Professor
Coroner	Personal Trainer	Researcher
Dermatoligist	Physician	Scientist
Geneticist		

ANCIENT GREEK LANGUAGES AND LITERATURE

Basics

Do you think Homer's *Iliad* is the greatest contribution ever made to literature? That Plato's *Republic* is the most important political book written in the last 2,370 years? Does Greek just happen to dance off your tongue in a way that Pop Rocks never did? If this sounds like you, it's time to start looking into a major in ancient Greek language and literature.

As the title suggests, a program in Ancient Greek language and lit is going to have two core components: language classes and literature classes. While you may come into the program with some modern Greek under your belt, you'll be asked to beef up your knowledge of the language, and develop a keen awareness of what distinguishes the Greek of Aristophanes (c. 407 B.C./B.C.E.) from the Greek of the guy who leads Parthenon tours (c. 2007 A.D./C.E.). You'll dedicate plenty of time to the literary, philosophical, dramatic, and religious texts that came out of ancient Greece—texts that form the foundations of contemporary Western arts and ideas.

This is not a major for the weak. These texts can be dense, and the concepts can be complex. The language can also be challenging to pick up. (After all, a word as simple as "sun" looks like this in ancient Greek: ἥλιος ο.) But this is also a major that, in the age-old tradition of liberal arts learning, will equip you with sharp analytic, reasoning, researching, and communication skills—the sort of talent prized by employers across the board.

SAMPLE COLLEGE CURRICULUM

Ancient Greek Myths

Aristotle

Beginning Greek

Ethics

History of Ancient Greece

The Iliad and *The Odyssey*

Intermediate Greek

Orators of Ancient Greece

Origins of Western Literature

Pindar

Reading and Writing Greek Prose

Studies in Greek Comedy

Studies in Greek Tragedy

The Three Theban Plays

If You Like Ancient Greek Languages and Literature, You May Also Like...

Ancient Near Eastern and biblical languages, literatures, and linguistics, ancient studies, archeology, art history, classics, comparative literature, Egyptology, great books, history, modern Greek

Suggested High School Prep for Ancient Greek Languages and Literature

Next time that weird English teacher with the thick glasses decides to offer an elective in Greek and Roman literature, take it! In fact, enroll in any literature course you can, particularly of the honors and AP varieties. Even if you're reading Dickens instead of Sophocles, these sorts of courses will help you build the reading and writing skills you'll need in college. And take language classes in modern Greek, if your high school offers them. If not, study another language. Simply wrestling with a foreign language will be a good experience.

Fun Facts

The Meat of the Matter

Vegetarians weren't always called "vegetarians". Until the recent centuries, people who shrugged off meat were often referred to as Pythagoreans. Why? Pythagoras, one of ancient Greece's prized philosophers and mathematicians, was founder of a sect of ascetic folks who believed, among other things, that killing animals made people more prone to kill each other. Thus, they passed on roast goat and filet o' pheasant.

It's All Ancient Greek to Me

There are three primary dialects of Ancient Greek: Aeolic, Doric, and Ionic. Homer composed his two legendary works, *The Iliad* and *The Odyssey*, in a form of Ionic Greek.

Good Things to Know About Greek

The Greek language has been written in the Greek alphabet—the first to introduce vowels—since the 9th century BC in Greece (before that in Linear B), and the 4th century BC in Cyprus (before that in Cypriot syllabary). Greek literature has a continuous history of nearly 3,000 years.

(Source: http://en.wikipedia.org/wiki/Greek_language)

Careers and Salary

Salaries can come in many sizes, depending on the career choices of the individual. A standard beginning salary falls between $24,000 and $30,000. It should be noted, though, that many Ancient Greek language and lit majors matriculate into graduate school.

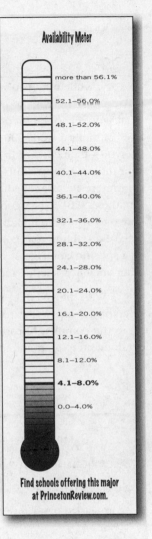

Availability Meter

more than 56.1%

52.1–56.0%

48.1–52.0%

44.1–48.0%

40.1–44.0%

36.1–40.0%

32.1–36.0%

28.1–32.0%

24.1–28.0%

20.1–24.0%

16.1–20.0%

12.1–16.0%

8.1–12.0%

4.1–8.0%

0.0–4.0%

Find schools offering this major at PrincetonReview.com.

CAREER OPTIONS

Editor	Political Scientist	Translator
Librarian	Professor	Travel Guide
Philosopher	Teacher	Writer

ANCIENT NEAR EASTERN AND BIBLICAL LANGUAGES, LITERATURES, AND LINGUISTICS

Basics

For a while now, you've been wondering what it would be like to complement those senior-year honors classes in Greek with some linguistic studies of Aramaic and Urartian. Or maybe you've been curious about what would happen if you mixed a dose of Egyptology with touch of numismatics, and then added a nice layer of biblical studies for good measure. If this sounds like you—strike that: If this sounds even remotely like you—then a major in ancient Near Eastern and biblical languages, literatures, and linguistics may be in your future. As an ANEBLLL major, you'll be given plenty of latitude to shape a course of study that best fits your interests. After all, there's a lot of territory you could cover under this academic umbrella. For this reason, the ANEBLLL is a good fit for students who are diligent and self-motivated. Whether you're primarily drawn to Armenian literature or Aramaic linguistics, cuneiform or Islamic studies, you can be sure that you'll receive a training that combines history, linguistics, archeology, and literature. While you'll probably focus on a specific language or culture, the ANEBLLL major will give you the basic tools you'll need to investigate other ancient societies and extinct languages.

With the ANEBLLL major, you'll be prepared to work in fields as varied as translation, archeology, lexicography, and as a librarian. As contemporary interest in the Middle East continues to grow, so does interest in the complex histories and languages of the region. If the topic really grips you, you may choose to continue on to graduate school, eventually becoming an ANEBLLL professor yourself.

SAMPLE COLLEGE CURRICULUM FOR ANEBLLL

Ancient Near Eastern Civilizations

Art and Archeology of the Ancient Near East

Biblical Inquiries

Classical Arabic Literature

Egyptology

Homer and His World

Intermediate Egyptian Language

Intro to Egyptian Language

Islam: A History

Qur'an in Context

Studies in Cuneiform

Survey of the Middle East

Women and Islam

If You Like ANEBLLL, You May Also Like...

Arabic, archeology, biblical studies, classics, Egyptology, Hebrew, historic preservation, history, Islamic studies, Jewish studies, Middle Eastern studies, religious studies, theology

Suggested High School Prep for ANEBLLL

Because you're likely to spend a lot of time familiarizing yourself with a language or two, it's a good idea to get plenty of experience with a foreign language before you graduate. Greek or Latin is ideal, but French, German, and Spanish will help as well. After all, the techniques involved in learning a foreign language will be fairly similar, even if you're trying to pick up ancient Hittite. Courses in history, literature, and religion will help you build the analytic muscles you'll need as an ANEBLLL major.

Fun Facts

Take a deep breath

Now, recite these names as quickly as possible:

Akkadian, Arabic, Aramaic, Armenian, Assyrian, Babylonian, Cannanite, Egyptian, Elamite, Ge'ez, Greek, Hebrew, Hittite, Hurrian, Latin, Luwian, Lycian, Lydian, Mandean, Palaic, Persian, Phonecian, Samarian, Sumerian, Turkish, Ugaritic, and Urartian.

These are among the languages you may encounter as an ANEBLLL major.

The Write Stuff

Cuneiform, invented by the Sumerians more than 5,000 years ago, is an advanced form of pictographs. Unlike pictographs, however, cuneiform is a more abstract written language that uses wedge-shaped symbols to convey ideas. Eventually, the Assyrians and the Babylonians decided that cuneiform was the way to go, and they adopted it.

Wonder what your name would look like in cuneiform? Visit the University of Pennsylvania Museum of Archeology and Anthropology online (www.upennmuseum.com/cuneiform.cgi) to find out.

Misunderstood Mesopotamia

The history of Mesopotamia begins at the emergence of urban societies in Southern Iraq in the 4th millennium BC and continues to the arrival of Alexander the Great in the 4th century BC, which is considered to be the hallmark of the Hellenization of the Near East, therefore supposedly marking the "end" of Mesopotamia. Even though a "cultural continuity" and "spatial homogeneity" for this entire historical geography, also known as "the Great Tradition", is popularly assumed, the assumption is problematic because Mesopotamia housed some of the world's most socially complex and highly developed ancient states.

(Source: http://en.wikipedia.org/wiki/Mesopotamia)

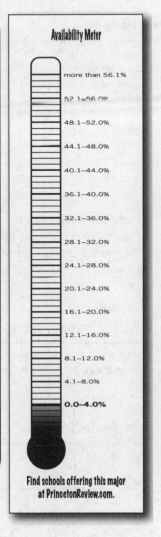

Availability Meter

more than 56.1%

52.1–56.0%

48.1–52.0%

44.1–48.0%

40.1–44.0%

36.1–40.0%

32.1–36.0%

28.1–32.0%

24.1–28.0%

20.1–24.0%

16.1–20.0%

12.1–16.0%

8.1–12.0%

4.1–8.0%

0.0–4.0%

Find schools offering this major at PrincetonReview.com.

Careers and Salary

Salaries vary widely and can be from $25,000 to $50,000. Careers in fields such as archeology will offer the competitive wages.

CAREER OPTIONS

Archeologist	Linguist	Translator
Editor	Missionary	Writer
Lexicographer	Teacher	

ANCIENT STUDIES

Basics

Are you intrigued by the Great Pyramids at Giza, the Code of Hammurabi, or the Mausoleum at Halicarnassus? Do you dream of dusting off the sands of time to examine the world of the past? Consider ancient studies as a possible major.

Ancient studies is the study of ancient civilization, religion, language, and literature. Whereas classical studies concentrate on Greece and Rome specifically, ancient studies also includes Egypt, Israel, Mesopotamia, and other parts of the ancient world. The coursework for an ancient studies major incorporates archaeology, literature, philosophy, art history, military history, architectural history, religious texts, and law. Ancient studies majors study Latin or Greek; they may also do work in another ancient language such as Egyptian, Coptic, biblical Hebrew, Syriac, or Targumic Aramaic.

Ancient studies is a classic liberal arts major. You'll read more 2,000- and 3,000-year-old texts than you thought was possible in four years and read many of the same material more than once. You'll develop a mind that can retain enormous amounts of information and an ability to synthesize ideas into cogent written arguments, a skill that will prove useful in whatever field of endeavor you choose to pursue.

If You Like Ancient Studies, You May Also Like . . .

Anthropology, archaeology, art history, biblical studies, classics, comparative literature, Hebrew, historic preservation, history, Islamic studies, philosophy

Suggested High School Prep for Ancient Studies

Latin or Greek is recommended or required for this major, so take any classes your school offers in those languages. If your school doesn't offer either of these languages, a romance language, such as French or Spanish, will help prepare you for Latin and its intricate declensions. Any and all classes in ancient history or art history will be useful. If you belong to a religious institution that offers classes in biblical Hebrew, you may want to consider taking those as well.

> **SAMPLE COLLEGE CURRICULUM FOR ANCIENT STUDIES**
>
> Ancient World History I–II
>
> Archaeology of Mesopotamia
>
> Classical Art and Architecture
>
> Classical Mythology
>
> Egyptian I–II
>
> Greek and Roman Religions
>
> History of Ancient Israel
>
> History of Egypt
>
> Latin (or Greek) I–III

Fun Facts

For More Information . . .

If you're interested in ancient studies, you may want to check out the following:

- NOVA's site on the seven wonders of the ancient world features a quiz and background on each structure (www.pbs.org/wgbh/nova/sunken/wonders).
- The British Museum has a site on ancient Egypt (www.ancientegypt.co.uk).
- Fordham University's Ancient History Sourcebook covers all areas of ancient history and provides links to online copies of ancient texts (www.fordham.edu/halsall/ancient/asbook.html).

In the Bible

"With the ancient is wisdom; and in length of days understanding."

—Job 12:12

World's Oldest Writing

Egyptologists consider Egyptian hieroglyphs to be the world's earliest known writing system. The hieroglyphic script was partly syllabic and partly ideographic.

(Source: http://en.wikipedia.org/wiki/Ancient_Egypt)

Careers and Salary

The starting salary for an ancient studies major fresh out of college ranges from $25,000 to $35,000.

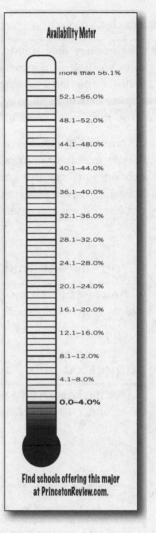

Availability Meter

more than 56.1%

52.1–56.0%

48.1–52.0%

44.1–48.0%

40.1–44.0%

36.1–40.0%

32.1–36.0%

28.1–32.0%

24.1–28.0%

20.1–24.0%

16.1–20.0%

12.1–16.0%

8.1–12.0%

4.1–8.0%

0.0–4.0%

Find schools offering this major
at PrincetonReview.com.

CAREER OPTIONS

Anthropologist	Archaeologist	Consultant
Antiques Dealer	Art Dealer	Philosopher

ANIMAL BEHAVIOR AND ETHOLOGY

Basics

Can dogs understand human language? Why do birds migrate? Do fish feel pain? These are some questions you'll seek to answer as an animal behavior and ethology major. Never heard of ethology? Merriam Webster's dictionary defines it as "the scientific and objective study of animal behavior." Animal behavior and ethology covers a range of scientific disciplines all concerned with what animals do and the neural mechanisms that enable them to do it.

A major in animal behavior and ethology piles on some serious science; you'll take classes like anatomy, biology, genetics, neurobiology, neuroscience, behavioral evolution, zoology, and cognition and sensory perception. You'll use this knowledge to observe and attempt to understand animal sensation, cognition, and behavior. By your junior or senior year, you'll undertake an independent research project in an area of special interest, such as animal communication or social evolution.

If You Like Animal Behavior and Ethology, You May Also Like . . .

Anatomy, artificial intelligence and robotics, biochemistry, biology, biopsychology, chemistry, ecology, entomology, genetics, marine biology, neurobiology, neuroscience, psychology, wildlife management, zoology

Suggested High School Prep for Animal Behavior and Ethology

For this major, you'll want to take biology, anatomy, and—if your school offers it—psychology. While you're at it, classes in chemistry, mathematics, and physics are also not a bad idea.

SAMPLE COLLEGE CURRICULUM FOR ANIMAL BEHAVIOR AND ETHOLOGY

Animal Behavior

Animal Physiology

Behavior of Social Insects

Conservation Biology

Mammalian Embryology

Marine Biology

Nature of Sensing and Response

Neuroscience

Sensation and Perception

Fun Facts

Dinner's Ready!

Honey bees are able to communicate to their hivemates the location, quality, and quantity of a food source through dances and sounds. When food is more than 35 yards away, the bee does a "waggle" dance, consisting of two loops with a straight run in the middle. The length of the straight run communicates the direction of the food, while the looping and buzzing indicate its distance away. When the food is fewer than 35 yards away, honey bees do what animal behaviorists have named the "round" dance. In this dance, the bee turns left and right in circles, and the richer the food source, the longer and more enthusiastic the dance.

(Source: www.discoverymuseum.net)

More About Mammals

There are three main types of mammals: monotremes, marsupials, and placental mammals. Monotremes are the most primitive, and there are only three species: the duck-billed platypus and two species of echidna. These mammals have hair and produce milk, but they also lay eggs. The eggs are leathery, similar to reptile eggs, and hatch into tiny young that are not well developed. The young cling to the fur on the mother's belly and suck at her milk, which comes from pores in the skin instead of from a nipple. Marsupials, such as koalas and kangaroos, have tiny, undeveloped young that grow inside the mother's body instead of in an egg. When they are born, they climb up the mother's fur to a pouch on her belly and settle inside. They latch onto a nipple and nurse almost continually until they have grown enough to leave the pouch.

(Source: http://www.sandiegozoo.org/animalbytes/a-mammal.html)

Otter Behavior

Otters are very energetic and playful. They are curious and intelligent, and they stay busy hunting, investigating, and playing with something. They like to throw and bounce things, wrestle, twirl, and chase their tails. They also chase each other, on land and in the water. Otters also make a variety of sounds, from whistles, growls, and screams to barks, chirps, and coos. All this activity is part of the otters' courtship, social bonding, and communication.

(Source: http://www.sandiegozoo.org/animalbytes/a-mammal.html)

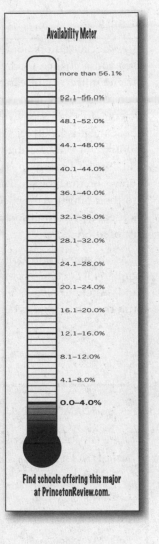

Availability Meter

more than 56.1%

52.1–56.0%

48.1–52.0%

44.1–48.0%

40.1–44.0%

36.1–40.0%

32.1–36.0%

28.1–32.0%

24.1–28.0%

20.1–24.0%

16.1–20.0%

12.1–16.0%

8.1–12.0%

4.1–8.0%

0.0–4.0%

Find schools offering this major at PrincetonReview.com.

Careers and Salary

Animal and behavior and ethology majors will need to do graduate work to advance in this field. However, the starting salary of a research assistant falls between $20,000 and $30,000 a year.

CAREER OPTIONS

Animal Behaviorist	Neuroscientist	Veterinarian
Animal Trainer	Professor	Veterinary Technician
Biologist	Researcher	Zoo or Museum Assistant

ANIMAL NUTRITION

Basics

A specialized offshoot of animal sciences, the animal nutrition major (sometimes called feed science), gives you a chance to chew on the challenging questions of animal diets and behaviors—questions that intrigue university researchers and livestock farmers alike. For instance, how do we gauge the nutritional value of one cattle feed versus another? In what ways do the dietary behaviors of those cattle affect human society? How can we change our feeding practices to reduce animal waste? And how can we raise animals whose meat is healthier for the humans who consume it? It's little wonder that, in a famously carnivorous country that is increasingly concerned with human nutrition and environmental protection, interest in the field of animal nutrition is growing. In a sense, animal nutrition has its fingers in a variety of pies. Obviously, it draws on the biological and veterinary sciences. It also draws on chemistry. (Just ask students a few weeks into their nutritional toxicology class how important chemistry is.) And let's not forget environmental science, economics, and sociology—all of which can play into an animal nutrition degree, depending on your area of interest.

As an animal nutrition major, you can expect to spend much of your time away from traditional classroom. You'll become very familiar with science labs, as well as the herds and flocks on the university's farms. Hands-on experience is a must in this field. With well-rounded training in animal nutrition, you'll be ready to hit the job market, where plenty of jobs await.

SAMPLE COLLEGE CURRICULUM

Animal Food Production and Emerging Technologies

Cattle Nutrition

Domestic Animal Physiology

Equine Nutrition

Ethics of Animal-based Agriculture

General Chemistry

Global Agriculture and Economics

Introduction to Animal Biology

Livestock vs. the Environment

Meat Science

Molecular Biology of Livestock

Nutritional Toxicology

Principles of Animal Nutrition

Swine Nutrition

If You Like Animal Science, You May Also Like...

Agricultural economics, agricultural education, agricultural journalism, agriculture, agriculture and biological engineering, animal science, biochemistry, biology, chemistry, ecology, feed science, food science, livestock management, range and livestock management, wildlife management, zoology

Suggested High School Prep for Animal Sciences

That's right: It's time to get your butt into all the science classes you can—and you'd better do it quick. Animal nutrition is no cake walk, and while it draws from a variety of disciplines, you'll need to have a particularly strong handle on the principles of science if you want to excel in this major. And really push yourself in those biology and chemistry classes. In fact, take the AP exams, if you can. This will show your future professors that you mean business—and it'll build your base of knowledge along the way.

Fun Facts

Holy Cow! Did You Know?

- According to Donna M. Amaral-Phillips, a dairy nutritionist from the University of Kentucky, most cows spend up to eight hours a day chewing on their cud. That's nearly 30,000 chews in a 24-hour period. What exactly is cud? It's food that a cow partially digests, regurgitates, and chews again. Why on earth would a cow do such a thing? Here's where a little knowledge in animal science comes in handy. A cow has four digestive compartments (often improperly called stomachs), and in order for the cow to move its food through the first compartment it needs a healthy dose of the antacids produced by its own saliva. Chewing cud generates saliva, which is swallowed, leading to healthy digestion and plenty of milk production.
- Ruminant = a cud-chewing, even-toed, hoof-footed, four-chamber-digestive-tracked creature. In other words, a cow is a ruminant. As is a bison, a buffalo, a camel, a deer, a giraffe, a llama, a sheep, and wildebeest.

The Hunt is on

Tigers often prefer deer and wild boar for prey. Depending on the habitat, tigers may also hunt antelope, buffalo, guar, domestic livestock, peafowl, monkeys, civets, porcupines, fish, frogs, crabs, large monitor lizards, pythons, and young elephants or rhinos. Grass, fruits, and berries can also be part of a tiger's diet.

(Source: http://www.seaworld.org/infobooks/Tiger/diettiger.html)

The Grizzly Truth

At one point in time, there were about 50,000 grizzly bears roaming through North America. Today, there are approximately 1,000 to 1,200 grizzly bears remaining in five separate populations in the continental 48 states. In Alaska, there are thought to be more than 30,000 grizzly bears, which are omnivorous and will eat vegetation and animals. A grizzly bear's diet will vary depending on what foods are available in a particular season.

(Source: http://www.defenders.org/wildlife_and_habitat/wildlife/grizzly_bear.php)

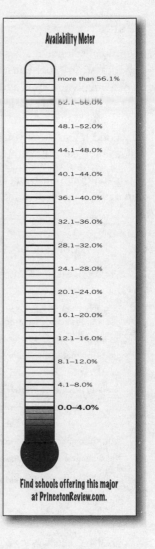

Availability Meter

more than 56.1%

52.1–56.0%

48.1–52.0%

44.1–48.0%

40.1–44.0%

36.1–40.0%

32.1–36.0%

28.1–32.0%

24.1–28.0%

20.1–24.0%

16.1–20.0%

12.1–16.0%

8.1–12.0%

4.1–8.0%

0.0–4.0%

Find schools offering this major at PrincetonReview.com.

Careers and Salary

With a degree in animal nutrition you're likely to catch the eye of employers in both the public and private sectors. Expect a starting salary between $30,000 and $35,000.

CAREER OPTIONS

Agricultural Salesperson/Marketer	Farmer	Product Developer
Animal Nutritionist	Livestock/Facility Inspector	Teacher
Ecologist	Lobbyist	Veterinary Assistant
Environmentalist/Environmental Scientist		

ANIMAL SCIENCE

Basics

Animal science majors enjoy a broad and extraordinarily flexible curriculum. In addition to animal biology, they study biochemistry, molecular biology, and other life sciences as well as animal breeding, anatomy, management, nutrition, and physiology. They apply what they learn to livestock, poultry, pets, laboratory animals, exotic creatures, and pretty much every organism that can be domesticated in any way. An animal science major will make you very appealing to employers even when you're straight out of college. It's also very good if you think you might want to go to graduate school or professional school. And if a major in animal science isn't the paramount training for veterinary school, it's definitely right up there.

In addition to learning about the basic principles of biology, biotechnology, and natural science, you'll likely gain a broad understanding of livestock operations and the agriculture industry. Most animal science curriculums are designed to provide plenty of practical instruction in the biological, physical, and economic aspects of animal management. In other words, when you graduate, you'll know your way around a barn.

If You Like Animal Science, You May Also Like . . .

Agricultural economics, agricultural education, agricultural and biological engineering, agricultural journalism, agricultural technology management, agriculture, agronomy and crop science, biochemistry, biology, chemistry, entomology, feed science, genetics, grain science, horticulture, wildlife management

Suggested High School Prep for Animal Science

If you think you might major in animal science, try to get as many physical sciences courses as you can while you are in high school. Courses in chemistry and biology are essential. Obviously, if your high school offers agriculture courses, you should take them.

SAMPLE COLLEGE CURRICULUM FOR ANIMAL SCIENCE

Most animal science majors specialize in something. Examples of specializations include specific animals (e.g., cattle, poultry, and sheep) as well as business, genetics, and nutrition. There's even a communication specialty at some schools. Whatever your specialization, you are likely to take several of the following classes:

Animal Growth and Development

Animal Nutrition

Animal Physiology

Animal Reproduction

Basic Concepts of Animal Science

Biology

Chemistry

Dairy Systems Management

Equine Science

Feeds and Feeding

Introduction to Agriculture

Livestock Selection and Evaluation

Meat Science

Physics

Fun Facts

A Few Interesting Facts About Cows

- About 3,000 cows give their lives to make the 22,000 footballs the NFL uses each season. This despite the fact that the football is sometimes called a pigskin, not a cowskin, but nevermind.
- The average California cow produces 19,825 pounds of milk each year, more milk per cow than any other state in the nation. That's enough for 128 people to have a glass of milk every day of an entire year!
- A typical cow lives to the ripe old age of seven. The oldest known cow was Big Bertha who was almost 49 when she passed away on New Year's Eve in 1993. Big Bertha produced 39 calves.
- In Sanskrit, the word for war can be translated as "the desire for more cows."

(Source: www.bluemoo.net/45cowfacts.html)

Know Your Pigs

There are eight main breeds of hogs ordinarily used for breeding in the United States.

Yorkshire: The most sought-after breed is white with a long, large frame and upright ears. They do have one drawback, though: they tend to get sunburned.

Chester White: This aggressive breed has droopy ears.

Berkshire: These are black with white noses, tails, and legs, and they have short snouts.

Duroc: These fast-growing hogs are reddish in color and have droopy ears.

Hampshire: This lean breed is black with a white belt that extends from one front leg, over the shoulder, and down the other front leg.

Poland China: Like the Berkshire, this breed has a black body and six white points.

Spot: These are white with black spots, and they grow fast.

Landrance: These have very big, floppy ears and long bodies.

Like Peas in a Pod

Bottlenose dolphins live in fluid social groups called pods, which can vary from 2 to 15 individuals. Several pods may join temporarily to form larger groups called herds or aggregations. Up to several hundred animals have been seen traveling in a herd.

(Source: http://www.seaworld.org/animal-info/Animal-Bytes/animalia/eumetazoa/coelomates/deuterostomes/chordata/craniata/mammalia/cetacea/bottlenose-dolphin.htm)

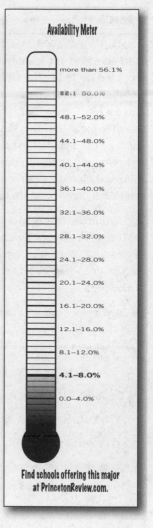

Availability Meter

more than 56.1%

52.1–56.0%

48.1–52.0%

44.1–48.0%

40.1–44.0%

36.1–40.0%

32.1–36.0%

28.1–32.0%

24.1–28.0%

20.1–24.0%

16.1–20.0%

12.1–16.0%

8.1–12.0%

4.1–8.0%

0.0–4.0%

Find schools offering this major at PrincetonReview.com.

Careers and Salary

The average starting salary for an animal science major just out of college ranges from $20,000 to $30,000 annually.

Career Options

Biochemist	Farmer	Teacher
Biologist	Journalist	Veterinarian
Ecologist	Lobbyist	Zoologist
Environmentalist/Environmental Scientist	Park Ranger	

ANIMATION AND SPECIAL EFFECTS

Basics

Many view 1993 as a watershed moment for visual effects in motion pictures. The seamless transition from Stan Winston's animatronic "creature creations" to the groundbreaking computer-generated dinosaurs provided by Industrial Light and Magic in Stephen Spielberg's *Jurassic Park* forever changed the scope of possibilities with regard to the stories filmmakers could convincingly tell—*and* show—to movie goers. There's more groundbreaking work being done every day in animation and special effects by people with amazing ideas and the skills to pursue them. Not all programs combine the two fields, but some do and much of the material overlaps. During your studies, you'll learn the basics of animation, such as stop-motion and two- and three-dimensional animation, as well as how to best integrate all the elements that make an animated character come alive—the drawing itself, the dialogue, and the sound effects. And the characters you create need something to do, so you'll also learn how to plot a story.

If your interest is special effects, you'll learn how to manipulate audiences' audiovisual senses to create your desired impact. You'll gain an understanding of how perception works and how this perception can be "tricked." With your new knowledge and technical skills, you'll be on your way to learning exactly how the jaw-dropping effects that you've always loved in the movies are created—and, eventually, you'll be able to create those effects on your own or with a team.

In your pursuit of a degree in animation and special effects, you'll also dabble in art history. By evaluating great animators and special effects artists of the past and present, you'll begin to perfect your own aesthetic and carry out your own creative visions.

SAMPLE COLLEGE CURRICULUM FOR ANIMATION AND SPECIAL EFFECTS

3-D Character Animation

Animation Storyboarding

Digital Video and Audio

Figure and Context

Figure and Dynamics

Historical and Contemporary Issues in Electronic Art

Image and Color

Motion for Computer Animation

Observation and Color

Perceptual Systems

Raster Imaging for Computer Graphics

Special Effects for Film and Video

Vector Imaging for Computer Graphics

Visual Programming

If You Like Animation and Special Effects, You May Also Like . . .

Advertising, art, art education, computer and information science, computer graphics, computer systems analysis, digital communications and media/multimedia, drawing, engineering design, entrepreneurship, film, graphic art, photography, printmaking, radio and television, visual communication

Suggested High School Prep for Animation and Special Effects

Your best preparation for a major in animation and special effects is to take as many art and computer courses as you can. The more computer programming you can learn now, the better. But don't neglect more traditional courses in the humanities and sciences—many programs in animation are very competitive, and having a broad knowledge base will work in your favor. Also, good writing and communication skills are vital to any career in the arts.

Fun Facts

The First Special Effects . . .

. . . appeared in the 1700s and were used by magicians to spook their audiences. These magicians would "summon the dead" by holding a semitransparent slide with the image of a dead historical figure in front of a light source. When projected onto a column of smoke or a piece of cloth, these figures appeared to be ghosts. Many magicians were condemned for doing this "satanic" work.

(Source: "History of Special Effects—70s" by Patrick James, www-viz.tamu.edu)

Animated Moments in History

- The first animated feature film was made by an American named Winsor McCay, called *Sinking of the Lusitania*. It was created in 1918.
- The first artist to add sound to an animated film was, of course, Walt Disney—he created *Steamboat Willie* in 1928.
- Disney produced the first full-length animated feature film in 1937, *Snow White and the Seven Dwarfs*.
- In 1985, Graphics Group created the first fully integrated CGI movie character for the film *Young Sherlock Holmes*. (The group would later change their name to Pixar Animation Studios and disappear into obscurity.)
- Disney's *Beauty and the Beast* became the first and—to this day—only animated film to ever be nominated for a Best Picture Oscar in 1992.
- Pixar animated *Toy Story* completely by computer in 1995, the first full-length feature film to be produced this way.

(Source: www.fi.edu/fellows/fellow5/may99/History/history.html)

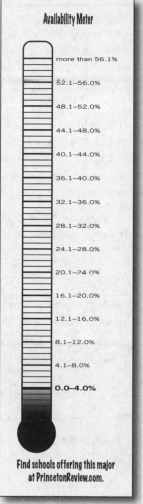

Availability Meter

more than 56.1%
52.1–56.0%
48.1–52.0%
44.1–48.0%
40.1–44.0%
36.1–40.0%
32.1–36.0%
28.1–32.0%
24.1–28.0%
20.1–24.0%
16.1–20.0%
12.1–16.0%
8.1–12.0%
4.1–8.0%
0.0–4.0%

Find schools offering this major at PrincetonReview.com.

Careers and Salary

The starting salary for animators and special effects artists varies widely and depends on what sort of company you work for or how you choose to use your skills. Artists and computer graphics folk usually earn in the $23,000 to $30,000 range, but make a name for yourself . . . and the sky's the limit!

CAREER OPTIONS

Animator	Entrepreneur	Media Specialist
Art Director	Film Editor	Product Designer
Artist	Graphic Designer	Software Developer
Computer Programmer	Internet/Intranet Technologies	Teacher
Content Creator	Manager	Web Master
Digital Artist	Map Maker	Website Designer

ANTHROPOLOGY

Basics

Anthropology is the broad study of humans and human cultures throughout the world and throughout history and prehistory. It's part natural science, part social science, and part humanistic study. If you major in anthropology, you'll compare and contrast biological, social, and cultural similarities and differences among humans and human societies. The topics you'll encounter are pretty much infinite. In one semester, you may study Neanderthals, politics in tribal New Guinea, chimpanzee language, Native American pottery, kinship and religion in Sub-Saharan Africa, or poverty in the large urban centers of the United States.

The field of anthropology is conventionally divided into the following four subfields: archaeology, biological anthropology, linguistic anthropology, and cultural anthropology. Archaeology deals primarily with the prehistoric origins of humankind. Biological anthropology includes the study of human and primate evolution as well as skeletal biology and genetics. Linguistic anthropology concentrates on the history of language and its relation to culture. Cultural anthropology deals with the functions of human societies all over the world.

A degree in anthropology can prepare you for graduate work (of course) and a number of professional activities in the fields of international affairs, medicine, environmental protection, social service, education, and historic preservation.

If You Like Anthropology, You May Also Like . . .

African American studies, African studies, American studies, ancient studies, Arabic, archaeology, art history, Asian American studies, Chinese, classics, comparative literature, criminology, East Asian studies, East European studies, economics, English, English literature, French, geography, German, great books, Hebrew, historic preservation, history, international studies, Islamic studies, Italian, Japanese, Jewish studies, Latin American studies, linguistics, Medieval and Renaissance studies, Middle Eastern studies, Modern Greek, music history, peace studies, philosophy, political science, Portuguese, psychology, public policy analysis, religious studies, Russian, Slavic languages and literatures, sociology, South Asian studies, Southeast Asian studies, Spanish, urban studies, women's studies

> ### SAMPLE COLLEGE CURRICULUM FOR ANTHROPOLOGY
>
> Anthropology of Religion
>
> Biological Anthropology
>
> Cultural Anthropology
>
> Evolution of the Human Species
>
> History of Anthropological Theory
>
> Human Biology
>
> Human Origins
>
> Human Skeletal Anatomy
>
> Indians of North America
>
> Introduction to Anthropology
>
> Linguistics
>
> Modern Human Physical Variation
>
> Origins of Civilization
>
> Peoples and Cultures of the Arctic
>
> Principles of Archaeology

Suggested High School Prep for Anthropology

If you are lucky enough to go to a high school that offers a course in anthropology, you should obviously take it. If not, geography and history-oriented courses are equally good, if not better, preparation for an anthropology major. Any advanced courses you can take in the social sciences, natural sciences, or humanities will be helpful as well. As with any liberal arts major, it's a virtual certainty that you'll be required to take several foreign language courses in college. Plan accordingly.

Fun Facts

Top 13 Movies for Students of Anthropology

At least according to Sharlotte Neely, PhD, Professor of Anthropology at Northern Kentucky University

1. Blade Runner
2. Dances with Wolves
3. The Dark Wind
4. The Emerald Forest
5. Gorillas in the Mist
6. Last of the Dogmen
7. Pathfinder
8. Raiders of the Lost Ark
9. Sarafina
10. Teahouse of the August Moon
11. The 13th Warrior
12. Three Kings
13. Walkabout

Did You Know?

Since World War II, the teaching and study of anthropology has grown tremendously. In fact, from the 1950s into the 1970s, anthropology grew more rapidly than any other academic major.

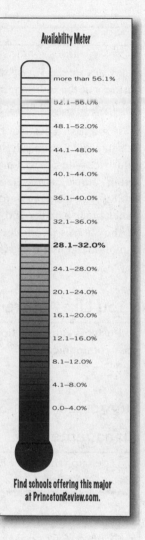

Availability Meter

more than 56.1%

52.1–56.0%

48.1–52.0%

44.1–48.0%

40.1–44.0%

36.1–40.0%

32.1–36.0%

28.1–32.0%

24.1–28.0%

20.1–24.0%

16.1–20.0%

12.1–16.0%

8.1–12.0%

4.1–8.0%

0.0–4.0%

Find schools offering this major at PrincetonReview.com.

Careers and Salary

The average starting salary for an anthropology major fresh out of college is approximately $25,000 to $30,000 per year.

CAREER OPTIONS

Advertising Executive

Anthropologist

Archaeologist

Curator

Diplomat/Attaché/Foreign Service Officer

Professor

Social Worker

Sociologist

APPAREL AND TEXTILE MARKETING MANAGEMENT

Basics

The fashion world is a much larger one than what ends up on the rack at Barneys, J.Crew, or Wal-Mart—as any devotee of *Vogue* will attest. Behind the designers, tailors, pattern makers, and celebrity models is the business of the industry: manufacturing, distributing, marketing, and consumer research. This is the realm of apparel and textile marketing management.

If you have a head for business and a heart for fashion, this major encompasses both aspects of the apparel industry. You'll primarily study marketing research and management as it pertains to the apparel and textile industries—design and manufacturing, sales and distribution, and every aspect of market research and marketing campaigns. You'll learn about textile manufacturing and distribution as well as its relationship to profitability; you'll also research issues of social responsibility and international trade relations. You'll study consumer buying habits and demographics, learning about the factors that explain why high-end denim flies off the shelves in one location but would never fly in another. After graduating, you'll work closely with fashion marketing experts and designers in this vibrant, vital industry.

If You Like Apparel and Textile Marketing Management, You May Also Like . . .

Business administration and management, economics, fashion design, fashion merchandising, marketing, mass communication

Suggested High School Prep for Apparel and Textile Marketing Management

Listen up when your English teacher assigns another five-paragraph essay—you'll need great writing and communication skills in any business program. Balance humanities with math (the more advanced, the better, but there's no need to go crazy). And a foreign language will help: for better or for worse, textile and apparel manufacturing is one of those industries where outsourcing, often to developing countries, is the name of the game.

> ### SAMPLE COLLEGE CURRICULUM FOR APPAREL AND TEXTILE MARKETING MANAGEMENT
>
> Apparel Buying I
>
> Apparel Importing and Exporting I
>
> Clothing Adornment and Human Behavior
>
> Fashion Illustration
>
> Fashion Industry
>
> Merchandising Policies and Strategies
>
> Principles of Marketing Management

Fun Facts

Employ Me!

"Together, the apparel and textile industries are the largest industrial employer in the world. The apparel sector represents about half that global industry. More than 23.6 million workers are employed in the garment industry worldwide. Close to 75 percent are women."

(Source: Maquila Solidarity Network. Check out www.maquilasolidarity.org for more information.)

Where Clothes are Sold

Wal-Mart sells more than $30 billion in apparel a year—more than all department stores combined.

(Source: http://www.oprah.com/tows/pastshows/tows_past_20010531_d.jhtml)

Buying the Brands

Does "more expensive" mean "better"? Consumer Reports tested different brands of cotton knit shirts. The top choice? A shirt from Target that cost nearly $53 less than the designer name brand came out on top.

(Source: http://www.oprah.com/tows/pastshows/tows_past_20010531_d.jhtml)

Careers and Salary

Jobs in the field run the gamut from creative to analytical, and salaries vary widely. Expect entry-level salaries anywhere between $22,000 and $32,000.

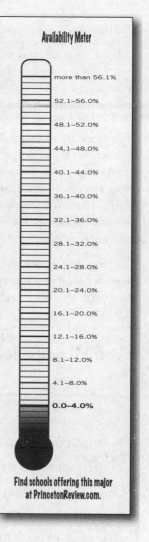

Availability Meter

more than 56.1%
52.1–56.0%
48.1–52.0%
44.1–48.0%
40.1–44.0%
36.1–40.0%
32.1–36.0%
28.1–32.0%
24.1–28.0%
20.1–24.0%
16.1–20.0%
12.1–16.0%
8.1–12.0%
4.1–8.0%
0.0–4.0%

Find schools offering this major at PrincetonReview.com.

CAREER OPTIONS

Advertising Manager	Import Specialist	Marketing Service Manager
Apparel Production Manager	Industry Journalist	Trend Analyst
Fashion Director		

APPLIED HISTORY AND ARCHIVAL ADMINISTRATION

Basics

Libraries, museums, schools, companies, governments—all of these are likely to house archives where documents, publications, photographs, artifacts, art work, and other miscellany from the organization's past are collected, preserved, stored, cataloged, and made available to the public. When you're dealing with thousands (sometimes millions!) of items, maintaining such a facility is no easy task, and this is why the applied history and archival administration major exists. As a student of applied history and archival administration, you'll begin by studying the research methods and ethical concerns of historians. How do historians collect information? How do they interpret it? Why does this matter? These sorts of questions will give way to a wider examination of the concerns and practices of archival work. You'll learn about creating and operating public records services and history-based facilities, archive and records management, preservation techniques, information-gathering procedures, and more. You'll also examine the brass tacks of public organizations, governmental agencies, foundations, and records facilities to get a clear sense of how archival work has been done, is being done, and might be done better in the future.

This is important work. The decisions archivists and applied historian make affect the ways in which we understand and remember the past. With a solid foundation in applied history and archival administration, you'll be able to find your own corner of history to preserve, protect, and enjoy.

If You Like Applied History and Archival Administration, You May Also Like...

American studies, anthropology, archeology, historic preservation, history, museum studies

SAMPLE COLLEGE CURRICULUM FOR APPLIED HISTORY AND ARCHIVAL ADMINISTRATION

American History to 1865

American History since 1865

Archives Administration

Historic Preservation

Historical Editing

History of Historians

Introduction to Historiography

Issues in Public History

The Media and Public History

Museums and Archives

Oral Histories

Technology and Historiography

Suggested High School Prep for Applied History and Archival Administration

History and sociology classes will school you in the subject matter and research methods that you'll be building on as an applied history and archival administration major. If your high school offers business electives, take one or two of those as well; after all, you'll need all the management skills you can muster when you're in charge of your own archive.

Fun Facts

Quick Facts...

About America's most prominent archive facility, the National Archives.

- The National Archives Building is in Washington, DC.
- There are 36 facilities across the country officially designated as National Archives facilities.
- A modest total of 3,000 people work in these 36 facilities.
- Since 1934, nine people have filled the position of U.S. Archivist.
- Since 1952, the Declaration of Independence, the Constitution, and the Bill of Right have been on display in the National Archives Building's rotunda.

(Source: www.archives.gov)

Where's the Paper Trail?

Only 1 percent to 3 percent of all documents used by the United States Federal government are so important for legal or historical reasons that they are archived.

(Source: http://www.archives.gov/about)

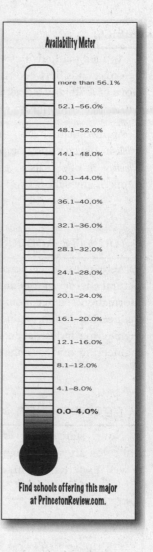

Availability Meter

more than 56.1%

52.1–56.0%

48.1–52.0%

44.1–48.0%

40.1–44.0%

36.1–40.0%

32.1–36.0%

28.1–32.0%

24.1–28.0%

20.1–24.0%

16.1–20.0%

12.1–16.0%

8.1–12.0%

4.1–8.0%

0.0–4.0%

Find schools offering this major at PrincetonReview.com.

Careers and Salary

Archivists and applied historians can expect to start between $30,000 and $40,000. Be aware though, that many employers may prefer candidates with an advanced degree.

CAREER OPTIONS		
Archivist	Consultant	Records Manager
Conservator	Historian	Writer

APPLIED MATHEMATICS

Basics

Applied mathematics is just what the name implies: mathematics applied to real-life situations. Found at the crossroads between theoretical academics and technical science, this major is a good choice if you have a love of math and a desire to do hands-on work. Applied mathematics majors are problem-solvers, creating mathematical models to resolve questions of a physical and theoretical nature.

Applied mathematics majors study more math than mere mortals can comprehend, while also completing work in physics and computer science. In some schools, this major is found under the subheading of engineering; in other cases, it falls under the jurisdiction of the mathematics department. Check both departments of any schools you are considering to find their applied mathematics major or concentrations.

If You Like Applied Mathematics, You May Also Like . . .

Actuarial science, aerospace engineering, agricultural and biological engineering, applied physics, architectural engineering, ceramic engineering, chemical engineering, chemistry, civil engineering, computer and information science, computer engineering, computer systems analysis, economics, electrical engineering, engineering design, engineering mechanics, environmental and environmental health engineering, geological engineering, industrial engineering, mathematics, mechanical engineering, metallurgical engineering, mineral engineering, nuclear engineering, ocean engineering, petroleum engineering, statistics, textile engineering

Suggested High School Prep for Applied Mathematics

Not to state the obvious, but . . . try to get as many advanced math courses under your belt as possible while you are still in high school. A background in physics couldn't hurt, as you'll be required to study it, as well. Experience with computers and programming languages is also good.

SAMPLE COLLEGE CURRICULUM FOR APPLIED MATHEMATICS

Abstract Algebra

Applied Probability

Calculus I–III

Complex Variables

Differential Equations

Discrete Mathematics for Computer Science

Physics I–II

Vector and Tensor Calculus

Fun Facts

For More Information . . .

Learn more about applied mathematics at www.siam.org, the website for the Society for Industrial and Applied Mathematics.

Famous People Who Majored in Applied Mathematics

Arthur C. Clark (University of London)

Euclid (probably studied under students of Plato)

Math Men

Sir Isaac Newton said, "If I have seen further it is by standing upon the shoulders of giants." Newton expanded upon the processes of those who had come before him, and he advanced every branch of mathematical science that was studied during that time. He is also credited for creating some new subjects. Newton is widely regarded as the inventor of modern calculus. In fact, that honor is correctly shared with Gottfried Leibniz, who developed his own version of calculus independent of Newton, resulting in a bitter dispute.

(Source: http://www.mathematicianspictures.com/Mathematicians/Newton.htm)

Careers and Salary

The starting salary for an applied mathematics major fresh out of college ranges from $45,000 to $50,000 annually.

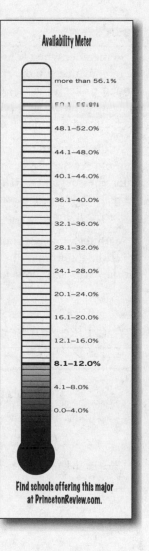

Availability Meter

more than 56.1%

52.1–56.0%

48.1–52.0%

44.1–48.0%

40.1–44.0%

36.1–40.0%

32.1–36.0%

28.1–32.0%

24.1–28.0%

20.1–24.0%

16.1–20.0%

12.1–16.0%

8.1–12.0%

4.1–8.0%

0.0–4.0%

Find schools offering this major at PrincetonReview.com.

CAREER OPTIONS		
Actuary	Computer Operator/Programmer	Nuclear Engineer
Auditor	Mathematician	Statistician

APPLIED PHYSICS

Basics

Remember when your high school physics teacher had you drop eggs out of a fourth-story window, trying to convince you the entire time that the little parachute you had built out of old straws and napkins was enough to keep the egg from breaking? (You really showed her, didn't you?) Well, now you have a basic understanding of the applied physics major; only instead of eggs, you'll be working on subjects such as fluid mechanics and vibration engineering.

At the center of the applied physics major is (as you may have already guessed) physics. And not just the plain old regular physics you may be used to, but quantum physics, lasers, and waves. The applied physics major goes beyond physics into highly specialized areas of concentration that have direct applications to the real world you'll be working in someday. Areas of concentration include, but are definitely not limited to, electrical engineering devices, nondestructive evaluation, and fluid mechanics.

With technology's constantly expanding influence in our society, a major in applied physics could place you at the forefront of the next technology revolution. Not only will your skills be in demand by employers, but they will also allow you the opportunity to help shape the way the future really looks.

If You Like Applied Physics, You May Also Like . . .

Aerospace engineering, applied mathematics, architectural engineering, astronomy, astrophysics, atmospheric science, biochemistry, bioengineering, chemical engineering, chemistry, civil engineering, computer and information science, computer engineering, computer systems analysis, electrical engineering, engineering design, engineering mechanics, environmental and environmental health engineering, mechanical engineering, nuclear engineering, petroleum engineering, statistics

Suggested High School Prep for Applied Physics

Algebra, trigonometry, geometry, chemistry, and physics are definite necessities toward becoming an applied physics major. In addition, you may want to throw in a little calculus, biology, and if you can find the time, advanced quantum mechanics (a sure way of impressing any admissions committee).

SAMPLE COLLEGE CURRICULUM FOR APPLIED PHYSICS

Calculus and Analytic Geometry

Differential Equations

Linear Algebra

Physics I–III

Physics Lab

Quantum Physics

Statistical Physics

Vector Analysis

And don't forget, you will also have to pick a concentration in fields such as the ones listed below.

Atmospheric Physics

Geophysics

Physical Oceanography

Quantum Optics

Fun Facts

Physics Humor

Heisenberg is out for a drive when he's stopped by a traffic cop. The cop says, "Do you know how fast you were going?" Heisenberg says, "No, but I know where I am." (What do you expect? It's a quantum physics joke.)

Applied Physics on the Missing Sock Theory: An Introduction

It has been argued that the act of doing laundry followed the discovery of clothing by only a few weeks. While this fact has been regarded to be fantastically trivial, one cannot ignore the enigmas that the act of doing laundry has created. This is especially true in the age of high-speed washers and dryers. In the early days, the disappearance of articles of clothing could simply be accounted for by saying that the sock was lost in the river. Unfortunately, such excuses can no longer be used today. The availability of high-speed automated washers and dryers has provided a number of fundamental questions that can not be answered using the classical laundry theory (i.e., the river washed the sock away). Such questions include the following: Where, exactly, does lint come from, and why does the quantity of lint change from load to load? If the washing machine is a closed system, how can socks disappear? When using public washing machines and dryers, why is it that every once in a while you will find someone else's socks in your load even when you checked the washer/dryer ahead of time?

The inability to answer these questions using the classical theory of laundry resulted in the development of new theories. This paper is a simple introduction to the quantum theory of laundry. As a result, it only deals with the simplest example in which a sock is analyzed in either a washer or dryer. The mathematics involved in the analysis of a sock in both a washer and dryer and in transition between the two is left for more advanced laundry courses. The first modern attempt to explain the fundamental questions of laundry involved the decay theory. The decay theory states that the quantity of socks in a load can be expressed as a decreasing exponential function of time, which is analogous to radioactive decay. The decay theory easily explains the origin of lint and why new socks tend to release more lint than old socks. However, according to this theory, socks should never completely disappear, or more importantly, reappear. This clearly contradicts everyday experience.

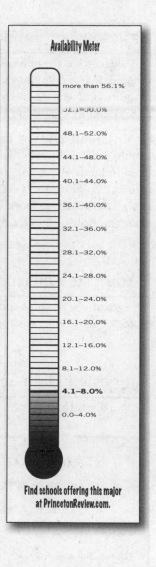

Availability Meter

more than 56.1%

52.1–56.0%

48.1–52.0%

44.1–48.0%

40.1–44.0%

36.1–40.0%

32.1–36.0%

28.1–32.0%

24.1–28.0%

20.1–24.0%

16.1–20.0%

12.1–16.0%

8.1–12.0%

4.1–8.0%

0.0–4.0%

Find schools offering this major at PrincetonReview.com.

Careers and Salary

Starting salaries for applied physics and physics majors are between $40,000 and $45,000.

CAREER OPTIONS

Aerospace Engineer	Electrical Engineer	Physicist
Astronaut	Geophysicist	Robotics Engineer
Astronomer	Nuclear Engineer	

AQUACULTURE

Basics

Aquaculture, the newest and fastest-growing sector of the agriculture business, is the fancy name for fish farming. If you didn't already know, much of the fish we eat is not caught in the wild. Instead, they are domesticated—raised and harvested in controlled environments specifically created for food production. As an aquaculture major, you'll learn the ins and outs of operating a successful fish farm.

First, you'll learn the fundamentals of aquatic and marine biology, as well as basic fish nutrition and health. You'll want your fish farm to replicate wild conditions (while also keeping out predators), so you'll need to know about wild fish, marine plants, and habitats. Next, you'll learn how to select, culture, propagate and harvest fish, shellfish, and marine plants. Finally, you'll take classes in the technical and business aspects necessary to work in this field—how to design and build fish farms, breeding facilities and culture beds, and finally, how to market your product.

If You Like Aquaculture, You May Also Like . . .

Agricultural business and management, agricultural economics, agriculture, animal science, aquatic biology, biology, engineering, environmental science, marine biology, microbiology

Suggested High School Prep for Aquaculture

You'll want to focus on math classes, including algebra, geometry, and trigonometry, as well as biology. In your spare time, get involved with your local 4-H chapter and start making some connections in the agricultural world.

SAMPLE COLLEGE CURRICULUM FOR AQUACULTURE

Agribusiness Systems

Aquatic Biology

Business Management

Cell Biology

Fish Growth and Development

Fish Pathology

Genetics and Stock Improvement

Marine Plants

Nutrition and Feeding

Seafood Technology

Technical Writing

Water Quality Management

Fun Facts

The Top 10 Most Frequently Eaten Types of Seafood in the United States (Pounds Per Capita):

1. Shrimp (3.40)
2. Tuna (2.90)
3. Salmon (2.02)
4. Alaska Pollock (1.20)
5. Catfish (1.15)
6. Cod (0.56)
7. Clams (0.46)
8. Crab (0.44)
9. Flatfish (0.39)
10. Tilapia (0.35)

(Source: www.worldseafoodmarket.com)

Did You Know?

In Louisiana, 50 times more water is used for fish farming than is used for animals that produce meat, poultry, and milk.

Calculating Contributions

In 2003, aquaculture contributed about 31 percent of the total world production of fisheries product. Approximately 90 percent of all shrimp consumed in the United States is farmed and imported.

(Source: http://en.wikipedia.org/wiki/Aquaculture)

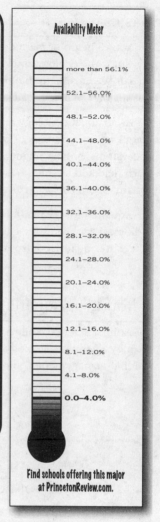

Availability Meter

more than 56.1%

52.1–56.0%

48.1–52.0%

44.1–48.0%

40.1–44.0%

36.1–40.0%

32.1–36.0%

28.1–32.0%

24.1–28.0%

20.1–24.0%

16.1–20.0%

12.1–16.0%

8.1–12.0%

4.1–8.0%

0.0–4.0%

Find schools offering this major at PrincetonReview.com.

Careers and Salary

Starting salaries for an aquaculture major still wet behind the ears earns roughly $24,000 a year.

CAREER OPTIONS

Agricultural Inspector	Fish Farmer	Fish Hatchery Owner
Biologist	Fish Hatchery Technician	Soil and Water Conservation Service Technician
Fish Conservation Aides		

AQUATIC BIOLOGY

Basics

You've heard of marine biology, but what's aquatic biology? Aquatic biology is like marine biology in that you study the ecology and behavior of plants, animals, and microbes living water; however, instead of focusing on salt water, aquatic biology majors study freshwater inland lakes, ponds, rivers, creeks, and wetlands. In this major, you'll cover all aspects of life in fresh water, from algae to salmon to plankton.

As an aquatic biology major, you'll take lots of science classes, including those that deal with the biology, chemistry, and physics of lakes and streams. You'll also learn the basics of geology and hydrology, aquatic ecosystems, botany, mammalogy, mycology (the study of fungi), and ichthyology (the study of fish). You'll learn field and lab methods used to gage environmental conditions of water, and measure the abundance of aquatic organisms such as plankton.

Aquatic biology majors often go on to pursue ecology-oriented careers; for example, they may conduct biological surveys, write environmental impact statements, work on natural resource conservation, or undertake water quality control studies.

If You Like Aquatic Biology, You May Also Like . . .

Animal science, animal behavior and ethology, aquaculture, biology, biotechnology, botany and plant biology, chemistry, ecology, environmental science, geology, marine biology, marine science, microbiology, wildlife management, zoology

Suggested High School Prep for Aquatic Biology

To prepare for this major, it's recommended that students load up on math and science courses, taking biology, chemistry, algebra, geometry, trigonometry, and physics.

SAMPLE COLLEGE CURRICULUM FOR AQUATIC BIOLOGY

Aquatic Plants

Coral Reef and Deep Sea Biology

Field and Laboratory Methods in General Ecology

Fisheries Management

Freshwater Invertebrates

Ichthyology

Limnology

Organic Chemistry

Organic Evolution

Standard Methods of Water Analysis

Fun Facts

Did You Know?

Adult Atlantic salmon average 30 inches in length and typically weigh 7 to 12 pounds. The Latin name for this fish, salmo salar, means "the leaper," and if conditions are right, they are able to jump up to 12 feet into the air!

(Source: www.fws.gov/r5crc/fish/za_sasa.html)

Careers and Salary

An aquatic biology major fresh out of college can expect to earn about $23,000 to $30,000 a year.

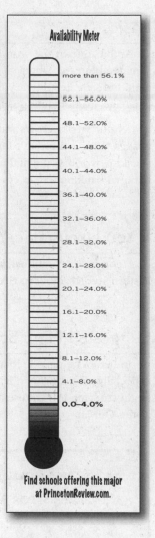

Availability Meter

more than 56.1%

52.1–56.0%

48.1–52.0%

44.1–48.0%

40.1–44.0%

36.1–40.0%

32.1–36.0%

28.1–32.0%

24.1–28.0%

20.1–24.0%

16.1–20.0%

12.1–16.0%

8.1–12.0%

4.1–8.0%

0.0–4.0%

Find schools offering this major
at PrincetonReview.com.

CAREER OPTIONS

Biochemist

Biologist

Consultant

Ecologist

Environmentalist/Environmental
Scientist

Zoologist

ARABIC

Basics

Arabic, one of the world's oldest and most widely spoken languages, is a perfect major for anyone passionate about the language and culture of the Middle East. A major in Arabic will take you through one of mankind's greatest literary traditions, as well as provide you with a thorough understanding of a remarkable language, from its unique alphabet to syntax.

As our world grows more connected, Arabic has established itself as one of its most important languages. With a thorough knowledge and appreciation of the culture, language, and history of the Arabic-speaking world, you will find yourself poised to enter a wide array of different professional fields, from international banking to careers in government and education.

If You Like Arabic, You May Also Like . . .

Hebrew, international business, international relations, international studies, Islamic studies, Middle Eastern studies, modern Greek

Suggested High School Prep for Arabic

In lieu of being able to actually study Arabic in your high school, a strong background in the humanities, especially world history, is excellent preparation for a major in Arabic. In addition, it's never too early to begin studying the culture and history of the Arab-speaking world, including reading such important works as the Qur'an.

SAMPLE COLLEGE CURRICULUM FOR ARABIC

Advanced Arabic Conversation and Composition

Arabic Grammar I–II

Contemporary Arabic Fiction

Contemporary Arabic Poetry and Drama

History of the Arabic Language

Intermediate Arabic Conversation and Composition

Intermediate Literary Arabic Reading

Intermediate Modern Standard Arabic

Introduction to the Qur'an

Modern Arabic Literature in Translation

Fun Facts

Did You Know?

Arabic is spoken in more than 20 countries and is the native language of almost 200 million people.

Did You Know?

How to say "I only speak a little Arabic," in Arabic:

"Anaa ataHaddath faqaT qaliil min aläArabiyya."

(Source: www.transparent.com/languagepages/Arabic/Arphrases.htm)

Alphabet Soup

"The Arabic alphabet derives from the Aramaic script (which variety, Nabataean or Syriac, is a matter of scholarly dispute), to which it bears a loose resemblance like that of Coptic or Cyrillic script to Greek script. Traditionally, there were several differences between the Western (Maghrebi) and Eastern version of the alphabet - in particular, the fa and qaf had a dot underneath and a single dot above respectively in the Maghreb, and the order of the letters was slightly different (at least when they were used as numerals.) However, the old Maghrebi variant has been abandoned except for calligraphic purposes in the Maghreb itself, and remains in use mainly in the Quranic schools (zaouias) of West Africa. Arabic, like Hebrew, is written from right to left. (note the "â" is in between "a" (car) and "e" (bed))."

(Source: http://www.languagehelpers.com/languagefacts/arabic.html)

Careers and Salary

Beginning salaries for Arabic majors range from $24,000 to $30,000 and higher depending upon the professions they choose.

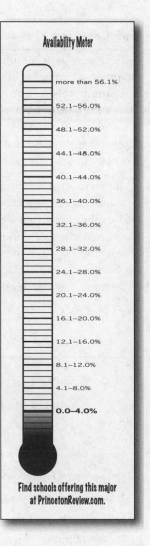

Availability Meter

more than 56.1%

52.1–56.0%

48.1–52.0%

44.1–48.0%

40.1–44.0%

36.1–40.0%

32.1–36.0%

28.1–32.0%

24.1–28.0%

20.1–24.0%

16.1–20.0%

12.1–16.0%

8.1–12.0%

4.1–8.0%

0.0–4.0%

Find schools offering this major
at PrincetonReview.com.

CAREER OPTIONS

Clergy—Priest, Rabbi, Minister	Foreign Exchange Trader	Translator
Diplomat/Attaché/Foreign Service Officer	Journalist	Writer

ARCHAEOLOGY

Basics

Archaeology is a multidisciplinary study of the material past. Archaeologists concern themselves with the physical remnants of ancient cultures and peoples. The things people use reveal much about their civilization, and this sort of revelation is the pursuit of archaeologists. The location of a discovered artifact, its historical context, what's been found near and around it, and our knowledge of customs and traditions are of primary concern to archaeologists. Many describe archaeology as "an anthropology of the past," and this implies that the field is not just about the physical. Together these factors offer a picture of ancient times and places.

If you're an archaeology major, you'll be dabbling in fields such as anthropology, classics, art history, history, and foreign languages. Many universities offer field programs all over the world, so you'll be gaining field experience in, as well as knowledge of, many disciplines—a great major if you have an adventurous spirit and insatiable curiosity. Your life as an archaeology major probably won't resemble Indiana Jones's. It's exact work; you'll spend more time dusting off potsherds with a toothbrush in blistering sun than swinging from vines and killing evil Nazis. But you will be helping to tell the ever-evolving story of how human civilizations have developed, flourished, and ultimately failed.

SAMPLE COLLEGE CURRICULUM FOR ARCHAEOLOGY

Ancient Cultures of South America

Archaeological Field Techniques

Archaeological Method and Theory

Archaeology of the Bible Lands

The Arts of Japan

Egyptian Architecture

Ethnohistory

Foreign language courses

Lost Cities and Ancient Empires

Origins of Human Society

Problems in Archaeology

The Rise of Civilization

Roman Art and Architecture

Settlements and Landscapes

Courses in anthropology, art history, and history

If You Like Archaeology, You May Also Like . . .

African American studies, African studies, ancient studies, anthropology, architectural history, art history, Asian American studies, East Asian studies, geology, historic preservation, history, Latin American studies, Middle Eastern studies, South Asian studies, Southeast Asian studies

Suggested High School Prep for Archaeology

You'll want to take as many science courses as you can—biology and chemistry especially. Writing and language courses will be useful, as will geography, history, and anthropology.

Fun Facts

Ten Novels About Archaeology

1. *Congo* by Michael Crichton
2. *The Professor's House* by Willa Cather
3. *Death Comes as the End* by Agatha Christie
4. *Icy Clutches* by Aaron Elkin
5. *Bridge of Sand* by Frank Gruber
6. *The Plumed Serpent (Quetzalcoatl)* by D. H. Lawrence
7. *Briefing for a Descent into Hell* by Doris Lessing
8. *The Source: A Novel* by James A. Michener
9. *Penny Royal* by Susan Moody
10. *Runestruck* by Calvin Trillin

(Source: Archaeology in Fiction Bibliography by Anita G. Cohen-Williams)

Archaeological Surprise

Thirty-seven years ago, Soviet archaeologists unearthed an amazing find: a ceramic figure of a reclining Buddha, the largest such statue in the world. Found in Nirvana, Afghanistan, among the ruins of the Adzhinatepe Buddhist monastery in 1964, it required nearly 37 years of restoration. The statue went on display in April 2001, at a time when Afghanistan's Islamic Taliban was systematically destroying other important Buddha statues.

Famous People Who Majored in Archaeology

Téa Leoni (Sarah Lawrence)

Glenn Close (College of William and Mary)

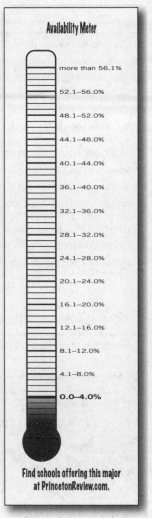

Availability Meter

more than 56.1%

52.1–56.0%

48.1–52.0%

44.1–48.0%

40.1–44.0%

36.1–40.0%

32.1–36.0%

28.1–32.0%

24.1–28.0%

20.1–24.0%

16.1–20.0%

12.1–16.0%

8.1–12.0%

4.1–8.0%

0.0–4.0%

Find schools offering this major at PrincetonReview.com.

Careers and Salary

Starting salaries depend largely on where you live and where and how you choose to practice your skills. The mid-30s is a typical starting point.

CAREER OPTIONS

Anthropologist	Curator	Professor
Archaeologist	Geologist	

ARCHITECTURAL ENGINEERING

Basics

As you know, architects design buildings. Architectural engineers on the other hand, specialize in designing the engineering systems within buildings. Architectural engineering is in many ways similar to civil and mechanical engineering, but it is specifically geared toward the building industry. There are only a handful of architectural engineering programs throughout the United States, and some of them require five years of fairly rigorous and diverse study. For the lucky few who graduate from these programs though, employment opportunities are exceptional and career opportunities are bright.

Architectural engineering majors study the planning, design, construction, and operation of engineered systems for all different kinds of buildings. What kind of engineered systems, you ask? In a nutshell, all those tremendously important things in every building that no one really notices, such as electrical systems, lighting, heating, ventilation, air conditioning, fire protection, plumbing, and structural systems.

If you decide to major in architectural engineering, you'll study the fundamentals of engineering and building construction as well as architectural history and design, math, the physical sciences, computer programming, and surveying.

If You Like Architectural Engineering, You May Also Like . . .

Architectural history, architecture, industrial design, interior architecture, interior design, mathematics, naval architecture, physics, sculpture, urban planning

---

SAMPLE COLLEGE CURRICULUM FOR ARCHITECTURAL ENGINEERING

Architectural Design

Architectural Graphics

Building Materials Science

Calculus

Computers in Engineering

Construction Contracting

Electronics and Electric Circuits

Engineering Systems Mathematics

History of Architecture

Physics

Plane Surveying

Statics and Dynamics

Structural Analysis

Structural Design

Suggested High School Prep for Architectural Engineering

In a word: math. You will do more math as an architectural engineering major (or as any kind of an engineering major) than you could ever shake a stick at in high school. So get used to it, and get good at it. You'll also want to be comfortable working with different kinds of computer applications, and you should take a few art classes to feel comfortable with different design elements.

Fun Facts

Penn State's Study Abroad Program

Penn State University and the University of Leeds in jolly old Leeds, England, have established a study abroad program specifically for architectural engineering majors. Penn State students who have declared a major in architectural engineering enroll at the University of Leeds during the fall semester for a special academic program that includes lectures, design studies, architectural history, and field trips.

Car Characteristics

The Chrysler Building in New York City, which is considered a masterpiece of Art Deco architecture, has distinctive ornamentation of the building that is based on features from Chrysler automobiles. The corners of the 61st floor are graced with eagle replicas of the 1929 Chrysler hood ornaments. On the 31st floor, the corner ornamentation has replicas of the 1929 Chrysler radiator caps.

(Source: http://en.wikipedia.org/wiki/Chrysler_Building)

A Marvel of its Time

The Flatiron Building in New York City was designed by Chicago's Daniel Burnham with John Wellborn Root in the Beaux-Arts style. Because it was one of the first buildings to use a steel skeleton, the building could be constructed to 285 feet (87 m), which would have been very difficult with other construction methods of that time.

(Source: http://en.wikipedia.org/wiki/Flatiron_Building)

Careers and Salary

Starting salaries range from about $30,000 annually at small firms in small cities to a little more than $40,000 at big firms in big cities.

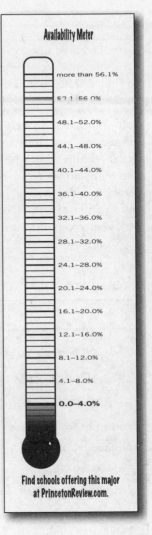

Availability Meter

more than 56.1%

52.1–56.0%

48.1–52.0%

44.1–48.0%

40.1–44.0%

36.1–40.0%

32.1–36.0%

28.1–32.0%

24.1–28.0%

20.1–24.0%

16.1–20.0%

12.1–16.0%

8.1–12.0%

4.1–8.0%

0.0–4.0%

Find schools offering this major at PrincetonReview.com.

CAREER OPTIONS

Architect	Construction Manager	Graphic Designer
Civil Engineer	Electrical Engineer	Interior Designer

ARCHITECTURAL HISTORY

Basics

Architectural history is a unique specialization that combines elements of art history and architecture. Unfortunately, it is offered as a distinct, structured major at only a handful of colleges and universities around the United States. Because of this, students at these schools often double major in architectural history and something else.

If you decide to major in architectural history, you'll gain a strong academic grounding in history (through the lens of its architecture), the growth of urban areas, and architectural theory across countless periods, cultures, and styles. You'll spend plenty of time studying grand monuments, famous palaces, and glorious temples (of course, of course), but you'll also have the opportunity to learn about the architecture of villages, farms, and small houses. And you'll develop technical skills. By the time you graduate, you'll know how to generate architectural graphics and three-dimensional computer models with the best of them, and you'll almost certainly have a working knowledge of the modern methods of historic preservation.

If You Like Architectural History, You May Also Like . . .

American history, architecture, art, civil engineering, engineering design, graphic design, industrial design, interior architecture, interior design, history, landscape architecture, naval architecture

SAMPLE COLLEGE CURRICULUM FOR ARCHITECTURAL HISTORY

Ancient Art and Architecture

Architectural Design

Architectural Drawing

Architectural Theory and Criticism

Asian Architectural History

Calculus

Construction Technology

Historical Preservation

Medieval Art and Architecture

Nineteenth-Century Architecture

Renaissance and Baroque Architecture

Seminar and Thesis

Specialized courses in the history of architecture

Twentieth-Century Architecture

Western Art and Architecture

Suggested High School Prep for Architectural History

Architectural history involves lots of critical thinking and a great deal of reading and writing. It also involves a flair for art and design. If you major in architectural history, take courses in history and different kinds of art. You should also take English composition so you can perfect your essay writing skills. Drafting wouldn't hurt either, if your high school offers it. Finally, take foreign language classes because you are almost certainly going to be required to take several of them to fulfill your general education requirements.

Fun Facts

Frank Lloyd Wright's Falling Water

This structure, which is located about an hour from Pittsburgh, is a beautiful home and a masterpiece by practically any standard. As the architectural historian Kenneth Frampton notes, "Falling Water defies photographic record. Its fusion with the landscape is total . . . its interior evokes the atmosphere of a furnished cave rather than that of a house in the traditional sense." As beautiful as it is to look at, Falling Water apparently wasn't as nice to live in. The original owner, Edgar Kaufman, Sr., called it Rising Mildew.

Did You Know?

Thomas Jefferson's home, Monticello, was built and rebuilt over a period of more than 20 years, and Jefferson's daughter once remarked that he loved to tear down the walls even more than build them up. The house was completely redesigned at least twice, reflecting Jefferson's evolving tastes and restless mind. He himself seemed to consider Monticello perpetually incomplete; he referred to it as his continuing architectural essay in brick and wood.

Famous People Who Majored in Architectural History

Martha Stewart (guru for stylish living, Barnard College)

Careers and Salary

Because architectural history is a very specific degree program, there isn't much data available. Art history is a pretty comparable subject area, though, and we can tell you that beginning salaries for art history majors who go straight to work after college range from $25,000 to $30,000 annually.

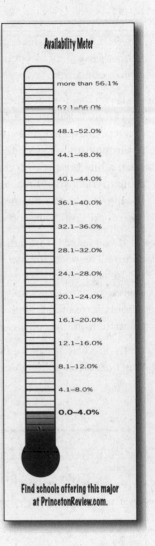

Availability Meter

more than 56.1%

52.1–56.0%

48.1–52.0%

44.1–48.0%

40.1–44.0%

36.1–40.0%

32.1–36.0%

28.1–32.0%

24.1–28.0%

20.1–24.0%

16.1–20.0%

12.1–16.0%

8.1–12.0%

4.1–8.0%

0.0–4.0%

Find schools offering this major at PrincetonReview.com.

CAREER OPTIONS

Archaeologist	Construction Manager	Professor
Architect	Curator	Real Estate Agent/Broker
City Planner	Interior Designer	

ARCHITECTURE

Basics

Architects are concerned with nothing less than the form of the physical environment and its effect on people's lives. Architecture is equal parts art and science, and encompasses technical, social, aesthetic, and ethical concerns.

If you major in architecture, your first year will be crucial as it will lay the foundation for the rest of your education. It will be intense, to say the least. The focus of the first year is training you to understand the conceptual, spatial, and abstract qualities of architecture. You'll learn how to communicate ideas graphically through drawings and models, as well as how to assess and research architectural questions. You'll also learn a bit about architectural history and theory. You'll take some pretty heavy doses of math too. Mostly though, you'll spend tremendous amounts of time agonizing over minuscule details in the studio—alone, in small groups, and one-on-one with faculty members (architecture professors are some of the most dedicated around). You'll also observe more advanced students while they work.

If you make it through your daunting first year, you'll be well on your way to one of two degrees in architecture. The bachelor of architecture requires a bare minimum of five years of study (expect to spend six). The master of architecture requires a minimum of three years of study following an unrelated bachelor's degree or two years following a four-year, pre-professional architecture program. There are about 110 schools across the fruited plain that offer accredited professional programs in architecture, and you need to graduate from one of these programs to become a licensed architect.

By the way, it can be pretty difficult to actually get into the school of architecture at most universities. You'll need to submit a convincing portfolio of creative work and a personal statement.

SAMPLE COLLEGE CURRICULUM FOR ARCHITECTURE

Architectural Design (numerous courses)

Architectural Drawing

Architectural History (numerous courses)

Architectural Theory

Architecture Structures

Calculus

Computer Graphics in Architecture

Construction

Design Fundamentals

Environmental Control Systems

Physics

Trigonometry and Analytic Geometry

If You Like Architecture, You May Also Like . . .

Architectural history, art, art history, ceramics, drawing, graphic art, industrial design, interior architecture, interior design, landscape architecture, mathematics, naval architecture, physics, sculpture, urban planning

Suggested High School Prep for Architecture

Keep in mind that if you want to major in architecture, it's not enough to simply get into a college with an architecture school; you must also be accepted into the architecture school. Take as much math as you can: algebra, geometry, trigonometry, and (if possible) calculus or pre-calculus. You also want to develop a strong background in the sciences (particularly physics) and art. Taking art classes—drawing, painting, sculpture, photography, and the like—will develop your ability to visualize, conceptualize, and create. Familiarity with computers is also a plus, as a lot of design is done with the assistance of software these days.

Fun Facts

From Bauhaus to Our House *by Tom Wolfe*

With his delightfully biting brand of journalism, the one and only Tom Wolfe explains exactly why modern architecture is hideous and yet all over the place. You can read it in one sitting; you'll laugh out loud; and you'll never look at any building constructed between about 1930 and 1990 quite the same way again.

Catholic University of America

This school boasts a bevy of study abroad programs relating to architecture. They include a landscape architecture program in France, a three-week summer seminar in Japan and China, and a design-build workshop in British Columbia. CUA students also have the opportunity to spend an entire semester of their senior year living and studying in Rome or an entire summer touring the architecture of Europe.

Famous People Who Majored in Architecture

Jimmy Stewart (movie star, Princeton University), Robert Venturi (Postmodern architect, Princeton University), John Katzman (founder of The Princeton Review, Princeton University)

Careers and Salary

New graduates with a pre-professional degree can expect internship salaries about $25,000 annually. People with professional degrees who have completed their internships and their registration exams may command salaries of $40,000 or more. Partners in large architecture firms earn considerably more, with income and benefits often exceeding $100,000. Just keep in mind that becoming a partner will probably come considerably later in your architecture career.

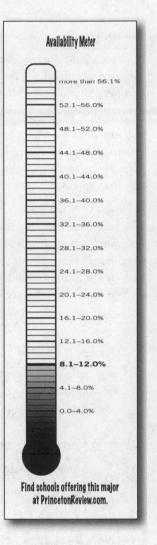

Availability Meter

more than 56.1%
52.1–56.0%
48.1–52.0%
44.1–48.0%
40.1–44.0%
36.1–40.0%
32.1–36.0%
28.1–32.0%
24.1–28.0%
20.1–24.0%
16.1–20.0%
12.1–16.0%
8.1–12.0%
4.1–8.0%
0.0–4.0%

Find schools offering this major at PrincetonReview.com.

CAREER OPTIONS

Architect	Graphic Designer	Professor
City Planner	Interior Designer	Structural Engineer
Civil Engineer	Landscape Architect	

ARMY R.O.T.C.

Basics

Uncle Sam's picture may not be staring you down at the local post office anymore, but you can bet that the army is still looking for a few good men and women who can do several hundred push-ups while reading *Hamlet*. After all, this is basic training, a college education, and much more all rolled into one.

You may be wondering what the heck R.O.T.C. stands for (Reserve Officer Training Corps), or perhaps you just can't get that "Be all that you can be . . ." jingle out of your head. Whatever it is, the army has a special appeal to you: the training, the discipline, the camaraderie, the uniforms. . . . If so, the Army R.O.T.C. program is the place to begin seeking answers to your questions, as well as get firsthand knowledge of what the army offers.

R.O.T.C. is not a major in its own right but an elective program that you can choose to take for one to four years. Participating in the program does not automatically bind you to a career in the army, but it does open up a whole new level of hands-on skills training that only R.O.T.C. could provide. Where else could you learn how to rappel from a Black Hawk helicopter while also taking courses in the art of military strategy? In addition to the training you receive, R.O.T.C. programs also provide as much as $60,000 in college scholarships for those who are dedicated to making an eight-year commitment to the army after graduation.

If You Like Army R.O.T.C., You May Also Like . . .

Air Force R.O.T.C., business administration and management, computer and information science, computer engineering, electrical engineering, Marine Corps R.O.T.C., mechanical engineering, military science, Navy R.O.T.C., physical education

SAMPLE COLLEGE CURRICULUM FOR ARMY R.O.T.C.

Administration and Operations

Basic Tactics and Soldier Skills

Contemporary Military Subjects

Introduction to the U.S. Army

Land Navigation and Map Reading

Military Justice and Officership

Military Leadership and Skills

Military Operations, Management, and Ethics

Military Survival Skills for the Small-Unit Leader

Small-Unit Actions

Suggested High School Prep for Army R.O.T.C.

If you haven't learned how to jump from a helicopter just yet, you'll want to start practicing. Aside from that, though, the Army R.O.T.C. program is looking for people with a wide array of skills, especially strong leadership and management skills demonstrated through activities in sports, student government, and public service.

Fun Facts

For More Information . . .

For all of the information you need, check out the Army's R.O.T.C. website at www.goarmy.com/rotc.

Serving Our Country

More than 1.4 million people serve in the active Army, Navy, Marine Corps, and Air Force, and more than 1.2 million serve in their Reserve components, and the Air and Army National Guard. The Coast Guard, which is also discussed in this Handbook statement, is now part of the U.S. Department of Homeland Security.

(Source: http://www.bls.gov/oco/ocos249.htm)

Careers and Salary

The starting salary for an Army R.O.T.C. graduate is that of a second lieutenant and is approximately $28,000 to $36,000; however, these numbers change from year to year. Visit www.goarmy.com to find out the most recent numbers. Free room and board and great medical benefits are included.

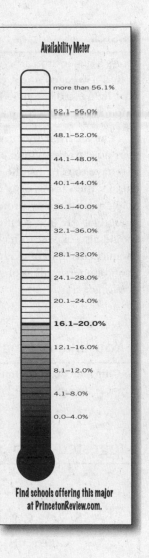

Availability Meter

more than 56.1%
52.1–56.0%
48.1–52.0%
44.1–48.0%
40.1–44.0%
36.1–40.0%
32.1–36.0%
28.1–32.0%
24.1–28.0%
20.1–24.0%
16.1–20.0%
12.1–16.0%
8.1–12.0%
4.1–8.0%
0.0–4.0%

Find schools offering this major at PrincetonReview.com.

CAREER OPTIONS

Aerospace Engineer

Army National Guard

Army (Officer)

Auto Mechanic

Avionics Technician

Career Counselor

Computer Engineer/Systems Analyst

Corrections Officer

Diplomat/Attaché/Foreign Service Officer

FBI Agent

Firefighter

Human Resources Manager

Information Manager

Lobbyist

Machinist

Management Consultant

Military Officer

Organizational Developer

Quality Control Manager

Technician

Telecommunications Specialist

Translator

AROMATHERAPY

Basics

As a major, aromatherapy is still relatively scarce in the traditional university setting. You're more likely to find it wedged into a course or reading assignment on alternative medicines than as a marquee degree. That being said, the field has garnered a substantial following, meaning that folks in the academy are beginning to take notice. In particular, vocational schools with a nutritional bent are hopping on aboard.

As an aromatherapy student, you're likely to learn more than you ever thought possible about how your nose works, where essential oils come from, and what major hurdles holistic medicine still faces. You'll also have to get a handle on the health concerns associated with essential oils, the proper storage of essential oils, the various uses of essential oils—basically, everything you'll need to know before you begin practicing aromatherapy professionally. As you can probably tell, this is not a degree that allows you to just sit around all day in a scented room practicing the art of massage. Well, there may be some of that, but you should also expect to have your nose in the science textbooks, studying the physiology of inhalation, and chemical makeup of tea tree oil. The goal is to not only give you thorough training in aromatherapy, but also a solid understanding of where aromatherapy fits within the matrix of holistic medicine and medical practice in general.

If You Like Aromatherapy, You May Also Like...

Chiropractic, community health and preventative medicine, dietetics, massage therapy, nursing, pharmacy, physical therapy, psychology, respiratory therapy

Suggested High School Prep for Aromatherapy

It's not likely that your high school offers an elective in aromatherapy, so you'll want to prepare yourself by taking courses in health, nutrition, and science. Because many people tout the spiritual benefits of aromatherapy, you might also take courses in philosophy and religion.

SAMPLE COLLEGE CURRICULUM

Anatomy

The Botany Behind the Oils

Herbal Studies

Holistic Medical Practices

Introduction to Biosciences

Massage Therapy

Naturopathy

Nutrition and Lifestyles

Nutritional Toxicology

(Re)Defining Health

Fun Facts

Aromatherapy is the practice of using essential oils to prevent illness and to relieve physical and mental displeasure. The oils are most often inhaled through the nose or massaged into the skin.

Essential oils are extracted from a wide variety of aromatic flowers, fruits, leaves, seeds, barks, and plants. Popular oils include cinnamon, lavender, and tea tree oil.

Balm for Cuts and Scrapes

Ingredients:

- 3 ounces vegetable carrier oil such as sweet almond oil or infused oil such as calendula (infused oil of calendula can supply added therapeutic benefit)
- 1 ounce grated beeswax (Many herbal stores and health food stores sell pure beeswax.)
- 40 drops lavender oil
- 40 drops tea tree oil
- 4 ounce wide-mouth jar

Directions: Place the beeswax in a microwave safe bowl and melt in the microwave using a reduced power setting if you have one. You can also melt the beeswax in a pan on the stove using a low heat setting. Beeswax is hard to remove from pans, so please keep that in mind. In a separate pan, slowly and gently heat your carrier or infused oil. Pour the warm carrier or infused oil into a bowl, add the melted beeswax and then stir very well. Add the lavender and tea tree essential oils and again stir well. Close the jar and wait until the ointment has cooled before using. Remember that all bowl, pans and utensils that you use will be hard to clean afterwards.

(Source: http://www.aromaweb.com/recipes/rbalm.asp)

Insomnia Aromatherapy Blend

Ingredients:

- 10 drops Roman Chamomile
- 5 drops Clary Sage
- 5 drops Bergamot

Directions: Blend the oils well in a clean dark-colored glass bottle. Add 1-2 drops to a tissue and place inside your pillow to aid you in falling asleep.

If you prefer to make a diffuser blend that you enjoy during the hour before bedtime, make a blend with a ratio of 2 drops Roman Chamomile to 1 drop Clary Sage to 1 drop Bergamot and add to your diffuser.

Lavender can also help provide relaxation and drowsiness, but using more than 1 or 2 drops can have the opposite effect.

(Source: http://www.aromaweb.com/recipes/sinsomnia.asp)

Availability Meter

more than 56.1%

52.1–56.0%

48.1–52.0%

44.1–48.0%

40.1–44.0%

36.1–40.0%

32.1–36.0%

28.1–32.0%

24.1–28.0%

20.1–24.0%

16.1–20.0%

12.1–16.0%

8.1–12.0%

4.1–8.0%

0.0–4.0%

Find schools offering this major at PrincetonReview.com.

Careers and Salary

An aromatherapist can expect to make between $25,000 and $30,000 a year. This can fluctuate, though, depending on where you live and the range of services you offer.

CAREER OPTIONS

Aromatherapist	Physical Therapist	Teacher
Massage Therapist		

ART

Basics

What is art? That's an age-old question. Ask just about anyone, and they'll have a unique answer. As an artist, you'll have to find your own definition of what it is. That's a big part of the job.

Art majors tend to be famous on campus for odd fashion, the weirdest dorm rooms, and generally strange behavior. Most enjoy perpetuating this reputation.

Don't be fooled by what seems like simply carefree expression. Most artists are absolutely dedicated to the perfection of their craft, and the art major is a rigorous program. Art majors basically live in studios where they paint, sculpt, design, draw, and illustrate their commentaries about the world in which we live. An art major's curriculum depends largely on the artist's medium, although certain core art classes in drawing, art history, and design are usually required for all concentrations.

Contrary to what you may hear about the starving artist, there is a great demand for people with artistic training, especially graphic designers and those with multimedia skills. Web and software companies hire thousands of artists each year. The advertising and publishing industries constantly need illustrators and photographers. All schools and small studios need art instructors, and museums recruit art majors for staff positions.

If You Like Art, You May Also Like . . .

Advertising, art education, art history, drawing, fashion design, graphic art, interior design, painting, photography, printmaking

Suggested High School Prep for Art

In most cases you will need to have a portfolio of work to be admitted to an art program. When reviewing portfolios, most schools look for strong observational drawing skills, so draw from life as often as you can. Use all resources available at your school. Check out local museums, community colleges, and universities for pre-college programs or seminars. Sometimes museums also offer volunteer opportunities for students.

SAMPLE COLLEGE CURRICULUM FOR ART

Art History I–II

Fundamentals of Design

Fundamentals of Drawing I–II

Fundamentals of Sculpture I–II

Studio (in your chosen medium) I–VI

Fun Facts

Ask Joan of Art!

The name alone makes this site a winner. Ask Joan of Art! is part of the Smithsonian American Art Museum website. You can submit a question or read the FAQ to get information on American artists.

Definitely Not Star Struck

"Well, not bad, but there are decidedly too many of them, and they are not very well arranged. I would have done it differently."

—James Abbott McNeill Whistler (on being asked about the stars one night)

(Source: http://americanart.si.edu/index3.cfm)

Quotable:

"So I said to myself, I'll paint what I see-what the flower is to me but I'll paint it big and they will be surprised into taking the time to look at it-I will make even busy New Yorkers take time to see what I see of flowers."

—Georgia O'Keeffe.

(Source: http://www.artquotes.net/masters/georgia-okeeffe-quotes.htm)

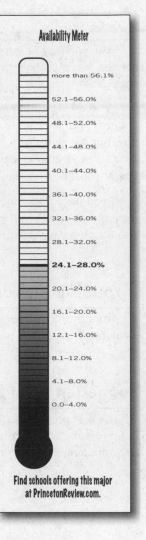

Availability Meter

more than 56.1%

52.1–56.0%

48.1–52.0%

44.1–48.0%

40.1–44.0%

36.1–40.0%

32.1–36.0%

28.1–32.0%

24.1–28.0%

20.1–24.0%

16.1–20.0%

12.1–16.0%

8.1–12.0%

4.1–8.0%

0.0–4.0%

Find schools offering this major at PrincetonReview.com.

Careers and Salary

The starting salary for an art major varies widely. An independent artist could make less than $20,000 a year, but a graphic artist could start at a little more than $40,000. A Web or multimedia artist could make as much as $50,000 to $70,000 fresh out of college. You should expect a range of between $20,000 to $34,000.

CAREER OPTIONS

Animator	Digital Artist	Set Designer
Art Dealer	Fashion Designer	Web Art Director
Artist	Graphic Designer	Website Designer
Clothing/Jewelry/Cosmetics Generalist	Interior Designer	Writer
	Product Designer	

ART EDUCATION

Basics

Now, you may be having flashbacks of field trips to your local art museum during which your teacher's guesses were probably no better than your own, but don't worry, those memories will go away soon enough.

As an art education major you will be responsible for helping to create the next generation of Jackson Pollocks and Mark Rothkos. Not only will you study different artistic methods such as painting and sculpture, but you will also receive the formal training necessary to becoming a great teacher. After all, knowing how to paint doesn't mean you can teach someone else to do the same, and as that old teacher of yours taught you, knowing how to teach doesn't mean you know anything about art.

If you have a genuine love of art and an irrepressible urge to communicate that love and appreciation to someone else, then this just may be the major for you. As you expand your understanding of art, you will also develop your skills as that rare and vital person—an exceptional teacher.

If You Like Art Education, You May Also Like . . .

Art, art history, drawing, education, education administration, education of the deaf, educational psychology, elementary education, painting, photography, physical education, printmaking

Suggested High School Prep for Art Education

The best preparation for an art education major is a strong background in the liberal arts, especially classes in fine art, including art history and studio classes in painting, sculpture, photography, and drawing. You can also supplement your education by making frequent trips to museums and attending art history lectures.

**SAMPLE COLLEGE
CURRICULUM FOR ART
EDUCATION**

Art Criticism

Art Education Core

Art Electives

Art Studio I–II

Art Survey

Introduction to Art Education

Fun Facts

Have Some Bad Art Humor

Sandy imagined herself a brilliant artist, but her teacher said she was so bad that it was a wonder she could draw a breath.

And Some More

Did you hear about the two little boys who found themselves lost in a modern art gallery? "Quick," said one, "run before they say we did it."

Did You Know?

Young people who participate in the arts for at least three hours on three days each week through at least one full year are:

- Four times more likely to be recognized for academic achievement.
- Three times more likely to be elected to class office within their schools.
- Four times more likely to participate in a math and science fair.
- Three times more likely to win an award for school attendance.
- Four times more likely to win an award for writing an essay or poem.

(Source: http://www.artsusa.org/public_awareness/facts)

Careers and Salary

The average starting salary for an art education major is between $27,000 and $31,000.

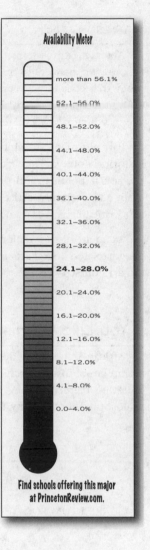

Availability Meter

more than 56.1%

52.1–56.0%

48.1–52.0%

44.1–48.0%

40.1–44.0%

36.1–40.0%

32.1–36.0%

28.1–32.0%

24.1–28.0%

20.1–24.0%

16.1–20.0%

12.1–16.0%

8.1–12.0%

4.1–8.0%

0.0–4.0%

Find schools offering this major at PrincetonReview.com.

CAREER OPTIONS		
Art Dealer	Curator	Teacher
Artist	Digital Artist	Writer
Auctioneer	Graphic Designer	

ART HISTORY

Basics

Abstract Expressionism or Post Impressionism? Surrealism or Dadaism? What's the difference? In addition to knowing answers to questions such as these, art history majors study both the history and aesthetic ideology that goes into a work of visual art. Whether it's painting, photography, architecture, film, sculpture, or multimedia projects, art historians are responsible for helping us to interpret art within the context of the age in which it was created.

Part historian, part cultural critic, art history majors help define a work of art by placing it into its proper historical context. They examine the layers of influences that go into the making of a piece of art, including the social, political, and personal forces underlying an artist's development. With each new artistic movement and each new artist arrives a new way of seeing and interpreting the world. Through the art historian's critical lens, our own ability to share in the artist's insight and vision is enhanced.

As an art history major you will also have the opportunity to cultivate your knowledge of a foreign language, related liberal arts majors, and if you're interested, explore your own artistic inclinations through studio art courses.

If You Like Art History, You May Also Like . . .

African American studies, African studies, American history, American studies, ancient studies, anthropology, architectural history, architecture, art, art education, Asian American studies, ceramics, classics, comparative literature, dance, drawing, East Asian studies, East European studies, English, history, Middle Eastern studies, philosophy, photography, theology

SAMPLE COLLEGE CURRICULUM FOR ART HISTORY

Asian Art

Contemporary Art

Hellenistic and Roman Art

History of Western Art I–III

Introduction to Artistic Media and Techniques

Japanese Art

Modern American Painting and Sculpture

Northern Renaissance Art

Survey of Art History

Writing Seminar in the History of Art

Suggested High School Prep for Art History

Classes in art history and fine arts, including painting, photography, sculpture, dance, and ceramics, are a great way to begin to develop your ability to think critically about art. But a solid background in the humanities and liberal arts as a whole is the best possible preparation if you're interested in majoring in art history. Classes in English, history, philosophy, science, and math are also necessary. In addition, a continued personal engagement with art through frequent museum visits, reading art history books, and study of your favorite artists and their works will help prepare you for this major.

Fun Facts

Did You Know?

In Tim Burton's *Batman* there are numerous works of art, including a Francis Bacon painting that Jack Nicholson's Joker likes so much that he stops one of his goons from defacing it.

That Mysterious Mona Lisa

Many of the paintings and drawings (more than 95 percent) that originate from the Renaissance are not signed or dated, including Leonardo da Vinci's "Mona Lisa." There is also no evidence that mentions the person who is depicted, so the date of its creation and the person that it depicts remain a mystery.

(Source: http://www.kleio.org/monalisa/mlnews_eng.html)

Careers and Salary

An entry-level position as an archivist or curator technician with only an undergraduate degree has an average starting salary range of $22,000 to $30,000 annually. People with advanced degrees can earn from $28,000 to $100,000.

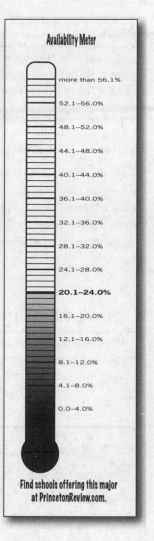

Availability Meter

more than 56.1%

52.1–56.0%

48.1–52.0%

44.1–48.0%

40.1–44.0%

36.1–40.0%

32.1–36.0%

28.1–32.0%

24.1–28.0%

20.1–24.0%

16.1–20.0%

12.1–16.0%

8.1–12.0%

4.1–8.0%

0.0–4.0%

Find schools offering this major at PrincetonReview.com.

CAREER OPTIONS

Anthropologist	Artist	Librarian
Antiques Dealer	Auctioneer	Photographer
Archaeologist	Curator	Professor
Art Dealer	Digital Artist	Web Art Director

ART THERAPY

Basics

This isn't therapy for artists—although given the lives of so many of them, they may need it more than anyone else. But trust us—or at least the psychologists—art can heal. No, it didn't do much for Vincent Van Gogh (or his ear), but it can work wonders for others dangling from a precipice.

It's a stressful world out there, and while a little Prozac and a comfortable leather couch may help some, for others they're just not enough. Consider art therapy, then, to be the merging of Freud and Picasso or the couch and the paintbrush.

Art therapy is a combination of the analytical and the creative. As an art therapy major you'll learn all the tools of the trade that come with being a therapist of those with mental, emotional, and developmental disorders. You'll get to tap into that creative vein of yours as you help your patients learn to communicate their thoughts and feelings through the stories they draw and pictures they paint. After all, the mind expresses itself in many ways, not just through words. Sometimes it takes a blank canvas, paintbrush, and therapist to figure that out.

If You Like Art Therapy, You May Also Like . . .

Art, art education, art history, ceramics, child development, counseling, drawing, educational psychology, human development, illustration, industrial psychology, music therapy, occupational therapy, painting, photography, physical therapy, physiological psychology, psychology, sculpture, social psychology, social work

---

SAMPLE COLLEGE CURRICULUM FOR ART THERAPY

Abnormal Psychology

Art History

Assessment in Art Therapy

Child Development

Clinical Applications in Art Therapy

Counseling

Foundations in Studio Art

Imagery and Metaphor

Painting and Drawing

Principles of Psychology

Psychology of Personality

Quantitative Reasoning

Theory of Art Therapy

Suggested High School Prep for Art Therapy

In addition to taking introductory psychology courses at your high school and having a strong background in art and art history, students should also prepare themselves by building a solid foundation in science, math, English, and computers. Volunteering at a local hospital or mental health clinic is also a great opportunity to gain firsthand experience in the field.

Fun Facts

Did You Know?

Art therapy has been developing for years, but it didn't emerge as a distinct profession until the 1930s. World War II and the trauma it brought to many soldiers' lives helped the field to burgeon in the second half of the century.

Did You Know?

There are more than 4,000 professionally recognized art therapists throughout the world, so you'll never be lonely.

Renoir's Self Therapy

Renoir battled severe rheumatoid arthritis and fought to overcome the disease so he could continue creating masterpieces. He experienced bouts of illness and bouts of excruciating pain. His joints became deformed and his skin dried up and by 1904, Renoir weighed only 105 pounds and was barely able to sit. By 1910 he could not even walk using crutches and became a prisoner in his wheelchair. His hands were completely deformed, and a gauze bandage was used to prevent his fingernails from growing into the flesh. He was unable to pick up a paintbrush, and it had to be wedged between his fingers. He continued to paint everyday unless an attack of arthritis prevented him from doing so. There were also episodes that completely paralyzed him. There were times when he could only move his arm in short, sudden motions to thrust the paintbrush forward. In 1912, another attack of rheumatoid arthritis left Renoir's arms paralyzed and left him unable to paint. By 1915, Renoir was carried to his easel every morning. Revived by his work, he was able to create paintings once again in the few years before his death.

(Source: http://arthritis.about.com/od/art/a/renoir.htm)

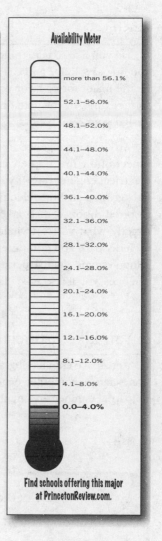

Availability Meter

more than 56.1%

52.1–56.0%

48.1–52.0%

44.1–48.0%

40.1–44.0%

36.1–40.0%

32.1–36.0%

28.1–32.0%

24.1–28.0%

20.1–24.0%

16.1–20.0%

12.1–16.0%

8.1–12.0%

4.1–8.0%

0.0–4.0%

Find schools offering this major at PrincetonReview.com.

Careers and Salary

The average starting salary for an art therapy major ranges from $27,000 to $28,000 a year in positions like those of a mental health specialist, consultant, or program director. These salaries increase with education and experience. To become a licensed art therapist, you'll need a master's degree, or you'll need to show you've taken enough classroom time to earn one.

CAREER OPTIONS

Animator	Artist	Digital Artist
Antiques Dealer	Auctioneer	Psychologist
Art Dealer		

ARTIFICIAL INTELLIGENCE AND ROBOTICS

Basics

Do you like to take things apart to see how they work? Have you been fascinated with robots ever since you first saw R2D2 and C3PO steal the spotlight in *Star Wars*? If so, artificial intelligence and robotics could be the major for you. For years, robots have been used in many fields, from manufacturing to transportation to medicine. In this exciting program, you'll gain the computer, engineering, and scientific know-how to design your own robots.

Artificial intelligence and robotics is a multidisciplinary field and the courses you pursue depend on which aspect of the major interests you most. If you want to design the robot body, take classes in mechanical and electrical engineering. If you're more interested in designing robot minds and behaviors, then you'll need a background in both electrical engineering and computer science. Finally, if you're interested in animal-inspired robotics, then take biology, animal behavior, and cognitive science classes, so you can understand exactly what you're trying to mimic. No matter what your specialty, an artificial and robotics major will include math and computer classes covering the basics of programming languages, algorithm design, operating systems, data structures, logic, and probability theory and statistics. And as with most experimental sciences, you'll also take classes in ethics and philosophy.

If You Like Artificial Intelligence and Robotics, You May Also Like . . .

Aerospace engineering, animal behavior and ethology, biology, cognitive psychology, computer and information science, computer engineering, computer science, electrical engineering, industrial design, engineering, industrial engineering, mathematics, mechanical engineering, neuroscience, physics, psychology

---

SAMPLE COLLEGE CURRICULUM FOR ARTIFICIAL INTELLIGENCE AND ROBOTICS

Advanced Computer Programming

Artificial Intelligence and Robotics

Automated Reasoning

Cognitive Modeling

Computing Theory

Cybernetics

Logistics

Practical Engineering Skills

Robot Design

Sensation and Perception

Suggested High School Prep for Artificial Intelligence and Robotics

To prepare yourself for this rigorous field, take all of the advanced math and science classes your school has to offer, especially calculus, physics, and anatomy. Sign up for computer classes and learn a programming language. In your spare time, tinker with electronic and mechanical devices to figure out how they work.

Fun Facts

Remote Surgery

A study by British doctors showed that a robot is superior to a human surgeon at carrying out a complex kidney operation—even when the robot is controlled by doctors thousands of miles away. Since unlike human arms, robot "arms" do not shake, they appear to make for a safer and more precise operation. With the help of video technology, robotics may open up a whole new field of medicine.

(Source: www.guardian.co.uk/medicine/story/0,11381,805662,00.html)

C-3PO is one of the few characters to appear in all six of the Star Wars feature films, and one of the very few to be played six times by the same actor. In all his various appearances, he is portrayed by Anthony Daniels. In one of the films, Anthony does not act in the C-3PO suit as the character is computer generated, however he does provide the voice.

(Source: http://en.wikipedia.org/wiki/C-3PO)

Careers and Salary

Artificial intelligence and robotics majors typically earn somewhere between $45,000 to $50,000 a year, depending upon what specific field they go into.

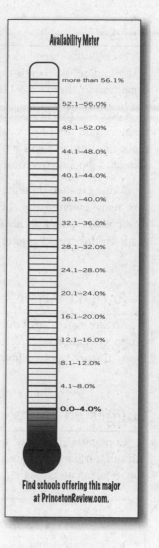

Availability Meter

more than 56.1%

52.1–56.0%

48.1–52.0%

44.1–48.0%

40.1–44.0%

36.1–40.0%

32.1–36.0%

28.1–32.0%

24.1–28.0%

20.1–24.0%

16.1–20.0%

12.1–16.0%

8.1–12.0%

4.1–8.0%

0.0–4.0%

Find schools offering this major at PrincetonReview.com.

CAREER OPTIONS

Aerospace Engineer	Inventor	Robotics Engineer
Computer Engineer/Systems Analyst	Mechanical Engineer	Software Developer
Computer Programmer	Professor	
Electronics Engineer	Research Technician	

ARTS MANAGEMENT

Basics

Even Picasso depended on galleries and foundations for his success, and the realm of arts management is the engine that keeps those gears turning. For every successful artist, gallery, theater, or high-profile art organization, there's most likely a successful arts manager behind it.

Careers in this field keep the art scene going on every imaginable level: organizing and managing museums, theaters, and nonprofits; taking care of business for galleries (or starting their own); promoting openings; managing budgets and writing grants; spearheading public relations efforts for all of the above; lobbying state and federal governments on behalf of arts advocacy groups—the list goes on.

While creative thinking—not to mention art-world savvy—definitely plays a role in the career life of an arts management major, the sharp organizational and analytical abilities valued by the business world are of tremendous worth in this field as well. Expect to manage much more than widgets: You'll be leaving your mark on the ever-changing landscape of the art world.

If You Like Arts Management, You May Also Like . . .

Art, art history, art education, advertising, business administration and management, business communication, education administration, marketing, mass communication, museum studies, music, music education, music history, public administration

Suggested High School Prep for Arts Management

Concentrate on your English classes and especially on your writing skills—you'll be using them a lot. Although it goes without saying, we'll say it anyway: Focus on your art classes, especially on art history (if you're fortunate enough to attend a school that offers this). Don't ignore the more left-brain-oriented classes (like math) that'll help with the business side of this major.

SAMPLE COLLEGE CURRICULUM FOR ARTS MANAGEMENT

Creative Theories and Criticism in Performing Arts

Elementary Statistics

Financial Management in the Arts

Introduction to Management

Marketing

Managing Nonprofit Organizations

Principles of Microeconomics

Survey of Arts Management

Fun Facts

Playing the Field

If you're looking for more information about arts management, check out the National Endowment for the Arts (www.nea.gov) or the American Association of Museums (www.aam-us.org); both are useful sites for beginning your research.

Van Broke

The cliché of the starving artist who achieves posthumous fame and fortune is typified in Vincent Van Gogh. The artist sold one painting in his lifetime. One hundred years after his death, his Portrait of Doctor Gachet sold for $82.5 million at Christie's—a new record at the time (now second only to Picasso's Garçon à la Pipe, which sold for $104.1 million in 2004).

Careers and Salary

It's hard to estimate starting salaries for a career in arts management, mostly because there are so many career paths you could take with this major. That said, expect starting salaries between $26,000 and $42,000. It all depends on where you work, and how you're putting your training to work for you.

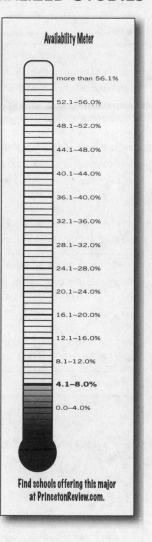

Availability Meter

more than 56.1%

52.1–56.0%

48.1–52.0%

44.1–48.0%

40.1–44.0%

36.1–40.0%

32.1–36.0%

28.1–32.0%

24.1–28.0%

20.1–24.0%

16.1–20.0%

12.1–16.0%

8.1–12.0%

4.1–8.0%

0.0–4.0%

Find schools offering this major at PrincetonReview.com.

CAREER OPTIONS

Archivist	Arts Program Coordinator	Literary Agent
Art Consultant	Dance Company Manager	Museum Art Educator
Art Curator	Director	Performing Arts Manager
Art Show Promoter		

ASIAN AMERICAN STUDIES

Basics

Asian American studies is a multidisciplinary major requiring courses in the humanities and social sciences. By majoring in it, you'll learn how Americans of Asian descent have affected and been affected by American culture. You'll learn about the difficulties and discrimination Asian Americans faced in the past and the problems they still face today. You'll study the changing roles of Asian American women, the implications of youth cultures, and the history of Asian American politics.

An Asian American studies major exposes you to Asian art, language, music, politics, psychology, and literature. You'll form your own ideas of what it means to be Asian American and how identity, gender, sexuality, and race have been defined, challenged, and consequently redefined.

If You Like Asian American Studies, You May Also Like . . .

African American studies, African studies, American history, American literature, American studies, anthropology, Chinese, East Asian studies, East European studies, Islamic studies, Japanese, Jewish studies, Latin American studies, South Asian studies, Southeast Asian studies

Suggested High School Prep for Asian American Studies

Load up on courses in English and history and, if they're available at your school, philosophy and religion as well. Most schools don't offer language classes in Korean, Japanese, and Chinese, but if they do, guess what? Yup. Take them.

SAMPLE COLLEGE CURRICULUM FOR ASIAN AMERICAN STUDIES

Asian American Literature

Asian American Women

Asian American Youth Cultures

Asian Americans and the Law

History of Asians in the Americas

Korean Foreign Relations

Literature and Film in Modern China

The Politics of Gender and Race

Race and Art

Women and Development in Asia

Women in Chinese History

Women in Japanese Literature: Love, Sexuality, and Gender

Fun Facts

Important Dates in Asian American History

1848—Gold discovered in California. Chinese begin to arrive.

1860—Japan first sends a diplomatic mission to United States.

1885—San Francisco builds segregated "Oriental School." Anti-Chinese violence at Rock Springs, Wyoming Territory. First group of Japanese contract laborers arrives in Hawaii under the Irwin Convention.

1893—Japanese in San Francisco form first trade association, the Japanese Shoemakers League. Attempts are made to expel Chinese from towns in Southern California.

1897—Nishi Hongwanji includes Hawaii as a mission field.

1909—Koreans form Korean Nationalist Association. Seven thousand Japanese plantation workers strike at major plantations on Oahu, Hawaii, for four months.

1925—Warring tongs in North America's Chinatowns declare truce. Hilario Moncado founds Filipino Federation of America.

1947—Amendment to 1945 War Brides Act allows Chinese American veterans to bring brides into the United States.

1952—One clause of the McCarran-Walter Act grants the right of naturalization and a small immigration quota to Japanese.

(Source: Asian Americans, an Interpretive History by Sucheng Chan)

Recommended Reading

Consider checking out one of these books in your local library or bookstore. All of them deal in some way with the Asian American experience.

Dogeaters by Jessica Hagedorn

Typical American by Gish Jen

The Joy Luck Club by Amy Tan

Obasan by Joy Kogawa

The Woman Warrior by Maxine Hong Kingston

Native Speaker by Chang-Rae Lee

Bone by Fae Myenne Ng

Availability Meter

more than 56.1%

52.1–56.0%

48.1–52.0%

44.1–48.0%

40.1–44.0%

36.1–40.0%

32.1–36.0%

28.1–32.0%

24.1–28.0%

20.1–24.0%

16.1–20.0%

12.1–16.0%

8.1–12.0%

4.1–8.0%

0.0–4.0%

Find schools offering this major at PrincetonReview.com.

Careers and Salary

As with most humanities majors, your studies may lead you in any number of directions. Most liberal arts majors can expect a starting salary of $24,000 to $30,000, but that can vary widely depending on the field.

CAREER OPTIONS

Anthropologist

Diplomat/Attaché/Foreign Service Officer

Fund-raiser/Institutional Solicitor

Journalist

Lobbyist

Sociologist

Writer

ASIAN HISTORY

Basics

From any angle you look at it—geographically, culturally, economically, historically—Asia has a tremendous influence on the world's stage. Asian history majors study the hows and whys of Asians' development, focusing (necessarily so, since Asia is such a vast region) on a specific culture, period, institution, or theme. Some of the world's first civilizations, technologies, religions, and art forms emerged and developed in Asia. This major covers a lot of ground.

After graduating, you'll be able to compare current Chinese domestic economic policies with those of Maoism; understand the Israeli/Palestinian situation by examining the history of Jewish/Arab relations; and talk about the Ainu displacement by Japanese. You'll study ancient trades routes through Central Asia, gender and sexuality in the Indus Valley civilization, and you'll ponder questions such as how North Korea is affecting the Six-Party Talks. You might continue onto law, medical, or business schools, with the intention of establishing your practice in Asia. People with a nuanced understanding of Asian cultures are also of great value in the nonprofit arena. Further—indeed, unending—research in graduate school is another career path you could take.

If You Like Asian History, You May Also Like . . .

American history, ancient studies, anthropology, archaeology, architecture, art history, Asian American studies, East Asian studies, European history, history, international relations, international studies, Islamic studies, South Asian studies, Southeast Asian studies

---

SAMPLE COLLEGE CURRICULUM FOR ASIAN HISTORY

As with the history major, Asian history—while more specific—is nevertheless a broad topic of study. You'll therefore, probably choose a major concentration on a specific period, culture, institution, or theme. That said, in some courses you might come across:

Asian American History

Chinese Literature

The Cultural Revolution

Hindu Art

History of Ancient Egypt

History of Islam

International Trade

Vietnam War

Suggested High School Prep for History Preservation

Definitely pay attention in history class and English. Take any philosophy and religious studies your school may offer, and if you're fortunate enough to be able to study an Asian language, seize that opportunity.

Fun Facts

Where We Live

About 60 percent of the world's population lives in Asia.

Did You Know?

The word "Asia" may derive from the Akkadian word "asu," meaning "to go out" or "to rise"—referring to the direction of the sun at sunrise in the Middle East.

Careers and Salary

Studying Asian history could result in any number of career paths. Your decision about if and where to pursue a graduate degree will certainly affect your earnings and earning potential. Look for starting salaries in the $24,000 to $30,000 range.

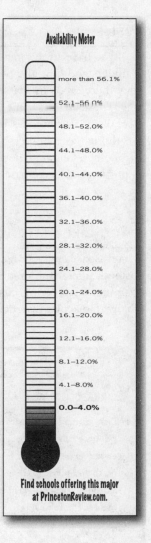

Availability Meter

more than 56.1%

52.1–56.0%

48.1–52.0%

44.1–48.0%

40.1–44.0%

36.1–40.0%

32.1–36.0%

28.1–32.0%

24.1–28.0%

20.1–24.0%

16.1–20.0%

12.1–16.0%

8.1–12.0%

4.1–8.0%

0.0–4.0%

Find schools offering this major at PrincetonReview.com.

CAREER OPTIONS

Anthropologist	Journalist	Sociologist
Diplomat/Attaché/Foreign Services Officer	Political Aide	Teacher
	Professor	Theologian
Historian	Researcher	Writer

ASTRONOMY

Basics

If you have always had your head in the clouds, astronomy could be the major for you. Astronomers seek to understand how the universe—the planets, stars, and galaxies—has evolved and functioned over time. They therefore help shape our understanding of the physical world. How old is the Earth? What is a black hole? These are just some of the questions that astronomers have tried to answer. Equipped with the latest technology, astronomers are dependent entirely on their abilities to observe and record. Unlike other scientists though, astronomers will never be able to come into direct contact with the objects they study. Instead, astronomers rely on a keen eye, incredibly large telescopes, and some theoretical physics to help interpret all of the electromagnetic rays (and numerous other invisible forces) that continually bombard Earth.

If You Like Astronomy, You May Also Like . . .

Aerospace engineering, architectural engineering, astrophysics, atmospheric science, biochemistry, biology, business administration and management, chemistry, civil engineering, computer and information science, computer engineering, computer systems analysis, geology, marine science, mechanical engineering, microbiology, molecular genetics, neurobiology, neuroscience, nuclear engineering, physics, statistics

SAMPLE COLLEGE CURRICULUM FOR ASTRONOMY

A basic curriculum in astronomy is going to be heavily based in the sciences, so be prepared for a lot of math and physics. General courses astronomy majors have to take include the following:

Astronomical Observations

Calculus and Analytic Geometry

Particles and Motion

Particles and Waves

Quantum Physics I–II

Solar System Astronomy

Statistical Physics

Stellar and Galactic Astronomy

Stellar Evolution of Cosmology

Theoretical Mechanics

Thermal Physics and Electrostatics

Vector Analysis

Suggested High School Prep for Astronomy

Two words: math and science. Take as much and to as high a level as your school offers. This means at least geometry and trigonometry. Calculus will also help a lot. As for science, absorb like a sponge all the chemistry and physics they throw at you. A good deal of computer experience will also prove extremely helpful.

Fun Facts

Astronomy Is One of the Oldest Sciences

The first astronomers were the Babylonians, who in 3000 B.C./B.C.E. made note of most of the stars and planets that we know today. Using this information, they developed one of the earliest calendars based on astronomical events.

Credit Where Credit Is Due

Even though Galileo gets much of the credit for developing a theory that places the Sun at the center of the universe, it was actually a Polish astronomer, Nicolaus Copernicus, who in 1543 published *Six Books Concerning the Revolutions of the Heavenly Orbs*, which gave us our understanding of the solar system.

There are probably more than one hundred billion (10^{11}) galaxies in the observable universe. (Source: http://en.wikipedia.org/wiki/Galaxy)

Careers and Salary

Starting salaries for astronomy majors depend upon their levels of education. Astronomers and physicists can range anywhere from $45,000 to upward of $132,000.

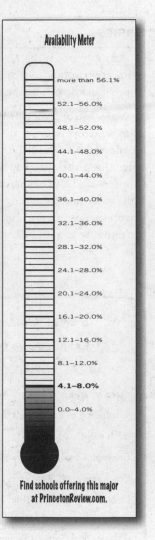

Availability Meter

more than 56.1%

52.1–56.0%

48.1–52.0%

44.1–48.0%

40.1–44.0%

36.1–40.0%

32.1–36.0%

28.1–32.0%

24.1–28.0%

20.1–24.0%

16.1–20.0%

12.1–16.0%

8.1–12.0%

4.1–8.0%

0.0–4.0%

Find schools offering this major at PrincetonReview.com.

CAREER OPTIONS
Astronomer

ASTROPHYSICS

Basics

Astrophysics is the physics of celestial bodies. Majoring in it involves learning about the physical properties and evolution of stars, planets, galaxies, and quasars—the stuff of the universe. Astrophysics is also closely linked with mathematics and computer science.

Many astrophysics programs put a great deal of emphasis on research. In Penn State University's program, students not only do research but also build the very instruments with which they do it. Besides your independent and collaborative research, astrophysics exposes you to processes of the birth and death of stars. Along the way you'll learn how to use instruments such as reflecting telescopes, gas proportional counters, and CCD cameras (big contraptions designed specifically to take pictures of the heavens). You'll walk away understanding the properties of active galactic nuclei. You'll master general relativity, galactic dynamics, cosmology, and the physics of space plasma. If these subjects sound mysterious, that's because the universe is a mysterious thing, and the goal of the astrophysics major is to help you understand it.

SAMPLE COLLEGE CURRICULUM FOR ASTROPHYSICS

Astrodynamics

Astronomy of the Distant Universe

Birth and Death of Stars

Computational Astrophysics

Cosmology

Electromagnetic Radiation and Plasma Physics

Galaxies and Galactic Dynamics

General Relativity

High Energy Astrophysics and Compact Objects

Molecular Astrophysics

Nuclear and Particle Physics

Physics of the Interstellar Medium

Quantum Physics and Relativity

Radio Astronomy

Stellar Structure and Evolution

Wind, Bubbles, and Explosions in Galaxies

If You Like Astrophysics, You May Also Like . . .

Applied mathematics, applied physics, astronomy

Suggested High School Prep for Astrophysics

Your best preparation in high school will be advanced-level courses in math and science—especially physics, calculus, trigonometry, and analytic geometry. Any courses your high school offers in statistics and computer science will also be valuable. The broader your science and math background, the better. Also, try to apply your physics knowledge. Be that nerd whose physics projects for science fairs blow the competition out of the water.

Fun Facts

A Little Astrophysics Humor

From Tom Comeau at the Space Telescope Science Institute:

"A coworker remarked yesterday that she had a master's in astrophysics in addition to her doctorate—of course she also has a bachelor's in physics. Her rationale was that it made perfect sense for an astronomer to have a three-degree background."

Did You Know?

Have you ever seen a meteor shower, or found a meteor in your yard after one happened? Meteors have usually been in orbit for about 4.5 billion years before they actually fall to the Earth.

In ancient times, astronomers noted how certain lights moved across the sky in relation to the other stars. These objects were believed to orbit the Earth, which was considered to be stationary. The lights were first called "πλανητς" (planïtïs), meaning "wanderer", by the ancient Greeks, and it is from this that the word "planet" was derived.

(Source: http://en.wikipedia.org/wiki/Planet)

Careers and Salary

Starting salaries for astrophysics majors generally fall in the $40,000 to $50,000 range but can be higher or lower depending on how you use your degree. Higher levels of education also play a large role in determining starting salaries, as many astrophysics majors go on to graduate school.

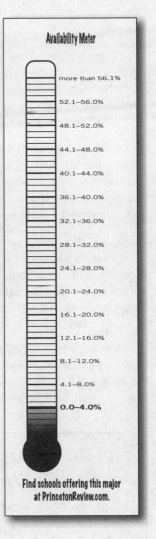

Availability Meter

more than 56.1%

52.1–56.0%

48.1–52.0%

44.1–48.0%

40.1–44.0%

36.1–40.0%

32.1–36.0%

28.1–32.0%

24.1–28.0%

20.1–24.0%

16.1–20.0%

12.1–16.0%

8.1–12.0%

4.1–8.0%

0.0–4.0%

Find schools offering this major at PrincetonReview.com.

CAREER OPTIONS		
Astronaut	Astronomer	Professor

ATHLETIC TRAINING/TRAINER

Basics

Athletic trainers have played an integral role in the lives of athletes since the time of first Olympiad. Today, athletic trainers are highly educated specialists who bear few similarities to their ancient counterparts. No longer the aging or sub-par athlete devoting his/her time to carrying the team's water or towels, the modern athletic trainer, in consultation with and under the supervision of physicians, has become an invaluable asset to men and women who've been injured on—or far off—the playing field.

An athletic trainer is a health professional, so expect the training to be as intense as it is fulfilling. As an athletic training major, you'll be getting instruction on how to identify, evaluate, and treat athletic injuries and illnesses. Additionally, you'll be well versed in first aid and emergency care, therapeutic exercise, anatomy and physiology, exercise physiology, kinesiology and biomechanics, nutrition, sports psychology, personal and community health, and the biomechanical and physiological demands of various sports.

Clearly, the knowledge gained as an athletic training major is applicable to all kinds of fields, athletic or otherwise. In addition to their work at all levels of student and professional sports, athletic trainers work in hospitals, clinics, the military, and industrial or commercial settings. Some schools might suggest that you enhance your training and eventual job placement with a minor or a double major in a field that would complement an athletic training degree: biology, business administration for health care, business communications, chemistry, exercise science, physical education, occupation therapy, physical therapy, and premedicine.

Plenty of schools offer an athletic training major, but if you're looking to become a certified athletic trainer, it's important that the school you choose is approved by the Commission on Accreditation of Allied Health Education Programs (CAAHEP).

SAMPLE COLLEGE CURRICULUM FOR ATHLETIC TRAINING/TRAINER

Anatomy and Physiology I–II

Athletic Training (Intro–Advanced)

Clinical Experience in Athletic Training

Conditioning of Athletics

Exercise Physiology

First Aid

Kinesiology

Medical Issues in Athletic Training

Sports Nutrition

Therapeutic Modalities

Therapeutic Rehabilitation

If You Like Athletic Training/Trainer, You May Also Like . . .

Biology, biopsychology, cell biology, chemistry, chiropractic, circulation technology, dietetics, health administrator, human development, medical technology, nursing, occupational therapy, pharmacology, pharmacy, physical therapy, premedicine, pre-optometry, pre-veterinary medicine, radiologic technology, recreation management, rehabilitation services, respiratory therapy

Suggested High School Prep for Athletic Training/Trainer

Like most programs that are heavy on science, it's a good idea to build a strong foundation in the physical sciences. Take Advanced Placement classes in biology, chemistry, and physics. See if your local hospital or clinic accepts high school volunteers. Oh, and you guessed it, go out for the team!

Fun Facts

Did You Know?

Founded in 1950, the National Athletic Trainers' Association (NATA) helped to unify athletic trainers across the country by setting a standard for professionalism, education, certification, research, and practice settings. It has been the driving force behind the recognition of the athletic training profession. For more information visit www.nata.org.

Code of Ethics

To assure high quality care, the NATA established a code of aspirational standards of behavior that all members should strive to achieve.

- Members should respect the rights, welfare, and dignity of all individuals.
- Members should comply with the laws and regulations governing the practice of athletic training.
- Members should accept responsibility for the exercise of sound judgment.
- Members should maintain and promote high standards in the provision of services.
- Members should not engage in any form of conduct that constitutes a conflict of interest or that adversely reflects on the profession.

Careers and Salary

Generally the most sought-after careers for athletic training majors are those in professional and Division I sports. While opportunities in these fields are limited, there are plenty of other arenas for job placement. Generally, the athletic training major can expect to receive an average salary of $30,000 per year.

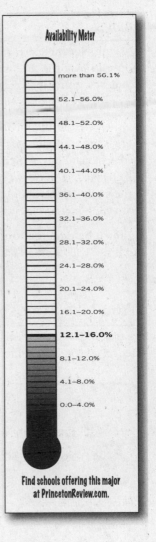

Availability Meter

more than 56.1%

52.1–56.0%

48.1–52.0%

44.1–48.0%

40.1–44.0%

36.1–40.0%

32.1–36.0%

28.1–32.0%

24.1–28.0%

20.1–24.0%

16.1–20.0%

12.1–16.0%

8.1–12.0%

4.1–8.0%

0.0–4.0%

Find schools offering this major at PrincetonReview.com.

CAREER OPTIONS		
Athletic Trainer	Recreational Therapist	Team Manager
Physical Therapist	Sports Manager	

ATMOSPHERIC SCIENCE

Basics

Nope. Not the exact same thing as meteorology, which is just one of the areas you'll learn about if you choose to major in atmospheric science. Atmospheric science, according to the University of Washington, includes "weather forecasting, air pollution and air chemistry, climate change, radiative transfer, and boundary layer processes." Not as simple as flinging magnetic disks shaped like suns onto a metal weatherboard.

Interested in the environment? You may want to concentrate on the study of air quality, health issues, energy, and pollution. Or you may choose to study atmospheric science as it relates to the ocean. Then there's climatology, which is the study of how the atmosphere in one area of the world has changed and will change over long periods of time. Still another specialization is aeronomy, which Britannica.com defines as the study of "the photochemical processes of the upper atmosphere." And, of course, you have the option of studying meteorology, where you'll learn how to analyze and predict the weather.

You'll be required to use advanced math and computer skills in your investigation of the atmosphere, and these will come in handy when searching for a job, even if it's not for a weather forecaster's position.

If You Like Atmospheric Science, You May Also Like . . .

Astrophysics, chemistry, ecology, environmental and environmental health engineering, environmental science, geological engineering, geology, natural resources conservation, ocean engineering

SAMPLE COLLEGE CURRICULUM FOR ATMOSPHERIC SCIENCE

Air Quality Modeling

Atmospheric Kinematics and Dynamics

Atmospheric Motions

Atmospheric Physics

Climates of the World

Global Environmental Chemistry

Long Range Forecasting

Meteorology of the Biosphere

Ocean Circulation

Physical Climatology

Remote Sensing for Meteorology and Natural Resources

Thermodynamics and Cloud Processes

Weather Briefing

Suggested High School Prep for Atmospheric Science

A wide range of math and science courses will be your best preparation for this major. Physics, chemistry, biology, and advanced math classes—as well as computer courses—will give you a strong foundation for what you'll be studying in college. Any courses your high school offers on environmental topics are also useful.

Fun Facts

A Near-Disaster in Naming

The first national weather service was developed by the U.S. Army in 1878. A few years later, in 1890, a civilian service was created. This service was almost named the Weather Reporting Office of the National Government—the acronym for which would be WRONG

(Source: The Hersh Website Observer)

Important Dates for the National Weather Service

1849—The Smithsonian Institution establishes an extensive observation network. Observations are made and sent by telegraph.

1894—Kite weather observations are begun with self-recording thermometers to make observations of temperature aloft.

1909—The Weather Bureau begins experiments with balloon observations.

1931—Regular aircraft observations begin at Chicago, Cleveland, Dallas, and Omaha. Altitudes as high as 16,000 feet are met, and the kite service ends.

1948—The first primitive computer numerical forecasts are made on the Electronic Numerical Integrator and Computer.

1960—TIROS 1, the world's first weather satellite, is launched.

1975—The first geostationary weather satellite, GOES 1, is launched.

(Source: NWS–Tulsa)

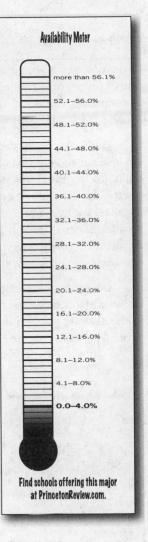

Availability Meter

- more than 56.1%
- 52.1–56.0%
- 48.1–52.0%
- 44.1–48.0%
- 40.1–44.0%
- 36.1–40.0%
- 32.1–36.0%
- 28.1–32.0%
- 24.1–28.0%
- 20.1–24.0%
- 16.1–20.0%
- 12.1–16.0%
- 8.1–12.0%
- 4.1–8.0%
- 0.0–4.0%

Find schools offering this major at PrincetonReview.com.

Careers and Salary

The starting salaries for most atmospheric science majors are in the $20,000 to $30,000 range but can be higher depending on how you choose to use your degree and what sort of experience you have in your field.

CAREER OPTIONS		
Biologist	Ecologist	Environmentalist/Environmental Scientist

AUSTRALIAN/OCEANIC/PACIFIC LANGUAGES, LITERATURES, AND LINGUISTICS

Basics

If you enjoy learning new (and somewhat obscure) languages and if you love reading about far-away cultures, you've come to the right page. Australia, New Zealand, Fiji, Tahiti, Tonga, Samoa, the Solomon Islands, the Marshall Islands, the Cook Islands, Hawaii, Kiribati, Pukapuka, Papau/New Guinea—these are just some of the places your studies will take you.

This is an area of the world with a rich fabric of indigenous traditions as well as a troubled history of colonialism and cultural abuse. As a major, you'll examine everything from the oral roots of Oceanic storytelling to the insightful stories of modern-day Maoris. You'll spend time analyzing books, films, plays, and poetry, and you'll wrestle with the evolutions occurring in these cultures today. In recent decades, for instance, young writers and artists have started to drift away from the theme of colonialism and toward broader issues of racism, economic hardship, and cultural identity. What does this tell us about the commerce, technology, governments, and global immersion of these cultures? These are the sorts of difficult questions you'll attempt to answer.

Obviously, you'll also need to be prepared to pick up a new language or two. The list of possibilities includes Maori, Mola, Naurun, Pidgin, Fijian, Tahitian, Tongan, and Somoan. And the work will pay off. Interest in the Australian, Oceanic, and Pacific cultures continues to grow; with fluency in a native tongue and a strong knowledge of the region, you'll be poised to become a major contributor to the field.

SAMPLE COLLEGE CURRICULUM FOR AUSTRALIAN/OCEANIC/PACIFIC LANGUAGES, LITERATURES, AND LINGUISTICS

Beginning Maori Language

Comparative Linguistics

Contemporary Oceania

Indigenous Aesthetics

Indigenous Film

Indigenous Literature

Intermediate Maori Language

Methodology of International Cultural Studies

Pacific Diaspora

Survey of Colonial Studies

If You Like Australian/Oceanic/Pacific Languages, Literatures, and Linguistics, You May Also Like...

African languages, literatures, and linguistics, African studies, anthropology, archaeology, East Asian studies, international relations, international studies, political science, South Asian studies, Southeast Asian studies

Suggested High School Prep for Australian/Oceanic/Pacific Languages, Literatures, and Linguistics

We know, we know: Your high school doesn't offer any courses in the Tongan language. No worries. For now, enroll in whatever language courses you can. This will at least give you good practice with those pesky foreign conjugations. And steep yourself in humanities classes from English to history to political science—courses that'll sharpen the analytic and communication skills you'll need when you enroll in Literature of New Zealand 101.

Fun Facts

Getting Started

In preparation for your future studies, here's a list of common phrases in Tahitian. Get practicing!

Hello

Ia Orana (yo-rah-nah)

Bye-bye

Nana (nah-nah)

What's your name?

O vai to oe i'oa? (oh vah-ee toh oh-ay ee-oh-ah)

My name is Jessica.

O Jessica to'u i'oa. (oh kris toh-oo ee-oh-ah)

Hurry up!

Ha'a viti viti! (ha-ah vee-tee vee-tee)

Let's go!

Haere tatou! (ha-ay-ray tah-toh-oo)

(Source: www.tahiti-explorer.com)

Talk, Talk

According to Ethnologue.com, Australia is home to 273 languages, of which 231 are still used as a primary language. In addition, 3 more of these languages are also in use, but not as a primary tongue, while the remaining 39 are now extinct.

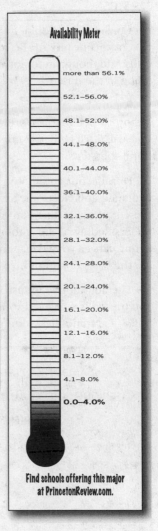

Availability Meter

more than 56.1%

52.1–56.0%

48.1–52.0%

44.1–48.0%

40.1–44.0%

36.1–40.0%

32.1–36.0%

28.1–32.0%

24.1–28.0%

20.1–24.0%

16.1–20.0%

12.1–16.0%

8.1–12.0%

4.1–8.0%

0.0–4.0%

Find schools offering this major at PrincetonReview.com.

Careers and Salaries

It's quite possible that before you begin drawing a salary, you'll matriculate to graduate school to extend your studies. Otherwise, you can expect a starting salary between $20,000 and $30,000.

CAREER OPTIONS

Anthropologist	Fundraiser	Sociologist
Archeologist	Journalist	Teacher
Diplomat/Attaché/Foreign Service Officer	Lobbyist	Translator
	Missionary	Writer

AUTOMOTIVE ENGINEERING

Basics

Consider the Cobra. In 1962, legendary car designer Carroll Shelby was the man behind the introduction of this beauty of the road—the fastest mass-produced car ever made. That's right: 0 to 60 in 3.9 seconds. And though automotive technology has since surpassed that feat, at the time it left Ferraris everywhere idling in the dust.

Shelby began his career as a chicken farmer in Leesburg, Texas, and pursued his hot-rod drag-racing hobby to become a world-class race driver and an automotive engineer. Shelby's career path was, well, unusual. You'll be better off sticking with an automotive engineering major if you plan to follow in his rubber-burnt footsteps.

During your automotive engineering studies, you'll examine the operating principles of the mechanical, hydraulic, and electronic systems of automobiles. You'll pick up the specialized vocabulary that accompanies these systems so that you can throw around terms like transaxle with true authority. You'll gain an insider's understanding of the automotive industry and learn the technological issues involved in designing and marketing cars as you take an in-depth look at the materials, manufacturing, ergonomics, and design testing that are the basis of automotive engineering.

The automotive industry is challenging and exciting, and your automotive engineering major will give you the skills you need to make a worthwhile contribution to it. You'll become familiar with the nuts and bolts of automobiles, so to speak, so you'll be able to identify and solve problems with current systems, as well as to design new ones that are reliable, functional, and innovative.

Some programs combine automotive engineering with courses in mechanical engineering, so be sure to research your prospective programs carefully if you think this is something you may like.

If You Like Automotive Engineering, You May Also Like . . .

Aerospace engineering, chemical engineering, civil engineering, computer programming, electrical engineering, engineering design, engineering mechanics, engineering systems, industrial engineering, mathematics, mechanical engineering, metallurgical engineering

Suggested High School Prep for Automotive Engineering

Courses in upper-level math, like calculus or trigonometry, will build a great foundation for your college studies. Science courses in physics and chemistry will be useful as well. Communication skills are vital to any engineer, so be sure to take courses in English, languages, and history, and work on your writing and reading skills.

SAMPLE COLLEGE CURRICULUM FOR AUTOMOTIVE ENGINEERING

Automotive Design and Manufacture

Basic Fuel and Emission Control Systems

Circuits and Electronics

Electromechanics

Engine Electrical Systems

Engine Principles

Fluid Mechanics and Heat Transfer

Manual Transmission and Transaxle Principles

Mechanical Vibrations

Motorsport Technology

Powertrain Systems

Steering and Suspension

Stress Analysis

Technical Drawing and Print Reading

Fun Facts

Can You Name Every Part of an Engine?

Intake valve, rocker arm and spring, valve cover, intake port, head, coolant, engine block, oil pan, oil sump, camshaft, exhaust valve, rocker arm and spring, spark plug, exhaust port, rod bearing, crankshaft

(Source: www.howstuffworks.com)

Tell It Like It Is

Here are some actual quotes from insurance forms where drivers attempted to explain the accidents they'd been involved in.

- In my attempt to kill a fly, I drove into a telephone pole.
- I had been driving for 40 years when I fell asleep at the wheel and had an accident.
- I told the police I was not injured, but upon removing my hair, I found that I had a fractured skull.
- I saw a slow-moving, sad-faced gentleman as he bounced off the hood of my car.
- I was thrown from my car as it left the road and was later found in a ditch by some stray cows.
- I thought my window was down, but I found out it was up when I put my head through it.
- The guy was all over the road. I had to swerve a number of times before I hit him.

(Source: *Toronto News*, July 26, 1977)

Careers and Salary

The starting salary for automotive engineers ranges from $26,000 to $35,000, but that figure depends heavily on where you live and how you choose to use your skills.

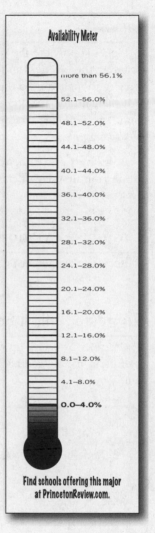

Availability Meter

more than 56.1%
52.1–56.0%
48.1–52.0%
44.1–48.0%
40.1–44.0%
36.1–40.0%
32.1–36.0%
28.1–32.0%
24.1–28.0%
20.1–24.0%
16.1–20.0%
12.1–16.0%
8.1–12.0%
4.1–8.0%
0.0–4.0%

Find schools offering this major at PrincetonReview.com.

CAREER OPTIONS

Auto Mechanic	Engineering Lab Technician	Product Developer
Automotive Engineer	Machinist	Race Car Driver
Designer	Professor	Stunt Driver

AVIATION

Basics

Picking up where the Wright brothers left off, an aviation major will cover almost every aspect of flying, including the business and economics behind the aviation industry. But this major is about more than just flying (although you do that too) since aviation is an entire industry in its own right. That means there is a high demand for aviation specialists who understand the logistics behind flying a plane from Point A to Point B, including federal regulations, management skills, and the physical happenings that allow an aircraft to defy gravity.

Be aware: Cool leather bomber jackets, sunglasses, and a copy of *Top Gun* probably won't be passed out during your first day of classes as an aviation major, so you better come prepared with your own.

If You Like Aviation, You May Also Like . . .

Aerospace engineering, Air Force R.O.T.C., applied physics, engineering design, engineering mechanics

Suggested High School Prep for Aviation

Consider brushing up on those math and science courses, particularly physics, geometry, and calculus. In addition, having good communication skills is a must, so make sure you know how to read and write very well.

SAMPLE COLLEGE CURRICULUM FOR AVIATION

Air Transportation Analysis

Airline Marketing

Airport Management

Aviation Communication

Aviation Law

Aviation Management

Calculus

Computer Science

Engineering Graphics

Geography of Transportation

National Aviation System

Physics

Principles of Macroeconomics

Private Pilot Fundamentals

Fun Facts

- American Airlines saved $40,000 in 1987 by eliminating one olive from each salad served in first-class.
- Chicago's O'Hare International Airport is the world's busiest airport. An airplane takes off or lands every 37 seconds.
- The first women flight attendants in 1930 were required to weigh no more than 115 pounds, be nurses, and unmarried.
- Average number of people airborne over the United States during any given hour: 61,000.
- Back in the 1920s a plane ticket cost $5. Barnstormers would give anyone willing and able a quick ride in their planes for $5 after performing their shows (a considerable sum in those days).
- Hijacking of airplanes was outlawed in 1961.

(Source: www.butlerwebs.com/travel/air.htm)

- Hartfield-Jackson Atlanta International Airport is the world's busiest airport by passenger traffic as well as landings and take-offs.

(Source: http://en.wikipedia.org/wiki/world's_busiest_airport)

Don't Forget the Directions

Featured on an American Airlines packet of peanuts:

"Instructions: Open packet, eat nuts."

Flying Food

LSG SKY CHEFS, the world's largest airline caterer, served 427 million meals for 260 airline customers worldwide in 2001.

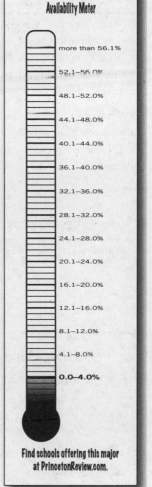

Availability Meter

more than 56.1%

52.1–56.0%

48.1–52.0%

44.1–48.0%

40.1–44.0%

36.1–40.0%

32.1–36.0%

28.1–32.0%

24.1–28.0%

20.1–24.0%

16.1–20.0%

12.1–16.0%

8.1–12.0%

4.1–8.0%

0.0–4.0%

Find schools offering this major at PrincetonReview.com.

Careers and Salary

The average starting salary for pilots and aviation majors ranges from $35,000 to $50,000, depending on experience and the sector of aviation you enter.

CAREER OPTIONS		
Aerospace Engineer	Astronaut	Avionics Technician
Air Force National Guard		

BAKERY SCIENCE

Basics

Bakery science is more complex than its name may suggest. If you major in it, you'll learn all about the intricate chemical processes involved in baking just about anything. You'll learn about production processes, the functions of various ingredients, and nutrition. This new knowledge will be important as you work on developing new baked products and perfecting your baking skills, which you'll be able to do in your university's bakery science laboratories.

A bakery science major also involves study of the business side of baking. You'll study government regulations for food products and production. You'll learn about management and other business concepts. You'll look at economic trends and changes that may affect your career, and you'll learn the maintenance and engineering skills you'll need to run your own successful bakery operation.

If You Like Bakery Science, You May Also Like . . .

Culinary arts, dietetics, food science, home economics, nutrition

Suggested High School Prep for Bakery Science

You can build a solid foundation for bakery science by taking courses in math, biology, chemistry, and English. A business course could be useful, if one is available at your high school. And embrace home economics—you may find more useful information here than you'd expect. Hands-on experience (and experiments) with your own baking will give you a taste—literally—of what you're in for.

SAMPLE COLLEGE CURRICULUM FOR BAKERY SCIENCE

Assuring Quality Baking Products

Baking and Frying Technology

Baking and Pastry

Basic Industry Standards

Bread and Roll Production

Chemically Leavened Pizzas

Cookie Ingredient Technology

Dealing with Flour Quality

Enzyme Usage for Bakers

Extending Shelf Life for Bakery Foods

Oven Technology

Process Engineering for Dough Systems

Restaurant Desserts

Wedding Cakes

Fun Facts

American Society of Baking

If bakery science is your field, you may eventually get involved with the American Society of Baking. The society encourages an exchange of ideas and information among people in the baking industry. It was founded in 1924 and now has close to 3,000 members worldwide.

A Brief History of Sourdough

Sourdough was developed nearly 6,000 years ago, after people figured out how to make a mixture of fermented grain and water. Fermentation occurs when yeasts and bacteria grow in a dough of grains and liquid, leavening and flavoring the dough. When a bit of fermented grain was saved for the next batch of bread, it was called a "sourdough starter." In the 1800s, people traveling west used starters to keep from starving. Some people, before heading further into the mountains, bought provisions in San Francisco. The bread produced from grains of these areas had an unusually sour taste—hence the term "sourdough" as we know it.

(Source: the American Society of Baking)

Careers and Salary

The starting salary for bakery science is difficult to predict because there are so many ways to use your degree. Salaries will depend on where you work, your position in the workplace, and what experience you've had. Some bakers earn hourly wages of about $10 to $14. Salaries for chefs or caterers are in the $20,000 to $30,000 area.

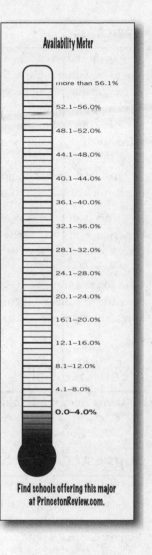

Availability Meter

more than 56.1%

52.1–56.0%

48.1–52.0%

44.1–48.0%

40.1–44.0%

36.1–40.0%

32.1–36.0%

28.1–32.0%

24.1–28.0%

20.1–24.0%

16.1–20.0%

12.1–16.0%

8.1–12.0%

4.1–8.0%

0.0–4.0%

Find schools offering this major at PrincetonReview.com.

CAREER OPTIONS

Caterer	Entrepreneur	Restaurateur
Chef		

BALLET

Basics

Nearly sixty years ago, poet W.H. Auden famously advised, "Anyone who has a child today should train him to be either a physicist or a ballet dancer." Well, if your parents took this advice, there's a decent chance you're thinking about becoming a ballet major when you head off to college. If so, prepare yourself to examine this exquisite art form from every angle. First and foremost, you'll dedicate many hours (and tired muscles) to practicing and improving your technique as a dancer. But it's not all practice. Many programs pride themselves on the public performance opportunities they offer their students. A little *Giselle* here, a little *Coppélia* there—all of it contributing to the professional resume you'll be able to take to dance companies when your degree is complete. In addition, you'll explore the art of choreography, the science of kinesiology, the history of ballet, and the role of dance in contemporary society.

This is not the sort of major you select on a whim. Most ballet majors arrive at college with plenty of experience in tow. While many ballet dancers skip college in order to turn pro in their late teens, others take advantage of the ballet major as a chance to grow as performers and to hone their skills in teaching, choreography, and other forms of dance. Focus is key. Professional competition can be cutthroat, so you'll want to get as much as possible out of your degree. Because ballet programs are looking for serious students, be ready to submit a recording of a past performance (or perhaps even to give a live audition) as part of the application process.

If You Like Ballet, You May Also Like...

Dance, film, music, music education, musical theater, visual communication, voice

Suggested High School Prep for Ballet

Unless you're one of the lucky ones, your high school probably doesn't offer dance classes, let alone ballet classes. Instead, check in with your school's drama and music programs, which may offer classes or performances that'll let you get comfortable with the stage. Heck, they may even be planning a run of *The Nutcracker* that's right up your alley. You should also look into summer programs that will give you a boost. Perhaps your college of choice even offers one.

SAMPLE COLLEGE

CURRICULUM FOR BALLET

Ballet I

Ballet II

Ballet III

Craft of Choreography

Kinesiology

Modern Technique

Theater Dance

Fun Facts

Hey Ladies!

During its first 100 years in existence, ballet was the domain of men—exclusively. It wasn't until 1681 that trained female dancers joined the party. The first ballet to feature women, called *Le Triomphe de l'Amour* (or *The Triumph of Love*) was performed in Paris, the headquarters of early ballet.

(Source: www.bartleby.com)

Getting Nutty

The Nutcracker, perhaps the world's most beloved ballet, was the first performance to include the celesta in its orchestral score. What's a celesta? It's a keyboard instrument on which a musician hits steel plates with mallets. The celesta produces a bell-like sound.

(Source: www.funtrivia.com)

Career and Salary

Because companies and circumstances vary so widely, it's tough to predict what you'll earn as a professional dancer. In most instances, you can expect $15,000 to $25,000 to start. Many ballet dancers perform seasonally, supplanting their income by teaching.

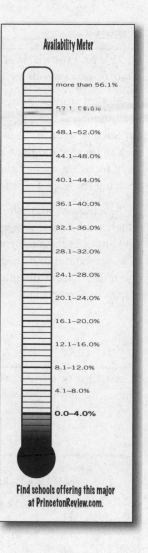

Availability Meter

more than 56.1%

52.1–56.0%

48.1–52.0%

44.1–48.0%

40.1–44.0%

36.1–40.0%

32.1–36.0%

28.1–32.0%

24.1–28.0%

20.1–24.0%

16.1–20.0%

12.1–16.0%

8.1–12.0%

4.1–8.0%

0.0–4.0%

Find schools offering this major at PrincetonReview.com.

CAREER OPTIONS

Actor	Costume Designer	Dancer
Artistic Director	Dance Company Owner/Operator	Publicist
Choreographer	Dance Instructor	Venue Manager

BIBLICAL STUDIES

Basics

This isn't the major of novitiates for the priest- or sisterhood, and biblical studies majors don't knock on doors or hand out fliers in airports.

Biblical studies is often a concentration within a broader religious studies major. The role religion plays in all human activity is immeasurable. Religion is often the source of the deepest ideas and values held by any society, addressing every human experience from birth to death. Religious studies majors as a whole seek to understand the ways in which the various religions of the world shape culture, society, and history. They focus on the religion itself, whether it's Christianity or Islam, Buddhism or Judaism, usually closely studying the sacred scriptures through which each tradition is maintained.

As a biblical studies major you'll have your work cut out for you since the Bible (besides being the most widely read, best-selling book ever) is one of the most complex works of literature in the world, prescribing laws about everything from property to the Godly diet. You will study and read the Bible closely, attempting to understand it in its historical context. In the process you will not only gain a depth of understanding of one of the most influential texts of all time, but also develop critical writing and thinking abilities that will help you interpret and understand any question you encounter.

If You Like Biblical Studies, You May Also Like . . .

Art history, classics, comparative literature, English, English literature, Hebrew, Islamic studies, Jewish studies, Medieval and Renaissance studies, philosophy, religious studies, teacher education, theology

Suggested High School Prep for Biblical Studies

The best preparation for a biblical studies major is a strong interest in the humanities. English AP classes will help you develop textual analysis skills, and that will be important since studying the Bible is all about textual analysis. If you go to a Christian or Jewish high school, take religion classes and pay attention. If your high school does not offer theology courses, history and art history are wonderful ways to begin exploring this major.

> ### SAMPLE COLLEGE CURRICULUM FOR BIBLICAL STUDIES
>
> Augustine
>
> Biblical Theology
>
> Christian Worldview
>
> Ethics
>
> Methods of Teaching the Bible
>
> New Testament Studies
>
> Old Testament Prophecy
>
> Old Testament Studies
>
> Plato
>
> The Teaching of Jesus
>
> The Wisdom Literature

Fun Facts

When Was the Bible Completed?

According to William F. Albright, there is no longer any solid basis for dating any book of the New Testament after about A.D./C.E. 80. Albright was the world's foremost biblical archaeologist. Important Dates in Biblical History B.C./B.C.E.

1800—Abraham, Patriarchs

1290—Exodus (some take an early date of 1440), Moses, Joshua

1050—Beginning of the Israelite monarchy, Samuel, Saul

1000—David, Nathan; Fall of Samaria, end of the Northern Kingdom; Ahaz, Isaiah

701—Assyrian invasion of Judah, deliverance from Sennacherib; Hezekiah, Isaiah, Micah

605—Battle of Carchemish, rise of the Babylonian empire, Jeremiah, Habakkuk

598—First deportation of Israelites to Babylon; Jeremiah, Ezekiel

586—Destruction of Jerusalem, second deportation, exile, Jeremiah, Ezekiel

538—Overthrow of Babylonian Empire by Persians, return from exile, Cyrus

520—Rebuilding of the Jerusalem temple; Haggai, Zechariah, Zerubbabel

450—Reforms of Ezra, beginning of Judaism, Nehemiah (date is disputed), Malachi

323—Death of Alexander the Great, Seleucids, Ptolomies

167—Macabbean Revolt; Judas Macabbee, Book of Daniel

63—Roman control of Palestine under the Roman general Pompey

5–3—Birth of Jesus, Herod the Great A.D./C.E.

27–30—Death and resurrection of Jesus the Christ

45—Council of Jerusalem, marking the break of Christianity from Judaism

50—Earliest New Testament writings: 1 and 2 Thessalonians, Paul, Silas

60–70—First Gospel written (Mark), death of Paul

70—Destruction of Jerusalem by the Roman general Titus

Famous People Who Majored in Biblical Studies

Paul Tillich, Mircea Eliade, Martin Marty, Christof Ernst Luthardt

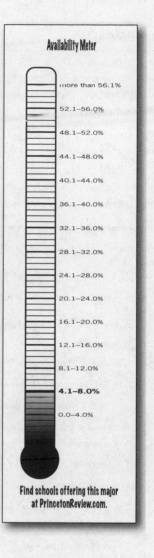

Availability Meter

more than 56.1%

52.1–56.0%

48.1–52.0%

44.1–48.0%

40.1–44.0%

36.1–40.0%

32.1–36.0%

28.1–32.0%

24.1–28.0%

20.1–24.0%

16.1–20.0%

12.1–16.0%

8.1–12.0%

4.1–8.0%

0.0–4.0%

Find schools offering this major at PrincetonReview.com.

Careers and Salary

The starting salaries for biblical studies and religious studies majors are $22,000 to $28,000.

CAREER OPTIONS

Anthropologist	Editor	Teacher
Archaeologist	Missionary	Theologian
Clergy—Priest, Rabbi, Minister	Philosopher	Writer

BILINGUAL/MULTICULTURAL EDUCATION

Basics

Spanish is the native language of many families in the United States, and a number of children grow up learning both Spanish and English at the same time. That's why K–12 schools in some regions are staffed with bilingual teachers who can relate to (and communicate with) a bilingual student population. These talented teachers not only speak two languages, but they also understand at least two different cultures.

If you're a pro at Spanish and think you'd enjoy working with bilingual kids, this major may be perfect for you. (A few colleges also offer a similar program for French.) Through a combination of coursework and student teaching, you will learn two important things: what it takes to be an amazing teacher, and how to lead a class in which your students may still be learning to speak, read, and write in English (their second language) while they also study subjects like math, science, and history. It's a demanding set of tasks for teachers and students alike—but it's also highly rewarding for all involved.

Your college classes will cover the culture and history of people from Mexico, Puerto Rico, and the Dominican Republic, among other countries. You'll discuss belief and value systems, as well as reasons for emigration. Once you graduate, you can help shape the intellectual development of multilingual students. You'll also have made a great career choice as bilingual teachers are in high demand across the United States.

SAMPLE COLLEGE CURRICULUM FOR MULTICULTURAL EDUCATION

Assessment of Bilingual and ESL Students

Classroom Management

Current Issues and Problems in Bilingual-Bicultural Education

Developing Literacy in the Bilingual Classroom

Foundations in Bilingual Education

Hispanic Cultural Perspectives

Language and Concept Development in Young Children

Language, Culture, and Communication

Linguistics for the Teacher of English Language Learners

Methods of Teaching English as a Second Language

Multicultural and Social Foundations of Education

Student Teaching Practicum

Teaching School Content in the Bilingual Classroom

Workshop: Cultural Awareness

If You Like Multicultural Education, You May Also Like . . .

Child care, child development, education, education administration, elementary education, English, Latin American studies, linguistics, Spanish, teacher education, teaching English as a second language

Suggested High School Prep for Multicultural Education

You should take the highest-level Spanish courses that your high school offers. Volunteering to teach ESL will also help you gain valuable experience.

Fun Facts

¿Habla Español?

Spanish is the second most spoken language in the United States (after English). In 2005, it was spoken natively by about 30 million people (about 12 percent of the population).

Spanish has the status of an official language (along with English) in the state of New Mexico. Spanish is the second most spoken language in 43 states as well as the District of Columbia.

(Source: www.wikipedia.com)

Did You Know?

A child born on U.S. soil is automatically a citizen of the United States even if their parents are not U.S. citizens.

Careers and Salary

The starting salary for a bilingual teacher usually falls within the range of $35,000 to $45,000.

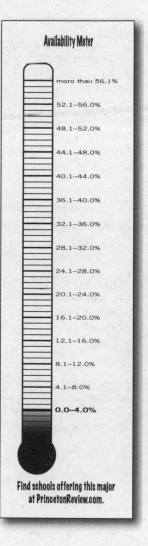

Availability Meter

more than 56.1%
52.1–56.0%
48.1–52.0%
44.1–48.0%
40.1–44.0%
36.1–40.0%
32.1–36.0%
28.1–32.0%
24.1–28.0%
20.1–24.0%
16.1–20.0%
12.1–16.0%
8.1–12.0%
4.1–8.0%
0.0–4.0%

Find schools offering this major at PrincetonReview.com.

CAREER OPTIONS

Child Care Worker	Professor	Translator
Journalist	Teacher	

BIOCHEMISTRY

Basics

Do you love chemistry? Do you go all soft and squishy in your biology class? Do you wish you could somehow take them both at once? Well, you can if you major in biochemistry.

Biochemistry majors study the chemistry of living things—the molecular compounds, substances, and physiology that make them tick. You can think of it as teeny biology. Biochemists study the minute, discrete characteristics of every organism and biological process. You'll be the envy of premed majors everywhere because you will actually understand organic chemistry. This major is also good preparation for medical school.

Remember that most college science classes require extensive lab time. Be prepared to do more bonding with your lab partner than with your roommate or significant other. (Unless, of course, your lab partner is your roommate or significant other.)

If You Like Biochemistry, You May Also Like . . .

Agricultural and biological engineering, biology, biopsychology, cell biology, chemistry, nursing, pharmacology, premedicine

Suggested High School Prep for Biochemistry

Do we even need to say it? Take chemistry and biology. Advanced math and physics are usually a part of the biochemistry curriculum as well, so classes in these areas will help.

SAMPLE COLLEGE CURRICULUM FOR BIOCHEMISTRY

Biochemistry I–II

Calculus I–II

General Biology I–II

General Chemistry I–II

Microbiology

Organic Chemistry I–II

Physics I–II

Fun Facts

I'd Like to Use a Lifeline . . .

Stuck on a problem? Ask an expert at *Scientific American* at sciam.com/askexpert/index.html. When you post a question, scientists from around the country offer answers. The archive contains helpful Q&A on biology, chemistry, physics, mathematics, medicine, astronomy, computers, geology, and the environment. Not a bad resource to bookmark.

Making a Difference

"The true men of action of our time, those who transform the world, are not the politicians and statesmen, but the scientists. Unfortunately, poetry cannot celebrate them, because their deeds are concerned with things, not persons and are, therefore, speechless."

—W. H. Auden

Careers and Salary

A biochemistry major right out of college can expect to make anywhere from $35,000 to $45,000.

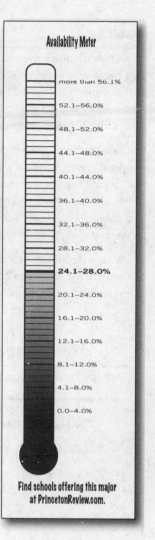

Availability Meter

more than 56.1%

52.1–56.0%

48.1–52.0%

44.1–48.0%

40.1–44.0%

36.1–40.0%

32.1–36.0%

28.1–32.0%

24.1–28.0%

20.1–24.0%

16.1–20.0%

12.1–16.0%

8.1–12.0%

4.1–8.0%

0.0–4.0%

Find schools offering this major at PrincetonReview.com.

CAREER OPTIONS

Biochemist	Chemist	Geneticist
Biologist	Doctor	Pharmacist
Chemical Engineer		

BIOETHICS

Basics

When it comes to medical research, each new development leaves a trail of moral questions in its wake. Just because we can do something, does that mean we should? Bioethics is the study of ethical issues in the fields of medical research and treatment. In a sense, bioethicists act as the conscience of science; they make sure society doesn't get too far in over its head. If you are a patient, philosophical person interested in medical issues and helping people, the rapidly growing field of bioethics may be for you.

As a bioethics major, you'll learn how to apply social and moral values to health issues. You'll study philosophical ethics, medical sociology, theology, spirituality, policy analysis, and decision theory; you'll research and debate the big questions, like cloning, stem cell research, and euthanasia. But you'll also deal with everyday health care issues like death and dying, therapeutic relationships, organ transplantation, human and animal subjects, reproduction and fertility, health care justice, cultural sensitivity, needs assessment, professionalism, and clinical or emergency procedures.

With a degree in bioethics, you might work in health care, education, public policy, or social work. Or, after further schooling, you might find employment at a university think tank. It seems that demand for people with backgrounds in bioethics will only increase in the years to come.

If You Like Bioethics, You May Also Like . . .

Biology, counseling, genetics, health administration, nursing, philosophy, premedicine, political science, public policy analysis, religious studies, social work, sociology, theology

SAMPLE COLLEGE CURRICULUM FOR BIOETHICS

Bioethics and the Law

Clinical Ethics

Empirical Research Methods in Bioethics

Feminism and Bioethics

Health and Human Values

Health Care Policy

Health Care Systems

The Human Body and Parts as Property

Human Genetics

Medical Sociology

Philosophical Foundations of Bioethics

Race, Gender, and Medical Science

Reproductive Ethics

Theology, Ethics, and Medicine

Suggested High School Prep for Bioethics

To prepare for this major, take biology, along with U.S. history and English. If your school happens to offer philosophy or religion, take those too.

Fun Facts

A Brief History of Bioethics

Medical ethics traces its roots back to the Hippocratic oath, the ancient Greek coda that required physicians, above all, to "do no harm." Centuries later, the first professional code of ethics was established in 1846 by the founders of the American Medical Association. More recently, the Nuremburg Code for research ethics on human subjects was established in response to the atrocities of human experimentation performed in the 1930s and 1940s in Nazi Germany.

(Source: www.bioethics.net/articles.php?viewCat=3&articleId=1)

Careers and Salary

Most careers in this field require at least a master's or other professional degree. Students straight out of a bioethics major in college will probably make between $20,000 and $30,000 a year.

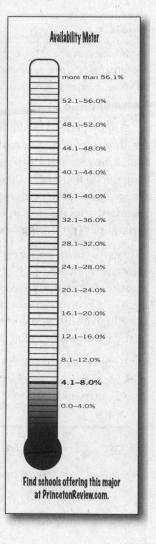

Availability Meter

more than 56.1%
52.1–56.0%
48.1–52.0%
44.1–48.0%
40.1–44.0%
36.1–40.0%
32.1–36.0%
28.1–32.0%
24.1–28.0%
20.1–24.0%
16.1–20.0%
12.1–16.0%
8.1–12.0%
4.1–8.0%
0.0–4.0%

Find schools offering this major at PrincetonReview.com.

CAREER OPTIONS

Bioethicist	Nurse	Public Health Educator
Counselor	Philosopher	Researcher
Lawyer	Professor	Social Worker
Medical Scientist	Psychologist	Sociologist

BIOINFORMATICS

Basics

Biology in the 21st century is home to a host of complicated questions and answers, and the field of bioinformatics is where those questions and answers live. As computer programs become more equipped to store, retrieve and analyze data, they also have been called upon to help scientists predict and simulate biological matter.

Strictly defined, bioinformatics, also known as computational molecular biology, is the "use of computers to characterize the molecular components of living things," according to Wikipedia. Most notoriously, bioinformatics is the driving force behind the Human Genome Project, a program that spent 13 years mapping the 20,000 to 25,000 human genes and the 3 billion chemical base pairs that make them. Now that the mapping has been completed, the second phase of analysis of the data will rely on the work of those with bioinformatics degrees. In fact, work in bioinformatics is characterized by its use of data resulting from high-throughput (producing large quantities of data) experiments.

The bachelor's, masters', and doctorate programs in bioinformatics look to meld several fields of study into one multi-faceted, highly technical skill set. In addition to heavy emphasis in biology, chemistry, math, statistics, computer programming and algorithms, students can expect ethics classes that specifically keep sight of the dynamic legal and social climate surrounding this type of research. Most programs look to produce individuals who combine the roles of scientist, engineer and computer analyst by overlapping several of the traditional training programs of each element.

Graduates of bioinformatics will be prepared for jobs conducting research for pharmaceutical companies, medical research and medical data analysis. A minor in Bioinformatics can be used to tailor a biology or chemistry major toward research or to expand computer engineering into biomedics.

SAMPLE COLLEGE CURRICULUM FOR BIOINFORMATICS

Advance Programming Concepts

Bioethics

Chemistry

Computational Biology

Data Structures

Discrete Structures

Evolution Biology

Genetics

High-Level Calculus

Molecular Biology

Organic Chemistry

Statistical Theory

If you like Bioinformatics, you may also like...

Chemical engineering, biological engineering, computer engineering, medical research, computational algorithms, statistics

Suggested High School Prep for Bioinformatics

Applicants to bioinformatics should take four years of math in high school at least through advanced algebra and trigonometry and three years of science including biology and chemistry. Other classes like statistics, physics and computer programming will give students an understanding of the basic principles on which their college training will build.

Fun Facts

The Human Genome project is a multi-national endeavor into a deeper understanding of what it means to be human. Humans are made up of 24 distinct chromosomal pairs, and the Human Genome project hopes to isolate specific factors on each that correlates with human characteristics. Scientists who have completed the mapping of the Human Genome, say that their research tells us that each chromosome is roughly 80 percent to 90 percent "junk DNA" meaning it serves no specific purpose as far as current research reports.

(Source: www.wikipedia.com)

Careers and Salary

Starting salary will vary depending on the level of degree a student achieves in bioinformatics. For a student with a bachelor's in bioinformatics starting salary can range from $55,000 to $75,000.

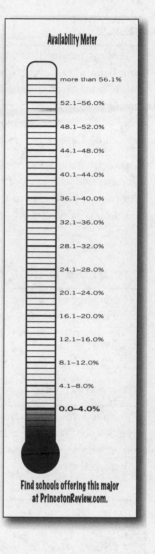

Availability Meter

more than 56.1%

52.1–56.0%

48.1–52.0%

44.1–48.0%

40.1–44.0%

36.1–40.0%

32.1–36.0%

28.1–32.0%

24.1–28.0%

20.1–24.0%

16.1–20.0%

12.1–16.0%

8.1–12.0%

4.1–8.0%

0.0–4.0%

Find schools offering this major at PrincetonReview.com.

CAREER OPTIONS

Biochemist	Geneticist	Physician
Biologist	Pharmacist	Researcher

BIOLOGY

Basics

Biology majors, in a sense, go straight to the heart of things. They focus on the living world, on everything from microscopic organisms to the human body. They look at all of the elements and questions surrounding life, from questions about reproduction to the ways in which our physical environment influences the way we grow and develop. Given the nature and scope of biology, the field is often divided into subcategories such as molecular biology, which studies the exchange and transfer of chemicals within living organisms, and cell biology, which examines the basic building blocks of living organisms.

Biology majors have at their disposal a vast array of skills and tools that can lead to careers and professions in a wide variety of fields. In addition to being a stepping stone to a career in medicine, a biology major offers the opportunity to explore careers in some of the hottest and most rapidly developing fields around, including genetics (think Human Genome Project), biotechnology, and medical research.

If You Like Biology, You May Also Like . . .

Chemistry, child care, food science, genetics, gerontology, home economics, human development, medical technology, microbiology, neurobiology, neuroscience, nursing, nutrition, pharmacology, pharmacy, physical therapy, physiological psychology, premedicine, pre-optometry, pre-veterinary medicine, public health

Suggested High School Prep for Biology

Immerse yourself as fully as possible in all of the sciences available to you in high school. General biology, physics, and chemistry classes are a good starting point, as is a background in math. Advanced placement courses in any of these subjects will certainly help you build a strong foundation before starting college.

SAMPLE COLLEGE CURRICULUM FOR BIOLOGY

Calculus

Cell Biology

Evolution

General Biology

General Chemistry

Genetics

Microbiology

Organic Chemistry

Organismal Biology

Physics

Fun Facts

That's Not Easy

"Trying to determine the structure of a protein by UV spectroscopy was like trying to determine the structure of a piano by listening to the sound it made while being dropped down a flight of stairs."

—Francis Crick, British molecular biologist

A Short History of Medicine

I have an earache.

2000 B.C./B.C.E.—Here, eat this root.

A.D./C.E. 1000—That root is heathen. Here, say this prayer.

A.D./C.E. 1850—That prayer is superstition. Here, drink this potion.

A.D./C.E. 1940—That potion is snake oil. Here, swallow this pill.

A.D./C.E. 1985—That pill is ineffective. Here, take this antibiotic.

A.D./C.E. 2000—That antibiotic is artificial. Here, eat this root.

Careers and Salary

Because of the breadth of opportunities available to biology majors, specific starting salaries are dependent on the careers they choose. The average starting salary for a biology major ranges from $23,000 to $32,000.

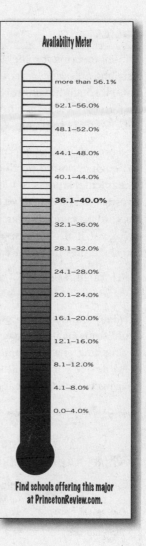

Availability Meter

more than 56.1%

52.1–56.0%

48.1–52.0%

44.1–48.0%

40.1–44.0%

36.1–40.0%

32.1–36.0%

28.1–32.0%

24.1–28.0%

20.1–24.0%

16.1–20.0%

12.1–16.0%

8.1–12.0%

4.1–8.0%

0.0–4.0%

Find schools offering this major at PrincetonReview.com.

CAREER OPTIONS

Biochemist

Biologist

Ecologist

Environmentalist/Environmental Scientist

Geneticist

Optometrist

Pharmaceutical Sales Representative

Pharmacist

Physician

Professor

Researcher

Teacher

Veterinarian

BIOMEDICAL ENGINEERING

Basics

"Engineering for Life" is a phrase Columbia University couples with its biomedical engineering program. It's right on target, of course. Biomedical engineers have saved and improved lives of people around the globe through breakthroughs and innovations that have helped solve problems that have baffled the industry for years. Patients who benefit from an artificial organ or a prosthetic limb, for example, have biomedical engineers to thank.

Through your major in biomedical engineering, you'll learn how to use physics, chemistry, mathematics, and engineering to produce solutions to important biological and medical problems. Topics span from the fundamental studies of biological structures to applied medical device design and evaluation. Many of your investigations will involve the design and development of implantable or indwelling devices such as orthopedic, cardiac, endovascular, drug delivery, or cell- and tissue-engineered systems. As a biomedical engineering major, you'll also be responsible for understanding laboratory techniques, concepts of engineering design, and the ethics involved when practicing the development of biomedical devices and systems.

Through research (both your own and that of others) you'll see practical applications of the laws of biology and how what you study leads to new advancements in fields far outside the realm of engineering.

Many biomedical engineering programs also cover the basics of our health care system, meaning you could study health management systems and legal and ethical issues in health care. The field of biomedical engineering changes rapidly, and many students choose to pursue advanced degrees to stay on top of the latest devices or techniques, which emerge practically daily. Graduates may find themselves working with pharmaceuticals, medical devices, artificial organs, prosthetics and sensory aids, diagnostics, medical instrumentation, or medical imaging.

SAMPLE COLLEGE CURRICULUM FOR BIOMEDICAL ENGINEERING

Biological Transport

Biomaterials

Biomedical Fluid Mechanics

Bioprocess Design

Biotechnology and Environmental Process

Cell Biology

Genetics

Heat Transfer in Biological Systems

Medical Devices

Physiology

Principles of Neuroanatomy

Tissue Engineering

If You Like Biomedical Engineering, You May Also Like . . .

Agricultural and biological engineering, applied mathematics, applied physics, biochemistry, biology, biopsychology, biotechnology, cell biology, chemical engineering, chemistry, engineering design, engineering mechanics, engineering physics, environmental and environmental health engineering

Suggested High School Prep for Biomedical Engineering

Math and science courses of every stripe are key preparation if you're considering this field. Biology, chemistry, physics, statistics, calculus . . . need we go on? Don't forget about English courses either; good engineers must also be good communicators. Courses in philosophy (especially ethics), history, and religion will also give you a strong foundation.

Fun Facts

Read Up

Indulge your interest in biomedical engineering with one of these scholarly journals. They might not be weekend reading, but you could learn some fascinating things about current research and debates.

- Annals of Biomedical Engineering
- BioTech Navigator
- Genetic Engineering News
- Journal of Molecular Microbiology and Biotechnology

Back in Touch

Imagine life without any physical contact—for people with the disorder called epidermolysis bullosa (EB), their skin can blister from even the slightest touch. But thanks to biomedical engineering advancements, these people have the opportunity to receive "new skin"—Apligraf. Apligraf was developed by biomedical engineers and is made from the living human skin cells of newborns. It's used mainly to help diabetic and venous leg ulcers heal when more conventional methods fail, although it is also considered a good short-term solution for treating chronic nonhealing EB wounds.

Virtual Stomach

A virtual stomach has been developed by researchers to aid in the discovery of how medicines are broken down and released into the body. Check it out at: www.whitaker.org.

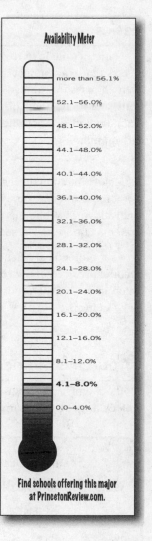

Availability Meter

more than 56.1%

52.1–56.0%

48.1–52.0%

44.1–48.0%

40.1–44.0%

36.1–40.0%

32.1–36.0%

28.1–32.0%

24.1–28.0%

20.1–24.0%

16.1–20.0%

12.1–16.0%

8.1–12.0%

4.1–8.0%

0.0–4.0%

Find schools offering this major at PrincetonReview.com.

Careers and Salary

Most engineering fields have starting salaries in the $37,000 to $45,000 range, although this number depends heavily on where you live and how you choose to use your degree. Advanced degrees usually greatly increase starting salaries.

CAREER OPTIONS

Biologist	Chemist	Researcher
Biomedical Engineer	Health Care Administrator	Technical Writer

BIOMEDICAL SCIENCE

Basics

Some people love to say, "At least you have your health." Biomedical science majors want to make sure it stays that way. Biomedical science combines the fields of biology and medicine to focus on the health of both animals and humans. As a biomedical science major, you'll study biochemical and physiological functions, anatomical and histological structures, epidemiology, and pharmacology. You'll learn how to both maintain and promote health in humans and animals with knowledge in the basics of nutrition, diseases, and immunology. Delve into fields such as cell and molecular biology, parasitology, and toxicology, and emerge with hands-on experience through laboratory work and research.

Majors in biomedical science are poised to make valuable contributions to the fields of both biology and medicine—and many move on to make discoveries in the field of biology that have important effects in the medical world. While there are copious careers available to students who obtain a bachelor of science, many students choose to pursue additional education in professional or graduate schools.

As a biomedical science major, you may go on to make advancements in the study of cancer or AIDS, become involved in the research of infectious diseases, or propel science toward improving the human condition in any of hundreds of other ways. Get set to make a scientifically sound difference in the health of living beings.

If You Like Biomedical Science, You May Also Like . . .

Biochemistry, biology, biopsychology, cell biology, chemical engineering, chemistry, genetics, medicine, molecular genetics, pharmacy, premedicine

SAMPLE COLLEGE CURRICULUM FOR BIOMEDICAL SCIENCE

Anatomy

Animal Science

Biology of Cell Tissues

Biomedical Aspects of Human Nutrition

Clinical Microbiology

Comparative Mammalian Neurology

Endocrine Physiology

Genetics

Organic Chemistry

Statistical Methods

Virology

Suggested High School Prep for Biomedical Science

Bulk up on as many science and math courses as you can handle, especially biology, chemistry, physics, calculus, and trigonometry. The more you can learn now, the better. Scientists must also be good communicators, so be sure to take classes such as English, history, and languages that will help polish your reading and writing skills. And of course, you should take advantage of any science courses or clubs that offer laboratory experience.

Fun Facts

Science Summed Up

Here are a few words from philosopher/sociologist Herbert Spencer (1820–1903).

"Science is organized knowledge."

"People are beginning to see that the first requisite to success in life is to be a good animal."

"Evolution . . . is—a change from an indefinite, incoherent homogeneity, to a definite coherent heterogeneity."

"Progress, therefore, is not an accident, but a necessity. . . . It is a part of nature."

Animal Lovers

Do you love animals and science? Sometimes it's hard to accept the idea of animal testing, even when that testing is considered necessary and may lead to valuable discoveries. The National Association for Biomedical Research (NABR) strives to ensure that animals are treated humanely in labs. It is the only national nonprofit organization of its kind, and it represents more than 300 institutions that use animals in research. The NABR believes that pain and distress should be minimized, no more animals than absolutely necessary should be used, and that alternatives to animals should be used whenever possible.

Careers and Salary

Starting salaries for biomedical science majors are difficult to determine and depend on how much education you pursue, how you choose to use your degree, and how much experience you've acquired. A reasonable estimate for science majors is in the $25,000 to $35,000 range.

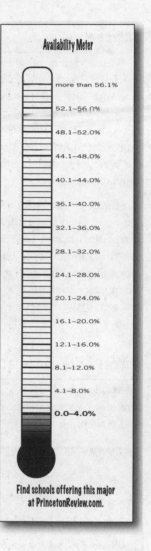

Availability Meter

more than 56.1%

52.1–56.0%

48.1–52.0%

44.1–48.0%

40.1–44.0%

36.1–40.0%

32.1–36.0%

28.1–32.0%

24.1–28.0%

20.1–24.0%

16.1–20.0%

12.1–16.0%

8.1–12.0%

4.1–8.0%

0.0–4.0%

Find schools offering this major at PrincetonReview.com.

CAREER OPTIONS		
Biochemist	Dentist	Professor
Biologist	Physician	Researcher

BIOMETRICS/BIOSTATISTICS

Basics

Which variety of wheat provides greater yield in an agricultural experiment? Which HIV therapies are most effective among poverty-stricken communities in Botswana? Why are death rates from heart disease in New York City and its suburbs among the highest in the nation? Why do three out of four dentists supposedly prefer one particular chewing gum over another? Biometrics refers to the statistical and mathmatical methods of data analysis that are aimed at solving real-world problems such as these—and ultimately, at improving individuals' qualities of life. This discipline is generally considered the nexus between statistics and biology/medicine, although lately it's come to encompass other fields such as ecology, agriculture, and population genetics.

Studying biometrics means solving complex analysis problems. As a result, this major places a significant emphasis on mathematics and statistics. You'll study such quant-heavy topics as computational biology, matrix algebra and applied calculus, spatial and temporal analysis, and sampling theory. This is not to suggest that biometrics is entirely theoretical—as we said, biometrics uses data analysis to tackle real-world issues that involve actual people, places, and issues. Results from this data analysis have concrete effects. When other students talk about changing the world, you'll be able to tell them, from a biometrics perspective, exactly what factors will come into play.

If You Like Biostatistics/Biometrics, You May Also Like . . .

Applied mathematics, biology, computer and information science, ecology, environmental science, epidemiology, experimental pathology, forestry, genetics, marine biology, natural resources conservation, premedicine, public health, sustainable resource management, wildlife management

SAMPLE COLLEGE CURRICULUM FOR BIOSTATISTICS/BIOMETRICS

Advanced Probability and Statistical Inference

Applied Stochastic Processes

Biostatistics

Computer Science

Epidemiology of Chronic Disease

Intermediate Linear Models

Principles of Experimental Analysis

Public Health Demography

Quantitative Methods

Theory and Methods of Survival Analysis

Suggested High School Prep for Biostatistics/Biometrics

Become a sciences rock star and take as many math courses as you can. You'll need to study biology and computer science too. Since much of your work in biometrics will be under public scrutiny, make sure you also excel in humanities courses so that you become the best possible communicator.

Fun Facts

Disaster Relief

Biostatistics has played a tremendous role in tracking the ongoing aftermath of the Chernobyl disaster, the worst nuclear accident of the twentieth century. Using biostatistical studies, international health organizations have helped Belarus, Ukraine, and Russia manage the remediation of the environment, evacuate and resettle civilians, develop uncontaminated food sources and food distribution channels, and implement effective public health measures.

Visiting Disney

At Walt Disney World, biometric measurements are taken from the fingers of guests to ensure that the same person uses the ticket from day to day. Walt Disney World is now the nation's largest single commercial application of biometrics, but the U.S. Visit program will very soon take over the No. 1 spot from Walt Disney World for the use of biometrics.

(Source: http://en.wikipedia.org/wiki/Biometrics)

Authentication at the ATM

Several banks in Japan use palm vein authentication technology on their ATMs. The technology was developed by Fujitsu among other companies and has proved to have low false rejection rate (about 0.01 percent) and a very low false acceptance rate (less than 0.00008 percent).

(Source: http://en.wikipedia.org/wiki/Biometrics)

Careers and Salary

Starting salaries for college graduates are approximately $40,000. Of course, the majority of biostatistics majors continue on to graduate school and earn that salary once they've earned their master's degrees.

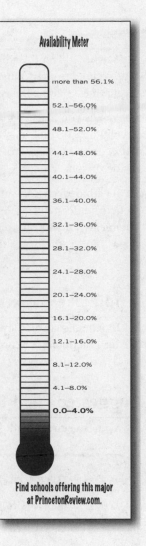

Availability Meter

more than 56.1%
52.1–56.0%
48.1–52.0%
44.1–48.0%
40.1–44.0%
36.1–40.0%
32.1–36.0%
28.1–32.0%
24.1–28.0%
20.1–24.0%
16.1–20.0%
12.1–16.0%
8.1–12.0%
4.1–8.0%
0.0–4.0%

Find schools offering this major at PrincetonReview.com.

CAREER OPTIONS

Professor	Researcher	Survey Researcher
Public Health Administrator	Scientist	Teacher

BIOPSYCHOLOGY

Basics

Maybe if Freud hadn't gotten so wrapped up in those dreams of his he would have gotten to biopsychology after polishing off psychoanalysis. Or maybe he would have just taken one look at the major requirements and gone right back to sleep.

Yes, as you may have already figured out, this major is a combination of biology and psychology. It's the psychology of biology—or is it the biology of psychology? Either way, this major is that missing link between the biology major that's been tempting you and that psychology major lurking somewhere deep inside of your id.

As a biopsychology major you will take courses in both fields, using the skills learned in one discipline to help understand the issues of the other. The relationship between our biological makeup (hormones, chemicals, and so on) and our behavior is a complicated one, so complicated that it demanded its own major. This is the major that trains its students to discover those relationships.

If You Like Biopsychology, You May Also Like . . .

Biochemistry, biology, chemistry, clinical psychology, counseling, experimental psychology, genetics, medical technology, neuroscience, nursing, nutrition, pharmacology, physics, premedicine, psychology

Suggested High School Prep for Biopsychology

You can start recording your dreams alongside what you ate for dinner the night before, but that probably won't help too much. Instead focus on those math and science classes, particularly biology, chemistry, physics, and calculus. The more advanced, the better.

> ### SAMPLE COLLEGE CURRICULUM FOR BIOPSYCHOLOGY
>
> Advanced Seminar in Physiological Psychology
>
> Animal Behavior
>
> Brain and Behavior
>
> Cells and Organisms
>
> Comparative Vertebrate Physiology
>
> Experimental Psychology
>
> General Genetics
>
> Human Neuropsychology
>
> Neurobiology
>
> Statistics

Fun Facts

Deductive Reasoning

Taking a well-earned break from the detective business, Sherlock Holmes and Watson were on a camping/hiking trip. They had gone to bed and were looking up at the sky.

Holmes said, "Watson, look up. What do you see?"

"Well, I see thousands of stars."

"And what does that mean to you?"

"Well, I suppose it means that of all the planets and suns and moons in the universe, that we are truly the one most blessed with the reason to deduce theorems to make our way in this world of criminal enterprises and blind greed. It means that we are truly small in the eyes of God but struggle each day to be worthy of the senses and spirit we have been blessed with. And, I suppose, at the very least, in the meteorological sense, it means that it is most likely that we will have another nice day tomorrow. What does it mean to you, Holmes?"

"To me, it means someone has stolen our tent."

Psychology Is Actually Math

Psychology is actually biology.

Biology is actually chemistry.

Chemistry is actually physics.

And physics is actually math.

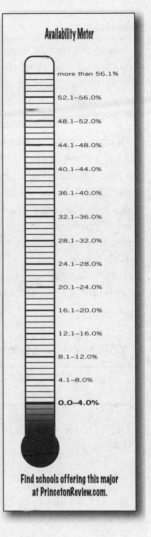

Availability Meter

more than 56.1%

52.1–56.0%

48.1–52.0%

44.1–48.0%

40.1–44.0%

36.1–40.0%

32.1–36.0%

28.1–32.0%

24.1–28.0%

20.1–24.0%

16.1–20.0%

12.1–16.0%

8.1–12.0%

4.1–8.0%

0.0–4.0%

Find schools offering this major
at PrincetonReview.com.

Careers and Salary

As a biopsychology major you will have a number of career paths open to you. The average starting salary for biopsychology majors hovers in the range of $23,000 to $34,000.

CAREER OPTIONS

Biologist	Guidance Counselor	Psychologist
Criminologist	Physician	Substance Abuse Counselor

BIOTECHNOLOGY

Basics

You have your biology major, and you have your chemistry major, and your biochemistry major, and your molecular biology major, and maybe someday your biochemicalmolecular major, but until then what you have is a biotechnology major. It's the best of all four worlds—assuming you believe in a best world when you're talking about analyzing and figuring out the genetic structure of everything from the human heart to the soybean.

Biotechnology is a new and very, very hot field. Building on the advancements made through molecular biology and biochemistry, biotechnology is centered on the ways we can manipulate and exploit genes (not the faded, slightly tight ones that make you look skinny, but the really tight ones that hang out on chromosomes). You'll learn about how genes operate and how those operations can be altered. By combining just about every science known to man (chemistry, biology, food science, animal science, earth science, and plant science for starters) this major is perfect for the student who wants to know how every living thing—everything—works. Whether you dream of spending thousands of hours researching as an academic or want to help figure out how to clone a monkey's heart, a biotechnology major is sure to keep you on your toes with rapid advancements and a world of developing opportunities. (Note: Trying to clone yourself in your basement is still illegal, so don't get any fancy ideas.)

If You Like Biotechnology, You May Also Like . . .

Agricultural and biological engineering, animal science, biochemistry, biology, botany and plant biology, genetics, horticulture, microbiology, molecular genetics, natural resources conservation, neurobiology, neuroscience, nutrition, pharmacology, pharmacy, plant pathology, zoology

> **SAMPLE COLLEGE CURRICULUM FOR BIOTECHNOLOGY**
>
> Animal Cell Culture
>
> Applications in Molecular Biology
>
> Biotechnology Seminar
>
> Botany
>
> Cell and Molecular Biology
>
> Entomology
>
> General Biology
>
> Human Heredity
>
> Immunology
>
> Microbiology
>
> Plant Pathology
>
> Virology
>
> Zoology

Suggested High School Prep for Biotechnology

If you're interested in studying biotechnology, it's important to immerse yourself as fully as possible in all of the sciences available to you in high school. General biology, physics, and chemistry classes are good starting points, as is a deep and solid background in math. If you want to hit the ground running as a biotechnology major, AP courses in these subjects aren't optional—they're a requirement.

Fun Facts

Did You Know?

The Department of Agriculture has stated that approximately 44 percent of soybeans and 36 percent of all corn grown in the United States in 1998 were grown from seeds enhanced with biotechnology.

Farmers and other experts have for years conducted outdoor testing for each crop variety enhanced through biotechnology. To date, 50 varieties of biotechnology-enhanced crops have been approved in the United States.

Daily Doses

The average person comes into contact with a million species of bacteria and about 5,000 viruses daily, according to the Centers for Disease Control.

(Source: http://www.junkscience.com/nov99/jenkins2.html)

Tougher Tomatoes

A gene from the Arctic flounder has been transferred to tomatoes to lessen their susceptibility to cold.

(Source: http://www.junkscience.com/nov99/jenkins2.html)

Careers and Salary

Starting salaries for biotechnology majors fall in the high twenties and low thirties. Master's and doctoral degrees will push those numbers up.

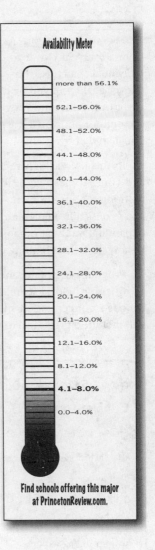

Availability Meter

more than 56.1%

52.1–56.0%

48.1–52.0%

44.1–48.0%

40.1–44.0%

36.1–40.0%

32.1–36.0%

28.1–32.0%

24.1–28.0%

20.1–24.0%

16.1–20.0%

12.1–16.0%

8.1–12.0%

4.1–8.0%

0.0–4.0%

Find schools offering this major at PrincetonReview.com.

CAREER OPTIONS

Biologist

Ecologist

Environmentalist/Environmental Scientist

Pharmaceutical Sales Representative

Professor

Researcher

BOTANY AND PLANT BIOLOGY

Basics

Like to dish the dirt? As a botany and plant biology major, you'll learn about every aspect of the plant world, from a four-leaf clover to the world's largest rain forests. Your passion for plants will lead you to study their individual structures, how plants are alike and different, and how to identify and classify plants of all kinds. (Never again will you be able to hike through the woods with friends without feeling the irresistible urge to point out, name, and provide factoids on every tree, plant, vine, and shrub.) Plants play an important part in our culture, and you'll learn about their many functions and roles in nutrition, medicine, and the environment. You'll study how plants have evolved, how they have affected us, and, in turn, how we have affected them.

In this increasingly technological world, advances in the field of botany and plant biology are abundant, and your studies may lead you to any number of careers—from a burgeoning field like biotechnology to working for environmental causes or firms. You may study the ways we can manipulate the growth of plants and genetically alter them for nutritional or environmental benefits. Or you may get involved in the rapidly expanding study of organic food products and the plants and herbs that make up homeopathic medicines. Botany and plant biology gives you the opportunity to study the very building blocks of plant life.

Programs in botany and plant biology vary from school to school. Some may offer a general overview of all different fields, leaving it up to you to specialize later, in graduate programs. Others may require you to choose a concentration such as cellular biology, genetics, or environmental biology. In all cases, your studies will include a great deal of research, field work, and lots of time in the laboratory and possibly a greenhouse, giving you hands-on experience in this exciting and significant field.

SAMPLE COLLEGE CURRICULUM FOR BOTANY AND PLANT BIOLOGY

Anatomy of Vascular Plants

Biology

Cell Biology

Chemistry

Ecology of Vegetation

Ecosystem Ecology

Evolutionary Survey of the Plant Kingdom

Flowering Plant Systematics

Microbiology

Mycology

Physiology and Biochemistry of Plants

Plant Molecular Genetics

Plant Morphology

Plants, Environment, and People

If You Like Botany and Plant Biology, You May Also Like . . .

Agriculture, agricultural and biological engineering, agronomy and crop science, biochemistry, biology, cell biology, chemistry, ecology, entomology, environmental and environmental health engineering, environmental science, forestry, genetics, grain science, horticulture, microbiology, molecular genetics, natural resources conservation, neurobiology, plant pathology, soil science, sustainable resource management, turfgrass science

Suggested High School Prep for Botany and Plant Biology

For a botany and plant biology major, your best preparation will be advanced-level courses in biology, chemistry, math, and computers. And don't forget your English courses; effective scientists must also be good communicators. Try to get involved in groups that deal with plants and the environment—besides being a great way to gain knowledge related to your field, you'll also be able to get a taste for what your college studies may lead to in the future.

Fun Facts

For More Information

For just about everything you'd ever want to know about studying botany, check out the Botanical Society of America's website at www.botany.org. You'll find information on the various specialized areas of botany studies, job opportunities, new research, current issues, and articles written by practicing botanists about working in the field of botany.

Man-Eating Plants?

You've probably heard of the Venus flytrap, a plant that can capture bugs and digest them. But did you know there are almost 600 species of plants that are classified as carnivorous? To be carnivorous, a plant must not only capture and kill its prey but also digest and absorb the prey's nutrients. These plants usually stick to eating bugs, but some are large enough to eat frogs—and some have even been reported to eat small birds and rodents! These large carnivorous plants are in the genus Nepenthes and can grow tens of meters long.

(Source: International Carnivorous Plant Society, www.carnivorousplants.org)

Careers and Salary

Starting salaries for biologists are typically about $25,000. Furthering your education and work/research experience will substantially raise this figure. Botany majors can expect to earn a starting salary of about $23,000 to $32,000.

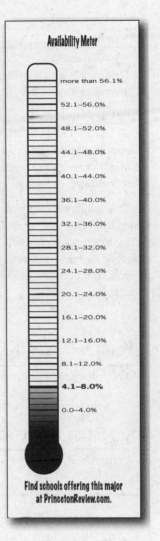

Availability Meter

more than 56.1%

52.1–56.0%

48.1–52.0%

44.1–48.0%

40.1–44.0%

36.1–40.0%

32.1–36.0%

28.1–32.0%

24.1–28.0%

20.1–24.0%

16.1–20.0%

12.1–16.0%

8.1–12.0%

4.1–8.0%

0.0–4.0%

Find schools offering this major at PrincetonReview.com.

CAREER OPTIONS		
Biochemist	Ecologist	Geneticist
Biologist	Environmentalist/	
Botanist	Environmental Scientist	

BUDDHIST STUDIES

Basics

A major in Buddhist studies allows you to approach the 2,500-year-old traditions of Buddhism via the academic path. You'll study the life and philosophy of Siddhartha Gautama, his enlightenment, and the consequent diaspora of the faith from ancient India across Asia and eventually, the West.

Besides studying sacred literature like the Dhammapada, the Lotus Sutra, or the Tripitaka, you'll study Buddhist ritual and culture, past and present, and you'll likely narrow your focus to (at least) one of the three schools of Buddhist thought: Theravada, Mahayana, and Vajrayana—and one or more of Buddhism's many permutations—Pure Land, Zen, Shingon, or Tibetan, for example—as each developed alongside the indigenous traditions of its host country.

This major will set you up to become an expert on a religion still taking root in America. If a job in academia interests you, you'll be on track for grad school and ultimately a career as a professor or scholar. If the clergy interests you, you'll have the background knowledge to supplement a rich spiritual life (although studying Buddhism is, as you'll learn in this major, vastly different from actually living it). In the private sector, you could end up pursuing a career as an anthropologist, archaeologist, historian, philosopher, journalist, and the like.

If You Like Buddhist Studies, You May Also Like . . .

Art history, Asian studies, history, philosophy, religious studies, theology

Suggested High School Prep for Buddhist Studies

Certainly philosophy classes will help you in high school, as will history and English. In fact, all courses in the humanities provide solid preparation for a major in Buddhist studies. Spend any free time studying the classic literature of Buddhism. If you live in an area with any Buddhist cultural centers or temples, make yourself a regular face at such places of worship and cultural exchange.

> ### SAMPLE COLLEGE CURRICULUM FOR BUDDHIST STUDIES
>
> Buddhist Ethics
>
> Buddhist Political and Social Theory
>
> Buddhism in America
>
> East Asia in the Early Buddhist Age
>
> The Life of the Buddha
>
> Meditation Traditions
>
> Religion in Human Experience
>
> Tibetan Ritual Life
>
> Zen Buddhism

Fun Facts

Sound of Silence

The Ch'an school of Buddhism traces its lineage to one of history's most succinct religious lectures: The story goes that the Buddha, surrounded by a crowd of patient monks waiting to hear his words, said nothing. He merely held up a single flower. Naturally, everybody was confused—everybody except one monk, Kashyapa. He understood that all the words ever spoken cannot convey the essence of the Buddha's message; receiving this transmission directly from the Buddha, he smiled. The Buddha smiled back. Thus, the meditative tradition of Silent Transmission—that of Ch'an, Dhyana, Son, or Zen—was born.

Telling the Truth

The Four Noble Truths of Buddhism teach the following:
- All worldly life is unsatisfactory, disjointed, containing of suffering.
- There is a cause of suffering, which is attachment or desire rooted in ignorance.
- There is an end of suffering, which is Nirvana.
- There is a path that leads out of suffering, known as the Noble Eightfold Path.

The Eightfold Path consists of:
- Right Understanding
- Right Thought
- Right Speech
- Right Action
- Right Livelihood
- Right Effort
- Right Mindfulness
- Right Concentration

Did You Know?

The Buddha isn't considered an omnipotent god by Buddhists; nor did the historical Buddha ever claim divine status or inspiration for himself. The seeds for enlightenment are present in every sentient being—one must merely awaken to them.

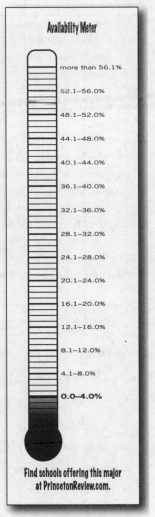

Availability Meter

more than 56.1%

52.1–56.0%

48.1–52.0%

44.1–48.0%

40.1–44.0%

36.1–40.0%

32.1–36.0%

28.1–32.0%

24.1–28.0%

20.1–24.0%

16.1–20.0%

12.1–16.0%

8.1–12.0%

4.1–8.0%

0.0–4.0%

Find schools offering this major at PrincetonReview.com.

Careers and Salary

If you opt to enter the workforce without a graduate degree, then you can expect starting salaries to be about $22,000 to $30,000.

CAREER OPTIONS		
Anthropologist	Historian	Teacher
Archaeologist	Journalist	Theologian
Clergyperson	Professor	Writer

BUSINESS ADMINISTRATION AND MANAGEMENT

Basics

Be the boss's boss. Or, at least, be a boss. While you may not be the head honcho on day one, this field offers enormous potential for growth. Organizational gurus with stellar people skills and a head for business will flourish in business administration and management.

Creating and perpetuating a successful business has always been a challenge. And in the only-the-strong-survive world of modern business—rampant with new, ever-advancing technology—managers need unshakable knowledge, top-notch training, and a serious set of skills.

Management, according to Penn State University, involves "the coordination of human, material, and financial resources to accomplish organizational goals." A major in business administration and management will provide that goal—focused training. You'll get a thorough grounding in the theories and principles of accounting, finance, marketing, economics, statistics, human resources functions, and decision making. You'll come away a whiz on how to budget, organize, plan, hire, direct, control, and otherwise manage various organizations.

As a major in business administration and management, expect to work in small groups—no room for wallflowers here. Count on problem solving, theorizing, and math-heavy number crunching too. You'll have your choice of areas in which to concentrate; many colleges and universities require you to focus on one, while others allow you to sample several. Options may include operations management, human resources management, and general management.

This major will also get you thinking about issues such as diversity, ethics, politics, and other dynamics that play a role in every work environment. As a manager-to-be, you'll also be required to develop a balance between sensitivity and fairness. You'll need to be innovative, creative, and a good problem solver. These qualities (and your winning personality) will put you on a path to successful management in any number of fields.

If You Like Business Administration and Management, You May Also Like . . .

Accounting, agricultural economics, business communications, computer and information science, data processing, entrepreneurship, finance, hospitality, human resources management, industrial management, international business, logistics management, managerial economics, marketing, mathematics, operations management, public administration, public policy analysis, recreation management, risk management, statistics

Suggested High School Prep for Business Administration and Management

Good businesspeople have great communication skills, so take your English courses seriously. You should also try to take as many advanced math and computer courses as you can. If your high school offers any business-related courses (such as business law), you should take them too. Keeping up with a foreign language will also help, particularly for a career in international business.

SAMPLE COLLEGE CURRICULUM FOR BUSINESS ADMINISTRATION AND MANAGEMENT

Employee Relations

Entrepreneurship

Human Resources Survey

Leadership and Motivation

Legal Environment of
 Business

Macroeconomics

Management Information Systems

Managerial Accounting

Managerial Skills

Microeconomics

Multinational Corporate Management

Operations Management

Organizational Behavior

Small Business Management

Women in Management

Fun Facts

Presidential Wisdom

"After all, the chief business of the American people is business."

—Calvin Coolidge, thirtieth president of the United States

Wet Behind the Ears

Being a first-time manager is tricky. When the time comes, you might find some useful information in one of these books.

- *96 Great Interview Questions to Ask Before You Hire* by Paul Facone
- *Action Tools for Effective Managers* by Margaret Mary Gootnick and David Gootnick
- *Effective Delegation* by Chris Roebuck
- *The First-Time Manager* by Loren B. Belker
- *The Four Elements of Successful Management* by Don R. Marshall
- *The Inner Work of Leaders* by Barbara Mackoff and Gary Wenet
- *Is It Always Right to Be Right?* by Warren H. Schmidt and B. J. Gallagher Hateley
- *The New Supervisor's Survival Manual* by William A. Salmon
- *The Rookie Manager* by Joseph T. Straub
- *The Successful New Manager* by Joseph T. Straub

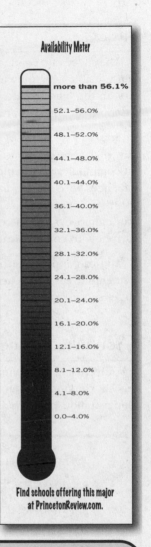

Availability Meter

more than 56.1%

52.1–56.0%

48.1–52.0%

44.1–48.0%

40.1–44.0%

36.1–40.0%

32.1–36.0%

28.1–32.0%

24.1–28.0%

20.1–24.0%

16.1–20.0%

12.1–16.0%

8.1–12.0%

4.1–8.0%

0.0–4.0%

Find schools offering this major at PrincetonReview.com.

Careers and Salary

Starting salaries for business administration and management majors can range anywhere from $30,000 to $50,000 and depend mostly on where you live, how you choose to use your degree, and how much experience you've had in your field.

CAREER OPTIONS

Accountant	Health Care Administrator	Plastics Manufacturer
Actuary	Hospital Administrator	Police Officer/Manager
Advertising Executive	Hotel Manager	Power Plant Manager
Auditor	Information Manager	Production Manager
Bank Officer	Management Consultant	Public Health Administrator
Bar/Club Manager	Manufacturing Executive	Quality Control Manager
Benefits Administrator	Market Researcher	Restaurateur
Business Valuator	Marketing Executive	Small Business Owner
Consultant	Mediator	Sports Manager
Entrepreneur	Performing Arts Administrator	Venture Capitalist/Investor

BUSINESS COMMUNICATIONS

Basics

The successful conduct of business demands effective communication, and you can hone your skills and gain valuable new knowledge with a major in business communications. What's the best way to communicate on the Internet? How do you effectively incorporate visual aids into a presentation? Answering these questions and many more will be part of your studies in business communications.

Speaking skills are of primary importance to a successful career in business. You'll learn how to interview, make presentations, deliver a ceremonial speech, or explain policy analysis. You'll get practice nonverbal communication methods such as visual aids, that you will use to underscore your points. You'll analyze audiences to compose an appropriate speech for them. You'll examine numerical data, such as survey results, and translate that data into helpful information. You'll learn how to communicate policy changes to your employees and discover the best ways to use the Internet for the dissemination of information. You'll learn how to communicate in a crisis and how to develop and maintain good public relations.

You can apply most of what you learn in your business communications major to dealings with your own employees, coworkers, or the public. A major in business communications could greatly expand your career success.

If You Like Business Communications, You May Also Like . . .

Advertising, agricultural journalism, business administration and management, creative writing, English, English composition, English literature, international business, marketing, mass communication, public administration, public policy analysis, radio and television, technical writing

SAMPLE COLLEGE CURRICULUM FOR BUSINESS COMMUNICATIONS

Analyzing Audiences

Argumentation Strategies for Business

Crisis Communication

Managerial Communication

Managing Corporate Communication on the World Wide Web

Persuasive Speeches

Public Relations Management

Public Speaking

Speech Writing for Business

Team Building

Web-based Communication

Suggested High School Prep for Business Communications

A broad background in courses such as speech, English, psychology, and computer science is great preparation for your college career. Any business courses are obviously helpful, as well as courses in statistics (you'll be looking at a lot of data and learning to analyze it).

Fun Facts

PowerPoint

No doubt you've heard of Microsoft PowerPoint, the software program that organizes presentations into neat, bulleted slides usually projected onto a screen. PowerPoint is now the most frequently used presentation aid in business.

The most popular graphics used in PowerPoint presentations are the Screen Beans—small black silhouettes that jump, point, scratch their heads, and perform a few other amusing actions. These icons were created by Cathleen Belleville, a designer who worked at PowerPoint from 1989–1995.

The original version of PowerPoint, created by Bob Gaskins, was called Presenter.

(Source: "Absolute PowerPoint" by Ian Parker. *The New Yorker*, May 28, 2001.)

Careers and Salary

Starting salaries for business communications majors are usually in the $25,000 to $40,000 range but can vary widely depending on where you live, how you choose to use your degree, and the company at which you work.

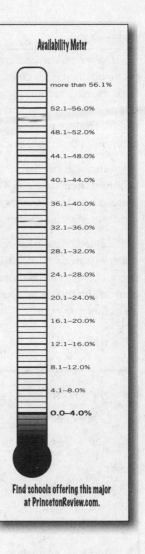

Availability Meter

more than 56.1%

52.1–56.0%

48.1–52.0%

44.1–48.0%

40.1–44.0%

36.1–40.0%

32.1–36.0%

28.1–32.0%

24.1–28.0%

20.1–24.0%

16.1–20.0%

12.1–16.0%

8.1–12.0%

4.1–8.0%

0.0–4.0%

Find schools offering this major at PrincetonReview.com.

CAREER OPTIONS

Advertising Executive	Investment Banker	Office Manager
Agent	Journalist	Public Relations
Attorney	Management Consultant	Publicist
Bank Officer	Marketing Executive	Radio Producer
Consultant	Media Planner	Television Producer
Corporate Lawyer	Media Specialist	Television Reporter
Editor	Music Executive	Web Editor

BUSINESS EDUCATION

Basics

If you're fascinated by the business world, but not the business dress code and late hours at the office, picture yourself in charge of a classroom. Business education majors learn the fundamentals of business, such as macroeconomics, microeconomics, accounting, and marketing, while also studying the fundamentals of education, such as the history and philosophy of education and some psychology. You're prepped to teach business classes to those who want in on the rat race. Student teaching gets you a dose of real life, and computer experience is emphasized. Business teachers will often teach computer courses too.

Some schools offer regular business majors an opportunity to become certified to teach after they've acquired their bachelor's degree in business. Usually, this will require an additional three semesters to complete education courses, student teaching, and additional business courses. This extra work can take the form of a second bachelor's degree or a certificate, depending on the program.

Business education majors have an important role in teaching high school and postsecondary students the fundamentals of business that will, perhaps, lead to business careers of their own—or at least some savvy business know-how. After completing most business education programs, you'll be qualified to teach courses, including accounting, computer applications, word processing, business economics, keyboarding, and other subjects.

SAMPLE COLLEGE CURRICULUM FOR BUSINESS EDUCATION

Computer Applications

E-Commerce

Entrepreneurship

Financial Accounting

History and Philosophy of Education

International Marketing

Macroeconomics

Marketing

Microeconomics

Office Systems Applications

Organization and Management

Psychological Foundations for Pre-Adolescent Learners

Student Teaching

Teaching Methods

If You Like Business Education, You May Also Like . . .

Accounting, business administration and management, business communications, computer and information science, education, education administration, educational psychology, managerial economics, mass communication, teacher education, technology education

Suggested High School Prep for Business Education

If your school offers business courses, take one or two to get an overall feel for the business world. Since any education major requires a solid background in a variety of fields, try to take courses in English, science, history, and languages in as great a depth as you can. Math courses are especially important to business majors. The more you know in all these fields, the more you'll feel prepared as a teacher.

Fun Facts

It's Educational

The National Business Education Association may become important to you as you move through your business education studies. The NBEA is, according to its website, "the nation's largest professional organization devoted exclusively to serving individuals and groups engaged in instruction, administration, research, and dissemination of information for and about business." Students are welcome to join as well. For more information, check out nbea.org.

But You Might Not Know This

"It is the business of the wealthy man To give employment to the artisan."

—Hilaire Belloc, from "Lord Finchley"

And You Should Hope to Know This

"To business that we love we rise betime, And go to 't with delight."

—William Shakespeare, from *Antony and Cleopatra*

Careers and Salary

The starting salary for teachers is about $20,000 to $30,000, but this figure depends on where you teach. Salaries often differ markedly between public and private institutions and between different parts of the country. Pursuing additional education will increase your salary; not to mention, some schools will even pay for their teachers to obtain master's degrees.

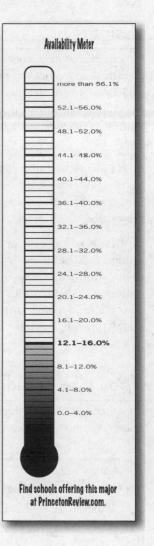

Availability Meter

more than 56.1%

52.1–56.0%

48.1–52.0%

44.1–48.0%

40.1–44.0%

36.1–40.0%

32.1–36.0%

28.1–32.0%

24.1–28.0%

20.1–24.0%

16.1–20.0%

12.1–16.0%

8.1–12.0%

4.1–8.0%

0.0–4.0%

Find schools offering this major at PrincetonReview.com.

CAREER OPTIONS

Administrative Assistant	Professor	Secondary School Teacher
College Administrator	School Administrator	Substitute Teacher
Elementary School Teacher		

CANADIAN STUDIES

Basics

Americans are notoriously clueless about their Northern neighbor. However, there's a great deal more to Canada than ice hockey, maple trees, and Celine Dion. As a Canadian studies major, you'll seek an in-depth understanding of all aspects of Canada—its people, cultures, history, and institutions. First established in the late 1960s, Canadian studies is an interdisciplinary field, incorporating history, sociology, literature, media studies, political science, geography, and fine arts.

In your first two years of this major, you'll take core classes in Canadian history and geography, covering topics like Native American pre-history, early European settlers, and the establishment of the Confederation. You'll also learn about contemporary Canadian government, economy, health care, and international relations. On the cultural side, you'll study Canadian literature, the politics of bilingualism, and Canada's ethnic minorities.

Unless you already go to school in Canada, it goes without saying that you'll want to spend at least a semester abroad there. If you plan to study in Quebec, then it's a good idea to have a few years of French under your belt. When your senior year as a Canadian studies major rolls around, you'll probably have the option of undertaking an independent research project, in which you'll work with an advisor on a topic of your choice. Possible subjects include "Canadian-American Relations," "Québécois Nationalist Movements," and "Women in Canadian Literature."

If You Like Canadian Studies, You May Also Like . . .

American history, American studies, anthropology, English, European history, French, history, international relations, Native American studies, sociology

SAMPLE COLLEGE CURRICULUM FOR CANDIAN STUDIES

Canada and Alaska in Circumpolar Perspective

Canada, the United States, and War

Canadian-American Relations

The Canadian Health Care System

French

Introduction to Canada

Literature of French Canada/Quebec

North American Indian History

United States and Canada in Comparative Perspective

Suggested High School Prep for Canadian Studies

For this major, you should concentrate on English and history classes. Since Canada is a bilingual country, you should also take at least three years of French.

Fun Facts

Some Canadianisms:

Loonie: A dollar. The Canadian $1 coin has a loon (the bird) on one side.

Toonie: Two dollars. It takes its name from the $1 coin, the loonie, and adds its value, two, to form "twonie" or, more easily read, "toonie."

Pogey: Unemployment benefits. "I'm getting pogey" means, as the British would say, "I'm on the dole."

Serviette: French for "napkin." This term is used by anglophones as well as francophones.

Housecoat: Robe, bathrobe

Chesterfield: A couch or sofa

Poutine: Québecois specialty: french fries covered in cheese curds and gravy.

Smarties: Not the ones like in the United States. In Canada, Smarties are a candy resembling M&Ms. They do melt in your hand, and they're a lot sweeter.

Kraft dinner or KD: macaroni and cheese

Back bacon: Canadian bacon, sometimes rolled in cornmeal (though referred to as "peameal," for the ground yellow peas that originally coated the product).

Keener: Brown-noser

Toque: A kind of wintertime hat.

The States: The United States of America. Canadians hate referring to the United States as "America" because Canadians are just as much (North) Americans as citizens of the United States are.

Chip trucks: These are like the vans driven by the ice cream man, only they sell French fries. They are most ubiquitous on the roads to "cottage country."

(Source: www.craigmarlatt.com/canada/symbols_facts&lists/canadianisms.html)

Can you name all thirteen Canadian provinces and territories?

Alberta	Labrador	Prince Edward Island
British Columbia	Northwest Territories	Quebec
Manitoba	Nova Scotia	Saskatchewan
New Brunswick	Nunavut	Yukon Territory
Newfoundland	Ontario	

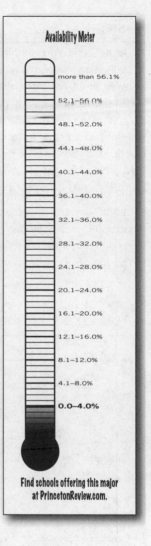

Availability Meter

more than 56.1%

52.1–56.0%

48.1–52.0%

44.1–48.0%

40.1–44.0%

36.1–40.0%

32.1–36.0%

28.1–32.0%

24.1–28.0%

20.1–24.0%

16.1–20.0%

12.1–16.0%

8.1–12.0%

4.1–8.0%

0.0–4.0%

Find schools offering this major at PrincetonReview.com.

Careers and Salary

The starting salary for the recently-graduated Canadian studies major ranges from $20,000 to $30,000. Don't worry, that's in U.S. dollars!

CAREER OPTIONS

Anthropologist	Historian	Public Relations Consultant
Archivist	Journalist	Sociologist
Curator	Market Research Analyst	Teacher
Economist	Political Scientist	Writer
Geographer	Professor	

CARIBBEAN STUDIES

Basics

From New York and Connecticut to Michigan, Indiana, and Illinois, there are plenty of cold-weather schools that will warm you up with a major in Caribbean studies. As a student in this major, you'll gain vast knowledge of the Caribbean culture and how it has affected and been affected by U.S. culture. You'll learn about the difficulties and discrimination Caribbean peoples have faced in the past and the array of problems they still face today. The changing roles of Caribbean women are crucial to developing your overall understanding, as are the stereotypes and implications of Caribbean religions. Caribbean history, economics, and politics will be covered in depth as you deal with such issues as slavery, urbanization, and education. You'll learn about the problems and effects of Caribbean migration to the United States. And most programs also require you to gain proficiency in Spanish, Portuguese, or possibly French.

Look forward to the exposure your studies will give you to the rich layers of Caribbean art, language, music, politics, psychology, and literature from pre-Columbian times (before 1492) to the present. You'll form ideas on what it means to be Caribbean and how identity, gender, and race have been challenged and defined in the region. Keep in mind that many schools combine this major with studies of Latin America.

If You Like Caribbean Studies, You May Also Like . . .

African American studies, African studies, American studies, comparative literature, French, history, international business, international relations, international studies, linguistics, peace studies, philosophy, Portuguese, religious studies, Spanish

> ### SAMPLE COLLEGE CURRICULUM FOR CARIBBEAN STUDIES
>
> Caribbean Cinema
>
> Caribbean Environment and Development
>
> Caribbean History
>
> Caribbean Migration
>
> The Caribbean: Peoples, History, and Culture
>
> Caribbean Religions
>
> Caribbean Writers
>
> Conflict and Change in the Caribbean
>
> Formation of Hispanic Caribbean Identities
>
> Latin America and the Caribbean
>
> Political Economy of the Caribbean
>
> Race, Gender, and Ethnicity

Suggested High School Prep for Caribbean Studies

You'll be best prepared for a major in Caribbean studies by taking courses in English, history, philosophy, and religion. Language courses will be useful as well. This major will expose you to many different disciplines, so feel free to explore any classes that interest you—a diverse background of knowledge will be your best preparation.

Fun Facts

Island-Style Fame

- A famous Caribbean actor: Sidney Poitier (Bahamas)
- A few famous Caribbean sports figures: Kareem Abdul-Jabbar (Trinidadian descent), Patrick Ewing (Jamaica), Tim Duncan (Bahamas)

Immortal Words

"If you know your history/Then you would know where you coming from."

—Bob Marley

Caribbean Origins

The name "Caribbean" is named after the Caribs, which was one of the dominant Amerindian groups in the region when Europeans made contact during the late 15th century. The analogous "West Indies" originates from Christopher Columbus' idea that he had landed in the Indies, which then meant all of south and east of Asia, when he had actually reached the Americas.

(Source: http://en.wikipedia.org/wiki/Caribbean)

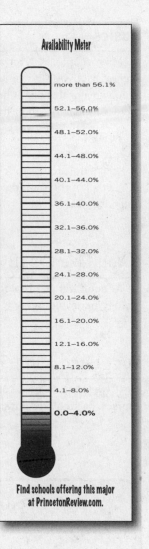

Availability Meter

more than 56.1%

52.1–56.0%

48.1–52.0%

44.1–48.0%

40.1–44.0%

36.1–40.0%

32.1–36.0%

28.1–32.0%

24.1–28.0%

20.1–24.0%

16.1–20.0%

12.1–16.0%

8.1–12.0%

4.1–8.0%

0.0–4.0%

Find schools offering this major at PrincetonReview.com.

Careers and Salary

As with most humanities majors, you'll have a vast selection of careers to choose from—your studies could lead you in any number of directions. Most liberal arts majors can expect a starting salary of $20,000 to $30,000, but that can vary widely depending on your field. Advanced degrees will also influence your starting salary.

CAREER OPTIONS

Archaeologist	Journalist	Teacher
Diplomat	Professor	Translator
FBI Agent	Sociologist	Writer

CELL BIOLOGY

Basics

Microscopic, and yet seemingly infinitely complicated, cells are at the heart of every living organism. Every day of your life you shed millions of them without the slightest thought or concern. If you were a cell biology major this might not be the case, since you would know a wealth of information about cells, including their composition, their function, their parts, and probably just about anything else you could think of.

Biology is essentially the study of life in all of its varied forms. As you can guess, that's a lot of territory for one major to cover, so fortunately there are specializations. Cell biology, as you've figured out, is one of those. It's the study of life pinpointed on a single, tiny, tiny, little world: the cell. As a cell biology major you will get all of the training of a normal biology major with an added focus on the internal and external functions of cells.

If You Like Cell Biology, You May Also Like . . .

Agricultural and biological engineering, biochemistry, biology, biopsychology, chemistry, ecology, microbiology, neurobiology

Suggested High School Prep for Cell Biology

If you want to be a cell biologist, you had better come prepared with a strong list of science and math courses, particularly physics, chemistry, biology, algebra, and trigonometry.

SAMPLE COLLEGE CURRICULUM FOR CELL BIOLOGY

Biology

Cell Biology

Developmental Biology

Genetics

Immunology

Mechanisms of Carcinogenesis

Molecular Biology

Receptors and Effectors

Tumor Cell Biology

Vascular Bilogy

Fun Facts

Biology Humor

Cell biology is the only science in which multiplication means the same thing as division.

More Biology Humor

A biologist was interested in studying how far bullfrogs can jump. He brought a bullfrog into his laboratory, set it down, and commanded, "Jump, frog, jump!"

The frog jumped across the room.

The biologist measured the distance, then noted in his journal, "Frog with four legs jumped eight feet." Then he cut the frog's front legs off. Again he ordered, "Jump, frog, jump!"

The frog struggled a moment, then jumped a few feet.

After measuring the distance, the biologist noted in his journal, "Frog with two legs jumped three feet." Next, the biologist cut off the frog's back legs. Once more, he shouted, "Jump, frog, jump!"

The frog just lay there.

"Jump, frog, jump!" the biologist repeated. Nothing. The biologist noted in his journal, "Frog with no legs—lost its hearing."

Careers and Salary

The average starting salary for a cell biology major ranges from $23,000 to $35,000.

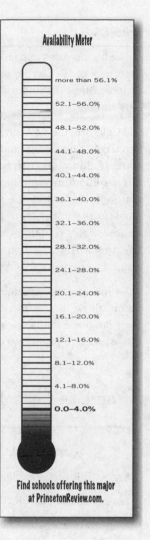

Availability Meter

more than 56.1%
52.1–56.0%
48.1–52.0%
44.1–48.0%
40.1–44.0%
36.1–40.0%
32.1–36.0%
28.1–32.0%
24.1–28.0%
20.1–24.0%
16.1–20.0%
12.1–16.0%
8.1–12.0%
4.1–8.0%
0.0–4.0%

Find schools offering this major at PrincetonReview.com.

CAREER OPTIONS

Biochemist	Geneticist	Physician
Biologist	Health Care Administrator	Psychologist
Ecologist	Paramedic	Researcher
Environmentalist/ Environmental Scientist		Teacher

CELTIC LANGUAGES, LITERATURES, AND LINGUISTICS

Basics

Celtic cultures expanded across Western Europe throughout the first millennium B.C./B.C.E.; Welsh, Irish, Breton, Scottish Gaelic, and the vibrant (and ongoing) literature of these languages constitute a significant proportion of the linguistic remains of this great period of Celtic expansion.

As a Celtic languages, literatures, and linguistics major, you'll gain an in-depth understanding of the historical Celts and their cultures; and you'll receive rigorous instruction in one or several extant or historical Celtic languages (like Manx and Cornish, the most recently extinct of the Celtic languages). You'll study Celtic myths, folklore, and narratives like the *Irish Lebor Gabála Érenn* or the *Book of Kells*. To say that Celtic languages, literatures, and linguistics remains a relatively untapped field—and therefore, one ripe with scholarly potential—wouldn't be an exaggeration. Despite the fact that about a million people speak a Celtic language as their primary tongue (easily twice that number could be considered fluent) and that records of the Celtic literary tradition extend far into the shadowy past, scholarly attention since the nineteenth century has primarily focused on collecting rather than studying this literature. There just aren't that many scholars trained to perform this type of analysis.

You'll have the chance to change all that. Important discoveries are waiting to be made, and many departments allow their students broad flexibility in determining their courses of study. Many programs overlap their language studies with other disciplines like anthropology, history, comparative literature, and linguistics which are just a few of the natural companions to this major.

If You Like Celtic Languages, Literatures, and Linguistics, You May Also Like . . .

Ancient studies, archaeology, anthropology, art history, classics, comparative literature, comparative linguistics, English, English literature, history, Medieval and Renaissance studies

Suggested High School Prep for Celtic Languages, Literatures, and Linguistics

Since much of what you'll study in this major is historical, you'll obviously want to concentrate on your history classes. Research depends on critical thinking and communication so English is essential. Train yourself for language study by focusing on a foreign language.

> **SAMPLE COLLEGE CURRICULUM FOR CELTIC LANGUAGES, LITERATURES, AND LINGUISTICS**
>
> Celtic Mythology and Oral Tradition
>
> Elementary Modern Irish
>
> History of Linguistics
>
> Introduction to Modern Welsh
>
> Irish Literature in Translation
>
> Medieval Celtic Folklore
>
> Medieval Welsh Language and Literature
>
> Old Irish
>
> Phonetics
>
> Voices of the Celtic World

Fun Facts

Lads and Lasses Are Celtic

Despite its historical stronghold in Ireland and Great Britain, Celtic words make up a miniscule proportion of the English language. Some of the few English words with Celtic origins are: *hubbub, gull, cart, dock, babe, griddle,* and, of course, *lad, lass* and *whiskey.*

Did You Know?

The *Book of Kells*, which consists of the four biblical gospels written in Latin, was produced by Celtic monks in Ireland, Scotland, and Northern Ireland around A.D./C.E. 800. This manuscript is considered one of the most technically brilliant, beautiful, and important pieces of work in medieval art.

Careers and Salary

If you don't head to grad school to pursue an advanced degree—as most students do—expect to earn a starting salary about $20,000 to $30,000.

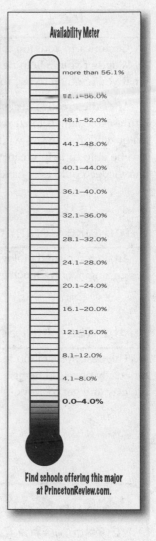

Availability Meter

more than 56.1%

52.1–56.0%

48.1–52.0%

44.1–48.0%

40.1–44.0%

36.1–40.0%

32.1–36.0%

28.1–32.0%

24.1–28.0%

20.1–24.0%

16.1–20.0%

12.1–16.0%

8.1–12.0%

4.1–8.0%

0.0–4.0%

Find schools offering this major at PrincetonReview.com.

CAREER OPTIONS		
Anthropologist	Teacher	Translator
Professor		

CERAMIC ENGINEERING

Basics

Ceramics, in addition to being a fine art, also requires a thorough working knowledge of certain materials. Whether you're helping to design a new office building or a vase for your bedroom, you'll need to know what you're going to use to construct your next project, and that's where the engineering comes in.

After the creative design part has been nailed down, someone has to figure out how to turn that design into a three-dimensional reality. In walks the engineer. By joining together ceramics and engineering, this major will provide you with more than just a working knowledge of the material used by ceramicists. You'll also be able to help create new and more interesting works with materials that only somebody with your knowledge could ever have dreamed.

If You Like Ceramic Engineering, You May Also Like . . .

Architectural and biological engineering, architectural history, architecture, civil engineering, engineering design, engineering mechanics

Suggested High School Prep for Ceramic Engineering

The best preparation for a ceramic engineering major is a very strong background in math and science, especially physics, chemistry, trigonometry, and calculus. You'll also need to practice as an artist, so break out the clay and get to work.

SAMPLE COLLEGE CURRICULUM FOR CERAMIC ENGINEERING

Chemistry

Electrical Engineering

Engineering Graphics

Engineering Mechanics

Introduction to Engineering

Materials Science and Engineering

Physics

Statistics

Technical electives

Fun Facts

For More Information . . .

For a really in-depth look at the ceramic industry, visit the American Ceramic Society's website at acers.org.

Did You Know?

Some of the oldest found ceramic works date back to at least 24,000 B.C./B.C.E.

Careers and Salary

The average starting salary for a ceramic engineering major is $38,000 to $45,000.

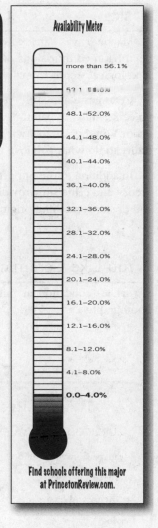

Availability Meter

more than 56.1%

52.1–56.0%

48.1–52.0%

44.1–48.0%

40.1–44.0%

36.1–40.0%

32.1–36.0%

28.1–32.0%

24.1–28.0%

20.1–24.0%

16.1–20.0%

12.1–16.0%

8.1–12.0%

4.1–8.0%

0.0–4.0%

Find schools offering this major at PrincetonReview.com.

CAREER OPTIONS		
Artist	Plastics Manufacturer	Product Designer

CERAMICS

Basics

Maybe it was Patrick Swayze's strong hands or Demi Moore's gentle touch. Whatever the case, you've been haunted by visions of spinning brown clay ever since you saw *Ghost*. You can't help yourself. The next logical step is to major in ceramics.

Ceramics is a mixture of sculpture, drawing, and the science behind the materials used in making ceramic objects. Similar to painting, sculpture, and other fine arts majors, ceramics may be listed under a broader art major. Whether on its own or part of a larger context, though, a major in ceramics will give you the opportunity to do what you love most: Create works of art.

In addition to the opportunity to learn your craft, your studies will require you to learn some art history, theory, and criticism, providing you with a solid conceptual background to make sure you can go out there and create something original.

If You Like Ceramics, You May Also Like . . .

Art, art education, art history, drawing, fashion design, interior design, landscape architecture, painting, photography

Suggested High School Prep for Ceramics

Don't think you can just sit down and begin making ornate jars and vases. This stuff takes a lot of practice, so if you're interested, begin developing and honing those skills as soon as possible. You can always supplement your art history knowledge by frequent trips to museums and lectures. You'll have to submit a portfolio when applying to college; most art schools value strong observational skills, so draw from life as often as you can.

SAMPLE COLLEGE CURRICULUM FOR CERAMICS

Advanced Ceramic Studio

Advanced Ceramics

Art Theory and Analysis

Carving

Drawing I–II

Introduction to Ceramics

Introduction to Chemistry

Sculpture Modeling

Survey of Western Art: Prehistoric to Medieval

Survey of Western Art: Renaissance to Postmodern

Technology of Ceramics

Three-Dimensional Design

Two Dimensional Design

Fun Facts

Did You Know?

Prior to the 1700s, potters were often criticized for digging holes in the road to find more clay, an offense so often committed it earned its own word: pothole.

For More Information . . .

If you want to learn how to "throw a pot," go to the Gladstone Pottery Museum for a nice visual guide.

Why Ceramic?

Most ceramics resist heat and chemicals and are poor conductors of heat and electricity. Traditional ceramics are made of clay and other natural occurring materials, while modern high-tech ceramics use other specially purified or synthetic raw materials. Ceramic products include cookware and dinnerware; art objects, such as figurines; building materials, such as brick; abrasives, such as alumina, and specialized cutting tools; electrical equipment, such as insulators in spark plugs; refractories, such as firebrick and the heat shield on the space shuttle; and artificial bones and medical devices. The oldest known fired ceramics date from the Paleolithic period some 27,000 years ago.

(Source: http://education.yahoo.com/reference/encyclopedia/entry/ceramics)

Careers and Salary

Ceramics majors entering the museum world can expect to earn about $25,000.

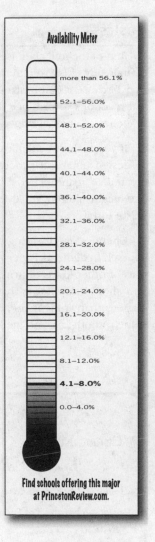

Availability Meter

more than 56.1%

52.1–56.0%

48.1–52.0%

44.1–48.0%

40.1–44.0%

36.1–40.0%

32.1–36.0%

28.1–32.0%

24.1–28.0%

20.1–24.0%

16.1–20.0%

12.1–16.0%

8.1–12.0%

4.1–8.0%

0.0–4.0%

Find schools offering this major at PrincetonReview.com.

CAREER OPTIONS		
Antiques Dealer	Artist	Teacher
Art Dealer	Curator	

CHEMICAL ENGINEERING

Basics

Run-of-the-mill chemists develop new compounds and determine the structures and properties of things that already exist. You knew that. Chemical engineering is different from and more complicated than chemistry because it emphasizes the commercial applications of chemical reactions; it involves harnessing chemical reactions to produce things people want. It's a very broad field that overlaps considerably with other branches of engineering, chemistry, and biochemistry.

If you major in chemical engineering, you'll learn how to reorganize the structure of molecules and how to design chemical processes through which chemicals, petroleum, foods, and pharmaceuticals can be created or manipulated. You'll learn how to build and operate industrial plants where raw materials are chemically altered. You'll learn how to keep the environment safe from potential pollution and hazardous waste too.

Chemical engineering is not an easy major, but if you can make it through to graduation day, you'll find yourself in demand. Paper mills, manufacturers of fertilizers, pharmaceutical companies, plastics makers, and tons of other kinds of firms will be looking for your expertise, and they'll pay you pretty handsomely for it. You should also know that, traditionally, more chemical engineering majors obtain master's and doctoral degrees than students in almost any other engineering field and this major makes for a wonderful stepping stone to both law and medicine.

SAMPLE COLLEGE CURRICULUM FOR CHEMICAL ENGINEERING

Chemical Reaction Engineering

Design and Analysis of Processing Systems

Differential Equations

Engineering Graphics

Engineering Mechanics

Heat and Mass Transfer

Internship

Organic Chemistry

Physical Chemistry

Physics

Reaction Kinetics

Thermodynamics

Transport Phenomena

If You Like Chemical Engineering, You May Also Like . . .

Aerospace engineering, agricultural and biological engineering, applied mathematics, astronomy, astrophysics, atmospheric science, biochemistry, biology, biopsychology, botany and plant biology, cell biology, chemistry, civil engineering, computer and information science, computer engineering, electrical engineering, engineering design, environmental and environmental health engineering, environmental science, genetics, industrial engineering, mathematics, mechanical engineering, microbiology, molecular genetics, neurobiology, neuroscience, nuclear engineering, petroleum engineering, physics, statistics

Suggested High School Prep for Chemical Engineering

A strong background in chemistry, biology, math, and physics is essential if you want to major in chemical engineering, as is extensive knowledge of computers and computer programming skills. Take AP chemistry and take calculus or the highest-level math class that your high school offers.

Fun Facts

Science Humor

Two hydrogen molecules are walking down the street. One of the hydrogen molecules says to the other one, "You know, I think I lost an electron."

The other hydrogen molecule asks, "Are you sure?"

"Yeah," responds the first one. "I'm positive."

The Big Four

The four main engineering fields are civil engineering, mechanical engineering, electrical engineering, and chemical engineering. Of these big four, chemical engineers make up the smallest percentage. This relatively small percentage of engineers holds a very prominent position in many industries, though, and chemical engineers are, on average, the highest paid of the big four.

Famous People Who Majored in Chemical Engineering

Cindy Crawford (Northwestern University)

Careers and Salary

Starting salaries for chemical engineers fresh out of college are about $53,000. One way to increase your odds of getting a great-paying job is to gain work experience through internships.

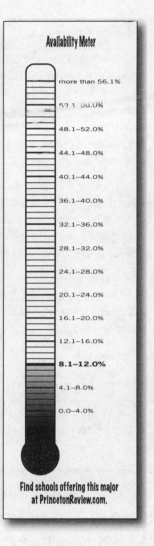

Availability Meter

more than 56.1%

52.1–56.0%

48.1–52.0%

44.1–48.0%

40.1–44.0%

36.1–40.0%

32.1–36.0%

28.1–32.0%

24.1–28.0%

20.1–24.0%

16.1–20.0%

12.1–16.0%

8.1–12.0%

4.1–8.0%

0.0–4.0%

Find schools offering this major
at PrincetonReview.com.

CAREER OPTIONS

Biochemist	Ecologist	Petroleum Engineer
Chemical Engineer	Inventor	Textile Manufacturer
Chemist		

CHEMICAL PHYSICS

Basics

Chemical kinetics. Molecular synthesis. Laser physics. If your heart's starting to beat a little faster, you're (a) in the minority of people who actually have a clue what these are, and (b) probably ready for the rigors of a major in chemical physics. The chemical physics major is concerned with the behavior of matter at molecular and nuclear scales. You'll focus on the behavior and structure of molecules and the unique characteristics of small molecular systems. Research topics will include the dynamics of chemical reactions and intermolecular forces such as strong, weak, electromagnetic, and gravitational. These forces are the basics of quantum theory, which you'll really dig into as you simultaneously master a great deal of math and statistics.

As a chemical physics major, you'll learn the vocabularies and philosophies of two distinct fields—physical chemistry and atomic/molecular physics—and how to communicate effectively within and between them. You'll learn how chemistry and physics affect and inform each other, and how the research and developments in one field have influenced those in the other. You'll learn how to integrate information, how to engage in effective problem solving, and how to design and participate in research projects. And those three terms we mentioned in the beginning? Yeah, those will be there too.

As in any scientific major, you'll study research from both the past and the present, and you'll gain a strong foundation in both the theoretical and practical knowledge of the field. Expect a great deal of computer work.

If You Like Chemical Physics, You May Also Like . . .

Applied mathematics, applied physics, astrophysics, biochemistry, botany and plant biology, chemical engineering, chemistry, engineering physics, genetics, medicine, molecular genetics, physics

---

SAMPLE COLLEGE CURRICULUM FOR CHEMICAL PHYSICS

Atoms, Molecules, and Spectroscopy

Inorganic Chemistry

Kinetics and Thermodynamics

Laser Physics

Materials Chemistry

Modern Physics and Mechanics

Organic Chemistry

Quantum Chemistry and Physics

Solid State Physics

Vector Calculus

Suggested High School Prep for Chemical Physics

Since the field of chemical physics involves so much science, try to take courses in biology, chemistry, and physics. Also important are math courses such as calculus and analytic geometry as well as computer science courses. Don't forget English—as a scientist you'll need exceptional reading and writing skills.

Fun Facts

Some Chemistry Humor

Q: What weapon can you make from the chemicals potassium, nickel, and iron?

A: KNiFe

You Might Be a Physics Major If

- You know vector calculus but you can't remember how to do long division.
- You avoid doing anything because you don't want to contribute to the eventual heat-death of the universe.
- You've calculated that the World Series actually diverges.
- You know how to integrate a chicken and can take the derivative of water.
- You have a pet named after a scientist.
- You hesitate to look at something because you don't want to break down its wave function.
- You'll assume that a "horse" is a "sphere" to make the math easier.
- You understood more than five of these indicators.

(Source: www.physlink.com)

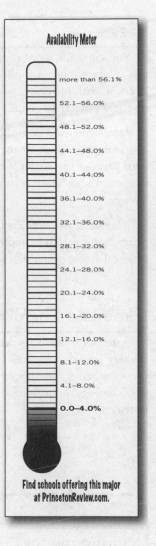

Availability Meter

more than 56.1%

52.1—56.0%

48.1—52.0%

44.1—48.0%

40.1—44.0%

36.1—40.0%

32.1—36.0%

28.1—32.0%

24.1—28.0%

20.1—24.0%

16.1—20.0%

12.1—16.0%

8.1—12.0%

4.1—8.0%

0.0—4.0%

Find schools offering this major
at PrincetonReview.com.

Careers and Salary

Starting salaries for chemical physics majors are generally in the $35,000 to $45,000 range, although this number varies widely depending on how much experience you've had, the research you've done, and how you use your skills. Advanced degrees usually make a big difference in salary in the scientific fields too.

CAREER OPTIONS

Chemical Engineer	Professor	Scientist
Chemist	Researcher	Teacher
Physicist		

CHEMISTRY

Basics

For some, the word chemistry conjures up images of a mad scientist hunched over a table full of beakers and tubes, concocting potions to change lead into gold or people into animals. That's *alchemy*, silly. The chemist, with his or her white lab coat and wild hair, is difficult to define and yet endowed with seemingly mystical powers to change the physical structure of the world.

Often referred to as the "central science", chemistry examines the composition, structure, properties, and reactions of matter, the stuff of the universe. It looks at the way the material world—petroleum, a tree, your hand—is arranged. What are the properties that make water? What do we need to sustain life? How do two chemicals react with each other? These are some of the basic questions a chemistry major tries to answer.

The skills you will learn as a chemistry major will be applicable to any number of fields, ranging from pharmaceuticals to biotechnology to environmentalism. You will gain a greater understanding as to how the physical world operates and what we can do to improve and advance the way we live and work.

If You Like Chemistry, You May Also Like . . .

Astronomy, astrophysics, atmospheric science, biochemistry, biology, biopsychology, botany and plant biology, business administration and management, cell biology, dietetics, economics, entomology, environmental science, forestry, genetics, geology, marine science, mathematics, microbiology, molecular genetics, neurobiology, neuroscience, nutrition, pharmacology, pharmacy, physics, plant pathology, public health, statistics

Suggested High School Prep for Chemistry

If you're interested in majoring in chemistry, it's important to have a strong background in the sciences—particularly physics, chemistry, and biology—as well as strong written and oral communications skills. Begin to cultivate and develop your own scientific curiosity as much as possible by taking advanced science courses and getting as much laboratory experience as you can.

SAMPLE COLLEGE CURRICULUM FOR CHEMISTRY

Advanced Chemistry Elective

Advanced Inorganic Chemistry

Calculus/Analytical Geometry

Calculus/Differential Equations

General Chemistry

Instrumental Analysis

Organic Chemistry

Physical Chemistry

Physics

Quantitative Analysis

Fun Facts

And Even More So for the Students

"It is disconcerting to reflect on the number of students we have flunked in chemistry for not knowing what we later found to be untrue."

(Source: quoted in Robert L. Weber's *Science With a Smile*, 1992)

Chemistry Humor

Have you heard the one about the chemist who was reading a book about helium and just couldn't put it down?

Famous People Who Majored in Chemistry

Louis Pasteur, Marie Curie, Alfred Nobel, Niels Bohr, George Washington Carver, Albert Einstein, Enrico Fermi

Careers and Salary

The average annual starting salary for a bachelor's degree in chemistry ranges from $35,000 to $44,000.

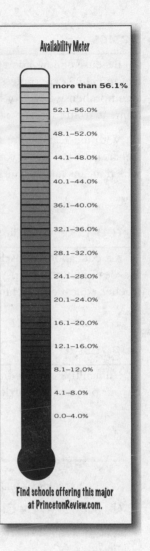

Availability Meter

more than 56.1%

52.1–56.0%

48.1–52.0%

44.1–48.0%

40.1–44.0%

36.1–40.0%

32.1–36.0%

28.1–32.0%

24.1–28.0%

20.1–24.0%

16.1–20.0%

12.1–16.0%

8.1–12.0%

4.1–8.0%

0.0–4.0%

Find schools offering this major at PrincetonReview.com.

CAREER OPTIONS

Biochemist	Optometrist	Professor
Chemical Engineer	Petroleum Engineer	Researcher
Chemist	Pharmacist	Teacher
Dentist	Physician	

CHILD CARE

Basics

Beacuse children don't come with manuals, we've had to formulate some innovative ways to help families and child care professionals maintain their sanity. In lieu of guidebooks, we've got the child care major, a comprehensive two- or four-year program that will take you through almost every stage of a child's development, from first baby steps to the first time they roll the car out of the garage at 3:00 A.M.

With more and more families in which both parents work, the need for well-trained child care professionals is on the rise. If you want a career in the child care industry, you're going to have to know your stuff, which means taking courses that cover child educational development, child abuse, and art for children.

If You Like Child Care, You May Also Like . . .

Art education, counseling, developmental psychology, education, education administration, education of the deaf, educational psychology, experimental psychology, psychology, social psychology, social work, teacher education, teaching English as a second language

Suggested High School Prep for Child Care

Humanities courses that emphasize clear communication skills, such as English and speech, should be in your preparatory curriculum. You should also take psychology if your school offers it.

SAMPLE COLLEGE CURRICULUM FOR CHILD CARE

Administration of Child Development Program

Art for Child Development

Child Growth and Development

Child, Family, and Community

Infant and Toddler Development

Introduction to Programs and Curriculum for Young Children

Language and Literature

Science and Mathematics for Child Development

Working with Children with Special Needs

Education/Nutrition, Home Economics, and Related Fields

Fun Facts

Working Mothers

Sixty-five percent of mothers with children under age 6 and 78 percent of mothers with children ages 6 to 13 are in the labor force. Fifty-nine percent of mothers with infants (younger than age 1) are in the labor force.

Did You Know?

In 1999, only 23 percent of all families with children younger than six and only one-third of married-couple families with young children had one parent who worked and one parent who stayed at home.

Bringin' Home the Bacon

The majority (55 percent) of working women in the United States bring home half or more of their family's earnings.

(Source: Children's Defense Fund)

Careers and Salary

The average starting salary for a child care worker is approximately $15,700 because many work only part-time.

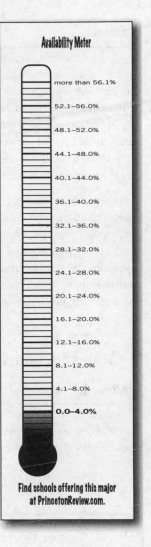

Availability Meter

more than 56.1%
52.1–56.0%
48.1–52.0%
44.1–48.0%
40.1–44.0%
36.1–40.0%
32.1–36.0%
28.1–32.0%
24.1–28.0%
20.1–24.0%
16.1–20.0%
12.1–16.0%
8.1–12.0%
4.1–8.0%
0.0–4.0%

Find schools offering this major at PrincetonReview.com.

CAREER OPTIONS

Child Care Worker	Human Resources Manager	Teacher

CHILD CARE AND SUPPORT SERVICES MANAGEMENT

Basics

Child care and support services management is an incredibly rewarding career—as many of those already in it will tell you—but it can be frustrating at times. As is often the case with satisfying work, child care and support services management presents a unique set of challenges. Children (and their parents) can be demanding souls. But if you're interested in having a direct impact on the life of another person—and in helping to shape his or her development and growth—then this is the career for you. If you opt to provide child care for social service organizations (governmental or nonprofit), you should be aware in advance that such social work has its own special set of trials, but also its own set of triumphs. All things considered, few career choices affect the lives of young people as directly as this one.

Besides managing a child care faciltity and creating a safe and healthy environment for those in their charge, child care professionals often find themselves working in home-based child care; developing child development or after-school programs in conjunction with certified teachers; managing parent and family relations; keeping abreast of child care- and family-related laws and policies; identifying diseases, injuries, and psychological trauma in children; and becoming a business management professional. As an effective and compassionate child care professional, you'll have an impact on the course of a young person's life in unimaginably positive ways.

If You Like Child Care and Support Services Management, You May Also Like . . .

Art education, counseling, developmental psychology, education, education administration, education of the deaf, educational psychology, experimental psychology, psychology, social psychology, social work, teacher education, teaching English as a second language

SAMPLE COLLEGE CURRICULUM FOR CHILD CARE AND SUPPORT SERVICES MANAGEMENT

Administration of Child Care Programs

Caring for Young Children

Children's Literature

Contemporary Families

Introduction to Psychology

Parent/Child Interactions

Social Problems

Suggested High School Prep for Child Care and Support Services Management

Study psychology if your high school offers it, and prepare yourself for a career of communication by building a solid base in English. If your school has a speech team, sign up.

Fun Facts

Did You Know?

According to the Children's Defense Fund, only one in seven children eligible for federal child care assistance actually receives it.

Shaping Young Minds

The most crucial period of brain development occurs before a child reaches the age of five. Many psychologists believe that the quality and tenor of the environment in which a child is raised—and the experiences that he or she has—profoundly affects the child's brain.

Careers and Salary

While most workers in child care are part-timers, managers of these programs often work longer hours and are consequently paid more. Expect between $28,000 to $32,000 to as a starting salary.

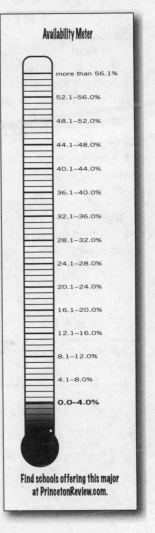

Availability Meter

more than 56.1%

52.1–56.0%

48.1–52.0%

44.1–48.0%

40.1–44.0%

36.1–40.0%

32.1–36.0%

28.1–32.0%

24.1–28.0%

20.1–24.0%

16.1–20.0%

12.1–16.0%

8.1–12.0%

4.1–8.0%

0.0–4.0%

Find schools offering this major at PrincetonReview.com.

CAREER OPTIONS

Child Care Worker	School Administrator	Teacher
Executive Director		

CHILD DEVELOPMENT

Basics

First steps, first words, the first day of school. A major in child development exposes you to all the details of a child's growth, from birth to adolescence. You'll learn about children's physical development, including their sensory and motor skills. You'll see how children progress socially. You'll study the theories of how children learn and how their intellectual understanding changes from year to year.

Because understanding the family is integral to learning about how children develop, your studies will expose you to family relationships so that you can observe how family members and other adults can help or hinder the developmental process. You'll look at peer groups and school environments to see how they influence children, and you'll study the complex issues of diversity and multiculturalism in educational settings.

Your coursework for a child development major will include classes in psychology, sociology, education, and the humanities. Most programs include a research component, and you'll get practice in different research methodologies. Many students choose child development because they are interested in becoming educators, and with this major you'll be getting a lot of hands-on experience working with children.

If You Like Child Development, You May Also Like . . .

Anthropology, child care, clinical psychology, counseling, developmental psychology, education, education administration, education of the deaf, educational psychology, elementary education, human development, psychology, social psychology, social work, sociology, special education, speech pathology, teacher education

SAMPLE COLLEGE CURRICULUM FOR CHILD DEVELOPMENT

Cognitive Aspects of Human Development

Developmental Psychology

Early Childhood Education

Ethical and Moral Development

Ethical Issues in Human Services

Experimental Methods

Family Development

Group Dynamics

Introduction to Language

Language of Representational Systems

Psychology of Thinking

Social and Personality Development

Statistical Analysis

Suggested High School Prep for Child Development

A broad spectrum of courses in the humanities—English, philosophy, languages, religion, and others—will give you a good foundation for your college career. Any courses offered in psychology will be especially helpful in giving you a head start in your studies.

Fun Facts

If My Baby Listens to Mozart, Will She Be Smarter?

The connection between intelligence and exposure to music may seem like urban legend, but in fact there is a good deal of evidence to support it. Exposing children to music early in their lives causes neurons in the brain to fire, thus linking them to other neurons, forming connections called synapses. The more synapses created, and the more precise the firings, the better the chance a baby has of performing well intellectually. The music area of the brain is close to the math area, and stimulation of either area helps in the development of complex thought processes. But synapses can't wait—birth to four years is the ideal time to expose children to music.

(Source: www.earlychildhood.com)

How About Reading?

Reading is key to raising an intelligent child. Children who are read to throughout their early lives are more likely to enjoy reading and perform better in school. About.com's site on parenting babies gives some suggestions for the best kinds of books to read to babies, including the following:

- Books with rhyme, rhythm, and repetition
- Books with pictures of other babies
- Informational books
- Poetry books
- Books with textures or touch-and-feel books
- Mother Goose and nursery rhyme books
- Concept books
- Folktales
- Books that feature familiar items or events in baby's world
- Books that feature sounds
- Books babies can manipulate, such as lift-the-flap books or books with holes (12 to 18 months)
- Books of different sizes and shapes (18 to 30 months)

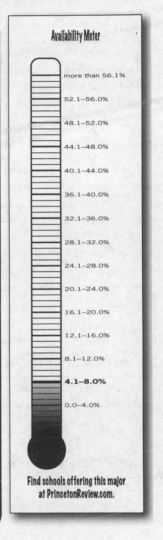

Availability Meter

- more than 56.1%
- 52.1–56.0%
- 48.1–52.0%
- 44.1–48.0%
- 40.1–44.0%
- 36.1–40.0%
- 32.1–36.0%
- 28.1–32.0%
- 24.1–28.0%
- 20.1–24.0%
- 16.1–20.0%
- 12.1–16.0%
- 8.1–12.0%
- **4.1–8.0%**
- 0.0–4.0%

Find schools offering this major at PrincetonReview.com.

Careers and Salary

Salaries for child development majors are difficult to predict because there are so many different ways to use your degree. Starting salaries for child care workers, for example, fall in the $10,000 to $20,000 range, while psychologists fall in the $20,000 to $30,000 range.

CAREER OPTIONS

Anthropologist	School Administrator	Sociologist
Child Care Worker	Social Worker	Teacher
Psychologist		

CHINESE

Basics

Question: What is the most spoken language in the world? Answer: While English and Spanish make a decent showing, Chinese makes them look like half-pints. Mandarin, or Modern Standard Chinese, is the native tongue of almost a billion people. There are several variations of the Chinese language, each spoken by millions of individuals.

As the global community comes closer together in the coming years, people who can speak and write Chinese will find themselves in high demand.

The Chinese major isn't to be underestimated. Don't think this is anything like studying a romance language, which offers the benefit of (almost) the same alphabet. With Chinese, you don't even get an alphabet. Students majoring in this language must complete intensive classes in written and spoken Chinese, as well as additional work in Chinese culture, language, and history. Confucianism, history of the People's Republic of China, Maoism, and the subtle art of calligraphy will probably be offered as part of the overall curriculum. Most Chinese programs also recommend or require study abroad. If you want to major in Chinese, plan on spending copious hours memorizing vocabulary and the minute differences of inflection that sometimes mean the difference between saying "Hello. How are you?" and "I poisoned that tea you're drinking."

If You Like Chinese, You May Also Like . . .

Asian American studies, East Asian studies, international business, international relations, international studies, Japanese, political science, South Asian studies, Southeast Asian studies

Suggested High School Prep for Chinese

If you are fortunate enough to go to a school that offers Chinese as a language, well . . . you know what to do. Any training in foreign languages will help you become accustomed to college-level language study. Courses in political science and Asian history will also be useful. Art could prove to be a practical thing to study as well since training the eye to observe delicate distinctions will be very useful when reading and writing calligraphy.

> ### SAMPLE COLLEGE
> ### CURRICULUM FOR CHINESE
> Advanced Chinese Conversation
>
> Chinese Calligraphy
>
> Chinese History
>
> Chinese I–IV
>
> Classical Chinese I–II
>
> Confucianism
>
> Intermediate Chinese Conversation

Fun Facts

It's Official

Modern Standard Chinese is one of the five official languages of the United Nations.

Chinese Literacy

There are several thousand characters in the Chinese language (each word generally being composed of two characters). Most Chinese readers know between 3,000 and 6,000 characters.

Famous People Who Majored in Chinese

Mira Sorvino (actress, Harvard University)

Careers and Salary

The starting salary for a Chinese major fresh out of college is about $30,000.

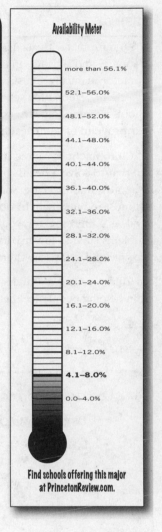

Availability Meter

more than 56.1%

52.1–56.0%

48.1–52.0%

44.1–48.0%

40.1–44.0%

36.1–40.0%

32.1–36.0%

28.1–32.0%

24.1–28.0%

20.1–24.0%

16.1–20.0%

12.1–16.0%

8.1–12.0%

4.1–8.0%

0.0–4.0%

Find schools offering this major at PrincetonReview.com.

CAREER OPTIONS		
Anthropologist	Diplomat/Attaché/Foreign Service Officer	Foreign Exchange Trader
Archaeologist		Translator

CHIROPRACTIC

Basics

A chiropractor treats disorders that affect the nerves, bones, joints, and muscles. It does not involve drugs or surgery and is hands-on ("chiropractic" derives from the Greek terms for "practical hand"), meaning a chiropractor manually adjusts a patient's body. Chiropractic is actually not an undergraduate major. Like medical school, osteopathic school requires that you complete college before you can be admitted. Though some schools require only two years of college, most require four. You can then look forward to a four- or five-year program of study leading to chiropractic certification.

Chiropractic is rooted in the philosophy that health is determined in large part by the nervous system, and that to solve a health problem the whole body must be evaluated and treated through nutrition, exercise, and emotional care. Some states allow chiropractors to include herbal drug regimes in their treatment, but most require that chiropractors work in tandem with family doctors to give their patients the care they need. As a chiropractor, you'll learn how to manipulate muscles, joints, and the spine to solve a variety of problems such as lower back pain, arthritis, and carpal tunnel syndrome. You'll learn the art of therapeutic massage and soft-tissue therapies.

Chiropractic is a growing field; almost 25 million Americans visit chiropractors each year. If you're interested in helping people feel better using non-drug methodologies, chiropractic may be the career path for you.

SAMPLE COLLEGE CURRICULUM FOR CHIROPRACTIC

Anatomy

Biomechanics

Chiropractic Procedures

Clinical Orthopedics

Community Health

Histology

History of Chiropractic

Imagining Interpretation

Normal Radiographic Anatomy

Nutritional Assessment

Pathology

Pharmacotoxicology

Physics of Clinical Imaging

Practice Management

If You Like Chiropractic, You May Also Like . . .

Biology, physical therapy, physiological psychology, premedicine, pre-veterinary medicine

Suggested High School Prep for Chiropractic

As with all medical majors, you should take as many math and sciences courses as you can. Biology, physics, and anatomy will be especially useful.

Fun Facts

Who Discovered Chiropractic?

Daniel David Palmer developed the fundamental theories for chiropractic care about a century ago. Five thousand years before that, manual therapies were practiced in China. The philosophies and therapies of chiropractic went through many changes over the years, and now we have new ideas about why these therapies work and how they should be executed.

When Did Chiropractic Come to America?

Although chiropractic care came to America long ago, it wasn't accepted as a legitimate form of care until very recently. It took about 77 years for all 50 states to establish licensing boards, and only a lawsuit prompted recognition and acceptance of the field by the American Medical Association in 1991. Now, most doctors and medical associations work with chiropractors for patient care, and the field is well on its way to shedding its stigma as the realm of quacks and becoming a fully accepted part of the medical world.

Careers and Salary

Starting salaries for new chiropractors are usually about $45,000, but that number fluctuates with their locations and the size of their practice.

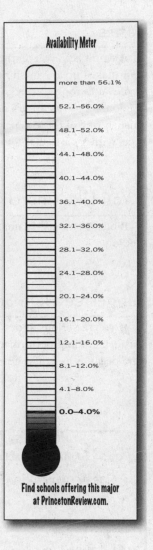

Availability Meter

more than 56.1%

52.1–56.0%

48.1–52.0%

44.1–48.0%

40.1–44.0%

36.1–40.0%

32.1–36.0%

28.1–32.0%

24.1–28.0%

20.1–24.0%

16.1–20.0%

12.1–16.0%

8.1–12.0%

4.1–8.0%

0.0–4.0%

Find schools offering this major
at PrincetonReview.com.

CHURCH MUSIC

Basics

It won't land you on the cover of *Rolling Stone*, but what church music lacks in popular content, it more than makes up for in spirituality. Church music has a very long, and definitely complicated history. From Medieval Europe to the gospel choirs of the South, music has always been a vital component of faith and religion. Music as an art has long been an intense academic discipline with multifarious genres. Church music is one of these genres. As a major, it combines the study of music, including composition and performance, with a particular focus on the music heard and performed in churches throughout the world.

If You Like Church Music, You May Also Like . . .

Biblical studies, Islamic studies, Jewish studies, Medieval and Renaissance studies, religious studies, theology

Suggested High School Prep for Church Music

If you're serious about becoming a church music major, you will have to have a strong background in music, including performance. So, as the old saying goes, practice, practice, practice. Since ability with the pipe organ is essential, get your hands on one and start listening to The Doors.

SAMPLE COLLEGE CURRICULUM FOR CHURCH MUSIC

Choral Arranging

Choral Methods and Repertoire

Church Music Administration

Church Music Methods

Conducting

Ensemble

History and Philosophy of Worship

Hymnology

Introduction to Church Music

Music Engraving

Principles of Organization and Management

Fun Facts

Church Humor

A man is struck by a bus on a busy street in New York City. He lies dying on the sidewalk as a crowd of on-lookers gathers around.

"A priest. Somebody get me a priest!" the man gasps. A policeman checks the crowd—no priest, no minister, no man of God of any kind. "A priest, please!" the dying man says again. Then out of the crowd steps a little old man dressed shabbily and at least 80 years of age.

"Mr. Policeman," says the man, "I'm not a priest. I'm not even a Catholic. But for 50 years now I've been living behind St. Elizabeth's Catholic Church on First Avenue, and every night I listen to the Catholic litany. Maybe I can be of some comfort to this man."

The policeman agrees and brings the octogenarian over to where the dying man lies. He kneels down, leans over the injured man and says slowly in a solemn voice: "B-4. I-19. N-38. G-54. O-72. . . ."

Something for Everyone

Dentist's Hymn: "Crown Him with Many Crowns"

Weatherman's Hymn: "There Shall be Showers of Blessing"

Contractor's Hymn: "The Church's One Foundation"

Tailor's Hymn: "Holy, Holy, Holy"

Golfer's Hymn: "There is a Green Hill Far Away"

Politician's Hymn: "Standing on the Promises"

Optometrist's Hymn: "Open Mine Eyes that I Might See"

I.R.S. Hymn: "All to Thee"

Gossip's Hymn: "Pass It On"

Electrician's Hymn: "Send the Light"

Shopper's Hymn: "Sweet By and By"

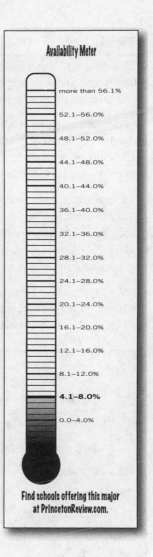

Availability Meter

more than 56.1%

52.1–56.0%

48.1–52.0%

44.1–48.0%

40.1–44.0%

36.1–40.0%

32.1–36.0%

28.1–32.0%

24.1–28.0%

20.1–24.0%

16.1–20.0%

12.1–16.0%

8.1–12.0%

4.1–8.0%

0.0–4.0%

Find schools offering this major at PrincetonReview.com.

Careers and Salary

The starting salary for a church music major is about $28,000.

CAREER OPTIONS

Clergy—Priest, Rabbi, Minister	Music Executive	Musician
Disc Jockey		

CINEMATOGRAPHY AND FILM/VIDEO PRODUCTION

Basics

Everyone, at some point, dreams of living the high life in Hollywood and making a big name for themselves in the glamorous industry of moviemaking. Gear yourself up to become the best of the best in a cinematography and film/video production program, and you may do just that.

For starters, you'll study the technical aspects of film production—lighting, editing, camera techniques, and sound equipment. You'll learn all the elements that go into making a film and how those elements affect one another—from directing and managing a film project to budgeting and marketing. Eventually you'll be able to develop an idea from start to finish and make it come alive through screenwriting and production.

A cinematography and film/video production major wouldn't be complete without an overview of the history of cinema: the advancements and innovations that got us where we are today and a look at the landmark films we hold sacred as "classics." Film theory and criticism will be studied as well, helping you to begin to develop your own analytical skills. Taking a more sociological perspective, you'll examine the role film plays in our culture and how it has shaped the world.

Most programs give students the opportunity to learn about cinematography and film/video production firsthand, with assignments to make their own short film or assisting with others' films. Some programs may ask you to choose a concentration in a specific area of film—such as directing or screenwriting—and produce a final project accordingly. Be sure to research the requirements and find a program that best suits you (and your star-studded goals).

SAMPLE COLLEGE CURRICULUM FOR CINEMATOGRAPHY AND FILM/VIDEO PRODUCTION
American Cinema
The Art of the Cinema
Digital Audio and Video
Digital Technologies
Directing for the Screen
Documentary Film
Film Criticism
Film Editing
Film History and Theory
International Cinema
Media Criticism
Multimedia Production
Narrative Video
Production and Direction
Script Writing for Cinema and TV

If You Like Cinematography and Film/Video Production, You May Also Like . . .

Advertising, art, art education, art history, computer graphics, creative writing, english, film, graphic design, playwriting and screenwriting, theater, visual communication

Suggested High School Prep for Cinematography and Film/Video Production

The world is your oyster when it comes to what you may end up filming someday, so the best high school preparation is a wide variety of challenging courses in math, science, and the humanities. Take courses that will strengthen your reading, writing, and communication skills. Courses in history, psychology, religion, and languages will give you perspectives on the world that may help you become a better filmmaker, and art classes could help hone your creative vision.

Fun Facts

History of the Oscars

- The first Academy Awards ceremony took place in 1929 to celebrate films from 1927 and 1928.
- "Sound" movies began that same year.
- In the beginning, there were two awards for Best Picture: one for "most outstanding motion picture production" and one for "most unique, artistic, worthy and original production." In 1929, the winner of the first was *Wings*, directed by William Wellman; the winner of the second was *Sunrise*, directed by F. W. Murnau.

(Source: www.filmsite.org/aa27.html)

Jazzed Up

The Jazz Singer was the first talking motion picture, and at the 1929 Academy Awards it won a Special Award for being the "pioneering talking picture which has revolutionized the industry." However, in the interest of fairness, it was not permitted to compete against silent films for the rest of the awards.

(Source: www.filmsite.org/aa27.html)

Careers and Salary

The starting salary for cinematography and film/video production majors varies widely and depends on how you use your skills. Beginning cinematographers and film/video producers often make very little ($25,000 to $30,000) until they garner experience and earn respect. Some work on a freelance basis, making salaries unpredictable. Where you live also makes a difference in how much you're paid.

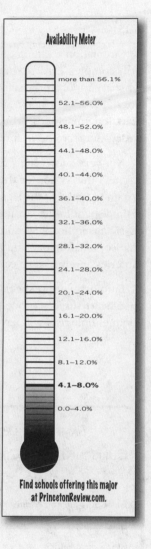

Availability Meter

more than 56.1%

52.1–56.0%

48.1–52.0%

44.1–48.0%

40.1–44.0%

36.1–40.0%

32.1–36.0%

28.1–32.0%

24.1–28.0%

20.1–24.0%

16.1–20.0%

12.1–16.0%

8.1–12.0%

4.1–8.0%

0.0–4.0%

Find schools offering this major at PrincetonReview.com.

CAREER OPTIONS

Animator	Documentary Filmmaker	Teacher
Cinematographer	Journalist	Various careers in advertising or television
Director	Producer	

CIRCULATION TECHNOLOGY

Basics

Circulation technologists—also called perfusion technologists—provide support to surgeons who perform complex cardiac surgery. Not just any kind of support, mind you. Specifically, they provide cardiopulmonary support in situations where it is necessary to temporarily suspend a patient's cardiac or respiratory functions. If you major in circulation technology, you'll learn more than you thought possible about heart/lung machines, artificial hearts, and a variety of other devices designed to keep patients alive during cardiac surgery and in intensive care.

Not very surprisingly, circulation technology is very hands-on. It's also a complex and highly specialized business that is not for the faint of heart (no pun intended). If you choose it as your major, you are almost certain to find that the significance of time spent in the classroom pales in comparison with the significance of time spent in the lab and in clinical training and internships. You will probably find yourself working with physicians in hospitals and clinics as a college student. While other students are writing papers and studying philosophical theory, you'll be helping to select and operate medical equipment used in quadruple bypass surgeries and intensive care units.

Employment prospects for circulation technology majors are pretty bright. So long as the occurrence of open-heart surgery procedures continues to increase throughout the United States and the world, circulation technologists will have plenty of job opportunities.

SAMPLE COLLEGE CURRICULUM FOR CIRCULATION TECHNOLOGY

Basic Surgery and Monitoring

Biochemistry

Biomedical Ethics

Cardiac Anatomy and Physiology

Cardiovascular Pathology

Chemistry

Clinical Internships

Human Anatomy

Perfusion Technology

Pharmacology

Physics

Physiological Management of Bypass

Statistics

If You Like Circulation Technology, You May Also Like . . .

Biochemistry, biology, cell biology, chemistry, genetics, gerontology, medical technology, mental health services, microbiology, neurobiology, neuroscience, nursing, occupational therapy, pharmacology, pharmacy, physical education, physiological psychology, premedicine, pre-optometry, pre-veterinary medicine, public health, radiologic technology, rehabilatation services, respiratory therapy

Suggested High School Prep for Circulation Technology

Circulation technology is pretty rigorous. If you are thinking about majoring in it, take the most advanced math courses you can. Also, take every chemistry and biology course your school offers. You also want to know your way around a lab as well as possible. Taking a job or a volunteer position at a local hospital or clinic isn't a bad idea either.

ALLIED MEDICAL AND HEALTH PROFESSIONS

Fun Facts

The Average Heart ...

- is a little larger than a fist.
- beats 100,000 times and pumps about 2,000 gallons of blood each day.
- beats more than 2.5 billion times over the course of a 70-year lifetime.

Feeling a Little Queasy?

Here are 10 of the best hospitals in the country, at least according to *U.S. News & World Report*.

- Johns Hopkins Hospital (Baltimore, Maryland)
- Mayo Clinic (Rochester, Minnesota)
- UCLA Medical Center (Los Angeles, California)
- Cleveland Clinic (Cleveland, Ohio)
- Massachusetts General Hospital (Boston, Massachusetts)
- New York Presbyterian University Hospital of Columbia and Cornell (New York, New York)
- Duke University Medical Center (Durham, North Carolina)
- University of California, San Francisco Medical Center (San Francisco, California)
- Barnes Jewish Hospital, Washington University (St. Louis, Missouri)
- Brigham and Women's Hospital (Boston, Massachusetts)

(Source: health.usnews.com/usnews/health/best-hospitals/honerroll.htm)

Careers and Salary

The average starting salary for a cardiopulmonary perfusionist is between $45,000 and $65,000 annually. Expect to be on call and work overtime.

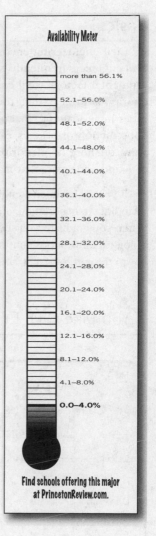

Availability Meter

more than 56.1%

52.1–56.0%

48.1–52.0%

44.1–48.0%

40.1–44.0%

36.1–40.0%

32.1–36.0%

28.1–32.0%

24.1–28.0%

20.1–24.0%

16.1–20.0%

12.1–16.0%

8.1–12.0%

4.1–8.0%

0.0–4.0%

Find schools offering this major at PrincetonReview.com.

CAREER OPTIONS

Health Care Administrator	**Paramedic**	**Physician Assistant**
Nurse	**Physician**	

CIVIL ENGINEERING

Basics

Civil engineering encompasses a broad combination of all the subdisciplines within engineering, and civil engineers frequently work on complex projects that involve many technical, economic, social, and environmental factors. Civil engineering majors who become professional civil engineers are responsible for enormous projects like the Golden Gate Bridge, the Sears Tower, the English Channel Tunnel, and every other huge structure that needs to withstand the forces of nature. Civil engineering involves the design and construction of bridges, earthquake-resistant high-rise buildings in high-seismic-risk areas, eight-lane highways, offshore oil platforms, transit systems, dams, airports, landfills, recycling plants—all the colossal, one-of-a-kind endeavors that make modern civilization what it is. They synchronize traffic lights too.

If you major in civil engineering, you'll probably choose from one of many different specialties in the field, including transportation, structures, materials, hydrosystems, geotechnical, environmental, and construction. When you graduate, you shouldn't have a problem getting a job. As environmental concerns grow and as technological innovations continue at a breakneck pace, the demand for civil engineers will rise. After all, somebody has to design, construct, and maintain the infrastructure and the facilities that are essential to our civilization.

If You Like Civil Engineering, You May Also Like . . .

Applied mathematics, applied physics, architectural engineering, chemical engineering, computer and information science, computer engineering, electrical engineering, engineering design, environmental and environmental health engineering, industrial engineering, mathematics, mechanical engineering, naval architecture, nuclear engineering, petroleum engineering, physics, statistics

> ### SAMPLE COLLEGE CURRICULUM FOR CIVIL ENGINEERING
>
> Calculus and Analytic Geometry
>
> Civil Engineering Ethics
>
> Differential Equations
>
> Dynamics
>
> Engineering Graphics
>
> Fluid Mechanics
>
> Geology
>
> Materials of Construction
>
> Physics
>
> Reinforced Concrete Design
>
> Structural Masonry Design
>
> Structural Principles
>
> Surveying and Measurement
>
> Thermodynamics
>
> Transportation Engineering

Suggested High School Prep for Civil Engineering

A very solid background in math and physics is essential if you want to pursue civil engineering, as is extensive knowledge of computers and computer programming skills. Take trigonometry and calculus (or the highest-level math class that your high school offers).

Fun Facts

The World's Tallest Buildings

You wouldn't believe the debate that rages over which building is the world's tallest. We don't pretend to know. Here is one list of the eight tallest, in alphabetical order, with the years in which they were completed.

Central Plaza, Hong Kong, China (1992)

Citic Plaza, Guangzhou, China (1997)

Empire State Building, New York, USA (1931)

Jin Mao Building, Shanghai, China (1999)

Petronas Tower 1, Kuala Lumpur, Malaysia (1998)

Petronas Tower 2, Kuala Lumpur, Malaysia (1998)

Sears Tower, Chicago, USA (1974)

Shun Hing Square, Shenzhen, China (1996)

Most People Put Stock in the Old Adage

If it ain't broke, don't fix it. Engineers, however, believe that if it ain't broke, it must not have enough features and gadgets yet.

Careers and Salary

Salaries for newly minted civil engineers average about $43,000 per year.

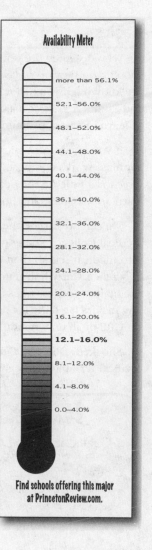

Availability Meter

more than 56.1%

52.1–56.0%

48.1–52.0%

44.1–48.0%

40.1–44.0%

36.1–40.0%

32.1–36.0%

28.1–32.0%

24.1–28.0%

20.1–24.0%

16.1–20.0%

12.1–16.0%

8.1–12.0%

4.1–8.0%

0.0–4.0%

Find schools offering this major at PrincetonReview.com.

CAREER OPTIONS

Architect	Construction Manager	Military Officer
Army National Guard	Developer	Robotics Engineer
Army (Officer)	Graphic Designer	Structural Engineer
City Planner	Inventor	Surveyor
Civil Engineer		

CLASSICS

Basics

Who designed the water faucet? How did a Caesarean section get its name? Was Homer really blind? Why should you beware of Greeks bearing gifts? The answers to these and many other questions are yours for the knowing if you major in classics—the study of the languages, literatures, and cultures of ancient Greece and Rome. A classics major offers the opportunity to explore the beliefs and achievements of antiquity and to learn just how profoundly they still affect contemporary civilization.

If you major in classics, you'll learn Greek or Latin (or both). You'll also read the great literary and philosophical works composed in these languages. Be forewarned, though: reading *The Odyssey* in the original Greek is a little on the demanding side. You'll study ancient art, architecture, and technology too, and you'll learn about Greek and Roman legal systems, social institutions, religious practices, and class distinctions.

We can't overstate the value of a classics major. Check this out: According to the Association of American Medical Colleges, students who have a major or double major in classics have a better success rate getting into medical school than do students who concentrate solely in biology, microbiology, and other branches of science. Crazy, huh? Furthermore, according to Harvard Magazine, classics majors (and math majors) have the highest success rates of any majors in law school. Believe it or not, political science, economics, and pre-law majors lag fairly far behind. Furthermore, classics majors consistently have some of the highest scores on GRE of all undergraduates.

Shocked? Don't be. One reason classics majors are so successful is that they completely master grammar. Medical terminology, legal terminology, and all those ridiculously worthless vocabulary words on the GRE (and the SAT) have their roots in Greek and Latin. Ultimately though, classics majors get on well in life because they develop intellectual rigor, communications skills, analytical skills, the ability to handle complex information, and above all, a breadth of view which few other disciplines can provide.

If You Like Classics, You May Also Like . . .

Anthropology, Arabic, archaeology, art history, ceramics, English, great books, history, Islamic studies, Italian, Jewish studies, library science, Medieval and Renaissance studies, Modern Greek, philosophy, religious studies, sociology, Spanish, theology

Suggested High School Prep for Classics

In a word: Latin. Take as much high school Latin as possible. If you don't want to take Latin or your school doesn't offer it, take some other foreign language class, so you can become familiar with grammatical structure and translating from one language to another. History and literature courses are important as well.

Fun Facts

College Year in Athens (www.cyathens.org)

This independent study abroad program based in Cambridge, Massachusetts, enrolls about 100 students every semester and offers courses conducted in English. In addition to tooling around Athens for a semester, students explore the development of Western civilization as well as Eastern Orthodox Christianity. Courses are available in archaeology, art history, classical languages, cultural anthropology, Greek literature, history, Modern Greek, philosophy, political science, and religious studies.

The Seven Wonders of the Ancient World

The Great Pyramid of Giza: A massive stone structure near the ancient city of Memphis. It was the tomb for the Egyptian Pharaoh Khufu.

The Hanging Gardens of Babylon: King Nebuchadnezzar II's palace on the bank of the Euphrates River was resplendent with profuse gardens.

The Statue of Zeus at Olympia: A colossal statue of the god of all Greek gods, carved by the great sculptor Pheidias.

The Temple of Artemis at Ephesus: A stunning temple in Asia Minor erected to honor the Greek goddess of hunting and nature.

The Mausoleum at Halicarnassus: An extravagant tomb constructed for King Maussollos, Persian governor of Caria.

The Colossus of Rhodes: A statue of ridiculously immense proportions honoring Helios, the sun god. The ancient Greeks erected it near the harbor of this Mediterranean island.

The Lighthouse of Alexandria: A Ptolemaic lighthouse on the island of Pharos off the coast of this capital city.

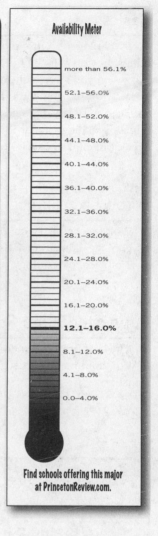

Availability Meter

- more than 56.1%
- 52.1–56.0%
- 48.1–52.0%
- 44.1–48.0%
- 40.1–44.0%
- 36.1–40.0%
- 32.1–36.0%
- 28.1–32.0%
- 24.1–28.0%
- 20.1–24.0%
- 16.1–20.0%
- **12.1–16.0%**
- 8.1–12.0%
- 4.1–8.0%
- 0.0–4.0%

Find schools offering this major at PrincetonReview.com.

Careers and Salary

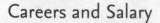

Salaries vary widely. Beginning salaries range from $24,000 at the low end to about $30,000. A very high percentage of classics majors head straight to graduate or professional school.

CAREER OPTIONS

Actor	Curator	Philosopher
Art Dealer	Editor	Physician
Artist	Journalist	Political Scientist
Attorney	Librarian	Professor
Book Publishing Professional	Lobbyist	Teacher
Clergy—Priest, Rabbi, Minister	Paralegal	Writer
Corporate Lawyer		

CLINICAL PSYCHOLOGY

Basics

Psychology is a discipline that focuses on behavior, on why people, and in some cases animals, do the things they do. Why do I dream of flying monkeys at night? Well, it may be because of that trip you took the zoo when you were eight where the monkeys . . . we'll leave that alone for now. Clinical psychology is one variation of the study and practice of psychology, and as a discipline its primary focus is on the practical application of psychological research and methods. This means, in simpler terms, that the focus is on putting a psychology major to use. Whether it's helping to diagnose a mental disorder or conducting research, a major in clinical psychology prepares you for direct work in the field.

If You Like Clinical Psychology, You May Also Like . . .

Biology, chemistry, child care, child development, communication disorders, counseling, developmental psychology, educational psychology, human development, industrial psychology, neurobiology, nursing, physiological psychology, psychology, social work, sociology

Suggested High School Prep for Clinical Psychology

The best preparation for a clinical psychology major is, obviously, psychology. Take it if your school offers it. You should also focus on those math and science classes, particularly biology, chemistry, physics, and statistics.

SAMPLE COLLEGE CURRICULUM FOR CLINICAL PSYCHOLOGY

Abnormal Psychology

Chemistry

Child Development

Clinical Methods

Introduction to Psychology

Research Methods in Clinical
    Psychology

Seminar Fieldwork

Seminar in Physiological Psychology

Statistics for the Behavioral Sciences

Fun Facts

A Joke

A man is walking along the street when he is brutally beaten and robbed. He lies unconscious, bleeding. While he is lying there, a police officer passes by but crosses to the other side of the road without trying to help. A Boy Scout troop does the same, as do a number of pedestrians. Finally, a psychologist walks by and runs up to the man. He bends down and says, "My God! Whoever did this needs help."

Top Ten Signs a Therapist Is Approaching Burnout

10. You think of the peaceful park you like as "your private therapeutic milieu."
9. You realize that your psychotic patient, who is picking invisible flowers out of mid-air, is probably having more fun in life than you are.
8. A grateful client, who thinks you walk on water, brings you a small gift, and you end up having to debrief your feelings of unworthiness with a colleague.
7. You are watching a rerun of *The Wizard of Oz*, and you start to categorize the types of delusions that Dorothy had.
6. Your best friend comes to you with severe relationship troubles, and you start trying to remember which cognitive behavioral technique has the most empirical validity for treating this problem.
5. You realize you actually have no friends; they have all become just one big caseload.
4. A coworker asks how you are doing, and you reply that you are a bit "internally preoccupied" and "not able to interact with peers" today.
3. Your spouse asks you to set the table, and you tell your spouse that it would be "counter-therapeutic to your current goals" to do that.
2. You tell your teenage daughter she is not going to start dating boys because she is "in denial," "lacks insight," and her "emotions are not congruent with her chronological age."
1. You are packing for a trip to a large family holiday reunion, and you take the DSM-IV with you just in case.

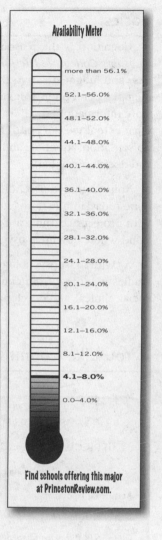

Availability Meter

more than 56.1%

52.1–56.0%

48.1–52.0%

44.1–48.0%

40.1–44.0%

36.1–40.0%

32.1–36.0%

28.1–32.0%

24.1–28.0%

20.1–24.0%

16.1–20.0%

12.1–16.0%

8.1–12.0%

4.1–8.0%

0.0–4.0%

Find schools offering this major at PrincetonReview.com.

Careers and Salary

For clinical psychology majors, the average starting salaries are similar to those of other psychology majors, which fall between $25,000 and $35,000.

CAREER OPTIONS

Career Counselor	Criminologist	Physician
Child Care Worker	Guidance Counselor	Psychologist

COGNITIVE PSYCHOLOGY

Basics

Cognition is the reason computers will never completely replace real, live human beings. *Merriam Webster's Collegiate Dictionary* defines cognition as "the act or process of knowing," including both awareness and judgment—two things your fancy laptop will never have. Cognitive psychology majors examine memory, perception, thinking, and intelligence. They study how our brains work to perceive, process, and store information. You'll learn how our mental processes—like mood swings—affect our behaviors and to what extent we can control and hone them. Cognitive psychology majors pay attention to details that make up sensation, attention, and reasoning. You'll also examine the many processes involved in problem solving and decision making.

Your cognitive psychology major will expose you to research from the past and research that is being done today; in most programs you'll even have a chance to do some research of your own or assist others with projects. Learning about the problems, advancements, and theories from the past will help you understand where cognitive psychology has been, where it is, and where you may lead it.

As with most psychology disciplines, cognitive psychology is interdisciplinary to a large degree, and your studies will draw from courses in philosophy, linguistics, statistics, and other areas of psychology such as social, clinical, and developmental psychology.

If You Like Cognitive Psychology, You May Also Like . . .

Biopsychology, clinical psychology, counseling, developmental psychology, educational psychology, experimental psychology, industrial psychology, physiological psychology, psychology, social psychology, sociology

SAMPLE COLLEGE CURRICULUM FOR COGNITIVE PSYCHOLOGY

Abnormal Behavior

Behavior Therapy

Childhood Behavior Disorders

Development of Human Behavior

History of Psychology

Human Memory

Human Neuropsychology

Intelligence

Learning

Motivation and Emotion

Research Design

Statistical Methods

Tests and Measurements

Suggested High School Prep for Cognitive Psychology

Since psychology requirements usually comprise a wide selection of both humanities and science courses, you should try to take a little of everything—English, history, languages, science, and math. It's important to take higher-level courses such as calculus; tough math courses will build a strong foundation for your college studies, since you'll be dealing with statistics in your research. And any psychology courses your school offers will give you a good introduction to your chosen field. Check out a book of Freud's theories for some leisure reading; you may be surprised at what you learn!

Fun Facts

Top Five

There have been many developments in the field of cognitive psychology over the years. The Center for Cognitive Sciences at the University of Minnesota has put together a list of the 100 most influential works in cognitive sciences from the twentieth century. Here are the first five.

1. *Syntactic Structures*, N. Chomsky, 1957
2. *Vision: A Computational Investigation into the Human Representation and Processing* of *Visual Information*, D. Marr, 1982
3. *Computing Machinery and Intelligence*, A. M. Turing, 1950
4. *The Organization of Behavior: A Neuropsychological Theory*, D. O. Hebb, 1949
5. *Parallel Distributed Processing: Explorations in the Microstructure of Cognition*, D. E. Rumelhart and J. L. McClelland, 1986

Find the rest at www.cogsci.umn.edu/OLD/calendar/past_events/millennium/top100.html.

Turing Point

Alan Turing, from Britain, is responsible for developing the first stirrings of what eventually came to be known as cognitive science. In 1950, Turing conceived of the idea of a computer and described his idea mathematically; not long after, "universal Turing machines" (i.e., digital computers) were created. Turing then discovered that computers could be programmed to do things that, until then, only humans could do, such as play chess. Check out www.cs.rochester.edu for more information.

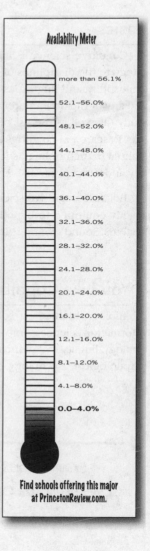

Availability Meter

more than 56.1%

52.1–56.0%

48.1–52.0%

44.1–48.0%

40.1–44.0%

36.1–40.0%

32.1–36.0%

28.1–32.0%

24.1–28.0%

20.1–24.0%

16.1–20.0%

12.1–16.0%

8.1–12.0%

4.1–8.0%

0.0–4.0%

Find schools offering this major at PrincetonReview.com.

Careers and Salary

Salaries for cognitive psych majors are usually in the $35,000 range. However, after obtaining advanced degrees, practicing psychologists have salaries as varied as $40,000 to $100,000.

CAREER OPTIONS

Counselor	Psychologist	Social Worker
Professor	Researcher	Teacher
Psychiatrist		

COGNITIVE SCIENCE

Basics

Cognitive science is inherently interdisciplinary. If you study this field, you'll have the opportunity to integrate the disciplines of psychology, artificial intelligence, neuroscience, biology, education, anthropology, philosophy, and linguistics. You'll also study computer science and mathematics, along with logic, robotics, and any of the other aforementioned disciplines that cognitive science overlaps. The list of available topics of study (as well as the list of potential applications of your cognitive science knowledge) is seemingly limitless. Research in cognitive science has led to developments in artificial intelligence, the emergence of a substantial branch of linguistics, the economic concept of behavioral finance, and new models of human memory and perception.

Because cognitive science ventures beyond the domain of human intelligence, cognitive scientists are readily equipped to hypothesize about intelligence in other animals or in (as yet undeveloped) computer systems. Sound exciting? It is.

If You Like Cognitive Science, You May Also Like . . .

Biology, biomedical science, biopsychology, clinical psychology, cognitive psychology, computer and information science, computer programming, computer science, developmental psychology, experimental psychology, linguistics, mathematics, molecular biology, neurobiology, neuroscience, pharmacology, psychology, physiological psychology, premedicine

Suggested High School Prep for Cognitive Science

Science is crucial to this major; biology, computer science, and any psychology you can study will get you on the right track. Mathematics is necessary as well. Since you'll eventually be conducting research, take advantage of every opportunity to hone your English skills.

SAMPLE COLLEGE CURRICULUM FOR COGNITIVE SCIENCE

Artificial Life

Cognitive Consequences of Technology

Cognitive Neuroscience

Everyday Cognition

Human Computer Interaction

Introduction to Cognitive Science

Language Development

Learning, Memory, and Attention

Neuroanatomy and Physiology

Neurobiology of Cognition

Neural Network Models of Cognition

Fun Facts

The Future of Cognition

Ray Kurtzweil—an inventor, programmer, author, and futurist—proposes a series of exponential paradigm shifts, one of which describes the point at which human cognition and computer cognition become indistinguishable, in his Law of Accelerating Returns. Some futurists predict this event taking place as early as the third decade of the twenty-first century.

Computer Speak (Getting Beyond the 1s and 0s)

The "Turing Test," named after Alan Turing, measures a machine's capacity to participate in human-like conversation. If a judge engaged in a natural language conversation with both a human and a machine and cannot discern which is which, the machine passes the test.

Careers and Salary

Computer-industry careers are common for undergraduate degrees in cognitive science, but outside of jobs in artificial intelligence, neural network applications, software design, and cognitive engineering, many cognitive science majors pursue graduate school. Expect starting salaries of about $45,000.

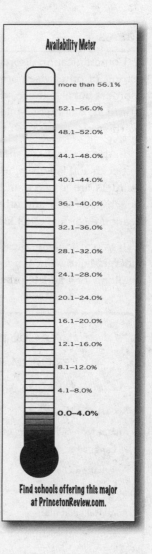

Availability Meter

more than 56.1%

52.1–56.0%

48.1–52.0%

44.1–48.0%

40.1–44.0%

36.1–40.0%

32.1–36.0%

28.1–32.0%

24.1–28.0%

20.1–24.0%

16.1–20.0%

12.1–16.0%

8.1–12.0%

4.1–8.0%

0.0–4.0%

Find schools offering this major at PrincetonReview.com.

CAREER OPTIONS

Computer Systems Designer	Researcher	Teacher
Professor	Software Designer	

COMMUNICATION DISORDERS

Basics

Communication disorders majors study just about any disorder that impairs language abilities, speaking, hearing, or otherwise normal communication with others. This field deals with not only people born with disorders but also those who become afflicted with them later in life. As a communication disorders major, your focus will be two-fold: you'll learn what fundamentally causes these disorders, as well as ways to manage them.

In this major, you'll study how language develops, the acoustics of speech, audiology, and the acquisition of speech and language. You'll learn the different ways disordered communication develops and how these disorders are affected and viewed by society. You'll learn about rehabilitation, American Sign Language, speech pathology, and other treatment services. You'll learn how to identify, manage, and prevent communication disorders of all kinds.

If you're looking ahead to a career in speech-language pathology or audiology, you should know that undergraduate work is not enough to become a professional in these fields; graduate work is required. There are plenty of graduate programs out there with great programs in these fields, so don't feel pressured . . . yet.

SAMPLE COLLEGE CURRICULUM FOR COMMUNICATION DISORDERS

Acoustics of Speech

Anatomy and Physiology of Speech and Language

Articulation Disorders

Audiological Assessment

Aural Rehabilitation

Communication Using Computers

Developmental Disorders of Communication

Language and Cognition

Language Development

Mind and Brain

Neurogenic Disorders of Communication

Psycholinguistics

Speech and Language Acquisition

Speech Pathology

Structure of English Words

If You Like Communication Disorders, You May Also Like . . .

Biology, biopsychology, counseling, education, education of the deaf, human development, mass communication, physical therapy, physiological psychology, psychology, special education, speech pathology, visual communication

Suggested High School Prep for Communication Disorders

To prepare for a major in communication disorders, try to take as many science courses as possible—biology, chemistry, anatomy, and others. Math courses will also be valuable. Writing and speaking will be important in your major, so also make an effort to take English and communication courses. It never hurts to acquire a second (or third or fourth) language while you're still in high school. If you have time, also consider becoming a volunteer to help people with communication disorders; your guidance counselor may have ideas for where to seek out this sort of opportunity.

Fun Facts

Did You Know?

Three of the most important components of verbal communication are voice, speech, and language. Problems with any of these can result in difficulties in communicating ideas to others. The National Institute on Deafness and Other Communication Disorders points out that 7.5 million people in the United States have problems with their voices, problems that affect such things as pitch, volume, and quality. Speech disorders are common in about 5 percent of children at the first-grade level. Between 6 million and 8 million people in the United States struggle with various forms of language problems.

A Sampling of What's Ahead

If you decide to study communication disorders, you may become familiar with many of the following speech-language disorders:

- Amyotrophic lateral sclerosis
- Aphasia
- Autism
- Bells palsy
- Cleft palate
- Cri du Chat syndrome
- Dysphagia
- Hydrocephalus
- Hyperlexia
- Elective mutism
- Rett syndrome
- Williams syndrome

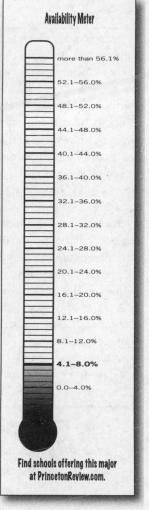

Availability Meter

more than 56.1%

52.1–56.0%

48.1–52.0%

44.1–48.0%

40.1–44.0%

36.1–40.0%

32.1–36.0%

28.1–32.0%

24.1–28.0%

20.1–24.0%

16.1–20.0%

12.1–16.0%

8.1–12.0%

4.1–8.0%

0.0–4.0%

Find schools offering this major
at PrincetonReview.com.

Careers and Salary

Starting salaries for communication disorders majors are difficult to estimate, since so much depends upon what sort of graduate work they choose to pursue or what type of career they select. A speech therapist, for instance, earns about $25,000. However, speech pathologists with graduate degrees usually earn from $42,000 to $82,000.

CAREER OPTIONS

Occupational Therapist	**Social Worker**	**Translator**
Psychologist	**Speech Therapist**	

COMMUNICATIONS STUDIES, SPEECH COMMUNICATION, AND RHETORIC

Basics

Ratings prove that television audiences prefer laugh tracks over silence. Now and then a new show will go experimental, opting to can the canned laughter, only to be promptly cancelled. So why do we want to laugh on cue? Why are shows funnier when a studio full of people laughs with us? You may soon have the answers as a major in communications studies, speech communication, and rhetoric. In this program, students learn how certain messages influence individual and group behavior—and why—as well as how our reactions reflect the underlying values of society. You'll spend a significant amount of time studying different kinds of speaking and writing and the strategies speakers and writers use to make their points and drive them home. You'll take a look at verbal and nonverbal messages, audience reaction, and the varied effects of different communication environments. Communication theory will play a part, too, as you delve into monumental speeches, revolutionary political campaigns, radical social movements, and the trends in styles of news reporting.

Rhetoric itself is about putting together good arguments—communication for the means of persuasion. People with fiery personalities, quick wits, and cunning will take pleasure in a major that includes rhetoric—mastering different types of appeals and how to craft those appeals and make them situation-specific, audience-tailored, and sharp as all get-out. Your studies will range from classical forms of rhetoric, like great Roman orations, to the modern-day places it rears its head, like websites, film, and television.

A major in communications studies, speech communication, and rhetoric makes for solid pre-professional training. It will prepare you for a wealth of careers in business, public relations, advertising, human resources, government, education, media, and social services. You won't come away with specific skills, such as putting together an ad campaign or producing a television show. However, it will give you a strong foundation from which to launch any number of careers and aspirations.

> ### SAMPLE COLLEGE CURRICULUM FOR COMMUNICATIONS STUDIES, SPEECH COMMUNICATION, AND RHETORIC
>
> Argumentative Writing
> Behavioral Research Methods in Communication
> Business Communication
> Communication and Society
> Communication Technology
> Electronic Media
> Greater Speakers and Speeches
> History of Rhetoric
> Interpersonal Communication
> Nonverbal Communication
> Propaganda and Persuasion
> Rhetoric of Film
> Rhetorical Theory and Analysis

If You Like Communications Studies, Speech Communication, and Rhetoric, You May Also Like . . .

American literature, business administration and management, classics, communication disorders, comparative literature, creative writing, economics, English, English composition, English literature, film, great books, journalism, mass communication, philosophy, political science, radio and television, speech pathology, technical writing, visual communication

Suggested High School Prep for Communications Studies, Speech Communication, and Rhetoric

Take all the English and writing-intensive courses you can—there's no better way to prepare for a communication or rhetoric major. Courses in literature, poetry, drama, and public speaking are all integral to these fields, and instruction in a foreign language would be extremely useful (especially Latin). Consider joining the forensics or debate team too or auditioning for a play. What better way to test audience reaction firsthand?

Fun Facts

Two Essential Primers

Aristotle's *Rhetoric* is pretty much the essential book on the subject. The classic text is now available in a handy online version at www.public.iastate.edu/~honeyl/Rhetoric/index.html. Also check out the electronic *Strunk and White: The Elements of Style*, the quintessential handbook on writing, at www.bartleby.com/141/index.html. You will be required to read this book for at least one class, and it will save your life when you are writing papers.

Famous Communication Majors

- Howard Stern (morning radio shock jock, Boston University)
- Barry Levinson (movie director, American University)

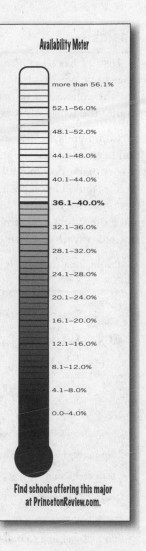

Availability Meter

more than 56.1%

52.1–56.0%

48.1–52.0%

44.1–48.0%

40.1–44.0%

36.1–40.0%

32.1–36.0%

28.1–32.0%

24.1–28.0%

20.1–24.0%

16.1–20.0%

12.1–16.0%

8.1–12.0%

4.1–8.0%

0.0–4.0%

Find schools offering this major at PrincetonReview.com.

Careers and Salary

Starting salaries for communication majors vary widely. Entry-level salaries in marketing, advertising, and public relations are about $25,000. Mid-level salaries are about $60,000, and top-level salaries are more than $100,000. Rhetoric majors who begin careers in writing after graduation can expect to earn about $27,000.

CAREER OPTIONS

Advertising Executive	Editor	Politician
Agent	Fund-raiser/Institutional Solicitor	Publicist
Attorney	Guidance Counselor	Speech Writer
Auctioneer	Journalist	Telecommunications Specialist
Bank Officer	Management Consultant	Television Reporter
Bar/Club Manager	Media Specialist	Web Editor
Benefits Administrator	Mediator	Writer
Disc Jockey	Motivational Speaker	

COMMUNITY HEALTH AND PREVENTIVE MEDICINE

Basics

History has shown that the ability for a society of people to withstand the onslaught of infectious diseases to be one of—if not the—most important factor in a civilization's success. Indeed, long before science had any concept of or name for microscopic infectors, germs were playing a key role in human evolution around the world, a process that continues to this day.

Community health and preventative medicine majors study the patterns and explanations for population health and disease and examine health policy on a local, national, and international scale. An interdisciplinary major, community health programs incorporate study of the social, political, and behavioral sciences, biology, and economics. They spend a great deal of time scrutinizing our national and international health care systems, resource allocation, and regional patterns of health and disease, while looking for ways to make the world a healthier place to live. Outside the classroom, students take part in field study at university and private research centers and at community outreach programs.

Public health is no less pressing an issue today than when the Black Death first decimated Europe in the fourteenth century. While wealthy countries have developed increasingly effective methods to combat illness, the future of much of the world's health is of constant concern. As a community health and preventive medicine major, you will be forming the basic knowledge and skill set to find solutions to the problems of disease that have plagued (literally) civilization since its outset.

SAMPLE COLLEGE CURRICULUM FOR COMMUNITY HEALTH AND PREVENTIVE MEDICINE

Applied Nutrition, Diet, and Exercise

Chronic and Communicable Diseases

Community Health Care and Services

Death and Dying

Drugs and Alcohol

Epidemiology

Ethical, Legal, and Critical Health Problems

Health Counseling Issues

Human Sexuality

Introduction to Grant Funding and Proposal Development in the Field of Health

Introduction to Research and Writing in Health

Personal and Community Health

Planning, Implementation, and Evaluation of Community Health Programs

---

If You Like Community Health and Preventive Medicine, You May Also Like . . .

Anthropology, biochemistry, biology, biopsychology, chemistry, clinical psychology, counseling, economics, experimental psychology, genetics, history, human development, medical technology, neuroscience, nursing, nutrition, pharmacology, political science, premedicine, psychology, social work, and sociology

Suggested High School Prep for Community Health and Preventive Medicine

As the field spans the gambit, it'd probably be a good idea that you focus on getting as well-rounded an education as possible. Clearly, you'll want to focus on biology and the social and behavioral sciences. Outside of school, look for avenues that will help you feel productive in the community. Volunteer! Your home town probably has innumerable organizations that cater to the sick and poor, and a helping hand is always welcomed.

Fun Facts

A Brief History of Health and Disease

1000 B.C./B.C.E.: The Chinese developed the process of variolation, in which a healthy individual may gain some immunity to small pox by inhaling the dried crust forming around lesions of the infected. During this same period, the Chinese performed the first known inoculations against the disease—a practice not documented in the West until the eighteenth century.

1347–1350: Black Death, called the "Great Mortality" by writers of the day, devastated Europe leaving an estimated one third of the continent dead. A true pandemic, before it was reined in, the Black Plague depopulated large portions of Africa, Asia, and the Middle East. Quarantining the dead and other failed attempts at preventing further infection were eventually replaced by the more effective method of burning whole portions of ravaged cities.

1680: Microorganisms were first observed by Anton van Leeuwenhoek. It would be another 200 years before the connection between germs and disease would gain acceptance.

1820: Edward Jenner coined the term "vaccination" for his revolutionary process of immunization to small pox through the infection of the similar—and curable—cow pox. ("Vacca" is Latin for cow.)

1854: John Snow developed the science of epidemiology when he identified a polluted water well as the source of a London cholera outbreak.

1862: Louis Pasteur and Claude Bernard performed the first "pasteurization" tests by which they heated milk and other liquids to kill molds and microorganisms present within them.

1876: Robert Koch published his findings on the connection between spores in the soil and as yet unexplained anthrax outbreaks.

(Source: www.absoluteastronomy.com)

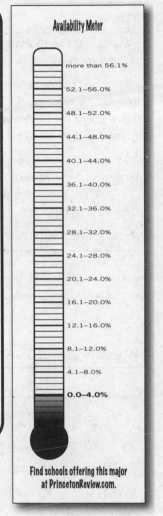

Availability Meter

more than 56.1%

52.1–56.0%

48.1–52.0%

44.1–48.0%

40.1–44.0%

36.1–40.0%

32.1–36.0%

28.1–32.0%

24.1–28.0%

20.1–24.0%

16.1–20.0%

12.1–16.0%

8.1–12.0%

4.1–8.0%

0.0–4.0%

Find schools offering this major
at PrincetonReview.com.

Careers and Study

Depending on the field, the salary for community health and preventive medicine major can vary quite a bit. Generally, salaries of people who are right out of school range from $25,000 to $40,000, but they can reach as high as six figures for some positions.

CAREER OPTIONS

Biologist	Health Care Manager	Physician Assistant
Child Care Worker	Hospital Administrator	Public Health Administrator
Ecologist	Nurse	Social Worker
Epidemiologists	Nutritionist	Statistician
Health Care Administrator	Occupational Therapist	Substance Abuse Counselor

COMPARATIVE LITERATURE

Basics

Would you like to dig into French decadence, African novels, Asian drama, Italian poetry, and countless other literary works of the world? If so, consider comparative literature.

While an English literature major concentrates on works originally written in English, a comparative literature major reads works originally written in a variety of languages, although usually in translation. The comp lit major then strives to put these works into context by comparing them against the art, history, political, and social climate of the country and time in which they were written.

Comparative literature majors often concentrate their studies in one area (such as African, Latin American, or Near Eastern literature). Some programs require fluency in at least one foreign language.

If You Like Comparative Literature, You May Also Like . . .

African studies, American literature, ancient studies, anthropology, art history, classics, creative writing, East Asian studies, East European studies, English, English composition, great books, history, international studies, Latin American studies, Slavic languages and literatures

Suggested High School Prep for Comparative Literature

Try to take as many classes in literature and composition as you can. Additional work in art history, music, philosophy, or social science will be helpful. Experience in a least one foreign language will prove extremely useful.

SAMPLE COLLEGE CURRICULUM FOR COMPARATIVE LITERATURE

Art History I

Classical Literature

The Enlightenment

Greek and Roman Mythology

History of Literary Criticism

Introduction to Asian Theater

Introduction to Comparative Literature

The Latin American Novel

Modernism

Realism

Romanticism

World Literature

World Mythology

Fun Facts

Delve Deeper

You can find lots of information about comparative literature and a large listing of programs all over the country at the University of Pennsylvania's thorough comparative literature website at http://cccat.sas.upenn.edu/Complit/Eclat.

Sex Sells

One of the greatest blockbusters of comparative literature was Camille Paglia's 1991 bestseller *Sexual Personae*.

Famous People Who Majored in Comparative Literature

Herman Wouk (Pulitzer Prize winning author of *The Caine Mutiny*, *The Winds of War*, *Don't Stop the Carnival*, and *War and Remembrance*, Columbia University)

Careers and Salary

The starting salary for a comparative literature major fresh out of college ranges from $22,000 to $30,000.

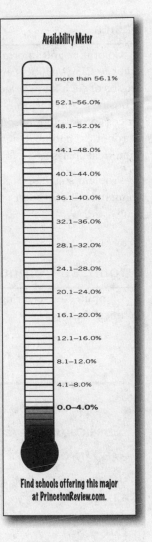

Availability Meter

more than 56.1%

52.1–56.0%

48.1–52.0%

44.1–48.0%

40.1–44.0%

36.1–40.0%

32.1–36.0%

28.1–32.0%

24.1–28.0%

20.1–24.0%

16.1–20.0%

12.1–16.0%

8.1–12.0%

4.1–8.0%

0.0–4.0%

Find schools offering this major at PrincetonReview.com.

CAREER OPTIONS

Diplomat/Attaché/Foreign Service Officer

Journalist

Philosopher

Political Scientist

Professor

Teacher

Translator

COMPUTER AND INFORMATION SCIENCE

Basics

Computer and information science is a branch of the more general field of computer science. If you major in CIS you'll be learning about computers and computer technology, with an emphasis on the applications of such knowledge. This means you'll focus on how computer technology can be applied to all fields of business. You'll learn how to develop business applications and perform system analysis; you'll study the process of developing software, from designing to programming to testing. You'll be exposed to areas such as robotics, natural language recognition programs, artificial intelligence, programming languages, and numerical analysis.

Problem solving is a major part of CIS, and graduates pursue careers in fields including business, management, and computer support. The knowledge you gain from a CIS major is absolutely applicable to the real world.

If You Like Computer and Information Science, You May Also Like . . .

Computer engineering, computer systems analysis, data processing, electrical engineering, statistics, technical writing

Suggested High School Prep for Computer and Information Science

Learn as much about computers as you can—take classes, read books, and explore subjects on your own. CIS also involves a great deal of math, so try to take higher-level courses such as calculus, trigonometry, and analytic geometry. A business class or two may also be useful, if your high school offers them.

SAMPLE COLLEGE CURRICULUM FOR COMPUTER AND INFORMATION SCIENCE

Algorithms and Programming

Calculus

Circuits and Electronics

Computer Systems Engineering

File Processing

Information Ethics

Micro- and Macroeconomics

Operating Systems

Spreadsheet Applications

Statistics

Systems Analysis

Systems Design

Techniques in Artificial Intelligence

Visual Basic Programming

Fun Facts

Quotable

"Computer science is no more about computers than astronomy is about telescopes, biology about microscopes, or chemistry is about beakers and test tubes. Science is not about tools. It is about how we use them, and what we find out when we do."

—Tracy Anne Hammond, Columbia University

A Joke

There was once a young man who, in his youth, professed his desire to become a great writer. When asked to define "great," he said, "I want to write stuff that the whole world will read; stuff that people will react to on a truly emotional level; stuff that will make them scream, cry, howl in pain and anger!" He now works for Microsoft, writing error messages.

Careers and Salary

Salaries typically fall in the $35,000 to $38,000 range but can rise to $60,000 or higher, depending on your field.

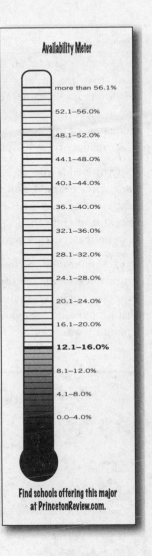

Availability Meter

more than 56.1%
52.1–56.0%
48.1–52.0%
44.1–48.0%
40.1–44.0%
36.1–40.0%
32.1–36.0%
28.1–32.0%
24.1–28.0%
20.1–24.0%
16.1–20.0%
12.1–16.0%
8.1–12.0%
4.1–8.0%
0.0–4.0%

Find schools offering this major at PrincetonReview.com.

CAREER OPTIONS

Air Force National Guard
Air Force (Officer)
Army National Guard
Army (Officer)
Bookkeeper
Coast Guard (Officer)
Computer Engineer/Systems Analyst

Computer Operator/Programmer
Internet/Intranet Technologies Manager
Marines (Officer)
Navy (Officer)
Network Engineer
Professor
Research Technician

Software Developer
Systems Administrator
Systems Analyst
Technical Support Specialist
Web Editor
Web Master
Website Designer

COMPUTER ENGINEERING

Basics

Assuming you haven't been living in a cave or under a rock for the last few decades, you are probably aware that an amazing computer revolution has rapidly changed the way much of the world works. Developments in radio, television, radar, transistors, computers, and robotics have fundamentally altered human life. The field of computer engineering is at the epicenter of this development. It encompasses a wide range of topics, including operating systems, computer architecture, computer networks, robotics, artificial intelligence, and computer-aided design.

If you major in computer engineering, you'll learn all about the hardware and software aspects of computer science. You'll gain a solid understanding of circuit theory and electronic circuits too. Also, because computer engineering is closely linked with electrical engineering, the fields are found in the same department at many universities. Consequently, many undergraduate programs incorporate most of the core curricula in both electrical engineering and computer science so graduates will be prepared to work in either field.

Computer engineering is a difficult major, but it's a major that's in demand. Software engineering companies, telecommunications firms, designers of digital hardware, and many other business enterprises hire computer engineering majors right out of college and pay them well. Computer engineering also makes great preparation for medical school, business school, and law school (particularly if you want to specialize in patent law).

SAMPLE COLLEGE CURRICULUM FOR COMPUTER ENGINEERING

Calculus

Circuit Analysis

Computer Programming

Data Structures and Algorithms

Differential Equations

Digital Logic

Electromagnetics

Fluid and Thermal Engineering

Microelectronic Circuits

Operating Systems

Physics

Programming Languages

Software Engineering

Statics and Dynamics

Technical Communication

If You Like Computer Engineering, You May Also Like . . .

Applied mathematics, applied physics, architectural engineering, chemical engineering, civil engineering, computer and information science, electrical engineering, engineering design, environmental and environmental health engineering, industrial engineering, mathematics, mechanical engineering, nuclear engineering, petroleum engineering, physics, statistics

Suggested High School Prep for Computer Engineering

Math and science courses will be the most important. A very solid background in math and physics is essential if you want to pursue computer engineering, as is extensive knowledge of computers and computer programming skills. Take trigonometry and calculus (or the highest-level math class that your high school offers). If at all possible, get a head start in the basics of the programming language C as it will really help you down the road.

Fun Facts

A (Very) Short History of the Mouse

Doug Engelbart invented and patented the computer mouse way back in the 1960s. He originally called his device the x–y position indicator. At Stanford University's MouseSite, you'll find a ton of photos of early mice, mouse prototypes, and the people who created them, including Engelbart.

(Source: http://sloan.stanford.edu/MouseSite)

First Things First

"The most important thing in the programming language is the name. A language will not succeed without a good name. I have recently invented a very good name and now I am looking for a suitable language."

—D. E. Knuth, 1967

Careers and Salary

Starting salaries for electrical and computer engineers with bachelor's degrees range from $50,000 to $52,000.

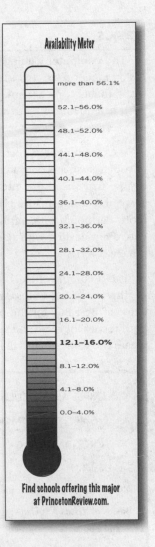

Availability Meter

more than 56.1%

52.1–56.0%

48.1–52.0%

44.1–48.0%

40.1–44.0%

36.1–40.0%

32.1–36.0%

28.1–32.0%

24.1–28.0%

20.1–24.0%

16.1–20.0%

12.1–16.0%

8.1–12.0%

4.1–8.0%

0.0–4.0%

Find schools offering this major at PrincetonReview.com.

CAREER OPTIONS

Aerospace Engineer

Air Force National Guard

Army National Guard

Army (Officer)

Avionics Technician

Computer Engineer/Systems Analyst

Computer Operator/Programmer

Information Manager

Internet/Intranet Technologies Manager

Inventor

Management Consultant

Marines (Officer)

Network Engineer

Professor

Quality Assurance Engineer

Research Technician

Robotics Engineer

Software Developer

Web Programmer

Web Master

Website Designer

COMPUTER GAMES AND PROGRAMMING SKILLS

Basics

The computer gaming industry draws more than $10 billion a year—and it shows no sign of slowing. It's no longer restricted to a bunch of teenage computer fanatics holed up in front of a monitor on a Friday night. In fact, a recent study by the NPD Group found that 87 percent of casual gamers are over the age of 25. It can no longer be denied: America loves computer games. If you want to be one of the people to develop these games, then consider a major in computer games and programming skills.

As you might expect, this is an extremely technical major that requires you to master the ins and outs of topics such as computer programming, software design, and informatics. But it's not all science. This is a degree that sits at the intersection of computer science and the creative arts, so when you're not slaving away in that informatics class, you're likely to be flexing your artistic muscles in a drawing studio, a photography darkroom, or a graphic design lab. You'll also need to be well versed in the craft of narrative. After all, you're not dealing with *Pac-Man* anymore; today's gaming programmers are at the cutting-edge of contemporary storytelling.

It is a complex field, but it's also a lot of fun. This is an ideal major for someone whose personality is a patchwork of Bill Gates, Andy Warhol, William Shakespeare, and that dude who's been hogging the Xbox demo at Best Buy for the past three hours now and shows no signs of fatigue. With a solid background in both technology and the arts, you'll have the skills you need to do more than simply play the games. You'll create the games that will keep millions of players on the edge of their computer chairs.

SAMPLE CURRICULUM FOR COMPUTER GAMES AND PROGRAMMING SKILLS

3-D Design

Algorithms and Programming

Basics of Visual Art: Drawing, Painting, and Photography

Calculus

Craft of Animation

Game Design

Graphic Design

Informatics

Introduction to Computer Science

Introduction to Software Design

Survey of Artificial Intelligence

Systems Design

Techniques in New Media

Technology and Ethics

If You Like Computer Games and Programming Skills, You May Also Like...

Animation and special effects, advertising, art, cinematography and film/video production, computer graphics, computer and information science, computer systems analysis, creative writing, digital communications and media/multimedia, engineering design, graphic communication, graphic design, visual communication, web design

Suggested High School Prep for Computer Games and Programming Skills

If your high school offers courses in computers and technologies, sign up fast! Otherwise, immerse yourself in those math and science classes—especially the math. You'll be surprised how well those trig and calc classes prepare you to tackle the complex problems ahead. On the other side of things, take all the art classes you can. Imagination goes a long way in this field.

Fun Facts

Drum roll, please....

Since 1998 the Games Critics Awards, an independent collective of journalists from across America, have dished out awards to the top dogs in gaming. In 2006, the "Best PC Game" category saw five nominees:

- *Crysis*
- *Enemy Territory: Quake Wars*
- *Hellgate: London*
- *Supreme Commander*
- *Spore*

Spore walked away with the grand prize.

The Skinny on Spore

So what exactly makes *Spore* so special? According to Jeff Green, editor of *Computer Gaming World* and a GCA judge, "No PC game at the show came close to matching *Spore*'s originality, scope, and breadth of design." You hear that, computer-game-developers-to-be? It's the mixture of strong technical design and unbridled imagination that rises to the top.

Careers and Salary

According to the International Game Developers Association, a game programmer with 1 to 2 years experience can expect to bring in at least $55,000.

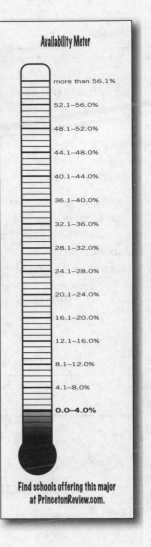

Availability Meter

more than 56.1%

52.1–56.0%

48.1–52.0%

44.1–48.0%

40.1–44.0%

36.1–40.0%

32.1–36.0%

28.1–32.0%

24.1–28.0%

20.1–24.0%

16.1–20.0%

12.1–16.0%

8.1–12.0%

4.1–8.0%

0.0–4.0%

Find schools offering this major at PrincetonReview.com.

CAREER OPTIONS

Animator	Content Creator	Software Developer
Artist	Digital Artist	Special Effects Programmer
Artificial Intelligence Programmer	Entrepreneur	Video Game Programmer
Audio Programmer/Engineer	Film Editor	Webmaster
Computer Game Programmer	Graphic Designer	Website Designer

COMPUTER GRAPHICS

Basics

Highly technical yet completely artistic, computer graphics blends elements of a computer science major and elements of an art major into one exciting four-year ride. Students will be expected to draw on aspects from both fields and use them to succeed. You'll learn the basics—and the not-so-basics—of computer programming and a variety of computer applications, and you'll practice computer-based graphic design and the programming of graphic systems. With the rapid advancements being made in this field, you'll never run out of new things to discover and use in your work. And it's not all about knowing the nuts and bolts of how to do it either; throughout this major, you'll be developing your own digital aesthetic so your graphic creations are truly yours.

Creative types will enjoy projects that incorporate computer-based imaging, two-dimensional and three-dimensional design, and photography. Different college programs offer different concentrations, such as animation, interactive multimedia, or construction graphics, which can lead computer graphics majors in any number of directions. You may use your skills to pursue engineering or architecture, develop Web technologies, produce spectacular CD-ROMs, or become specialists in computer-aided design (CAD). Whatever your job, you'll use your background in both computers and art to create computer graphics that entertain, persuade, assist, and inform your intended audience.

If You Like Computer Graphics, You May Also Like . . .

Advertising, art, art education, computer and information science, computer systems analysis, digital communications and media/multimedia, drawing, engineering design, entrepreneurship, film, graphic art, photography, printmaking, radio and television, visual communication

> **SAMPLE COLLEGE CURRICULUM FOR COMPUTER GRAPHICS**
>
> Color Photography
> Computer Graphics
> Computer Programming
> Digital Photography
> Fundamentals of Drawing
> Mathematics
> Multimedia Authoring
> Three-Dimensional Design
> Two-Dimensional Design
> Web Development
> Web Page Design
> Windows-Based Application Development

Suggested High School Prep for Computer Graphics

Since many computer graphics programs are tied to math, computer, and art departments, getting a strong foundation in upper-level math courses (like calculus) and computer courses is essential. Art courses would strengthen your abilities in original thought, visual harmony, and effective design. Since much of computer graphics is about communication, you should also polish your reading and writing skills in English and language courses. The best preparation of all may actually be the work you do on your own—experimenting with your own computer, drawing, and creating up a storm.

Fun Facts

Additional Reading

Want to get a look inside the world of computer graphics? Check out http://cgw.pennnet.com/home.cfm to read the online magazine *Computer Graphics World: The Magazine for Digital Content Professionals.*

And the Winners Are . .

Computer Graphics World offers Innovation Awards each year to products that have demonstrated true creativity and usefulness. Here are a few of the 2002 winners.

- Maya Unlimited 4.5: Its computational fluid dynamics technology allows designers to better simulate things like viscous liquids and pyrotechnics.
- FaceStation 1.5: Digital artists can manipulate the expressions of their computerized faces by using their own expressions.
- Softimage XSI 3.0: Allows digital artists to work with large data sets, such as crowd scenes, manipulating behaviors and controlling thousands of characters.

Careers and Salary

Starting salaries for computer graphics majors are generally about $30,000 to start. The sort of company you work for will make a huge difference. Also, some computer graphics majors choose to work on a freelance basis, making salaries unpredictable.

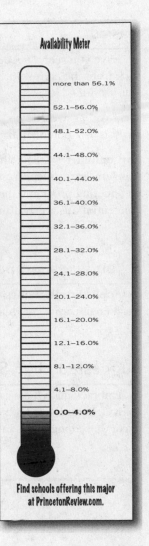

Availability Meter

more than 56.1%

52.1–56.0%

48.1–52.0%

44.1–48.0%

40.1–44.0%

36.1–40.0%

32.1–36.0%

28.1–32.0%

24.1–28.0%

20.1–24.0%

16.1–20.0%

12.1–16.0%

8.1–12.0%

4.1–8.0%

0.0–4.0%

Find schools offering this major at PrincetonReview.com.

CAREER OPTIONS

Animator	Entrepreneur	Product Designer
Art Director	Film Editor	Set Designer
Artist	Graphic Designer	Software Developer
Computer Programmer	Internet/Intranet Technologies Manager	Teacher
Content Creator		Web Master
Digital Artist	Map Maker	Website Designer
	Media Specialist	

COMPUTER SYSTEMS ANALYSIS

Basics

Have you seen *The Matrix* more than ten times? Do you think *Tron* was more than just a fluffy Disney flick from the early 1980s? Is your computer your portal to the outside world? Do you believe in the outside world?

If you answered "yes" to any of the first three questions or "no" to the last, consider computer systems analysis as a potential major.

Computer systems analysis majors examine how computer systems work together. They determine problem areas, identify security risks, and improve overall performance. This major is often part of an engineering program. Check with your prospective school to see what kinds of computer systems analysis concentrations are available.

If You Like Computer Systems Analysis, You May Also Like . . .

Applied mathematics, applied physics, computer and information science, computer engineering, electrical engineering, mathematics, physics

Suggested High School Prep for Computer Systems Analysis

Embrace math. Take as much as you can. A background in physics couldn't hurt, as you'll be required to study it. Experience with computers and programming languages is also essential. So now's your chance to make those long hours in front of the screen pay off!

SAMPLE COLLEGE CURRICULUM FOR COMPUTER SYSTEMS ANALYSIS

Calculus I–II

Computing Network Principles

Data Structures

Introduction to Digital Systems

Mathematical Modeling

Physics I–II

Programming Languages

Software Engineering

Statistics

Switching Theory

Fun Facts

Computers at the Movies

Go on, feed the need. The Internet Movie Database has tons of information on the making of *The Matrix* movies, including a full page of trivia, a list of goofs, and all of the shooting locations. Oh, go on. You know you want to look. Just go to imdb.com, and enter the film title in the search box.

To Fit In

You have to speak the language. The geek.com technical glossary (www.geek.com) will have you sounding like a pro in minutes!

Careers and Salary

The starting salary for a computer systems analysis major fresh out of college is about $40,000.

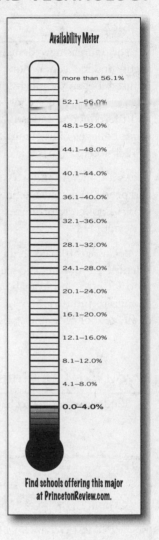

Availability Meter

more than 56.1%

52.1–56.0%

48.1–52.0%

44.1–48.0%

40.1–44.0%

36.1–40.0%

32.1–36.0%

28.1–32.0%

24.1–28.0%

20.1–24.0%

16.1–20.0%

12.1–16.0%

8.1–12.0%

4.1–8.0%

0.0–4.0%

Find schools offering this major at PrincetonReview.com.

CAREER OPTIONS

Computer Engineer/Systems Analyst	Navy (Officer)	Systems Analyst
Consultant	Network Engineer	Technical Support Specialist
Information Manager	Systems Administrator	Web Programmer

CONCRETE INDUSTRY MANAGEMENT

Basics

The increasingly demanding schedules and advancement in building and construction require more highly trained supervisors to coordinate tight schedules and large crews. To fill that need, the concrete industry began the push for a college curriculum that could produce individuals who have strong knowledge and skills that are job specific. As a result of a joint venture between Middle Tennessee State University and the concrete industry, a uniform curriculum was established and served as a model for programs at other colleges like Arizona State University, California State University, Chico, and the New Jersey Institute of Technology.

As a Concrete Industry Manager, graduates can expect to fill such roles as sales representatives, project and production management, and technical services such as equipment manufacturing. In the field they may work as concrete producers, developing various cement and admix mixtures, or in general contracting roles as developers.

Because this major is an up-and-coming program it may not be available at every college, but the applied sciences supporting the major like construction materials and management will be easier to find. Students who wish to find availability for the program can contact the colleges of their choice or visit the CIM's (Concrete Industry Management) initiative website at concretedegree.com. The site includes information about school programs, job possibilities and scholarship opportunities.

If you like Concrete Industry Management, you may also like...

Building science, mechanical engineering, architecture, drafting and design

SAMPLE COLLEGE CURRICULUM FOR CONCRETE INDUSTRY MANAGEMENT

Blueprint Reading

Concrete Application

Concrete Construction Methods

Concrete Problems Diagnosis Prevention and Problem Solving

English Composition

Fundamentals of Concrete Testing and Properties

Science

Statistics

Understanding Concrete Construction

Suggested High School prep for Concrete Industry Management

A strong knowledge of math and physics is essential, as well as good reading, writing, and computer skills. Foreign languages are always helpful, and any courses in business—if offered—will definitely prove to be beneficial. It will be important for you to develop people and communication skills in order to be an effective manager.

Fun Facts

Concrete as we know it consists of varying levels of four agents: cement for bonding; sand or gravel for rigidity, water for malleability, and admixtures. One of the earliest uses of a similar mixture dates to the remains of a crude hut in Serbia that has a floor made of red lime, sand and gravel. The approximate dating on the hut is 5600 B.C.E.

Careers and Salary

Starting salaries for a management position in the concrete industry will be on the lower end of the $40,000 to $70,000 range that a supervisor can expect. Increases will depend upon the size of the crew and company.

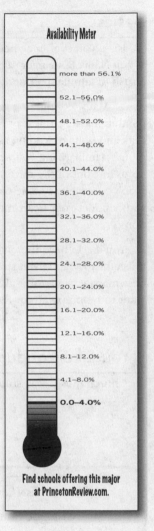

Availability Meter

more than 56.1%

52.1–56.0%

48.1–52.0%

44.1–48.0%

40.1–44.0%

36.1–40.0%

32.1–36.0%

28.1–32.0%

24.1–28.0%

20.1–24.0%

16.1–20.0%

12.1–16.0%

8.1–12.0%

4.1–8.0%

0.0–4.0%

Find schools offering this major at PrincetonReview.com.

CAREER OPTIONS		
Concrete Specialist	Contractor	Inspector
Construction Manager		

CONDUCTING

Basics

Have you ever imagined yourself as Leonard Bernstein standing at the podium conducting an orchestra? When Nadia Boulanger says, "Do not take up music unless you would rather die than not do so," do you feel a rush of adrenaline flood through your body? If so, a major in conducting might be your cup of tea.

Many conducting programs will allow you to select a focus, such as choral, orchestral, or band conducting. Regardless of which focus you opt for, the conducting major will move you carefully through the nuts and bolts of leading an ensemble. You'll devote time to reading musical scores, learning rehearsal techniques, familiarizing yourself with instruments and technologies, and, in your private moments, taking deep bows in front of the mirror while imaginary crowds call, "Bravo, Maestro! Bravo!" Before long, those crowds won't be imaginary. The conducting major promises a range of opportunities to step in front of an orchestra and conduct your heart out. As you might expect, performance will be a strong component of your education.

You'll also have the chance to play the liberal arts field. Conducting draws heavily on music education, music history, and even stretches into the realms of general education, psychology, and, in some cases, business management. After all, you're going to be asked to teach and then lead a large group of musicians. You want to be prepared for that responsibility—right, Maestro?

If You Like Conducting, You May Also Like...

Church music, jazz studies, music, music education, music history, musical theater

Suggested High School Prep for Conducting

First and foremost, join your high school orchestra. For that matter, join any other music-related activity your school sponsors. Conducting requires a thorough knowledge of how music "works," so the more exposure you have, the better. Along these lines, take whatever music classes your guidance counselor will let you enroll in. You might try some drama classes too, as these will get you close to that beloved stage and may even land you a role in a musical. Finally, if you haven't done so already, choose an instrument (or two, or three), sign up for private lessons, and get practicing.

SAMPLE COLLEGE CURRICULUM

Band Conducting

Beginning Conducting

Choral Conducting

Ensemble Performance

Instrumental Conducting

Introduction to Composition

Music Education

Orchestration

Stravinsky

Survey of Music History

Twentieth Century Music

Fun Facts

Felix the Pioneer

Felix Mendelssohn, the nineteenth century German composer and pianist, was one of the pioneers of conducting. He believed the role of the conductor was to interpret the work and then guide the performance according to his interpretation. This was a very new idea in 1833, when Mendelssohn went to the Leipzig Gewandhaus to lead a series of concerts. There was grumbling among the musicians. Here's how an eyewitness described Mendelssohn as a conductor:

"Mendelssohn's fiery glance surveyed and dominated the entire orchestra. Reciprocally, all eyes were on the tip of his conductor's baton. Thus he was able, with sovereign freedom, to lead the masses at all times according to his will."

Lenny the Conductor

"I'm not interested in having an orchestra sound like itself. I want it to sound like the composer."

—Leonard Bernstein

Careers and Salary

Salaries for conductors vary widely. (Just imagine the different salaries earned by big-city symphony conductors and small-town choir directors.) Conductors can expect to start between $25,000 and $30,000 a year, and that's usually with some teaching or instrument performance on the side. Be advised that it's not typically possible to conduct as a full-time profession early in a career.

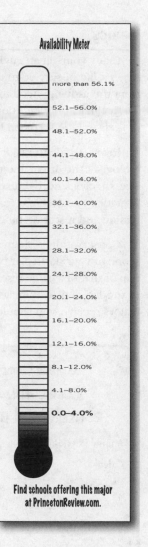

Availability Meter

more than 56.1%

52.1–56.0%

48.1–52.0%

44.1–48.0%

40.1–44.0%

36.1–40.0%

32.1–36.0%

28.1–32.0%

24.1–28.0%

20.1–24.0%

16.1–20.0%

12.1–16.0%

8.1–12.0%

4.1–8.0%

0.0–4.0%

Find schools offering this major at PrincetonReview.com.

CAREER OPTIONS

Band Conductor	Journalist	Music Executive
Choral Conductor	Music Critic	Musician
Instrumental Conductor	Music Director	Teacher

CONSERVATION BIOLOGY

Basics

Fancy yourself an environmentalist? There are many options out there to help the conscientious student begin a life of service to the world at large. Conservation biology is a relatively new field that has emerged from the growing need to combat the loss of biological diversity in the ecosystem. Conservation biologists are distinct from practitioners of similar fields like wildlife management and environmental biology because of their unique focus on biodiversity.

If you decide to major in conservation biology, you'll quickly identify the chief concerns of conservation biologists: the origin and maintenance of biodiversity; the effects of habitat loss, habitat fragmentation, invasive species, and overexploitation; the design and implementation of nature reserves; the restoration of degraded ecosystems (restoration ecology); and the use of zoos, botanical gardens, and aquariums in maintaining and restoring biodiversity.

Conservation biology majors should expect to spend much of their time on the field. Depending on the scope of your particular program, you may find yourself either studying the biodiversity of your local ecosystem or that of a game reserve in Kenya. Fieldwork is key, but it's also important to make the most of your time in the lab and in the classroom. In addition to the hard science instruction that all conservation biology majors receive, you should also expect to find a curriculum heavy on the social sciences and public policy.

SAMPLE COLLEGE CURRICULUM FOR CONSERVATION BIOLOGY

Animal Physiology

Calculus

Chemistry

Conservation Biology I–III

Fundamentals of Ecology

General Biology I–II

Genetics

Global Environment

Introduction to Probability and Statistics

Organic Chemistry

Problem Solving in Conservation Biology

Techniques in Wildlife Conservation Biology

The United States and Transnational Issues

If You Like Conservation Biology, You May Also Like . . .

Agricultural and biological engineering, agronomy and crop science, biology, botany and plant biology, ecology, environmental and environmental health engineering, forestry, geology, horticulture, international agriculture, plant pathology, soil science, sustainable resource management, wildlife management

Suggested High School Prep for Conservation Biology

It's a good idea to begin with a firm foundation in the sciences. Take as many chemistry, biology, and physics classes as you can. You should also have a strong background in mathematics, so take trigonometry and calculus in high school. Get involved! Your community may be home to all kinds of green organizations that could use your help.

Fun Facts

The Global 200

The World Wildlife Fund (WWF) has identified what it considers to be the 200 areas most critical in the fight for global conservation. The regions include some of the most richly beautiful ecosystems on the planet; some of the most remarkable places on Earth are also the most threatened. The flora and fauna there are among the world's most endangered terrestrial, marine, and freshwater species. To learn more, visit www.wwf.org.

Biodiversity Benefits

Water purification: Plants, animals and microorganisms in wetlands act as sponges to filter sediments and toxins from inflowing waters.

Pollination: Insects pollinate crops worth $6 to 12 billion a year in the United States.

Disease control: Natural enemies (predators and parasites) of disease-carrying organisms (for example, ticks and mosquitoes) control diseases such as malaria, Lyme disease, hantavirus, and cholera.

Careers and Salary

Just out of college, conservation biology majors can expect a salary of about $28,000. Some positions require a master's degree, and these positions tend to pay more.

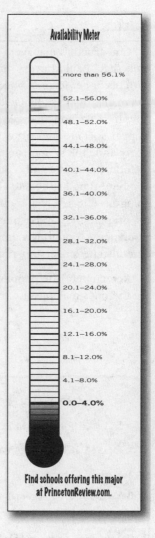

Availability Meter

more than 56.1%

52.1–56.0%

48.1–52.0%

44.1–48.0%

40.1–44.0%

36.1–40.0%

32.1–36.0%

28.1–32.0%

24.1–28.0%

20.1–24.0%

16.1–20.0%

12.1–16.0%

8.1–12.0%

4.1–8.0%

0.0–4.0%

Find schools offering this major at PrincetonReview.com.

CAREER OPTIONS

Biochemist

Biologist

Conservation Biologist

Restoration Ecologist

Park Ranger

Environmentalist/ Environmental Scientist

Public Policy Maker at the local, state, and federal levels

CONSTRUCTION MANAGEMENT

Basics

Construction managers are able to walk the streets of their cities and say with a smile to themselves, "I built that." Behind every amazing building is one fine construction manager running a smooth operation with his or her team of builders. Construction management combines two separate areas of study: trade skills and management skills. On the trade side, you'll study the processes and materials involved in building—from how to make and analyze construction plans and drawings to how to interpret construction site data and inspect specific sites. Your major will verse you on construction tools and machinery as well as codes for safety and ethics. Then, on the management side, you'll learn how to actually run a construction operation, including resource and cost control and every aspect of site safety. As a construction manager, your days will combine time at the site—controlling the execution of building plans and ensuring that the building is going up effectively and efficiently—with time behind a desk, where you'll oversee contracts and proposals, prepare bids and estimates, and make sure you're squared away with accident prevention and quality assurance. Accounting, communication, and directing will be all under your command. You'll be required to demonstrate leadership, problem solving, and great responsibility.

Remember: The people actually doing the building are important, but the managers behind the scenes are the ones making sure the job is done right.

SAMPLE COLLEGE CURRICULUM FOR CONSTRUCTION MANAGEMENT

Analysis of Commercial Prints

Basic Construction Estimating

Business Law

Construction Codes and Documents

Construction Law

Construction Project Financing

Construction Safety Management

Construction Surveying

Construction Working Drawings

Principles of Management

Production Control

Quality Assurance and Inspection

Residential Development

Temporary Structures

If You Like Construction Management, You May Also Like . . .

Business administration and management, human resources management, industrial management, logistics management, operations management, risk management

Suggested High School Prep for Construction Management

A strong knowledge of math is key to construction management, as are good reading, writing, and computer skills. Foreign languages are always a plus. Consider courses in business if they're offered, but most important is developing the communication skills you'll need to be an effective manager.

Fun Facts

Built-In Fun

Here's some construction management humor from www.chanen.com.

Six Phases of a Project

1. Enthusiasm
2. Disillusionment
3. Panic
4. Search for the Guilty
5. Punishment of the Innocent
6. Praise & Honors for the Nonparticipants

(Surely your newfound construction management skills will help you avoid all but the first of these phases!)

Construction Terminology Humor

- Project Manager—the conductor of an orchestra in which every musician is in a different union
- Contractor—a gambler who never gets to shuffle, cut, or deal
- Delayed Payment—a tourniquet applied at the pockets
- Critical Path Method—a management technique for losing your shirt under perfect control

(Source: www.netfunny.com)

Careers and Salary

The starting salary in most management fields is in the $20,000 to $40,000 range, but this number can go higher or lower depending on how you use your skills, where you live, and the type of company you're managing.

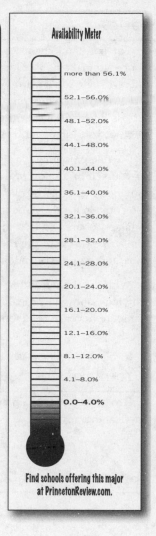

Availability Meter

more than 56.1%

52.1–56.0%

48.1–52.0%

44.1–48.0%

40.1–44.0%

36.1–40.0%

32.1–36.0%

28.1–32.0%

24.1–28.0%

20.1–24.0%

16.1–20.0%

12.1–16.0%

8.1–12.0%

4.1–8.0%

0.0–4.0%

Find schools offering this major at PrincetonReview.com.

CAREER OPTIONS

Construction Manager	Contractor	Manager
Building Inspector		

COSMETOLOGY

Basics

The cosmetology major is an extremely vocation-minded course of study suited to students who harbor an urge to make people look and feel pretty darn good. You'll learn how to cut, comb, bleach, dye, tint, trim, and style hair. You'll learn how to clean, polish, soften, lubricate, and manicure nails. You'll get the skinny on cuticles, on split ends, on wigs, and, yes, on a whole bunch of cosmetics. If a product is out there, you can bet you'll hear about it—the good and the bad—as well as how exactly it's used. As you can probably guess, much of your time will be spent in the studio developing your skills.

While grooming is a significant aspect of the cosmetology trade, it's not the only one. Whether working for yourself or a salon, you'll need to have the people skills to chat with your customers and, hopefully, to convince them that the almond oil cuticle balm on the shelf would be a great purchase. Business skills will also come in handy, as the minds of salon owners and managers are never far from the budget books. Expect to take a course or two in interpersonal communication and business management. The major will also familiarize you with the theoretical premises of cosmetology, applicable professional/governmental regulations, and state certification requirements.

With the degree and necessary certifications in hand, you'll be prepared to step into a job market that's growing—and will probably continue to grow for years to come. This isn't surprising. After all, a paraffin manicure never hurt anybody.

If You Like Cosmetology, You May Also Like...

Aromatherapy, chiropractic, community health and preventative medicine, massage therapy, nursing, physical therapy

Suggested High School Prep for Cosmetology

SAMPLE COLLEGE CURRICULUM

Advanced Cosmetology

Basics of Business Management

Cosmetology Brush-Up

Esthetics

Fundamental Techniques of Cosmetology

Nail Technology

Principles of Cosmetology

Speech Communications

If your school district has a vocational-technical school, check to see if it offers any courses in cosmetology or related fields. You should also sign up for courses in anatomy, biology, health, and business management. Some of your best prep, though, may come in the after-school hours, when you convince your best friends to let you cut their hair, wax their eyebrows, treat their cuticles, and talk their ears off. Of course, you'll first need to read up on the techniques—otherwise, you may put those friendships at risk!

Fun Facts

The Numbers

According to the Bureau of Labor Statistics, in 2004 around 790,000 Americans worked as cosmetologists, barbers, or some other type of personal-appearance professionals. Of these:

- 670,000 were cosmetologists or barbers/hair stylists
- 60,000 were manicurists or pedicurists
- 30,000 were skincare specialists
- 27,000 were shampooers

Approximately 48 percent (or 379,200) of these workers were self-employed.

The Clients

Supermodel Cheryl Tiegs has said, "Like anyone else, there are days I feel beautiful and days I don't, and when I don't, I do something about it." Want to know what she does? Well, you should ask a cosmetologist.

Styling License

In the United States, all states require barbers, cosmetologists, and most other personal appearance workers, with the exception of shampooers, to be licensed. Applicants for a license usually are required to pass a written test and demonstrate an ability to perform basic barbering or cosmetology services.

(Source: http://en.wikipedia.org/wiki/Cosmetology)

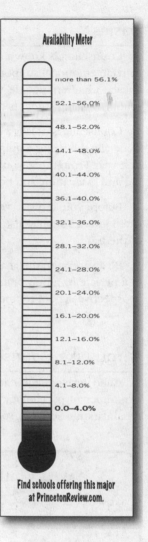

Availability Meter

more than 56.1%

52.1–56.0%

48.1–52.0%

44.1–48.0%

40.1–44.0%

36.1–40.0%

32.1–36.0%

28.1–32.0%

24.1–28.0%

20.1–24.0%

16.1–20.0%

12.1–16.0%

8.1–12.0%

4.1–8.0%

0.0–4.0%

Find schools offering this major at PrincetonReview.com.

Careers and Salary

Rookies in the field can expect to pull in between $13,000 and $25,000 annually.

CAREER OPTIONS

Beauty Salon Owner/Operator	Manicurist	Skincare Specialist
Cosmetologist	Pedicurist	Stylist
Hair Stylist	Shampooers	Wig Maker

COUNSELING

Basics

Counseling is known as one of the helping professions. Counselors assist in behavior modification and provide emotional support and guidance to people in all walks of life. As a counselor, you might work with abused children, people with drug and alcohol dependencies, or the homeless. Or you might work in a school advising students on college decisions and teaching stress-reduction techniques.

Counseling is usually a concentration within a psychology major or is overseen by a psychology department. Generally, this major requires a foundation in biology and statistics. You'll begin with general psychology in your first year. From there, you'll move on to the classes in abnormal psychology, personality, psychological testing and evaluation, and behavior modification.

Before you know it, you'll be rushing to the aid of everyone in your hall who gets dumped or has pre-exam jitters. You may also get roped into volunteering as a test subject for the graduate students. It's all part of the fun.

Be aware: with this major, you will probably need an advanced degree to operate as a licensed counselor in a private or group practice. In some states, you must have a PhD to obtain this license. Check with your prospective school to find out more about state requirements and graduate study opportunities.

If You Like Counseling, You May Also Like . . .

Child development, clinical psychology, communication disorders, criminology, developmental psychology, experimental psychology, industrial psychology, mental health services, occupational therapy, psychology, rehabilatation services, social psychology, social work

SAMPLE COLLEGE CURRICULUM FOR COUNSELING

Abnormal Psychology

Adolescence Psychology

Behavior Modification

Biology I–II

Cognitive Psychology

General Psychology

Group Psychology

Physiological Psychology

Psychological Testing

Psychology of Personality

Statistics

Theory of Counseling

Suggested High School Prep for Counseling

A good background in arts and sciences will serve you well. If your school offers it, take psychology and strive to excel in it. Pick up classes in statistics if you can. Other than that, you can gain experience volunteering your time to hospitals, crisis lines, shelters, and other organizations that offer counseling services.

Fun Facts

Online Resources

Check out Psych Web (www.psywww.com) for links to psychology resources on the net. Also, the site Psychlinks (www.psychlinks.cjb.net) has information on psychology, famous psychologists, college papers (don't copy; just read 'em), online research, and graduate programs.

Careers and Salary

The starting salary for a counseling major fresh out of college ranges from $25,000 to $30,000.

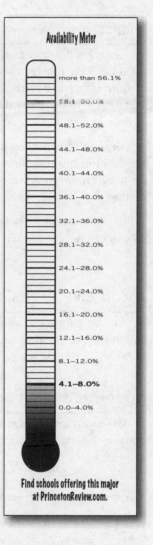

Availability Meter

more than 56.1%

52.1–56.0%

48.1–52.0%

44.1–48.0%

40.1–44.0%

36.1–40.0%

32.1–36.0%

28.1–32.0%

24.1–28.0%

20.1–24.0%

16.1–20.0%

12.1–16.0%

8.1–12.0%

4.1–8.0%

0.0–4.0%

Find schools offering this major at PrincetonReview.com.

CAREER OPTIONS

Career Counselor	Mediator	Substance Abuse Counselor
Guidance Counselor	Social Worker	

CRAFTS

Basics

Crafts is a fine arts major with one eye on utility; you'll study the aesthetics and techniques of handcrafting, including ceramics, glassware, baskets, jewelry, metalwork, furniture, textiles, and wax molding. By second or third year, you'll start to specialize in a specific handicraft. Much time will be spent in the studio, experimenting with materials, developing your artistic vision, perfecting your technique, working closely with an advisor, and having frequent peer critiques.

As a crafts major, you'll also study the history and methods of handicrafts, gaining an understanding of the relationship of your work to the long line of folk art traditions. You may take art history courses in anything from Native American basket-weaving, to ancient Greek pottery design, to traditional East Asian textiles.

Because it can be tricky to make a career out of crafts, many programs offer retail and business classes, so you can be savvy when it comes time to market your work in a professional environment.

If You Like Crafts, You May Also Like . . .

Art, art education, art history, ceramics, drawing, furniture design, interior design, jewelry and metal-smithing, textile and weaving arts, painting, sculpture

Suggested High School Prep for Crafts

Obviously, you'll want to take whatever studio art and art history classes your high school offers. Also consider taking a ceramics, weaving, or jewelry-making course with a local artist.

SAMPLE COLLEGE CURRICULUM FOR CRAFTS

Candles and Waxworks

Crafts Technical Drawing

Drawing

Glass and Glass Structure

Independent Study in Clay

Intro to Jewelry Making

Materials and Processes Metals

Methods in Fibers

Planning a Career in the Crafts

Woodworking Techniques

Fun Facts

Basketry

Basketry is one of the most ancient crafts, preceding and influencing cloth weaving, pottery, and carpentry. Ancient people made baskets out of anything available—grasses, reeds, stalks, twigs, and leaves were all common materials. The Hopi Indians still weave a style of plaited ring basket that is part of an uninterrupted basket-making tradition 15 centuries old!

(Source: www.nau.edu/~hcpo-p/arts/bas2.htm)

A Cool Website

Part of the Smithsonian, the White House Collection of American Crafts, has an extensive website with examples of ceramics, fiber, glass, metal, and wood handicrafts, as well as artists' bios and interviews. Check it out at http://americanart.si.edu/collections/exhibits/whc.

Careers and Salary

It's difficult to predict the salary of a crafts major, but an independent artist just starting out may make $20,000 a year or less.

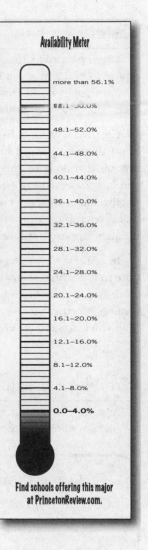

Availability Meter

more than 56.1%

52.1—56.0%

48.1—52.0%

44.1—48.0%

40.1—44.0%

36.1—40.0%

32.1—36.0%

28.1—32.0%

24.1—28.0%

20.1—24.0%

16.1—20.0%

12.1—16.0%

8.1—12.0%

4.1—8.0%

0.0—4.0%

Find schools offering this major
at PrincetonReview.com.

CAREER OPTIONS

Artist	Entrepreneur	Potter
Cabinetmaker	Glass Blower	Retail Manager
Curator	Jewelry Designer	

CREATIVE WRITING

Basics

Often pictured sitting in dark little cafés, scrawling furiously on a piece of paper, or sitting alone at a typewriter punching out the next great American novel, the creative writer always seems to stand alone in his or her own world. How do you get to be the next Ernest Hemingway, William Faulkner, or Toni Morrison? Well, you write a lot, and, if you can, you major in creative writing.

Creative writing is frequently listed as a concentration within a broader English major program since opportunities to major specifically in creative writing do not exist at every university or college. For those schools that do have creative writing programs, expect a course of study that will involve a lot of reading, and of course, writing. Creative writing majors blend the love and study of books that come with being an English major with the creative freedom and expression of being an artist. It is the best of both worlds, one that gives you the opportunity to read the greatest works of literature and in the process develop your own unique response to those works.

In addition to reading everything from William Shakespeare to Virginia Woolf, creative writing allows you time to focus on your own development as a writer. At the heart of the creative writing major is the writing workshop, the small and intimate courses in which students and faculty read and criticize one another's writing. Whether you are writing short stories, poetry, or novels, the creative writing major is designed to help you learn and develop your skills as a writer in your chosen genre.

If You Like Creative Writing, You May Also Like . . .

American literature, comparative literature, English, English composition, English literature, film, journalism, technical writing, theater

SAMPLE COLLEGE CURRICULUM FOR CREATIVE WRITING

American Literature Since 1865

British Literature: 1800 to Present

Contemporary World Literature

Craft of Fiction

Craft of Nonfiction

Craft of Poetry

Creative Writing

Early American Literature

Literary Criticism

Romantic and Victorian Literature

Writing Workshop I–IV

Suggested High School Prep for Creative Writing

Creative writing majors, in addition to loving to write, should also love to read. If you are interested in majoring in creative writing, begin by reading everything you can get your hands on. Advanced English courses will help to enhance your ability to read and write critically. In addition, a solid background in the humanities and liberal arts will expand your vision and understanding of the world, as well as prepare you for the rigors of college academics.

Fun Facts

T. S. Eliot

Before going on to write *The Waste Land* and win the Nobel Prize for literature, Eliot worked in a bank.

Jack Kerouac

Kerouac wrote his most famous work, *On the Road*, in a stretch of three weeks, all on the same scroll of paper.

Careers and Salary

In the absence of a six-figure advance for their first novels, starting salaries for creative writing majors depend on the career paths they choose. Creative writing majors can expect their starting salaries to be similar to those of English majors entering the same fields, with an average starting salary of $30,000.

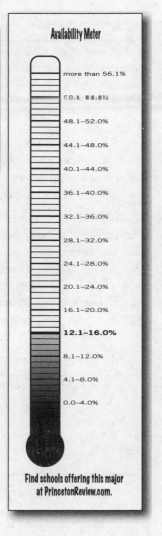

Availability Meter

more than 56.1%

52.1–56.0%

48.1–52.0%

44.1–48.0%

40.1–44.0%

36.1–40.0%

32.1–36.0%

28.1–32.0%

24.1–28.0%

20.1–24.0%

16.1–20.0%

12.1–16.0%

8.1–12.0%

4.1–8.0%

0.0–4.0%

Find schools offering this major at PrincetonReview.com.

CAREER OPTIONS

Actor	Comedian	Teacher
Advertising Executive	Editor	Web Editor
Artist	Journalist	Writer
Book Publishing Professional	Professor	

CRIMINAL JUSTICE

Basics

The field of criminal justice is tremendously broad; you could spend the better part of your career studying and working in corrections, criminal science, law enforcement administration, juvenile corrections, or even securities services administration, and only scratch the surface of all that this diverse major covers. To succeed in any of these specialties, however, you'll need to take an interdisciplinary approach toward the study of crime, social control, and the legal system.

Criminal justice is a major geared primarily toward professional training. Some graduates ultimately take jobs as corrections officers in public or private incarceration facilities. Others focus on the criminal justice system and work together with police and attorneys to ensure that the law is applied justly. Criminal scientists reconstruct crime scenes and analyze physical evidence; if you're a CSI junky, this could be your dream job.

Whatever you eventually end up doing, you'll begin your career by studying the theories and principles of correctional science. Depending on your academic focus, that could mean getting instruction in anything from law enforcement management to loss prevention services and from laboratory science to witness interviewing. Criminal justice courses cross paths with anthropology, sociology, political science, biology, and even business management. All told, you'll need a sharply analytical—not to mention inquisitive—mind and a strong sense of justice to shine in criminal justice.

If You Like Criminal Justice, You May Also Like . . .

Clinical psychology, criminology, forensic science, public policy analysis, sociology

Suggested High School Prep for Criminal Justice

Pay attention in your social studies and English classes; criminal justice, at its heart, concerns itself with every aspect of the human condition. Don't shirk your math and science courses either, as you never know what form evidence will take.

SAMPLE COLLEGE CURRICULUM FOR CRIMINAL JUSTICE

Asset Protection

Criminal Justice Policy

Crime and Punishment

Introduction to Criminalistics

Juvenile Delinquency

Multicultural Justice

Police in Society

Psychology of Criminal Behavior

Sociology of Law

Fun Facts

Did You Know?

"Today there are more than 2 million people incarcerated [in the United States] on any given day. About 600,000 adults enter prison each year, and there are upwards of 9 million jail admissions annually (some individuals account for multiple entries). When probation and parole caseloads are included, about 4 percent of the adult population is under some form of state penal control today. At no time in history has there been such a long-term, sustained reliance upon growing the mechanisms of formal social control in any society: democratic, capitalist, or otherwise."

(Source: Todd Clear, *Harvard University Talk*, September 2, 2003.)

Careers and Salary

Depending on the area of study, expect to earn starting salaries between $28,000 and $34,000.

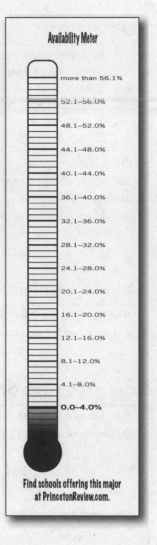

Availability Meter

more than 56.1%

52.1–56.0%

48.1–52.0%

44.1–48.0%

40.1–44.0%

36.1–40.0%

32.1–36.0%

28.1–32.0%

24.1–28.0%

20.1–24.0%

16.1–20.0%

12.1–16.0%

8.1–12.0%

4.1–8.0%

0.0–4.0%

Find schools offering this major at PrincetonReview.com.

CAREER OPTIONS

Border Patrol Agent	FBI Agent	Police Officer/Manager
Correctional Counselor	Inmate Records	Prisoner Classification
Corrections Officer	Interviewer	Probation Officer
Criminologist	Paralegal	Social Worker
Customs Agent	Parole Officer	Warden
Facility Manager	Penologist	

CRIMINAL SCIENCE

Basics

"There is nothing so important as trifles," once said Sherlock Holmes; most criminal science majors would certainly agree. This is a field whose main focus is the reconstruction of crimes through the characterization of trace evidence. As a criminal science major, you'll take chemistry and clinical laboratory classes where you'll learn how to analyze potential physical evidence of a crime, including fire debris, gunshot residues, bodily fluids, metals, glasses, hair, fibers, paint, and drugs.

While criminal science is very much a chemistry-based field, it's important to understand the larger context of the evidence you'll be working with. Outside the crime lab, you'll study research methods, juvenile justice, corrections, criminology, and court systems. You'll also take classes like psychology, sociology, and behavioral science. Though perhaps it's less exciting than DNA matching or dusting for fingerprints, this major will also teach you practical skills like computer applications, record-keeping, and evidence handling and storage.

If You Like Criminal Science, You May Also Like . . .

Biochemistry, biology, chemistry, clinical psychology, criminology, forensic psychology, forensic science, genetics, molecular genetics, pre-law, pharmacology, psychology, social work, sociology

Suggested High School Prep for Criminal Science

For this major, just sit back and watch as many episodes of *CSI* and *Law & Order* as you can . . . just kidding. Take math, biology, advanced chemistry, physics, and English.

SAMPLE COLLEGE CURRICULUM FOR CRIMINAL SCIENCE

Abnormal Personality

Analysis of Criminal Behavior

Chemistry and Crime

Court Systems and the Judicial Process

Introduction to Sociology

The Juvenile Offender

Principles of Investigation

Survey of Forensic Science

Fun Facts

Fingerprinting

In 1892, an Argentine police officer named Juan Vucetich was the first to solve a crime using fingerprint matching. Although it had been known for centuries that no two individuals had the same fingerprints, Vucetich was the first to implement a system for print identification. He was able to use it successfully to prosecute a woman named Francesca Rojas, who had murdered her two sons, and had no reason to think to wear gloves while doing it.

(Source: www.bbc.co.uk/history/historic_figures/faulds_henry.shtml)

A Chilling Site

Court TV's riveting crime library website includes profiles and pictures of dozens of notorious crime cases. Check it out at www.crimelibrary.com.

Careers and Salary

Although you may want to get a master's degree to pursue this field, the average starting salary for someone with a bachelor's in criminal science is between $23,000 and $33,000 a year.

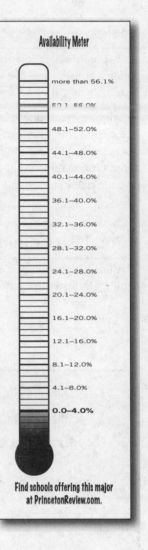

Availability Meter

more than 56.1%

52.1–56.0%

48.1–52.0%

44.1–48.0%

40.1–44.0%

36.1–40.0%

32.1–36.0%

28.1–32.0%

24.1–28.0%

20.1–24.0%

16.1–20.0%

12.1–16.0%

8.1–12.0%

4.1–8.0%

0.0–4.0%

Find schools offering this major
at PrincetonReview.com.

CAREER OPTIONS		
Chemist	Criminal Investigator	Detective/Private Investigator
Customs Agent	Criminalist	Drug Enforcement Agent
CIA Agent	Criminologist	FBI Agent

CRIMINOLOGY

Basics

Criminology is an enriching and engaging major well worth pursuing as an end in itself. It's also good if you are considering law school or if you want to apprehend criminals or work in some facet of the legal system right out of college.

Any way you slice it, however, if you major in criminology you'll learn all about the administration of justice within the American criminal justice system. In classes, you'll explore the different causes and consequences of different kinds of crime, reasons for the prevalence of crime in society, and more than a little about criminal psychology. You'll also learn all about law enforcement, probation and parole systems, prisons, juvenile delinquency, and the many federal, state, and local agencies that exist to combat all things illegal.

If You Like Criminology, You May Also Like . . .

Clinical psychology, communication disorders, counseling, developmental psychology, experimental psychology, industrial psychology, psychology, public policy analysis

Suggested High School Prep for Criminology

There's not a lot you can take in high school that will especially prepare you for a major in criminology. Stick to a solid, meat-and-potatoes college preparation curriculum that includes several courses in English, math, and the sciences.

SAMPLE COLLEGE CURRICULUM FOR CRIMINOLOGY

Criminal Justice Policy

Criminology

Drug Addiction and Alcoholism

Gender, Crime, and Justice

Internship

Introductory Sociology

Juvenile Justice

Police and Policing

Probation and Parole

Research Methods in Criminology

Sociological Aspects of Deviance

Sociology of Law

Sociology of Youth and Crime

Statistical Analysis in Criminology

Theories of Crime

Fun Facts

A Joke

A police officer spots a man driving down the road with 25 penguins in the back seat of his car. The officer stops the man and orders him to take the penguins to the city zoo immediately. The man agrees and drives off in the direction of the zoo.

The next day the officer sees the same man once again driving down the road with 25 penguins in the back seat. The officer is infuriated and stops the man once again.

"I thought I told you to take those penguins to the zoo!" yells the angry officer.

"I did," replies the man. "And we had so much fun that today I'm taking them to the movies."

Remember, Kids: Crime Doesn't Pay

Here's what happened to seven of the most notorious criminals in American history.

Clyde Barrow: Clyde Barrow, Bonnie Parker, and the Barrow Gang instigated what may be the most famous crime spree in history. They robbed banks and other places. They killed people. They died in an ambush on the outskirts of Gibsland, Louisiana.

Ted Bundy: Ted Bundy charmed women with his good looks and law school background and then murdered them. He was eventually arrested for attacking women at a sorority house at Florida State. Bundy was convicted for several murders across the United States. He received the death penalty.

Al Capone: Public Enemy Number 1, Al (Scar Face) Capone was a bootlegger during Prohibition. He ran one of the most ruthless and successful enterprises in U.S. history. The FBI never convicted him for any of the seriously awful crimes he committed. He was, however, sentenced to eight years in a federal penitentiary for failure to pay income taxes, and he died in 1947 from syphilis.

Jeffrey Dahmer: The bizarre Jeffrey Dahmer sadistically murdered, dismembered, and in some cases, ate several young men in the Milwaukee area. He was sentenced to 15 successive life terms in prison. A few years into his prison sentence, another prisoner beat Dahmer to death.

Albert Henry De Salvo: The Boston Strangler raped and strangled 13 women in Boston. He died in prison, thanks to 16 stab wounds inflicted by fellow inmates in Walpole State Prison.

John Herbert Dillinger: John Dillinger was a bank robber and a multiple murderer during the Great Depression. On Sunday evening, July 22, 1934, FBI agents shot Dillinger to death outside the Biograph Theater in Chicago.

Charles Manson: Cult leader Charles Manson masterminded the gruesome murders of Sharon Tate and several other people in 1969. He was sentenced to life imprisonment. Although he is periodically up for parole, it is a good bet that Manson will die in prison.

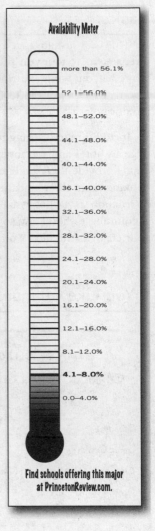

Availability Meter

more than 56.1%

52.1–56.0%

48.1–52.0%

44.1–48.0%

40.1–44.0%

36.1–40.0%

32.1–36.0%

28.1–32.0%

24.1–28.0%

20.1–24.0%

16.1–20.0%

12.1–16.0%

8.1–12.0%

4.1–8.0%

0.0–4.0%

Find schools offering this major at PrincetonReview.com.

Careers and Salary

A typical starting salary for a criminology major with a bachelor's degree ranges from $25,000 to $35,000 per year.

CAREER OPTIONS

Attorney	Crisis Negotiator	Police Officer/Manager
Bodyguard	Detective/Private Investigator	Psychologist
Child Care Worker	FBI Agent	Social Worker
Court Reporter	Paralegal	Trial Lawyer
Criminologist		

CULINARY ARTS

Basics

This isn't just advanced home economics or an opportunity to create abstract art with food. It's also an intense two- to four-year program for people who are serious about cooking. Yeah, you'll get to wear a funny white hat, but while wearing it, you'll learn all the finer details of making everything deliciously edible, from lasagna to a crepe soufflé. Plus you'll graduate knowing the difference between a cabernet sauvignon and a pinot noir.

In addition to learning how to become a first-class chef, a culinary arts major also gains practical knowledge in hotel and restaurant management, facilities management, and hospitality. Many culinary arts programs provide their students with hands-on experience through internships at restaurants. There's a lot of cooking, from the mundane to the elegant, but the major doesn't end in the kitchen. To complement your instruction as a chef, you'll take courses designed to prepare you in basic business administration, from accounting to hotel law, so that by the time you complete your degree you will be ready to begin staking your claim as the next Wolfgang Puck.

If You Like Culinary Arts, You May Also Like . . .

Art, bakery science, dietetics, food science, home economics, hospitality, nutrition

SAMPLE COLLEGE CURRICULUM FOR CULINARY ARTS

Baking I

Basic Cooking

Catering Operations and Sales

Dining Room Service

Facilities Management

Food Service Operations

Food Service Sanitation

Hospitality Accounting

Hospitality Marketing

Hotel Law

Labor Management Relations

Nutrition

Personnel Administration

Practical Work Experience

Purchasing

Saucier

Suggested High School Prep for Culinary Arts

The best preparation for a career in the culinary arts is, of course, a love of cooking. It's never too early to begin developing your skills as a chef, whether it's learning how to bake brownies or make a crème brûlée that leaves your taster begging for more. On a more practical level, take some home economics and business courses. You may also want to hang out with your grandma in the kitchen; you just never know what family secrets will turn into blue-ribbon-winning dishes.

Fun Facts

How Do You Cut Onions Without Breaking Into Tears?

Cut them either under cold water, or wet several times with cold water the knife you are using.

NUTRITION, HOME ECONOMICS, AND RELATED FIELDS/ SPECIALIZED STUDIES

Cooking Brownies With Kids

Remove teddy bear from oven and preheat to 375 degrees.

Melt 1 cup margarine in saucepan.

Remove teddy bear from oven and tell Billy, "No, no."

Add margarine to 2 cups sugar.

Measure cup cocoa.

Take shortening can away from Billy and bathe cat.

Apply antiseptic and bandages to scratches sustained while removing shortening from cat's tail.

Combine 4 eggs, 2 teaspoons vanilla, and 1 cups sifted flour.

Take smoldering teddy bear from oven and open all doors and windows for ventilation.

Take telephone away from Billy and assure party on the line the call was a mistake. Call operator and attempt to have direct dialed call removed from bill.

Measure in 1 teaspoon salt and cup nuts and beat all ingredients well.

Let cat out of refrigerator.

Pour mixture into well-greased 9 x 13-inch pan.

Bake 25 minutes.

Rescue cat and take razor away from Billy. Explain that you have no idea if shaved cats will sunburn.

Frosting:

Mix the following in saucepan:

    1 cup sugar

    1 ounce unsweetened chocolate

    cup margarine

Take the %&*$#@! teddy bear out of the %&*$#@! broiler and throw it away. Far away.

Answer the door and meekly explain to nice policeman that you didn't know Billy had slipped out of the house and was heading for the street. Put Billy in playpen.

Add cup milk, dash of salt, and boil, stirring constantly for 2 minutes.

Answer door and apologize to neighbor for Billy having stuck garden hose in man's front door mail slot. Promise to pay for ruined carpet.

Tie Billy to clothesline.

Remove burned brownies from oven.

(Source: www.basicjokes.com)

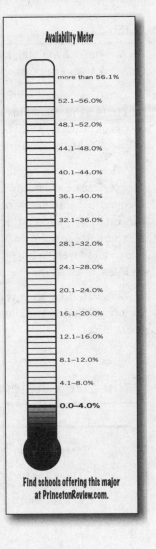

Availability Meter

more than 56.1%

52.1–56.0%

48.1–52.0%

44.1–48.0%

40.1–44.0%

36.1–40.0%

32.1–36.0%

28.1–32.0%

24.1–28.0%

20.1–24.0%

16.1–20.0%

12.1–16.0%

8.1–12.0%

4.1–8.0%

0.0–4.0%

Find schools offering this major at PrincetonReview.com.

Careers and Salary

Culinary arts is a hot field, with a lot of different opportunities. Current starting salaries for chefs and those working in the hotel/restaurant industry are between $20,000 and $35,000.

CAREER OPTIONS

Bar/Club Manager	Consultant	Sommelier
Caterer	Hotel Manager	Wedding Consultant
Chef	Restaurateur	

CYTOTECHNOLOGY

Basics

Are you drawn to the medical sciences? Do you enjoy scientific research? Do you like the idea of working each day with a microscope? If so, then we have six syllables for you: cytotechnology.

Often associated with biology or health services programs, the cytotechnology major provides specialized training in examining cells and tissues for abnormalities. The work of a cytotechnologist is perhaps the first significant step in the diagnosis and subsequent treatment of severe afflictions, particularly cancer. Cytotechnologists are expected to be meticulous, self-disciplined, and very well-trained.

With a major in cytotechnology, you'll learn how to operate laboratory equipment, stain cell and tissue samples, create slides, and interpret what you see. Your coursework will range from cellular biology to organic chemistry, with likely forays into physics, mathematics, zoology, and even ethics. Many programs will also ask you to step outside the university gates, where you'll do internships that allow you to garner professional experience in the field. This combination of academic and real-world education will not only look impressive to employers in hospitals and research labs, but, should you decide to continue on for a higher degree, it's likely to catch the eye of med school and PhD program admissions committees as well.

Be aware that after you have the degree in hand, you'll have one more hurdle ahead: the American Society of Clinical Pathologists Exam. With this certification in hand, you'll be prepared to join the professional ranks.

If You Like Cytotechnology, You May Also Like...

Anatomy, biochemistry, biology, bioethics, biomedical engineering, biomedical science, cellular biology, chemistry, diagnostic medical sonography, epidemiology, genetics, gerontology, medical illustration, microbiology, molecular biology, molecular genetics, nursing, premedicine, public health, zoology

SAMPLE COLLEGE CURRICULUM FOR CYTOTECHNOLOGY

Bench Chemistry

Biochemistry

Biotechnology

Calculus

Cellular Biology

Genetics

Immunology

Introduction to Botany and Zoology

Medical Ethics

Microbiology

Molecular Biology

Organic Chemistry

Suggested High School Prep for Cytotechnology

It's pretty simple: science, science, science; math, math, math. Rinse, wash, repeat.

Fun Facts

What They Look At

Cytotechnologists most commonly examine samples taken during a Pap smear, a procedure that collects cell and tissue samples from a female's cervix. The Pap smear got its name from Dr. George Papanicolaou, a Greek doctor who conducted a wealth of important research at the Cornell Medical School in the 1920s, 1930s, and 1940s. His work led to groundbreaking theories and procedures—e.g., the Pap smear—that aided in the detection and treatment of uterine cancer.

(Source: www.papsociety.org/drpap.html)

Eye, Eye

Because cytotechnology requires the careful and frequent examination of tiny cellular objects, healthy eyesight is a virtue.

Careers and Salary

A cytotechnologist's starting salary is typically about $35,000. With several years experience under your belt, you can expect to rise to an annual salary between $45,000 and $60,000.

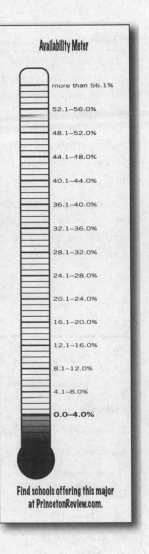

Availability Meter

more than 56.1%

52.1–56.0%

48.1–52.0%

44.1–48.0%

40.1–44.0%

36.1–40.0%

32.1–36.0%

28.1–32.0%

24.1–28.0%

20.1–24.0%

16.1–20.0%

12.1–16.0%

8.1–12.0%

4.1–8.0%

0.0–4.0%

Find schools offering this major
at PrincetonReview.com.

CAREER OPTIONS		
Hospital/Laboratory Cytotechnologist	Pathologist Assistant Researcher	Teacher

DANCE

Basics

There is a certain mystique to women and men who can move their bodies in amazing and beautiful ways. Dance is as much a part of the world's artistic history as literature, music, or the visual arts, and its beauty is just as varied and complex. If you're a dance major, you'll study many forms of dance, including ballet, modern, jazz, and various ethnic forms. You will also study dance as an art—its role in history and its influences on different cultures. Dance is a performance art, and much of your college experience will include performance. You may choose from many concentrations of study as you move toward your degree—choreography or technology, for example. Many students choose to focus their study on dance education.

Dance majors are usually already devoted to their art, having taken dance classes from a young age. Dance programs are generally competitive, as is the case with most performance programs. Be prepared to submit a videotape of your past performances. You'll probably also have to give a live audition to be accepted to a dance program.

If You Like Dance, You May Also Like . . .

Art, art education, music, physical therapy, theater, visual communication, voice

Suggested High School Prep for Dance

Many high schools don't offer dance classes but if yours does, jump on them! Another good outlet for dance in high school is with the drama club. Musicals often require skilled dancers and choreographers and are a great way to get experience on stage. Marching band may also offer dance opportunities. You may also look into various art and music classes to broaden your artistic horizons.

SAMPLE COLLEGE CURRICULUM FOR DANCE

Choreography

Classical Indian Dance

Classical Spanish Dancing

Dance Composition: Form and Content

Dance Criticism

Dance History

Dance in East Asia

Dance Technologies

Dynamic Postural Alignment

Ensemble Dance Repertory

Kinesiology

Movement Analysis

Music for Dance

Musical Theater Dance

Solo Repertory

Somatic Practices

Technique courses in ballet, modern dance, jazz, and tap

Fun Facts

Fame! I'm Gonna Live Forever!

If you love the art of dance, be sure to participate in next year's National Dance Week. According to the Voice of Dance website, "National Dance Week's ongoing mission is to heighten awareness of dance and the art form's contributions to the national culture." That should put some spring in your step!

Words to Dance By

"He that lives in hope danceth without musick."

—George Herbert

"O body swayed to music, O brightening glance, How can we know the dancer from the dance?"

—W. B. Yeats

"A dance is a measured pace, as a verse is a measured speech."

—Francis Bacon

Famous People Who Majored in Dance

Kay Cummings (Julliard), Joy Kellman (California Institute of the Arts), James Martin (California Institute of the Arts), Faruk Ruzimatov (Leningrad's Vaganova Ballet Academy), Tiekka Schofield (Houston Ballet Academy)

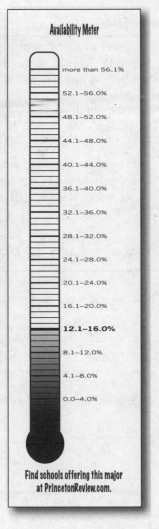

Availability Meter

more than 56.1%

52.1–56.0%

48.1–52.0%

44.1–48.0%

40.1–44.0%

36.1–40.0%

32.1–36.0%

28.1–32.0%

24.1–28.0%

20.1–24.0%

16.1–20.0%

12.1–16.0%

8.1–12.0%

4.1–8.0%

0.0–4.0%

Find schools offering this major at PrincetonReview.com.

Careers and Salary

Salaries for dancers vary widely and depend mostly on the sizes of their dance companies or the fields they plan to pursue. According to Ohio State University, the salaries for dance company members range from $8,000 to $25,000, and dance educators can earn up to $35,000.

CAREER OPTIONS

Actor	Dancer	Teacher
Artist		

DATA PROCESSING

Basics

If the words "data processing" bring to mind images of a roomful of monkeys typing away into infinity, or fond memories of *Star Trek: The Next Generation*, then it's probably about time to update your understanding of this major.

As computers and technology continue to become the cornerstone for just about every business, data processors will be in constant demand to help corporations, individuals, and government offices adapt and more effectively use technology in the office and in the home.

From creating computer networks within a company that allow offices to share files and data to working as a computer service administrator, data processing majors will be invested with a wide array of computer and office skills that have real practical applications to the job market.

If You Like Data Processing, You May Also Like . . .

Accounting, business administration and management, business communications, computer and information science, computer systems analysis

Suggested High School Prep for Data Processing

The best preparation is a strong general background in statistics and the most complex math available to you in addition to special courses in computer science.

SAMPLE COLLEGE CURRICULUM FOR DATA PROCESSING

Computer Applications Practicum

Computer Science

File Processing

Introduction to Computing

Introduction to Microcomputer Spreadsheets

Microcomputer Word Processing

Principles of Accounting

Principles of Economics

Fun Facts

A Data Processing Joke

Typing teacher to a student named Tom: "Tom, your work has certainly improved. There are only 10 mistakes here."

Tom: "Great."

Teacher: "Now let's look at the second line."

Careers and Salary

The average starting salary for a data processing major is between $18,000 and $27,000.

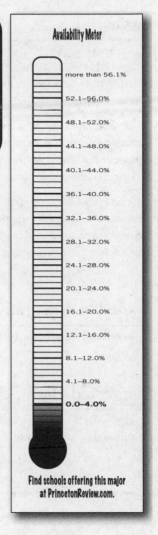

Availability Meter

more than 56.1%

52.1–56.0%

48.1–52.0%

44.1–48.0%

40.1–44.0%

36.1–40.0%

32.1–36.0%

28.1–32.0%

24.1–28.0%

20.1–24.0%

16.1–20.0%

12.1–16.0%

8.1–12.0%

4.1–8.0%

0.0–4.0%

Find schools offering this major
at PrincetonReview.com.

CAREER OPTIONS

Accountant	Bookkeeper	Quality Assurance Engineer
Auditor	Computer Operator/Programmer	Research Technician

DECISION SCIENCES

Basics

Students who are interested in decision sciences must have strong passion for statistical analysis and decision theory. Majoring in decision sciences as an undergraduate course of work is not available at most colleges, but makes an excellent addition to degrees in psychology, business management and administration, or computer engineering.

In general decision science is the active use of decision theory which can be either normative or prescriptive meaning it focuses on the ability of a rational, fully-informed decision maker's ability to make the best decision. Those who work in decision sciences analyze data from surveys of social or group decision making, relative value, and commodities that cannot be measured in the same units.

The application of such science is highly technical and jobs in the field are highly competitive. Those who work in decision sciences must be able to integrate several fields of study into concrete answers that are supported by statistical data. Such work will require a wide range of expertise in areas like statistics, economics, computer analysis and psychology in addition to any industry-specific knowledge.

If you like Integrative Decision Science, you may also like...

Economics, statistics, business theory, actuarial analysis

Suggested High School prep for Decision Science

High levels of math including calculus, microeconomics, statistics and probability as well as computer programming and analysis.

SAMPLE COLLEGE CURRICULUM FOR DECISION SCIENCE

Applied Decision Analysis

Applied Regression Analysis

Business Statistics

Decision Analysis for Negotiation Problems

Non parametric Statistics

Production Systems Analysis

Quality Management

Simulation of Business Operations

Fun Facts

The father of decision science Blaise Pascal. He was a child genius who was home schooled. His writings have strongly influenced modern economics and social science theory; he clarified the concepts of pressure and vacuums and shaped the study of fluids all before he died at the age of 39.

Careers and Salary

Since most students will have to pursue decision science in the course of master's studies, the salary range will depend more heavily on the industry in which the student works, but in general should fall between $40,000 and $85,000.

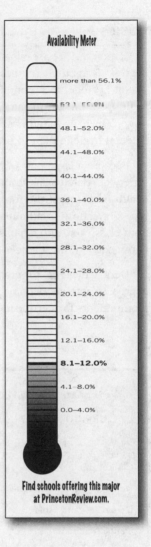

Availability Meter

more than 56.1%

52.1–56.0%

48.1–52.0%

44.1–48.0%

40.1–44.0%

36.1–40.0%

32.1–36.0%

28.1–32.0%

24.1–28.0%

20.1–24.0%

16.1–20.0%

12.1–16.0%

8.1–12.0%

4.1–8.0%

0.0–4.0%

Find schools offering this major at PrincetonReview.com.

CAREER OPTIONS

Actuary	Financial Planner	Statistician
Financial Analyst	Investment Banker	

DENTAL HYGIENE

Basics

"Open up!" Those words instill panic in the hearts of many. But you can be the hero who calms their nerves, cleans their teeth, and urges them to become more diligent flossers when you enter the world of dental hygiene. As a dental hygiene major, you'll learn the fundamentals of oral health and nutrition, the anatomy of the mouth, and how to promote oral safety and care. You'll also learn about dental care laws and how to manage patients safely. And you'll come away armed with the knowledge to help patients develop a dental hygiene plan to protect and care for their teeth, thus making this world a cleaner, brighter place.

Because a large part of being a dental hygienist is educating patients about oral health, you'll gain a wide variety of related skills. Primarily, you'll be providing your patients with preventive care—ensuring their dental health now and in the future. To that end, you'll learn how to screen for oral cancer, how to take and analyze x-rays, how to administer fluoride, and how to remove deposits from the teeth. Your learning will be both classroom- and lab-based, and eventually you'll practice your newfound skills on real patients. A strong knowledge in the sciences as well as good communication skills are vital for success in dental hygiene.

Dental hygiene programs are generally two years in length, and you'll graduate with an associate's degree. To actually become a dental hygienist, you must pass a national written exam and fulfill your state's requirements for certification.

SAMPLE COLLEGE CURRICULUM FOR DENTAL HYGIENE

Clinical Dental Hygiene

Dental Hygiene Techniques

Dental Law and Ethics

Dental Materials

Dental Radiology

Infection and Hazard Control

Medical Emergencies

Oral Health and Nutrition

Oral Histology

Pain Control

Pathology

Patient Management

Periodontics

Preventive Dentistry

Tooth Morphology

If You Like Dental Hygiene, You May Also Like . . .

Dietetics, health administration, medical technology, nursing, nutrition, pharmacy, pre-dentistry, premedicine, pre-optometry, public health

Suggested High School Prep for Dental Hygiene

Becoming solidly versed in the sciences—especially biology and chemistry—will give you a great head start on your college studies. And since you'll need to be a great communicator, don't neglect humanities courses like English and languages, where you'll perfect your written and oral skills. Take advantage of any health or anatomy courses your school offers too—and pay close attention when talk turns to teeth.

ALLIED MEDICAL AND HEALTH PROFESSIONS/
SPECIALIZED STUDIES

Fun Facts

On the Bright Track

According to the American Dental Association, dental hygiene is one of the 30 fastest grow-ing occupations. Your future looks as bright as your teeth!

Show Those Teeth

Yet another reason to promote a perfect smile:
"Better by far that you should forget and smile
Than that you should remember and be sad."

—Christina Rossetti

Careers and Salary

Dental hygienists are usually paid by the hour, with an average hourly wage of about $25. However, your salary will depend on where you work and how much experience you've had. Many private practices will pay on a salary basis ranging from $30,000 to $33,000 per year.

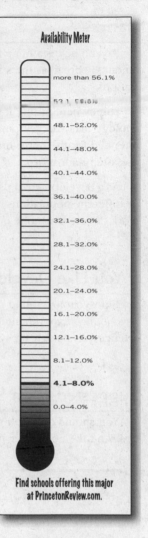

Availability Meter

more than 56.1%

52.1–56.0%

48.1–52.0%

44.1–48.0%

40.1–44.0%

36.1–40.0%

32.1–36.0%

28.1–32.0%

24.1–28.0%

20.1–24.0%

16.1–20.0%

12.1–16.0%

8.1–12.0%

4.1–8.0%

0.0–4.0%

Find schools offering this major
at PrincetonReview.com.

CAREER OPTIONS

Dental Equipment Salesperson	Health Care Administrator	Researcher
Dental Hygienist	Public Health Administrator	Teacher
Dental Lab Technician		

DEVELOPMENTAL PSYCHOLOGY

Basics

Psychology is a huge field, and it's no wonder. Anytime a discipline has as its focus something as monumentally broad as the study of behavior, you had better expect a whole lot of concentrations and specializations.

Somewhere in that long list of psychology majors is developmental psychology. Just like a general psychology major, developmental psychology is concerned with human behavior. As a specialized major, it is intended for the brave man or woman who is looking to put his or her education into direct practice and use after graduation.

As a developmental psychology major, you'll be prepared to work as a psychologist with a wide number of different populations, including children, the elderly, and families. Many developmental psychologists work directly with one or more of these groups, focusing on the causes and reasons behind behavior.

If You Like Developmental Psychology, You May Also Like . . .

Biopsychology, child care, child development, clinical psychology, counseling, criminology, educational psychology, experimental psychology, human development, industrial psychology, neurobiology, neuroscience, physiological psychology, psychology, social psychology, social work, special education

Suggested High School Prep for Developmental Psychology

You should focus on those math and science classes, particularly biology, chemistry, physics, and statistics. And the no-brainer part: If your school offers psychology classes, enroll and excel in them.

SAMPLE COLLEGE CURRICULUM FOR DEVELOPMENTAL PSYCHOLOGY

Behavior Modification

General Psychology

Introduction to Psychobiology

Learning Memory and Cognition

Psychology in Childhood

Psychopathology and Psychotherapy

Quantitative and Statistical Methods

Research in Psychology

Social Psychology

Statistics

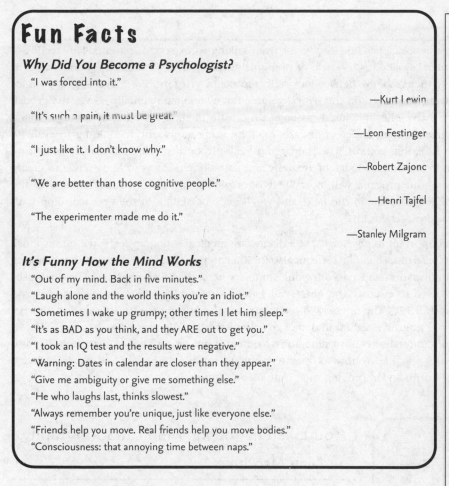

Fun Facts

Why Did You Become a Psychologist?

"I was forced into it."

—Kurt Lewin

"It's such a pain, it must be great."

—Leon Festinger

"I just like it. I don't know why."

—Robert Zajonc

"We are better than those cognitive people."

—Henri Tajfel

"The experimenter made me do it."

—Stanley Milgram

It's Funny How the Mind Works

"Out of my mind. Back in five minutes."

"Laugh alone and the world thinks you're an idiot."

"Sometimes I wake up grumpy; other times I let him sleep."

"It's as BAD as you think, and they ARE out to get you."

"I took an IQ test and the results were negative."

"Warning: Dates in calendar are closer than they appear."

"Give me ambiguity or give me something else."

"He who laughs last, thinks slowest."

"Always remember you're unique, just like everyone else."

"Friends help you move. Real friends help you move bodies."

"Consciousness: that annoying time between naps."

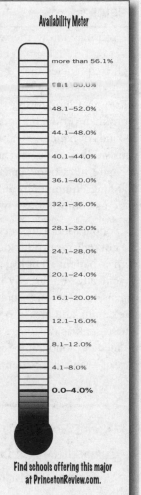

Availability Meter

more than 56.1%

56.1—56.0%

48.1—52.0%

44.1—48.0%

40.1—44.0%

36.1—40.0%

32.1—36.0%

28.1—32.0%

24.1—28.0%

20.1—24.0%

16.1—20.0%

12.1—16.0%

8.1—12.0%

4.1—8.0%

0.0—4.0%

Find schools offering this major at PrincetonReview.com.

Careers and Salary

The average starting salary for a psychology major ranges from $23,000 to $30,000.

CAREER OPTIONS

Career Counselor	Detective/Private Investigator	Social Worker
Corrections Officer	Psychologist	Substance Abuse Counselor
Criminologist		

DIAGNOSTIC MEDICAL SONOGRAPHY

Basics

You may know the words ultrasound and sonogram from talking to expectant parents. This testing—described by Trident Technical College as the "use of nonionizing equipment to transmit sound waves at high frequencies into the patient's body, then collect reflected echoes to form an image"—gets couples excited to start picking out names based on the baby's gender. But a sonogram actually serves the crucial purpose of monitoring the baby's health. Plus, a major in diagnostic medical sonography involves much more than producing images of a fetus to detect disease. You'll be using ultrasound techniques to evaluate all kinds of patients' health situations and you'll be prepared to help physicians form their diagnoses. During your studies, you'll gain an in-depth knowledge of anatomy and pathology, using your knowledge to create accurate ultrasound images. Your program will most likely offer plenty of hands-on experience with the scanning equipment you'll someday use in the field, and you'll become skillful in the art of dealing with patients compassionately and professionally.

Sonographers are very important to physicians. As a diagnostic medical sonographer, you'll be responsible not only for producing these ultrasound images but also for interpreting them. You'll integrate the images with a patient's clinical information and pass on your summary to a qualified physician for diagnosis. Specifically, sonography is used to evaluate the heart, gallbladder, kidneys, liver, blood vessels, and pelvic organs, in addition to unborn babies. The ultrasound technique involves forming a two-dimensional image to examine and measure your internal organs and detect any abnormalities. You may choose to specialize in a field such as obstetrics, abdominal, or echocardiography. No matter what your chosen path, as a diagnostic medical sonography major you'll learn how to operate highly technical equipment, and you'll be a vital part of evaluating patients' health and improving their outlook and future.

SAMPLE COLLEGE CURRICULUM FOR DIAGNOSTIC MEDICAL SONOGRAPHY

Abdominal Sonography

Cardiac Sonography

Case Studies

Clinical Education

Imaging Pathophysiology

Instrumentation Registry

Medical Ethics and Law

Obstetric and Gynecologic Sonography

Sectional Anatomy

Sonographic Physics and
   Instrumentation

Superficial Structure

If You Like Diagnostic Medical Sonography, You May Also Like . . .

Anatomy, child care, chiropractic, dental hygiene, health administration, medical technology, nursing, physical therapy, physician assistant, pre-dentistry, premedicine, public health

Suggested High School Prep for Diagnostic Medical Sonography

A broad familiarity with the sciences is vital to a career in diagnostic medical sonography, so fill your schedule with upper-level biology, chemistry, and physics courses. Math courses are also important. This career requires good communication skills as well, so take courses in the humanities—such as English and languages—that will help you improve your reading, writing, and oral communication. Any health or anatomy courses your high school offers will give you a great head start for college.

Fun Facts

Ultrasound in History

A Swiss physicist named Daniel Colladen was the first to calculate the speed of sound underwater. In 1822, he rang a bell underwater in Lake Geneva, Switzerland, and ignited gunpowder at the same time. The flash was seen 10 miles away, and the time it took for the sound to arrive—heard through a special device—was measured. He determined that the speed of sound underwater was 1,435 meters per second, and that number is still considered fairly accurate.

(Source: www.ob-ultrasound.net/history.html)

SONAR Savvy

- SONAR is short for sound navigation and ranging.
- Underwater detection systems began to be used in 1912, after the Titanic sank. The first patent for underwater sonar was filed just one month after this tragedy.
- Submarines in World War I also used underwater detection systems for underwater navigation.

(Source: www.ob-ultrasound.net/history.html)

Careers and Salary

In general, starting salaries for sonographers are about $30,000 to $40,000. However, this number depends on where you live and in what capacity you use your skills.

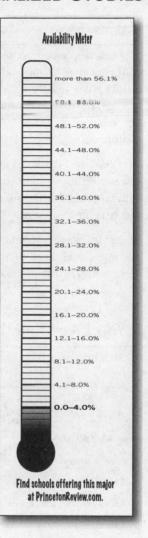

Availability Meter

more than 56.1%

52.1–56.0%

48.1–52.0%

44.1–48.0%

40.1–44.0%

36.1–40.0%

32.1–36.0%

28.1–32.0%

24.1–28.0%

20.1–24.0%

16.1–20.0%

12.1–16.0%

8.1–12.0%

4.1–8.0%

0.0–4.0%

Find schools offering this major at PrincetonReview.com.

CAREER OPTIONS

| Diagnostic Medical Sonographer | Physician Assistant | Public Health Administrator |

DIETETICS

Basics

Dietetics is a burgeoning professional field that combines practical skills and research in food and health with education about food intake and food choices. Think of dietetics as the psychology of food. Sure, dietetics majors study nutrition. In fact, they study it a lot. But they also study people's attitudes, beliefs, and behaviors toward food and eating habits. And what with the swift innovations in medical research—not to mention perpetually rising health care costs and consumer demands—it's a field that has become increasingly complex.

Registered dietitians assess nutritional needs, treat dietary problems, and help prevent diseases through counseling about sound dietary practices and fitness. They also manage food service in health care and commercial settings. They are educators, therapists, consultants, and managers who work in hospitals, cafeterias, and large corporations.

Any dietetics program worth its salt is going to be accredited by the American Dietetic Association. To become a registered dietitian, you've got to complete an ADA-approved curriculum and pass the National Registered Dietitian Exam. Once you do, you should find a solid and growing job market waiting for you.

If You Like Dietetics, You May Also Like . . .

Biochemistry, biology, cell biology, chemistry, child care, food science, genetics, gerontology, home economics, human development, medical technology, microbiology, neurobiology, neuroscience, nursing, nutrition, occupational therapy, pharmacology, pharmacy, physical therapy, physiological psychology, premedicine, pre-optometry, pre-veterinary medicine, public health, respiratory therapy

> **SAMPLE COLLEGE CURRICULUM FOR DIETETICS**
>
> Biochemistry
> Community Nutrition
> Cultural and Social Aspects of Food
> Economics
> Food Preparation
> Food Service Administration
> Human Anatomy
> Internship
> Nutrition
> Nutrition Therapy
> Organic Chemistry
> Pediatric Nutrition
> Physiology
> Statistics
> Therapeutic Nutrition

Suggested High School Prep for Dietetics

If you are thinking about majoring in dietetics, take chemistry and biology courses as well as a home economics course or two. You also want to know your way around a lab as well as possible.

ALLIED MEDICAL AND HEALTH PROFESSIONS/ NUTRITION, HOME ECONOMICS, AND RELATED FIELDS

Fun Facts

These People Don't Mess Around

Qualifications for becoming a registered dietitian

- Bachelor's degree in dietetics, nutrition, food-service management, institutional management, or related field
- American Dietetic Association-accredited dietetic internship or approved professional experience
- Passing score on the National Dietetic Examination
- Mandatory continuing education to retain professional registration

Cyberdiet

For tons of tremendous information regarding eating right and living a healthy lifestyle, check out www.cyberdiet.com.

Careers and Salary

Typical starting salaries for dietetics majors range from $25,000 to about $35,000 annually. Raises will come as well. Salaries for experienced dietitians can exceed $63,000.

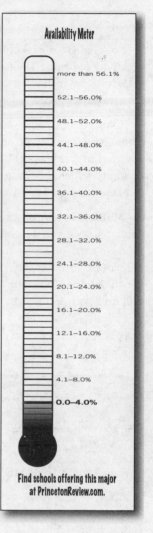

Availability Meter

more than 56.1%

52.1–56.0%

48.1–52.0%

44.1–48.0%

40.1–44.0%

36.1–40.0%

32.1–36.0%

28.1–32.0%

24.1–28.0%

20.1–24.0%

16.1–20.0%

12.1–16.0%

8.1–12.0%

4.1–8.0%

0.0–4.0%

Find schools offering this major at PrincetonReview.com.

CAREER OPTIONS

Caterer	Hospice Nurse	Physician
Chef	Nurse	Physician Assistant
Health Care Administrator	Nutritionist	

DIGITAL COMMUNICATIONS AND MEDIA/MULTIMEDIA

Basics

So what are digital communications and media/multimedia anyway? That's for you and your tech-heavy creativity to decide. Digital communications are just what they sound like: Communications performed with and by digital technology. Multimedia developers and managers use digital communications methods to create an endless variety of entertainment, graphic design, and artistic productions.

In this major, you'll start with the fundamentals: computer programming, teleprocessing, graphic design, photography, and audio and video production. You'll move on to build websites and create 3-D animation in addition to tackling CD-ROM production and computer imaging. All of these methods of digital communication together constitute the "multi" nature of multimedia. You'll also learn about the laws and regulations in place for digital communications and what our role is in the development and use of new technologies.

Multimedia, as you probably know, is a rapidly expanding field. Been to a museum lately? Then you've probably seen video installations and interactive works of art. Heard about e-books? A hardcover paper volume isn't the only way to publish or read novels anymore. Multimedia is evident on websites that involve animation, virtual reality, photography, and audio. The field is new, exciting, and evolving; it's nearly impossible to define or set boundaries for it because your major in digital communications and media/multimedia will be largely defined by your own ideas and experiments.

Sample College Curriculum for Digital Communications and Media/Multimedia

CD-ROM Production

Classes in computer applications such as Access, Excel, Java, JavaScript, etc.

Computer Literacy and Productivity

Computer-Aided Graphic Arts

Digital Illustration

Information Architecture

Internet and Electronic Commerce

Multimedia Design

Visual Design

Web Programming

Web Publishing

Website Construction and Design

If You Like Digital Communications and Media/Multimedia, You May Also Like . . .

Advertising, art, computer and information science, computer systems analysis, drawing, entrepreneurship, graphic design, photography, printmaking, radio and television, visual communication

Suggested High School Prep for Digital Communications and Media/Multimedia

Learning as much as you can about computers is your most pertinent preparation. Software, programming, the Internet—being versed to some degree in all these areas will help you once you begin your studies in college. Strong reading, writing, and communication skills are also vital to these fields, so take advantage of your school's humanities courses. Also, any art classes you can fit into your schedule will be helpful—everyone in multimedia, even a programmer, is involved in some way with design.

Fun Facts

Tune In

Ever wonder who invented wireless communication? It was Guglielmo Marconi, who won the Nobel Prize in physics in 1909 for his equipment that transmitted electrical signals through the air—what we now know as radio.

Get Hip to That

If you're interested in digital communications and/or media/multimedia, check out threeoh.com. It is, as the site puts it, an online "digital design journal." It always has links to the newest and best sites by some of the hippest designers in the biz.

Careers and Salary

Starting salaries for digital communications and media/multimedia majors are generally in the upper twenties to upper thirties, although this estimate varies widely depending on how you use your skills. Since you can work for or with just about any company that advertises or does its primary business over any kind of digital media, it's unusually difficult to predict starting salaries for this major.

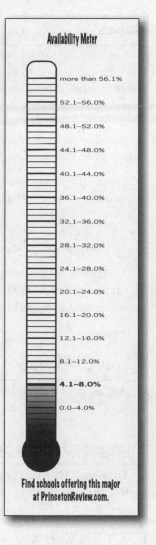

Availability Meter

more than 56.1%

52.1–56.0%

48.1–52.0%

44.1–48.0%

40.1–44.0%

36.1–40.0%

32.1–36.0%

28.1–32.0%

24.1–28.0%

20.1–24.0%

16.1–20.0%

12.1–16.0%

8.1–12.0%

4.1–8.0%

0.0–4.0%

Find schools offering this major at PrincetonReview.com.

CAREER OPTIONS

Animator	Film Editor	Media Specialist
Artist	Graphic Designer	Software Developer
Computer Programmer	Internet/Intranet Technologies Manager	Web Master
Entrepreneur		Website Designer

DRAWING

Basics

Drawing, like all fine arts majors, requires exceptional self-motivation and discipline. If you major in it, you'll be challenged to find your own artistic vision and apply it to your art. You'll experiment with a variety of techniques and explore both traditional (still life, landscape, and the figure) and nontraditional subjects. Chances are your notions of drawing will be challenged through the materials you'll be encouraged to use. Drawing majors equip themselves with the knowledge of a number of mediums through a variety of two-dimensional art-related courses, particularly printmaking. You'll learn how mediums inform and affect one another and how you can incorporate them.

One of the most valuable aspects of a major in drawing is the opportunity to see the work of faculty and other students. Visiting faculty programs, outside lectures, and student exhibitions are essential to see where artists are taking the art of drawing. Most programs offer regular student and faculty critiques, so you'll have the chance to hear what others think of your work. You'll also learn how to critique others (a fine art in itself), which is absolutely necessary to becoming a better artist.

Location is an important consideration with a drawing major. You may want to choose a college or university located in a thriving art community, where there will be ample opportunity for visits to galleries, museums, and private shows.

If You Like Drawing, You May Also Like . . .

Art, art education, art history, graphic art, painting, printmaking

Suggested High School Prep for Drawing

Drawing expertise comes only with practice, so draw, draw, draw—those doodles in your notebooks may be just the practice you need. But be warned: Art schools tend to frown upon copied photos and portfolios full of drawings from the imagination. Draw from life as much as possible. Buy a full range of pencils to ensure strong gradation from light to dark in all of your drawings. Learning about different artistic mediums will make your drawing endeavors richer and your artistic vision broader. History and English classes may also give your art new perspectives.

> **SAMPLE COLLEGE CURRICULUM FOR DRAWING**
>
> Anatomy
>
> Art History
>
> Color
>
> Drawing Into Painting
>
> Drawing Materials and Techniques
>
> Figure Drawing
>
> Painting
>
> Studio Drawing
>
> Two-Dimensional Design

Fun Facts

Words on Drawing

"To draw, you must close your eyes and sing."

—Pablo Ruiz y Picasso

"The essence of drawing is the line exploring space."

—Andy Goldsworthy

"My contribution to the world is my ability to draw. I will draw as much as I can for as many people as I can for as long as I can. Drawing is still basically the same as it has been since prehistoric times. It brings together man and the world. It lives through magic."

—Keith Haring

About Leonardo da Vinci

Leonardo da Vinci was left-handed. You may not think this is so extraordinary, but during Leonardo's time, superstitious people considered left-handedness bad. Children who showed left-handed tendencies were forced to use only their right hands. More extraordinary, when Leonardo wrote in his notebooks, he wrote from right to left—if you held his notebooks up to a mirror, you could read them perfectly. Some people think he did this to prevent smudging the ink (any lefties out there will understand that!). Others think he wanted to prevent people from copying his ideas, and still others think he was trying to hide his ideas from the Roman Catholic Church, since he often disagreed with their teachings.

(Source: The Museum of Science, www.mos.org)

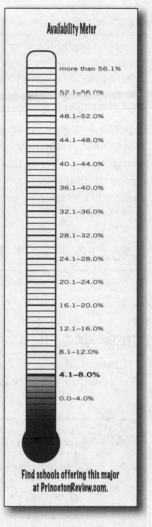

Availability Meter

more than 56.1%

52.1–56.0%

48.1–52.0%

44.1–48.0%

40.1–44.0%

36.1–40.0%

32.1–36.0%

28.1–32.0%

24.1–28.0%

20.1–24.0%

16.1–20.0%

12.1–16.0%

8.1–12.0%

4.1–8.0%

0.0–4.0%

Find schools offering this major at PrincetonReview.com.

Careers and Salary

Career options for artists vary widely—they may find themselves in any number of places after graduation, including working as a freelancer or in a corporation. For this reason, a starting salary is difficult to predict. An independent artist could make less than $20,000 a year. Salaries for artists entering art administration range from $30,000 to $35,000.

CAREER OPTIONS

Animator	Graphic Designer	Tattoo Artist
Artist	Interior Designer	Teacher
Fashion Designer	Set Designer	Website Designer

DUTCH/FLEMISH LANGUAGE AND LITERATURE

Basics

According to the University of California—Berkeley, approximately 40 million people around the globe speak Dutch. You can find Dutch speakers in the Netherlands, the Netherlands Antilles, Belgium, French Flanders, Indonesia, and Suriname. You can also find Dutch speakers at a handful of American institutions (UC Berkeley among them) where some version of the Dutch/Flemish language and literature major exists. The major provides thorough language training, as well as careful examination of Dutch literature, art, and society. You'll spend time gazing at the works of Rembrandt, Van Gogh, and Vermeer. You'll explore the culture's expansive literature, from its medieval roots to its seventeenth century renaissance to its World War I resurgence and beyond. Keep your fingers crossed, as you might get the chance to study abroad. Yep, that means strolling the canals of Amsterdam, visiting the political hotspots in The Hague, and relaxing in the medieval city center of Brussels—all in the name of education.

If You Like Dutch/Flemish Language and Literature, You May Also Like...

Comparative literature, European history, German, Scandinavian studies

Suggested High School Prep for Dutch/Flemish Language and Literature

Chances are your high school doesn't offer a Dutch language course—but that doesn't mean you're out of luck. Studying any foreign language will get you used to studying vocabulary, thinking about grammar, and wrestling with frustrations like unfamiliar conjugations. German is the language most likely to offer some crossover. You should also enroll in plenty of literature and history classes, which will sharpen your reading, researching, and writing skills.

> **SAMPLE COLLEGE CURRICULUM FOR DUTCH/FLEMISH LANGUAGE AND LITERATURE**
>
> Advanced Dutch
>
> Contemporary Netherlands
>
> Conversation and Composition
>
> Dutch Art
>
> Dutch Culture and the Great War
>
> Dutch History
>
> The Dutch Resistance
>
> Early Dutch Literature
>
> Elementary Dutch
>
> Literatures of the Colonizers and Colonized

Fun Facts

What's it Called?

The Netherlands, often referred to as Holland, is the home of Dutch culture. Why all the names? Isn't it easier when, say, Ireland is simply called Ireland and it's the home of Irish culture?

The Netherlands is, in fact, the correct term. Well, it's almost the correct term. To natives, the country is simply known as Nederland (meaning "low country"). In English, however, this is pluralized as The Netherlands (meaning "the low countries"). Why the discrepancy? The plural name refers to the Republic of the Seven United Netherlands, which ended in 1795 but lives on in the English tongue.

So what about Holland? Holland is actually a powerful region of the Netherlands. People often use Holland to refer to the Netherlands as a whole. In literary terms, this is synecdoche. What's synecdoche? You have some studying to do!

Career and Salary

The starting salary for a Dutch/Flemish language and literature major can vary depending specific job. Generally, you should expect to between $25,000 and $30,000.

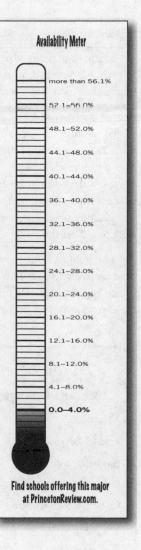

Availability Meter

more than 56.1%

52.1–56.0%

48.1–52.0%

44.1–48.0%

40.1–44.0%

36.1–40.0%

32.1–36.0%

28.1–32.0%

24.1–28.0%

20.1–24.0%

16.1–20.0%

12.1–16.0%

8.1–12.0%

4.1–8.0%

0.0–4.0%

Find schools offering this major at PrincetonReview.com.

CAREER OPTIONS

Diplomat/Attaché/Foreign Service Officer

Editor

Historian

Journalist

Teacher

Translator

Travel Agent/Guide

Writer

E-BUSINESS/E-COMMERCE

Basics

In the digital age where consumers are often just as likely to visit a company's website as they are likely to visit a brick and mortar store, business training has had to take on a new specialization to meet digital demands. That specialization is e-business, an off-shoot of traditional business modeling that focuses on the specific challenges associated with conducting and attracting business on the Web.

E-Business has become a higher demand job now that its expertise is needed not only by companies such as Google Inc., Yahoo Inc., or eBay Inc., that exist chiefly or conduct business only on the Internet, but also by older companies like daily newspapers, Ford Motor Company and Wal-Mart. Modern business models pressure companies to make their information available to an increasingly technology savvy generation of customers, and that means creating Web services for information, advertising and communication. Companies need employees who can adapt the traditional business model of a company and make it an effective Web tool.

The goal of E-Business educators is to prepare students for jobs where they may be asked to build and manage websites or Web campaigns that strive to achieve the same results as older business practices within the parameters of a new medium. Students can choose to pursue a bachelor's degree in e-business from business administration programs or to specialize an MBA with e-business focus.

SAMPLE COLLEGE CURRICULUM FOR E-BUSINESS

Advertising

Applied Database

Business Law

Communication

Computer Programming

Computers and Society

Digital Graphics

Economics

Finance

Hardware and Basic Networking

Marketing

Principles of Management

Production/Operations Management

Statistics

Systems Development

Web Design

Web Systems Analysis and Design

If you like E-Business, you may also like

Business administration, computer sciences, marketing, advertising, finance, computer design, economics

Suggested High School Prep for E-Business

Students who want to expose themselves to e-business principles should try courses that begin with traditional business practices but also try their hands at some computer-specific classes. Courses such as economics, statistics and pre-business are more traditional ways of stepping into business shoes, and coupling those classes with computer graphics, programming, or applications will well prepare students for their collegiate education. Technical writing classes, if available will also help students begin to bridge the gap between the two arenas and to improve communication skills.

Fun Facts

Did you know there is a difference between the Internet and the World Wide Web? While the two terms are used almost synonymously, there is a subtle distinction between the two terms. The term Internet refers to a network of computer networks that share data using packet switching under the common Internet Protocol (IP). Underlying the Internet are more groupings of smaller networks that host information services such as e-mail and file-transfers. It is these inter-linked Web pages that comprise the World Wide Web.

(Source: http://en.wikipedia.org/wiki/Internet)

Careers and Salary

E-Business/E-Commerce business analysts can expect to earn from $25,000 to $40,000 with a bachelor's degree depending on location and company and from $35,000 to $55,000 with an MBA that denotes an E-Business specialization.

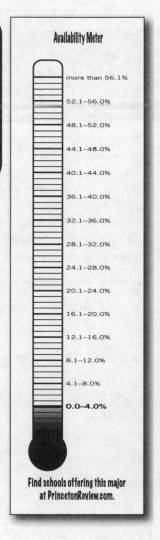

Availability Meter

more than 56.1%

52.1–56.0%

48.1–52.0%

44.1–48.0%

40.1–44.0%

36.1–40.0%

32.1–36.0%

28.1–32.0%

24.1–28.0%

20.1–24.0%

16.1–20.0%

12.1–16.0%

8.1–12.0%

4.1–8.0%

0.0–4.0%

Find schools offering this major at PrincetonReview.com.

CAREER OPTIONS

Advertising Executive	E-Commerce Business Analyst	Web Master/Manager
Computer Engineer	Marketing Executive	Web Programmer
Consultant	Salesperson	

EARLY CHILDHOOD EDUCATION

Basics

Like kids? As obvious a question as it sounds, it's a serious one. The ideal early childhood education major will have, aside from good grades and possibly some experience babysitting or volunteering with little ones, a genuine love for and devotion to children. He or she will be a person drawn to this field not solely during the summer! Stretching far beyond supervising distribution of cookies and milk or coloring within the lines, you'll play a vital role in the development of children both individually and as a class. As an early childhood education major, you'll learn how to be an effective teacher of kids in preschool, kindergarten, and first through third grades. These young learners have needs markedly different from kids even a year or two older. You'll learn how children develop and what their educational needs are at each stage of their lives. You'll study children's literature (remember *Harold and the Purple Crayon*?), how to teach mathematics and reading, and the importance—and significance—of play. You'll study the history of early childhood education so that you can recognize the unique challenges that have faced teachers in this field and how they've been overcome successfully. Most important, you'll study children—how they operate, what they think, and how you can ensure that they reach their full potential.

Being a student teacher is an important part of your college experience—this is how you'll get substantial hands-on experience in the classroom. As a student teacher, you'll work with a supervising teacher to build a curriculum, organize the classroom, and of course, teach. You'll also take part in classroom observation or less intensive hands-on experiences. Education is by nature interdisciplinary, and you'll be studying elements of psychology, sociology, science, and various fields in the humanities.

Different states have different certification requirements, so be sure to do your research when you're applying to education programs—and also when it's time to look for a teaching job.

If You Like Early Childhood Education, You May Also Like . . .

Child care, child development, education, education administration, education of the deaf, educational psychology, music education, physical education, special education, teacher education, teaching english as a second language, technology education

Suggested High School Prep for Early Childhood Education

High school allows you to get a strong foundation in the many fields you'll touch on in your early childhood education studies. Fill your schedule with a variety of challenging courses in math, science, English, history, and languages. Take courses that will improve your reading, writing, and communication skills. And since computers are becoming a more prominent part of the classroom, a computer class or two may be valuable. Put your heart into it before college even starts by volunteering with a community organization that works with young children.

SAMPLE COLLEGE CURRICULUM FOR EARLY CHILDHOOD EDUCATION

Child Guidance

Child, Family, and Community Relations

Childhood Growth and Development

Children's Literature

Computers in the Classroom

Cultural Anthropology

Curriculum and Classroom Organization

Educational Psychology

History of Early Childhood Education

Introduction to Special Education

Mathematics for Elementary Teachers

Methods of Teaching Reading

Music Methods

Pedagogical Techniques

Philosophy of Education

Reading Foundations

Sociology of the Family

Fun Facts

Movie Break

Don't think you're cut out for elementary school teaching? Not so fast! Sometimes the most unlikely people become the best teachers, at least that's how it is in the movies. Check out Arnold Schwarzenegger's transformation from tough guy to tough kindergarten teacher in *Kindergarten Cop*.

Baby Talk

Sign language isn't just for deaf babies; many parents have started teaching signs to their babies who hear just fine. Research has shown that young children who learn signs have higher IQs and better language skills. Before they even learn to talk, babies have the ability to sign—pretty amazing! Two books about signing for babies are published by Gallaudet University Press: *Word Signs* and *Animal Signs*.

(Source: www.deafness.about.com)

Careers and Salary

The starting salary for early childhood teachers is about $25,000 to $30,000, but that figure depends on where you live and whether you choose to teach in a public or private institution. Obtaining a master's degree will put your salary closer to the low to mid-thirties.

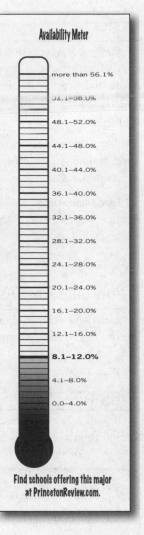

Availability Meter

more than 56.1%

52.1–56.0%

48.1–52.0%

44.1–48.0%

40.1–44.0%

36.1–40.0%

32.1–36.0%

28.1–32.0%

24.1–28.0%

20.1–24.0%

16.1–20.0%

12.1–16.0%

8.1–12.0%

4.1–8.0%

0.0–4.0%

Find schools offering this major at PrincetonReview.com.

CAREER OPTIONS		
Professor	School Administrator	Teacher

EAST ASIAN STUDIES

Basics

Many analysts predict that East Asia will soon be the most powerful economic force in the world, a very compelling reason to consider East Asian studies as your major. Not any less compelling is the fact that East Asian studies students also learn about many of the richest cultural traditions in the world. The art, theater, language, music, literature, and religion of the region are becoming more and more influential in the Western Hemisphere.

East Asian studies combines language study with work in sociology, history, literature, and political science. Majors graduate from the program with a firm grasp on the culture and history of the region, as well as a command of at least one additional language.

East Asian studies majors sometimes combine their studies with work in business, economics, or political science departments. (Alternatively, you can often incorporate an East Asian studies minor into these majors.)

If You Like East Asian Studies, You May Also Like . . .

Asian American studies, Chinese, comparative literature, international agriculture, international business, international relations, international studies, Japanese, South Asian studies, Southeast Asian studies

Suggested High School Prep for East Asian Studies

If your school offers classes in Japanese, Chinese, or Korean, you should take them, but any training in foreign languages will help you become accustomed to the intensity of college-level language study. Courses in political science and Asian history will also be useful.

SAMPLE COLLEGE CURRICULUM FOR EAST ASIAN STUDIES

Chinese Politics and Government

Chinese, Korean, or Japanese I–IV

East Asian Foreign Policy

East Asian Political Economy

History of Hong Kong

Introduction to Buddhism

Japanese Politics and Government

Postwar Japanese Society

Survey of Japanese Literature

Twentieth-Century Chinese History

Fun Facts

For More Information . . .

Keep on top of current events in East Asia. Check out Asian news at AsiaOne, (www.Asia1.com). Yahoo! also offers area guides to Asia, China, Japan, Korea, Singapore, Taiwan, and Hong Kong. Scroll down to the bottom of the main page to the Asian Pacific line of the local guide section. The Asia and Singapore sites are in English; you will need to download language programs for the others. This is not a difficult process, and Yahoo! provides instructions and links to guide you through the procedure.

Asia Via the United Kingdom

Want to know more about East Asian studies? Why not join a newsgroup? The University of Sheffield, England, has an extensive list of newsgroups that you can join. Find it at www.shef.ac.uk.

Careers and Salary

The starting salary for an East Asian studies major fresh out of college is about $24,000 to $30,000.

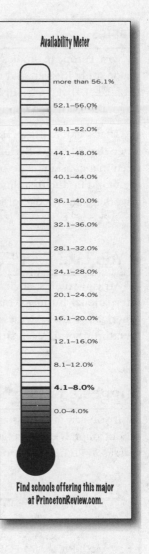

Availability Meter

more than 56.1%
52.1–56.0%
48.1–52.0%
44.1–48.0%
40.1–44.0%
36.1–40.0%
32.1–36.0%
28.1–32.0%
24.1–28.0%
20.1–24.0%
16.1–20.0%
12.1–16.0%
8.1–12.0%
4.1–8.0%
0.0–4.0%

Find schools offering this major at PrincetonReview.com.

CAREER OPTIONS

Anthropologist

Antiques Dealer

Archaeologist

Consultant

Diplomat/Attaché/Foreign Service Officer

Foreign Exchange Trader

Journalist

Lobbyist

Translator

EAST EUROPEAN STUDIES

Basics

East European studies is, as the name implies, a fairly broad course of study. Students who choose this major study Russian and often another Eastern European language (Azeri, Czech, Polish, Romanian, Serbo-Croatian, Uzbek, or Yiddish are just a few). This work is combined with the study of the literature, culture, art, politics, law, geography, history, and society of Eastern Europe.

That's a lot to grasp. However, the time has never been better to consider this major as a course of study. Since the fall of the Berlin Wall and the splitting and reorganization of the Soviet Union, Eastern Europe has been in a constant state of change. In the past ten years, many Westerners have come to know this part of the world for the first time. Political analysts, language specialists, historians, journalists, and translators with a working knowledge of Eastern Europe may find themselves in great demand in the coming years.

If You Like East European Studies, You May Also Like . . .

African studies, ancient studies, anthropology, comparative literature, East Asian studies, great books, international business, international relations, international studies, Islamic studies, Jewish studies, Latin American studies, Medieval and Renaissance studies, Middle Eastern studies, Russian, Slavic languages and literatures, South Asian studies, Southeast Asian studies

Suggested High School Prep for East European Studies

If you can take Russian or Polish (or by some chance, Czech, Serbo-Croatian, Uzbek, or Yiddish) at your school, do it. If these languages are not offered, start getting your experience in another foreign language. Classes in European history and world literature will be useful.

SAMPLE COLLEGE CURRICULUM FOR EAST EUROPEAN STUDIES

Czech I–II

Eastern European Political Culture

History of Poland

Russian I–IV

Russian Modernist Theater

Socialist Economies in Transition

Survey of Russian Literature

Twentieth-Century Eastern Europe

World War I

Fun Facts

The Spooky Side

Learn a little more about Eastern Europe and one of its most famous residents—Prince Vlad, otherwise known as Dracula at en.wikipedia.org/wiki/Dracula.

Careers and Salary

The starting salary for an Eastern European studies major fresh out of college ranges from $24,000 to $30,000.

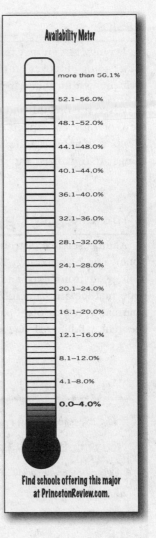

Availability Meter

more than 56.1%

52.1–56.0%

48.1–52.0%

44.1–48.0%

40.1–44.0%

36.1–40.0%

32.1–36.0%

28.1–32.0%

24.1–28.0%

20.1–24.0%

16.1–20.0%

12.1–16.0%

8.1–12.0%

4.1–8.0%

0.0–4.0%

Find schools offering this major at PrincetonReview.com.

CAREER OPTIONS

Anthropologist

Consultant

Diplomat/Attaché/Foreign Service Officer

Foreign Exchange Trader

Lobbyist

Political Aide

Professor

Translator

ECOLOGY

Basics

Ecology, as you may have already guessed, is a science closely related to biology, psychology, and chemistry. Ecology focuses on the relationships between individual living things, like humans, and the chemical elements within their environment. You could call it a holistic approach to understanding nature.

Given the breadth and scope of ecology it's often necessary to break it down into smaller categories that focus on different aspects of this relationship. For example, there's population ecology, which studies the distribution of animals and plants; community ecology, which studies the ways in which communities of living things are organized and relate to one another; and paleoecology, which studies the ecology of fossils.

If You Like Ecology, You May Also Like . . .

Animal science, astronomy, astrophysics, atmospheric science, biochemistry, biology, biopsychology, botany and plant biology, business administration and management, cell biology, dietetics, economics, entomology, environmental and environmental health science, forestry, genetics, geology, horticulture, marine science, mathematics, microbiology, molecular genetics, neurobiology, neuroscience, nutrition, pharmacology, pharmacy, physics, plant pathology, public health, soil science, statistics, surveying, sustainable resource management, wildlife management, zoology

Suggested High School Prep for Ecology

If you're interested in majoring in ecology it's important to have a strong background in the sciences—particularly physics, chemistry, and biology—as well as strong written and oral communications skills.

SAMPLE COLLEGE CURRICULUM FOR ECOLOGY

Analytical Geometry and Calculus

Animal Ecology

Aquatic Ecosystems

Birds

Environmental Physiology

Evolutionary Biology

Fish and Amphibians

General Physics I–II

Genetics

Organic Chemistry

Plant Ecology

Principles of Chemistry I–II

Reptiles and Mammals

Terrestrial Ecosystems

Fun Facts

Did You Know?

Ecology evolved from the natural history of the Greeks, particularly Theophrastus, a friend of Aristotle, who was the first to describe the interrelationships between organisms and other organisms, and organisms and their nonliving environment.

Distress Signals

New research from the Max Planck Institute for Chemical Ecology in Jena, Germany, has shown that plants emit a chemical cry for help when being attacked by bugs.

Careers and Salary

The starting salary for an ecologist usually ranges from $23,000 to $30,000 a year, depending upon the field and the level of education.

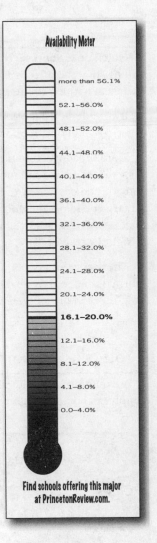

Availability Meter

more than 56.1%

52.1–56.0%

48.1–52.0%

44.1–48.0%

40.1–44.0%

36.1–40.0%

32.1–36.0%

28.1–32.0%

24.1–28.0%

20.1–24.0%

16.1–20.0%

12.1–16.0%

8.1–12.0%

4.1–8.0%

0.0–4.0%

Find schools offering this major at PrincetonReview.com.

CAREER OPTIONS

| Ecologist | Environmentalist/ Environmental Scientist | Park Ranger |

ECONOMICS

Basics

Quick quiz: Suppose several producers of your favorite product suddenly go out of business, causing a serious shortage of your favorite product. Nonetheless, everyone still wants to buy the same amount of it. What will happen to the price of your favorite product?

If you predicted a price increase, you may have a knack for economics: the study of the production, distribution, and consumption of goods and services.

More broadly, economics is the study of how individuals, businesses, governments, and societies choose to spend their time and money and otherwise allocate their resources. Even more broadly, economics is the study of choices. When the federal government decides to allocate a certain part of the national budget to military spending and another part to funding for the arts, that decision and its consequences are part of what economists study. Similarly, when you decide to buy a CD instead of a fancy new shirt (or watch Nick at Night instead of MTV or take the bus instead of your car), that's economics too.

Knowledge of economics is an invaluable component of any liberal arts education, not to mention an indispensable tool for making sense of the intricacies of the modern world. It is also excellent preparation for a future in business, as well as for graduate studies in law, public policy, and international studies.

If You Like Economics, You May Also Like . . .

Accounting, agricultural economics, applied mathematics, business administration and management, computer and information science, entrepreneurship, history, international business, international relations, political science, public policy analysis, statistics

SAMPLE COLLEGE CURRICULUM FOR ECONOMICS

Accounting

Calculus

Economic History of the United States

Economics

Intermediate Macroeconomics

Intermediate Microeconomics

International Business

Labor Economics

Money and Banking

Principles of Macroeconomics

Principles of Microeconomics

Statistics

Wage and Price Theory

Suggested High School Prep for Economics

Economics involves lots of critical thinking and at times, heavy doses of math. Try to get as many advanced math courses under your belt as possible while you are still in high school. Experience with computers is good too, as is any introduction you can get to formal logic. Obviously, if your high school offers economics as an elective, you should take it.

Fun Facts

Give Me a One-Handed Economist!

"All my economists say, 'On one hand . . . on the other.'"

—President Harry Truman

A Joke

A mathematician, an accountant, and an economist apply for the same job. The interviewer calls in the mathematician and asks, "What does two plus two equal?" The mathematician replies, "Four." The interviewer asks, "Four, exactly?" The mathematician looks at the interviewer incredulously and says, "Yes, four, exactly." Then the interviewer calls in the accountant and asks the same question. "What does two plus two equal?" The accountant says, "On average, four—give or take 10 percent." Then the interviewer calls in the economist and poses the same question. "What does two plus two equal?" The economist gets up, locks the door, closes the shade, sits down next to the interviewer, and says, "What do you want it to equal?"

Famous People Who Majored in Economics

Ronald Reagan (United States president, Eureka College), Ted Turner (media magnate, Brown University), Scott Adams (creator of Dilbert, Hartwick College), John Elway (NFL quarterback, Stanford University), Sandra Day O'Connor (former United States Supreme Court justice, University of California—Berkeley), Jane Pauley (television journalist, Indiana University)

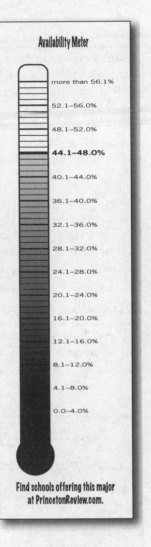

Availability Meter

more than 56.1%

52.1–56.0%

48.1–52.0%

44.1–48.0%

40.1–44.0%

36.1–40.0%

32.1–36.0%

28.1–32.0%

24.1–28.0%

20.1–24.0%

16.1–20.0%

12.1–16.0%

8.1–12.0%

4.1–8.0%

0.0–4.0%

Find schools offering this major at PrincetonReview.com.

Careers and Salary

The starting salary for an economics major fresh out of college ranges from $35,000 to $50,000.

CAREER OPTIONS

Accountant/Auditor

Actuary

Attorney

Bank Officer

Bookkeeper

Buyer

Corporate Lawyer

Diplomat/Attaché/Foreign Service Officer

Economist

Insurance Agent/Broker

Investment Banker

Labor Relations Specialist

Management Consultant

Market Researcher

Marketing Executive

Researcher

Small Business Owner

Statistician

Stockbroker

Trader

Venture Capitalist/Investor

EDUCATION

Basics

As an education major you'll learn the skills you need to become an effective and inspirational teacher—someone who has the ability to influence young children and teenagers in life-changing ways. A teacher's job is all-important in our increasingly fast-paced society because the knowledge each student needs is constantly evolving. For example, while just a decade ago they were more of an exception than the rule, computers are very much a part of today's classroom. At a time when schools are being blamed for poor test scores and problem children, good teachers are needed more than ever. If you are creative, dedicated, enthusiastic, and compassionate, schools need you.

Although much of your coursework will be general education material, most states require you to choose a specific grade level you'd like to teach. Choices usually include some variation of early childhood education (pre-school), primary education (kindergarten through eighth grade), secondary education (ninth through twelfth grade), and special education. Your student teaching experience, in which you spend a semester or more in a sponsoring classroom, will be in the field of your choice.

If You Like Education, You May Also Like . . .

Agricultural education, art education, child care, child development, developmental psychology, education administration, education of the deaf, educational psychology, physical education, teacher education, teaching English as a second language

Suggested High School Prep for Education

You're doing it! By being in school for twelve years you've already seen the nuts and bolts of how things work. Consider discussing education with your teachers to get their perspectives and learn from their experiences. And because teachers need knowledge in such a variety of fields, make sure your class schedule is rounded out with plenty of math, English, and science courses.

SAMPLE COLLEGE CURRICULUM FOR EDUCATION

Basic Media Skills

Counseling

Courses in specific subject areas such as math, science, reading, and English

Curriculum Studies

Education and American Culture

Educational Psychology

History of Modern Education

Instructional Systems Technology

Methods of Teaching

Special Education

Student Teaching for a semester in an elementary or secondary school

Teaching in a Pluralistic Society

Fun Facts

Words of Wisdom

"It takes a village to raise a child."

—African proverb

Good News

According to an article in the April 23, 2001 issue of *Newsweek*, we're getting smarter. Intelligence test scores have risen steadily and significantly over the years. In the United States, for example, scores have risen 24 points since 1918—a rise so large that what used to be considered a genius score is now pretty common. The scores have puzzled psychologists, who at one time believed that IQ was gene-related and not influenced by environment. Now, however, researchers are beginning to believe that both genes and environment can shape IQ, a theory known as the Flynn effect. Library, anyone?

(Source: "Are We Getting Smarter?" by Sharon Begley)

Careers and Salary

Teachers' salaries depend mainly on the school's locations and whether they are private or public. Generally, public school teachers with master's degrees receive about $30,000 to $40,000.

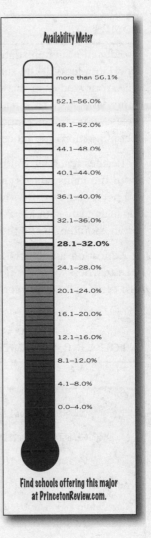

Availability Meter

more than 56.1%

52.1–56.0%

48.1–52.0%

44.1–48.0%

40.1–44.0%

36.1–40.0%

32.1–36.0%

28.1–32.0%

24.1–28.0%

20.1–24.0%

16.1–20.0%

12.1–16.0%

8.1–12.0%

4.1–8.0%

0.0–4.0%

Find schools offering this major at PrincetonReview.com.

CAREER OPTIONS

College Administrator	Professor	Teacher
Guidance Counselor		

EDUCATION ADMINISTRATION

Basics

Education administrators usually serve in educational management positions, mostly as principals or superintendents. To be successful as an administrator, you must have great communication and leadership skills. Your studies in this major will expose you to the fundamentals of management, and you'll learn how to mobilize resources, supervise personnel, and handle school finance and law. You'll learn the basics of organizational change, and you'll study international perspectives on education. Computer applications are becoming more and more important to schools, and this major will expose you to many of them.

Besides teaching you how to be a good leader, a major in education administration will also teach you about the many factors that impact education—factors such as economics and politics. You'll share ideas and perspectives with other administrators to expand your conceptions of education. If you're considering this major, you should have a strong desire to serve and an even stronger vision of what the future of education should be—and the practical ideas to help take it there.

Education administration programs are generally offered as master's programs, where students have been teachers for some period of time and need administrative degrees to move further in their careers or turn them in a new direction.

If You Like Education Administration, You May Also Like . . .

Business administration and management, child care, child development, education, education of the deaf, educational psychology, elementary education, health administration, human resources management, public administration, teacher education

SAMPLE COLLEGE CURRICULUM FOR EDUCATION ADMINISTRATION

Administration of School Personnel

Curriculum and Instruction in Learning Centered Schools

Diversity and Governance in Learner-Centered Schools

Educational Facility Planning

Futuristic Leadership Roles in School Administration

Legal Aspects of Education

Organizational Development in School Settings

Principalship in Elementary and Secondary Schools

Problems of Educational Finance

School-Community Relations

Suggested High School Prep for Education Administration

Communication skills are vital to any administration major, so make an effort to take classes in English, languages, writing, and the rest of the humanities. Take speech. Computer skills are also important, so take computer science classes if they're offered in your school. As an administrator, you're responsible for the bottom line, so take as much math as you can. And learn how to type.

Fun Facts

Murphy's Law for School Administrators

- Your friends come and go, but your enemies accumulate.
- Never fight with anyone who buys ink by the barrel.
- If you think you are wrong . . . you're right.
- If you think you are right . . . you're wrong.
- The grass is brown on both sides of the fence.
- In education, the shortest distance between two points is a downward spiral.
- Every cow is sacred to its mother.
- When you stand in the middle of the road, you get hit by traffic going in both directions.
- Doing things the right way isn't necessarily the right way.
- You can't lead from behind.

A Little Education Administration Humor

Early one morning, a mother went in to wake up her son.

"Wake up, son. It's time to go to school!"

"But why, Mom? I don't want to go."

"Give me two reasons why you don't want to go."

"Well, the kids hate me for one, and the teachers hate me too!"

"Oh, that's no reason not to go to school. Come on now and get ready."

"Give me two reasons why I should go to school."

"Well, for one, you're 52 years old. And for another, you're the principal!"

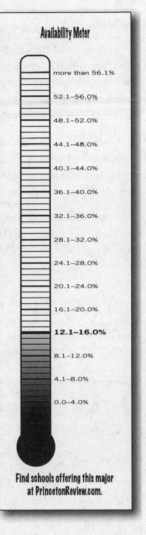

Availability Meter

more than 56.1%

52.1–56.0%

48.1–52.0%

44.1–48.0%

40.1–44.0%

36.1–40.0%

32.1–36.0%

28.1–32.0%

24.1–28.0%

20.1–24.0%

16.1–20.0%

12.1–16.0%

8.1–12.0%

4.1–8.0%

0.0–4.0%

Find schools offering this major at PrincetonReview.com.

Careers and Salary

Education administrators' salaries range from $28,000 to $35,000, although they are greatly influenced by where you live and in what capacity you use your degree.

CAREER OPTIONS

Benefits Administrator	Hospital Administrator	Politician
College Administrator	Human Resources Manager	Public Health Administrator
Consultant	Performing Arts Administrator	School Administrator
Guidance Counselor		

EDUCATION OF THE DEAF

Basics

Education of the deaf combines the fields of education, language instruction, speech development, communication disorders, and psychology. As an education of the deaf major, you'll learn the basics of education—classroom management, education psychology, and others—while adapting these basics to accommodate the hearing impaired students you'll eventually be teaching. You'll develop curriculum for mathematics, English, and other subject areas while learning how you'll teach these fields to deaf students.

Your studies in education of the deaf will include American Sign Language, and you'll learn the basics of speech development, language development, and the fundamentals of hearing. You'll study the cultural, social, and psychological implications of deafness. You'll learn how to work with deaf students and their families. You'll use your communication and people-skills in brand new ways.

Many colleges require students to major in traditional education and become certified to teach the deaf by taking extra courses. These extra courses may or may not extend your degree; be sure to inquire about the requirements when you begin searching for schools.

If You Like Education of the Deaf, You May Also Like . . .

Child development, communication disorders, counseling, education, education administration, educational psychology, physical education, rehabilatation services, special education, speech pathology, teacher education

SAMPLE COLLEGE CURRICULUM FOR EDUCATION OF THE DEAF

American Deaf Culture

American Sign Language

Audiology

Classroom Behavior and Management

Curriculum and Instruction for the Deaf

Educational Psychology

Equality, Exceptionality, and Excellence

Fundamentals of Hearing

Human Relations in Education

Language Development

Phonetic Theory and Transcription

Psychosocial Aspects of Deafness

Speech Acoustics

Speech Development

Suggested High School Prep for Education of the Deaf

Being serious about your own education will give you a good preparation for a major in education of the deaf. English and other humanities courses will be a good foundation, as will anything your high school offers in communication. If your school offers them, take sign language courses. Some high schools have clubs or programs that will teach you sign language and have you work with the deaf in your community—being involved in something along these lines will be invaluable. Experience with teaching and tutoring peers or younger students will give you a taste of what teaching's about too.

Fun Facts

Celebrating the Deaf

Get out your calendars . . . and pencil in Deaf Awareness Week, which is always the last full week of September. Also known as the International Week of the Deaf, this time is used to focus on the advancements of deaf people and educate the public on various issues of the hearing impaired. If this is an area that interests you, check out what your local establishments are doing to mark the week.

Did You Know?

American Sign Language was first developed around 1817, after the first American school for the deaf opened in Connecticut. American Sign Language was adapted from the French system of signing by Thomas Gallaudet and Laurent Clerc.

Careers and Salary

The average starting salary for teachers ranges from $26,000 to $38,000, but this can vary depending on the type of school in which they choose to work (if they choose a school at all), in what capacity they use their degrees, and how much experience they've had.

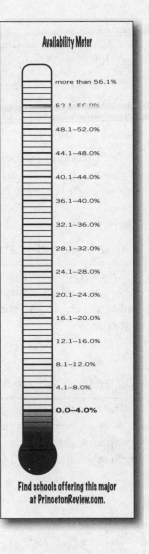

Availability Meter

more than 56.1%

52.1–56.0%

48.1–52.0%

44.1–48.0%

40.1–44.0%

36.1–40.0%

32.1–36.0%

28.1–32.0%

24.1–28.0%

20.1–24.0%

16.1–20.0%

12.1–16.0%

8.1–12.0%

4.1–8.0%

0.0–4.0%

Find schools offering this major at PrincetonReview.com.

CAREER OPTIONS

Professor	Teacher	Translator
Speech Therapist		

EDUCATIONAL PSYCHOLOGY

Basics

At the heart of the educational psychology major are the whys and hows of human learning.

Education doesn't occur in a vacuum. We learn in classrooms, office environments, parks and museums. However, how we learn—under what conditions, under what circumstances—is the mystery, the research, and the major. It's much more complicated than this, though; there is a whole batch of other issues and questions that surround the educational psychology major and the learning process in general.

The practical applications of an educational psychology major are numerous, especially with today's great focus on education. You can expect that your degree will be in high demand and that the research and the studies you perform have the potential of shaping how the next generation learns.

If You Like Educational Psychology, You May Also Like . . .

Art education, biopsychology, child development, clinical psychology, counseling, criminology, developmental psychology, education, education administration, education of the deaf, experimental psychology, human development, mental health services, physiological psychology, social psychology, technology education

Suggested High School Prep for Educational Psychology

The best preparation you can get for any psychology major is to have a solid background in the liberal arts, with a strong focus on math and science classes—particularly biology, chemistry, physics, and statistics. Having strong reading and writing skills will help you get through all of that research you'll be putting together. You'll also need to take psychology courses if your school offers them.

SAMPLE COLLEGE CURRICULUM FOR EDUCATIONAL PSYCHOLOGY

Adolescent Development

Applied Cognition and Learning

Human Sexuality

Individual Learning Skills

Introduction to Statistics

Problems in Educational Psychology

Psychological Foundations of Education

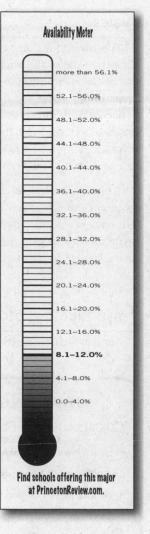

Availability Meter

more than 56.1%

52.1–56.0%

48.1–52.0%

44.1–48.0%

40.1–44.0%

36.1–40.0%

32.1–36.0%

28.1–32.0%

24.1–28.0%

20.1–24.0%

16.1–20.0%

12.1–16.0%

8.1–12.0%

4.1–8.0%

0.0–4.0%

Find schools offering this major
at PrincetonReview.com.

Fun Facts

Psychology Joke

One day a guy went to a psychologist for the first time. After telling him his troubles, the man says, "So doc, what's wrong with me?"

The doctor replies, "Well, you're crazy.

Indignant, the man replies, "I am not. I want another opinion."

To which the doctor replies, "Okay. You're also ugly."

Another Psychology Joke

A psychology PhD student, a postdoc, and their professor are walking through a city park, and they find an antique oil lamp. They rub it, and a genie comes out in a puff of smoke. The genie says, "I usually only grant three wishes, so I'll give each of you just one."

"Me first! Me first!" says the PhD student. "I want to be in the Bahamas, driving a speedboat with a gorgeous woman who sunbathes topless." Poof! He's gone.

"Me next! Me next!" says the postdoc. "I want to be in Hawaii, relaxing on the beach with a professional hula dancer on one side and a mai tai on the other." Poof! He's gone.

"You're next," the genie says to the professor.

The professor says, "I want those guys back in the lab after lunch."

Careers and Salary

The average starting salary for most psychology majors is between $25,000 and $35,000.

CAREER OPTIONS

Career Counselor	Guidance Counselor	Substance Abuse Counselor
Child Care Worker	Psychologist	Teacher
Criminologist	School Administrator	

EGYPTOLOGY

Basics

The mysterious and compelling culture of ancient Egypt has fascinated laypeople and scholars alike since the time of the ancient Greeks. If you wonder who built the pyramids and whether Queen Nefertiti was really as beautiful as her statue implies, then consider majoring in Egyptology, the study of ancient Egypt. In this major, you'll study all aspects of ancient Egypt, including language, culture, society, history and archaeology. To interpret original writings and inscriptions firsthand, you'll embark on a vigorous language program, studying the five distinct language phases encompassing Old Egyptian, Middle Egyptian, Late Egyptian, Demotic, and Coptic. Fluency in at least one of the following is necessary to read scholarly publications: Greek, Latin, French, or German.

Through extensive class instruction and your own reading of original texts, you'll learn a great deal about ancient Egyptians' political, social, religious, economic, legal, and medical histories. You'll also get a firm background in Egyptian art, architecture, and archaeology. You'll learn about the different periods of Egyptian art, and gain the skills to understand and interpret Egyptian artifacts. If you're lucky, you'll even have a chance to participate in an excavation at an Egyptian archaeological site.

If You Like Egyptology, You May Also Like . . .

Ancient studies, anthropology, archaeology, biblical studies, art history, classics, Hebrew, historic preservation, history, Islamic studies, linguistics, Medieval and Renaissance studies, Modern Greek

SAMPLE COLLEGE CURRICULUM FOR EGYPTOLOGY

Ancient Egyptian Art and Architecture

Ancient Egyptian Literature

Ancient Egyptian Religion and Magic

Archaeology of Ancient Egypt I, II

History of Egypt I: The History and Society of Ancient Egypt

History of Egypt II: The New Kingdom

History of Egypt III: Libyans, Nubians, and Persians in Egypt

Introduction to Coptic

Introduction to Demotic

Introduction to Late Egyptian

Introduction to Old Egyptian History of Egypt IV: The Age of Cleopatra

Selection from Middle Egyptian Hieroglyphic Texts

Suggested High School Prep for Egyptology

Take all the history and art history classes your school offers. Take three or four years of French, and consider taking German or Latin as well. These languages will come in handy when reading scholarly publications, since they won't all be in English.

Fun Facts

Deciphering Hieroglyphics

Hieroglyphics, the Egyptian pictorial language dating back to 3,000 B.C./B.C.E., remained unreadable for hundreds of years after its rediscovery. For many years, scholars assumed that each picture (e.g. a bird, sun, or man) represented a whole idea. Then, in 1799, the Rosetta Stone, the most famous archaeological discovery of all time, was unearthed by French scholars working for Napoleon. This slab contained the same text written in three scripts: hieroglyphics, Demotic, and Greek. A few small breakthroughs were made following the discovery, but it wasn't until 20-odd years later that a young prodigy and Egyptologist, Jean-Francois Champollion (who had been made a professor at the French Academy of Grenoble at age 17) finally cracked the code. Champollion, who had learned 13-plus languages including Syrian, Ethiopic, Arabic, and Chinese to prepare for the task of tackling hieroglyphics, discovered that the language was, in fact, a phonetic one (each character represented a sound), and using his knowledge of Coptic, was able to successfully assign sound values for each picture. For the first time in 14 centuries, the history of the pharaohs could again be understood.

(Source: *The Code Book*, by Simon Singh, Anchor Books, 2000)

Careers and Salary

An Egyptology major will most likely need to attend graduate school to work in this field. As a liberal arts graduate with only a bachelor's degree, you can expect to find a job making about $25,000 to $30,000 a year.

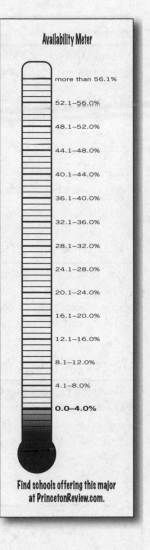

Availability Meter

more than 56.1%

52.1–56.0%

48.1–52.0%

44.1–48.0%

40.1–44.0%

36.1–40.0%

32.1–36.0%

28.1–32.0%

24.1–28.0%

20.1–24.0%

16.1–20.0%

12.1–16.0%

8.1–12.0%

4.1–8.0%

0.0–4.0%

Find schools offering this major at PrincetonReview.com.

CAREER OPTIONS

Archaeologist	Curator	Historian
Art Dealer	Egyptologist	Professor
Consultant		

ELECTRICAL ENGINEERING

Basics

Think *MacGyver* here: Is it the red or yellow wire that deactivates the bomb? Does the answer seem obvious to you? Perhaps you're an electrical engineer in the rough.

Electrical engineers design, develop, and test electrical equipment. They figure out ways to generate and control electrical energy. Electrical engineers work with every kind of device imaginable, from computers to clock radios to global positioning devices. They also really know the difference between amperage (strength), voltage (force), and wattage (power) of a current, and can toss off these terms and others with ease.

A major in electrical engineering requires extensive work in math and science. You can expect to take several classes in physics and calculus before moving into the more detailed study of electrical systems.

If You Like Electrical Engineering, You May Also Like . . .

Aerospace engineering, applied mathematics, applied physics, computer and information science, computer engineering, computer systems analysis, engineering design, engineering mechanics, mechanical engineering, nuclear engineering

Suggested High School Prep for Electrical Engineering

Electrical engineering is a math- and science-heavy field. Take physics and as many advanced math classes as you can. Additional experience in programming languages is very helpful but certainly not required. And be sure to watch a lot of *MacGyver* reruns.

SAMPLE COLLEGE CURRICULUM FOR ELECTRICAL ENGINEERING

Calculus I–III

Circuit Theory

Electromagnetics

Electronics I–II

Foundations of Electrical Engineering

General Chemistry

Physics I–II

Signals and Systems

Fun Facts

Engineering Humor

A mechanical engineer, an electrical engineer, and a computer engineer were riding down the street in a car. Suddenly, the car made a loud popping noise and ground to a halt.

"Something's broken," said the mechanical engineer. "Maybe a rod."

"No, no," the electrical engineer assured his friends. "Did you hear that noise? Clearly there is a problem with the electrical system."

The two turned to the computer engineer, who just shrugged. "Well," said the computer engineer, "I suggest we just all get out, then get back in and start the car up again."

Famous People Who Majored in Electrical Engineering

Herbie Hancock (musician, Grinnell College)

Careers and Salary

The starting salary for an electrical engineering major fresh out of college is about $50,000.

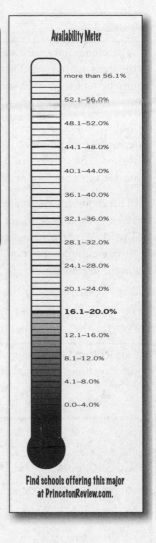

Availability Meter

more than 56.1%

52.1–56.0%

48.1–52.0%

44.1–48.0%

40.1–44.0%

36.1–40.0%

32.1–36.0%

28.1–32.0%

24.1–28.0%

20.1–24.0%

16.1–20.0%

12.1–16.0%

8.1–12.0%

4.1–8.0%

0.0–4.0%

Find schools offering this major
at PrincetonReview.com.

CAREER OPTIONS

Aerospace Engineer	Coast Guard (Officer)	Network Engineer
Air Force National Guard	Electrical Engineer	Power Plant Manager
Army National Guard	Electrician	Quality Assurance Engineer
Army (Officer)	Marines (Officer)	Technician
Avionics Technician	Navy (Officer)	

ELEMENTARY EDUCATION

Basics

The elementary education major learns how to preside over what is essentially a one-room schoolhouse. In the early grades, teachers are responsible for giving instruction in all the basic subjects (reading, writing, 'rithmetic—plus science, social studies, and the basics of health and physical education), as well as overseeing the general development of each of their charges. It's a challenging and very rewarding field.

Some programs offer (or require) an area of specialization, such as early childhood, language arts, mathematics, or middle school instruction. When the academic work is complete, elementary education majors move into the classroom for the trial by fire known as student teaching. This practicum lasts at least one semester but could go on for a full academic year.

The requirements for teacher certification vary from state to state. Check with the education department of your college to see if its requirements meet the standards of the state in which you want to reside and work. When you successfully complete the elementary education program, you have to take any certification examinations required by the state in which you want to work. Again, your school should help you make these transitions.

If You Like Elementary Education, You May Also Like . . .

Agricultural education, art education, education, education administration, education of the deaf, educational psychology, special education, teacher education, technology education

---

SAMPLE COLLEGE CURRICULUM FOR ELEMENTARY EDUCATION

Child Growth and Development

Children's Literature

Classroom Management

Curriculum Planning

Educational Psychology

Foundations of Education

Methods of Teaching Mathematics

Methods of Teaching Reading

Methods of Teaching Science

Methods of Teaching Social Studies

Student Teaching

Technology for Teachers

Suggested High School Prep for Elementary Education

A firm background in English, math, and science is required for all education majors. If your school offers classes in psychology or sign language, try to take them too.

Fun Facts

Quotable

"There is divine beauty in learning, just as there is human beauty in tolerance. To learn means to accept the postulate that life did not begin at my birth. Others have been here before me, and I walk in their footsteps. The books I have read were composed by generations of fathers and sons, mothers and daughters, teachers and disciples. I am the sum total of their experiences, their quests. And so are you."

—Elie Wiesel

For More Information . . .

Check out *The New York Times* learning network (www.nytimes.com/learning). You'll find lesson plans, summaries of current events, and sample handouts.

Careers and Salary

Salaries usually depend on the area in which teachers work. An elementary education major could make from $26,000 to $35,000 a year to start, depending on location.

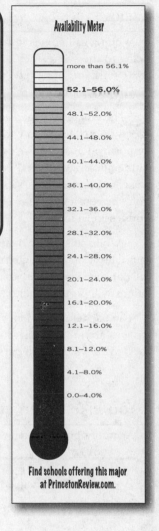

Availability Meter

more than 56.1%

52.1–56.0%

48.1–52.0%

44.1–48.0%

40.1–44.0%

36.1–40.0%

32.1–36.0%

28.1–32.0%

24.1–28.0%

20.1–24.0%

16.1–20.0%

12.1–16.0%

8.1–12.0%

4.1–8.0%

0.0–4.0%

Find schools offering this major at PrincetonReview.com.

CAREER OPTIONS

Librarian	School Administrator	Teacher
Professor		

EMERGENCY MEDICAL TECHNOLOGY

Basics

When a call comes in to 911, emergency medical technicians (EMTs) are often the first to know. After racing to the scene, they have to make a series of split-second decisions: What's the problem? Who needs help? What sort of help do they need? What medicines or procedures should be administered immediately? What must not be done?

The emergency medical technology major will prepare you to answer these questions swiftly and confidently. You'll learn how to evacuate and transport injured persons, select medicines, and provide basic life support (open airways, stop bleeding, and get hearts pumping again). You'll become an expert at working with emergency medical equipment—sirens and flashing lights, yes, but also extrication vests, petrolatum gauze, pulse oximeters, stethoscopes, syringes, catheters, tourniquets, defibrillators, and more. This training won't be restricted to the classroom; many programs ensure that you will get on-the-job experience through a professional internship.

While this major demands enrollment in a spectrum of specialized courses, you should also expect your education to extend into the liberal arts and sciences. A basic understanding of biology and chemistry will enhance your ability to make sound and well-reasoned decisions. A background in ethics and communications will prepare you to interact with victims, witnesses, and colleagues, often in high-pressure situations.

The Bachelor of Science in emergency medical technology offers the solid training emergency medical services are looking for. (Some schools also offer a two-year associate's degree in paramedics.) It's worth noting you will need to pass a state certification exam before finally making it onto the payroll.

If You Like Emergency Medical Technology, You May Also Like...

Anatomy, biology, community health and preventative medicine, medical technology, nursing, pharmacology, physician assistant, pre-medicine, rehabilitation services, respiratory therapy

SAMPLE COLLEGE CURRICULUM FOR EMERGENCY MEDICAL TECHNOLOGY

Aeromedical Emergency Services

Cardiac Care

Emergency Medical Services Internship

EMT Basic

EMT Rescue

Ethics and Medicine

Introduction to Emergency Medicine

Pre-hospital Pharmacology

Trauma Management

Wilderness Survival

Suggested High School Prep for Emergency Medical Technology

Let's begin with the obvious: A strong, broad understanding of math and science will give you a definite edge. If possible, takes honors and AP courses. You should also enroll in humanities courses (English, history, etc.), because these will force you to sharpen your communications skills and improve your ability to assess situations analytically. Electives in speech communications, psychology, and ethics will also be a help.

Fun Facts

A Bright Future

The Bureau of Labor Statistics predicts that job opportunities in the EMT field will be plentiful through, at the very least, 2014. The majority of these jobs will be in metropolitan areas as rural EMS services tend to be staffed by volunteer workers.

Beat it!

You're watching a movie. There's a scene in an ambulance. The victim is unconscious. The EMTs are working feverishly. They grab a pair of handheld paddles and press them against the victim's chest. His body leaps and suddenly the monitor on the wall shows that the victim's heartbeat has returned.

The equipment the EMTs are using is called a defibrillator. In essence, a defibrillator is a device that sends a targeted electrical shock right through the chest and into the non-beating heart. Ideally, the defibrillator will cause the heart's muscles to contract, thus jumpstarting the body's blood flow.

(Source: http://columbia.thefreedictionary.com/defibrillator)

Careers and Salary

Depending on location and employer, an EMT's starting salary will range between $19,000 and $30,000.

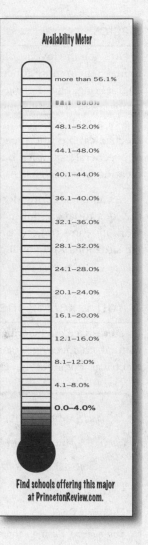

Availability Meter

more than 56.1%

52.1–56.0%

48.1–52.0%

44.1–48.0%

40.1–44.0%

36.1–40.0%

32.1–36.0%

28.1–32.0%

24.1–28.0%

20.1–24.0%

16.1–20.0%

12.1–16.0%

8.1–12.0%

4.1–8.0%

0.0–4.0%

Find schools offering this major
at PrincetonReview.com.

CAREER OPTIONS

Emergency Medical Technician	Paramedic	Researcher
Emergency Medical Service Director	Physician Assistant	Teacher

ENGINEERING DESIGN

Basics

Are you the inventor in your group of friends? Do you constantly modify or improve things in your house to make them more functional? Then consider a major in engineering design. Part of the field of mechanical engineering, engineering design is a major that requires its students to constantly exercise their practical problem-solving skills and creativity. Wonder about the best way to protect an egg that's thrown from the top of a building? You might be required to design a device that will preserve it. Have a bag of random mechanical bits and pieces? You might be given a time limit in which to create a robotic device. These are only general examples, but you get the picture—you'll apply the principles of engineering to the process of creating new designs.

As an engineering design major, you'll be involved in all aspects of product development, from forming the idea to laying out its specifications to fabricating it to testing the finished device. You'll learn how to work in teams to get a project together. You'll use your problem-solving and decision-making skills in real-life situations. And you'll get hands-on experience with the actual nuts and bolts of engineering.

If You Like Engineering Design, You May Also Like . . .

Aerospace engineering, agricultural and biological engineering, applied mathematics, applied physics, architectural engineering, ceramic engineering, chemical engineering, civil engineering, computer engineering, electrical engineering, engineering mechanics, environmental and environmental health engineering, geological engineering, industrial engineering, mechanical engineering, metallurgical engineering, mineral engineering, nuclear engineering, ocean engineering, petroleum engineering

SAMPLE COLLEGE CURRICULUM FOR ENGINEERING DESIGN

Electrical Circuits

Electronic Devices

Engineering Design Laboratory

Engineering Graphics and Programming

Kinematics

Materials Science

Math courses such as calculus and analytic geometry

Mechanical Design

Science courses such as chemistry and physics

Statics and Strength of Materials

Thermodynamics

Suggested High School Prep for Engineering Design

Courses in advanced math such as calculus, analytic geometry, and trigonometry will be great preparation for your major in engineering design. Science courses will be useful as well. And don't forget your English classes—good engineers must also be good communicators.

Fun Facts

Einstein on Engineering

"Scientists investigate that which already is; engineers create that which has never been."

Albert Einstein

A Few Famous People Who Have Engineering Backgrounds

- Scott Adams, creator of the cartoon strip *Dilbert*
- Alfred Hitchcock, film director
- Montel Williams, talk show host
- Leonardo da Vinci, artist
- Herbert Hoover, thirty-first president of the United States

Careers and Salary

The starting salary for most engineering majors is in the $44,000 to $50,000 range, although their experience, level of education, and area of concentration will influence their levels of income.

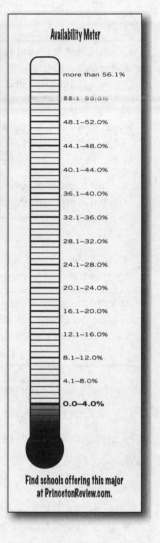

Availability Meter

more than 56.1%

52.1—56.0%

48.1—52.0%

44.1—48.0%

40.1—44.0%

36.1—40.0%

32.1—36.0%

28.1—32.0%

24.1—28.0%

20.1—24.0%

16.1—20.0%

12.1—16.0%

8.1—12.0%

4.1—8.0%

0.0—4.0%

Find schools offering this major at PrincetonReview.com.

CAREER OPTIONS

Aerospace Engineer	Avionics Technician	Quality Assurance Engineer
Architect	Civil Engineer	Robotics Engineer
Auto Mechanic	Navy (Officer)	

ENGINEERING MECHANICS

Basics

Linked closely to the field of civil engineering, engineering mechanics deals with the behavior of matter. If you major in it, you'll learn how matter reacts to stresses, strains, and thermal effects. You'll learn about resultants, equilibrium, and centers of gravity. You'll learn about the strength of materials, the mechanics of motion, statics, and dynamics. You'll study engineered structures to analyze their stability, design, and safety.

Since you'll use computers and applied mathematics on a daily basis, much of your studies will consist of mathematics courses—eventually you'll be using this knowledge to predict matter's response to forces, show the behavior of matter mathematically, and perform other such tricks of the trade.

As with most engineering majors, you'll have laboratory work to supplement your coursework, and you may have the opportunity to participate in a cooperative education program. This is a great way to get valuable hands-on experience in your field.

If You Like Engineering Mechanics, You May Also Like . . .

Aerospace engineering, agricultural and biological engineering, applied mathematics, applied physics, architectural engineering, ceramic engineering, chemical engineering, civil engineering, computer engineering, electrical engineering, engineering design, environmental and environmental health engineering, geological engineering, industrial engineering, mechanical engineering, metallurgical engineering, mineral engineering, nuclear engineering, ocean engineering, petroleum engineering

SAMPLE COLLEGE CURRICULUM FOR ENGINEERING MECHANICS

Analysis of Structures

Construction Engineering

Construction Engineering Design

Design of Steel Structures Civil
   Engineering Design

Dynamics

Finite Element Applications

Hydraulics

Mechanics of Deformable Solids

Soil Mechanics

Statics and Mechanics of Materials

Strength of Materials

Surveying

Thermodynamics

Dynamics

Suggested High School Prep for Engineering Mechanics

Advanced math courses such as calculus, analytic geometry, and trigonometry will be your best preparation for your engineering mechanics major. Computer courses will also give you a good head start. And don't forget your English classes—good engineers must also be good communicators.

Fun Facts

A Few Famous Engineers

- Alexander Graham Bell, inventor of the telephone
- Armand Bombardier, manufacturer of the first snowmobile
- Ray Dolby, audio system innovator
- Bonnie Dunbar, shuttle astronaut
- William Hewlett and Dave Packard, cofounders of Hewlett-Packard

(Source: www.asee.org)

Measurements

Engineering is full of measurements and standards, and the *Communications Standards Review* has a few humorous measurements of its own.

- Unit of beauty required to launch one ship: milli-Helen
- 2,000 pounds of Chinese soup: Won ton
- 1 millionth mouthwash: 1 microscope
- 1,000,000 aches: 1 megahurtz
- 1,000 grams of wet socks: 1 literhosen
- 8 nickels: 2 paradigms

Careers and Salary

The starting salary for most engineering majors ranges from $40,000 to $50,000. Their experience, levels of education, and capacity in which they use their degrees will all play a role in determining how much money they make.

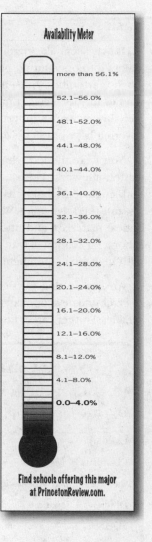

Availability Meter

| more than 56.1% |
| 52.1–56.0% |
| 48.1–52.0% |
| 44.1–48.0% |
| 40.1–44.0% |
| 36.1–40.0% |
| 32.1–36.0% |
| 28.1–32.0% |
| 24.1–28.0% |
| 20.1–24.0% |
| 16.1–20.0% |
| 12.1–16.0% |
| 8.1–12.0% |
| 4.1–8.0% |
| 0.0–4.0% |

Find schools offering this major at PrincetonReview.com.

CAREER OPTIONS

Aerospace Engineer	Demolition Expert	Quality Assurance Engineer
Architect	Navy (Officer)	Researcher
Civil Engineer	Professor	Robotics Engineer
Construction Manager		

ENGINEERING PHYSICS

Basics

It may seem like engineering physics is someone's idea of a cruel joke—combining two of the toughest majors into one. But no pain, no gain, my friend! Gains in this field come in the form of a wide blanket of job opportunities and—if you play your cards right—a pretty nice-looking starting salary. Engineering physics majors blend courses from engineering, physics, and math to build an understanding of how these areas interact and support one another. You'll boost your knowledge of the physical environment while discovering how physics is applied to problem solving in our rapidly changing high-tech world.

You were the kid who took first prize at the science fair? You secretly liked helping friends with their math homework? Perfect. As an engineering physics major, you'll study the fundamentals and intricacies of both engineering and physics, including electricity, magnetism, statics, strength of materials, thermodynamics, and fluid dynamics. Want more? Some programs include research in space science, superconductivity, optical materials, and nuclear engineering. You'll also take courses in calculus and differential equations. Laboratory work will teach you how to use experimental techniques and will give you hands-on experience with high-tech equipment.

An engineering physics major comes in handy for a range of job opportunities, including positions in research and development ("R&D") at high-technology industries as well as jobs in national laboratories and universities. Further career development may lead to a position as a staff engineer, scientist, or technical director.

SAMPLE COLLEGE CURRICULUM FOR ENGINEERING PHYSICS

Calculus

Chemistry of Materials

Circuits and Instrumentation

Differential Equations

Electricity and Magnetism

Engineering Graphics and Programming

Fields and Waves

Fluid Dynamics

Heat and Thermodynamics

Physical and Solid State Electronics

Physics

Solid State and Digital Electronics

Statics and Strength of Materials

Statistical Mechanics

Vector Analysis for Engineers

If You Like Engineering Physics, You May Also Like . . .

Aerospace engineering, applied mathematics, applied physics, chemical engineering, civil engineering, computer engineering, electrical engineering, engineering design, engineering mechanics, mechanical engineering, metallurgical engineering, nuclear engineering

Suggested High School Prep for Engineering Physics

If you're thinking of majoring in engineering physics, you'd better like science—because you'll need to take a lot of it in high school to prepare for your college studies. Take courses in physics, chemistry, biology, calculus, and any other math and science courses you can, and take advanced-level classes if they're offered. Scientists must also be good communicators, so be sure to take English, language, and other humanities courses that will help you strengthen your reading, writing, and speaking skills.

Fun Facts

Certainly Not You

"Very strange people, physicists—in my experience the ones who aren't dead are in some way very ill."

—Mr. Standish in *The Long Dark Tea-Time of the Soul* by Douglas Adams

(Source: www.xs4all.nl/~jcdverha/scijokes/2_2.html)

Who Invited the Engineer?

"It is not uncommon for engineers to accept the reality of phenomena that are not yet understood, as it is very common for physicists to disbelieve the reality of phenomena that seem to contradict contemporary beliefs of physics."

—H. Bauer

(Source: www.xs4all.nl/~jcdverha/scijokes/2_2.html)

"It would be a poor thing to be an atom in a universe without physicists, and physicists are made of atoms. A physicist is an atom's way of knowing about atoms."

—George Wald, biochemist

(Source: www.bartleby.com)

Careers and Salary

Engineering physics majors generally earn about $40,000 to $50,000 to start. The amount of experience you've had, where you live, and the type of company you work for will all have an effect on this number.

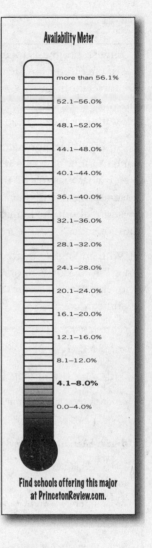

Availability Meter

more than 56.1%

52.1–56.0%

48.1–52.0%

44.1–48.0%

40.1–44.0%

36.1–40.0%

32.1–36.0%

28.1–32.0%

24.1–28.0%

20.1–24.0%

16.1–20.0%

12.1–16.0%

8.1–12.0%

4.1–8.0%

0.0–4.0%

Find schools offering this major at PrincetonReview.com.

CAREER OPTIONS		
Engineer	Researcher	Teacher
Professor		

ENGLISH

Basics

English programs focus on literature, language, and writing, and an English major provides the opportunity to encounter a wide array of absorbing works of fiction, poetry, and nonfiction from around the world and throughout history. A few years of analyzing the works of the greatest minds and imaginations that human civilization has produced will assuredly sharpen your critical, emotional, creative, and moral faculties. With any luck, a little greatness may rub off on you as well.

An English major accords the unique opportunity to engage with different societies, different eras, and come to think of it, different societies from different eras. It enables you to share the experiences of others, to feel what was felt by people in earlier eras, distant lands, entirely other patterns of life, and to juxtapose those feelings with your own. The study of literature also beautifully and powerfully conveys the enduring questions about the human condition, and—if you look especially hard—sheds light on the answers to those questions.

With an English degree, you can certainly become a starving author. Or you can become an affluent one. Just ask Toni Morrison or Amy Tan. You can also become a legendary football coach like Joe Paterno or a governor like Mario Cuomo. These and many other people used a degree in English as a springboard to a successful career.

A working knowledge of literature is an invaluable component of any liberal arts education. It is tremendous preparation for a future in law (or any professional training that requires interpreting written material), journalism, publishing, graduate studies, and just about anything else.

> ### SAMPLE COLLEGE CURRICULUM FOR ENGLISH
>
> American Literature Since 1865
>
> Ancient Literature
>
> British Literature: Medieval through 1800
>
> British Literature: 1800 to Present
>
> Contemporary World Literature
>
> Creative Writing
>
> Early American Literature
>
> Electives devoted to specific authors such as Chaucer, Shakespeare, Tolstoy, and Austen
>
> Electives devoted to specific books such as James Joyce's *Ulysses*
>
> Electives devoted to specific periods and genres such as the Harlem Renaissance and feminist theater
>
> Literary Criticism
>
> Medieval and Renaissance Literature
>
> Modern Drama

If You Like English, You May Also Like . . .

African American studies, art history, classics, creative writing, film, French, German, Hebrew, journalism, Latin American studies, radio and television, Slavic languages and literatures, technical writing, theology

Suggested High School Prep for English

As you might have guessed, English involves a ton of reading, and thinking and writing about what you have read. Take all the English and writing-intensive courses you can. Advanced Placement classes are especially good because you'll concentrate more on reading in those classes and (hopefully) less on things like spelling and grammar, which are more or less taken for granted by English professors in college. If your high school has a limited number of English courses available, don't worry. Just head over to the library. Getting immersed in the stacks is probably the best possible preparation for an English major anyway.

Fun Facts

The 2:00 A.M. Paper

"I am returning this otherwise good typing paper to you because someone has printed gibberish all over it and put your name at the top."

—anonymous English professor

The Ten Best English Language Novels of the Twentieth Century

(At least according to the Modern Library Association's distinguished Board of celebrated authors, historians, critics, and a scientist)

1. *Ulysses* by James Joyce
2. *The Great Gatsby* by F. Scott Fitzgerald
3. *A Portrait of the Artist as a Young Man* by James Joyce
4. *Lolita* by Vladimir Nabokov
5. *Brave New World* by Aldous Huxley
6. *The Sound and the Fury* by William Faulkner
7. *Catch-22* by Joseph Heller
8. *Darkness at Noon* by Arthur Koestler
9. *Sons and Lovers* by D. H. Lawrence
10. *The Grapes of Wrath* by John Steinbeck

Famous People Who Majored in English

David Duchovny (star of *The X-Files*, fighter of evil, Princeton University), Douglas Adams (author of *The Hitchhiker's Guide to the Galaxy* trilogy, Cambridge University), Christopher Reeve (*Superman*, Cornell University), Chris Isaak (rock star, University of the Pacific), Dave Barry (humorist, Haverford College), Joseph Heller (author of *Catch-22*, New York University), Arthur Miller (author of *Death of a Salesman*, University of Michigan), Allen Ginsburg (beat poet, Columbia University)

Availability Meter

more than 56.1%
52.1–56.0%
48.1–52.0%
44.1–48.0%
40.1–44.0%
36.1–40.0%
32.1–36.0%
28.1–32.0%
24.1–28.0%
20.1–24.0%
16.1–20.0%
12.1–16.0%
8.1–12.0%
4.1–8.0%
0.0–4.0%

Find schools offering this major at PrincetonReview.com.

Careers and Salary

The average starting salary for an English major fresh out of college ranges from $26,000 to about $33,000. It's worth noting, however, that averages are a bit misleading in this case because an English degree can lead to such an array of career paths.

CAREER OPTIONS

Actor	Book Publishing Professional	Television Producer
Advertising Executive	Corporate Lawyer	Television Reporter
Artist	Editor	Theologian
Attorney	Film Director	Trial Lawyer
Auctioneer	Public Relations Professional	Web Editor
Bar/Club Manager	Teacher	Writer

ENGLISH COMPOSITION

Basics

Normally located within a broader English major, composition specifically focuses on the construction of thoughts and ideas into written words. Composition is the way we write—the rules of grammar that we follow and the styles we use to express our thoughts effectively.

How do you construct an effective essay or story? What are some of the different tools you can employ in writing? What exactly is a dangling participle, and why are you not supposed to end your sentences with a preposition? These are just some of the principal questions you will encounter as you learn how to become an effective and thoughtful writer, able to express your deepest thoughts and ideas in language so finely honed that you'll be the envy of your old high school English teachers.

One of the best ways to learn how to write is by reading, and as with any English concentration, you will do plenty of that here. All of the classics, both old and contemporary, await you in the English composition major, from William Shakespeare to Virginia Woolf, Ernest Hemingway to T. S. Eliot. You will find in the books you read not only great works of composition but also some of the most significant artistic expressions dealing with everything from death to war to history.

If You Like English Composition, You May Also Like . . .

Advertising, African American studies, African studies, American history, American literature, American studies, ancient studies, Asian American studies, biblical studies, classics, comparative literature, creative writing, East Asian studies, East European studies, English, English literature, film, Islamic studies, Jewish studies, journalism, Medieval and Renaissance studies, Middle Eastern studies, teacher education

SAMPLE COLLEGE CURRICULUM FOR ENGLISH COMPOSITION

British Literature: Medieval through 1800

Colonial and U.S. Literature

Critical Writing

Introduction to Chaucer

Introduction to Poetry

Nineteenth-Century English Novel

Romantic Poetry and Poetics

Shakespeare

Studies in Critical Theory

Twentieth-Century U.S. Fiction

U.S. Literature: 1830–1865

Suggested High School Prep for English Composition

There are enough great books out there to make for a lifetime's worth of reading, so why not begin early and build upon the English classes you have already taken? In addition, writing is something you can always do, from your own creative short stories to writing for your high school newspaper. The opportunity to develop your compositional skills are widely available.

Fun Facts

Precision of Language

Henry Watson Fowler's *A Dictionary of Modern Usage*, first published in 1926, was the first in what has become a long series of modern usage dictionaries outlining the rules of language.

William Safire's Rules for Writers

- Remember to never split an infinitive.
- The passive voice should never be used.
- Do not put statements in the negative form.
- Verbs has to agree with their subjects.
- Proofread carefully to see if you words out.
- If you reread your work, you can find on rereading a great deal of repetition can be avoided by rereading and editing.

Careers and Salary

The average starting salary for an English composition major is $23,000 to $30,000. Given the broad range of fields that English majors enter, though, starting salaries can fluctuate dramatically depending on career choice.

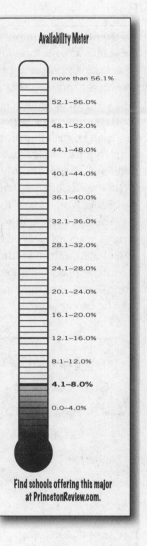

Availability Meter

more than 56.1%

52.1–56.0%

48.1–52.0%

44.1–48.0%

40.1–44.0%

36.1–40.0%

32.1–36.0%

28.1–32.0%

24.1–28.0%

20.1–24.0%

16.1–20.0%

12.1–16.0%

8.1–12.0%

4.1–8.0%

0.0–4.0%

Find schools offering this major at PrincetonReview.com.

CAREER OPTIONS

Attorney	Editor	Radio Producer
Book Publishing Professional	Film Director	Web Editor
Consultant	Film Editor	Writer
Corporate Lawyer		

ENGLISH LITERATURE (BRITISH ISLES AND COMMONWEALTH)

Basics

Do Anglophile books engulf your bedroom, making it appear less like sleeping quarters and more like the stacks at your local library? Readers like you will rejoice with a major in English literature. Plenty of theorizing, analyzing, and critiquing goes into an English literature degree—you'll consume tome after tome before you process them through your intellectual wringer. Here's your justified chance to decode centuries' worth of English conjecture on every topic under the sun. English literature is often offered as a concentration within a larger English major; at some colleges, however, it is offered as a major on its own.

As an English lit major, you'll be studying literature from the British Isles and the British Commonwealth, from its earliest incarnation to the present day. Your studies will include close reading of authors such as William Shakespeare, John Milton, and Geoffrey Chaucer. You'll become familiar with many different genres, including fiction, nonfiction, drama, and poetry, as well as areas of literature such as folklore and regional specialties. You'll learn the basics of literary criticism and how to analyze style and content with a critical eye. You'll also gain an understanding of the history and society in which these writers were living—how various wars influenced the literature of the time, for example, or how English writers have absorbed and reflected American culture in their stories. Through your reading and analyzing, you'll get a broad picture of the values, preoccupations, customs, politics, and trends that inspired these English writers and shaped their world—and how they, in turn, inspired and shaped the writers (and societies) that came after them.

The canon of great literature is constantly evolving, and gaining a solid foundation in the great works and authors of English literature will give you the thinking, writing, reading, and communication skills that are highly valued in countless careers. Building up your background in English literature is a great way to prepare for further studies in other major blocks of literature.

SAMPLE COLLEGE CURRICULUM FOR ENGLISH LITERATURE (BRITISH ISLES AND COMMONWEALTH)

British Drama to 1800

British Literature: Medieval through 1800

The British Novel

The Critical Canon

Critical Theory

Introduction to Chaucer

Medieval English Literature

Milton's Major Poetry

Nineteenth-Century English Novel

Renaissance English Literature

Restoration and Eighteenth-Century English Literature

Romantic Poetry and Poets

Shakespeare

Shakespeare's Contemporaries

Studies in History and Literature

Victorian and Modern Authors

If You Like English Literature (British Isles and Commonwealth), You May Also Like . . .

American history, American literature, American studies, art history, classics, creative writing, English, English composition, film, history, journalism, philosophy, technical writing

Suggested High School Prep for English Literature (British Isles and Commonwealth)

To prepare for the years of reading and writing ahead, AP courses in English and history are essential if your high school offers them. Other humanities courses—like philosophy, religion, and languages—will also help you start building a foundation of knowledge that will come in handy when you begin to analyze texts. There are tons of great books out there, so some of the best preparation can be done on your own. Walk into a library and lose yourself for hours. Read everything you can get your hands on. Then dabble a bit on the writing side—whether it's a journal or a summer writing workshop, none of it will hurt you down the road.

Fun Facts

A Writer of Excess

Christopher Marlowe, one of William Shakespeare's contemporaries, was accused of blasphemy, was rumored to have been a government spy, and died in a bar fight in Davenport, England.

Borne of the Bard

William Shakespeare, in his plays, sonnets, and poems, made use of about 17,677 different words. Of those 17,677 words, 1,700 were brand-new—meaning that Shakespeare coined them. Most of these Shakespeare-created words are surprisingly common: accommodation, amazement, assassination, dwindle, frugal, exposure, courtship, eventful, critic, and auspicious are just a few. There's even a book, titled *Coined by Shakespeare: Words and Meanings First Used by the Bard*, by Jeffrey McQuain and Stanley Malless, that gives a complete listing. You just may be quoting Shakespeare without even knowing it!

Careers and Salary

The average starting salary for an English literature major is about $23,000 to $30,000. Given the broad range of fields that English lit majors enter, however, starting salaries can fluctuate dramatically depending upon career choice.

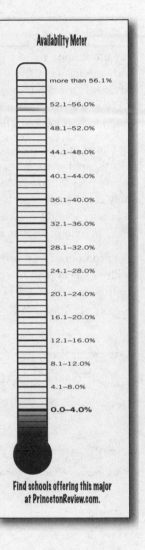

Availability Meter

more than 56.1%

52.1–56.0%

48.1–52.0%

44.1–48.0%

40.1–44.0%

36.1–40.0%

32.1–36.0%

28.1–32.0%

24.1–28.0%

20.1–24.0%

16.1–20.0%

12.1–16.0%

8.1–12.0%

4.1–8.0%

0.0–4.0%

Find schools offering this major at PrincetonReview.com.

CAREER OPTIONS		
Advertising Executive	Journalist	Teacher
Attorney	Librarian	Trial Lawyer
Book Publishing Professional	Politician	Web Editor
Corporate Lawyer	Professor	Writer
Editor	Public Relations Professional	

ENTOMOLOGY

Basics

Entomology majors gain a vast knowledge of all aspects of the insect world. First and foremost they study the insects themselves—the many different types of them, their differences and similarities, and how we classify them into major groups (a practice known as taxonomy). You'll study the evolution of insects and see how they've been affected by changes in the environment and human society. You'll learn the ways in which insects are both harmful and helpful to our health and the many methods available to control them.

The scope of your studies will vary widely. For instance, you'll learn about the biological aspects of insects, such as their anatomy, biochemical processes, and growth. You'll learn about various problems that insects present to agriculture and urban life and how we can best manage insects in these realms. You'll study relatives of insects such as spiders, ticks, and mites. And you'll gain an understanding of environmental concerns and how insects, the environment, and humans are connected. (Bonus: You'll understand Elton John's "Circle of Life" at a much deeper level as an entomology major.)

Entomology, like any other scientific field, requires a great deal of research and laboratory work. Fieldwork is also an integral part of many programs. This is an exciting way to get hands-on experience and see how your studies relate to the real world.

SAMPLE COLLEGE CURRICULUM FOR ENTOMOLOGY

Aquatic Insects

Arthropods Affecting Urban Life and Public Health

Biology

Ecology

Evolution and Classification of Insects

Field Ecology of Disease Vectors

Fundamentals of Pesticides

Inorganic Chemistry

Insect Ecology

Insect-Plant Disease Relationships

Insects, Science, and Society

Livestock Entomology

Microbiology

Molecular Genetics

Organic Chemistry

If You Like Entomology, You May Also Like . . .

Agriculture, animal science, biology, ecology, environmental and environmental health engineering, environmental science, microbiology, natural resources conservation, neurobiology, plant pathology, wildlife management, zoology

Suggested High School Prep for Entomology

If you're considering a major in entomology, you should try to take as many biology, chemistry, and math courses as you can. These will be your best preparation. Computer courses will be good as well. And don't forget your English classes—good researchers must also be good communicators.

Fun Facts

Did You Know . . .

There are more than 1 million species of insects on the planet—some scientists claim there might even be 10 million—and one out of every four animals is a beetle. That lowly can of Raid doesn't seem quite so powerful now, does it?

Some Facts About Ants from Earth-Life Web Productions

- Ant colonies sometimes contain as few as 50 ants.
- Some ant colonies, like one discovered on the coast of Japan, contain as many as 1,080,000 queens and 306,000,000 workers.
- The animal biomass in the Amazon Basin, according to some scientists, is 30 percent ants.
- The animal biomass of the whole world is 10 percent ants.
- An ant is considered a social insect.

Careers and Salary

Starting salaries for entomology majors are generally in the $20,000 to $40,000 range, varying widely according to the field in which the entomologist chooses to work. Further education in graduate school will raise starting salaries substantially as well.

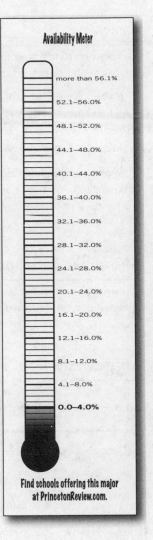

Availability Meter

| more than 56.1% |
| 52.1–56.0% |
| 48.1–52.0% |
| 44.1–48.0% |
| 40.1–44.0% |
| 36.1–40.0% |
| 32.1–36.0% |
| 28.1–32.0% |
| 24.1–28.0% |
| 20.1–24.0% |
| 16.1–20.0% |
| 12.1–16.0% |
| 8.1–12.0% |
| 4.1–8.0% |
| **0.0–4.0%** |

Find schools offering this major at PrincetonReview.com.

CAREER OPTIONS		
Biochemist	Ecologist	Pest Technician
Biologist	Environmentalist/ Environmental Scientist	Zoologist

ENTREPRENEURSHIP

Basics

You used to tell your family that one day you wanted to own your own business. Well, guess what, you've grown up and now it's time to put your money where your mouth is.

If you love the idea of starting a company of your own, there is probably no better place to begin than here. Entrepreneurship is a major dedicated to helping you become the next celebrity CEO. Starting, running, and managing a company, whether it's three employees or a thousand, is a lot of hard work and requires someone with some serious business skills.

As an entrepreneurship major you'll learn many of those business skills, including accounting, economics, and management. Your course of study will take you straight into the heart of the business world, preparing you for days of power lunches and power ties and million-dollar bonuses.

If You Like Entrepreneurship, You May Also Like . . .

Business administration and management, business communications, economics, hospitality, logistics management, operations management, real estate, recreation management, risk management

Suggested High School Prep for Entrepreneurship

Plan on building those analytical skills, particularly through math courses, including algebra, calculus, and statistics. In addition, you'll need strong reading and writing skills, so don't slack off in your English and history classes.

SAMPLE COLLEGE CURRICULUM FOR ENTREPRENEURSHIP

Accounting Information for Entrepreneurial

Decision-Making

Economics

Entrepreneurship in the Global Economy

Financial Management

Introduction to Entrepreneurship Law

Marketing Strategies and Small Business Managers

Software Applications in Business

Special Issues in Entrepreneurship

Fun Facts

The Business End of the Monkey

An organization is like a tree full of monkeys. They are all on different limbs at different levels. Some are climbing up. Some are climbing down. The monkeys on the top look down and see a tree full of smiling faces. The monkeys on the bottom look up and see nothing but a bunch of . . .

Careers and Salary

The average starting salary for entrepreneurship majors can vary widely depending upon what they do when they graduate. If they're entering the business world, starting salaries average about $35,000.

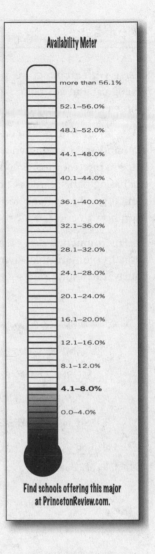

Availability Meter

more than 56.1%

52.1–56.0%

48.1–52.0%

44.1–48.0%

40.1–44.0%

36.1–40.0%

32.1–36.0%

28.1–32.0%

24.1–28.0%

20.1–24.0%

16.1–20.0%

12.1–16.0%

8.1–12.0%

4.1–8.0%

0.0–4.0%

Find schools offering this major at PrincetonReview.com.

CAREER OPTIONS

Bar/Club Manager	Entrepreneur	Stockbroker
Buyer	Small Business Owner	Venture Capitalist/Investor
Consultant		

ENVIRONMENTAL DESIGN/ARCHITECTURE

The Basics

As its name suggests, the environmental design/architecture major combines aspects of landscape design with architecture. In this program, you'll learn how to design indoor and outdoor spaces that are in ecological and aesthetic harmony with their surroundings. You'll study the principles of architecture, landscape architecture, and urban planning that involve math, physics, drawing, and computer classes.

As an environmental design/architecture major, your task is to consider the larger aesthetic picture when planning and creating your spaces, structures and other projects. Each of four variables (and their relationships to one another) will be considered when engineering your designs: architecture (buildings); landscape (including parks, gardens, and recreational surfaces); interiors (spaces within existing buildings); and environmental graphics (signs and information boards). As an environmental design/architecture major, you'll also learn how to construct structures and spaces that are both ecologically sustainable and environmentally safe.

Environmental designers and architects work on both public and private spaces, used for leisure, recreational, commercial, or living purposes. Examples of their work include parks, garden centers, green roofs, courtyards, and public squares.

SAMPLE COLLEGE CURRICULUM FOR ENVIRONMENTAL DESIGN/ARCHITECTURE

Air Pollution Control

Biology of Populations

Biostatistics

Calculus

Environmental Biology

Environmental Engineering Processes

Environmental and Environmental Health Engineering

Environmental Toxicology

Fluid Mechanics Hydrology

Hazardous Materials Management

Health Effects and Risk Management

Parasites

Pollution Prevention

Water and Wastewater Plant Design

Water Contaminants

If You Like Environmental Design/Architecture, You May Also Like . . .

Architectural engineering, architectural history, architecture, ecology, engineering, environmental science, geography, graphic design, industrial design, interior architecture, interior design, landscape architecture, landscape horticulture, urban planning

Suggested High School Prep for Environmental Design/Architecture

Programs in environmental design/architecture draw from many different disciplines. Take geometry, calculus and physics, as well as drawing and art history. Finally, computer and computer graphics courses will be helpful, since much of your planning and designing will be done on computer.

Fun Facts

What's a Green Roof?

A green roof, also called a living roof, is a roof that has been covered with a dense mat of low-growing plants. Far from just looking good, a green roof performs a number of ecological services in urban settings that lack natural greenery, including absorbing heat, humidity, and pollution particles from the air. It also provides insulation for a building, preventing the escape of heat in the winter, while keeping the building cool in the summer.

(Source: www.greenroofs.com)

Careers and Salary

An environmental design/architecture major can expect a starting salary of about $30,000 to $40,000 a year.

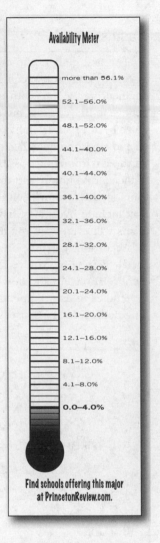

Availability Meter

more than 56.1%

52.1–56.0%

48.1–52.0%

44.1–40.0%

40.1–44.0%

36.1–40.0%

32.1–36.0%

28.1–32.0%

24.1–28.0%

20.1–24.0%

16.1–20.0%

12.1–16.0%

8.1–12.0%

4.1–8.0%

0.0–4.0%

Find schools offering this major at PrincetonReview.com.

CAREER OPTIONS		
Contractor	Landscape Architect	Urban Planner
Environmental Designer/Architect	Regional Planner	

ENVIRONMENTAL AND ENVIRONMENTAL HEALTH ENGINEERING

Basics

The first grader who organizes his or her family's recycling bins, sets up a backyard compost unit, and swears by daily sunscreen usage is almost destined for a major in environmental and environmental health engineering. People with a devoted interest in these causes know it long before college; they not only believe in these ideals, but also live them out. Keeping our air and water clean, developing systems to minimize health risks from hazardous waste, and promoting regulations for industries all fall under environmental and environmental health engineering. In this major, you'll learn about the impact of different industries on the environment, possible strategies for reversing damaging effects, ways to provide potable water and reduce air pollution, and the safest methods of waste disposal. You'll tackle the specific ways that our environment affects our health and what measures we can take individually and as a society. Special interests may include hydrology, hazardous substance treatment, hydraulics, or geostatistical modeling. Some programs will even have you drafting mock legislation that, for example, protects wildlife reserves.

According to Tufts University, environmental health has three components: biological, physical, and social. By the time you've completed your studies, you'll be able to better understand the health-to-environment relationship and how it can (and should be!) optimized.

Studies in environmental and environmental health engineering involve many different, often overlapping fields: infectious disease, biology, chemistry, biostatistics, epidemiology, toxicology, nutrition, and math. In most programs, you'll enhance your classroom knowledge with hands-on research and laboratory work.

SAMPLE COLLEGE CURRICULUM FOR ENVIRONMENTAL AND ENVIRONMENTAL HEALTH ENGINEERING

Air Pollution Control

Biology of Populations

Biostatistics

Calculus

Environmental Biology

Environmental Engineering Processes

Environmental Toxicology

Fluid Mechanics

Hazardous Materials Management

Health Effects and Risk Management

Hydrology

Parasites

Pollution Prevention

Water and Wastewater Plant Design

Water Contaminants

If You Like Environmental and Environmental Health Engineering, You May Also Like . . .

Agricultural and biological engineering, biochemistry, biology, botany and plant biology, chemical engineering, chemistry, ecology, engineering design, environmental science, geological engineering, geology, industrial engineering, mineral engineering, natural resources conservation, ocean engineering, petroleum engineering, plant pathology, public health, sustainable resource management

Suggested High School Prep for Environmental and Environmental Health Engineering

You'll best prepare yourself to be an engineer with courses in math, chemistry, physics, biology, and other sciences. The higher the level, the better—you'll get a head start in your college coursework by taking calculus and trigonometry. Computer courses are also important. Look into environmental clubs at your school or local volunteer work that would give you experience with environmental concerns.

Fun Facts

One Man's Trash, Another Man's Treasure

Environmental engineers came to the rescue for Boston's Spectacle Island. Spectacle Island, located in Boston Harbor, had been nothing but a landfill for years—until Boston's Central Artery/Tunnel Project came along. The project faced a major problem: what to do with the nearly 3 million cubic yards of dirt, clay, and gravel that the tunnel would displace. Various environmental groups found a solution: Bring the dirt, clay, and gravel to Spectacle Island and create a city park.

Un-Sanitary

The name environmental engineering is a fairly new label for this field. Until the mid-1960s, it was called sanitary engineering. It was changed when the activities and concerns of engineers began reaching beyond issues of sanitation.

Careers and Salary

A career in environmental and environmental health engineering can bring a starting salary ranging from the upper thirties to about $50,000. Location, area of employment, and previous experience (such as co-ops or internships) will impact where starting salaries fall within that range—or beyond it.

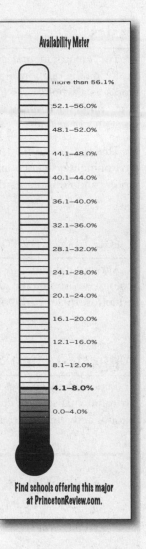

Availability Meter

more than 56.1%

52.1–56.0%

48.1–52.0%

44.1–48.0%

40.1–44.0%

36.1–40.0%

32.1–36.0%

28.1–32.0%

24.1–28.0%

20.1–24.0%

16.1–20.0%

12.1–16.0%

8.1–12.0%

4.1–8.0%

0.0–4.0%

Find schools offering this major at PrincetonReview.com.

CAREER OPTIONS

Chemical Engineer	Farmer	Park Ranger
Ecologist	Hazardous Waste Manager	Professor
Environmentalist/	Lobbyist	Public Health Administrator
Environmental Scientist		

ENVIRONMENTAL SCIENCE

Basics

The environmental science major combines study in biology, chemistry, physics, and mathematics, exploring the relationships between these areas to acquire a greater understanding of how our environment works as a whole. Unlike the environmental engineering major, the environmental science major concentrates on general scientific principles and analysis, rather than design and application. Bottom line: It's a whole lot of science.

This is a great time to get involved in environmental work. As concern for the environment increases, environmental science majors will be in increasing demand. Environmental science majors work as policy writers and consultants, developers, conservationists, educators, and ecologists.

If You Like Environmental Science, You May Also Like . . .

Agricultural and biological engineering, agronomy and crop science, biology, botany and plant biology, ecology, environmental and environmental health engineering, forestry, geology, horticulture, international agriculture, plant pathology, soil science, sustainable resource management, wildlife management

Suggested High School Prep for Environmental Science

Take as many courses in chemistry, biology, and physics as you can. Advanced math is usually a part of the environmental science curriculum, so courses in calculus and trigonometry are also useful. Experience with outdoor activities is extremely useful, as almost all environmental science programs require field experience.

SAMPLE COLLEGE CURRICULUM FOR ENVIRONMENTAL SCIENCE

Biochemistry

Calculus I–II

Environmental Policy

General Biology

General Chemistry

Geology

Inorganic Reactions

Organic Chemistry

Physics

Plant Pathology

Statistics

Fun Facts

It's All Connected

"When one tugs at a single thing in nature, he finds it attached to the rest of the world."

John Muir

"A human being is part of a whole, called by us the 'Universe,' a part limited in time and space. He experiences himself, his thoughts and feelings, as something separated from the rest—a kind of optical delusion of his consciousness. This delusion is a kind of prison for us, restricting us to our personal desires and to affection for a few persons nearest us. Our task must be to free ourselves from this prison by widening our circles of compassion to embrace all living creatures and the whole of nature in its beauty."

—Albert Einstein

Careers and Salary

The starting salary for an environmental science major fresh out of college ranges from $23,000 to $30,000.

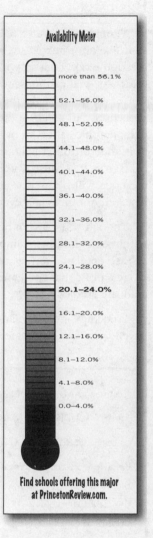

Availability Meter

more than 56.1%

52.1–56.0%

48.1–52.0%

44.1–48.0%

40.1–44.0%

36.1–40.0%

32.1–36.0%

28.1–32.0%

24.1–28.0%

20.1–24.0%

16.1–20.0%

12.1–16.0%

8.1–12.0%

4.1–8.0%

0.0–4.0%

Find schools offering this major at PrincetonReview.com.

CAREER OPTIONS

Biochemist	Environmentalist/	Hazardous Waste Manager
Biologist	Environmental Scientist	Park Ranger
Ecologist	Farmer	

EPIDEMIOLOGY

Basics

Though we haven't yet found a cure for AIDS, we do know some of the things that lead to its transmission, like unprotected sex and shared hypodermic needles, and we have reason to believe that it originated through blood contact with monkeys in West Africa that were consumed as food. Those important discoveries—as well as thousands of others—were made by epidemiologists. Epidemiology is, according to the University of Alabama, "the study of the distribution and determinants of diseases in human populations." If you choose to major in epidemiology, you'll be studying the origins and causes of diseases, as well as the demographics affected by them and those most at risk. You'll study factors such as environment, occupation, and nutrition to determine their relationships to specific diseases. Through an exploration of the external factors that cause disease, you'll learn how to identify, prevent, and control infectious diseases. Statistical methods will be used to investigate health issues as you develop the ability to analyze and interpret the research of others and eventually perform independent research of your own.

Though you may not be asked to specialize as an undergraduate, knowing some of the specialized fields within epidemiology is important. The University of Pittsburgh, for example, offers specializations in chronic disease epidemiology, women's health epidemiology, infectious disease epidemiology, psychiatric epidemiology, and alcohol epidemiology. You'll gain a basic understanding of some or all of these areas in your undergraduate studies.

Epidemiology is in many ways a multidisciplinary field, dealing heavily with biology, chemistry, pathology, psychology, and medicine. You'll draw from these fields during your studies and interact and work with experts in these fields once you begin your career. Epidemiology deals with humans from preconception through old age—the whole life span is rich with opportunities for research and study. Your efforts in college and beyond may pave the way for vast improvements in our quality of life.

If You Like Epidemiology, You May Also Like . . .

Biology, biomedical engineering, biomedical science, cell biology, chemistry, genetics, molecular genetics, neurobiology, neuroscience, pharmacology, pharmacy, premedicine, public health

Suggested High School Prep for Epidemiology

Building a strong foundation in the sciences is vital to getting a head start on your epidemiology major. Bulk up with courses in biology and chemistry, and be sure to take advantage of any laboratory components offered. Math courses will be valuable as well—you'll be doing a lot of work with statistics in college. Health courses may be useful, as well as humanities courses that will help you improve and strengthen your reading, writing, and communication skills.

SAMPLE COLLEGE CURRICULUM FOR EPIDEMIOLOGY

Behavioral Factors in Disease

Biostatistics

Clinical Epidemiology

Control of Chronic Disease

Environmental Epidemiology

Epidemiology of Aging

Epidemiology of Chronic Disease

HIV/AIDS and STDs

Infectious Disease

Nutrition, Immunity, and Infection

Occupational Epidemiology

Pathophysiology of Human Disease

Public Health Demography

Quantitative Methods

Tropical Infectious Diseases

Vaccinology

Fun Facts

Further Reading

Interested in learning more about epidemiology and some of the current issues at stake? Check out the *American Journal of Epidemiology*. You'll be able to read about some of the problems epidemiologists are addressing, and it will give you an idea of the wide scope of your chosen field.

Did You Know?

The word epidemic was being used as early as 1603, meaning "common unto all people, or to the most part of them."

(Source: Oxford English Dictionary online, www.oed.com)

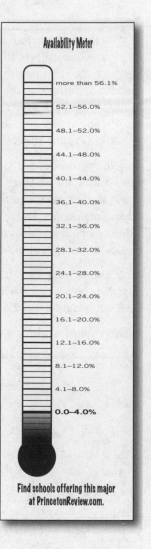

Availability Meter

more than 56.1%

52.1–56.0%

48.1–52.0%

44.1–48.0%

40.1–44.0%

36.1–40.0%

32.1–36.0%

28.1–32.0%

24.1–28.0%

20.1–24.0%

16.1–20.0%

12.1–16.0%

8.1–12.0%

4.1–8.0%

0.0–4.0%

Find schools offering this major at PrincetonReview.com.

Careers and Salary

Epidemiologists generally earn about $54,000 per year, although this figure will most likely be lower if you do not pursue a degree beyond your bachelor's.

CAREER OPTIONS

Epidemiologist	Public Health Administrator	Scientist
Physician	Researcher	Teacher
Professor		

EQUINE STUDIES

Basics

You know those movie scenes with an elegant horse running free on a deserted beach? Someone carefully trained that horse to run down that beach and appear spontaneous and carefree, yet stay perfectly in line with the tide and throw off just the right amount of spray while taking great care not to create an ugly shadow or bump into the camera crew. Someone else groomed him, fed him, cared for him, and was ready to nurse him back to health should he happen to get sick. And chances are that someone else trained the actor who's riding him, should there be one. Those are exactly some of the things you could be doing after a major in equine studies.

During your studies, you'll start off learning about horse anatomy and physiology, various breeds, and diseases and illnesses. You'll learn how to care for horses through proper nutrition, health care, and fitness. You'll also examine equine lameness and how it's treated. Then there's equipment—how to choose it and how to maintain it. And of course, the fun part: how to ride, train, and handle horses skillfully. You may learn about jumping and dressage, how to "cut" a horse, or how to rope calves. Some programs include courses on horse showmanship. You may even get a little experience in rodeo.

Your studies will also lead you into the arena of stable and horse management—the business side of horses—including how to keep accurate records, how to manage a farm or stable, and the accompanying safety concerns. In addition, you'll develop the ability to give instruction to others and pass on the joy of riding.

An equine studies major is as specific as they come—most students enter with at least tentative goals in mind for postgraduation pursuits. Jobs in this field vary from region to region, which is another aspect of this major to consider. The skills you learn will make you a valuable asset to any horse institution, and you'll be prepared to someday, perhaps, set up a business of your own.

If You Like Equine Studies, You May Also Like . . .

Agricultural business and management, animal sciences, forestry, pre-veterinary medicine, wildlife management, zoology

Suggested High School Prep for Equine Studies

Building a strong foundation in the sciences—especially biology—will give you a good head start in your equine studies major. Math courses will be valuable as well. A good selection of humanities courses—English, history, languages, religion, psychology—will also be useful. Good reading, writing, and oral communication are vital to any future business career, so be sure to take courses that will help you strengthen your skills. If your community offers any opportunities for volunteer work with animals, take advantage!

SAMPLE COLLEGE CURRICULUM FOR EQUINE STUDIES

Basic Horse Care

Basic Roping

Equine Breeding

Equine Business Management

Equine Fitting and Showing Techniques

Equine Health

Equine Lameness

Equine Nutrition

Equine Sales and Service

Exercise Physiology

Farm Records Management

Horse Anatomy Equine Industry

Horseshoeing

Rodeo Timing Events

Stable Management

Training and Handling

Zoology

Fun Facts

From the Horse's Mouth

"Horses and children, I often think, have a lot of the good sense there is in the world."

—Josephine Demott Robinson, U.S. circus performer

"Good people get cheated, just as good horses get ridden."

—Chinese proverb

(Source: www.bartleby.com)

Did You Know?

Horses were domesticated in central Asia somewhere between 4000 B.C./B.C.E. and 3000 B.C./B.C.E., and were originally kept for their meat and milk.

(Source: www.ansi.okstate.edu/breeds/horses/Horses-w.htm)

Careers and Salary

The starting salary for equine managers is about $20,000 to $35,000, but this number varies widely depending on how you use your skills and what sort of career you aspire to. As you get more experience in your field, your salary will increase.

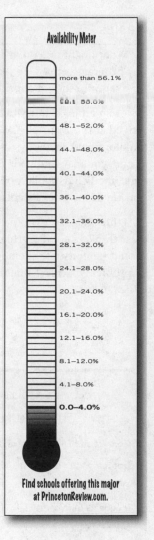

Availability Meter

more than 56.1%

52.1—56.0%

48.1—52.0%

44.1—48.0%

40.1—44.0%

36.1—40.0%

32.1—36.0%

28.1—32.0%

24.1—28.0%

20.1—24.0%

16.1—20.0%

12.1—16.0%

8.1—12.0%

4.1—8.0%

0.0—4.0%

Find schools offering this major at PrincetonReview.com.

CAREER OPTIONS		
Breeder	Horse Trainer	Stable or Farm Manager
Competitive Horse Rider	Riding Instructor	Stable Owner

ETHICS

Basics

What ought one do in any given situation? Usually contained under the umbrella of the greater philosophy programs, ethics is a major that anyone interested in future leadership positions (in politics or business, for example) should consider.

As an ethics major, you'll be trained to find answers to difficult problems—and also to justify how you've arrived at those answers. While all ethics programs are going to give you a healthy dose of philosophy, epistemology, and metaphysics, not all ethics majors are the same. Depending on the school you choose to attend, you may find your course load weighted toward one of a series of concentrations: business, history, logic, medicine, public policy, or religion. Additionally, a degree in ethics could lead you to a specialization outside of the ones listed; many ethics majors go on to be effective members of the bar and media.

Ethics majors are expected to demonstrate a capacity to view issues holistically. This group of careful, clear thinkers should bring an historical perspective to modern problems. But above all else, ethics majors should demonstrate the ability to impose rational and ethical criteria when considering possible solutions to problems. Critical thinking is not so much a lesson learned (though it is) as it is a prerequisite for any ethics major.

Sample College Curriculum

Conflict and Dispute Resolution

Contemporary Ethics

Ethical Theory

Inequality in Everyday Life

Material Culture

Modern Moral Philosophy

Philosophy and Law

Philosophy, Politics, and Economics

Political Philosophy

Professional Ethics

Social and Political Philosophy

Social Structure, Public Policy, and Ethical Dilemmas

Technology, Nature, and Values

Women's Studies

World Religions In Everyday Life

If You Like Ethics, You May Also Like . . .

Anthropology, art, art history, classics, comparative literature, creative writing, economics, history, international studies, journalism, peace studies, philosophy, political science, sociology, technical writing, theology, women's studies

Suggested High School Prep for Ethics

While your high school probably doesn't have a specific class in ethics or philosophy, a great way to get a head start on your ethics degree is to load up on as many classes in the humanities as possible. Of specific importance are higher-level history, sociology, and literature classes, as well as a logic class, if your high school offers one.

Fun Facts

Words on Ethics

"Ethics and religion differ herein; that the one is the system of human duties commencing from man; the other, from God. Religion includes the personality of God; Ethics does not."

—Ralph Waldo Emerson

"Moralities, ethics, laws, customs, beliefs, doctrines-these are of trifling import. All that matters is that the miraculous become the norm."

—Henry Miller

"Ethics is in origin the art of recommending to others the sacrifices required for cooperation with oneself."

—Bertrand Russell

"Ethics, too, are nothing but reverence for life. That is what gives me the fundamental principle of morality, namely, that good consists in maintaining, promoting, and enhancing life, and that destroying, injuring, and limiting life are evil."

—Albert Schweitzer

"What I have observed of the pond is no less true in ethics. It is the law of average. Such a rule of the two diameters not only guides us toward the sun in the system and the heart in man, but draw lines through the length and breadth of the aggregate of a man's particular daily behaviors ... and where they intersect will be the height or depth of his character. Perhaps we need only to know how his shores trend and his adjacent country or circumstances, to infer his depth and concealed bottom."

—Henry David Thoreau

"Laws, religions, creeds, and systems of ethics, instead of making society better than its best unit, make it worse than its average unit, because they are never up to date."

—George Bernard Shaw

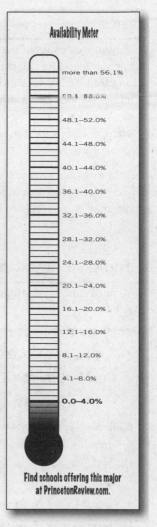

Availability Meter

more than 56.1%

52.1–56.0%

48.1–52.0%

44.1–48.0%

40.1–44.0%

36.1–40.0%

32.1–36.0%

28.1–32.0%

24.1–28.0%

20.1–24.0%

16.1–20.0%

12.1–16.0%

8.1–12.0%

4.1–8.0%

0.0–4.0%

Find schools offering this major at PrincetonReview.com.

Careers and Salary

The average starting salary for an ethics major is between $25,000 and $35,000, depending on the field of focus. Pursuing an advanced degree (in law, for example) will significantly increase your earning potential.

CAREER OPTIONS

Attorney	Mediator	Professor
Editor	Philosopher	Public Relations Professional
Journalist	Political Scientist	Writer

ETHNIC STUDIES

Basics

Ethnic studies grew out of the civil rights movements and growing social consciousness of the 1960s. Ethnic studies majors take a multidisciplinary approach to studying the lives and experiences of groups originating from Africa, Asia, and the Americas. You'll take classes in the social sciences to achieve a better understanding the socioeconomic, historical, and political context of people of color in the United States, as well as explore the subjective experiences of minority groups through literature and art. The objective is to heighten society's awareness of the gifts, struggles, and needs of ethnic communities; the ultimate goal is to improve living conditions and balance social power.

Ethnic studies majors definitely develop and hone writing, researching, and critical thinking skills. Expect to undertake an independent project during senior year on a topic of your choice. If you focus on a community where English is a second language, you'll learn to speak and write in that language.

If You Like Ethnic Studies, You May Also Like . . .

African American studies; American studies, anthropology; Asian American studies; Caribbean studies; comparative literature; gay and lesbian studies; Hispanic American, Puerto Rican, and Chicano studies, history; Latin American studies; mass communication; Native American studies; peace studies; philosophy; psychology; public policy analysis, sociology; urban studies; women's studies

> ### SAMPLE COLLEGE CURRICULUM FOR ETHNIC STUDIES
>
> Community Research in a Multicultural Context
>
> Film-Video Images of Communities of Color:
>
> Analysis and Video Production
>
> History of Race and Ethnicity in Western
>
> North America
>
> Introduction to Ethnic Studies
>
> The Making of Multicultural America:
>
> A Comparative Historical Perspective
>
> People of Mixed Race Descent
>
> Race, Ethnicity, and Immigration in the United States
>
> Racialization and Empire
>
> Social Science Methods
>
> The Southern Border

Suggested High School Prep for Ethnic Studies

To get ready for this major, focus on English and history classes. Taking three or four years of Spanish (or another language) would also be smart.

Fun Facts

Useful Websites for the Ethnic Studies Major

- Bureau of the Census: www.census.gov
  Online U.S. census data can be searched by specific region, race or ethnicity, age, and more.
- Center for Multilingual Multicultural Research: www.usc.edu/dept/education/CMMR
  Full text articles, research, and websites on minorities and language issues, compiled by the University of Southern California's Center for Multilingual Multicultural Research.
- Diversity Database: www.inform.umd.edu
  Searchable database with definitions, resources, bibliographies, and more.

Careers and Salary

Career options for ethnic studies major vary widely, but you can expect to make about as much as the average liberal arts graduate fresh out of college—$20,000 to $30,000 a year.

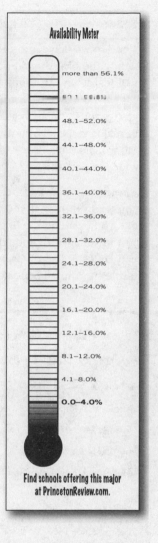

Availability Meter

more than 56.1%

52.1–56.0%

48.1–52.0%

44.1–48.0%

40.1–44.0%

36.1–40.0%

32.1–36.0%

28.1–32.0%

24.1–28.0%

20.1–24.0%

16.1–20.0%

12.1–16.0%

8.1–12.0%

4.1–8.0%

0.0–4.0%

Find schools offering this major at PrincetonReview.com.

CAREER OPTIONS

Community Organizer/Outreach Worker	Labor Relations Specialist	Radio and Television Producer
Consultant	Lawyer	Sociologist
Filmmaker	Lobbyist	Social Worker
Health Care Worker	Professor	Teacher
Journalist	Politician	Writer
	Radio and Television Writer	

EUROPEAN HISTORY

Basics

Before we delve into the European facet, let's say that as a history major, generally speaking, your goal is to study the past to gain perspective on the present—pretty straightforward, but not as easy as it sounds. You'll learn how to think critically about historical events and cultures and apply what you learn to the analysis of our world. History isn't set in stone—it's always open to new interpretations, critiques, questions, investigations, and analysis. As a student of history, you'll be involved in those processes. As with any humanities major, you'll learn how to communicate your ideas, both spoken and written, persuasively and skillfully. History majors become experts on the world and how it has taken shape—and they use their expertise in a wide variety of fields.

Your studies in European history may take the form of a major in some colleges and as a concentration or minor in others. If you're romanced by the Renaissance and the Reformation, you'll be right at home while you examine the lingering effects of each. War, conflict, angst, pain, triumph, and victory will all play a part in your whirlwind education, spanning from the rise and fall of the Napoleonic Empire, the Versailles Treaty, and the rise of fascism through the French Revolution, World War I, and World War II. You'll dissect the role the United States has played in European affairs and vice versa. By studying these and other fascinating aspects of European history, you'll gain a new understanding of the culture, attitudes, and politics of modern Europe.

Summers in Europe may not be a mandatory, or even optional, part of your studies in this major, but it's a great excuse to get away anyway. Field trip!

If You Like European History, You May Also Like . . .

American history, ancient studies, anthropology, archeology, architecture, art history, classics, education, English, history, international relations, international studies, music history, peace studies

Suggested High School Prep for European History

A solid background in the humanities will be your best preparation for a European history major. Fill your schedule with challenging courses in English, philosophy, religion, and of course, history. Take classes that will help you improve your writing and speaking skills. Language courses will be a great addition to your schedule—some European history programs may even require several semesters of a foreign language, so getting a head start now is a good idea.

SAMPLE COLLEGE CURRICULUM FOR EUROPEAN HISTORY

Anglo-Irish Relations

Europe 1400–1600

Europe Since 1945

The French Revolution and the Napoleonic Empire

The Holocaust

Ireland Since 1600

Nineteenth-Century Germany

Politics and Economics in Western Europe

Reading, Writing, and Research for History

The Renaissance

Twentieth-Century France

Western Civilizations

World Civilizations

World War I

World War II

Fun Facts

European Countries (Say Them Five Times Fast)

Albania, Andorra, Austria, Belarus, Belgium, Bosnia and Herzegovina, Bulgaria, Croatia, Cyprus, Czech Republic, Denmark, Estonia, Finland, France, Germany, Greece, Hungary, Iceland, Ireland, Italy, Latvia, Liechtenstein, Lithuania, Luxembourg, Macedonia, Malta, Moldova, Monaco, Netherlands, Norway, Poland, Portugal, Romania, Russia, San Marino, Serbia and Montenegro, Slovakia, Slovenia, Spain, Sweden, Switzerland, Ukraine, United Kingdom, Vatican City

(Source: http://geography.about.com)

European Union Refresher (or, In a Nutshell)

- The European Union began in 1993.
- Fifteen countries are members: Austria, Belgium, Denmark, Finland, France, Germany, Greece, Ireland, Italy, Luxembourg, Netherlands, Portugal, Spain, Sweden, and United Kingdom.
- The euro is the currency used throughout the European Union.
- The European Union flag is a circle of 12 gold stars on a background of blue.

(Source: http://geography.about.com)

Careers and Salary

Most liberal arts majors with bachelor's degrees can expect to earn in the $20,000 to $30,000 range. However, since you'll have a wide range of career options open to you, that number can vary widely. Pursuing an advanced degree will also make a difference in the level of your salary.

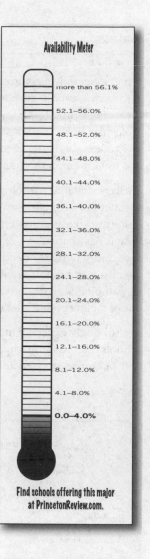

Availability Meter

more than 56.1%

52.1–56.0%

48.1–52.0%

44.1–48.0%

40.1–44.0%

36.1–40.0%

32.1–36.0%

28.1–32.0%

24.1–28.0%

20.1–24.0%

16.1–20.0%

12.1–16.0%

8.1–12.0%

4.1–8.0%

0.0–4.0%

Find schools offering this major at PrincetonReview.com.

CAREER OPTIONS

Historian	Professor	Teacher
Journalist	Researcher	Writer
Lawyer		

EXPERIMENTAL PATHOLOGY

Basics

Pathology is the study of diseases and what goes wrong within the body because of them. This may not sound inherently glamorous, but a major in experimental pathology may pave the way for a future of amazing discoveries, even a cure for cancer. You'll be studying the nature of diseases and how they can attack tissues, organs, and the body as a whole. You'll become knowledgeable about diseases on all levels, from the molecular to the cellular and more. And by learning about diseases in such great depth—and the factors and processes that lead to them—you'll be on your way to helping create more effective ways to prevent and treat them in the future.

Experimental pathology majors learn how to perform skillful research so that they can someday make advances in the field. How to use laboratory equipment, how to interpret and analyze data, and how to communicate your findings effectively are all topics that will be covered. You'll study research from the past and how it has shaped the field, and you'll gain an understanding of exactly where we are in the realm of disease and where we need to go. Pathologists pursue careers involving molecular genetics, tumors, neurochemistry, immunotoxicology, and cancer, to name a few possibilities. It's strange to think that if experimental pathologists got so good at their jobs that they wiped out all disease, they'd actually perform themselves out of a career—but that's the goal!

Although experimental pathology is frequently a specialization in graduate or medical school, many schools offer undergraduates the chance to pursue studies in this area. The depth and breadth of your study will, of course, deepen and widen as you move further in your schooling.

SAMPLE COLLEGE CURRICULUM FOR EXPERIMENTAL PATHOLOGY

Biochemistry

Biomedical Research

Cell Biology

Ethics

Gene Targeting in Transgenic Mice

Genetics

Medical Immunology

Molecular Biology

Neurobiology

Pharmacology

Radiation Biology

Statistics

Virology

If You Like Experimental Pathology, You May Also Like . . .

Biology, biomedical science, cell biology, chemistry, epidemiology, genetics, molecular biology, molecular genetics, neurobiology, neuroscience, pharmacology, pharmacy, premedicine, public health, toxicology

Suggested High School Prep for Experimental Pathology

To best prepare for a major in experimental pathology, get a solid foundation in science and math courses including calculus, biology, chemistry, and physics. Courses that include laboratory work are especially valuable. Scientists must also be good communicators, so take humanities courses like English and languages to strengthen your reading, writing, and speaking skills.

Fun Facts

Read All About It

Check out *The International Journal of Experimental Pathology*. This journal was founded in 1920 as a forum for research and new thoughts on the cause and cure of human disease. You can find more information as well as current and archived tables of contents at blackwellpublishing.com.

Say It Ain't So

Here are a few words about pathology.

"Unrecognized alcoholism is the ruling pathology among writers and intellectuals."

—Diana Trilling

"Every age develops its own peculiar forms of pathology, which express in exaggerated form its underlying character structure."

—Christopher Lasch

"The shock of unemployment becomes a pathology in its own right."

—Robert Farrar Capon

"Lying just for the fun of it is either art or pathology."

—Mason Cooley

Careers and Salary

The starting salary for experimental pathologists is about $35,000, though that number heavily depends on how much experience you've had, your level of education, and in what sort of capacity you choose to use your skills.

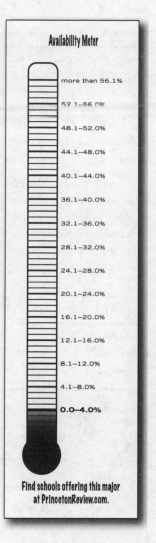

Availability Meter

more than 56.1%

52.1–56.0%

48.1–52.0%

44.1–48.0%

40.1–44.0%

36.1–40.0%

32.1–36.0%

28.1–32.0%

24.1–28.0%

20.1–24.0%

16.1–20.0%

12.1–16.0%

8.1–12.0%

4.1–8.0%

0.0–4.0%

Find schools offering this major at PrincetonReview.com.

CAREER OPTIONS

Experimental Pathologist	Professor	Scientist
Physician	Researcher	Teacher

EXPERIMENTAL PSYCHOLOGY

Basics

Are you curious about the relationship between video games and violent children? Do you suspect that computers and road rage may be connected? Well, if you're intrigued by these ideas, consider a major in experimental psychology. As an experimental psychology major you will focus primarily on research. Topics of research are limitless—they're bound only by your imagination and curiosity. Students often work with one or more faculty members on research projects, but as your experience grows, many programs will give you the opportunity to begin projects of your own choosing. In all cases, you'll be involved with conceptualizing the experiment, designing it, running it, and eventually, documenting and analyzing your findings.

In addition to your research, experimental psychology will also expose you to the world of psychology in general. You may take courses in cognitive psych, social psych, biology, chemistry, child psych, or any number of other fields. Once you learn the basics of each psychological field, you'll be able to design relevant and valuable experiments, and you'll begin to see what your research and the research of psychologists from the past and present contribute to the discipline.

If You Like Experimental Psychology, You May Also Like . . .

Anthropology, biopsychology, clinical psychology, counseling, developmental psychology, educational psychology, industrial psychology, mental health services, neurobiology, neuroscience, physiological psychology, psychology, rehabilitation services, social psychology, social work

---

SAMPLE COLLEGE CURRICULUM FOR EXPERIMENTAL PSYCHOLOGY

Adult Psychology and Aging

Behavior Modification

Cognitive Psychology

Engineering Psychology

Ergonomics

Experimental Design and Statistics

Experimental Social Psychology

Human Factors in Systems Development

Human Information Processing

Psychological Disorders of Children

Psychology of Reading

Psychology of the Self

Team and Group Processing

Suggested High School Prep for Experimental Psychology

If your high school offers any psychology courses, taking them would be a great way to learn the basics of the field—the kinds of stuff you'll learn in Psych 101. Other science courses, such as chemistry and biology, will be valuable, as will math courses, especially statistics. Since you'll be doing a lot of research, hone your reading and writing skills so you can write up your findings in impressive papers.

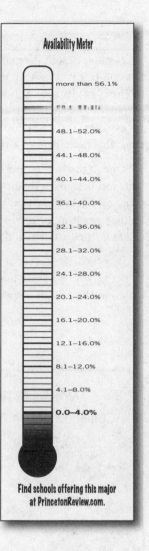

Availability Meter

more than 56.1%

52.1–56.1%

48.1–52.0%

44.1–48.0%

40.1–44.0%

36.1–40.0%

32.1–36.0%

28.1–32.0%

24.1–28.0%

20.1–24.0%

16.1–20.0%

12.1–16.0%

8.1–12.0%

4.1–8.0%

0.0–4.0%

Find schools offering this major
at PrincetonReview.com.

Fun Facts

The Ethics of Psychology

Psychological experiments often raise sticky questions of morality and ethics. One experiment that caused a great deal of controversy was one that tested the theory of obedience, developed by Stanley Milgram in 1974. In this experiment, Milgram instructed participants—the "teachers"—to give electric shocks to "learners" every time a learner answered a question incorrectly. The learners were also involved in the experiment, and no shocks were actually given. However, the teachers didn't know that, and Milgram instructed them to give shocks of larger and larger voltages to the learners. Even though in ordinary situations most people would not administer painful shocks to strangers, 65 percent of the teachers obeyed Milgram and gave shocks of, eventually, 450 volts. The mental anguish of the teachers gave rise to many questions of psychology ethics.

Where Did Experimental Psychology Begin?

The exact roots of experimental psychology are difficult to trace—there are many possible histories that have been and continue to be amended. The origins of this field reach back to the seventeenth and eighteenth centuries, when psychologists and philosophers, such as John Locke, George Berkeley, Immanuel Kant, and many others, debated the reliability of the mind and the legitimacy of psychology as an empirical science.

(Source: an essay by Robert H. Wozniak)

Careers and Salary

Starting salaries for psychology majors are generally in the $25,000 to $35,000 range, but depend greatly on how psych majors use their skills and how much experience they've had. A graduate degree plays a role in increasing the salary range.

CAREER OPTIONS

Professor	Social Worker	Sociologist
Psychologist		

FASHION DESIGN

Basics

Fashion design programs are perfect for anyone fascinated by the creative and outrageous possibilities of fashion. If you have an eye for style, color, trends, and flair, you may want to consider this field. According to The New Parsons School of Design, though, fashion design is about more than beautiful clothes, it is a barometric gauge of our society and culture. If you pursue a career in fashion design you'll also design shoes, accessories, and even costumes. You'll be sketching and designing on both paper and computer, and most programs culminate in a publicly attended fashion show of student work.

One of the best aspects of a fashion design program is the potential for internships, travel, and close work with top designers. When choosing a school, keep location in mind. A school in New York, for example, will give you far better opportunities for schmoozing with the best designers than, say a school in Idaho. The Fashion Institute of Technology, for instance, is located right on Seventh Avenue—or Fashion Avenue, as it's called in the business. It'd be hard to get any closer to the heart of fashion than that.

Be prepared for lots of hands-on work. As with most creative fields, the core of fashion design is learning by doing. You won't be hitting the books like your liberal arts-majoring friends; you'll be hitting the sewing machine, the design software, and eventually, the runway.

SAMPLE COLLEGE CURRICULUM FOR FASHION DESIGN

Accessories Design

Apparel Design

Design

Design Illustration

Electronic Retailing

Fashion Art and History

Fashion Illustration

Historical Theatrical Costume

History of Dress

Knitting

Merchandising and Manufacturing

Model Drawing

Patternmaking

Shoe Design

Textiles

If You Like Fashion Design, You May Also Like . . .

Advertising, art, art education, art history, graphic art, interior design, photography, theater, visual communication

Suggested High School Prep for Fashion Design

Because most fashion design programs encourage emphasis on fine arts including drawing and sculpture, take advantage of your high school art department. It goes without saying that a home economics class or two would be on the right track. And don't forget history and English courses—any good designer knows that fashions are greatly influenced by society and culture.

Fun Facts

What Is Haute Couture?

Haute couture, in the hard, technical sense, is the business of designing and selling high-fashion, exclusive women's clothing. Not every designer can be considered haute couture—he or she must belong to the Syndical Chamber for Haute Couture in Paris. Coco Chanel and Pierre Cardin are among the elite 18 members. Because each article of clothing is custom-made and requires an average of three fittings, dress prices can range from $26,000 to $100,000.

We Do Love Our Fashion

Sixty percent of the 2,000 women in the world who buy haute couture clothes are American. (Source: www.infoplease.com)

Fashion Quotes

"Fashion is architecture: It is a matter of proportions."

—Coco Chanel

"My shoes are special . . . shoes for discerning feet."

—Manolo Blahnik

"Fashion changes—style remains."

—Coco Chanel

"I don't design clothes. I design dreams."

—Ralph Lauren

"Dressing is a way of life."

—Yves Saint-Laurent

Famous People Who Majored in Fashion Design

Susan Ekahn, Nicole Miller, Michael Leva, Leo Narducci, and Monique Robidoux are among those who have graduated from the Rhode Island School of Design apparel design program.

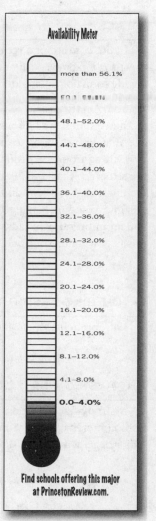

Availability Meter

more than 56.1%

52.1–56.0%

48.1–52.0%

44.1–48.0%

40.1–44.0%

36.1–40.0%

32.1–36.0%

28.1–32.0%

24.1–28.0%

20.1–24.0%

16.1–20.0%

12.1–16.0%

8.1–12.0%

4.1–8.0%

0.0–4.0%

Find schools offering this major at PrincetonReview.com.

Careers and Salary

How and where they choose to use their skills will greatly determine their salary, but people in graphic design–related fields can usually expect to start in the $20,000 to $30,000 range.

CAREER OPTIONS

Artist

Clothing/Jewelry/Cosmetics
   Generalist

Fashion Designer

IMage Consultant

Photographer

Retail Salesperson

Seamstress/Tailor

Stylist

Wedding Consultant

FASHION MERCHANDISING

Basics

Haute couture or a return to the leg-warmer days of 1985? (Definitely 1985.) Will people actually spend $100 for a pair of designer socks? (Of course.) What's up with those new GAP ads? (Who cares?) If you decide to major in fashion merchandising, you'll spend much of your time answering questions like these.

Yours is the world of fashion: the beautiful models, the runways, the photographers, and oh yeah, the clothes. Fashion is a billion-dollar industry that requires not only a little business savvy but also a well-trained eye that knows how to help spot the hottest trends before they show up on *Desperate Housewives*. Everything from the production to the marketing, design, and delivery of the clothes and products hitting the street in Milan and New York is going to be covered by fashion merchandising. Your courses will be both technical and creative, and you can bet that new Hermes bag of yours that great internship opportunities will give you the chance to learn the biz firsthand. All this instruction and professional experience will make you an impresario of fads, a barker of brands. So you may not make the next cover of *Glamour*, but with this major under your belt, you'll be able to predict what will.

If You Like Fashion Merchandising, You May Also Like . . .

Entrepreneurship, fashion design, marketing, mass communication

Suggested High School Prep for Fashion Merchandising

A strong background in the liberal arts, focusing on the humanities, is good preparation for a major in fashion merchandising. Some art or design classes could prove helpful. Although the fashion merchandising major deals with the business side of the industry, the ability to see how designs can be altered for a particular client or market can be invaluable in the heat of the moment.

SAMPLE COLLEGE CURRICULUM FOR FASHION MERCHANDISING

The Business of Fashion

Catalog Development and Usage

Fashion Design for the Apparel Industry

Fashion Sales Promotion

Introduction to Retailing I

Introduction to Visual Merchandising

Merchandise Buying

Merchandise Mathematics

Retail Internship Seminar

BUSINESS, MARKETING, AND RELATED FIELDS

Fun Facts

Off the Average

Some 65 million, or 40 percent, of American women wear a size 12 or higher. Yet only 26 percent of all women's clothing sales are in the plus-size category.

Women and Models

Today's fashion models weigh 23 percent less than the average female, and a young woman between the ages of 18 and 34 has a 7 percent chance of being as slim as a catwalk model and a 1 percent chance of being as thin as a supermodel.

Careers and Salary

Average entry-level positions range from $20,000 to $32,000, but with extensive experience, fashion merchandisers can more than $80,000.

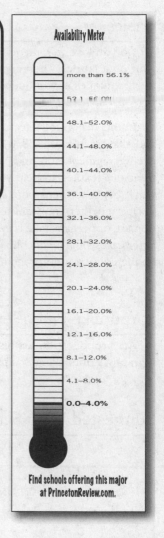

Availability Meter

more than 56.1%

52.1–56.0%

48.1–52.0%

44.1–48.0%

40.1–44.0%

36.1–40.0%

32.1–36.0%

28.1–32.0%

24.1–28.0%

20.1–24.0%

16.1–20.0%

12.1–16.0%

8.1–12.0%

4.1–8.0%

0.0–4.0%

Find schools offering this major at PrincetonReview.com.

CAREER OPTIONS

Advertising Executive	Entrepreneur	Product Designer
Auctioneer	Fashion Designer	Retail Salesperson
Consultant	Market Researcher	Service Sales Representative
Costume Designer	Marketing Executive	Small Business Owner

FIBER, TEXTILES, AND WEAVING ARTS

Basics

Do you love to knit, quilt, or crochet? Do you silkscreen T-shirts for your friends or dream of designing your own fabrics? Then consider fiber, textiles, and weaving arts, a fine arts major which teaches students the techniques of working with woven and non-woven fabrics and fibers, while helping them develop their personal styles and artistic visions.

In this major, you'll learn how to weave and use a loom; how to knit, coil, and crochet; and how to print and silkscreen fabrics. You'll learn both traditional hand processes and the technology-based methods of dyeing, pigmentation, and pattern design. Outside the studio, you'll be taught historical and contemporary trends in textiles, to help you gain an understanding of the larger context of the industry. By junior year, you'll begin to focus on a specific medium or technique and start to develop your own concepts. You'll decide whether you want to use the fiber, textiles, and weaving arts major to create sculptural and installation art, or perhaps take it in a more technical direction, preparing to enter the textile design industry. In the latter case, you'll be encouraged to do an internship in a design studio, textile production studio, museum, or textile conservation program.

If You Like Fiber, Textiles, and Weaving Arts, You May Also Like . . .

Art, art education, art history, crafts, drawing, fashion design, graphic art, interior design, painting, photography, printmaking, sculpture, visual communication

Suggested High School Prep for Fiber, Textiles, and Weaving Arts

You'll obviously want to take all the art and art history courses you can to prepare for this major. Consider taking up knitting or crocheting in your spare time.

SAMPLE CURRICULUM FOR FIBER, TEXTILES, AND WEAVING ARTS

Figure, Nature or Object

History of Textiles

Introduction to Computers for Fashion and Textile Design

Introduction to Textile Design

Machine Knitting

Print Design

Screen Print and Block Print on Fabric

Weaving

Woven Design

Fun Facts

Sew What?

The world's largest historical quilt, which covers some 11,390 square feet, is a faithful reproduction of the state of North Dakota. Sewn by a woman named Leona Tennyson to commemorate her state's one-hundredth anniversary of statehood, this gigantic work of art's appreciation for North Dakota is sadly not reciprocated. Why won't the state display the quilt? According to a North Dakota official, "She should've asked us before she made it that big."

(Source: www.roadsideamerica.com)

Careers and Salary

Starting salary for students with a degree in fiber, textiles, and weaving arts range from about $25,000 to $35,000 a year.

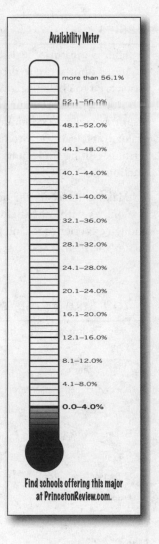

Availability Meter

more than 56.1%

52.1–56.0%

48.1–52.0%

44.1–48.0%

40.1–44.0%

36.1–40.0%

32.1–36.0%

28.1–32.0%

24.1–28.0%

20.1–24.0%

16.1–20.0%

12.1–16.0%

8.1–12.0%

4.1–8.0%

0.0–4.0%

Find schools offering this major
at PrincetonReview.com.

CAREER OPTIONS		
Artist	Costume and Wardrobe Specialist	Textile Designer
Curator	Fashion Designer	

FILM

Basics

Film is a form of artistic expression that involves moving images, sound, color, and light projected in front of a human eye to produce a desired effect. Film is a record of the human condition, and over the years has served to challenge, remind, move, and entertain us. Film is inextricably linked to society and culture—it is both a product and a reflection of our time. Majoring in film involves a dedication to your own artistic vision, as well as a commitment to learning about the great filmmakers from the past and present. As a film major you'll learn how to turn your vision into a work of art through studies in acting, directing, producing, writing, editing, and sound mixing. You'll learn about what goes into making a film, from pre- to post-production.

Making films isn't the only goal of film majors. They also study animation, cinematography, radio, and television. As with other fields of art, film is very competitive—an undergraduate degree probably won't yield enough experience to land you in the Sundance Film Festival unless you're extraordinarily talented or have the luck o' the Irish. If you're serious about becoming a filmmaker, graduate work will probably be a necessity.

If You Like Film, You May Also Like . . .

Advertising, art, art education, art history, creative writing, dance, English, graphic art, photography, theater, visual communication

SAMPLE COLLEGE CURRICULUM FOR FILM

Business of Film

Cinematography

Directing the Actor

Documentary Film

Film Development

Film Noir

Frame and Sequence

Introduction to Animation

The Language of Film

Script Analysis

Sound and Image

Storytelling Strategies

Studies in New Media

Various in-depth courses featuring one filmmaker, writer, or topic, such as Elia Kazan, Martin Scorsese, Film Noir, or Holocaust Film

Suggested High School Prep for Film

If your high school has any classes on film, take advantage; if not, you can prepare for a film degree by taking English, philosophy, art, music, and history classes. Film involves the expression of ideas and culture, and the best way to prepare is to expose yourself to great thinkers and artists of the past.

Fun Facts

From the American Film Institute

The AFI's Greatest American Films of the Past 100 Years

1. *Citizen Kane*
2. *Casablanca*
3. *The Godfather*
4. *Gone with the Wind*
5. *Lawrence of Arabia*
6. *The Wizard of Oz*
7. *The Graduate*
8. *On the Waterfront*
9. *Schindler's List*
10. *Singin' In the Rain*

Those First Tentative Steps

In 1895, Auguste and Louis LumiFre of Lyon invented the first movie camera, the cinematograph. The first film made with this camera was titled *La Sortie des Usines LumiFre* (*Leaving the LumiFre Factory*), and it marked the first time that men captured other men on film. The street where this historic event took place is called the Rue du Premier Film.

Famous People Who Majored in Film

Spike Lee (writer/director/actor, New York University), Chris Columbus (director, New York University), Martin Brest (director, New York University), Joel Coen (director, New York University), Billy Crystal (actor/producer, New York University), Harry Elfont (writer/director, New York University), Martin Scorsese (writer/director/producer, New York University), Oliver Stone (writer/director/producer, New York University), Kim Peirce (writer/director, Columbia University)

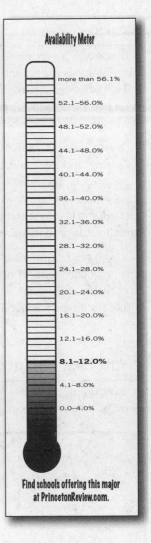

Availability Meter

more than 56.1%

52.1–56.0%

48.1–52.0%

44.1–48.0%

40.1–44.0%

36.1–40.0%

32.1–36.0%

28.1–32.0%

24.1–28.0%

20.1–24.0%

16.1–20.0%

12.1–16.0%

8.1–12.0%

4.1–8.0%

0.0–4.0%

Find schools offering this major at PrincetonReview.com.

Careers and Salary

Although salaries vary depending on location and project, actors, directors, and producers can expect to receive between $20,000 and $30,000 a year.

CAREER OPTIONS		
Actor	Artist	Film Director
Agent	Comedian	Film Editor
Animator	Film Critic	Photographer

FINANCE

Basics

Finance is a very professionally oriented major designed to prepare you for a career in financial management, which is the art and science of managing money or, if you like, the way people, institutions, markets, and countries generate and transfer wealth. It's a good major and potentially a very lucrative one because, these days, everybody—small businesses, monolithic corporations, charities, and governments—needs effective financial management.

If you major in finance, you'll study things such as commercial and investment banking, forecasting and budgeting, and asset and liability management. You'll learn more than you may ever want to know about money, stocks and bonds, and the way markets function. You'll learn how to determine what fraction of a firm's assets (or your own assets) to put into different kinds of investment vehicles to obtain the highest return for a justifiable level of risk. When you graduate, all those baffling indexes at the back of the Wall Street Journal will make sense to you.

Upon graduation, your career can take many paths (naturally), but most finance majors find jobs in the finance departments of firms; with banks, mutual funds, and other kinds of financial institutions; or in government or some kind of charitable organization. Some schools offer specialized areas of concentration within the finance major as well—in insurance and real estate, for example.

If You Like Finance, You May Also Like . . .

Accounting, actuarial science, advertising, applied mathematics, business administration and management, business communications, computer and information science, computer systems analysis, data processing, entrepreneurship, hospitality, human resources management, industrial management, international business, logistics management, managerial economics, marketing, public administration, public policy analysis, real estate, statistics

---

SAMPLE COLLEGE CURRICULUM FOR FINANCE

- Business Ethics
- Calculus
- Corporate Finance
- Cost Accounting
- Financial Accounting
- Human Resources Management
- Intermediate Accounting
- International Business
- Investment Management
- Macroeconomics
- Marketing
- Microeconomics
- Money and Capital Markets

Suggested High School Prep for Finance

If you want to major in finance, take math classes—preferably four or five years of college preparatory math. You'll take calculus as a first-year student, and let us just tell you, it's not for the squeamish. Experience with computers and business software programs will prove mighty helpful too, as will a strong background in writing and speaking.

Fun Facts

A Joke

A man walks into a Silicon Valley pet store looking to buy a monkey. The storekeeper points toward three identical monkeys in identical cages.

"The one on the left costs $500," says the storekeeper.

"Why so much?" asks the man.

"Because it can program in C," answers the storekeeper.

The man inquires about the next monkey. "That one costs $1,500 because it knows Visual C++." The startled man then asks about the third monkey.

"That one costs $3,000," answers the storekeeper.

"Wow!" exclaims the man. "What can it do?"

The owner replies, "To be honest, I've never seen it do a single thing, but it calls itself a financial consultant."

The Nugget Investment Club

This club at Northwestern University was founded in 1996, when a small group of students invested a minimum of $500 into a group portfolio. Since then, The Nugget has been featured twice on CNN and taken several trips to New York City (and nearby downtown Chicago) to investigate financial markets firsthand. Most importantly, though, members of The Nugget have succeeded in their primary objective, which is obviously to make a bit of cash. Best of all, Nugget membership looks really nice on a resume, which often leads to plum jobs.

Famous People Who Majored in Finance

Kevin Costner (actor, California State University—Fullerton)

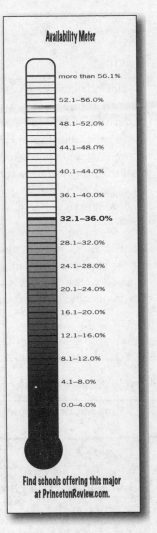

Availability Meter

more than 56.1%

52.1–56.0%

48.1–52.0%

44.1–48.0%

40.1–44.0%

36.1–40.0%

32.1–36.0%

28.1–32.0%

24.1–28.0%

20.1–24.0%

16.1–20.0%

12.1–16.0%

8.1–12.0%

4.1–8.0%

0.0–4.0%

Find schools offering this major at PrincetonReview.com.

Careers and Salary

Starting salaries for finance majors average about $38,000 to $40,000.

CAREER OPTIONS

Accountant/Auditor	Financial Analyst	Music Executive
Actuary	Financial Planner	Real Estate Agent/Broker
Agent	Foreign Exchange Trader	Restaurateur
Attorney	Fund-raiser/Institutional Solicitor	Small Business Owner
Bank Officer	Insurance Agent/Broker	Sports Manager
Bar/Club Manager	Investment Banker	Stockbroker
Bookkeeper	Manufacturing Executive	Trader
Business Valuator	Market Researcher	Venture Capitalist/Investor

FINNISH AND RELATED LANGUAGES, LITERATURES, AND LINGUISTICS

Basics

Finland occupies an extraordinarily interesting geographical position. Nestled in the Scandinavian countries, it's just north of Western Europe and at the edge of Russia and the Slavic world. The result of this position has been a complex and compelling history—linguistically, artistically, and culturally. A major in Finnish and related languages, literatures, and linguistics will allow you to plumb the depths of this society as it was in the past and as it is today. You'll have the opportunity to choose from several areas of concentration: Finnish, Estonian, or Hungarian. From there, you'll begin learning the language and exploring the literature it has produced. You'll also examine the culture with a wider lens. This means you'll spend time looking at art, listening to music, watching films, reading about architecture, and debating politics.

When you step away from the program, you'll be the proud owner of a firm knowledge of all things Finnish, Estonian, or Hungarian. This is a rarity in North America, which means you'll rise to the top of the list for teaching, translating, and other related jobs in the field. If you decide to continue on to graduate school—where you can convert that "firm" knowledge into "expert" knowledge—you'll have the opportunity to become one of the major players in the field.

If You Like Finnish and Related Languages, Literatures, and Linguistics, You May Also Like...

Comparative literature, European history, German, Russian, Scandinavian studies, Slavic languages and literatures

SAMPLE COLLEGE CURRICULUM FOR FINNISH AND RELATED LANGUAGES, LITERATURES, AND LINGUISTICS

Advanced Finnish

Classics in Scandinavian Literature

Contemporary Finnish Literature

Finnish Diaspora

Finnish Film

Finnish Language for Beginners

Introduction to Finnish Linguistics

The Kalevala

Literature of Finland

Survey of Scandinavian Art

Suggested High School Prep for Finnish and Related Languages, Literatures, and Linguistics

Though you're not going to find any electives in Finnish at your high school, you most certainly have the chance to study other languages. Choose one and dig in—it'll be terrific practice for your college days. Enroll in all the literature, history, political science, and art appreciation courses you can. The ability to read and respond (intelligently) to complex texts will come in handy.

Fun Facts

The Most Important Book in the Land

Known as the Finnish national epic, *The Kalevala* is a book that any student of Finnish literature is certain to become intimately acquainted with. *The Kalevala*, which is a collection of folk poems from Finland and Karelia, was initially compiled by folklorist/linguist/doctor/professor Elias Lönnrot in 1835. The book is divided into fifty sections.

The Man Behind the Book

This same year that he compiled and published the first edition of *The Kalevala*, Elias Lönnrot spent an exorbitant 100 rubles on alcohol. A man of healthy thirst and occasional affairs, he was no poster child for restraint. Later in life, however, influenced by a pious new wife, Lönnrot pushed aside the bottle and actually started Selveys-Seura (or Clearheads Club), Finland's first temperance organization.

(Sources: http://virtual.finland.fi/netcomm/news/showarticle.asp?intNWSAID=27015 and www.kirjasto.sci.fi/lonnrot.htm)

Careers and Salary

Finnish and related languages, literatures, and linguistics can expect a starting salary between $25,000 and $30,000 a year.

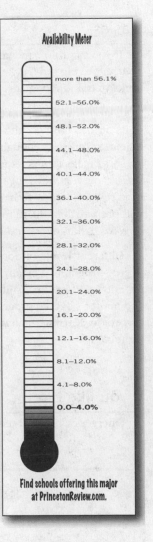

Availability Meter

more than 56.1%

52.1–56.0%

48.1–52.0%

44.1–48.0%

40.1–44.0%

36.1–40.0%

32.1–36.0%

28.1–32.0%

24.1–28.0%

20.1–24.0%

16.1–20.0%

12.1–16.0%

8.1–12.0%

4.1–8.0%

0.0–4.0%

Find schools offering this major at PrincetonReview.com.

CAREER OPTIONS

Diplomat/Attaché/Foreign Service Officer	Historian	Translator
	Journalist	Travel Agent/Guide
Editor	Teacher	Writer

FIRE SCIENCE

Basics

If you can think and act quickly in an emergency situation, have a commitment to public service, and of course love big red trucks, then fire science might be a perfect program for you. Fire science is a degree that seeks to train individuals to approach fighting fire with a sophisticated arsenal of training.

Like so much else, professional fighting fire has become much more modern and technical than the days of its birth. So too has the training and certification that are required to work in the field. No longer is it sufficient to be close enough to respond within minutes or strong enough to hold a hose and point it a fire. Today's qualifications require fire fighters to be able to understand the movement of and to put out existing fires, to prevent new ones in buildings or nature, to investigate fires, to clear smoke-filled buildings efficiently, to rescue victims, to handle hazardous materials, and to manage response teams. A degree in fire science will prepare a graduate for jobs as inspectors, fire fighters, fire chiefs, emergency response teams, national forestry park rangers and as fire fighting instructors.

Different levels of education are available in most programs. Undergraduate certificate and associates degree programs typically take less than a year to two years to complete and require a high school degree for entry and are best suited for volunteers or those who want entry-level fire fighting positions. Bachelor and master's degree programs are generally sought by fire fighting professionals who wish to advance their careers by learning managerial skills or specializing in areas like fire protection engineering or explosion protection.

If you like Fire Science, you may also like

Emergency medical technician, public emergency response, building science, arson investigation

SAMPLE COLLEGE CURRICULUM FOR FIRE SCIENCE

Algebra

Emergency Management

Fire Chemistry

Fire Dynamics

Fire Investigation

Fire Fighting Techniques and Strategy

Fire Modeling

Fire Prevention

Rescue Procedure

Writing Composition

Suggested High School Prep for Fire Science

All of the certificate programs and degrees in fire science require completion of a high school diploma. Courses that will build up a candidate's application are CPR certification, physical strength, good communication skills and basic algebra.

Fun Facts

Controlling fire is a skill mankind has long struggled with, especially within some of the largest most sophisticated cities. Some of history's cities that have been destroyed by fire and rebuilt on their ruins include Rome in 64 AD, London in 798, 982, 989 and 1666; Jamestown, Virginia, in 1608; and Chicago in 1871.

(Source: www.wikipedia.com)

Careers and Salary

Your starting salary falls with in the wide $30,000 to $65,000 salary range in the field of fire science, and it will depend heavily upon the degree level you earn as well as the level of public service your job covers. The lower end of the range will start with someone who has a one-year undergraduate certificate and works for a small city or municipality, and the higher end will refer to those who have master's or graduate degrees and work for larger cities or national organizations.

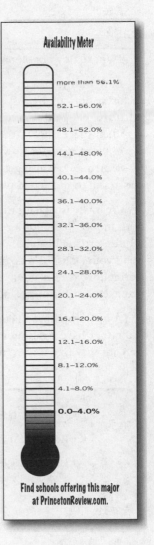

Availability Meter

- more than 56.1%
- 52.1–56.0%
- 48.1–52.0%
- 44.1–48.0%
- 40.1–44.0%
- 36.1–40.0%
- 32.1–36.0%
- 28.1–32.0%
- 24.1–28.0%
- 20.1–24.0%
- 16.1–20.0%
- 12.1–16.0%
- 8.1–12.0%
- 4.1–8.0%
- **0.0–4.0%**

Find schools offering this major at PrincetonReview.com.

CAREER OPTIONS

Emergency Medical Technician	Fire Fighter	Paramedic
Emergency Response Manager	Fire Investigator	Park Ranger
Fire Chief		

FLORICULTURE

Basics

"Where flowers bloom, so does hope."

Lady Bird Johnson was fond of that saying—and floriculture majors will probably enjoy it as well. A major in floriculture just seems to imply a career of making people happy. And chances are that that's just what will happen! Everyone loves getting flowers, and in this major you'll learn exactly what goes into growing them successfully—their appropriate environments, their needs, and their individual characteristics. You'll learn about types of flowers and other ornamental plants and the varying challenges faced by those who grow them. You'll also get experience working in greenhouses, so you can apply what you've learned in the classroom to the actual plant world, cultivating different varieties of plants and monitoring your success.

Creativity is vital for the floriculture major. You'll explore the art of floral design and landscaping, studying both indoor and outdoor plants and how to create attractive arrangements of each. Beautiful floral designs require artistic vision and innovation—arrangements differ throughout the seasons of the year, and you'll build your skills for recognizing artful and unusual combinations of colors and types of flowers. Since many floriculture majors go on to work in greenhouses, nurseries, or flower shops, you'll also learn the basics of management, business, and sales, which include purchasing, storage, and delivery.

Your floriculture major will lay the groundwork for your future in flowers. Emma Goldman once said, "I'd rather have roses on my table than diamonds on my neck." If others are inclined to agree, you'll be well on your way to a rewarding career!

SAMPLE COLLEGE CURRICULUM FOR FLORICULTURE

Basic Floral Design

Botany

Greenhouse Management

Herbaceous Plants

Horticulture

Houseplants

Landscaping

Plant Breeding

Plant Identification

Plant Physiology

Plant Propagation

Retail Flower Shop Operation

Small Business Management

Vegetable and Fruit Production

If You Like Floriculture, You May Also Like . . .

Agriculture, agronamy and crop science, biology, botany and plant biology, ecology, entomology, environmental science, forestry, grain science, horticulture, landscape horticulture, natural resources conservation, plant pathology, soil science, turfgrass science

Suggested High School Prep for Floriculture

You can prepare for a major in floriculture by taking courses in the sciences, especially biology. As with any major, a strong foundation in a variety of subjects, including math and the humanities, will be valuable. Good communication skills are vital to a successful career, so take courses that will strengthen your writing and speaking skills. Getting experience in gardening or flower arranging will give you great preparation for college—check out opportunities for volunteering in your community or start a flower garden of your own.

Fun Facts

Plant Food

Ever eaten a flower? Like some mushrooms, flowers can be poisonous, but there are plenty that are edible. These include carnations, chrysanthemums, cloves, daisies, dandelions, garlic flowers, hibiscus, honeysuckle, lotus blossoms, marigolds, nasturtium, pansies, primroses, roses, squash blossoms, tulips, and violets.

(Source: www.foodreference.com)

Roses Are . . . Purple?

Did you know that the color of the roses you buy for your sweetie has great significance? Keep these in mind next time you set out to win someone's heart.

- Red: "Creative spirit of love," true love, passion
- Pink: Grace, refinement, sweetness
- Yellow: Once jealousy, now friendship
- White: Loyalty and platonic love
- Purple: Enchantment, majesty, but also caution
- Orange: Pride, warmth
- Blue: "Fantasy and impossibility"
- Black: "The color of the crone," "the promise that soon you will know something you did not know before"

(Source: www.rosegathering.com)

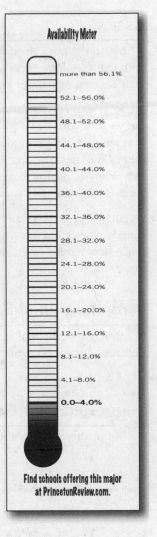

Availability Meter

more than 56.1%

52.1–56.0%

48.1–52.0%

44.1–48.0%

40.1–44.0%

36.1–40.0%

32.1–36.0%

28.1–32.0%

24.1–28.0%

20.1–24.0%

16.1–20.0%

12.1–16.0%

8.1–12.0%

4.1–8.0%

0.0–4.0%

Find schools offering this major at PrincetonReview.com.

Careers and Salary

The starting salary for floriculture majors is in the $20,000 to $30,000 range, but it depends on how you choose to apply your skills. Floral designers, for example, make less than floral shop owners. Those who specialize in upscale weddings may improve their income.

CAREER OPTIONS

Floral Designer	Floriculturist	Teacher
Floral Shop Owner/Manager	Researcher	

FOOD SCIENCE

Basics

No, this is not a major for someone who wants to eat their face off. Yes, this is a real science, complete with math, biology, chemistry, and the rest of the gang. No, this probably won't improve your cooking abilities. Yes, you may never want to eat fast food again after completing this major.

So, now that we got that cleared up, what is a food scientist? Many things. From learning how to develop the world's strongest soybean to administering food and safety standards, food scientists deal with almost every aspect of food production. They are the brains behind the genetically engineered ear of corn, the doctors of the meat-packing industry. Food scientists shape the way we eat by helping to create and enforce new safety standards, expand our understanding of what constitutes a balanced meal, and improve the ways we produce and consume food.

All of this involves a lot of hard science. You'll take a combination of premed and engineering courses aimed at providing you with a basic understanding of the chemical and biological world, as well as the nitty-gritty facts behind food and nutrition.

If You Like Food Science, You May Also Like . . .

Agricultural and biological engineering, biochemistry, biology, chemistry, dietetics, genetics, pharmacology, physical therapy, premedicine

Suggested High School Prep for Food Science

Get in a lot of math and science courses, particularly biology, chemistry, and calculus.

SAMPLE COLLEGE CURRICULUM FOR FOOD SCIENCE

Biochemistry

Biology

Chemistry

Data Analysis

Food Additives

Food Chemistry Analysis

Introduction to Food Processing

Microbiology

Nutrition

NUTRITION, HOME ECONOMICS, AND RELATED FIELDS

Fun Facts

Did You Know?
Food technology is America's largest industry.

Did You Know?
According to the Center for Disease Control, 97 percent of food-related illness occurs not at farms, but after the commodities have left the distribution center.

Careers and Salary

The average starting salary is between $30,000 and $40,000 for a food science major and for those with advanced degrees, the average salary is $59,000.

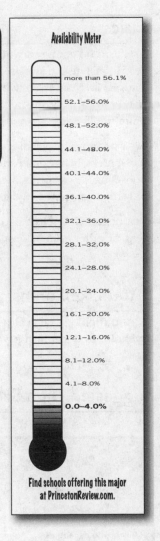

Availability Meter

more than 56.1%

52.1–56.0%

48.1–52.0%

44.1–48.0%

40.1–44.0%

36.1–40.0%

32.1–36.0%

28.1–32.0%

24.1–28.0%

20.1–24.0%

16.1–20.0%

12.1–16.0%

8.1–12.0%

4.1–8.0%

0.0–4.0%

Find schools offering this major at PrincetonReview.com.

CAREER OPTIONS

Biochemist

Geneticist

Nutritionist

Biologist

FORENSIC PSYCHOLOGY

Basics

Not to be confused with forensic science, forensic psychology is the application of psychology within the criminal justice system. Forensic psychologists perform psychological evaluations, counsel the mentally ill, advise lawyers, assist with juror selection, and provide courtroom testimonial. They deal with legal issues ranging from analyzing public policy, to determining whether a defendant was insane at the time he or she committed a crime.

As a forensic psychology major, you'll take psychology classes covering a range of topics including mental disorders, behavioral patterns, and risk factors for violence and criminality. You'll learn practical skills like counseling, assessment, intervention methods, and psychological testing. Forensic psychology majors also study the legal system, judicial processes, the basics of public policy, and professional standards and ethics.

A degree in forensic psychology can be used to pursue a career in psychology, social work, law enforcement, or other criminal justice positions.

If You Like Forensic Psychology, You May Also Like . . .

Anthropology, clinical psychology, cognitive psychology, criminal science, criminology, developmental psychology, educational psychology, forensic science psychology, social psychology, social work, sociology

Suggested High School Prep for Forensic Psychology

Pay special attention in math, science, and English classes, as a strong background in these areas will be necessary in the field. If your school offers any psychology courses, take it.

> **SAMPLE COLLEGE CURRICULUM FOR FORENSIC PSYCHOLOGY**
>
> Abnormal Psychology
>
> Criminology
>
> Ethics and Law
>
> Experimental Psychology
>
> The Family: Change, Challenges, and Crisis Intervention
>
> Psychology and the Law
>
> Psychology of Adolescence and the Adolescent Offender
>
> Psychology of Alcoholism
>
> Psychology of Criminal Behavior
>
> Theories of Personality

Fun Facts

Criminal Profiling

Some forensic psychologists also act as criminal profilers. Profilers analyze a perpetrator's behavior to deduce information about him/her—including motives, probable location, and appearance—to help authorities identify and capture their suspect.

Criminal profilers sometimes work with very subtle clues to deduce surprisingly accurate information. One of the best-known profiles was performed by a New York psychiatrist, James Brussels, who profiled "The Mad Bomber of New York." Back in the 1940s and 1950s, the Mad Bomber left 32 explosive packages around the city over a period of about 8 years. After reviewing the case file, which consisted primarily of letters the suspect had mailed over a 16-year period, Brussels suggested that the person the police were after was "a heavy man. Middle aged. Foreign-born. Roman Catholic. Single. Lives with a brother or sister." He also added that he was paranoid, lived in Connecticut, and when found would be "wearing a double-breasted suit. Buttoned." Sure enough, when authorities eventually located George Metesky, they found him to be an unmarried, overweight, 54-year-old Lithuanian-born Catholic, and living with his two unmarried sisters in Connecticut. The only detail that didn't match up was his clothes—when the Bomber came to the door, he was wearing pajamas, not a suit. Upon seeing the police, Metesky asked if they would wait while he changed. He returned wearing a double-breasted suit—buttoned.

(Source: www.crimelibrary.com)

Careers and Salary

A typical forensic psychology major earns a starting salary of about $25,000 to $35,000 a year.

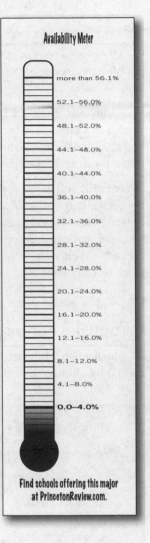

Availability Meter

more than 56.1%

52.1–56.0%

48.1–52.0%

44.1–48.0%

40.1–44.0%

36.1–40.0%

32.1–36.0%

28.1–32.0%

24.1–28.0%

20.1–24.0%

16.1–20.0%

12.1–16.0%

8.1–12.0%

4.1–8.0%

0.0–4.0%

Find schools offering this major at PrincetonReview.com.

CAREER OPTIONS

Detective	Psychiatrist	Social Worker
FBI Agent	Psychologist	Sociologist
Police Officer	Public Policy Writer	Trial Lawyer
Probation/Parole Officer	Researcher	Youth Counselor

FORENSIC SCIENCE

Basics

All right, so technically, it may be impossible to speak with the dead, but as anybody who's ever seen a couple of episodes of *NYPD Blue* or *Law & Order* will tell you the dead can speak, we just have to know how to listen.

Forensic science teaches us how to listen to the dead and to everything and everyone in any way connected to a crime. It is the eyes and ears behind the dead and the missing. It picks up where the crystal ball and the candles leave off, and—with a little molecular and biological testing, perhaps a pattern analysis or two—it can reveal the past to us.

Forensic science is aptly named because to uncover the missing links of crimes, forensic scientists need a working knowledge of almost every science. They're not just trying to figure out what happened, but also how, when, why, and because of whom. They are one part pathologist, one part dentist, one part psychologist, one part chemist, one part anthropologist, and one part criminologist. They get to show up at crime scenes in their own vans, and you can bet that when they speak, everyone listens. An easy major/profession? Not a chance. But rest assured that the work you do will be invaluable and possibly very lucrative.

If You Like Forensic Science, You May Also Like . . .

Biochemistry, biology, biotechnology, cell biology, chemistry, clinical psychology, criminology, developmental psychology, genetics, microbiology, molecular genetics, neurobiology, pharmacology, pharmacy, premedicine, psychology, sociology

SAMPLE COLLEGE CURRICULUM FOR FORENSIC SCIENCE

Forensic Anthropology

Biochemistry

Calculus

Concepts of Bioscience

Crime Scene Investigation

Criminal Justice and Community Law

Criminology

Forensic Anthropology

Genetics

Human Physiology

Molecular Genetics

Organic Chemistry

Social Psychology

Suggested High School Prep for Forensic Science

Science, science, and if you have time, a little more science. Think hard about biology, chemistry, physics, anatomy, advanced algebra, and if you can, take calculus and AP science courses to help prepare you for the rigors of this major.

Fun Facts

You Can Run, But You Can't Hide

Glass is often broken during a crime, and tiny fragments are commonly caught in clothing. These fragments can remain hidden in the clothes even if the criminal washes the clothes many times over. The fragments can then be recovered by police and analyzed to see whether they match the broken glass at the crime scene.

They Can See All That?

Experts can discover all sorts of things from even a microscopic piece of fiber evidence, including whether it was cut, what with, and whether by a right- or left-handed person.

Careers and Salary

The starting salary is between $28,000 and $38,000, but that could go as high as $80,000 for those working in a major city.

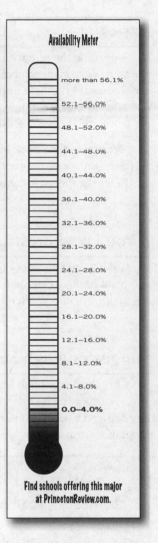

Availability Meter

more than 56.1%

52.1–56.0%

48.1–52.0%

44.1–48.0%

40.1–44.0%

36.1–40.0%

32.1–36.0%

28.1–32.0%

24.1–28.0%

20.1–24.0%

16.1–20.0%

12.1–16.0%

8.1–12.0%

4.1–8.0%

0.0–4.0%

Find schools offering this major
at PrincetonReview.com.

CAREER OPTIONS

Anthropologist	Paramedic	Private Investigator
Attorney	Physician	Sociologist
FBI Agent	Police Officer/Manager	Trial Lawyer

FORESTRY

Basics

Forestry is the science of wilderness management, incorporating the study of trees, crops, soil, wildlife, plant life, park management, and other environmental issues. Forestry majors divide their time between the classroom and the field, and most forestry programs require an extended stay in a camp setting. You probably won't spend much time roasting marshmallows or playing touch football at forestry camp, but you will get hands-on experience in the field.

Forestry majors work in many areas. Some work for the government as soil scientists, crop specialists, and park and forest rangers. Others work for private firms as growers, assessors, and consultants. As concern for the environment increases, forestry majors may find themselves in increasing demand.

If You Like Forestry, You May Also Like . . .

Agricultural education, agricultural and biological engineering, agriculture, animal science, biology, botany and plant biology, cell biology, ecology, environmental and environmental health engineering, environmental science, horticulture, microbiology, molecular genetics, plant pathology, wildlife management, zoology

Suggested High School Prep for Forestry

A firm background in science will serve you well. Take as many courses in chemistry, biology, and physics as you can. Advanced math is usually a part of the forestry curriculum, so courses in calculus and trigonometry are also useful. And don't forget about P.E., baby. You'd better like being outside because most forestry programs are physically demanding, and you don't always get to stay indoors when the elements aren't cooperative.

SAMPLE COLLEGE CURRICULUM FOR FORESTRY

Calculus

Environmental Policy

Forest Biology and Dendrology

Forest Measurements

General Biology

General Chemistry

Geology

Organic Chemistry

Silviculture

Soils

Statistics

Tree Taxonomy, Growth, and Structure

Fun Facts

Dig Deeper

Prospective forestry majors can find a wealth of information on college programs, scholarships, and careers at www.forestry.com, the official forestry site. You can also make contact with forestry professionals, learn about new developments in forestry equipment and policy, and read forestry publications via the site.

Thanks, Teddy!

The United States Forest Service was established in 1905 by President Theodore Roosevelt. It currently employs about 30,000 people and protects national forests that encompass 191 million acres of land.

Careers and Salary

The starting salary for a forestry major fresh out of college is about $25,000 to $30,000.

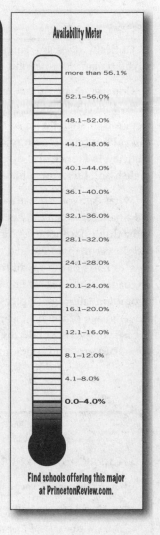

Availability Meter

more than 56.1%

52.1–56.0%

48.1–52.0%

44.1–48.0%

40.1–44.0%

36.1–40.0%

32.1–36.0%

28.1–32.0%

24.1–28.0%

20.1–24.0%

16.1–20.0%

12.1–16.0%

8.1–12.0%

4.1–8.0%

0.0–4.0%

Find schools offering this major at PrincetonReview.com.

CAREER OPTIONS

Biologist

Ecologist

Environmentalist/
Environmental Scientist

Florist

Park Ranger

FRENCH

Basics

Honestly, does any language sound cooler, more romantic, or more sophisticated than French? (Okay, maybe Italian.) But beyond sounding cool, French is also a great college major.

Undergraduate programs in French are primarily designed to ensure that you gain a substantial level of competence in speaking and writing the language (advanced courses are often conducted in French), so be prepared to spend a lot of time studying the nuts and bolts of grammar and translation. In addition, you'll learn about French culture, history, and literature and the throng of exotic locales where French is spoken. Majoring in French also offers abundant opportunities to take classes in other departments such as history, English and literature, philosophy, international studies, film, and art history.

What can you do with a French major besides teach? A lot. French speakers are in demand in banking and finance, foreign market analysis, diplomacy, and hotel management, just to name a few fields. But if you don't think corporations hire language majors, take note of what BP-Amoco (one of the most monolithic and powerful multinational corporations in the world) has to say: "It took us far too long to realize that 'business' in parts of the world outside North America is about 'relationships.'" While many will tell you that the language of business is English, relationships are forged through common experiences and respect, and in a common language (typically not English). Even the most basic efforts to understand and communicate in the language of the host are greatly appreciated, and often form the basis for a business deal to be struck." In case you were wondering, France boasts the world's fourth largest economy, and its gross domestic product (GDP) growth is one of the highest among European economies.

SAMPLE COLLEGE CURRICULUM FOR FRENCH

Advanced Business French

Advanced Spoken and Written French

Analysis of Literary and Cultural Texts

Basic French

Contemporary French Culture

French African Literature

French Culture and Writing

French Poetry

Intermediate French Composition

Intermediate French Conversation

Modern French Grammar and Syntax

Revolutionary France

Seventeenth- and Eighteenth-Century French Literature

If You Like French, You May Also Like . . .

Art history, Chinese, classics, English, German, Hebrew, history, Italian, Japanese, Modern Greek, Portuguese, Russian, Slavic languages and literature, Spanish

Suggested High School Prep for French

The more high school French you take, the better because taking foreign language placement tests is one of the first things you will probably do when you embark on your college career. The farther you can place yourself above French 101, the more time and money you will save.

Fun Facts

A Moveable Feast

There are several schools and agencies that offer study abroad programs in France. And here's good news: You don't necessarily have to be a student at the school that offers the program to sign up. (You will need to pony up some additional cash, though.)

- CUPA in Paris
- Hamilton College Program in Paris
- Institute of European Studies in Paris
- Knox College Program in Besancon
- Middlebury College Program in Paris
- New York University in Paris
- Smith College Junior Year in Paris
- Swarthmore College in Grenoble
- Sweet Briar College Junior Year Abroad
- Vassar-Wesleyan in Paris

Did You Know?

In addition to France, of course, French is at least one of the primary languages in more than 25 countries, including the following:

Burundi	Luxembourg
Cameroon	Madagascar
Canada	Monaco
Chad	Niger
Djibouti	Rwanda
Guinea	Senegal
Haiti	Togo
Ivory Coast	

Famous People Who Majored in French

Brooke Shields (actress and model, Princeton University)

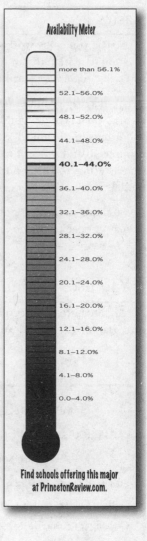

Availability Meter

more than 56.1%

52.1–56.0%

48.1–52.0%

44.1–48.0%

40.1–44.0%

36.1–40.0%

32.1–36.0%

28.1–32.0%

24.1–28.0%

20.1–24.0%

16.1–20.0%

12.1–16.0%

8.1–12.0%

4.1–8.0%

0.0–4.0%

Find schools offering this major at PrincetonReview.com.

Careers and Salary

The average starting salary received by foreign language majors is in the $22,000 to $30,000 range.

CAREER OPTIONS

Book Publishing Professional	Foreign Exchange Trader	Speech Therapist
Curator	Professor	Teacher
Diplomat/Attaché/Foreign Service Officer	Public Relations Professional	Translator
Film Director	Sommelier	Writer

FURNITURE DESIGN

Basics

Maybe you enjoy working with your hands and building things, or perhaps have a keen sense of aesthetics that you're itching to put to a practical use. Then again, maybe you dream of creating the world's most comfortable couch. If so, furniture design could be the major for you.

In this major, your course of study will encompass the skill, theory, and context of furniture design. This means you'll take drawing, design, and history of furniture to help develop and refine your aesthetic, while acquiring the technical knowledge needed to execute your projects. These skills include woodworking, using hand and power tools; metalworking, including welding and fabricating; finishing and veneering; and upholstering. You'll spend much time in the studio, experimenting with techniques and materials, building models, and testing pieces.

Students of furniture design may pursue a career designing mass-produced furniture destined for retail, or may choose to design and build one-of-a-kind pieces for a more upscale clientele.

If You Like Furniture Design, You May Also Like . . .

Architecture, architectural engineering, art, art history, drawing, illustration, environmental design/architecture, graphic design, industrial design, interior architecture, interior design, jewelry, metalsmithing, sculpture

SAMPLE COLLEGE CURRICULUM FOR FURNITURE DESIGN

Advanced Furniture Studio

Custom Cabinet and Furniture Design

Drawing for Furniture 2-D + 3-D

Historic Buildings and Interior Structures

History of Furniture

Interior Design

Interior Finishes and Design Application

Materials and Processes Wood

Media for Design Development

Preservation and Restoration

Professional Practice and Portfolio

Spatial Composition

Suggested High School Prep for Furniture Design

To prepare for the design part of the program, you'll want to take art history, geometry, drawing, and, if they are offered, sculpture and ceramics. A shop class will be helpful for the building and assembly part of the major.

Fun Facts

Would You Sit in a Paper Chair?

In the 1960s, there was such a thing! Developed by designer Peter Murdoch, the paper chair was covered in bright Op-art and Pop-art designs. The chairs were sold cheaply, and were meant to last about three to five months.

(Source: www.bbc.co.uk/homes/design/period_1960s.shtml)

Furniture Fortune

Ingvar Kamprad founded Ikea when he was just a teenager. Today he is ranked thirteenth on Forbes "World's Richest People" list.

(Source: www.forbes.com)

Careers and Salary

Starting salaries for those with a degree in furniture design are about $25,000.

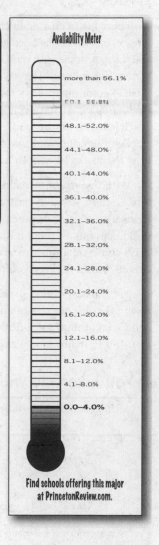

Availability Meter

more than 56.1%

52.1–56.0%

48.1–52.0%

44.1–48.0%

40.1–44.0%

36.1–40.0%

32.1–36.0%

28.1–32.0%

24.1–28.0%

20.1–24.0%

16.1–20.0%

12.1–16.0%

8.1–12.0%

4.1–8.0%

0.0–4.0%

Find schools offering this major at PrincetonReview.com.

CAREER OPTIONS

Architect	Carpenter	Product Designer
Antiques Dealer	Furniture Designer	Structural Engineer
Artist	Interior Designer	Woodworker

GAY AND LESBIAN STUDIES

Basics

There has been a significant number of high-impact jobs working with the gay and lesbian population much longer than there has been an entire major on which to build a foundation for those jobs. Times do change. Gay and lesbian studies is a multidisciplinary major that will give you a strong body of knowledge in gay and lesbian history and culture. The gay and lesbian community—often called the lesbian, gay, bisexual, and transgendered (LGBT) community—has faced many challenges over the years and still does today. You'll study how this culture has affected and been affected by heterosexual culture and the conflicts that have arisen between them. You'll learn about the LGBT population's concerns with civil rights in the workplace and home, struggles with public policy, and battles over legal issues. Media portrayal of the LGBT community will be discussed, as well as how the media have both harmed and helped LGBT efforts to establish a place in the culture.

With this major, sexuality will be treated as an important element of the humanities and social sciences. You'll study sexuality critically, examining its role in history, art, literature, and psychology, among other fields. The relationship between identity and sexuality has changed over the years, and you'll gain a deeper understanding of what it means to be LGBT today, the intricacies of LGBT relationships, and the number of ways those relationships are viewed by society. You'll also spend time on how LGBT relationships are perceived within different cultures and social classes.

Art, music, politics, psychology, philosophy, and literature will all be part of your gay and lesbian studies major. If you plan to obtain a master's degree in psychology, social work, or sociology, this major offers a solid background for a career working with this population. You don't have to be involved in a LGBT relationship to major in gay and lesbian studies—this major is open to all.

If You Like Gay and Lesbian Studies, You May Also Like . . .

African American studies, African studies, American history, American literature, American studies, anthropology, art history, comparative literature, East Asian studies, east European studies, history, Islamic studies, Jewish studies, linguistics, Medieval and Renaissance studies, Middle Eastern studies, peace studies, philosophy, psychology, South Asian studies, Southeast Asian studies

> ### Sample College Curriculum for Gay and Lesbian Studies
>
> Asian American Gender and Sexuality
> Cultural History of Queer Studies
> Feminist Theory and Research
> Gay and Lesbian Civil Rights
> Gay and Lesbian Perspectives in History
> Gender, Race, and Sexuality
> Lesbian and Gay Literature
> Lesbian and Gay Politics
> Philosophy of Gender and Sexuality
> Psychology of the Lesbian Experience
> Religion in the Gay and Lesbian Population
> Sexual Orientation and Health

Suggested High School Prep for Gay and Lesbian Studies

As with other humanities majors, your best preparation will be a broad spectrum of courses in all disciplines. Take upper-level courses in science and math, such as calculus and physics. Good reading, writing, and spoken communication skills will be vital to your success in a gay and lesbian studies major, so be sure to take advanced courses in English, languages, history, and other humanities disciplines. If your school or community has any gay and lesbian organizations, becoming involved might give you some good perspectives with which to begin your college studies. Volunteer work is another good option.

Fun Facts

Something to Celebrate

Each Sunday in *The New York Times*, several pages, once titled "Weddings," are devoted to the marriage announcements of the well-to-do. In autumn of 2002, the *Times* changed the heading from "Weddings" to "Weddings/Celebrations" and began including gay and lesbian couples who celebrated their own devotion in commitment ceremonies.

What Is Queer Theory?

Queer theory became popular in the late 1970s, when critics began reading texts with the intention of finding evidence of sexual identities that the author may not have intended to portray or realized he or she was portraying. This form of criticism turns the text into a kind of "coming-out narrative." The critic assumes responsibility for defining the characters and for completing a narrative that the author supposedly failed to finish.

(Source: *Queer Theory: An Introduction*, by Annamarie Jagose)

Careers and Salary

As with most humanities majors, you'll be able to choose from a wide variety of careers after graduation. Most humanities majors have starting salaries in the $20,000 to $30,000 range.

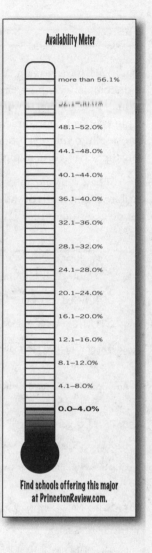

Availability Meter

more than 56.1%

52.1–56.0%

48.1–52.0%

44.1–48.0%

40.1–44.0%

36.1–40.0%

32.1–36.0%

28.1–32.0%

24.1–28.0%

20.1–24.0%

16.1–20.0%

12.1–16.0%

8.1–12.0%

4.1–8.0%

0.0–4.0%

Find schools offering this major at PrincetonReview.com.

CAREER OPTIONS		
Philosopher	Teacher	Writer
Professor		

GENERAL STUDIES AND HUMANITIES

Basics

Let's say that you're a travel writing fan—like, you've read *A Walk in the Woods* eleven times and can't wait to get started again. You especially like travel writing that involves a lot of nature. You also like this type of documentary. And website. Maybe this is a passion you'd like to develop in college. If so, you might want to major in general studies and humanities, where you can weave together a curriculum that lets you explore "travel communications" from all sorts of angles. This of course, will give you a special edge when you step into the real world. Check out the "Sample College Curriculum" below to see what sorts of classes you, the travel guru, might take.

Whatever your interests, the general studies and humanities major guarantees you plenty of room to explore the breadth of the humanities. That said, this is not a Gee-I-can't-quite-make-up-my-mind-so-I-think-I'll-just-do-gen-studies major. Instead, this is a major for self-motivated students who are interested in shaping a curriculum that matches their specific educational ambitions. Before you're even admitted to the major, you'll probably be asked to sit down with an advisor to articulate your goals and devise a rough course of study that'll help you meet those goals. The course of study will need to include core requirements in areas such as composition and foreign languages. You'll also need to select a major and a minor area of emphasis, which ensures you won't be pulled in too many directions. The bulk of your major and minor courses will be drawn from the humanities, but should you want to pair that literary theory class with a computer science lab, go for it. By the time you finish the degree, you'll be able to interact intelligently with people and ideas in many disciplines, and we all know how welcome a trait this is with employers.

> ### SAMPLE COLLEGE CURRICULUM FOR GENERAL STUDIES AND HUMANITIES
>
> Advanced Creative Nonfiction Workshop
>
> American History and Geography since the Automobile
>
> Basics of Graphic Design
>
> Beginning Spanish
>
> Creative Nonfiction Workshop
>
> Ethnographic Studies
>
> Expository Travel Writing
>
> Historical Geology
>
> Intermediate Spanish
>
> Introduction to Film Studies
>
> New Journalism and American Literature
>
> On the Road: The Beat Generation
>
> The Politics of Place
>
> Principles of Composition
>
> Romanticism
>
> Socrates, Plato, and Aristotle
>
> Theories in Visual Communications
>
> World Geography

If You Like General Studies and Humanities, You May Also Like...

Anthropology, classics, English, ethics, great books, history, peace studies, political science, religious studies, sociology

Suggested High School Prep for General Studies and Humanities

General studies and humanities majors must have strong communications skills and a keen ability to master a range of subjects. Taking a broad spectrum of humanities classes—English, history, government, etc.—will best prepare you for the college days ahead.

Fun Facts

The Name Game

Trying to locate the general studies and humanities program at your college of choice? It's possible that the program is wearing one of its many alternative titles. Here are some of the other names the major goes by:

- General Studies
- General Humanities
- General Studies in the Humanities
- Humanities and General Studies
- Humanities
- Interdisciplinary Studies in the Humanities
- Interdisciplinary Studies
- Liberal Studies
- Liberal Arts
- Create a Program

Careers and Salary

Because the potential career choices of general studies and humanities majors vary so widely, starting salaries are difficult to predict. However, majors in the humanities can typically expect to earn between $24,000 and $30,000.

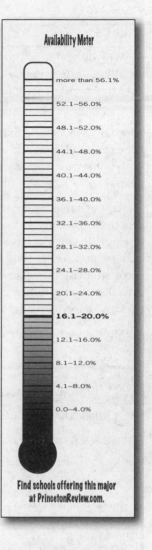

Availability Meter

more than 56.1%
52.1–56.0%
48.1–52.0%
44.1–48.0%
40.1–44.0%
36.1–40.0%
32.1–36.0%
28.1–32.0%
24.1–28.0%
20.1–24.0%
16.1–20.0%
12.1–16.0%
8.1–12.0%
4.1–8.0%
0.0–4.0%

Find schools offering this major at PrincetonReview.com.

CAREER OPTIONS

Activist	Film Maker	Salesperson
Artist	Historian	Social Worker
Businessperson	Journalist	Teacher
Consultant	Politician	Writer
Editor	Researcher	And the list goes on....
Entrepreneur		

GENETICS

Basics

Why do you have brown eyes, while your brother's are blue? Jeans, baby. Wait, we mean genes, which are all the little chemical components that make up you, from the color of your hair to the shape of your nose to whether your middle toe is longer than your big toe.

Genetics is the science of heredity. In other words, it's the study of which genes are responsible for which traits in humans and other organisms. Genetics is often broken down into more specialized areas of study. For example, Washington State University divides genetics into transmission genetics, molecular genetics, and evolutionary genetics. As an undergraduate, you'll most likely become well versed in all of three of these fields.

As a genetics major, you're in a position to do a great deal of good, medically and scientifically. Many geneticists eventually choose to focus on molecular genetics, which includes, among other things, cancer research. In this field, you would study how cell growth, reproduction, and mutation leads to cancer and how to stop (or reverse) the process. You may eventually concentrate on human gene therapy, in which you'd study the possible treatments and cures for currently incurable diseases such as cystic fibrosis. You may also choose to become involved in genetic engineering, which uses the fundamentals of genetics to alter and improve plants, animals, and other organisms.

Most genetics majors choose to continue their studies in graduate or medical school.

SAMPLE COLLEGE CURRICULUM FOR GENETICS

Biochemical Genetics

Classical Human Genetics

Clinical Implications of the Human Genome Project

Developmental Genetics

Genes and Cancer

Genes, Race, and Evolution

Genes: Clinical and Social Issues

Genetics of Common Disorders

Genomics

Medicine in the New Millennium

Modern Human Genomics

New Molecular Techniques in Cytogenetics

Prenatal Diagnosis

Red Cell Membranes

If You Like Genetics, You May Also Like . . .

Biology, botany and plant biology, cell biology, microbiology, molecular genetics, pharmacology, pharmacy, zoology

Suggested High School Prep for Genetics

Because the field of genetics involves a great deal of science, try to take courses in biology, chemistry, physics, and anything else involving research that your high school offers. Also important are math courses such as calculus, statistics, analytic geometry, and computer courses. And don't forget English. As a scientist you'll need good reading and writing skills.

Fun Facts

Like Two Peas in a Pod

Who would have thought that a complex field like genetics would have begun by studying garden peas? Gregor Mendel, an Augustinian monk and scientist, discovered the rudiments of genetics by cross-breeding peas in the garden of his monastery. He observed how plants differed from one another in size, color, and other qualities and suggested that these characteristics were the results of heredity. He also suggested that heredity followed simple statistical laws. The significance of Mendel's discoveries was not realized until many years after his death, when other botanists arrived at similar conclusions.

Bad Blood

In 500 B.C./B.C.E., the Greek philosopher Pythagoras suggested that male and female "fluids" were responsible for creating life. Aristotle furthered this idea and suggested that these fluids, or "semens," were actually purified blood—therefore, blood must be part of heredity. Though our knowledge is now far more advanced, Aristotle's concept lives on whenever we use phrases such as "blue blood," "blood relative," "bad blood," or "royal blood."

(Source: www.Britannica.com)

Careers and Salary

Genetics majors' starting salaries will depend mainly on how they choose to use their degrees. Engineering fields generally have salaries in the $40,000 to $50,000 range; other science fields are about the same, perhaps beginning about $30,000. Their salaries will increase as they continue their studies in graduate or medical school.

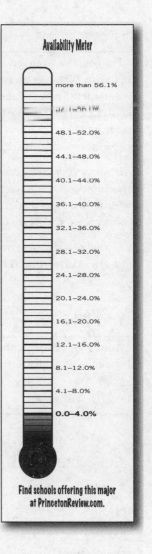

Availability Meter

more than 56.1%

42.1–56.1%

48.1–52.0%

44.1–48.0%

40.1–44.0%

36.1–40.0%

32.1–36.0%

28.1–32.0%

24.1–28.0%

20.1–24.0%

16.1–20.0%

12.1–16.0%

8.1–12.0%

4.1–8.0%

0.0–4.0%

Find schools offering this major at PrincetonReview.com.

CAREER OPTIONS		
Biochemist	Geneticist	Researcher
Biologist	Physician	

GEOGRAPHY

Basics

Do you lose yourself in maps or have an interest in the weather or the environment that your friends don't share? If so, geography may be a field to explore. There's more to geography than locating state capitals and identifying mountain ranges. Geographers predict the weather and analyze environmental changes, and they deal with issues of population such as where population is greatest and why and how populations change and have changed. If you have an interest in foreign affairs, you may be interested to know that many geographers focus on specific parts of the world such as Europe or Africa.

Human geography and physical geography are two main branches of this field, and both offer many opportunities for interesting study. According to the Association of American Geographers, human geography deals with the spatial aspects of human existence such as where we live and work, how we use space—basically how we create our worlds. Physical geographers, however, focus more on the land and climate.

Geography majors usually become familiar with geographic information systems, so be prepared for a lot of science, math, and computer work.

If You Like Geography, You May Also Like . . .

American history, anthropology, archaeology, ecology, forestry, history, natural resources conservation, soil science, statistics, urban planning, urban studies

Suggested High School Prep for Geography

Because geography involves quite a bit of science, take as many courses as you can in physics, chemistry, or biology. Math courses—especially statistics—will certainly help you out, as will computer classes. A drawing class or two couldn't hurt, nor could courses in history and social studies.

SAMPLE COLLEGE CURRICULUM FOR GEOGRAPHY

Air Pollution Meteorology

Applied Spatial Statistics

Computer Cartography

Environmental Change

Environmental Remote Sensing

Geographic Information Systems (GIS)

Geographic Methods

Hydroclimatology

Internships, such as in geographical analysis

Physical Geography of the City

Urban Meteorology

Weather and Climate

World Regional Geography

Fun Facts

What Is the Most Remote Place on Earth?

According to the *Guinness Book of World Records*, it is Bouvet Island in the South Atlantic Ocean. The nearest island, besides being uninhabited, is 1,020 miles away. The island is 23 square miles of black lava and glacial ice.

(Source: www.infoplease.com)

Famous People Who Majored in Geography

Michael Jordan (basketball phenom, University of North Carolina)

Careers and Salary

Salaries for geography majors typically start at $25,000 to $36,000.

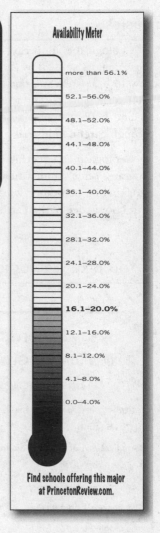

Availability Meter

more than 56.1%

52.1–56.0%

48.1–52.0%

44.1–48.0%

40.1–44.0%

36.1–40.0%

32.1–36.0%

28.1–32.0%

24.1–28.0%

20.1–24.0%

16.1–20.0%

12.1–16.0%

8.1–12.0%

4.1–8.0%

0.0–4.0%

Find schools offering this major at PrincetonReview.com.

CAREER OPTIONS		
Anthropologist	Professor	Teacher
Archaeologist	Surveyor	Website Designer

GEOLOGICAL ENGINEERING

Basics

Geological engineering combines the fields of geology and engineering in a way that makes a lot of sense; majors study how human beings can put the earth to safe and efficient use. For example, they learn how to evaluate a site on which a tunnel, dam, or road might be built. They learn about geologic hazards, such as earthquakes and volcanoes and how to best protect people from them. They examine ways to search for and harvest energy resources. They also discover ways to protect the earth while still developing it through careful industrial practices.

Geological engineering is very field work-oriented; much of your study will be hands-on research. Many programs offer summer field study programs in various parts of the country. Your studies will involve laboratory work, computer work, and problem-solving. The practical nature of geological engineering—using your knowledge of the Earth to solve engineering problems—can make for a rewarding and exciting career.

If You Like Geological Engineering, You May Also Like . . .

Agricultural and biological engineering, applied mathematics, applied physics, architectural engineering, chemical engineering, civil engineering, engineering design, engineering mechanics, environmental and environmental health engineering, geology, metallurgical engineering, mineral engineering, petroleum engineering, physics

Suggested High School Prep for Geological Engineering

As with most engineering majors, you'll be taking a heavy load of math and science courses. Your best preparation will be advanced courses in calculus, analytic geometry, trigonometry, physics, chemistry, biology, and geology (if your high school offers it). And since most colleges require you to take a certain number of humanities courses, don't forget about English, history, and foreign languages.

SAMPLE COLLEGE CURRICULUM FOR GEOLOGICAL ENGINEERING

Airphoto Interpretation for Terrain Evaluation

Applications of Geographic Information Systems

Environmental Geology

Explosives Engineering

Geologic Hazards

Hydrogeology

Mining and Exploration Geophysics

Properties of Geosynthetics

Regional Geological Engineering Studies

Retaining Structures

Rock Mechanics

Seepage and Slopes

Soil Dynamics

Tunneling

Waste Geotechnics

Fun Facts

Do You Know Who Founded Stratigraphy?

William Smith, an Englishman born in 1769. Throughout his life, he worked to identify layers of rock throughout England and Wales, developing his theories so carefully that his techniques are still used today. By the end of his life he had composed *A Delineation of the Strata of England and Wales, with Part of Scotland*, a geologic map so rich and accurate in detail that it served as the standard for all subsequent geologic maps.

Careers and Salary

Although starting salaries depend a great deal on where they live and how they use their degree, geological engineering majors can expect to earn an average salary in the mid-forties. Salaries can be higher and lower depending on the engineers' levels of education and how much experience they've had through internships or cooperative learning programs.

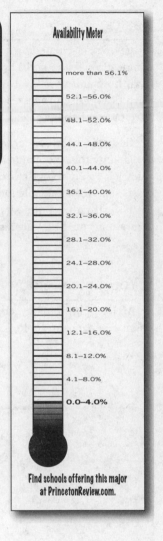

Availability Meter

more than 56.1%

52.1–56.0%

48.1–52.0%

44.1–48.0%

40.1–44.0%

36.1–40.0%

32.1–36.0%

28.1–32.0%

24.1–28.0%

20.1–24.0%

16.1–20.0%

12.1–16.0%

8.1–12.0%

4.1–8.0%

0.0–4.0%

Find schools offering this major at PrincetonReview.com.

CAREER OPTIONS

| Geologist | Geophysicist |

GEOLOGY

Basics

If you're fascinated by how the environment affects us and vice versa, or if you're concerned about maintaining clean water and a healthy environment, geology may be the major for you. As a geology major, you'll learn how and why the Earth has evolved. You'll study natural and artificial environmental processes and learn how those processes should be improved. You'll study the history of the Earth and see how humans have brought about change for better or for worse.

Geologists are concerned with the entire physical makeup of the Earth, and many specializations are available within the major. Mineralogists study the formation and structures of minerals while glaciologists study ice. Paleontologists are concerned with what fossils can tell us about our history while economic geologists search for valuable minerals like crystallized carbon. Other areas of study include the formation of the Earth's crust, the continents, the planets, chemical elements of rocks, and water. No matter what your concentration, you'll be learning how all aspects of the Earth relate to one another—and to us.

If You Like Geology, You May Also Like . . .

Archaeology, biology, chemistry, environmental and environmental health engineering, environmental science, geography, geological engineering, marine science, ocean engineering, petroleum engineering

Suggested High School Prep for Geology

The more science courses, the better. Try physics, biology, chemistry, physical science, and whatever else your high school offers. Math courses will be valuable as well, especially upper-level ones. Also important are computer courses—much of a geologist's work involves computers and other technological equipment.

SAMPLE COLLEGE CURRICULUM FOR GEOLOGY

Environmental Geology

Field Geology

Geochemistry

Geomorphology

Glacial Geology

Igneous Petrology

Mineralogy and Crystallography

Paleontology

Physical Geology

Stratigraphy and Sedimentation

Structural Geology

Surface and Groundwater Hydrology

Various math, computer, and engineering courses

Fun Facts

Mnemonics are Fun

There are 13 different periods to geologic history: Quaternary, Tertiary, Cretaceous, Jurassic, Triassic, Permian, Pennsylvanian, Carboniferous, Mississippian, Devonian, Silurian, Ordovician, and Cambrian. Obviously, remembering them all in the correct order can be tricky; here are a few mnemonic devices to help you remember most of them.

- Quit Telling Crummy Jokes to People Playing Competitive Monopoly During School or Card-playing.
- Could Oscar Sprint Down Mary Poppins Path to Just Carry the Quail?

The epochs of geologic history aren't quite as numerous, but still tricky: Holocene, Pleistocene, Pliocene, Miocene, Oligocene, Eocene, Paleocene. Here are some mnemonic devices to help you out.

- Happy People Play Music; Others Eat Pizza.
- Happy Plump Pregnant Mothers Only Eat Pickles.

Careers and Salary

The average starting salary depends a great deal on their location, but geology majors can most likely expect to make about $30,000 to $40,000. Salaries also depend on the degree—if geology majors pursue advanced degrees their salaries will increase a great deal; those with doctorates earn close to upwards of $70,000.

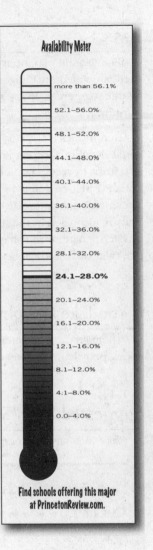

Availability Meter

more than 56.1%

52.1–56.0%

48.1–52.0%

44.1–48.0%

40.1–44.0%

36.1–40.0%

32.1–36.0%

28.1–32.0%

24.1–28.0%

20.1–24.0%

16.1–20.0%

12.1–16.0%

8.1–12.0%

4.1–8.0%

0.0–4.0%

Find schools offering this major at PrincetonReview.com.

CAREER OPTIONS

Archaeologist	Geologist	Petroleum Engineer
Biologist	Geophysicist	Professor
Ecologist		

GEOPHYSICS

Basics

The ground may pretty feel solid to you, but there's a lot happening under your feet. The Earth's outer shell is divided into huge sections called tectonic plates, which float on the hotter, softer rocks of Earth's mantle, or center. Every year, these plates move between 0.4 and 4 inches a year. How do we know? Geophysics.

Geophysics is the study of the physical characteristics of Earth and other planets. As a geophysics major, you'll develop a strong background in physics, mathematics, Earth sciences, and computer science. You'll also learn to recognize and measure the subtle features and movements of Earth that human senses cannot detect. You'll be trained in how to take electrical, magnetic, radioactive, and gravitational measurements. These techniques are used by geophysicists to explore for oil, natural gas, minerals, and groundwater. They're also used in the related field of seismology, the study of earthquakes. The small measurements geophysicists take of the shape, motion, and energy of the Earth are used to understand big geologic events, like tidal waves, volcanoes, landslides, and of course—earthquakes.

If You Like Geophysics, You May Also Like . . .

Chemistry, environmental science, geography, geological engineering, geology, mathematics, natural sciences, petroleum engineering, physical sciences, physics

Suggested High School Prep for Geophysics

Take as many advanced math and science classes as possible, including algebra, calculus, physics, and chemistry. Familiarity with at least one computer programming language will also be helpful.

SAMPLE COLLEGE CURRICULUM FOR GEOPHYSICS

Applied Vector and Tensor Mathematics

Chemistry and Biochemistry

Civil and Environmental Engineering

Differential Equations

Earth and Space Sciences

Earth Dynamics

Electricity and Magnetism

Electronics for Scientists

Plate Tectonics and Global Geophysics

Seismology

Stratigraphy

Structural Geology

Fun Facts

A Whole Lot of Shakin' Goin' On

1. A magnitude 1 seismic wave releases as much energy as blowing up 6 ounces of TNT. A magnitude 8 earthquake releases as much energy as detonating 6 million tons of TNT

2. It has been estimated that over 75 million people have been killed by earthquakes.

3. Of the ten strongest earthquakes ever recorded in the world, three have occurred in Alaska.

4. The largest earthquake ever recorded occurred in Chile on May 22, 1960, with a magnitude of 9.5.

5. Before electronics allowed recordings of large earthquakes, scientists built large spring-pendulum seismometers in an attempt to record the long-period motion produced by such quakes. The largest one weighed about 15 kg.

6. It is thought that more damage was done by the resulting fire after the 1906 San Francisco earthquake than by the earthquake itself.

7. Most earthquakes occur at depths of less than 80 km (50 miles) below the Earth's surface. The world's deadliest recorded earthquake occurred in 1557 in central China where people lived in soft-rock caves which collapsed killing an estimated 830,000 people.

8. The earliest recorded evidence of an earthquake has been traced back to 1831 B.C./B.C.E. in the Shandong province of China.

9. Eleven people are known to have died from British earthquakes dating from 1580 to 1940. Six were killed by falling stones, two fell from upper floors, two died of shock, and one committed suicide.

10. More than 3 million earthquakes occur every year. That's about 8,000 a day, or one every 11 seconds.

(Source: www.planet-science.com)

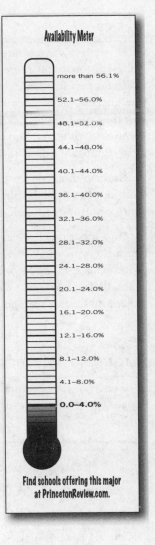

Availability Meter

more than 56.1%

52.1–56.0%

48.1–52.0%

44.1–48.0%

40.1–44.0%

36.1–40.0%

32.1–36.0%

28.1–32.0%

24.1–28.0%

20.1–24.0%

16.1–20.0%

12.1–16.0%

8.1–12.0%

4.1–8.0%

0.0–4.0%

Find schools offering this major at PrincetonReview.com.

Careers and Salary

Most careers in this field require a master's degree, many a PhD For geophysics majors right out of college, starting salaries range from $30,000 to $40,000.

CAREER OPTIONS

Geologist	Natural Sciences Manager	Physicist
Geophysicist	Petroleum Engineer	Professor

GERMAN

Basics

If you've always wanted to read Goethe's Faust in its original language, can't stand your translation of Nietzsche, or simply dream of going off to the Bavarian Alps to listen to Mozart, German may be the right major for you. In addition to learning the language inside and out, German majors also explore the rich culture and history of Germany. Here you can learn about everything from Martin Luther and the Protestant Reformation, to Frederick Barbarossa and the Holy Roman Empire, to Otto von Bismarck and the Prussian Empire, to Wilhelm II and the German Empire. In the process, you'll expand your knowledge of some of the most significant events in world history.

German thinkers, writers, and artists have played pivotal roles in defining all aspects of Western culture. From music to philosophy to science to literature, you'll find a German influence. A major in German is your opportunity to understand those influences in an up-close and personal way.

On a more practical level, with the global economy becoming more tightly interwoven, more and more national corporations are becoming multinational, creating a greater demand for people with foreign language skills and knowledge of foreign cultures. Germany is the largest, most powerful European economy (think BMW and DaimlerChrysler here), which means that the prospects for young German majors looking to get into business are good.

If You Like German, You May Also Like . . .

French, history, international business, international relations, international studies, Italian, Medieval and Renaissance studies, Portuguese, Russian, Slavic languages and literatures, Spanish

SAMPLE COLLEGE CURRICULUM FOR GERMAN

Advanced German I–II

Cultural Events in German-Speaking Countries

Elementary German

German Culture Survey

Government and Politics of Western Europe

Intermediate German

Introduction to Stylistics

Practice of Translation

Studies in German Literature

Weimar and Fascism in German Literature and Film

Suggested High School Prep for German

You don't have to be fluent or even know any German before entering college, but we're going to state the obvious anyway; take some German classes if they're at all available to you. Lots of Western civilization or history classes will also be helpful, as Germany (or the area and people of what became Germany) happened to play a pretty important role in the last couple thousand years or so. A tough English class will help, since English itself is a Germanic, rather than a Latinate language.

Fun Facts

Did You Know?

It took Goethe more than 60 years to complete both parts of his masterpiece *Faust*, now considered a hallmark of German and Western literature.

Did You Know?

The Berlin Wall, which separated Soviet and Western-protected sectors of a partitioned Berlin after World War II, was more than 13 feet high and 100 miles long.

Careers and Salary

German majors can expect $20,000 to $30,000 fresh out of college, depending on their field.

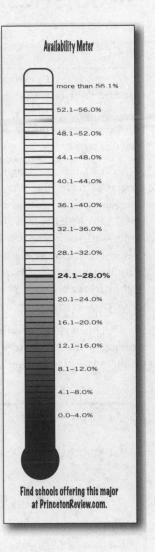

Availability Meter

more than 56.1%

52.1–56.0%

48.1–52.0%

44.1–48.0%

40.1–44.0%

36.1–40.0%

32.1–36.0%

28.1–32.0%

24.1–28.0%

20.1–24.0%

16.1–20.0%

12.1–16.0%

8.1–12.0%

4.1–8.0%

0.0–4.0%

Find schools offering this major at PrincetonReview.com.

CAREER OPTIONS

Consultant	Editor	Professor
Diplomat/Attaché/Foreign Service Officer	Foreign Exchange Trader	Translator

GERMANIC LANGUAGES, LITERATURES, AND LINGUISTICS

Basics

So you've been taking some German classes in high school and—admit it—you've actually enjoyed stocking your linguistic arsenal with words like Aufheregtheit and Geschwendigkeitsüberschreitung. You simply can't wait until your next opportunity to translate another Bertolt Brecht short story. If this sounds like you—even remotely like you—the Germanic languages, literatures, and linguistics major might be calling your name.

The Germanic languages, literatures, and linguistics major is closely linked to standard German language programs. In fact, the two majors draw from a common pool of courses. But this major takes you deeper into Germanic philology, history, commerce, and art. As you explore the long evolution of the German language, you'll gain insights into the cultures that evolved with it. *Grimm's Law*, Mozart, *Faust*, World War II, the Berlin Wall—all these will factor into the curriculum. Many programs will allow you to specialize in, say, linguistics or literature or commerce. In addition, programs often offer complementary courses in Slavic, Scandinavian, and Austrian language and society. In other words, whatever your primary focus, you'll have a healthy roster of courses to choose from. And you'll most likely have the chance to study abroad for a semester or two—a great opportunity to explore the culture and put your language skills to the test.

This well-rounded education will prepare you to continue on to graduate school or jump into the working world. Germany's high-powered economy is a major player in world markets, and this means the business world is looking for keen young minds with fluency in German language and culture.

SAMPLE COLLEGE CURRICULUM FOR GERMANIC LANGUAGES, LITERATURES, AND LINGUISTICS

Advanced German

After the Fall: Society Since 1989

Composition and Conversation

Contemporary German Literature

Early German Literature

Elementary German

Germanic Mythology

German Pedagogy

Grimm's Fairy Tales

Henrik Ibsen

Intermediate German

Introduction to German Linguistics

If You Like Germanic Languages, Literatures, and Linguistics, You May Also Like...

Comparative literature, East European studies, economics, European history, German, history, international business, international relations, international studies, linguistics, medieval and renaissance studies, political science, Scandinavia studies, Slavic languages and literatures

Suggested High School Prep for Germanic Languages, Literatures, and Linguistics

Though it's not imperative, diving into German courses will certainly give you a leg up as you head into college. Take English courses too. (After all, English is a Germanic language, so the better you understand how English works, the easier it'll be to pick up German.) English courses will also prepare you to read, analyze, and respond to difficult texts. History classes—especially Western civilization or European history classes—should also be on the list.

Fun Facts

Wordy

The quest for the longest German word is ongoing. Just surf the web—you'll see forums and sites devoted to debates over the spelling, legitimacy, and meaning of the longest words in German (and other languages, for that matter). At 39 letters, Rechtsschutzversicherungsgesellschaften (meaning, "insurance companies that offer legal protection") seems to be the longest word that's commonly used. More obscure words, however, make this list. For instance: Donaudampfschiffahrtselektrizitätenhauptbe-triebswerkbauunterbeamtengesellschaft. At 79 letters, this word means "the association for subordinate officials of the head office management of the Danube steamboat electrical services" (with thanks to www.Answers.com for that definition).

And the Winners Are...

Since its inception in 1901, the Nobel Prize for Literature has been awarded to nine German writers. They are:

> Theodor Mommsen (1902)
>
> Rudolf Eucken (1908)
>
> Paul Heyse (1910)
>
> Gerhart Hauptmann (1912)
>
> Thomas Mann (1929)
>
> Hermann Hesse (1946)
>
> Heinrich Böll (1972; West Germany)
>
> Günter Grass (1999)
>
> Elfriede Jelinek (2004)

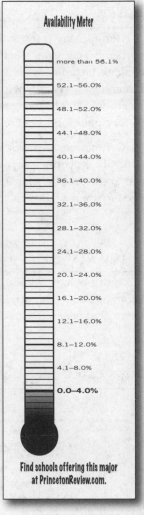

Availability Meter

more than 56.1%

52.1–56.0%

48.1–52.0%

44.1–48.0%

40.1–44.0%

36.1–40.0%

32.1–36.0%

28.1–32.0%

24.1–28.0%

20.1–24.0%

16.1–20.0%

12.1–16.0%

8.1–12.0%

4.1–8.0%

0.0–4.0%

Find schools offering this major at PrincetonReview.com.

Careers and Salary

Germanic languages, literatures, and linguistics grads should earn a starting salary about $25,000 a year—though if you land in the bustling business sector, you may be able to draw in more.

CAREER OPTIONS

Businessperson	Editor	Teacher
Consultant	Foreign Exchange Trader	Translator
Diplomat/Attaché/Foreign Service Officer	Journalist	Travel Agent
	Marketing Executive	

GERONTOLOGY

Basics

Gerontology is the study of aging and old age. Unlike geriatrics, which focuses mainly on the medical problems and issues associated with aging, gerontology is highly interdisciplinary. You'll study the biology of aging, including what happens physically and how bodies change. You'll learn how aging affects psychology and what psychological issues are associated with the elderly. You'll learn how society views aging and what societal roles aging people play. And you'll study aging and old age from the perspectives of literature, history, philosophy, and religion.

Gerontology involves a good deal of science, and you'll do a lot of research in your coursework. You'll apply the scientific process to various topics and problems, and you'll learn how to effectively document and communicate your findings. Most important, your studies in gerontology will give you the skills you need to apply your knowledge in ways beneficial to the aged in our society.

If You Like Gerontology, You May Also Like . . .

Anthropology, clinical psychology, counseling, developmental psychology, dietetics, human development, mental health services, nursing, nutrition, physical therapy, premedicine, psychology, public health, rehabilitation services, social work, sociology

Suggested High School Prep for Gerontology

AP courses in math and science will be solid preparation for your gerontology major. Also, because gerontology is multidisciplinary, you'll also benefit from courses in history, English, psychology, philosophy, and government. If you can, consider volunteering at a local nursing home to become familiar with issues involving older folks.

> ### SAMPLE COLLEGE CURRICULUM FOR GERONTOLOGY
>
> Administrative Problems in Aging
>
> Adult Development and Instruction
>
> Aging and Health
>
> Biology of Adult Development
>
> Developmental and Motor Assessment
>
> Human Physical Aging
>
> Power, Values, and Politics in an Aging Society
>
> Psychology of Adult Development
>
> Service Learning with the Elderly
>
> Society and Adult Development
>
> Working with the Elderly

Fun Facts

Who Is the Oldest Person in the World?

Jeanne Louise Calment is listed in the *Guinness Book of World Records* as being the absolute oldest person known—she lived to be 122 years and 164 days old.

A Little Old-Age Humor

An elderly lady was filling out the registration form at a doctor's office. After the address the form inquired about her "ZIP." She answered, "Not bad for my age."

Careers and Salary

The starting salary for gerontology majors is almost impossible to predict, since they can use their degree in so many different ways. A reasonable estimate is about $30,000, but again, this can vary widely depending on the field, amount of experience, and level of education.

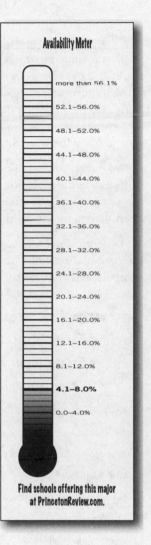

Availability Meter

more than 56.1%

52.1–56.0%

48.1–52.0%

44.1–48.0%

40.1–44.0%

36.1–40.0%

32.1–36.0%

28.1–32.0%

24.1–28.0%

20.1–24.0%

16.1–20.0%

12.1–16.0%

8.1–12.0%

4.1–8.0%

0.0–4.0%

Find schools offering this major at PrincetonReview.com.

CAREER OPTIONS		
Health Care Administrator	Nurse	Teacher
Hospice Nurse	Social Worker	

GOVERNMENT

Basics

If you fancy picturing yourself striding down the halls of the White House someday—or you're simply fascinated by what goes on there—welcome to a major in government. As a government major, you'll kick off with government basics such as the legislative process, political parties, and our judicial system. You'll move on to comparing different political systems and learning how the government operates on the state and municipal levels. You'll gain an understanding of political theory and begin to develop ideas of your own about what government is and should be—though you probably have plenty of those already.

An understanding of our government is crucial to understanding our country, but the reverse is also true. With a government major, you'll study American history, and you'll see how our civilization has changed over the years. When you study the history of law in our country, it becomes evident just how our society has been shaped by it. Civil rights, and the challenges still posed in that area, will be part of the curriculum too.

Different programs may ask you to choose a concentration in a specific realm of government, such as international relations or comparative politics. You may study the governments of different countries to compare and contrast the politics at work, or analyze U.S. involvement with foreign countries. You may be asked to examine the role government plays in business, the environment, and the press. No matter where your college studies lead you, you'll gain a deep understanding of our government, and you'll acquire the skills necessary to critique, evaluate, and eventually contribute to it.

SAMPLE COLLEGE CURRICULUM FOR GOVERNMENT
American Civilization
American Legal History
American Political Philosophy
Civil Rights
Criminal Justice Systems
Ethics and Law
International Relations
Legislative Process
Minority Politics
Political Parties
Principles of Constitutional Government
Public Opinion and Voting
Sociology of Law
State Constitutional Law
U.S. Foreign Policy
Urban Politics
Western Political Thought

If You Like Government, You May Also Like . . .

African American studies, anthropology, Asian American studies, business administration and management, economics, international business, international relations, international studies, Middle Eastern studies, peace studies, philosophy, political science, pre-law, public policy analysis

Suggested High School Prep for Government

Needless to say, any courses your school offers in politics, government, or history would be especially useful. But since government touches every aspect of our society, a solid foundation in many disciplines will be the best preparation for your college studies. Take courses in science, math, and the humanities; the more challenging, the better. A government major requires excellent communication skills, so take courses that will strengthen your reading, writing, and speaking abilities.

Fun Facts

Differences of Opinion

Here are a few wise and witty words on government:

"The government does not concern me much, and I shall bestow the fewest possible thoughts on it. It is not many moments that I live under a government, even in this world. If a man is thought-free, fancy-free, imagination-free . . . unwise rulers or reformers cannot fatally interrupt him."

—Henry David Thoreau

"Government is an evil; it is only the thoughtlessness and vices of men that make it a necessary evil. When all men are good and wise, government will of itself decay."

—Percy Bysshe Shelley

"Government is either organized benevolence or organized madness; its peculiar magnitude permits no shading."

—John Updike

"Royalty is a government in which the attention of the nation is concentrated on one person doing interesting actions. A Republic is a government in which that attention is divided between many, who are all doing uninteresting actions. Accordingly, so long as the human heart is strong and the human reason weak, Royalty will be strong because it appeals to diffused feeling, and Republics weak because they appeal to the understanding."

—Walter Bagehot, British economist

(Source: www.bartleby.com)

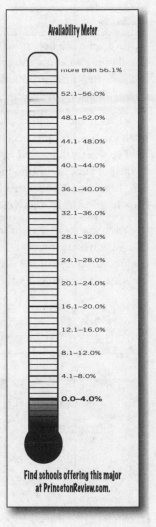

Availability Meter

more than 56.1%

52.1–56.0%

48.1–52.0%

44.1–48.0%

40.1–44.0%

36.1–40.0%

32.1–36.0%

28.1–32.0%

24.1–28.0%

20.1–24.0%

16.1–20.0%

12.1–16.0%

8.1–12.0%

4.1–8.0%

0.0–4.0%

Find schools offering this major at PrincetonReview.com.

Careers and Salary

The starting salary for government majors is about $30,000; it's generally lower if you're working in the nonprofit sector.

CAREER OPTIONS

Diplomat	Political Aide	Public Administrator
FBI Agent	Politician	Teacher
Journalist	Professor	Writer
Lawyer		

GRAIN SCIENCE

Basics

As a grain science major, you'll learn about the many techniques, processes, and problems of grain growing. You'll come to know the basic properties of cereals and other grains and the many ways that they are used in foods and other products. You'll get hands-on experience in the science; most programs have a wide array of facilities such as bakeries, flour and feed mills, grain storage facilities, and laboratories.

As its name suggests, this major requires some serious science. Most schools include biology, chemistry, mathematics, and physical science in the grain science curriculum, and you'll apply what you learn in each field to your studies and research. In your laboratory work you'll learn exactly how to use a freezedryer, an ultracentrifuge, a thermo-mechanical analyzer, dynamic rheometers, a starch viscometer, and maybe even a flux capacitor. You'll learn about the chemistry of cereals and other grains, and see firsthand how to clean, classify, grind, mix, and weigh raw materials.

Your studies as a grain science major don't stop with mastery of all these gizmos. Nutrition, environmental issues, management techniques, and technologies of specialized fields, such as the breakfast cereal industry, are only a few of the other topics you may encounter, making grain science a complex, challenging, and endlessly interesting field.

If You Like Grain Science, You May Also Like . . .

> ### SAMPLE COLLEGE CURRICULUM FOR GRAIN SCIENCE
>
> Air Handling in Grain Processing
>
> Biochemistry
>
> Cereal and Feed Analysis
>
> Cereal Food Plant Design and Construction
>
> Cereal Science
>
> Design of Experiments
>
> Electricity and Its Control
>
> Food and Feed Product Production
>
> Grain Processing
>
> Management Applications
>
> Milling Science
>
> Nutritional Properties of Cereals and Legumes

Agricultural business and management, agricultural economics, agricultural education, agricultural and biological engineering, agricultural journalism, agricultural mechanization, agricultural technology management, agriculture, agronomy and crop science, animal science, bakery science, environmental and environmental health engineering, environmental science, feed science, food science, genetics, international agriculture, landscape horticulture, plant pathology

Suggested High School Prep for Grain Science

Courses in biology, chemistry, and other life sciences will be the best preparation for a major in grain science. Math courses—preferably advanced-level ones—will also give you a great foundation. And, if your schedule permits, it may help to get some experience with groups dealing with environmental or agricultural concerns.

Fun Facts

Kaboom

Did you know that the grain dust in grain elevators is prone to explode? These dust explosions are caused by the right combination of dust, oxygen, and a spark. When grain dust is kept under pressure—as it is in a grain silo—an explosion is likely to happen, and the primary explosion then ignites more grain dust, making the explosion even more damaging and dangerous. According to a Kansas State University professor, Dr. Robert W. Schoeff, wheat and corn starch are the most likely grains to explode. Other dust explosions have been caused by walnut hulls, coal dust, sugar, modeling dough, and other substances.

(Source: "Exploding Elevators" by C. Claiborne Ray, *New York Times*, July 1998)

Breakfast: An Investigation

Many cereal companies add iron to their products to make them more nutritious. Curious about what, exactly, this iron looks like? Gather some fortified cereal, a magnet, a bowl, and a spoon, then try the following experiment from the About.com chemistry guide:

1. Pour the cereal into a bowl.
2. Mash it with a spoon or other utensil. The more finely ground the cereal is, the easier it will be to see the iron.
3. Stir the magnet through the crushed cereal.
4. Pull the magnet out and look for the black "fuzz" or iron.

Careers and Salary

The starting salary for most grain science majors is between $28,000 and $32,000.

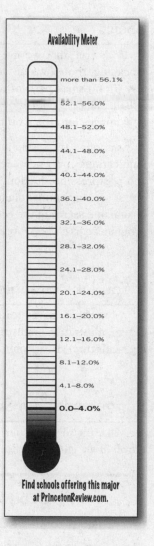

Availability Meter

more than 56.1%
52.1–56.0%
48.1–52.0%
44.1–48.0%
40.1–44.0%
36.1–40.0%
32.1–36.0%
28.1–32.0%
24.1–28.0%
20.1–24.0%
16.1–20.0%
12.1–16.0%
8.1–12.0%
4.1–8.0%
0.0–4.0%

Find schools offering this major
at PrincetonReview.com.

CAREER OPTIONS		
Biochemist	Farmer	Geneticist
Biologist		

GRAPHIC COMMUNICATIONS

Basics

If it's true that we live in a visual world, then graphic communications is our lingua franca. Pictures "speaking" thousands of words are all around you—on your T-shirt or your cereal box, in this book—courtesy (in no small part) of the hard-working souls who produce graphics for advertising, informational, and artistic value. A course of study in graphic communications will give you the tools and know-how to get new images into the world.

Straddling the disciplines of industrial education and studio arts, the courses of study in graphic communications cover new technologies and processes that generate new graphics. You'll learn prepress, press, and postpress production. You'll get hands-on experience in offset lithography, flexography, gravure, letterpress, screenprinting, digital imaging, and other methods of image reproduction. Since just about every imaginable sector of the economy depends on visuals to market itself, graduates of graphic communications programs can end up working in virtually every type of industry.

If You Like Graphic Communication, You May Also Like . . .

Advertising, art education, art history, ceramics, computer graphics, drawing, fashion design, graphic design, illustration, industrial design, interior architecture, interior design, painting, photography, printmaking, sculpture, visual communication, web design

Suggested High School Prep for Graphic Communication

Make the most of your school's art department: Take drawing, painting, art history, and ceramics classes. Enroll in art clubs or other relevant extracurricular activities. Develop your artist's eye.

SAMPLE COLLEGE CURRICULUM FOR GRAPHIC COMMUNICATION

Basic Typography

Design Fundamentals

Digital Illustration

Drawing

Intermediate Graphic Communication

Introduction to the Flexographic Process

Offset Print Operations

Press Technology I

Silkscreen

Fun Facts

The Making of Moveable Type

Johann Gutenberg, a German goldsmith, is typically credited with inventing moveable type in the 1450s. But moveable type can be traced further back to China in A.D./C.E. 1041, when Di Sheng, a cloth vendor by trade, invented a clay type. It never really took off though, partly because using moveable type with thousands of Chinese characters wasn't much faster than writing them.

Just Imagine If You Paid Attention to Them...

The average American is exposed to somewhere between 250 to 3,000 advertising "impressions" per day (the number varies according to which public-interest or marketing source is doing the measuring). Assuming that even half of those ads are visual, you'll start to get an idea how important printing is to advertising!

Careers and Salary

Starting salaries depend on the industry in which you launch your career, but graduates can expect entry-level salaries between $30,000 and $50,000.

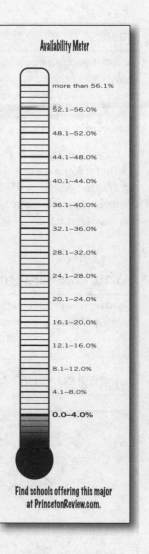

Availability Meter

more than 56.1%

52.1–56.0%

48.1–52.0%

44.1–48.0%

40.1–44.0%

36.1–40.0%

32.1–36.0%

28.1–32.0%

24.1–28.0%

20.1–24.0%

16.1–20.0%

12.1–16.0%

8.1–12.0%

4.1–8.0%

0.0–4.0%

Find schools offering this major at PrincetonReview.com.

CAREER OPTIONS

Color Specialist	Estimator	Printer
Digital Artist	Marketing Specialist	Sales Representative
Graphic Designer	Press Operator	Screen Printer
Educator		

GRAPHIC DESIGN

Basics

Are you fascinated by the visual world? Are you drawn to logos, illustrations, cartoons, and advertisements? You may be on your way to a graphic design major. Graphic designers find innovative ways to communicate ideas visually, incorporating a range of media, including digital imaging, photography, and illustration. As a graphic design major, you may explore Web design, product development, or advertising, using a wide variety of artistic skills and perspectives to create your own personal vision.

Developing your personal artistic vision involves critically studying both your own work and the work of others. You'll share your work, receive feedback, and in turn, learn the art of critiquing others. By studying graphic design you'll learn how creative ideas have changed and developed, and the concepts and creations of practicing graphic designers will help you see where the field of graphic design is now and where you may lead it.

If You Like Graphic Design, You May Also Like . . .

Advertising, art education, art history, ceramics, drawing, fashion design, interior architecture, interior design, painting, photography, printmaking, sculpture, visual communication

Suggested High School Prep for Graphic Design

SAMPLE COLLEGE CURRICULUM FOR GRAPHIC DESIGN

Art History

Artist Books

Color Theory

Computers and Design

Electronic Imaging

Figure Drawing

Graphic Design

Illustration

Painting

Printmaking

Sculpture

Typography

Web Design

Take advantage of your high school art department. Take as many art classes as you can, and get involved in extracurricular art clubs. Since graphic design majors are required to take the same foundation curriculum as fine arts majors, brush up on your drawing skills. Most likely, you'll be required to present a portfolio for admission. Although you'll be majoring in graphic design, the majority of your portfolio should consist of drawings from life. For feedback or a review of your portfolio by several schools at once, visit a National Portfolio Day (www.npda.org).

Fun Facts

Do You Know Who Invented Italics?

Italic type was invented by Aldus Manutius in 1501, and was known early on as the Aldine. In 1490 Aldus had begun a printing press in Venice, producing great works of Greek, Latin, and Italian literature at affordable prices. These works were printed in italic type, which is said to have been based on Petrarch's slanted handwriting.

Famous People Who Majored in Graphic Design

Eva Anderson, Tobias Frere-Jones, Michael McPherson, Eric Pike, Tyler Smith, and Michael Rock, all at the Rhode Island School of Design

Careers and Salary

Salaries for graphic design majors vary widely, since artists work both as freelancers and in many professional fields. They could start at more than $40,000. However, a good estimate would be in the $25,000 to $35,000 range.

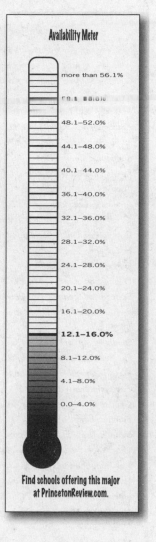

Availability Meter

more than 56.1%

52.1–56.0%

48.1–52.0%

44.1–48.0%

40.1–44.0%

36.1–40.0%

32.1–36.0%

28.1–32.0%

24.1–28.0%

20.1–24.0%

16.1–20.0%

12.1–16.0%

8.1–12.0%

4.1–8.0%

0.0–4.0%

Find schools offering this major at PrincetonReview.com.

CAREER OPTIONS

Animator	Digital Artist	Product Designer
Antiques Dealer	Graphic Designer	Web Art Director
Art Dealer	Printer	Website Designer
Artist		

GREAT BOOKS

Basics

What better way to learn about history, science, mathematics, art, music, and civilization than by reading the actual texts by the very people responsible for each? That's the basic idea behind the handful or so of great books programs that are scattered throughout the United States. So long as you are honestly motivated and self-disciplined enough for four years of voracious reading and sustained confrontation with the books in which the greatest minds of our civilization have expressed themselves, you'd be hard-pressed to find a more satisfying or more illuminating education.

If you major in great books, or if you go to a school that specializes in them, you'll read, dissect, mull over, and write papers about the most influential books in human history. You'll also discuss them in small, seminar-style classes with other students and your professors (sometimes called tutors). You'll learn the world's intellectual traditions from the ground up.

But what can you do with this kind of a degree? Can you walk into an advertising firm or a consulting firm or Bear Stearns and get a job? Well, yeah. You can also go on to get a PhD in just about anything. You can go to law school, medical school, or business school. You can become a farmer, architect, journalist, screenwriter, or member of the Peace Corps, too. Trust us: If there's one thing a great books major won't do, it's limit your options.

If You Like Great Books, You May Also Like . . .

African American studies, African studies, American studies, ancient studies, anthropology, Arabic, art history, Asian American studies, Chinese, classics, comparative literature, East Asian studies, East European studies, economics, English, English literature, French, geography, German, Hebrew, historic preservation, history, international studies, Islamic studies, Italian, Japanese, Jewish studies, Latin American studies, linguistics, Medieval and Renaissance studies, Middle Eastern studies, modern Greek, music history, peace studies, philosophy, political science, Portuguese, psychology, public policy analysis, religious studies, Russian, Slavic languages and literatures, sociology, South Asian studies, Southeast Asian studies, Spanish, urban studies, women's studies

Suggested High School Prep for Great Books

You should become a good reader as quickly as possible. Take English and history courses that require you to read actual texts by actual people, as opposed to traditional high school textbooks. Also, take at least one foreign language (more, if you are allowed and feel comfortable). Don't skimp on math and science either, as you'll be reading plenty about these topics, too.

Fun Facts

A Few Schools That Offer a Great Books Curriculum

- Central Washington University
- College of Saint Thomas More
- Gutenberg College
- St. John's College (New Mexico)
- Thomas Aquinas College
- University of Chicago

Careers and Salary

Salaries vary widely. Many students who major in great books go on directly to graduate school.

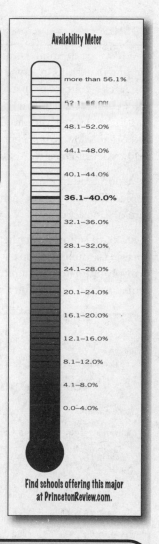

Availability Meter

more than 56.1%

52.1–56.0%

48.1–52.0%

44.1–48.0%

40.1–44.0%

36.1–40.0%

32.1–36.0%

28.1–32.0%

24.1–28.0%

20.1–24.0%

16.1–20.0%

12.1–16.0%

8.1–12.0%

4.1–8.0%

0.0–4.0%

Find schools offering this major
at PrincetonReview.com.

CAREER OPTIONS

Anthropologist	Editor	Political Scientist
Antiques Dealer	Film Director	Politician
Archaeologist	Journalist	Professor
Art Dealer	Librarian	Public Relations Professional
Artist	Lobbyist	Sociologist
Attorney	Paralegal	Sommelier
Book Publishing Professional	Philosopher	Stockbroker
Clergy—Priest, Rabbi, Minister	Physician	Teacher
Corporate Lawyer	Physicist	Trial Lawyer
Curator	Political Aide	Writer

HEALTH ADMINISTRATION

Basics

Most health administration curricula combine a liberal arts background with management theory and the practical skills involved in planning and delivering health services. If you major in health administration, you'll take courses in management, health care administration, epidemiology, health law, and health finance and economics. You'll learn how to manage the finances of huge organizations, how to deal with personnel, and how to interpret and comply with the maze of laws that affect health care providers, administrators, and organizations. It's a good bet that you'll participate in an internship or some other kind of professional field experience as well, so as to build your professional credentials.

Upon graduation, you'll be prepared for entry-level management positions in hospitals, clinics, nursing homes, mental health organizations, insurance companies, public agencies, and many other types of health care organizations.

A lot of schools offer health administration as a master's or doctoral program only, which means that you must get an undergraduate degree before you can actually specialize in the field. It's a pretty good idea to plan on ultimately obtaining a graduate degree anyway because you'll make a lot more money and you'll probably find significantly more employment opportunities.

SAMPLE COLLEGE CURRICULUM FOR HEALTH ADMINISTRATION

Accounting

Administration of Health Care Organizations

Biology

Business Law

Business Math

Economics

Ethics and the Health Sciences

Financial Management of Health Institutions

Health Care Economics

Health Care of the Aged

Health Planning

Health Policy

Health Regulation

Internship in Health Administration

Principles of Management

Public Health Administration

If You Like Health Administration, You May Also Like . . .

Accounting, actuarial science, business administration and management, business communications, entrepreneurship, finance, food science, gerontology, human development, human resources management, logistics management, managerial economics, marketing, medical technology, operations management, pharmacy, premedicine, pre-optometry, public administration, public health

Suggested High School Prep for Health Administration

What you want to do is develop a strong background in mathematics and written and oral communication. If you are thinking about majoring in health administration, take courses in English, math, and science, as well as a business law course or two.

Fun Facts

Salary Info

According to Salary.com, the world leader in online compensation information, a typical health administrator working in Flagstaff, Arizona, earns a median base salary of approximately $56,000. The average salary range in Flagstaff is between $48,000 and $65,500.

Did You Know?

More than 10 million American families spend more than 10 percent of their total income on health insurance and health-related expenses.

(Source: National Coalition on Health Care)

Careers and Salary

The average starting salary for a newly minted health administration major is about $28,000 annually. Starting salaries range from $22,000 to approximately $36,000.

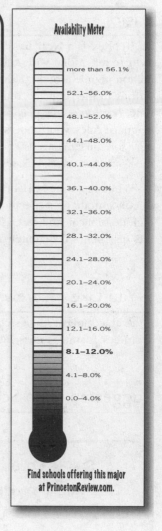

Availability Meter

more than 56.1%

52.1–56.0%

48.1–52.0%

44.1–48.0%

40.1–44.0%

36.1–40.0%

32.1–36.0%

28.1–32.0%

24.1–28.0%

20.1–24.0%

16.1–20.0%

12.1–16.0%

8.1–12.0%

4.1–8.0%

0.0–4.0%

Find schools offering this major
at PrincetonReview.com.

CAREER OPTIONS

Bank Officer	Hospital Administrator	School Administrator
Benefits Administrator	Human Resources Manager	Social Worker
College Administrator	Pharmaceutical Sales Representative	Substance Abuse Counselor
Health Care Administrator	Public Health Administrator	

HEBREW

Basics

Hebrew is a Near Eastern language—the language of Judaism—with an alphabet that is written from right to left. Along with Arabic, Hebrew is one of the two official languages in Israel and is spoken by 4.6 million people around the world. If you major in Hebrew you'll of course master the reading, speaking, and writing of the language. You'll also be introduced to Hebrew literature, including the best-selling book of all time, *The Bible*. Why major in a foreign language? There are many good reasons. For one, by studying foreign language rules, your understanding and usage of English will grow stronger and more effective. Also, studying a foreign language is a great way to immerse yourself in another culture, opening up doorways all around the world for travel, business, and friendships.

While majoring in Hebrew, expect to take courses in history, religion, and Jewish studies. You may want to concentrate on a specific area—indeed, many colleges may require you to do so. Possible concentrations include biblical studies, classical Jewish literature, and Hebrew literature. An appreciation for many liberal arts disciplines is definitely necessary if you plan to major in Hebrew.

If You Like Hebrew, You May Also Like . . .

Arabic, biblical studies, classics, East European studies, French, German, international relations, international studies, Islamic studies, Italian, Jewish studies, Middle Eastern studies, modern Greek, Spanish, theology

Suggested High School Prep for Hebrew

The more foreign languages you know, the easier it is to pick up another one, so take advantage of whatever your high school offers, be it French, Spanish, German. Since Hebrew is a multidisciplinary field, you'll benefit from English, history, and religion classes.

SAMPLE COLLEGE CURRICULUM FOR HEBREW

The Bible as Literature

Comparative Semitics

Composition in Hebrew

Conversation in Hebrew

Hebrew Grammar

Hebrew Literary and Cultural Texts

Hebrew Morphology

Hebrew of the Israeli Communications Media

History of Hebrew

Modern Hebrew Short Story

Structure of Modern Hebrew Grammar

Fun Facts

Brought Back from the Brink

Although Hebrew began as a spoken language, it faded into disuse for nearly 2,000 years. A Lithuanian medical student named Eliezer Ben-Yehuda revived the language only a century ago.

What's Your Lucky Number?

Hebrew numbers are formulated similarly to Roman numerals—using letters to represent numbers—and the number 18 is considered lucky because its letters form the word *khay*, which means life.

(Source: www.Transparent.com)

Careers and Salary

Starting salaries depend mainly on whether Hebrew is a primary or secondary tool in the career, but they can range from $25,000 to $32,000 or higher.

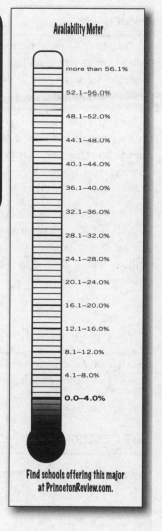

Availability Meter

more than 56.1%

52.1–56.0%

48.1–52.0%

44.1–48.0%

40.1–44.0%

36.1–40.0%

32.1–36.0%

28.1–32.0%

24.1–28.0%

20.1–24.0%

16.1–20.0%

12.1–16.0%

8.1–12.0%

4.1–8.0%

0.0–4.0%

Find schools offering this major at PrincetonReview.com.

CAREER OPTIONS		
Clergy—Priest, Rabbi, Minister	Theologian	Translator

HINDI

Basics

Question: What's the most spoken language in the world? All right, so it's Chinese by a long shot. But with close to half a billion speakers, Hindustani (and Hindi, its most widely spoken dialect) is the primary language of what will soon become the world's most populous nation. (India is one of today's fastest growing economies too.) There's never been a better time to consider Hindi as your college major.

As India has aggressively entered the global marketplace, Hindi is becoming a more widely recognized tongue than ever before. Hindi majors track the history of the language from its Sanskrit origins through the poetry, literature, and entertainment that have been the hallmark of modern Hindi for hundreds of years. Like movies? There's a good chance you'll have a class entirely devoted to the cinema of Bollywood—one of India's prime exports.

Of course, the best way to learn a foreign language is to find a way to immerse yourself in it. Many schools provide programs that allow Hindi majors to study in India. While it's true that in today's India one can get by on English alone, to have a greater insight into the country and her people, there is no greater path to follow than that which leads to an understanding of their language and their literature. Plus, the movies are really good!

If You Like Hindi, You May Also Like . . .

African American studies, African studies, anthropology, Arabic, Chinese, East Asian studies, East European studies, Islamic studies, Japanese, Jewish studies, South Asian studies, Southeast Asian studies

Suggested High School Prep for Hindi

> ### SAMPLE COLLEGE CURRICULUM FOR HINDI
>
> Bilingualism
>
> Contemporary Culture in South Asia
>
> Dance/Dance Theater of Asia
>
> Hindi I–IV
>
> Hinduism, Texts, Practices, and
>   Performance
>
> Indian Cinema
>
> Indian Dance and Hindu Cosmology
>
> Introduction to Asian/African
>   Literature—Voices of War
>
> Kundalini Yoga and Sikh Dharma

Chances are you don't go to a school that offers classes in South Asian languages, but there are ways to prepare for majoring in Hindi that don't necessarily involve that part of the world. It's true that once you've learned your second language, the third and fourth are easier to master, so load up on whatever foreign languages your school offers. It's probably a good idea to get a foundation in Indian literature—read modern Indian fiction or classic texts in English translations to get a real sense of the culture and history.

Fun Facts

Hooked on Phonetics

There are a ton of helpful books and online sources that can help you to translate English words to their phonetic equivalent in Hindi—and vice versa. With more than 46,000 words in its dictionary, Word Anywhere is one of the premiere online English to Hindi translation tools. Find the meaning of just about any word at www.WordAnywhere.com.

The Bare Essentials

Here's a quick list of common English phrases and their Hindi counterparts.

Hello/Namaskar

My name is John/Mera naam John hai

I am hungry/Mein bukha hun

Thank you/Dhanya-waadh

Planet Bollywood

The common name for the Mumbai-based film industry, "Bollywood" was recently added to the Oxford English Dictionary. In addition to Mumbai, the Indian film industry has hubs in Tamil/Kollywood, Telugu, Bengali, Kannada, and Malayalam. In terms of number of films produced and tickets sold, it is the largest film industry in the world.

Careers and Salary

Hindi majors can expect to earn between $24,000 and $30,000 right out of college.

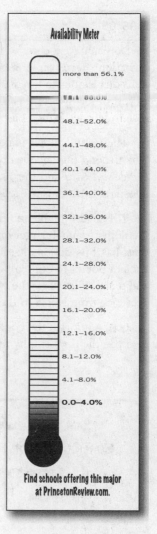

Availability Meter

more than 56.1%

52.1–56.0%

48.1–52.0%

44.1–48.0%

40.1–44.0%

36.1–40.0%

32.1–36.0%

28.1–32.0%

24.1–28.0%

20.1–24.0%

16.1–20.0%

12.1–16.0%

8.1–12.0%

4.1–8.0%

0.0–4.0%

Find schools offering this major at PrincetonReview.com.

CAREER OPTIONS

Anthropologist	Foreign Exchange Trader	Sociologist
Curator	Journalist	Teacher
Diplomat/Attaché/Foreign Service Officer	Lobbyist	Translator

HINDU STUDIES

Basics

Do you have a copy of the *Bhagavad Gita* on your nightstand? Are you intrigued by the notion of reincarnation? Have you long been fascinated with Indian culture? If so, you're experiencing the classic symptoms of a Hindu-studies-major-to-be. This is a good time to get the Hindu studies bug. After all, India (which, as you probably know, is the primary home of Hinduism) has seen its population and economy boom in recent decades, which has spurred renewed academic interest in Indian and Hindu culture.

The Hindu studies major will expose you to the philosophies and theologies at the heart of Hinduism. You'll spend time acquainting yourself with Brahma, Vishnu, and Shiva; you'll get lost in the pages of the *Bhagavad Gita* and the *Vedas*; you'll study the beliefs and practices of Hinduism; you'll debate the sticky question: Is Hinduism a religion or a way of life? And what's the difference, anyway?

This is just the beginning, though. As a Hindu studies major, you'll use this foundation in philosophy and theology to launch larger investigations into Hinduism and its relationship to Indian culture. In other words, how has this dominant set of beliefs affected its host culture, historically and today? You'll move from ancient poetry to contemporary Bollywood, tackling questions of art, commerce, environmentalism, health, and technology along the way. You'll also move beyond India's border to consider the impact of Hinduism's presence from Nepal to the United States.

Let's not forget the coolest part of the Hindu studies major: There's a good chance that your studies will give you the opportunity to go to India for a semester or two.

> ### SAMPLE COLLEGE CURRICULUM FOR HINDU STUDIES
>
> Contemporary Hinduism
>
> Elementary Hindi/Urdu
>
> Hinduism and Ayurvedic Medicine
>
> Hinduism and Jain Mythology
>
> Hindu-Muslim Relations
>
> Hindu Texts
>
> Indian Cinema
>
> Indian Philosophy
>
> Inside the Vedas and the Bhagavad Gita
>
> Introduction to Eastern Religions
>
> Kundalini Yoga and Sikh Dharma
>
> Religion and Politics in Hinduism
>
> Survey of Hinduism

If You Like Hindu Studies, You May Also Like...

African languages, literatures, and linguistics, Australian/Oceanic/Pacific languages, literatures, and linguistics, African studies, anthropology, archeology, Asian American studies, Asian history, biblical studies, Chinese, East Asian studies, Hindi, Islamic studies, Jewish studies, religious studies, South Asian studies, Southeast Asian studies

Suggested High School Prep for Hindu Studies

Hindu studies is a major steeped in the humanities, so to prepare you should steep yourself in the humanities too. That means you should enroll in history, literature, and political science courses—all courses that ask you to read, analyze, and write a lot. A class or two in world history could be especially helpful.

Fun Facts

Did You Know?

- That nearly 80 of India's 1 billion people are Hindu.
- About 30 million Hindus live outside of India.
- Shaivism, one of three primary strains of Hindiusm, is considered the world's oldest continuing form of religion.

(Source: www.hindugateway.com/library/quickfacts/)

The Holidays

Mahashivarati (February)

Holi (March)

Ramnavami (March)

Dusserah (November)

Diwali (November)

(Source: www.religionfacts.com)

Careers and Salary

Starting salaries will typically fall between $25,000 and $30,000.

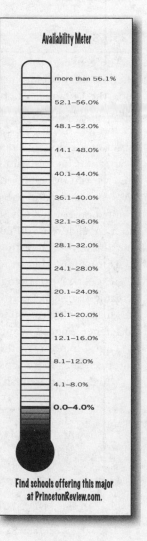

Availability Meter

more than 56.1%

52.1–56.0%

48.1–52.0%

44.1 48.0%

40.1–44.0%

36.1–40.0%

32.1–36.0%

28.1–32.0%

24.1–28.0%

20.1–24.0%

16.1–20.0%

12.1–16.0%

8.1–12.0%

4.1–8.0%

0.0–4.0%

Find schools offering this major at PrincetonReview.com.

CAREER OPTIONS

Anthropologist	Documentary Filmmaker	Sociologist
Businessperson	Editor	Teacher
Consultant	Historian	Travel Agent
Curator	Journalist	Writer
Diplomat/Attaché/Foreign Service Officer	Lobbyist	

HISPANIC AMERICAN, PUERTO RICAN, AND CHICANO STUDIES

Basics

The general issues addressed in Hispanic American, Puerto Rican, and Chicano studies remain similar, whether the people you're studying are native to (or descendants of people from) Mexico, Puerto Rico, Cuba, the Dominican Republic, or most other Latin American countries. Although they have dealt in some way with the problems of identity, race, national recognition, and changing culture, each of these nationalities has had distinctive experiences in their own countries and in the United States. In this major (or one subset of it—not all schools group them together as we've done here), you'll learn how Hispanic, Puerto Rican, and Chicano cultures have affected and been affected by U.S. culture, and how those effects have been viewed by society throughout the nations' histories. You'll study the diverse challenges these groups have encountered in the past and the problems they're facing today, including economic and political discrimination. You'll study the constantly evolving roles of Hispanic, Puerto Rican, and Chicano women—and the men, children, and families they belong to. And you'll learn about the substantial artistic and literary contributions each of these groups has made.

Throughout your studies, you'll gain exposure to Hispanic, Puerto Rican, and Chicano art, language, music, politics, psychology, and literature. You'll begin to form ideas of what it means to identify oneself as Hispanic American, Puerto Rican, or Chicano, and how the relationship between identity and race has evolved. This major will give you the opportunity to become knowledgeable in many different fields, including political science, English, women's studies, psychology, sociology, history, and others. Hispanics recently became the largest minority of the U.S. population, so learning about the past, present, and future of these different cultures makes more sense every day.

You do know Spanish, don't you? Start now if you don't. Chances are that your career may at some point involve working with these unique populations, either directly or indirectly. It is difficult to understand any culture before you understand its language.

SAMPLE COLLEGE CURRICULUM FOR HISPANIC AMERICAN, PUERTO RICAN, AND CHICANO STUDIES

Classism, Racism, and Sexism

Constitutional Relations Between Puerto Rico and the United States

Dominican Identity Formation

Hispanic Communities in the United States

The History of Cuba

History of the Dominican Republic

Puerto Rican Cultural Heritage

The Puerto Rican Educational Experience

Race, Gender, and Ethnicity

Social Class Development in Puerto Rico

If You Like Hispanic American, Puerto Rican, and Chicano Studies, You May Also Like . . .

African American studies, American studies, art history, Asian American studies, Caribbean studies, comparative literature, history, international business, international relations, international studies, linguistics, peace studies, philosophy, religious studies, Spanish

Suggested High School Prep for Hispanic American, Puerto Rican, and Chicano Studies

You'll be best prepared for this major by taking courses in English, history, philosophy, and religion. Language courses, especially Spanish, are recommended. This major will expose you to many different disciplines, so feel free to explore any classes that interest you. A diverse background of knowledge will be your best preparation.

Fun Facts

Some Facts on Puerto Rico

- Ninety percent of Puerto Rico's food is imported.
- Puerto Rico has a population of 3.9 million.
- Thirty-four percent of Puerto Rico is covered by forests, but 82 percent of those forests are privately owned, which means that owners can destroy or protect them as they wish.

Word to the Wise

The word Chicano became popular only in the 1960s. At the time, Hispanic Americans of Mexican origin sought a more specific label to define themselves and their roots. The word remains problematic, however, because in some regions of the country Mexican American Hispanics use it with pride, while in others it is considered offensive.

Careers and Salary

As with most liberal arts majors, you'll have a vast selection of careers to choose from, and your studies may lead you in any number of directions. Most liberal arts majors can expect a starting salary of $24,000 to $30,000, but that can vary widely depending on your field. Advanced degrees will also influence your starting salary.

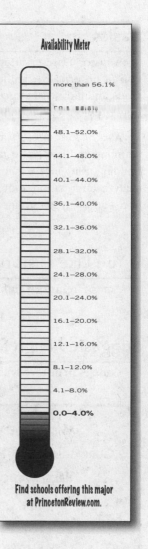

Availability Meter

more than 56.1%

52.1—56.0%

48.1—52.0%

44.1—48.0%

40.1—44.0%

36.1—40.0%

32.1—36.0%

28.1—32.0%

24.1—28.0%

20.1—24.0%

16.1—20.0%

12.1—16.0%

8.1—12.0%

4.1—8.0%

0.0—4.0%

Find schools offering this major
at PrincetonReview.com.

CAREER OPTIONS

Archaeologist	Journalist	Teacher
Diplomat	Professor	Translator
FBI Agent	Sociologist	Writer

HISTORIC PRESERVATION

Basics

A historic preservation major will expose you to the practical and theoretical aspects of the preservation of historically significant buildings. You'll study the history of architecture, including residential, religious, and industrial structures. You'll learn about landscape architecture and urban planning. And you'll see how preserving historic buildings creates appreciation in a community for social and cultural history.

As a historic preservation major, you'll learn the nuts and bolts of the profession, such as preservation planning and law, real estate development, and economics. You'll learn how to investigate the history of a building using local archives, architectural taxonomy, and physical evidence. You'll learn how to collect and analyze information about possibly significant structures, and you'll learn about the history of preservation—and why it's so important to our world.

If You Like Historic Preservation, You May Also Like . . .

American history, anthropology, archaeology, architecture, art history, classics, history

Suggested High School Prep for Historic Preservation

Courses in history will be the best preparation for your major in historic preservation. Also useful to this field are courses in foreign languages, English, philosophy, and art history. In your spare time you might try to visit museums, read books that deal with architecture and historic preservation, and investigate historic structures in your town or community.

> **SAMPLE COLLEGE CURRICULUM FOR HISTORIC PRESERVATION**
>
> American Architecture
>
> Architectural Conservation
>
> Community Public History
>
> Design Approaches to an Existing Context
>
> Documentation for Preservation
>
> Historic Preservation Law
>
> Perspectives of Preservation
>
> Policy Statement and Guidelines
>
> Preservation Planning and Law
>
> Researching Historic Structures and Sites
>
> Technology, Materials, and Conservation of Traditional Buildings

Fun Facts

In Honor of Architecture

Every city, large or small, has history in their buildings—and some cities choose to celebrate it. St. Louis, Missouri, for example, celebrates with Historic Preservation Week, held every year in May. The Landmarks Association hosts the event and its purpose is "preserving, enhancing, and promoting St. Louis's architectural heritage as well as encouraging 'sound planning and good contemporary design.'" The celebration has been held now for 40 years.

(Source: http://stlouis.about.com)

Wonder Why Historic Preservation Is Really That Important?

Here is an excerpt from Section I of The National Historic Preservation Act of 1966:

The Congress finds and declares that 1) the spirit and direction of the Nation are founded upon and reflected in its historic heritage; 2) the historical and cultural foundations of the Nation should be preserved as a living part of our community life and development in order to give a sense of orientation to the American people; 3) historic properties significant to the Nation's heritage are being lost or substantially altered, often inadvertently, with increasing frequency; 4) the preservation of this irreplaceable heritage is in the public interest so that its vital legacy of cultural, educational, aesthetic, inspirational, economic, and energy benefits will be maintained and enriched for future generations of Americans.

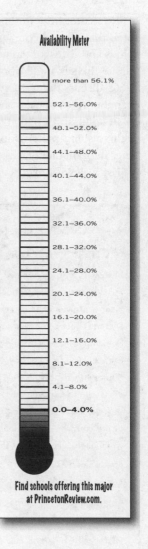

Availability Meter

more than 56.1%

52.1–56.0%

48.1–52.0%

44.1–48.0%

40.1–44.0%

36.1–40.0%

32.1–36.0%

28.1–32.0%

24.1–28.0%

20.1–24.0%

16.1–20.0%

12.1–16.0%

8.1–12.0%

4.1–8.0%

0.0–4.0%

Find schools offering this major at PrincetonReview.com.

Careers and Salary

There are many different ways to use a historic preservation degree, and starting salaries depend largely on the field chosen. Working for a museum, the government, a nonprofit organization, or a private organization all yield different levels of income. The level of education and amount of experience will also make a difference. A reasonable estimate for a starting salary is in the upper thirties to lower forties.

CAREER OPTIONS

Anthropologist	Architect	Curator
Antiques Dealer	Art Dealer	Professor
Archaeologist	Artist	

HISTORY

Basics

No matter how thrilling (or dull) your high school history classes have been, we can pretty much guarantee that history courses in college will be a lot more exciting. You won't have to memorize a bunch of names and dates, though there will be few matching quizzes in college-level history courses. Instead, you'll pursue the silk trade from Beijing to Baghdad, analyze the Civil Rights Movement and the New Left of the 1960s, discuss the writings of American conservatives from the founders to the New Right, or delve into the changing roles of class and gender in nineteenth-century France.

In addition to becoming good readers, writers, and communicators, history majors become experts at distinguishing patterns in information. What they really study is change: Why change occurs at particular times in particular places, why other things stay the same, and how individuals and groups deal with change.

For a slew of excellent reasons, the history major has endured and history departments remain large in spite of pressures on students to concentrate on more practical job training. For starters, history is interesting. We're not saying other majors are boring, but history deals with actual people and factual events. Everything has a history—nations, wars, ethnic groups, sexuality, jazz, gambling, postage stamps, you name it. One real plus about majoring in history is that you can stay engrossed in the subject matter long after you graduate.

On a broader scale, knowledge of history is important. As the philosopher George Santayana observed, "Those who cannot remember the past are condemned to repeat it. If anything holds the key to understanding warfare, famine, and social crises, it's the analysis and understanding of history. It's not a recitation of facts. It's the sum total of the human experience—a dramatic, never-ending, entirely uncensored adventure."

If You Like History, You May Also Like . . .

American studies, anthropology, archaeology, architectural history, art history, Asian American studies, biblical studies, classics, East Asian studies, East European studies, economics, English, geography, great books, historic preservation, international studies, Islamic studies, Jewish studies, Medieval and Renaissance studies, Middle Eastern studies, peace studies, philosophy, political science, public policy analysis, religious studies, Slavic languages and literatures, sociology, South Asian studies, Southeast Asian studies, theology, urban studies, women's studies

Suggested High School Prep for History

History involves lots of critical thinking and a great deal of reading and writing. If you think you might major in history, you obviously want to take as many courses in American history, civics, world history, and geography as you can. You should also take English composition, so you can get good at writing essays. And finally, take foreign language classes because you are almost certainly going to be required to take several foreign language classes as a history major.

Fun Facts

Some Essential Developments in Twentieth-Century History

1906—William Kellogg invents Corn Flakes.

1916—Coca-Cola introduces its curvaceous bottle.

1925—Yale students accidentally invent the Frisbee.

1934—The cheeseburger is unveiled in Louisville, Kentucky.

1942—Tony the Tiger debuts as the Kellogg's Frosted Flakes mascot.

1956—Elvis Presley's "Heartbreak Hotel" hits number one on Billboard's pop singles chart.

1965—The biggest power failure in history causes a sustained blackout in the eastern United States and Canada. There is a notable surge in national birthrates some nine months later.

1977—*Star Wars* is released.

1982—*Time* magazine names *Pac-Man* as its Man of the Year.

Careers and Salary

History majors who look for jobs directly out of college earn salaries ranging from $20,000 to about $33,000.

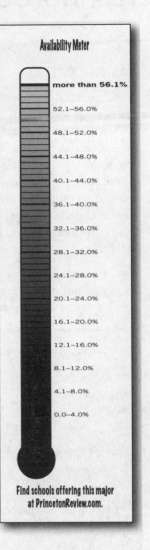

Availability Meter

more than 56.1%

52.1–56.0%

48.1–52.0%

44.1–48.0%

40.1–44.0%

36.1–40.0%

32.1–36.0%

28.1–32.0%

24.1–28.0%

20.1–24.0%

16.1–20.0%

12.1–16.0%

8.1–12.0%

4.1–8.0%

0.0–4.0%

Find schools offering this major at PrincetonReview.com.

CAREER OPTIONS

Mediator	Politician	Stockbroker
Military Officer	Professor	Teacher
Paralegal	Public Relations Professional	Theologian
Political Aide	Researcher	Trial Lawyer
Political Campaign Worker	Social Worker	Writer
Political Scientist		

HISTORY AND PHILOSOPHY OF SCIENCE AND TECHNOLOGY

Basics

Nature abhors a vacuum, so humankind had to pick up the slack in creating things. Starting with the halcyon days of cavemen figuring out how to make fire, discoveries in the physical, biological, and technological sciences have had huge impacts on human beings. Many of our contemporary concerns and controversies—weapons of mass destruction, euthanasia, artificial intelligence, abortion, oil drilling, and so on—demonstrate the complex overlap of scientific progressions and human systems of belief. It is this relationship between science and humanity that defines the study of history and philosophy of science and technology. The major explores both the causes and the consequences of scientific developments, calling on sources as wide-ranging as Plato and Nintendo. This is a highly interdisciplinary major; don't be surprised to find yourself drawing on courses in history, philosophy, anthropology, sociology, ethics, environmental science, cognitive science, and a host of other science- and technology-based disciplines.

By the end of the degree, you'll have a solid understanding of methodologies common to both philosophers and historians. This, along with keen skills in analytic reading and writing, will allow you to offer a strong voice to a conversation that promises to become even more complex in the decades ahead.

> ### SAMPLE COLLEGE CURRICULUM FOR HISTORY AND PHILOSOPHY OF SCIENCE AND TECHNOLOGY
>
> Android Epistemology—And Other A.I. Questions
>
> Art and Technology
>
> Change in the Twentieth Century
>
> Computers and Beyond
>
> Gender and Science
>
> History of Science
>
> Ideas in Classical Science
>
> Ideas in Contemporary Science
>
> Introduction to Historiography of Science and Technology
>
> Introduction to Philosophy of Science
>
> Methods of Philosophic Inquiry
>
> The Nature of Scientific Fact
>
> Philosophy and Biology
>
> The Scientific Revolution

We should note: This is not a science degree. You won't be spending your days dissecting rats in the bio lab and making volatile concoctions in bench chem. You're more likely to wander over to the biology department for a course in bioethics than a course in biochem.

If You Like History and Philosophy of Science and Technology, You May Also Like...

Anthropology, bioethics, ethics, public health, sociology

Suggested High School Prep for History and Philosophy of Science and Technology

As we mentioned above, this is highly interdisciplinary major with a heavy emphasis on the humanities courses. To prepare for a degree such this, you'll want to take all the humanities courses you can cram into your schedule. That means history, literature, philosophy, political science—you name it. These sorts of courses will help you sharpen the reading, writing, and researching skills you'll need as a history and philosophy of science and technology major.

Fun Facts

Listen Up

"Science is an integral part of culture. It's not this foreign thing, done by an arcane priesthood. It's one of the glories of the human intellectual tradition."

—the late Stephen Jay Gould, a famed evolutionary biologist

Join Up

To get the skinny on everything going on in the field, you'll want to become acquainted with the History of Science Society. Founded in 1924, the society is, in its own words, "the world's largest society dedicated to understanding science, technology, medicine, and their interactions with society in historical context." The HSS publishes two esteemed journals: the quarterly *Isis* and the annual Osiris.

Go to www.hssonline.org to check out the History of Science Society for yourself.

Careers and Salary

Starting salaries will typically range between $20,000 and $30,000 a year.

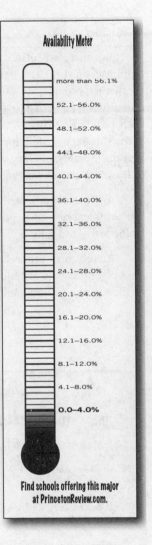

Availability Meter

more than 56.1%

52.1–56.0%

48.1–52.0%

44.1–48.0%

40.1–44.0%

36.1–40.0%

32.1–36.0%

28.1–32.0%

24.1–28.0%

20.1–24.0%

16.1–20.0%

12.1–16.0%

8.1–12.0%

4.1–8.0%

0.0–4.0%

Find schools offering this major at PrincetonReview.com.

CAREER OPTIONS

Archivist	Lobbyist	Teacher
Curator	Politician	Writer
Journalist	Researcher	

HOLOCAUST AND RELATED STUDIES

Basics

Holocaust and related studies examines the atrocities and complexities of genocide, laying particular emphasis on the 1915 Armenian genocide and the Nazi Holocaust of World War II. As a major, you'll draw on history, politics, art, literature, religion, philosophy, and psychology in an attempt to better understand this difficult subject. The major's interdisciplinary approach will allow you to construct unique answers to such basic questions as, "What circumstances allowed the Nazi Holocaust to take place?" Or, more simply, "Why does genocide happen?" These questions will lead you to investigate issues as wide ranging as propaganda, morality, military, and cult of personality. You'll look at other instances of genocide as well, such as in Bosnia, Bangladesh, Burma, Cambodia, East Timor, Rwanda, Sudan, and Ukraine, among others.

You'll also study the lingering effects of genocide. How have survivors coped? What are the psychological ramifications of genocide? What is the cultural impact? How have art and literature portrayed the Holocaust—and why does this matter?

A Holocaust and related studies major wrestles with formidable questions that remain imperative in the present day. As instances of genocide continue to mark our history, research in Holocaust studies offers us the chance to understand our past and shape our future.

SAMPLE COLLEGE CURRICULUM FOR HOLOCAUST AND RELATED STUDIES

Art and Literature of the Weimar Republic

European History: Early Twentieth Century

The First World War and the Armenian Genocide

History of the Holocaust

Introduction to Holocaust Studies

Literature After the Holocaust

Meaning of Genocide

Memory and Culture

Modern Jewish History

Nazi Germany

Survivor Studies

World War II

If You Like Holocaust and Related Studies, You May Also Like...

African studies, anthropology, Asian history, East European studies, European history, history, Jewish studies, peace studies, political science, Southeast Asian studies

Suggested High School Prep for Holocaust and Related Studies

Take any course in European history that is likely to devote significant time to the Holocaust. Courses in American and world history will likely touch on it as well. Otherwise, look for courses that'll give you a chance to build your writing and researching muscles. These will include English, history, and political science classes.

Fun Facts

From the Diary

Among the most significant books to emerge from the Holocaust was *The Diary of a Young Girl*, Anne Frank's first-hand account of her family's fight for survival. On July 15, 1944, more than two years after she began the diary, Anne Frank wrote:

"It's really a wonder that I haven't dropped all my ideals, because they seem so absurd and impossible to carry out. Yet I keep them, because in spite of everything, I still believe that people are really good at heart. I simply can't build up my hopes on a foundation consisting of confusion, misery, and death. I see the world gradually being turned into a wilderness, I hear the ever approaching thunder, which will destroy us too, I can feel the sufferings of millions and yet, if I look up into the heavens, I think that it will all come right, that this cruelty too will end, and that peace and tranquility will return again."

Careers and Salary

The starting salary for a Holocaust and related studies major is likely to be about $25,000. Nonprofit jobs might start at less than this.

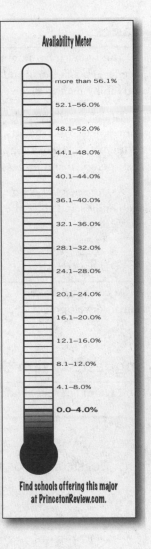

Availability Meter

more than 56.1%

52.1–56.0%

48.1–52.0%

44.1–48.0%

40.1–44.0%

36.1–40.0%

32.1–36.0%

28.1–32.0%

24.1–28.0%

20.1–24.0%

16.1–20.0%

12.1–16.0%

8.1–12.0%

4.1–8.0%

0.0–4.0%

Find schools offering this major at PrincetonReview.com.

CAREER OPTIONS

Activist	Diplomat/Attaché/Foreign Service Officer	Journalist
Consultant		Lobbyist
Curator	Editor	Politician
	Fundraiser	Teacher

HOME ECONOMICS

Basics

You won't learn how to make flapjacks or darn stockings with this major. Home economics at the college level teaches real and practical economic skills necessary to be sage when it comes to personal finance and family management.

Home economics borrows from several related fields in the humanities to provide a broad base of knowledge to its students. Home economics majors have the opportunity to take courses in everything from mathematics to sociology, providing them with a strong set of critical and analytical tools helpful in both their personal and professional careers.

As our society becomes increasingly complicated, a major in home economics prepares students to manage families and solve the problems they must face daily.

If You Like Home Economics, You May Also Like . . .

Accounting, bakery science, child care, child development, culinary arts, fashion design, food science, human development

Suggested High School Prep for Home Economics

If your high school offers them, take economics courses (both micro and macro), as well as mathematics courses such as statistics and accounting. Don't neglect your humanities, either, as you'll be digging in to a wide group of subjects about which you'll have to think critically.

> **SAMPLE COLLEGE CURRICULUM FOR HOME ECONOMICS**
>
> Consumer Economics
>
> Consumer Sciences
>
> Design Fundamentals
>
> Electives in the social sciences, including economics, psychology, and sociobiology
>
> Family Finance
>
> Family Relationships
>
> Family Resource Sciences
>
> Introduction to Apparel Construction
>
> Nutrition Today
>
> Professional Development and Careers in Home Economics

NUTRITION, HOME ECONOMICS, AND RELATED FIELDS

Fun Facts

Did You Know?

Ellen Henrietta Swallow, born in 1842 and the first woman to be admitted into the Massachusetts Institute of Technology, was the founder of the Home Economics movement in the United States, spending a lifetime encouraging and educating women in the discipline.

You Owe Me Big-Time, Kid

The average cost of raising a child born in 1999 to the age of seventeen in the United States is $160,000 ($237,000 when adjusted for inflation).

(Source: The U.S. Department of Agriculture)

Careers and Salary

Home economics starting salaries range all the way from $20,000 to $30,000.

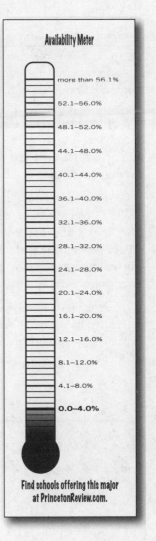

Availability Meter

more than 56.1%

52.1–56.0%

48.1–52.0%

44.1–48.0%

40.1–44.0%

36.1–40.0%

32.1–36.0%

28.1–32.0%

24.1–28.0%

20.1–24.0%

16.1–20.0%

12.1–16.0%

8.1–12.0%

4.1–8.0%

0.0–4.0%

Find schools offering this major at PrincetonReview.com.

CAREER OPTIONS

Bookkeeper	Guidance Counselor	Teacher
Child Care Worker	Social Worker	Wedding Consultant

HOMEOPATHIC MEDICINE

Basics

The homeopathic medicine major allows you to build a serious foundation in the field of—you guessed it!—homeopathic medicine. And what exactly does that mean? Homeopathic medicine is a branch of alternative medical science that uses natural substances to stimulate autoimmune (or self-healing) responses in the body. As a student of homeopathic medicine you'll learn all about these substances (or "materia medica," as they're called in the trade)—how they're derived, administered, and why they have the effects that they do. You'll also study the techniques of examination, diagnosis, and long-term treatment. This is science-heavy stuff, which means you'd better prepare yourself to pick through some chemistry, biology, physiology, and anatomy textbooks.

Homeopathy isn't all science. As a major, you'll examine the theories and philosophies that homeopathic medicine was founded on, and you'll trace the evolution of those ideas over the past two centuries. You'll look at the modern industry of homeopathic medicine and try to figure out where you'd like to fit in it. Because so many students move on to become homeopathic practitioners, you can expect to spend class time going over the nitty-gritty of client-practitioner relationships, professional expectations, private practice management, and legal requirements and certifications.

Programs in homeopathic medicine often give you the opportunity to check out other facets of alternative medicine as well. So you may find yourself taking a course in massage therapy, acupuncture, or herbology—complementary practices that can lend added dimensions to your practice of homeopathic medicine.

Sample College Curriculum for Homeopathic Medicine

Anatomy and Physiology

Biology

Body and Mind: Holistic Medicine

Fundamentals of Naturopathy

Homeopathy and Ethics

Homeopathy: History and Theory

Holistic Health

Introduction to Herbology

Managing a Practice

Materia Medica

Nutrition

Pathology

If You Like Homeopathic Therapy, You May Also Like...

Anatomy, aromatherapy, biology, chiropractic, community health and preventative medicine, counseling, dietetics, massage therapy, nursing, nutrition, pharmacology, physician assistant, physical therapy, public health, toxicology

Suggested High School Prep for Homeopathic Medicine

First things first: Sign up for those science courses pronto. This means biology, chemistry, physics—anything and everything your high school offers that will acquaint you with the laws of science. Keep in mind homeopathic medicine also has a strong philosophical component. So, if your high school offers some philosophy or religious studies courses, take a seat in the front row.

Fun Facts

The Vital Details

The father of homeopathic medicine is Samuel Hahnemann (1755–1843), a German physician who also introduced the concept of "quarantine." Homeopathic medicine first gained credibility during the Napoleonic Wars of the early nineteenth century, when it was used to treat cholera patients.

As homeopathic medicine made its way to America in the early decades of the nineteenth century, Constantine Herring was its largest advocate. In 1836, Herring founded the nation's first homeopathic medical college.

(Source: www.naturalhealers.com/qa/homeopathy.html)

Careers and Salary

The possible starting salaries can range from $20,000 to $50,000, and sometimes even higher. Why such a spread? The homeopathic medicine degree is often earned by students who already have training in some other area of holistic or allopathic medicine. Pursuing a graduate degree in the field can also add dimensions to your education and dollars to your wallet.

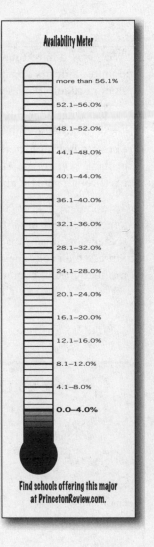

Availability Meter

more than 56.1%

52.1–56.0%

48.1–52.0%

44.1–48.0%

40.1–44.0%

36.1–40.0%

32.1–36.0%

28.1–32.0%

24.1–28.0%

20.1–24.0%

16.1–20.0%

12.1–16.0%

8.1–12.0%

4.1–8.0%

0.0–4.0%

Find schools offering this major at PrincetonReview.com.

CAREER OPTIONS

Counselor	Researcher	Teacher
Homeopathic Medicine Practitioner		

HORTICULTURE

Basics

Who would have thunk it? An authority no less than *Forbes* magazine has reported that horticulture is a booming industry for entrepreneurs and a profession in which six-figure incomes are feasible. If you thought horticulture was a backyard hobby, think again; it's a lucrative business.

So just what does this thriving enterprise involve, you ask? Basically, horticulture is the art, science, and business of growing fruits, vegetables, ornamental plants, and turfgrasses. Horticulturists arrange plants and flowers around the exterior landscapes of residences, office buildings, baseball fields, and virtually every respectable golf course. They also grow, maintain, market, and distribute all manner of plants. They improve plants through genetic manipulation, too.

If you major in horticulture, you'll learn a lot about agriculture and the biological sciences. In fact, you'll become an expert in all things plant-related: plant structures, plant diseases, plant genetics, soils, and the insects and organisms that affect plants. You are likely to specialize in an area as well, such as landscape horticulture, which combines plant science and principles of design to create cheerful environments, ornamental production, and commercial fruit and vegetable production.

SAMPLE COLLEGE
CURRICULUM FOR
HORTICULTURE

Biology

Chemistry

Entomology

Floral Design

Forestry

Genetics

Landscape Horticulture

Ornamental Plants

Plant Pathology

Plant Physiology

Plant Propagation

Plant Taxonomy

Soil Science

Vegetable and Fruit Crops

Weed Science

If You Like Horticulture, You May Also Like . . .

Agricultural economics, agricultural and biological engineering, agricultural technology management, agriculture, agronomy and crop science, animal science, biochemistry, biology, botany and plant biology, cell biology, chemistry, ecology, entomology, environmental science, feed science, forestry, genetics, geology, grain science, interior architecture, landscape architecture, landscape horticulture, microbiology, natural resources conservation, plant pathology, soil science, sustainable resource management

Suggested High School Prep for Horticulture

You'll need a strong foundation in the basic sciences. Having an endearing love of biology and the physical sciences will help you immensely as well. If you are planning to major in horticulture in college, you should take courses in biology, chemistry, algebra, trigonometry, physics, and vocational agriculture. Everything that you can learn about climate, soil, water, and plants will be helpful. Also, get used to working outdoors and in laboratories. Familiarity with business won't hurt, either.

Fun Facts

Did You Know?

Chili peppers are grown pretty much everywhere in the world. Asian nations are the world's largest producers. In the United States, New Mexico produces the most capsica (their fancy scientific name); more than 21,000 acres are dedicated to growing hot peppers in the Land of Enchantment.

Did You Know?

Horticulture is a $10 billion industry in the United States.

Careers and Salary

The average starting salary for a horticulture major fresh out of college is about $25,000 per year.

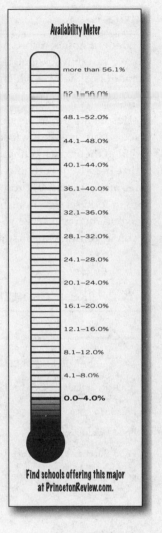

Availability Meter

more than 56.1%

52.1–56.0%

48.1–52.0%

44.1–48.0%

40.1–44.0%

36.1–40.0%

32.1–36.0%

28.1–32.0%

24.1–28.0%

20.1–24.0%

16.1–20.0%

12.1–16.0%

8.1–12.0%

4.1–8.0%

0.0–4.0%

Find schools offering this major at PrincetonReview.com.

CAREER OPTIONS		
Biologist	Farmer	Horticulturist

HOSPITALITY

Basics

Modern hotels, resorts, restaurants, and convention centers are huge, intricate, and diverse business entities. We can only imagine the confusion that would ensue if capable professionals weren't running them. A major in hospitality—which is alternatively called hospitality services, hospitality management, and tourism at various colleges and universities—will prepare you for a career managing these kinds of places.

Hospitality programs are very professionally oriented in nature. They integrate management theory with practical business knowledge. If you major in hospitality, you'll also learn quite a bit about basic nutrition and food theory, marketing, statistics, and even geography. One of the best things about hospitality programs is that they frequently incorporate one or more internships into their curricula as well—in fancy restaurants, major hotels, and resorts. In an internship, you'll gain on-the-job experience in real-world work situations in food service, human resources and employee relations, public relations, and management. This kind of experience will serve you well in your first job and—probably more important—it will be a great help to you in getting your first job.

If You Like Hospitality, You May Also Like . . .

Accounting, business administration and management, business communications, culinary arts, entrepreneurship, human resources management, industrial management, logistics management, marketing, operations management, recreation management, sport and leisure studies

Suggested High School Prep for Hospitality

A solid college preparatory curriculum will serve you adequately. Math is important (because you'll probably be required to take accounting and statistics), as is anything you can do to improve your organizational skills.

SAMPLE COLLEGE CURRICULUM FOR HOSPITALITY

Finance

Food Production

Food Purchasing and Cost Control

Food Service Layout, Design, and Catering

Global Tourism Geography

Internship

Legal Issues in the Hospitality Industry

Management Principles

Marketing

Nutrition

Personnel and Organization

Principles of Accounting

Principles of Economics

Resort, Cruise, and Entertainment Operations

Statistics

Fun Facts

Best Restaurant

According to *Wine Spectator* magazine, Charlie Trotter's restaurant in Chicago is the best restaurant in the United States.

Best Amusement Parks

Here is a list of the best amusement parks in the world, as rated by participants in www.ThemeParkInsider.com's How Readers Rate the Parks. (Note: The ratings might change by the time you visit the site).

1. Universal's Islands of Adventure (Orlando, Florida)
2. Busch Gardens (Williamsburg, Virginia)
3. Disneyland (Paris, France)
4. Tokyo DisneySea (Tokyo, Japan)
5. Disney-MGM Studios (Orlando, Florida)
6. Sea World Orlando (Orlando, Florida)
7. Cedar Point (Sandusky, Ohio)
8. Universal Studios Florida (Orlando, Florida)
9. Kennywood (Pittsburgh, Pennsylvania)
10. Gardaland (Gardaland, Italy)

Careers and Salary

Starting salaries in the burgeoning hospitality industry range pretty widely—from $20,000 to about $31,000 annually.

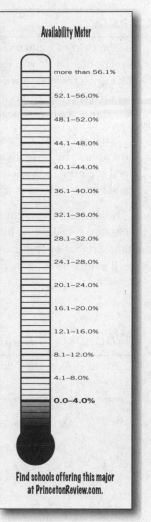

Availability Meter

more than 56.1%
52.1–56.0%
48.1–52.0%
44.1–48.0%
40.1–44.0%
36.1–40.0%
32.1–36.0%
28.1–32.0%
24.1–28.0%
20.1–24.0%
16.1–20.0%
12.1–16.0%
8.1–12.0%
4.1–8.0%
0.0–4.0%

Find schools offering this major at PrincetonReview.com.

CAREER OPTIONS

Accountant/Auditor	Chef	Sommelier
Advertising Executive	Hotel Manager	Tour Guide
Bar/Club Manager	Restaurateur	Travel Agent
Casino Host	Retail Salesperson	Wedding Consultant
Caterer	Secretary	

HUMAN DEVELOPMENT

Basics

The field of human development is concerned with the entire life span of human beings, from infancy through old age. If you major in it, you'll study the biological processes that characterize each stage of life and learn how we move physically from one stage to the next. You'll learn how these biological factors affect psychology and how social behavior changes over time. You'll study the concepts of work, school, and community. And you'll learn how the views of human development vary among cultures.

Many programs combine human development with course work in family studies. In this case, you'll learn about the formation of the family, family interactions, adult-child relationships, and family problems. You'll see how individuals and families interact in a community. And you'll discover how families change as people grow older and members are gained and lost.

Human development is a multidisciplinary major encompassing fields such as psychology, philosophy, sociology, social work, biology, and education. You may be required to specialize in a certain area such as aging services or community human services; other programs offer a more general track. Whatever the case, you'll gain a broad understanding of how humans change and grow and what is important to them along the way.

If You Like Human Development, You May Also Like . . .

Anthropology, child development, clinical psychology, developmental psychology, education, experimental psychology, psychology, social psychology, sociology

SAMPLE COLLEGE CURRICULUM FOR HUMAN DEVELOPMENT

Adolescent Development

Adult-Child Relationships

Adulthood Through Older Years

Biological Behavioral Development

Communities and Families

Death and Dying

Developmental Problems

Family Development

Gerontology

Infant and Child Development

Sexual Identity

Theories of Human Development

Transition to Adulthood

Suggested High School Prep for Human Development

Your best preparation for a human development major will be math and science courses. Biology, chemistry, physics, and advanced-level math courses will give you a good foundation, as will courses in anatomy and psychology. Courses in English, history, and philosophy will also be good preparation.

NUTRITION, HOME ECONOMICS, AND RELATED FIELDS

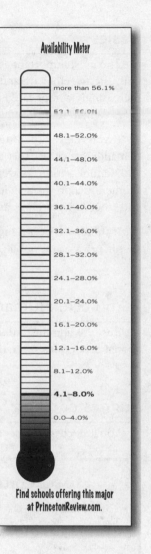

Fun Facts

Interested in Human Development?

Eventually, you might want to check out the scholarly journal *Human Development*, which features articles pertaining to human development from the fields of biology, psychology, history, and more.

What Makes People Grow?

The human growth hormone (HGH) is responsible for normal development. It is especially important for children, who develop at a rapid pace. This hormone is found in the pituitary gland, located at the base of the brain. Although there are many speculations about HGH's potential to prolong life, no conclusive findings about it have been made yet.

Careers and Salary

Since human development majors have so many options open to them, a starting salary is difficult to predict. Their salary will vary greatly depending on the capacity in which they use their degree—some options are as a psychologist, biologist, social worker, and teacher. Check out the starting salaries for those professions to get an idea of what they would make.

Availability Meter

more than 56.1%

52.1–56.0%

48.1–52.0%

44.1–48.0%

40.1–44.0%

36.1–40.0%

32.1–36.0%

28.1–32.0%

24.1–28.0%

20.1–24.0%

16.1–20.0%

12.1–16.0%

8.1–12.0%

4.1–8.0%

0.0–4.0%

Find schools offering this major at PrincetonReview.com.

CAREER OPTIONS

Anthropologist	Nutritionist	Social Worker
Biologist	Professor	Sociologist
Nurse	Psychologist	Teacher

HUMAN RESOURCES MANAGEMENT

Basics

The most important assets of any business are its employees. Employees need to be kept happy, trained, enthusiastic, efficient, and maybe even out of trouble. As businesses grow and as labor relationships grow increasingly complicated and demanding, more and more companies are turning to human resource managers to help them communicate with, reward, and enthuse their employees.

If you've ever spent ten minutes by the proverbial office water cooler, then you can imagine just how demanding a career this can be. It requires someone who has a clear knowledge of business management and administration, as well as someone who knows how to deal with people. As a human resources management major, you will learn about business administration as well as gain an understanding of corporate and labor law, planning, and psychology.

If there was ever a high-growth field, this is it. Human resources managers are needed in almost every sector, private and public, from *Fortune* 500 corporations to the next generation of startups.

If You Like Human Resources Management, You May Also Like . . .

Business administration and management, hospitality, industrial management, industrial psychology, managerial economics, operations management

Suggested High School Prep for Human Resources Management

You'll need some decent accounting skills when you're determining bonus scales, so pay attention in algebra and your other math classes. Any knowledge you can get out of a high school economics class or two will also prove valuable in college. And since human resources management is really a specialization within business administration, you should take some business classes if your high school offers them. And then there's psychology. Yes, managing humans will require a little understanding of their needs and desires. So if you can find a psychology class at your school, dig into it.

> **SAMPLE COLLEGE CURRICULUM FOR HUMAN RESOURCES MANAGEMENT**
>
> Compensation Management
>
> Cost Accounting
>
> Human Resource Policy, Planning, and Information Systems
>
> Industrial Psychology
>
> Labor Economics
>
> Labor Relations
>
> Law of the Management Process
>
> Organizational Behavior—Micro Perspective
>
> Recruitment, Selection, and Appraisal

Fun Facts

High Expectations

"I don't want any yes-men around me. I want everyone to tell me the truth—even if it costs him his job."

—Samuel Goldwyn

Quotes from Employee Appraisal Reports

"Since my last report, he has reached rock bottom and has started to dig."

"His men would follow him anywhere, but only out of morbid curiosity."

"I would not allow this associate to breed."

"Works well when under constant supervision and cornered like a rat in a trap."

"When she opens her mouth, it seems that this is only to change whichever foot was previously in there."

"He would be out of his depth in a puddle."

"This young lady has delusions of adequacy."

"She sets low personal standards and then consistently fails to achieve them."

Careers and Salary

The average starting salary for a human resources manager is between $30,000 and $40,000.

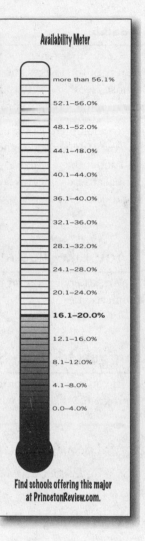

Availability Meter

more than 56.1%

52.1–56.0%

48.1–52.0%

44.1–48.0%

40.1–44.0%

36.1–40.0%

32.1–36.0%

28.1–32.0%

24.1–28.0%

20.1–24.0%

16.1–20.0%

12.1–16.0%

8.1–12.0%

4.1–8.0%

0.0–4.0%

Find schools offering this major at PrincetonReview.com.

CAREER OPTIONS

Bar/Club Manager

Consultant

Hospital Administrator

Human Resources Manager

Labor Relations Specialist

Management Consultant

Mediator

Office Manager

Organizational Developer

Small Business Owner

ILLUSTRATION

Basics

Remember when you were a kid and you picked up one children's book after another, marveling at the beauty of the images, the colors, the detail, and what you would now call the vividness of the characters at whose faces you were staring? The author created those characters, but it was the illustrator that let you see them, and in doing so brought them to life.

In addition to being a major that will help prepare you for a career as a professional illustrator—whether you're working for designers on websites or trying to become the next Dr. Seuss—illustration will also teach you about the aesthetics, philosophy, and business of the art world. Your classes will take into consideration formal artistic concerns faced by illustrators, as well as the ethics and law behind the profession you're preparing to join. So, pull out your pencils and sketch pads and prepare to enter an exciting and interesting world.

If You Like Illustration, You May Also Like . . .

Art, art education, art history, fashion design, film, interior design, photography, printmaking, visual communication

Suggested High School Prep for Illustration

If you want to major in illustration, you will need to have a portfolio of work in order to be admitted to a program. When reviewing portfolios, most schools look for strong observational drawing skills, so draw from life as often as you can. Use all resources available at your school. Check out local museums, community colleges, and universities for pre-college programs or seminars. Sometimes museums also offer volunteer opportunities for students.

SAMPLE COLLEGE CURRICULUM FOR ILLUSTRATION

Advanced Photography

Art History I–II

Graphic Communications

Introduction to Graphic Design

Introduction to Philosophical Aesthetics

Law of Mass Communication

Photo Design Techniques

Photo-Illustration Techniques

Photo Technology

Photography

Photojournalism I

Visual Design

Fun Facts

A Name to Remember

Felix Octavius Carr Darley (1821–1888) was the best-known American illustrator of the nineteenth century. During a highly successful career that spanned four decades, he illustrated the works of Edgar Allan Poe, James Fenimore Cooper, Washington Irving, Charles Dickens, Henry Wadsworth Longfellow, Nathaniel Hawthorne, and many others.

Did You Know?

Nearly 60 percent of all visual artists are self-employed—about six times the proportion for all professional occupations.

Careers and Salary

Starting salaries for artists vary dramatically depending upon the career and success of the artist. Introductory salaries for artists range anywhere from $20,000 to $35,000.

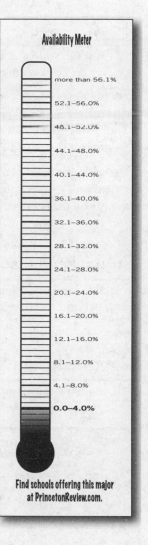

Availability Meter

more than 56.1%

52.1–56.0%

48.1–52.0%

44.1–48.0%

40.1–44.0%

36.1–40.0%

32.1–36.0%

28.1–32.0%

24.1–28.0%

20.1–24.0%

16.1–20.0%

12.1–16.0%

8.1–12.0%

4.1–8.0%

0.0–4.0%

Find schools offering this major at PrincetonReview.com.

CAREER OPTIONS

Animator	Graphic Designer	Web Art Director
Art Dealer	Photographer	Website Designer
Artist		

INDUSTRIAL DESIGN

Basics

As you flip your way through the newest Ikea catalog, you find yourself cringing, thinking, "How could they ever design something like that?" You know (or think you know) that you can do what they do better.

Behind every new piece of furniture, shoe, coffeemaker, and television stands an industrial designer. They are the men and women who help to fashion the objects around us, including that hideous coffee table in your living room. Industrial design takes the creativity behind a broader design major and focuses it on how some of the most basic objects that we take for granted are created. It's art for the practical world.

As an industrial design major you will have the chance to explore that creative energy within you. You can take your own particular aesthetic, which will expand through courses in art and art history, and bring it to bear on that perfect refrigerator you've been imagining.

If You Like Industrial Design, You May Also Like . . .

Architecture, art, ceramic engineering, civil engineering, drawing, engineering design, graphic art, interior architecture, interior design, painting, printmaking

Suggested High School Prep for Industrial Design

If you have the chance to take drafting, drawing, and design courses, run with it; otherwise, build up those drawing skills as much as you can on your own, along with math, art, and physics. You'll probably need a portfolio to get into any design program, so draw from life as much as possible. Buy a full range of pencils to ensure strong gradation from light to dark in all of your drawings. Learning about different artistic media will make your drawing endeavors richer and your artistic vision broader. History and English classes might also give your art new perspectives.

> **SAMPLE COLLEGE CURRICULUM FOR INDUSTRIAL DESIGN**
>
> Art History
>
> Conceptual Drawing for Industrial Design
>
> Graphic Presentation
>
> Industrial Design Practices
>
> Industrial Technology Education
>
> Introduction to Industrial Design
>
> Mathematics
>
> Product Design
>
> Statistics
>
> Three-Dimensional Graphics
>
> Visual Thinking and Problem-Solving

Fun Facts

Quotable

"An industrial designer should have direct involvement in any proposed project where the end user is expected to interact with the proposed product."

—Ed Cahill, senior designer

Careers and Salary

Starting salaries for those with a bachelor's degree in industrial design are about $30,000 to $35,000, but expect those numbers to go up with experience and an advanced degree.

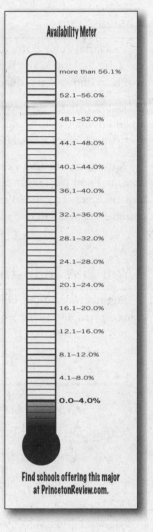

Availability Meter

more than 56.1%

52.1–56.0%

48.1–52.0%

44.1–48.0%

40.1–44.0%

36.1–40.0%

32.1–36.0%

28.1–32.0%

24.1–28.0%

20.1–24.0%

16.1–20.0%

12.1–16.0%

8.1–12.0%

4.1–8.0%

0.0–4.0%

Find schools offering this major at PrincetonReview.com.

CAREER OPTIONS

Architect	Fashion Designer	Set Designer
Art Dealer	Graphic Designer	Web Art Director
Artist	Product Designer	Website Designer
Digital Artist		

INDUSTRIAL ENGINEERING

Basics

Industrial engineering challenges you to improve, design, manage, evaluate, and test production systems. You'll be looking at the hows of the economy—how a product is made or a service is given. Your ultimate goal is to improve the quality of those products and services.

Unlike other engineering majors, industrial engineering focuses on people. You'll have classes in ergonomics and human factors and study how people are a part of a production system, of course investigating how they can do work more efficiently or how a production system can be designed to better serve them.

Although industrial engineers originally only dealt with manufacturing, today they have a wider range of options. Food, banking, health care, and commercial aviation are only a few of the sectors that rely on industrial engineers to make them more effectively deliver their wares. The skills of industrial engineers improve countless aspects of our society.

If You Like Industrial Engineering, You May Also Like . . .

Engineering design, engineering mechanics, human resources management, industrial design, industrial management, industrial psychology, logistics management, operations management

SAMPLE COLLEGE CURRICULUM FOR INDUSTRIAL ENGINEERING

Ergonomics

Facilities Design

Industrial Practice in Systems Design

Introduction to Simulation

Linear Programming

Musculoskeletal Mechanics

Network Flows

Occupational Biomechanics

Quality Design and Control

Solid Mechanics

Theory of Activity Networks

Work Analysis and Design

Work Physiology and Biomechanics in Work Design

Suggested High School Prep for Industrial Engineering

A strong background in advanced math and science courses (calculus, trigonometry, physics, biology, chemistry) will be the best preparation for your college courses. Computer proficiency is also very useful, as well as social sciences such as history and psychology.

Fun Facts

Who Started Industrial Engineering, Anyway?

In the early 1900s, Lillian and Frank Gilbreth, an American couple, developed many of the theories that shaped the tenets of industrial engineering. The idea of the industrial workplace's efficiency fascinated Frank and Lillian, and they developed a method of "time and motion study" to analyze how well workers were using their time. They applied social sciences to industry—that is, they focused on the worker instead of on outside factors. Their publications include *Motion Study*, *Fatigue Study*, and *Applied Motion Study*.

(Source: www.Britannica.com)

Ergonomics and Design

Studies in industrial engineering often include ergonomics. Ever have a tube of toothpaste you couldn't figure out how to open? Arrive at an intersection only to have no idea which traffic light belongs to you? Choose the wrong kind of tuna fish because all the cans look alike? You might want to take a look at baddesigns.com, which not only describes instances of unsuccessful product designs, but also suggests ways that those designs could be improved for better ergonomics.

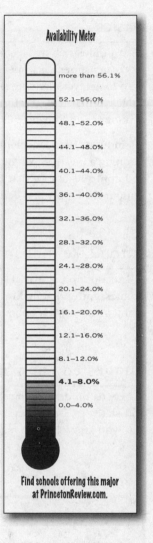

Availability Meter

more than 56.1%

52.1–56.0%

48.1–52.0%

44.1–48.0%

40.1–44.0%

36.1–40.0%

32.1–36.0%

28.1–32.0%

24.1–28.0%

20.1–24.0%

16.1–20.0%

12.1–16.0%

8.1–12.0%

4.1–8.0%

0.0–4.0%

Find schools offering this major at PrincetonReview.com.

Careers and Salary

According to Ohio State University, starting salaries for industrial engineers range from $42,000 to $52,000. Salaries depend heavily on where they live and how they choose to use their degree.

CAREER OPTIONS

Industrial Engineer	Power Plant Manager	Quality Assurance Engineer
Organizational Developer	Production Manager	Quality Control Manager

INDUSTRIAL MANAGEMENT

Basics

An industrial management major, similar to its counterparts, which include risk management and logistics management, is a specialized entry into corporate America. Industrial management majors are the folks with long-term planning skills. They're the ones who help to plan and manage a corporation's production strategy. This means that they have to have a keen sense of business in addition to a great understanding of economics and finance. Either those, or a very accurate crystal ball.

Industrial management majors are always in demand by companies and government organizations. Running a business can be a rollercoaster ride, and industrial management majors are there to help prepare and control some of that fickleness with long-term strategic planning that takes into consideration everything from supply and demand to last year's gross revenues.

If You Like Industrial Management, You May Also Like . . .

Accounting, actuarial science, business administration and management, business communications, economics, entrepreneurship, finance, human resources management, international business, logistics management, managerial economics, public administration, risk management, statistics

Suggested High School Prep for Industrial Management

Focus on developing those strong quantitative skills through advanced math courses such as calculus and statistics. Don't forget that managers have to be able to speak and communicate effectively, so make sure you know how to read and write clearly by taking tough English courses.

SAMPLE COLLEGE CURRICULUM FOR INDUSTRIAL MANAGEMENT

Business Information Systems

Business Operational Planning

Career Orientation: Management

Management Project

Organizational Behavior and Leadership Skills

Production and Operations Analysis

Production Planning and Control

Quality Management and Control

Fun Facts

Stock Market Definitions

Stock: A magical piece of paper that is worth $33.75 until the moment after you buy it. It will then be worth $8.50.

Bond: What you had with your spouse until you pawned his/her golf clubs to invest in Amazon.com.

Broker: The person you trust to help you make major financial decisions. Please note the first five letters of this word spell "Broke."

Bear: What your trade account and wallet will be when you take a flyer on that hot stock tip your secretary gave you.

Bull: What your broker uses to explain why your mutual funds tanked during the last quarter.

Margin: Where you scribble the latest quotes when you're supposed to be listening to your manager's presentation.

Short Position: A type of trade where, in theory, a person sells stocks he doesn't actually own. Since this also works in reality, a short position is what a person usually ends up being in (i.e., "The rent, sir? Hahaha, well, I'm a little short this month.").

Commission: The only reliable way to make money on the stock market, which is why your broker charges you one.

Yak: What you do into a pail when you discover your stocks have plunged and your broker is making a margin call.

Recent Headlines and the Hidden Truth Behind the Story!

Headline 1: Number of Companies Bidding on Janitorial Contracts for Law Firms in New York Down 50 Percent

Translation: Significant Reduction of Mergers and Acquisitions Expected This Year

Headline 2: SEC Says Securities Convictions Are Expected to Drop Next Year

Translation: Jails Are Overcrowded, Nowhere to Put the Violators

Headline 3: Yahoo! Reports Stock Message Posts Have Dropped Significantly

Translation: SEC Had a Banner Year in Convicting Posters, Which Caused the Current Overcrowding Situation in Headline 2

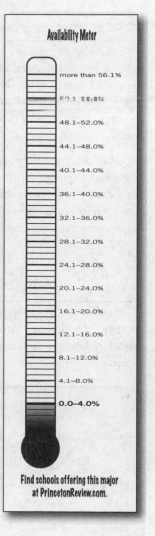

Availability Meter

more than 56.1%

52.1–56.0%

48.1–52.0%

44.1–48.0%

40.1–44.0%

36.1–40.0%

32.1–36.0%

28.1–32.0%

24.1–28.0%

20.1–24.0%

16.1–20.0%

12.1–16.0%

8.1–12.0%

4.1–8.0%

0.0–4.0%

Find schools offering this major at PrincetonReview.com.

Careers and Salary

The average starting salary for an industrial management major is between $35,000 and $45,000.

CAREER OPTIONS

Accountant/Auditor	Consultant	Management Consultant
Bank Officer	Financial Planner	Manufacturing Executive
Bookkeeper	Human Resources Manager	Organizational Developer
Business Valuator	Investment Banker	Stockbroker

INDUSTRIAL PSYCHOLOGY

Basics

Industrial psychology majors study psychology as it applies to the workplace—attitudes of employees and employers, organizational behavior, workplace environment and its effects, and much, much more. You'll study such things as personality, cognition, perception, and human development. You'll learn about the biological side of behavior (which means you'll also really know what chemicals aren't at proper levels in a person with a chemical imbalance). You might be given the option to take relevant business courses, such as management, since you will focus on organizational settings.

As an undergraduate, you can expect to get well acquainted with the basics of psychology in addition to the more specific field of industrial psychology. And as with all psychological fields, you'll be doing a lot of research, experimentation, and documentation. You'll learn—and use—statistics and other methods for data analysis. You'll also learn about the great psychologists of the past and present, and how you might use, adapt, contradict, or support their findings with your own ideas.

If You Like Industrial Psychology, You May Also Like . . .

Anthropology, biopsychology, clinical psychology, counseling, developmental psychology, educational psychology, experimental psychology, industrial engineering, industrial management, mental health services, neurobiology, neuroscience, physiological psychology, psychology, rehabilitation services, social psychology, sociology

SAMPLE COLLEGE CURRICULUM FOR INDUSTRIAL PSYCHOLOGY

Biological Bases of Behavior

Ethics

Evaluating Psychological Interventions

History of Modern Psychology

Organizational Theory

Performance Appraisal

Psychometrics

Stress and Well-Being

Training and Development

Understanding Jobs and Job Performance

Work Attitudes and Social Processes

Work Motivation

Work Teams and Groups

Suggested High School Prep for Industrial Psychology

If your high school offers them, psychology courses are a great way to learn the basics you'll cover in college. Science courses such as biology and chemistry are very important, as are math courses, especially statistics. And since you'll most likely be doing some research, hone your reading and writing skills so you can communicate your ideas effectively.

Fun Facts

Who Invented Industrial Psychology?

In 1911, Hugo Munsterberg began using psychology to solve problems in practical situations. The term "industrial psychology," however, was first used in 1903—by accident. A psychologist named W. L. Bryan used the term in an essay he wrote, but he'd meant to write "individual" psychology—not "industrial."

The Beginnings of Industrial Psychology, Pre-WWI

- The first professional management school was established at the University of Pennsylvania in 1881.
- Frederick W. Taylor began the experiments that would lead to his philosophy of scientific management.
- Walter Dill Scott applied psychology to advertising, then to the workplace.
- Hugo Munsterberg encouraged funding for research in industrial psychology.
- Frederick W. Taylor wrote *The Principles of Scientific Management* and was accused of exploitation of workers.

(Source: Middle Tennessee State University)

Careers and Salary

Psychologists earn starting salaries in the $25,000 to $35,000 range, but that depends greatly on how they apply their skills and what experience they've had. Graduate degrees also increase the salary range.

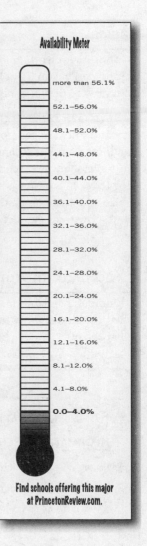

Availability Meter

more than 56.1%

52.1–56.0%

48.1–52.0%

44.1–48.0%

40.1–44.0%

36.1–40.0%

32.1–36.0%

28.1–32.0%

24.1–28.0%

20.1–24.0%

16.1–20.0%

12.1–16.0%

8.1–12.0%

4.1–8.0%

0.0–4.0%

Find schools offering this major
at PrincetonReview.com.

CAREER OPTIONS		
Labor Relations Specialist	Professor	Social Worker
Management Consultant	Psychologist	Sociologist

INFORMATION TECHNOLOGY

Basics

Those who work in information technology provide a crucial link between technology and those who use and depend on it but have little more than a superficial understanding of computers. In this major, you'll learn how to design computing systems based on a business' research, data, and communication needs.

In an information technology program, you'll learn all the basics of computer science, including hardware and software components, programming, algorithms, databases, operating systems, and network administration. Computer design and editing existing systems and software will also be part of your program. Once you understand how computers work and the technology behind them, you'll learn how to apply this knowledge in a business setting. You'll study how to solve a wide range of problems, including how to customize and integrate systems to meet business and individual user needs, how to maintain day-to-day operations, how to design networking systems, and how to handle security problems.

If You Like Information Technology, You May Also Like . . .

Computer and information science, computer engineering, computer graphics, computer systems analysis, digital communications and media/multimedia, information resources management, web master and web management

SAMPLE COLLEGE CURRICULUM FOR INFORMATION TECHNOLOGY

Applications Programming

Business Application Program Development

Client/Server Database Utilization

Computer Hardware Components

Computer Networks

Computer Systems and Architecture

Data Communication and Networking

Database Management Systems

Information Systems Design and Implementation

Programming Languages

Software Development

Systems Analysis

Web Development

Suggested High School Prep for Information Technology

To prepare for this major, take physics, advanced algebra, trigonometry, calculus, and whatever your school offers in computer classes.

Fun Facts

Computers Can Be So Confusing

Tech Support (over the phone): "Ok, in the bottom left hand side of the screen, can you see the 'OK' button displayed?"

Customer: "Wow. How can you see my screen from there?"

Tech Support: "I need you to right-click on the Open Desktop."

Customer: "OK."

Tech Support: "Did you get a pop-up menu?"

Customer: "No."

Tech Support: "OK. Right click again. Do you see a pop-up menu?"

Customer: "No."

Tech Support: "OK, sir. Can you tell me what you have done up until this point?"

Customer: "Sure, you told me to write 'click' and I wrote 'click.'"

(Source: www.desiboyzmasala.com)

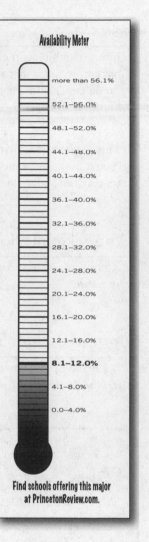

Availability Meter

more than 56.1%
52.1–56.0%
48.1–52.0%
44.1–48.0%
40.1–44.0%
36.1–40.0%
32.1–36.0%
28.1–32.0%
24.1–28.0%
20.1–24.0%
16.1–20.0%
12.1–16.0%
8.1–12.0%
4.1–8.0%
0.0–4.0%

Find schools offering this major at PrincetonReview.com.

Careers and Salary

Starting salaries for information technology majors range from $33,000 to $47,000 a year.

CAREER OPTIONS

Computer Engineer

Computer Programmer

Computer Security Specialist

Consultant

Database Administrator

Data Communication Analyst

Information Manager

Network Administrator

Systems Administrator

Systems Analyst

Technical Support Specialist

Web Developer

Webmaster

Web Programmer

INTERIOR ARCHITECTURE

Basics

Interior architects pick up where the other guys (the architects) leave off. They are the ones who fill in all that empty space that architects design. Now don't be fooled: this is more than just telling someone where to place a couch and what color patterns look best with the carpet. Whether it's the new corporate headquarters of the widget factory, or Bill Gates's new country home, interior architects help shape the way we live and work. And who knows, maybe with enough time they can help us figure a way out of the office cubicle.

This major looks a lot like an architecture major, complete with courses in planning, design, and drafting. You'll be using some of the hottest new technology out there, including computer-aided design programs that can show you how to turn that bedroom of yours into the hottest spot in the neighborhood.

If You Like Interior Architecture, You May Also Like . . .

Architectural engineering, architectural history, architecture, civil engineering, interior design, landscape architecture

Suggested High School Prep for Interior Architecture

If you have the chance to take drafting and architecture courses, run with it and consider yourself lucky. Otherwise, build up those drawing skills, along with math, art, and psychology.

SAMPLE COLLEGE CURRICULUM FOR INTERIOR ARCHITECTURE

Architectural Drafting

Architecture I

Art History

Computer Applications

Drawing

History of Decorative Arts

Interior Architecture I–V

Lighting Design

Materials, Finishes, and Technology

Presentation Techniques

Textiles

Three-Dimensional Design

Fun Facts

Did You Know?

The Mughal emperor Shah Jahan built the Taj Mahal, considered one of the world's most beautiful buildings, to immortalize his wife who had died in childbirth. The interior design took at least 15 years to complete.

Careers and Salary

The placement rates for interior architecture majors are fantastic. Starting salaries for a bachelor's in interior architecture are about $25,000 to $30,000, but expect those numbers to go way up with experience and an advanced degree.

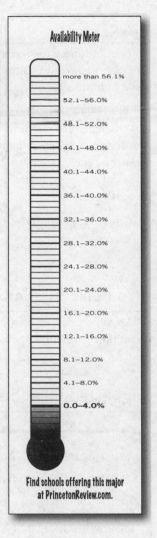

Availability Meter

more than 56.1%

52.1–56.0%

48.1–52.0%

44.1–48.0%

40.1–44.0%

36.1–40.0%

32.1–36.0%

28.1–32.0%

24.1–28.0%

20.1–24.0%

16.1–20.0%

12.1–16.0%

8.1–12.0%

4.1–8.0%

0.0–4.0%

Find schools offering this major at PrincetonReview.com.

CAREER OPTIONS		
Antiques Dealer	Architect	Structural Engineer
Archaeologist	Interior Designer	

INTERIOR DESIGN

Basics

Look around. Every contained space has some kind of an interior design: homes, offices, hospitals, stores, offices, hotels, resorts, theaters, restaurants, and everything else with four walls. Some of it is tasteful and some of it hideous, but it is interior design nonetheless.

As a college major, interior design is heavily pre-professional and very hands-on (expect a lot of projects that simulate on-the-job situations). It falls into the broader category of design. If you decide to major in interior design, you'll study light, color, form, space, furnishings, and pretty much all other aspects of built environments. You'll study the basics of three-dimensional design, space planning, and perspective. You'll also study color theory, different kinds of materials and patterns, and computer-aided design, which is all the rage these days.

Once you get into the major a bit, you'll probably have the choice of specializing in residential design or commercial design.

If You Like Interior Design, You May Also Like . . .

Architectural history, architecture, art, art history, ceramics, drawing, graphic art, industrial design, interior architecture, landscape architecture, naval architecture, sculpture, urban studies

Suggested High School Prep for Interior Design

Obviously, take art classes—drawing, painting, sculpture, photography, and the like—because it will develop your ability to visualize, conceptualize, and create. Familiarity with computers is also a plus, as a lot of interior design is done with the assistance of software these days.

SAMPLE COLLEGE CURRICULUM FOR INTERIOR DESIGN

Advanced Residential Design

Architectural Drafting

Art History

Basic Design Principles

Building Construction and Codes

Computer-Aided Drafting and Design

History of Architecture

Industrial Design

Interior Drawing

Interior Lighting

Textiles Design

Three-Dimensional Design

Fun Facts

Did You Know?

According to people in the know, combining yellow and black produces the most visually conspicuous color combination.

Did You Know?

If you mix blue and yellow paint, you'll get green paint.

Careers and Salary

It depends a lot on what interior designers do and where they find their first job. Starting salaries for interior design majors range between $22,000 and about $40,000.

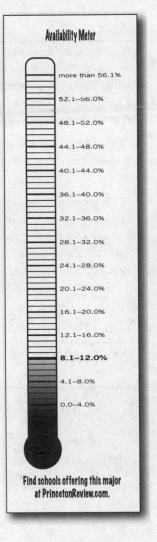

Availability Meter

more than 56.1%

52.1–56.0%

48.1–52.0%

44.1–48.0%

40.1–44.0%

36.1–40.0%

32.1–36.0%

28.1–32.0%

24.1–28.0%

20.1–24.0%

16.1–20.0%

12.1–16.0%

8.1–12.0%

4.1–8.0%

0.0–4.0%

Find schools offering this major
at PrincetonReview.com.

CAREER OPTIONS

Antiques Dealer	Art Dealer	Interior Designer
Archaeologist	Artist	Product Designer
Architect	Bar/Club Manager	Website Designer

INTERNATIONAL AGRICULTURE

Basics

Ever wonder why there are perpetual shortages of food in some parts of the world while tons upon tons of tasty, healthy chow goes to waste every day in the United States? Ever wonder what you could really do about it? One very constructive thing that you could do is major in international agriculture. If you do, you'll gain an understanding of the political, economic, social, and natural factors that interactively affect agricultural production and distribution everywhere on the planet.

A lot of the schools with international agriculture curricula offer only certificate programs, which are very similar to minors. In these programs, you usually concentrate on a specific country or region of the world.

With a degree or a certificate in international agriculture, you'll be prepared to help change the world, and as a bonus, you'll have experiences and knowledge that will make you an attractive employment candidate in the global job market. You can work for the United Nations, the U.S. State Department, multinational agricultural corporations, or the World Bank. You can also seek overseas employment with the Foreign Service, Peace Corps, charities and nonprofit assistance agencies, and a host of other international programs.

If You Like International Agriculture, You May Also Like . . .

Agricultural economics, agricultural and biological engineering, agricultural technology management, agriculture, animal science, atmospheric science, biochemistry, biology, botany and plant biology, cell biology, chemistry, ecology, economics, entomology, environmental science, forestry, genetics, geology, grain science, horticulture, microbiology, natural resources conservation, peace studies, plant pathology, public administration, soil science, sustainable resource management

---

SAMPLE COLLEGE CURRICULUM FOR INTERNATIONAL AGRICULTURE

Agriculture in Tropical Areas

Biology

Chemistry

Cultural Anthropology

Entomology

Foreign Language (several courses)

Forestry

Geography

Introduction to International Agriculture

Plant Pathology

Soil Science

Topics in International Agriculture

World Food Production and Distribution

Suggested High School Prep for International Agriculture

International agriculture is broad, and if you think you might want to make it your major, you should plan accordingly. You'll obviously need to take several years of a foreign language. In addition, take all the biology and chemistry courses that your high school offers. Everything that you can learn about climate, soil, water, and plants will be helpful. If your high school offers agriculture courses, you should take a few. Finally, you'll want to take social sciences courses (such as history and economics), too, because you will almost assuredly be required to take a few mid- to upper-level social science courses to complete a major in international agriculture.

Fun Facts

Study Abroad

Many schools with international agriculture programs offer—or, in some cases, require—study abroad opportunities that relate to agriculture. Texas A&M University, for example, offers a study abroad program in Vietnam that takes place between the fall and spring semesters. The University of Georgia offers a similar program in Guatemala. Students at Iowa State can learn about agriculture and work in the fields of Ghana, China, and Costa Rica, among other exotic places.

Did You Know?

As wealth increases in developing nations, more people eat meat (because they can). Consequently, more land is used to feed animals. In China, for example, the amount of grain used for animal feed in 1960 was less than 10 million tons. By about 1995, though, nearly 100 million tons of grain was used to feed animals per year.

Careers and Salary

Starting salaries for international agriculture majors vary fairly widely depending on what they choose to do. If they take a job for a huge agribusiness corporation, they are likely to start out somewhere between $30,000 and $40,000 annually. Peace Corps volunteers receive a stipend that covers basic necessities only (though they arguably feel better about themselves).

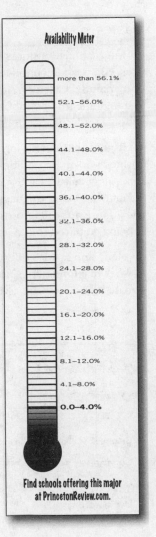

Availability Meter

more than 56.1%

52.1–56.0%

48.1–52.0%

44.1–48.0%

40.1–44.0%

36.1–40.0%

32.1–36.0%

28.1–32.0%

24.1–28.0%

20.1–24.0%

16.1–20.0%

12.1–16.0%

8.1–12.0%

4.1–8.0%

0.0–4.0%

Find schools offering this major at PrincetonReview.com.

CAREER OPTIONS

Biologist

Diplomat/Attaché/Foreign Service Officer

Ecologist

Environmentalist/ Environmental Scientist

Farmer

Foreign Exchange Trader

Park Ranger

INTERNATIONAL BUSINESS

Basics

International business is an extension of a business program. You'll learn about standard business practices, ethics, and economics, and you'll generally focus on a subset of the field such as accounting, finance, or marketing. A major in international business will lead you to use your business skills in a global context. You might learn about business transactions between and within countries, the laws and logistics of international trade, or investments made in foreign markets.

It goes without saying that knowledge of other cultures is crucial to being a successful international businessperson. In addition to your studies in business, finance, banking, and the like, you will also learn about new cultures and societies and strange laws and perspectives. You might be required to become proficient in a foreign language. Even if a language isn't required for your degree, however, it will certainly make you a more appealing prospective employee. If you're successful mastering all this, you've got a good shot at being admitted to the jetsetter crowd.

Many universities offer internships at overseas companies, so you'll be able to actually see what it's like to work in a foreign business environment. Keep in mind, too, that an appreciation for travel and a compassionate world view are assets in this field.

SAMPLE COLLEGE CURRICULUM FOR INTERNATIONAL BUSINESS

Business Skills and Environment

Comparative Economic Systems

Comparative Management

Decision Theory

Economic Development and Growth

International Accounting

International Business Finance

International Economics

International Policy

International Tourism

Law of International Trade

Multinational Corporate Management

Multinational Marketing

Organizational Behavior

Small Business Policy

Statistics

If You Like International Business, You May Also Like . . .

Accounting, advertising, business administration and management, business communications, entrepreneurship, finance, international relations, international studies, logistics management

Suggested High School Prep for International Business

To be a successful international business major, you should have excellent writing, reading, mathematics, and communication skills. You can develop all of these skills in high school courses such as English, history, political science, speech, and math. Also consider courses in foreign languages, any and all of them.

Fun Facts

The World Factbook

Find out all about international business and other affairs in *The World Factbook*, published by the CIA. The *Factbook* contains facts and figures for hundreds of countries; topics include geography, people, government, economy, transportation, military, and transnational issues. Perhaps of most interest to international business majors, the economy category includes information on household income, the inflation rate, labor force, currency, industries, budget, and much more.

Academy of International Business

The field of international business is growing at many colleges and universities, thanks in part to the Academy of International Business. Developed in 1981, the AIB strives to gather and spread knowledge about international business, and supports education and research in the field.

Careers and Salary

International business majors can expect a starting salary between $35,000 and $45,000. Salaries will depend greatly on location of employment, previous skills, and type of field in which they choose to work.

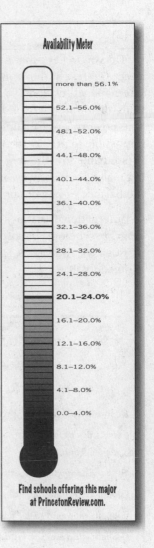

Availability Meter

more than 56.1%

52.1–56.0%

48.1–52.0%

44.1–48.0%

40.1–44.0%

36.1–40.0%

32.1–36.0%

28.1–32.0%

24.1–28.0%

20.1–24.0%

16.1–20.0%

12.1–16.0%

8.1–12.0%

4.1–8.0%

0.0–4.0%

Find schools offering this major
at PrincetonReview.com.

CAREER OPTIONS

Accountant/Auditor	Economist	Investment Banker
Bank Officer	Entrepreneur	Small Business Owner
Bookkeeper	Financial Analyst	Stockbroker
Buyer	Foreign Exchange Trader	Venture Capitalist/Investor

INTERNATIONAL RELATIONS

Basics

Do you believe that societies and cultures are linked in such a way that changes made in one society affect the rest of the world? If you do, international relations might be the major for you. With a major in international relations, you'll study the relationships among countries, governments, peoples, and organizations all around the world. You'll learn about global issues from a variety of perspectives—issues including war, poverty, disease, diplomacy, democracy, trade, economics, and globalization. Though it is, of course, impossible to predict the future, you'll be attempting to predict the consequences of international decisions by studying how the past has influenced the present. As an international relations major, you'll be integrating many points of view in an effort to work with others for a better world. Topics of study might include the balance of power, fair distribution of wealth, and the economic gap between rich and poor.

International relations is a multidisciplinary major that draws from politics, history, economics, law, sociology, psychology, philosophy, ethics, and geography. You'll be dealing with foreign cultures, languages, worldviews, and values. The study of foreign languages is a necessity, as is a sense of empathy, compassion, and good will.

SAMPLE COLLEGE CURRICULUM FOR INTERNATIONAL RELATIONS

Business Strategy

Economics of Regional Trade Agreements

Global Change and Security

Global Environmental Policy and Law

Globalization and Its Critics

Globalization and the Future of the Welfare State

International Norms

International Politics

Peace-Maintenance Operations

Political Philosophy

Politics of Race and Class

Preventing Ethnic Violence

Public International Law

Security in Post-Communist Regions

Technology in National Security

Understanding the Cold War

If You Like International Relations, You May Also Like . . .

African American studies, African studies, anthropology, Asian American studies, business administration and management, Chinese, East Asian studies, East European studies, economics, French, German, international agriculture, international business, international studies, Jewish studies, Latin American studies, Middle Eastern studies, peace studies, philosophy, political science, Portuguese, pre-law, public policy analysis, Russian, Slavic languages and literatures, South Asian studies, Southeast Asian studies, Spanish, teaching English as a second language

Suggested High School Prep for International Relations

Learning a foreign language or two is the best way to prepare for a major in international relations. Also important are courses in history, politics, philosophy, religion, and English—they'll expose you to ideas from around the world.

Fun Facts

Celebrate Peace

The International Day of Peace, so named by the United Nations General Assembly, is celebrated annually on the third Tuesday of September. The holiday began in 1981, and every year the General Assembly observes a minute of silence—a Moment of Peace—when they begin their convention.

Other peace days:

- A Day of Peace: May 10
- Peace Day: the third Sunday in May
- World Peace and Prayer Day: June 21
- World Peace Day: November 17

Notable Words

"Where, after all, do universal human rights begin? In small places, close to home . . . the world of the individual person . . . [and] unless these rights have meaning there, they have little meaning anywhere."

—Eleanor Roosevelt, in a 1958 address to the United Nations Commission on Human Rights

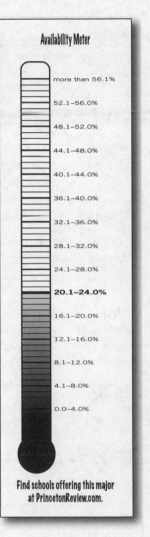

Availability Meter

more than 56.1%

52.1–56.0%

48.1–52.0%

44.1–48.0%

40.1–44.0%

36.1–40.0%

32.1–36.0%

28.1–32.0%

24.1–28.0%

20.1–24.0%

16.1–20.0%

12.1–16.0%

8.1–12.0%

4.1–8.0%

0.0–4.0%

Find schools offering this major
at PrincetonReview.com.

Careers and Salary

Starting salaries vary widely and range from $20,000 to about $35,000.

CAREER OPTIONS

Anthropologist

Bank Officer

CIA Agent

Diplomat/Attaché/Foreign Service Officer

Journalist

Public Relations Professional

INTERNATIONAL STUDIES

Basics

From knowing who the president of France is to understanding how the global economy really works, international studies majors are immersed in the politics, culture, and history of various parts of the world.

As an international studies major, your focus is more on depth than breadth, so while you'll gain a greater appreciation for the commerce of the world as a whole, you will probably concentrate on a specific region of the globe, studying in detail its unique history, economy, and political structure. Whether it's Africa, Asia, or Western or Eastern Europe, you will have the opportunity to focus on the region or countries that interest you most, learning their language and perhaps even spending a semester studying abroad. In addition to focusing on a specific region, international studies majors concentrate on some of the most pressing political and social issues of the contemporary world. For example, you might choose to focus on economic development issues around the globe or problems of diplomacy.

Drawing upon other fields of study such as economics, history, and political science, international studies will equip you with a greater understanding of how other cultures live and govern themselves.

If You Like International Studies, You May Also Like . . .

African studies, anthropology, archaeology, East Asian studies, East European studies, French, German, international agriculture, international business, international relations, Islamic studies, Italian, Japanese, Jewish studies, Latin American studies, South Asian studies, Southeast Asian studies, Spanish

SAMPLE COLLEGE CURRICULUM FOR INTERNATIONAL STUDIES

Area studies in your chosen region

Conceptual Approaches to International Studies

Econometrics

Economic Development

Introduction to Sociology

Macroeconomics

Political Analysis

Sociological Inquiry

Sociological Theory

Statistics

Don't forget that as an international studies major you will also need to be fluent in at least one foreign language.

Suggested High School Prep for International Studies

Foreign language: Find one that you love early and stick with it through high school. The higher levels of a language usually incorporate more study of the culture of the countries in which the language is spoken than lower-level classes do. World history and Western civilization classes lay the foundation of how the world has shaped up so far. If you have the means and can spend an extended period of time living in another country, immerse yourself in the culture. Believe us, you won't regret it.

Fun Facts

Did You Know?

According to the U.S. State Department, there are 191 independent countries in the world.

For More Information . . .

The U.S. State Department maintains a Digital Diplomacy website for students; the site can be found at www.State.gov/www/digital_diplomacy/index.html.

Careers and Salary

The starting salary for international studies majors ranges from $20,000 to $31,000, depending on the field they choose to enter.

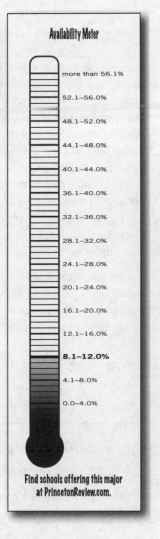

Availability Meter

more than 56.1%

52.1—56.0%

48.1—52.0%

44.1—48.0%

40.1—44.0%

36.1—40.0%

32.1—36.0%

28.1—32.0%

24.1—28.0%

20.1—24.0%

16.1—20.0%

12.1—16.0%

8.1—12.0%

4.1—8.0%

0.0—4.0%

Find schools offering this major at PrincetonReview.com.

CAREER OPTIONS

Anthropologist	Economist	Political Campaign Worker
Archaeologist	Foreign Exchange Trader	Political Scientist
Diplomat/Attaché/Foreign Service Officer	Lobbyist	Politician
	Paralegal	

IRANIAN/PERSIAN LANGUAGES, LITERATURES, AND LINGUISTICS

Basics

Have you ever heard of the extinct languages known as Parthian, Median, or Khwarezamian? How about the modern languages called Dari, Baluchi, or Ossetian? Each of these is a relative of Persian (or Farsi), the primary language spoken in Iran. As a major in Iranian/Persian languages, literatures, and linguistics, you'll study Persian and, if the urge strikes, you'll also have the chance to study any number of related languages, including those listed above. Your language studies will be the first of many doors that you'll open into this ancient and storied Middle Eastern culture. Through another door, you'll enter the world of Persian literature, which stretches back thousands of years and includes the likes of Ferdowski, Rumi, Omar Khayyam, Nuema Yooshij, and a strong collection of Iranian-born female poets that has emerged during the past half-century. Your examinations of the language and literature will lay the foundation for a wider consideration of the culture's fascinating and oftentimes turbulent past, as well as its complex role on the contemporary Middle Eastern and global stages. You'll look at social practices and norms, art and film, science and technology, government and religion—all forces that shape and interpret modern Iran.

Ultimately, the Iranian/Persian languages, literatures, and linguistics major will give you a solid linguistic, literary, and cultural background in all things Iranian. This background will prepare you to continue in academics or to fill any number of the increasing positions in private or governmental agencies that are looking for expertise in Middle Eastern cultures.

If You Like Iranian/Persian Languages, Literatures, and Linguistics, You May Also Like...

African languages, literatures, and linguistics, African studies, ancient studies, Arabic, comparative literature, Egyptology, Hebrew, international relations, international studies, Islamic studies, Jewish studies, Middle Eastern studies, peace studies

Suggested High School Prep for Iranian/Persian Languages, Literatures, and Linguistics

Studying one language makes it easier to study another language, because regardless of the language you pick, the process is the same—memorizing new words, producing unfamiliar sounds, relying on a foreign system of grammar. Since your high school probably doesn't offer training in Farsi, sign up for Spanish, German, French, whatever you can. The experience will pay off. Enroll in humanities courses too. Literature, history, and government courses will help you hone those all-important reading and writing skills that will be crucial during your college years.

SAMPLE COLLEGE CURRICULUM FOR IRANIAN/PERSIAN LANGUAGES, LITERATURES, AND LINGUISTICS

Advanced Farsi

Ancient Persia

Elementary Farsi

History of the Middle East

Intermediate Farsi

Iranian Film

Literature of Persia/Iran

Lyrical Poetry of Persia

Middle Eastern Politics

Modern Islam

Persian Linguistics

Fun Facts

In This Year...

1750 B.C./B.C.E.–550 B.C./B.C.E.: The Persian Empire begins.

331 B.C./B.C.E.–330 B.C./B.C.E.: Persia is conquered by Alexander.

572: Persia overtakes Arabia, which it controls for the next sixty years.

1048: Omar Khayyam, author of the Rubaiyat, is born.

1907: A new constitution curbs the royal absolutism that had existed in Persia for hundreds of years.

1935: Persia decides to change its name to Iran.

1951: The oil industry is nationalized by the Iranian congress.

1979: Ayatollah Khomeini comes to power. This is also the year that 52 American hostages are taken at the U.S. Embassy in Tehran. Khomeini stays in power until his death in 1989.

1980: Iraq invades Iran, which marks the beginning of the Iran-Iraq War.

1988: The Iran-Iraq War concludes with a ceasefire.

1990: Film director Abbas Kiarostami releases *Close-Up*, which quickly becomes a classic of Iranian cinema.

1999: Student-led protests in support of democracy lead to scores of arrests and days of rioting.

2003: An earthquake in southeast Iran causes nearly 40,000 deaths.

2006: Iran's announcement that it has successfully enriched uranium generates interest and concern worldwide.

Did You Know?

The modern-day Persian language actually comes in three varieties:

1) Farsi, which you'll find in Iran.
2) Dari, which you'll find in Afghanistan.
3) Tajiki, which you'll find in Tajikistan and Uzbekistan, among other Central Asian nations.

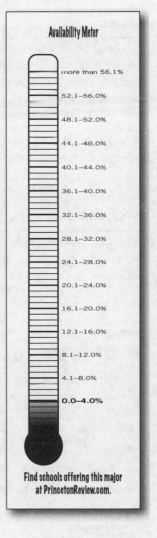

Availability Meter

more than 56.1%

52.1–56.0%

48.1–52.0%

44.1–48.0%

40.1–44.0%

36.1–40.0%

32.1–36.0%

28.1–32.0%

24.1–28.0%

20.1–24.0%

16.1–20.0%

12.1–16.0%

8.1–12.0%

4.1–8.0%

0.0–4.0%

Find schools offering this major at PrincetonReview.com.

Careers and Salaries

The job you choose can cause variation, but generally an Iranian/Persian languages, literatures, and linguistics can expect a starting salary about $25,000 a year.

CAREER OPTIONS

Consultant	Historian	Teacher
Diplomat/Attaché/Foreign Service Officer	Journalist	Translator
	Lobbyist	Writer
Editor	Politician	

ISLAMIC STUDIES

Basics

Islamic studies is a multidisciplinary major incorporating the fields of art, politics, religion, history, philosophy, literature, international studies, and others. As an Islamic studies major, you'll be gaining a solid humanities-based education with an emphasis on Islamic languages such as Arabic, Persian, and Turkish. You'll study Islamic literature both in its original languages and in translation, and like most majors in the liberal arts, your studies will touch upon what it means to be human and how we define our world.

Almost a billion people worldwide are of the Islamic faith, and through Islamic studies you'll gain an understanding of this religious culture that has influenced so much of modern society.

If You Like Islamic Studies, You May Also Like . . .

African studies, ancient studies, Arabic, biblical studies, East European studies, international business, international relations, international studies, Jewish studies, Middle Eastern studies, peace studies, religious studies, theology

Suggested High School Prep for Islamic Studies

You'll benefit from history and political science courses, of course, and language work will prepare for learning more difficult Middle Eastern languages such as Arabic. Since Islamic studies is based so firmly in a liberal arts education, any courses you can take in literature, art, religion, and other humanities will be worthwhile as well.

SAMPLE COLLEGE CURRICULUM FOR ISLAMIC STUDIES

Arabic Fiction

Canon and Communities in the Near East

Contemporary Arab Culture

Humanities courses such as philosophy,

international studies, art history

Islamic Architecture and Heritage

Islamic History

Islamic Law

Language courses in Persian or Turkish

Literary Arabic Reading

Middle East in the Modern Era

Modern Standard Arabic

Near Eastern Literature

Religion and Politics in the Islamic World

Fun Facts

Prayer for Guidance

Confused about what major to choose in college? Unsure about what career you might want to pursue? Undecided about what city to move to? When Muslims need guidance for making important decisions, they turn to Allah, whom they believe knows what is best. Here is the Salat I-Istikhara, or "prayer for guidance," that they recite in times of indecision:

Oh Allah! I seek Your guidance by virtue of Your knowledge, and I seek ability by virtue of Your power, and I ask You of Your great bounty. You have power; I have none. And You know; I know not. You are the Knower of hidden things. Oh Allah! If in Your knowledge, (this matter) is good for my religion, my livelihood and my affairs, immediate and in the future, then ordain it for me, make it easy for me, and bless it for me. And if in Your knowledge, (this matter) is bad for my religion, my livelihood and my affairs, immediate and in the future, then turn it away from me, and turn me away from it. And ordain for me the good wherever it may be, and make me content with it.

A Smidgen of Islamic Doctrine

Islam is a religion of many customs and traditions. Here are a few facts about Islam.

- The Arabic roots of the word Islam mean peace and submission.
- A believer and follower of the Islam faith is called a Muslim.
- The traditional Muslim greeting is "Salaam alaykum," which means "Peace be with you."
- The God of the Islamic faith is Allah, and Muslims devote their lives to obeying and serving him.
- The Islamic holy book is the Qur'an (Koran).
- There are five important tenets that Muslims follow to strengthen their faith. They're called the Five Pillars of Islam. They are: Testimony of Faith, Prayer, Fasting, Almsgiving, and Pilgrimage (to Mecca, Saudi Arabia).

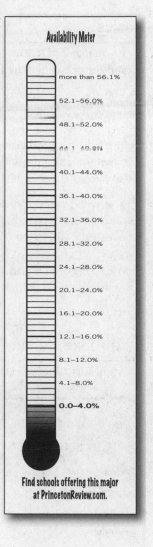

Availability Meter

more than 56.1%

52.1–56.0%

48.1–52.0%

44.1–48.0%

40.1–44.0%

36.1–40.0%

32.1–36.0%

28.1–32.0%

24.1–28.0%

20.1–24.0%

16.1–20.0%

12.1–16.0%

8.1–12.0%

4.1–8.0%

0.0–4.0%

Find schools offering this major at PrincetonReview.com.

Careers and Salary

The starting salary for Islamic studies majors will depend mostly on where they choose to live and how they use their degree, but expect somewhere between $24,000 and $30,000.

CAREER OPTIONS

Anthropologist	Clergy—Priest, Rabbi, Minister	Philosopher
Antiques Dealer	Consultant	Theologian
Archaeologist	Diplomat/Attaché/Foreign Service Officer	

ITALIAN

Basics

If you major in Italian, you will, of course, become fluent in speaking the language. You'll probably spend a semester or two in Italy, too. Or at least, you should. But all that is just the tip of the iceberg.

The study of a language at the college level is not limited to the memorization of words and verb conjugations. If you major in Italian (or any other language) in college, you'll study history, art, politics, and everything else that characterizes the culture of the places where it's spoken. After completing several required courses in Italian grammar, composition, and conversation, you'll choose from a variety of classes in Italian literature, advanced translation, and civilization. In a nutshell, your courses will cover everything Italian—from Dante to Fellini, from Spartacus to Mussolini.

You won't run out of topics. The people and culture of Italy have contributed a great deal to the arts, political theory, literature, and religion of the world. There's Michelangelo (who painted the Sistine Chapel), Leonardo da Vinci (who painted the Mona Lisa), Galileo (one of the most important scientists ever), Machiavelli (who wrote *The Prince*), and Dante (who wrote *The Divine Comedy*), just to name a few. If you choose to major in Italian, you will spend four years studying the great works of Italian culture—in the original Italian no less—which have greatly influenced the history and culture of the world.

If You Like Italian, You May Also Like . . .

Art history, Chinese, classics, English, French, German, great books, Hebrew, history, Japanese, Latin American studies, library science, Medieval and Renaissance studies, Modern Greek, philosophy, Portuguese, Russian, Slavic languages and literatures, Spanish, theology

SAMPLE COLLEGE CURRICULUM FOR ITALIAN

Advanced Italian Conversation and
  Composition

Dante

Petrarch

History of Catholicism

Italian Cinema

Italian I–IV

Italian Syntax

Italian Translating

Medieval and Renaissance Italian
  Literature

Modern Italian Culture

Modern Italian Literature

Modern Italian Poetry

Renaissance Art

Suggested High School Prep for Italian

This is obvious, but if your high school offers Italian as a subject, you should take as many courses as you can. Most high schools don't offer Italian though, so don't be surprised if yours doesn't. If you can't take Italian, take Latin, or if you prefer, Spanish, which is the next best thing because the languages are very similar. You should also take English composition and literature courses and European history courses. Also, remember that as a liberal arts major in college, you'll almost certainly be required to take a few courses in math and science, so don't ignore those topics.

Fun Facts

Did You Know?

Rome is located almost along 42 degrees north latitude. That's just about exactly due east of Chicago.

Did You Know?

Italy boasts the fifth largest economy on the planet.

Sorry, I Don't Speak Italian Well.

Mi dispiace, ma non parlo l'Italiano molto bene.

Would you like to dance with me?

Vuoi ballare con me?

My hotel room is on fire.

La mia stanza dell'hotel é su fuoco.

Which restaurant has the best ravioli in this city?

Quale ristorante ha i ravioli migliori in questa citta?

I am shocked! The Sistine Chapel is really small. It seems larger in photographs.

Ho una scossa! La Capella di Sistine é realmente piccola. Sembra piú grande in fotografie.

Careers and Salary

Starting salary for foreign language majors averages between $25,000 and $33,000 per year.

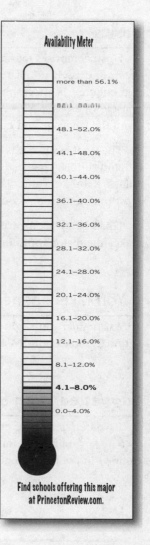

Availability Meter

more than 56.1%

52.1–56.0%

48.1–52.0%

44.1–48.0%

40.1–44.0%

36.1–40.0%

32.1–36.0%

28.1–32.0%

24.1–28.0%

20.1–24.0%

16.1–20.0%

12.1–16.0%

8.1–12.0%

4.1–8.0%

0.0–4.0%

Find schools offering this major at PrincetonReview.com.

CAREER OPTIONS

Curator	Editor	Sociologist
Diplomat/Attaché/Foreign Service Officer	Film Director	Teacher
	Professor	Translator

JAPANESE

Basics

Japan comprises four main islands and about 1,000 small islands. These slivers and dots of land are among the most densely populated in the world, and the amount of activity on them—in business, engineering, and pop culture—is astonishing. Japanese products, design, thought, and film play a major role in the American consciousness and marketplace. Japanese majors have the opportunity to bridge East and West, to understand the language and culture of this remarkable country.

The Japanese major is a challenging course of study. Japanese majors go through intensive classes in written and spoken Japanese, as well as additional work in Japanese culture and history. Classes in Buddhism, Shinto, Kabuki theater, Japanese film, and Noh drama might be offered as part of the overall curriculum. Most programs also recommend or require students to study abroad in Japan.

Japanese speakers are in demand in business, technology, and law. Japan's rich cultural heritage also makes the major appealing to those who are interested in visual and performing arts.

If You Like Japanese, You May Also Like . . .

Asian American studies, Chinese, East Asian studies, international business, international relations, international studies, South Asian studies, Southeast Asian studies

Suggested High School Prep for Japanese

If you are fortunate enough to go to a school that offers Japanese as a language, obviously you should take it. Any training in foreign languages will help you become accustomed to college-level language study. Courses in political science and Asian history will also get you ahead of the game.

SAMPLE COLLEGE
CURRICULUM FOR JAPANESE

Classical Japanese I–II

History of Buddhism

Japanese History

Japanese I–IV

Japanese Linguistics

Japanese Literature I–II

Noh Theater

Technical Japanese

Fun Facts

More Than the ABCs

There are three alphabets in Japanese: kanji, hiragana, and katakana. Each has a different use. A fourth system, romaji, can be used by foreigners who have no knowledge of Japanese writing systems.

You Can't Live in the Future

Japanese verbs have only two tenses, present and past.

Careers and Salary

The starting salary for a Japanese major fresh out of college is usually between $25,000 to $30,000.

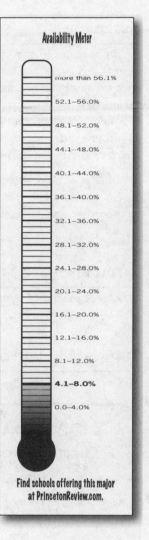

Availability Meter

more than 56.1%

52.1–56.0%

48.1–52.0%

44.1–48.0%

40.1–44.0%

36.1–40.0%

32.1–36.0%

28.1–32.0%

24.1–28.0%

20.1–24.0%

16.1–20.0%

12.1–16.0%

8.1–12.0%

4.1–8.0%

0.0–4.0%

Find schools offering this major at PrincetonReview.com.

CAREER OPTIONS

Consultant

Diplomat/Attaché/Foreign Service Officer

Foreign Exchange Trader

Teacher

Translator

JAZZ STUDIES

Basics

If you major in jazz studies, you'll study in depth the history and literature of the unique American art form that is jazz. You'll learn about contemporary trends in jazz and the storied history of jazz and its influence on American culture. More importantly, you'll learn how to really play jazz—in a professional kind of a way. You'll become a master of improvisation and reading on sight, of arrangement and composition, and of jazz theory. You'll get four years of music lessons from people who have dedicated their very lives to the study of jazz. Over the course of your jazz studies major, you'll learn all about melodies and rhythms, harmony and scales, transcription of jazz chords, and arranging and improvisation.

Outside of class, you can participate in an incredible wealth of opportunities to perform in jazz combos, ensembles, and big bands. It is in these extracurricular programs that you'll be able to hone and polish your own creative and professional style.

If You Like Jazz Studies, You May Also Like . . .

American studies, dance, film, music, music therapy, piano, voice

Suggested High School Prep for Jazz Studies

Get in your high school jazz band and become an expert on a particular instrument. If you want to major in jazz studies, your overriding goal needs to be developing the performance skills necessary for a successful audition (in person or via a recording) with your future college instructors. You'll also need recommendations from instructors, so make nice with those people. Piano lessons are a good thing, too, if you can get them, as is knowledge of basic music theory. In addition, you should complete a solid college preparatory curriculum. They aren't going to let you into college based on your saxophone-playing skills alone.

> ### SAMPLE COLLEGE CURRICULUM FOR JAZZ STUDIES
>
> Advanced Music Theory
>
> Applied Music
>
> Aural Training
>
> Basic Music Theory
>
> Conducting
>
> Instrument Lessons
>
> Jazz Composition
>
> Jazz Improvisation
>
> Jazz Theory and History
>
> Large Ensembles
>
> Music History
>
> Piano
>
> Small Ensembles

Fun Facts

Like Jazz?

Check out the Ford Detroit International Jazz Festival, home to hundreds of musicians and free performances on several stages during Labor Day weekend. It's the largest free music event in the United States

Ten Essential Jazz Albums

From one test-prep company's point of view.

- John Coltrane. *A Love Supreme* (1965)
- Miles Davis. *Birth of the Cool* (1956)
- Miles Davis. *Kind of Blue* (1959)
- Eric Dolphy. *At The Five Spot*, Volume 1 (1961)
- Dizzy Gillespie and Friends. *Sonny Side Up* (1958)
- Billie Holiday. *Lady in Satin* (1958)
- Charles Mingus. *The Black Saint & The Sinner Lady* (1963)
- Thelonious Monk. *Brilliant Corners* (1956)
- Oliver Nelson. *Blues and the Abstract Truth* (1961)
- Sonny Rollins. *Saxophone Colossus* (1956)

Careers and Salary

Starting salaries for musicians vary considerably, particularly for professional musicians. We can tell you that assistant professors in jazz studies start out between $45,000 to $50,000.

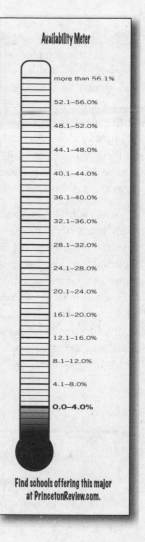

Availability Meter

more than 56.1%

52.1–56.0%

48.1–52.0%

44.1–48.0%

40.1–44.0%

36.1–40.0%

32.1–36.0%

28.1–32.0%

24.1–28.0%

20.1–24.0%

16.1–20.0%

12.1–16.0%

8.1–12.0%

4.1–8.0%

0.0–4.0%

Find schools offering this major
at PrincetonReview.com.

CAREER OPTIONS		
Journalist	Musician	Professor
Music Executive	Performing Arts Administrator	Teacher

JEWELRY AND METALSMITHING

Basics

A major in jewelry and metalsmithing means more than designing fabulous pieces with which to adorn yourself or the object of your every desire. But that would be a nice perk! As a jewelry and metalsmithing major, you'll gain all the skills you need to design jewelry and create other works of art from metals. You'll learn a wide range of techniques, including casting, forging, and raising, plus how to enamel and how to set stones. You'll learn the art of fabrication and master the use of jewelry and metalsmithing equipment such as ultrasonic cleaners, buffing machines, ring sizers, sandblasters, enameling kilns, and rolling mills. And as with any art major, you'll study the forms jewelry and metalsmithing have taken in the past in order to gain perspective on their current state and to get an idea of where your own art might fit in—even how it might push the field in brand-new directions.

Your major in jewelry and metalsmithing can lead you down any number of paths, and you'll acquire the skills you'll need to pursue a career in retail, design, and many other fields. Bonus skills include those required for jewelry repair and restoration, the ability to create work for retail or exhibition, and the fundamentals of setting up your own studio or shop. Most important, this major will give you the opportunity to focus on your own creative vision. You'll be able to experiment with forms and techniques you may not have even known about while being surrounded by faculty and students who can critique your work and offer advice and inspiration. Your imagination will be limited only by the materials you can afford to work with. That is, most freshmen aren't making eighteen-karat solitaire bands—but there's nothing wrong with sketching designs of them for later.

If You Like Jewelry and Metalsmithing, You May Also Like . . .

Art, art education, art history, fashion design, floriculture, graphic design, interior design, photography, visual communication

Suggested High School Prep for Jewelry and Metalsmithing

To prepare for a major in jewelry and metalsmithing, you should take a well-rounded selection of courses including math, science, English, history, and languages. Because much of this major requires you to produce your own works of art, art classes will get you thinking creatively. Computer proficiency is a must for any major, so if your skills are weak, take a computer class or two. You can do some of the best preparation on your own: drawing, thinking, and even making mock-up samples of the kinds of art you might like to make someday.

SAMPLE COLLEGE CURRICULUM FOR JEWELRY AND METALSMITHING

Art History

Critical Issues in Contemporary Art

Enameling

Forging and Forming

History of Adornment

Hollowware Techniques

Jewelry Making

Jewelry Sales and Marketing

Metal Fabrication

Mold Making

Three-Dimensional Rendering

Wax Carving and Casting

Fun Facts

Breakfast at . . .

The robin's-egg blue of Tiffany & Co. boxes have been the stuff many dreams were made of. Here are a few facts on that famous store.

- Charles Lewis Tiffany and John B. Young established Tiffany & Young at 259 Broadway in September 1837. The total sales for the day: $4.98.
- That famous blue was chosen to represent "quality and craftsmanship."
- Charles Tiffany renamed the store "Tiffany & Co." in 1853.
- Tiffany & Co. moved to their current location on Fifth Avenue in 1940.
- In 1950, *Breakfast at Tiffany's* by Truman Capote was published.

(Source: www.tiffany.com)

The Hope Diamond

The Hope Diamond is believed to have been found in a mine in Golconda, India. Originally, it was 112 3/16 carats. It was sold to King Louis XIV in 1668, and in 1673 it was recut and became 67 1/8 carats. After passing through many hands over many years, the diamond was donated to the Smithsonian Institution in 1958. The stone is now 45.52 carats.

(Source: www.si.edu)

Careers and Salary

The starting salary for jewelry and metalsmithing majors varies widely because students choose to use their skills in all sorts of ways. The life and finances of an artist are unpredictable, and students find many unique ways to make a living while they work to establish themselves.

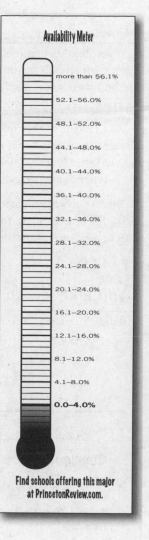

Availability Meter

more than 56.1%

52.1–56.0%

48.1–52.0%

44.1–48.0%

40.1–44.0%

36.1–40.0%

32.1–36.0%

28.1–32.0%

24.1–28.0%

20.1–24.0%

16.1–20.0%

12.1–16.0%

8.1–12.0%

4.1–8.0%

0.0–4.0%

Find schools offering this major at PrincetonReview.com.

CAREER OPTIONS

Fashion Consultant	Metalsmith	Retail Manager
Fashion Designer	Professor	Teacher
Jewelry Designer		

JEWISH STUDIES

Basics

If you think a lifetime of eating matzo balls and going to synagogue means you know it all, think again. The Jewish studies major is everything you wanted to know about Jewish culture, history, language, literature, and then some. It's thousands of years of history, religion, and language (maybe now you can figure out the etymology of "schmuck") all rolled into one intensive major.

As a Jewish studies major, you'll make use of all of the traditional methods of study that accompany the humanities. In short, that means you're going to be reading and writing a lot. You'll take classes in Hebrew and Yiddish, *The Bible*, history, and if you're lucky and creative enough, you'll have the chance for some serious independent research that expands our knowledge and understanding of Jewish history and culture.

When you've graduated, you'll have all the makings of a serious scholar (or at least a serious young scholar with a lot of potential). You'll have the benefits of a strong liberal arts background, which means that your skills at writing, researching, and communicating effectively can be applied to dozens of fields.

If You Like Jewish Studies, You May Also Like . . .

Biblical studies, classics, East European studies, Hebrew, history, Islamic studies, philosophy, religious studies, theology

Suggested High School Prep for Jewish Studies

The best high school preparation for a major in Jewish studies is a strong background in Jewish culture and history and experience with the Hebrew language. In the event that you can't take any of these at your school, though, a strong background in the humanities (especially English, history, and philosophy and/or theology) will help prepare you for the major as well.

SAMPLE COLLEGE CURRICULUM FOR JEWISH STUDIES

Ancient and Medieval Jewish Civilization

Introductory and Intermediate Hebrew I–II

Introduction to Jewish Philosophy

Introduction to Jewish Studies

Jewish Mysticism

Jewish Settlement in Palestine

Modern Hebrew Grammar, Composition, and Conversation

Modern Hebrew Short Story

Modern Jewish Civilization

Yiddish Literature in Translation

Fun Facts

Some Important Dates and Biblical Events

1900 B.C./B.C.E.—Abraham of Ur turned away from the gods of his family and began to worship one God. "I will make of you a great nation," promised God. He led Abraham and his family to the Land of Israel and told him, "Unto your seed have I given this land."

1750 B.C./B.C.E.—In a time of famine Abraham's great-grandchildren left Israel and went south to live in Egypt. Many years later the pharaoh of Egypt enslaved them.

1450 B.C./B.C.E.—God forced the pharaoh to free Abraham's descendants, the Jews. Moses led them into the desert, where they received the Torah. After years of wandering they reached the Land of Israel.

1410–1050 B.C./B.C.E.—The Jews conquered the land and settled down in separate tribes led by judges.

1050–933 B.C./B.C.E.—Saul unified all the tribes and became the first king of Israel. David, the next king, made the kingdom larger and stronger. David's son Solomon built the Holy Temple in Jerusalem.

Did You Know?

The word Jew originates from the name of one of Jacob's twelve sons, Judah.

Careers and Salary

The starting salary for Jewish studies majors is $20,000 to $30,000, depending of course on the field they choose to enter.

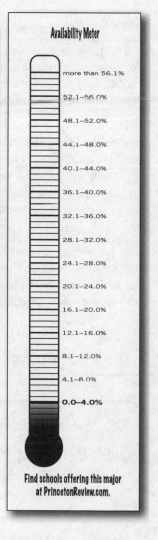

Availability Meter

more than 56.1%

52.1–56.0%

48.1–52.0%

44.1–48.0%

40.1–44.0%

36.1–40.0%

32.1–36.0%

28.1–32.0%

24.1–28.0%

20.1–24.0%

16.1–20.0%

12.1–16.0%

8.1–12.0%

4.1–8.0%

0.0–4.0%

Find schools offering this major at PrincetonReview.com.

CAREER OPTIONS

Anthropologist

Archaeologist

Clergy—Priest, Rabbi, Minister

Diplomat/Attaché/Foreign Service Officer

Professor

Theologian

Translator

JOURNALISM

Basics

Journalism is a hands-on, professionally oriented major that involves gathering, interpreting, distilling, and reporting information to audiences through a variety of media. Journalism majors learn about every conceivable kind of journalism (including magazine, newspaper, online journalism, photojournalism, broadcast journalism, and public relations).

That's not all, though. In addition to specialized training in writing, editing, and reporting, journalism requires a working knowledge of history, culture, and current events. You'll more than likely be required to take a broad range of courses that runs the gamut from statistics to the hard sciences to economics to history. There will also be a lot of lofty talk about professional ethics and civic responsibility as well—and you can bet you'll be tested on it. To top it all off, you'll probably work on the university newspaper or radio station, or perhaps complete an internship with a magazine or a mass media conglomerate.

We know it goes without saying but you'll also have to write an awful lot of articles if you decide to make journalism your major. This is true even if you ultimately want to work in radio or television. If you don't enjoy writing, you probably won't like journalism very much. Finally, take note: At universities with elite journalism programs, time-consuming weed-out courses abound, and you must be formally accepted into the journalism program, which can be ridiculously difficult and competitive.

If You Like Journalism, You May Also Like . . .

American studies, communication disorders, counseling, English, film, history, mass communication, psychology, radio and television, speech pathology, technical writing, visual communication

SAMPLE COLLEGE CURRICULUM FOR JOURNALISM

Broadcast Journalism

Communications Law and Ethics

Editing

Editorial Writing and Methods

Feature Writing

History of American Journalism

Investigative Reporting

Legislative Politics

Media Production

Photojournalism

Public Policy Issues

Radio and Television Reporting

Reporting and News Writing

Statistics

Suggested High School Prep for Journalism

Obviously, any experience you can get with your high school newspaper or television or radio station will be helpful. You might take several English courses and join the yearbook staff so as to further polish your writing skills. Beyond that, try to develop a solid understanding of current events. Believe it or not, many journalism programs require you to take a course in statistics and several foreign language classes. So in addition to writing courses, take mathematics and a foreign language all four years.

Fun Facts

Journalistic Integrity

Herewith, a few of the hilarious headlines from *The Onion*, journalism parody at its finest.

- Clinton Deploys Vowels to Bosnia
- Nine Drawn and Quartered at Out-of-Hand Renaissance Fair
- IOC Clears Pros to Wrestle in Summer Olympics
- U.S. Population at 13,462: 'We Don't Think Everybody Sent In Their Census Forms,' Say Officials

The Ten Most Widely Read Newspapers in the United States

- *Wall Street Journal*
- *USA Today*
- *New York Times*
- *Los Angeles Times*
- *Washington Post*
- *New York Daily News*
- *Chicago Tribune*
- *New York Newsday*
- *Houston Chronicle*
- *San Francisco Chronicle Examiner*

Famous People Who Majored in Journalism

Dennis Miller (acerbic comedian, Point Park College), Connie Chung (television journalist, University of Maryland)

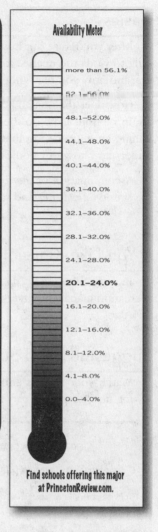

Availability Meter

more than 56.1%

52.1–56.0%

48.1–52.0%

44.1–48.0%

40.1–44.0%

36.1–40.0%

32.1–36.0%

28.1–32.0%

24.1–28.0%

20.1–24.0%

16.1–20.0%

12.1–16.0%

8.1–12.0%

4.1–8.0%

0.0–4.0%

Find schools offering this major at PrincetonReview.com.

Careers and Salary

It can be tough going early. The average starting salary for a newly minted journalism major with a bachelor's degree is about $21,000 per year. Graduates who take jobs with weekly newspapers and in radio and television can earn significantly less, particularly in nonurban locations. Of course, once they make it to the top, they can expect something of a raise. A premiere news anchor for a huge television network, for instance, can expect to make a cool $6 million per year.

CAREER OPTIONS

Advertising Executive	Lobbyist	Sports Announcer
Court Reporter	Media Specialist	Teacher
Disc Jockey	Photographer	Television Producer
Editor	Political Campaign Worker	Television Reporter
Graphic Designer	Public Relations Professional	Website Designer
Journalist	Publicist	Writer

KINESIOLOGY

Basics

After you figure out how to say this major, you'll probably want to know what it is, so you'll go off running towards the nearest kinesiology department, where, in turn, you will be asked how you ran, why you ran, and how you felt while running. This will constitute your introduction to kinesiology.

How does the human body move, and why does it move the way it does? What happens when our bodies are in motion? How do they respond to exercise? And how can we use it to help heal ourselves after sustaining an injury? Kinesiology answers, or tries to answer, these questions in an attempt to help us better understand how our bodies function.

A combination of physiology and health science, the kinesiology major will help prepare you to make the world a healthier and safer place.

If You Like Kinesiology, You May Also Like . . .

Biology, chiropractic, dance, dietetics, nutrition, occupational therapy, physical education, physical therapy, recreation management, rehabilitation services, sport and leisure studies

Suggested High School Prep for Kinesiology

Watch your friends and family in motion, take detailed notes, and then tell them what they're doing wrong and how they can improve their health and life. Also stay up on those math and science classes because you will definitely need a strong background in them, particularly algebra, biology, and chemistry.

SAMPLE COLLEGE CURRICULUM FOR KINESIOLOGY

Activity courses in aquatics, dance, technique, sports, and outdoor activities

Adapted Physical Activity

Biomechanics

Cellular and Biochemical Effects of Exercise

Exercise Physiology

Human Physiology Lab

Introduction to Kinesiology

Mechanics of Human Locomotion

Motor Learning

Science of Nutrition

Statistics and Evaluation

Fun Facts

Want to Visit the Largest Forum for Kinesiology in the World?

Then go to the Web page of the University of Illinois at Urbana-Champaign's kinesiology department (www.als.uiuc.edu) to stay connected to the world of kinesiology.

He Had a Good Heart, He Did

Kinesiology was introduced by an American chiropractor, Dr. George Goodheart, in 1964.

Careers and Salary

The average starting salary for a freshly minted kinesiology major is between $30,000 to $35,000.

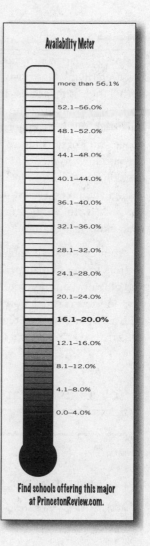

Availability Meter

more than 56.1%

52.1–56.0%

48.1–52.0%

44.1–48.0%

40.1–44.0%

36.1–40.0%

32.1–36.0%

28.1–32.0%

24.1–28.0%

20.1–24.0%

16.1–20.0%

12.1–16.0%

8.1–12.0%

4.1–8.0%

0.0–4.0%

Find schools offering this major at PrincetonReview.com.

CAREER OPTIONS

Athlete	Nutritionist	Personal Trainer
Coach	Occupational Therapist	Physical Therapist

KOREAN

Basics

In 1945, Japan surrendered to the Allies and withdrew from the Korean Peninsula. The Korean Peninsula has then divided into two zones, South Korea and North Korea. Your Korean major, of course, will focus on both—their similarities, their differences, their troubled relationship, and their individual plights and progress. It's an area the world is constantly watching, and you'll delve into its turbulent history and its uncertain future. A major in Korean will give you a wide spectrum of knowledge about both Korean language and Korean culture. The language will serve as your main focus, and you'll learn the grammar, the syntax, and how to read and write characters in modern written Korean. Through consistent reading, listening, speaking, and writing in Korean, you'll soon reach an impressive degree of proficiency. Becoming fluent in a language takes a great deal of work, but after four years of study, students in most programs are able to converse with a high level of success. Many colleges use multimedia centers so that students can work on their skills using computer programs and audiovisual aids.

Your courses will include Korean politics, society, economics, culture, and government. You'll learn what matters to the Korean people—plus those people in the related island groups and borderlands—personally and globally. Your newfound abilities to speak and write in Korean will open you up to appreciate and interpret in their context Korean texts, films, art, and music. You'll truly gain a perspective on what it means to be Korean and how Koreans see the world. Whether it's international business, foreign relations, news journalism, or teaching abroad, a major in Korean offers plenty of new opportunities.

If You Like Korean, You May Also Like . . .

SAMPLE COLLEGE CURRICULUM FOR KOREAN

Advanced Modern Korean

Cultural History of Korea

Korean American Literature

Korean Cinema

Korean Confucian Texts

Korean Conversation

Korean Folklore

Korean language courses

Korean Literature

Performance Traditions

Reading Korean Texts

Structure of Korean

Traditional Korean Thought

African American studies, African studies, anthropology, Asian American studies, business administration and management, Chinese, East Asian studies, East European studies, economics, French, German, international business, international relations, international studies, Latin American studies, Middle Eastern studies, peace studies, philosophy, political science, portuguese, pre-law, Russian, Slavic languages and literature, South Asian studies, Southeast Asian studies, Spanish, teaching English as a second language

Suggested High School Prep for Korean

The best preparation you can have for a major in Korean is the experience of learning another foreign language, even if it's not Korean. Courses in English, history, and other humanities will strengthen your reading and writing skills and will be of great value. A strong foundation in math and science courses will give you a solid background with which to enter any liberal arts program.

Fun Facts

Where Is Korea?

The Korean Peninsula is in the northeastern part of Asia; China and Russia share its border to the north. The East Sea is to the east of the Korean Peninsula. The Peninsula is 1,100 kilometers long, but Korea also includes about 3,000 islands.

The Korean Meal

A Korean meal consists of not only the main course but also many side dishes, rice, and soup. One of the most prevalent side dishes is kimchi, which is a fermented vegetable. Usually cabbage kimchi is served, but there can also be kimchi with radishes, green onions, cucumbers, and other vegetables. It's spicy hot and sometimes more of an acquired taste for those not used to it.

Rice is also an important dish; Koreans started growing rice around 1500 B.C./B.C.E.

(Source: www.korea.net)

Careers and Salary

Starting salaries for Korean majors vary widely and depend on where and how you apply your skills. A salary in the $20,000 to $30,000 range is a reasonable estimate. Pursuing further education is a good way to raise your salary.

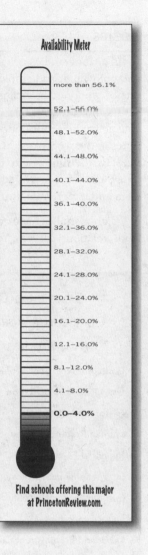

Availability Meter

more than 56.1%

52.1–56.0%

48.1–52.0%

44.1–48.0%

40.1–44.0%

36.1–40.0%

32.1–36.0%

28.1–32.0%

24.1–28.0%

20.1–24.0%

16.1–20.0%

12.1–16.0%

8.1–12.0%

4.1–8.0%

0.0–4.0%

Find schools offering this major at PrincetonReview.com.

CAREER OPTIONS

Corporate Executive	Immigration Administrator	Professor
Economist	Journalist	Social Worker
Embassy Official	Lawyer	Teacher
FBI Agent	Librarian	Translator
Foreign Diplomat	Politician	Writer
Foreign Exchange Trader		

LABOR STUDIES

Basics

In a labor studies program, you will not only study such large-scale fields as the job market, the economy, unemployment, and employer-employee relations; but you will also track the day-to-day experiences and interests of working Americans. Since people in many types of occupations—from police officers and nurses to actors and teachers—are in labor unions, the study of unions and how they operate will also factor into your college studies. Your courses will touch on managing people by maintaining fair labor practices, settling disputes in the workplace, and understanding occupational safety, health care, pensions, and management practices. By the time you're done, you'll have a grasp on the history of work, the problems in the labor force today, and what it will take to shape the future of employment in the United States. By using your knowledge and experience, you'll be able to help shape that future.

A labor studies major will prepare you to take on a leadership role in the labor movement or many other labor relations careers. Your understanding of the rapidly changing workforce and of the relationships among workers, labor unions, and management will also prepare you for a position in business (particularly human resources), government, labor law, teaching, or a labor union.

> **SAMPLE COLLEGE CURRICULUM FOR LABOR STUDIES**
>
> Contemporary Labor Problems
>
> Grievance Representation
>
> History of Labor
>
> Human Resources Management
>
> Industrial Psychology
>
> International Economics
>
> Introduction to Labor Studies
>
> Labor Economics
>
> Labor and Employment Law
>
> Litigation and Alternate Dispute Resolution
>
> Organizational Psychology
>
> Race Relations in the United States
>
> Social Inequality
>
> Survey of Unions and Collective Bargaining
>
> Work, Alienation, and Power in Social Life
>
> Workplace Discrimination and Fair Employment

If You Like Labor Studies, You May Also Like . . .

History, human resources management, logistics management, managerial economics, operations management, political science, pre-law, psychology, public policy analysis, sociology

Suggested High School Prep for Labor Studies

Because the field of labor studies encompasses a wide range of disciplines, any courses your school offers in history, economics/finance, sociology, and political science will be helpful for this major. Classes like English or public speaking that improve your communication skills will also benefit you. If your studies are going well, consider taking on a part-time job. After all, there's nothing like some first-hand experience to help you gain a real understanding of labor, the workplace, and the value of the dollar.

Fun Facts

Making the Minimum

Just because the U.S. government sets a minimum wage doesn't mean that it's enough to live on. And when the cost of living goes up dramatically, the minimum wage does not automatically increase to compensate for the difference. Congress must pass a bill that the president must then sign into law in order for the minimum wage to be increased.

As of this book's publication...

- The federal minimum wage for covered nonexempt employees is $5.15 an hour.
- Employees that receive tips as part of their wages may only receive a minimum wage of $2.13 an hour (plus tips).
- Workers under age 20 may receive as little as $4.25 per hour during their first 90 consecutive calendar days of employment with an employer. After 90 consecutive days, or after the employee turns 20 (whichever happens first), the employee must receive a minimum wage of $5.15 per hour.

(Source: www.dol.gov/elaws/esa/flsa/screen75.asp)

Think You Had It Hard?

If you've ever griped about having to vacuum the living room or mow the lawn, imagine how difficult the lives of some kids were before the enactment of labor laws. During the mid-nineteenth century, children were often hired to work in the fiery furnaces of glass factories, in dark textile mills, and in coalfields breathing in lung-blackening coal dust for 10 hours at a time.

The Fair Labor Standards Act of 1938, which for the first time set national minimum wage and maximum hour standards for workers in interstate commerce, also placed limitations on child labor. Finally, children under 16 were prohibited from working in manufacturing and mining.

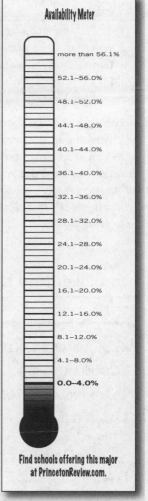

Availability Meter

more than 56.1%

52.1–56.0%

48.1–52.0%

44.1–48.0%

40.1–44.0%

36.1–40.0%

32.1–36.0%

28.1–32.0%

24.1–28.0%

20.1–24.0%

16.1–20.0%

12.1–16.0%

8.1–12.0%

4.1–8.0%

0.0–4.0%

Find schools offering this major at PrincetonReview.com.

Careers and Salary

The starting salary for a labor studies graduate will likely range from $29,000 to $40,000, though it may dip lower if you take a job in the nonprofit sector. Those who choose to pursue graduate studies often look at programs in labor and industrial relations, or in the related areas of business, education, law, public administration, and the social sciences.

CAREER OPTIONS

Economist	Journalist	Policymaker
Historian	Lawyer	Politician
Human Resources Manager	Lobbyist	

LAND USE PLANNING AND MANAGEMENT

Basics

The land use planning and management major teaches students how public and private land can be used, developed, and preserved in the best interest of society's social, economic, and environmental needs. Would a particular neighborhood benefit more from the building of a playground or a housing complex? Would it be ecologically conscionable for a certain forest to be cultivated for wood and paper products? These are the kinds of problems that a land use planner seeks to evaluate and resolve.

This major covers topics such as natural resource management and economics, public policy, regional and city planning, environmental impact assessment, cost analysis, and land laws and regulations. You'll learn the technical ins and outs of developing master plans for public and private development, drafting policies and regulations on land use zones, and critiquing new development proposals. Not all the information you learn will be specialized—you'll also explore and discuss relevant ethical considerations and an understanding of social dynamics. After all, the drive to determine what decisions will most benefit the common good lies at the heart of this discipline.

If You Like Land Use Planning and Management, You May Also Like . . .

Architecture, civil engineering, ecology, economics, environmental and environmental health engineering, environmental design/architecture, environmental science, forestry, natural resources conservation, public policy analysis, range science and management, surveying, sustainable resource management, urban planning, wildlife management

SAMPLE COLLEGE CURRICULUM FOR LAND USE PLANNING AND MANAGEMENT

Advanced Land Use Planning and Design

Business Management

Engineering Graphics

Environmental Impact Assessments

Environmental Policies and Administration

Environmental Sustainability: Theory, Issues, and Management

Introduction to Land Use Theory and Practice

Introductory Soil Science

Multicultural Perspectives on the Environment

Remote Sensing of Natural Resources

Site Planning and Development

Wildlife Science

Suggested High School Prep for Land Use Planning and Management

For this major, load up on math and science classes. Take algebra, geometry, biology, physical science, and chemistry.

Fun Facts

I Heart New York

For facts about New York City's land use and future projects and proposals, check out the New York City Department of City Planning website: www.nyc.gov/html/dcp.

Careers and Salary

Many planning jobs require a master's degree. In general, starting salaries for land use planning and management majors range from $30,000 to $35,000 a year.

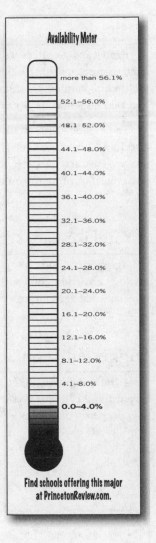

Availability Meter

more than 56.1%

52.1–56.0%

48.1–52.0%

44.1–48.0%

40.1–44.0%

36.1–40.0%

32.1–36.0%

28.1–32.0%

24.1–28.0%

20.1–24.0%

16.1–20.0%

12.1–16.0%

8.1–12.0%

4.1–8.0%

0.0–4.0%

Find schools offering this major at PrincetonReview.com.

CAREER OPTIONS

Conservation Scientist	Land Use Planner	Regional Planner
Ecologist	Natural Sciences Manager	Urban Planner
Forester	Park Naturalist	

LANDSCAPE ARCHITECTURE

Basics

Landscape architecture is the design of open space. Landscape architects determine where to put things such as trees, bushes, buildings, paths, and roads. It is quite an old occupation. In ancient times, landscape architects planned great gardens and public spaces. The Renaissance saw the creation of wondrous villas and piazzas. Andre le Notre, the designer of the gardens of Versailles, became famous for his work.

Today landscape architects are in constant demand. They design public esplanades and promenades, hotel and resort grounds, housing developments, parks, bike trails, and hundreds of other kinds of open spaces. Part art, part science, the landscape architecture major has a challenging and diverse curriculum structured to prepare you to create outdoor spaces that will take many a person's breath away.

If You Like Landscape Architecture, You May Also Like . . .

Agricultural and biological engineering, agronomy and crop science, biology, botany and plant biology, ecology, environmental and environmental health engineering, environmental science, geology, horticulture, international agriculture

Suggested High School Prep for Landscape Architecture

As landscape architecture combines both art and science, classes in both areas are useful. Take biology, physics, and calculus if you can. Art classes, such as drawing and design, and computer graphics classes will also prepare you to tackle all of the visual material you'll have to produce in college.

SAMPLE COLLEGE CURRICULUM FOR LANDSCAPE ARCHITECTURE

Biology I–II

Chemistry

Civil Engineering

Computer Graphics

Drafting

Horticulture

Landscape Design I–IV

Materials and Methods I–II

Fun Facts

For More Information . . .

To find out more about careers in landscape architecture, go to the American Society of Landscape Architects website at www.Asla.org.

The Next Best Thing

Check out one of the greatest examples of landscape architecture in the world. See the gardens of Versailles by taking the virtual tour at www.Virtourist.com/europe/versailles/versailles.htm.

Careers and Salary

A freshly degreed landscape architecture major can expect to make about $23,000 to $32,000.

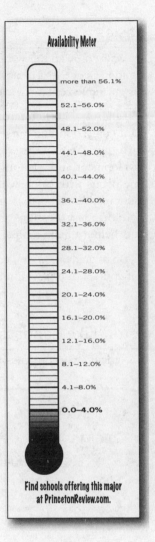

Availability Meter

more than 56.1%

52.1–56.0%

48.1–52.0%

44.1–48.0%

40.1–44.0%

36.1–40.0%

32.1–36.0%

28.1–32.0%

24.1–28.0%

20.1–24.0%

16.1–20.0%

12.1–16.0%

8.1–12.0%

4.1–8.0%

0.0–4.0%

Find schools offering this major at PrincetonReview.com.

CAREER OPTIONS

Construction Manager	Landscape Architect	Set Designer
Florist	Park Ranger	

LANDSCAPE HORTICULTURE

Basics

Want to make the world a happier, more colorful place? Consider majoring in the interesting blend of art and science that is landscape horticulture, which is also a multibillion-dollar industry that involves the design, implementation, management, and conservation of urban and rural landscapes.

Landscape horticulture includes a range of specialty areas such as plant identification, landscape design, plant cultivation, and nursery and garden-center management. If you major in landscape horticulture, you'll learn more about trees, shrubs, vines, and every other kind of plant—their optimal growing conditions, development, and relationships with other organisms—than pretty much anyone. You'll learn how to combine plants with brick, wood, stone, concrete, and other construction materials. You'll also be able to put your creative talents to work by designing eye-catching environments. And, by the way, you'll be doing a lot more than just dressing up the surroundings. The designs of landscape horticulturists and landscape architects help maintain temperature, reduce noise and glare, and provide increased security.

Upon graduation, you can set about the laudable task of making residences, businesses, roadways, parks, golf courses, and playgrounds prettier, healthier, and more usable.

If You Like Landscape Horticulture, You May Also Like . . .

Agricultural economics, agricultural and biological engineering, agricultural technology management, agriculture, agronomy and crop science, art, biology, botany, ecology, environmental science, forestry, genetics, grain science, interior architecture, landscape architecture, natural resources conservation, plant health management, plant pathology, sculpture, soil science, sustainable resource management

SAMPLE COLLEGE CURRICULUM FOR LANDSCAPE HORTICULTURE

- Agricultural Economics
- Biology
- Chemistry
- Data Analysis
- Entomology
- Genetics
- Introduction to Landscape Horticulture
- Landscape Horticulture Internship
- Plant Pathology
- Plant Physiology
- Plant Propagation
- Plant Taxonomy
- Soil Science
- Weed Science

Suggested High School Prep for Landscape Horticulture

You'll need a strong foundation in the basic sciences. Having an endearing love of biology and the physical sciences will help you immensely as well. If you are planning to major in landscape horticulture in college, you should take courses in biology, chemistry, algebra, and trigonometry. And don't forget about art. You want to develop an adequate understanding of design elements. Everything that you can learn about climate, soil, water, and plants will be helpful.

Fun Facts

Did You Know?

Gardening is one of the most popular leisure activities in the United States. More than 74 million American households participate in gardening activities.

America's 10 Greatest Golf Courses

1. Pine Valley Golf Course (Pine Valley, New Jersey)
2. Augusta National Golf Course (Augusta, Georgia)
3. Shinnecock Hills Golf Course (Southampton, New York)
4. Cypress Point Club (Pebble Beach, California)
5. Oakmont Golf Course (Oakmont, Pennsylvania)
6. Pebble Beach Golf Links (Pebble Beach, California)
7. Merion Golf Course (East) (Ardmore, Pennsylvania)
8. Winged Foot Golf Course (Mamaroneck, New York)
9. National Golf Links of America (Southampton, New York)
10. Seminole Golf Course (Juno Beach, Florida)

(Source: http://sports.espn.go.com/travel/news/story?id=2360187)

Careers and Salary

The average starting salary for a landscape horticulture major fresh out of college ranges from $23,000 to $30,000.

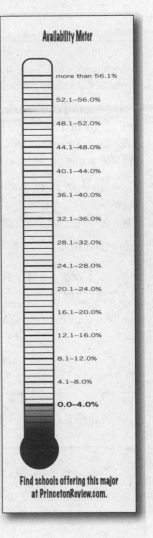

Availability Meter

more than 56.1%
52.1–56.0%
48.1–52.0%
44.1–48.0%
40.1–44.0%
36.1–40.0%
32.1–36.0%
28.1–32.0%
24.1–28.0%
20.1–24.0%
16.1–20.0%
12.1–16.0%
8.1–12.0%
4.1–8.0%
0.0–4.0%

Find schools offering this major at PrincetonReview.com.

CAREER OPTIONS		
Ecologist	Environmentalist/ Environmental Scientist	Landscape Architect

LATIN AMERICAN STUDIES

Basics

Zapata, García Márquez, Khalo, Peron, Che, Rigoberta Menchú. Do you know who these people are? Do you want to know how they have impacted the culture and politics of the lands that lie south of the United States? Then this is the major for you.

Latin American Studies is an interdisciplinary field, reaching over many academic areas. Students combine language course work with work in almost all of the humanities, focusing, of course, on Latin America. Many Latin American studies programs offer areas of concentration within the major, such as twentieth-century literature, gender issues, or history of the Caribbean.

Students in Latin American studies generally must become proficient in Spanish or Portuguese. Most programs strongly suggest (if not require) that students in this major spend some time studying in Mexico, South America, or the Caribbean.

If You Like Latin American Studies, You May Also Like . . .

Archaeology, comparative literature, history, international agriculture, international business, international relations, international studies, Portuguese, Spanish

Suggested High School Prep for Latin American Studies

Courses in Spanish are the best preparation for a major in Latin American studies. Additional work in history and sociology will be useful. Obviously, if your school offers any classes on Latin America, you should take them.

> **SAMPLE COLLEGE CURRICULUM FOR LATIN AMERICAN STUDIES**
>
> Democracy in Latin America
>
> Gender and Society in Latin America
>
> History of Mexico
>
> History of the Caribbean
>
> Latin America to 1930
>
> Latin American Fiction
>
> Native Peoples of South America
>
> Pre-Colombian Art
>
> Spanish (or Portuguese) I–IV
>
> Survey of Latin American Culture and Civilization

Fun Facts

For More Information . . .

Find out more about Latin American studies through the Latin American Studies Association (http://lasa.international.pitt.edu). The site contains information on conferences, internships, and scholarships, plus many useful links.

Another Option

Schools that do not offer the Latin American studies major may offer a Latin American studies concentration within another major, such as Spanish, Portuguese, history, sociology, or political science. When considering a school, look through these areas to check for a Latin American studies track.

Careers and Salary

The starting salary for a Latin American studies major fresh out of college is between $20,000 to $30,000.

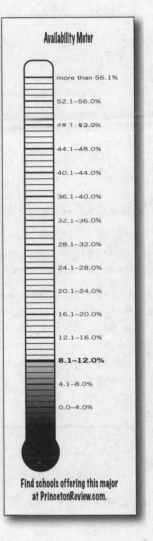

Availability Meter

more than 56.1%

52.1–56.0%

48.1–52.0%

44.1–48.0%

40.1–44.0%

36.1–40.0%

32.1–36.0%

28.1–32.0%

24.1–28.0%

20.1–24.0%

16.1–20.0%

12.1–16.0%

8.1–12.0%

4.1–8.0%

0.0–4.0%

Find schools offering this major at PrincetonReview.com.

CAREER OPTIONS

Anthropologist	Diplomat/Attaché/Foreign Service Officer	Political Aide
Antiques Dealer		Political Scientist
Archaeologist	Foreign Exchange Trader	Politician
Consultant	Lobbyist	Teacher

LATIN LANGUAGE AND LITERATURE

Basics

Quidquid latine dictum sit, altum viditur.

If you know what this means, then you're well on your way to a major in Latin language and literature. (If you don't, don't worry—we'll tell you in the "Fun Facts" section on the next page.) While experience with Latin isn't necessary to enroll in the major, it is a big help. Experienced or not, a decent portion of your coursework will be devoted to perfecting your skills in the language and linguistics of Latin. You'll examine Latin in a variety of contexts: the language of ancient Rome, when both vulgar and classical Latin enjoyed everyday usage; Latin's linguistic roots and principles, from which all modern romance languages are derived; literature produced in Latin; and Latin's present-day use in ecclesiastical settings. To further forge the connection between this ancient language and the twenty-first century, programs may also require you to take a course or two in contemporary Italian. If you play your cards right, that Italian training will come in handy when you spend a semester studying abroad in Rome.

Because many Latin programs are paired with Greek or classics programs, you may also have the options of pursuing a single degree in Greek and Latin, a double major in Greek and in Latin, or simply a Latin major supplemented by a few courses in Greek language or literature.

According to Indiana University, there's currently a shortage of Latin teachers in American high schools. A degree in Latin language and literature will prepare you to help diminish this shortage. If teaching's not your thing, there are plenty of other options. With its rigorous education in language and analysis, the major is an ideal training ground for thinkers prepared to matriculate into any number of fields. In fact, the folks at Indiana say that most of their Latin majors end up leaving classical studies altogether. Where do they go? Law school, med school, and business school are all popular degree destinations.

SAMPLE COLLEGE CURRICULUM FOR LATIN LANGUAGE AND LITERATURE

Advanced Latin

Art and Architecture of Ancient Rome

Beginning Latin

Classical Archeology

History of the Roman Empire

Intermediate Italian

Intermediate Latin

Introduction to Italian

Literature of the Silver Age

Roman Drama

Roman Mythology

Roman Satire

If You Like Latin Language and Literature, You May Also Like...

Ancient Greek languages and literature, Ancient Near Eastern and biblical languages, literatures, and linguistics, anthropology, archaeology, classics, European studies, great books, history, Italian, medieval and renaissance studies, Modern Greek, philosophy

Suggested High School Prep for Latin Language and Literature

If your high school is not currently affected by the shortage of Latin teachers, it's a no-brainer: Study Latin! Though there are more than 40 romance languages currently spoken in the world, your high school probably only offers courses in a few—Italian, Spanish, and French are the big ones. Try one of these. Also, sign up for classes in the traditional humanities, such as history and literature. These courses will give you a base of knowledge and communication skills that you can take to college with you.

Fun Facts

And the Answer Is...

Quidquid latine dictum sit altum viditur = Whatever is said in Latin sounds profound.

You May Also Need To Say...

Non plaudite. Modo pecuniam jacite = Don't applaud. Just throw money.

Labra lege = Read my lips.

Fac ut vivas = Get a life.

Braccae tuae aperiuntur = Your fly is open.

Die dulci freure = Have a nice day.

Careers and Salary

Though starting salaries vary by job, Latin language and literature majors can expect to earn between $20,000 and $30,000 a year. The many majors who continue on to graduate or professional school will obviously have to wait a little while before paychecks come their way.

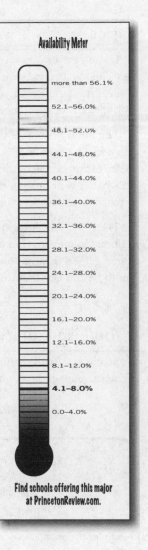

Availability Meter

more than 56.1%

52.1–56.0%

48.1–52.0%

44.1–48.0%

40.1–44.0%

36.1–40.0%

32.1–36.0%

28.1–32.0%

24.1–28.0%

20.1–24.0%

16.1–20.0%

12.1–16.0%

8.1–12.0%

4.1–8.0%

0.0–4.0%

Find schools offering this major at PrincetonReview.com.

CAREER OPTIONS

Archeologist	Librarian	Teacher
Curator	Linguist	Translator
Editor	Philosopher	Writer
Historian	Priest	

LIBRARY SCIENCE

Basics

If you've ever done research, then you probably already know the value of a great librarian. With the way they can locate any book or know what resources are available to you as you begin your search, they seem to have the answers to your questions before you even ask them. All of that knowledge comes, of course, with time and experience, and also with a degree in library science.

The library is one of our greatest cultural and social institutions, serving as a vast warehouse of information and a locus where bookworms can meet and fall in love. The men and women responsible for running these institutions, whether it's your local public library or the Library of Congress, are librarians. Any librarian worth his or her salt needs to be an organizational virtuoso, know what research resources are available to patrons, and understand how technology continues to change the face of libraries in America.

The library science major covers a wide range of topics and issues ranging from the history of libraries to library administration to media for children and young adults. A combination of both practical field experience gained through internships and rigorous academic course work, the library science major prepares you to be the key that unlocks the great reserves of America's information.

If You Like Library Science, You May Also Like . . .

Business administration and management, education administration, historic preservation, logistics management, managerial economics, public administration

Suggested High School Prep for Library Science

With libraries becoming increasingly dependent on technology, a strong background in computers is excellent preparation for the library science major. In addition, you can also volunteer or work at your local public library, reading to children or providing assistance to the librarians. It's a great way to get firsthand experience before entering the classroom.

SAMPLE COLLEGE CURRICULUM FOR LIBRARY SCIENCE

Administration of Libraries

Automation in the Library Media Center

Basic Information Source and Services

Introduction to Librarianship

Library Materials and Services for Special Audiences

Library Practice in the Secondary School

Media for Young Adults

Media Methods and the Curriculum

Organization of Information

Selection of Library Materials

Student Teaching Seminar

Fun Facts

Did You Know?

Thomas Jefferson is considered the founder of the Library of Congress in Washington, DC. It was his personal library that served as the seed for the LOC.

Did You Know?

The first book to be copyrighted in the United States was *The Philadelphia Spelling Book* by John Barry, registered in the U.S. District Court of Pennsylvania on June 9, 1790.

Careers and Salary

The average starting salary for librarians is $24,000 to $30,000.

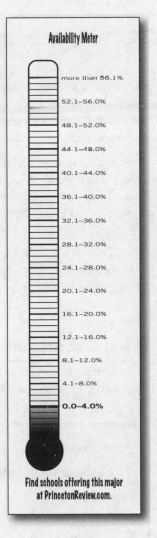

Availability Meter

more than 56.1%

52.1–56.0%

48.1–52.0%

44.1–48.0%

40.1–44.0%

36.1–40.0%

32.1–36.0%

28.1–32.0%

24.1–28.0%

20.1–24.0%

16.1–20.0%

12.1–16.0%

8.1–12.0%

4.1–8.0%

0.0–4.0%

Find schools offering this major at PrincetonReview.com.

CAREER OPTIONS

Book Publishing Professional	Information Manager	Researcher
Bookkeeper	Librarian	Teacher
Consultant		

LINGUISTICS

Basics

Linguistics is the study of language. It's not simply the learning of another language, although that may be part of your studies. As a linguistics major, you'll learn about the nature of language—its role in our life and thinking, its impact on society, and the ways in which it serves our needs. You'll discover how different languages relate to and inform each other, what they have in common, and why. You'll also be learning about the development of language—how it changes over time, how its speakers come to learn it, and how we ourselves affect its development.

Scientific study is a large part of linguistics. While you'll certainly be learning about language as a phenomenon of culture and society, you'll also study humans' cognitive abilities, perception, and organs of speech production. You'll do a great deal of research, and much of your study will include gathering, analyzing, and presenting material. You'll also use computer systems to analyze data and explore language processing programs.

Linguistics is a multidisciplinary field. Language has ties to nearly all fields of study, including but not limited to psychology, philosophy, and anthropology. This is a diverse and exciting field, and if you're fascinated by language in all its many forms and functions, this major may be the one for you.

If You Like Linguistics, You May Also Like . . .

American literature, anthropology, Arabic, Chinese, communication disorders, comparative literature, counseling, French, German, Italian, Japanese, mass communication, Modern Greek, Russian, sociology, Spanish, special education, speech pathology

SAMPLE COLLEGE CURRICULUM FOR LINGUISTICS

Advanced Hausa

Advanced Zulu

Elementary Xhosa

Field Methods

History of Linguistics

Intermediate Swahili

Introduction to Syntax

Language and Religion

Language and Style

Phonetics

Phonology

Semantics

Structure of Sino-Tibetan

Suggested High School Prep for Linguistics

As a linguistics major you'll be immersed in language, so devour all courses in English, literature, and any foreign languages—especially speaking-intensive courses—your high school offers. These will give you the best head-start for your college studies.

Fun Facts

Dead Languages

There are more than 6,000 languages spoken throughout the world. In her article "Language Connection," however, Cristina L'Homme points out that one language disappears every month, 12 each year. A language can disappear for many reasons: war, lack of speakers, depopulation, and the appearance of a more dominant language. "Culture and language form an inseparable couple," writes L'Homme. "So long as a culture is robust, the language persists. When a language is in danger, so is the culture."

(Source: "Language Connection," UNESCO Sources, September 1998)

Quotable

"Language is called the garment of thought: however, it should rather be, language is the flesh-garment, the body, of thought."

—Thomas Carlyle

Careers and Salary

Depending on where they live and how they use their linguistics knowledge, linguistics majors can expect a salary ranging from $20,000 to $30,000, perhaps higher.

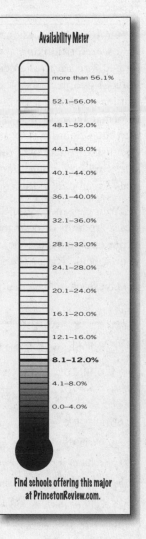

Availability Meter

more than 56.1%

52.1–56.0%

48.1–52.0%

44.1–48.0%

40.1–44.0%

36.1–40.0%

32.1–36.0%

28.1–32.0%

24.1–28.0%

20.1–24.0%

16.1–20.0%

12.1–16.0%

8.1–12.0%

4.1–8.0%

0.0–4.0%

Find schools offering this major at PrincetonReview.com.

CAREER OPTIONS		
Anthropologist	Radio Producer	Speech Therapist
Editor	Sociologist	Translator

LIVESTOCK MANAGEMENT

Basics

On the first occasion you had the chance to pet a fleecy sheep or hold a fluffy yellow chick, you probably weren't thinking about how these animals are part of a thriving industry—livestock—but they are indeed integral to the economy. The business of raising animals for meat and other products sustains millions of people across the world each day—and results in the production of meat, dairy, textile fiber, and leather goods. A major in livestock management will take you through the many facets of animal production, management, and care that apply to livestock, dairy cattle, poultry, and horses. Your classes will delve into the scientific side of this field with coursework in animal science, range science, nutrition, and biochemistry; you'll cover the business aspect of livestock management in economics, marketing, accounting, sales, and communications courses. Reproduction, population genetics, productivity, and the health of animals are all part of the curriculum. Sound like sex ed about pigs? Well it is, sort of—but it's also much more.

Your classroom studies will be complemented by lab experiments as well as hands-on work with real livestock. Students often manage animals for credit or as an extracurricular activity; and an off-campus learning experience may also be required for graduation. Many schools offer a choice of specializations based on your specific career goals.

Livestock management students seek employment in the fields of livestock production, management, and processing. They work for land management agencies as managers of swine, poultry, and farms; as salespeople for feed and farm equipment; or as research technicians. Other career opportunities include land resource consulting and jobs with communication and service organizations, such as breed associations, commodity groups, livestock publications, and government agencies.

SAMPLE COLLEGE CURRICULUM FOR LIVESTOCK MANAGEMENT
Agribusiness Law
Agribusiness Marketing
Agricultural and Environmental Policy
Agricultural Business Management
Agricultural Records and Accounting
Animal Reproduction and Breeding
Animal Feeds and Nutrition
Beef Production
Community Leadership
Introduction to Agricultural Economics
Livestock and Poultry Disease Management
Management of Personnel
Poultry Production
Principles of Sales
Principles of Soil Science
Swine Production

If You Like Livestock Management, You May Also Like . . .

Agricultural business and management, agricultural economics, agricultural journalism, agricultural mechanization, agricultural technology management, agricultural/biological engineering and bioengineering, agriculture, agronomy and crop science, animal behavior and ethology, animal science, aquaculture, feed science, pre-veterinary medicine

Suggested High School Prep for Livestock Management

Science is going to be essential in your college studies, so take as many high school science courses as your school offers. Good grades in biology, chemistry, and other science classes will look great on your college application. Strong math and writing skills are important, too. Be sure to stay in top physical condition: Work on a farm can be strenuous and tiring if you're not in good shape. Join your local 4-H group if you haven't already.

Fun Facts

Getting to the Meat of the Issue

Ever since humans began eating animals for food, they have come up with ways to waste as little of the animal as possible. Check out these creative dishes from across the globe. Some are common, while others are a more acquired taste.

Braunschwieger (BROWN-shvi-ger; BROWN-shi-ger): A soft German sausage made from pork liver and enriched with eggs and milk.

Hog Jowl: The cheek of a hog. It is usually cut into squares, then cured and smoked. Also called jowl bacon.

Hog Maw: A hog's stomach stuffed with sausage, then simmered and baked.

Pigs' Feet: The front feet of a hog that have been removed from the shoulder slightly below the knee joints. Pigs' feet are available fresh, cured, cooked, or pickled.

Scrapple: A Pennsylvania Dutch dish made from chopped "scraps" of pork simmered with cornmeal and seasonings, then packed into a loaf pan and chilled. Scrapple is usually sliced and fried in butter or bacon fat before serving.

Spam: A registered trademark name for a canned ground pork shoulder and ham product introduced by the Hormel Company in 1937.

Sweetbreads: The thymus gland or pancreas of calves or lambs and sometimes young hogs.

Tripe: The stomach lining from cattle and sometimes hogs and sheep. It has a subtle flavor and tender texture.

(Source: National Pork Board and www.otherwhitemeat.com)

Stock Pick

Want to keep up on what's making the news in livestock management? Check out *Livestock Weekly*, published every Thursday since 1949 and based in San Angelo, Texas. On Livestockweekly.com, you graze the week's headlines or order a full subscription. It's pretty in-depth and often peppered with industry jargon.

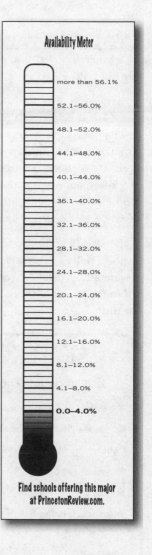

Availability Meter

more than 56.1%

52.1–56.0%

48.1–52.0%

44.1–48.0%

40.1–44.0%

36.1–40.0%

32.1–36.0%

28.1–32.0%

24.1–28.0%

20.1–24.0%

16.1–20.0%

12.1–16.0%

8.1–12.0%

4.1–8.0%

0.0–4.0%

Find schools offering this major at PrincetonReview.com.

Careers and Salary

Starting salaries for livestock management majors vary greatly, but generally range from $22,000 to $33,000. This increases at least another $10,000 per year with a master's degree in a related field.

CAREER OPTIONS

Biochemist	Farmer	Teacher
Biologist	Journalist	Veterinarian
Ecologist	Lobbyist	Zoologist
Environmentalist	Park Ranger	

LOGIC

Basics

If you're good at finding the loopholes in your parents' arguments about why you aren't old enough to stay out until 4 A.M., then a major in logic might be a solid choice for you.

As a student of logic, or a logician, you'll learn how to evaluate arguments to see whether they hold water. Logic helps us to reason, and without a foundation of good reasoning, we don't have the means for developing sound beliefs or finding truth. Your studies will include exercises in constructing arguments, inspecting claims and the evidence used to support them, using science and philosophy to support an argument, and identifying weaknesses in arguments. But you'll need more than words alone: Courses in computer and information science, statistics, mathematics, linguistics, philosophy, and even physics and psychology will help you recognize the many forms that logical arguments take. You'll never accept something as true based on its face value again.

Beyond helping you talk yourself out of difficult situations, logic will sharpen your analytic and communication skills. These skills might lead you to a technical career related to information security, computer programming, database technology, networking, or software engineering. Alternatively, you might find yourself in the world of business, law, or education—or on the road to becoming the next great philosopher of our time.

SAMPLE COLLEGE CURRICULUM FOR LOGIC

Arguments and Mathematical Inquiry

Casual and Statistical Reasoning

Concepts of Mathematics

Constructive Logic

Economics

Introduction to the Theory of Knowledge

Linear Logic

Logic and Computation

Logic and Proofs

Logic in Artificial Intelligence

Minds, Machines, and Knowledge

Philosophy of Mathematics

Physics

Probability and Artificial Intelligence

Proof Theory

Psychology

Statistical Reasoning

If You Like Logic, You May Also Like . . .

Applied mathematics, business administration/management, cognitive psychology, computer and information science, computer engineering, economics, linguistics, mathematics, philosophy, physics, pre-law, statistics

Suggested High School Prep for Logic

Such a dynamic major calls for a well-rounded high school program of study. Take as many math, physics, psychology, and computer courses as you can. Join the debate team, and read books about great philosophers. In your free time, keep an eye (and an ear) out for any logical loopholes on courtroom TV shows and movies.

Fun Facts

Two Ways to Reason

Deductive reasoning works from the general to the more specific. Inductive reasoning works the other way, moving from specific observations to broader generalizations and theories. Arguments based on experience or observations are usually expressed inductively; whereas arguments based on laws, rules, or other widely accepted principles are best expressed deductively. For example, if you start out with the proposition that all objects that come into contact with water will become wet, then you can deduce from that the conclusion that if you toss an object into a pool of water, it will become wet. On the other hand, if you start out with the observation that every time you put an object into water it becomes wet, then you might induce from that the hypothesis that the next time you put an object in water, it will become wet.

Some Logical Things to Say

"Religion is love; in no case is it logic."   —Beatrice Potter Webb

"A mind all logic is like a knife all blade: It makes the hand bleed that uses it."

—Rabindranath Tagore

"Better to be without logic than without feeling."   —Charlotte Brontë

"Logic, like whiskey, loses its beneficial effect when taken in too large quantities."

—Lord Dunsany

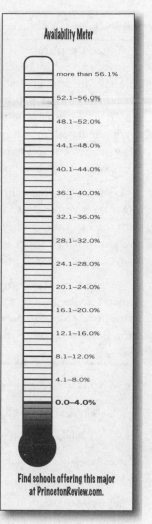

Availability Meter

more than 56.1%

52.1–56.0%

48.1–52.0%

44.1–48.0%

40.1–44.0%

36.1–40.0%

32.1–36.0%

28.1–32.0%

24.1–28.0%

20.1–24.0%

16.1–20.0%

12.1–16.0%

8.1–12.0%

4.1–8.0%

0.0–4.0%

Find schools offering this major at PrincetonReview.com.

Careers and Salary

The starting salary for a logic graduate can vary widely depending on the field. The higher-paying jobs are those in computer, technical, and business fields, while careers having to do with teaching, writing, and philosophy tend to pay less. The average starting salary falls between $25,000 and $40,000. Making the decision to continue on to law school will vastly improve your salary outlook.

CAREER OPTIONS

Attorney

Computer Operator/Programmer

Corporate Lawyer

Information Manager

Journalist

Lobbyist

Mediator

Philosopher

Political Scientist

Politician

Private Investigator

Systems Analyst

Teacher

Technical Support Specialist

Trial Lawyer

Writer

LOGISTICS MANAGEMENT

Basics

You're the planner of the group, the one who sets the time, date, place, and number of cars needed for the road trip to the beach. You know the absolute latest time you can drop your date off and still make it home before your curfew, partly because you know how many stoplights lie between her house and yours. (Or maybe you know how to use the back roads to avoid said stoplights altogether.) You've mapped it all out on your laptop or in your personal digital assistant. Some people say that you're bossy, controlling, and detail-orientated. You know better, though. You know that this is all just preparation for that future in logistics management you've been planning since you timed how long it would take to get from the cafeteria to the playground in kindergarten.

Logistics management, as you've probably already figured out, is the science behind the way businesses move their materials. Closely related to transportation management, logistics management is concerned with the management of product delivery. It's UPS, FedEx, and the U.S. Post Office all rolled into one intensive study that provides you with a strong background in business and business management, as well as an analytical approach to processing and using information.

By the time you complete this major, not only will you find yourself highly marketable and in great demand by the business world, but you'll also be able to figure out if train A, traveling 65 miles an hour en route from Boston to New York, will be able to beat train B, traveling 60 miles an hour en route from the same Boston station to the same New York station, that left 12 minutes earlier than train A on a route that is 7.5 miles longer but includes 3 miles of downhill track, which increases the speed of train B to 68 miles an hour.

SAMPLE COLLEGE CURRICULUM FOR LOGISTICS MANAGEMENT

- Accounting
- Analytical Marketing
- Business Statistics
- Information Management
- International Management
- International Trade and Banking
- Introduction to Logistics
- Location of Economic Activity
- Logistics Operations
- Logistics Strategy
- Marketing
- Retail Marketing and Distribution
- Strategic Logistics Management
- Strategic Management
- Transport Economics

If You Like Logistics Management, You May Also Like . . .

Accounting, actuarial science, business administration and management, business communications, economics, finance, human resources management, international business, marketing, operations management, public administration, sociology, statistics

Suggested High School Prep for Logistics Management

Keep those math and analytical skills finely honed and ready if you want a career in logistics management. Statistics and advanced math courses are excellent preparation for the intense courses you'll be taking.

Fun Facts

UPS

United Parcel Service, the shipping giant, delivered 3.5 billion packages and documents in 2000—all of this for a combined total revenue of $29.8 billion.

Versus the U.S. Postal Service

And to top that, the U.S. Postal Service delivers 107 billion pieces of first class mail each year. It does this through 15,000 commercial airline flights and more than a billion miles driven annually.

Careers and Salary

The average starting salary for a logistics management major is $26,000 to $40,000.

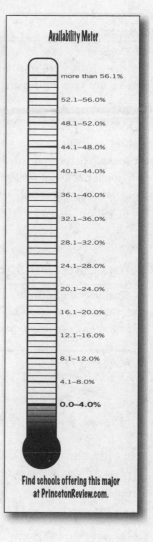

Availability Meter

more than 56.1%

52.1–56.0%

48.1–52.0%

44.1–48.0%

40.1–44.0%

36.1–40.0%

32.1–36.0%

28.1–32.0%

24.1–28.0%

20.1–24.0%

16.1–20.0%

12.1–16.0%

8.1–12.0%

4.1–8.0%

0.0–4.0%

Find schools offering this major at PrincetonReview.com.

CAREER OPTIONS

Accountant/Auditor	Casino Host	Management Consultant
Actuary	Coast Guard (Officer)	Navy (Officer)
Air Force (Officer)	Human Resources Manager	Office Manager
Bank Officer	Information Manager	Organizational Developer
Bookkeeper	Investment Banker	Wedding Planner

MANAGEMENT INFORMATION SYSTEMS

Basics

Companies and organizations depend on computerized information for almost every aspect of their business. How is all this data organized? Enter the field of management information systems. In this major, you'll learn how to design computer systems to help people and organizations function more effectively.

As you might expect, management information systems entails a whole slew of computer courses, including languages and programming, information technology and security, and systems planning and integration. A major in management information systems will also provide a solid grounding in all aspects of business management, including human resources, business law, and contracting. You'll learn how to analyze individual needs, as well as the larger economic and social priorities of a company, so you can most effectively structure and organize its data. Because you'll frequently be planning and problem-solving in teams, it's important that you possess good communications skills and enjoy working with people as well.

If You Like Management Information Systems, You May Also Like . . .

Business administration and management, business communications, computer and information science, computer systems analysis, human resources management, information technology, mathematics, operations management, organizational behavioral studies, statistics, webmaster/web management

SAMPLE COLLEGE CURRICULUM FOR MANAGEMENT INFORMATION SYSTEMS

Advanced Data Analysis

Computer Algorithms

Database Program Development

Decision Support Systems

Human Computer Interaction

Information System Auditing and Security

Information Systems Architecture and Technology

MIS Foundations

Principles of Organization and Management

Project Management

Systems Analysis and Design

Systems Programming II (C Language)

Suggested High School Prep for Management Information Systems

For this major, it's recommended that you take calculus and any computer science or programming courses your school offers. If a public speaking elective is available, take that too.

Fun Facts

Computer History Museum

If you're ever in Silicon Valley, check out the Computer History Museum. Established in 1996, the museum is, according to their website, "a public benefit organization dedicated to the preservation and celebration of computing history." Making up one of the most comprehensive collections of computing artifacts in the world, the Computer History Museum houses over 4,000 artifacts, 10,000 images, and 4,000 linear feet of cataloged documentation and gigabytes of software. Cool items in the collection include a Hollerith census machine, a Cray-3 supercomputer, a World War II Enigma machine, a see-through PalmPilot, parts of MIT's Whirlwind computer, and a computer-generated Mona Lisa.

(Source: www.computerhistory.org)

Careers and Salary

Typical starting salaries for those who major in management information systems are about $40,000 a year.

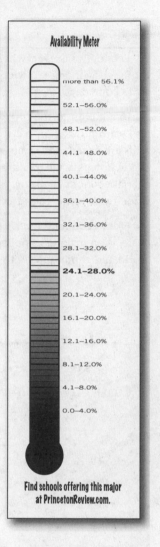

Availability Meter

more than 56.1%

52.1–56.0%

48.1–52.0%

44.1 48.0%

40.1–44.0%

36.1–40.0%

32.1–36.0%

28.1–32.0%

24.1–28.0%

20.1–24.0%

16.1–20.0%

12.1–16.0%

8.1–12.0%

4.1–8.0%

0.0–4.0%

Find schools offering this major at PrincetonReview.com.

CAREER OPTIONS

Chief Information Officer

Chief Technology Officer

Computer and Software Marketing Manager

Computer Programmer

Computer Security Specialist

Computer Systems Auditor

Computer and Information Systems Manager

Data Communications Analyst

Database Administrator

Information Systems Manager

Management Analyst

Network Administrator

Office Automation Specialist

Operations Research Analyst

Systems Analyst

Systems Consultant

MANAGERIAL ECONOMICS

Basics

Economics is everywhere. From the bursting of the dot-com bubble to federal interest rate standards, a thorough working knowledge of how economics shapes businesses is necessary if you're going to become a CEO one day.

In addition to the broad economic skills that you'll receive as a managerial economics major, you will also learn how to appreciate the intricate details behind specific economic contexts. No two economic systems are exactly the same, and so what works best in the United States for a company might not fly so well in, say, Romania, where different regulations can determine the way a company conducts business. As a managerial economics major, your job will be to analyze those contexts and figure out how policy decisions made by governments affect your company or business.

From economic forecasts (which are occasionally worse than the forecasts of your local weatherman) to decision making to policy analysis, a major in managerial economics is a great way to enter the business world and climb quickly to the top of that corporate ladder.

If You Like Managerial Economics, You May Also Like . . .

Accounting, actuarial science, business administration and management, business communications, economics, finance, international business, international relations, international studies, logistics management, public administration, statistics

Suggested High School Prep for Managerial Economics

The best way to get ready for this major is to strengthen those math and analytical skills. Advanced courses in math, such as calculus, along with economics, are great preparation. This field isn't just about numbers though, so keep those critical reading and writing skills sharp with AP English classes and some history. The latter will come in useful when you need to make historical arguments to support whatever outlandish theory it is that you're feeding to people.

SAMPLE COLLEGE CURRICULUM FOR MANAGERIAL ECONOMICS

Calculus

Corporate Finance

Decision Support Systems

Econometrics

Economic Statistics

Financial Accounting

Forecasting

Industrial Organization

Intermediate Macroeconomics

Intermediate Microeconomics

Labor Economics

Macroeconomics

Managerial Accounting

Microeconomics

Monetary Theory and Policy

Principles of Accounting

Fun Facts

Newlan's Truism

An "acceptable" level of unemployment means that the government economist to whom it is acceptable still has a job.

Cow Distribution

Socialism: You have two cows. State takes one and gives it to someone else.

Communism: You have two cows. State takes both of them and gives you milk.

Fascism: You have two cows. State takes both of them and sells you milk.

Nazism: You have two cows. State takes both of them and shoots you.

Bureaucracy: You have two cows. State takes both of them, kills one, and spills the milk in sewer system.

Capitalism: You have two cows. You sell one and buy a bull.

Feudalism: You have two cows. Your lord takes some of the milk.

Pure socialism: You have two cows. The government takes them and puts them in a barn with everyone else's cows. You have to take care of all the cows. The government gives you as much milk as you need.

Careers and Salary

The average starting salaries for managerial economics majors range from $35,000 to $45,000. Expect these numbers to increase dramatically with advanced degrees and experience.

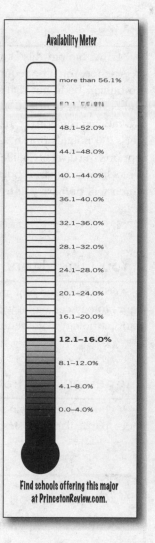

Availability Meter

more than 56.1%

52.1–56.0%

48.1–52.0%

44.1–48.0%

40.1–44.0%

36.1–40.0%

32.1–36.0%

28.1–32.0%

24.1–28.0%

20.1–24.0%

16.1–20.0%

12.1–16.0%

8.1–12.0%

4.1–8.0%

0.0–4.0%

Find schools offering this major at PrincetonReview.com.

CAREER OPTIONS

Accountant/Auditor	Consultant	Management Consultant
Actuary	Financial Planner	Stockbroker
Bank Officer	Human Resources Manager	Trader
Bookkeeper	Investment Banker	Venture Capitalist/Investor
Business Valuator		

MARINE BIOLOGY

Basics

Marine biology (also known as biological oceanography), just like every other biology major, is heavy on the science. You'll be required to learn all the nuts and bolts of biology—from cells and microorganisms to the human body, but that's not what's really at the heart of this major. Forget humans; what you want to study can only be found 500 fathoms under the sea (or maybe just one fathom down). From the reproductive mechanisms of the tiniest saltwater microbes to the killer whale's dietary habits (300 pounds of sea lions, 200 pounds of fish, 1 cup of coffee), you'll learn how the greatest ecosystem in the world (the ocean) supports the diversity of life forms that thrive on and because of each other. Specific instruction in subjects such as biochemistry, marine botany, ichthyology, and mammalogy are par for the course in the marine biology major, which will prepare you to delve into the broader mysteries of the life that exist between seafloor and the surface.

If You Like Marine Biology, You May Also Like . . .

Agricultural and biological engineering, animal science, biochemistry, biology, biopsychology, botany and plant biology, cell biology, environmental science, genetics, marine science, microbiology, molecular genetics, plant pathology, wildlife management, zoology

Suggested High School Prep for Marine Biology

If you're interested in majoring in marine biology, it's important to have a strong background in the sciences, particularly physics, chemistry, and biology, as well as strong written and oral communication skills.

> **SAMPLE COLLEGE CURRICULUM FOR MARINE BIOLOGY**
>
> Calculus
>
> Cell Biology
>
> General Biology
>
> General Chemistry
>
> Genetics
>
> Ichthyology
>
> Invertebrates
>
> Mammalogy
>
> Marine Ecosystems
>
> Physics

Fun Facts

Did You Know?

There are 275,000 species of organisms that live in the ocean. The largest animal and marine mammal in the world is the blue whale. It grows up to 33 meters long and weighs as much as 49 rhinoceroses.

Did You Know?

The sea provides the biggest source of wild or domestic protein in the world. Each year some 70 to 75 million tons of fish are taken from the ocean.

Careers and Salary

Biologists can expect a starting salary ranging from $20,000 to $30,000 a year depending on the industry they enter and their level of education.

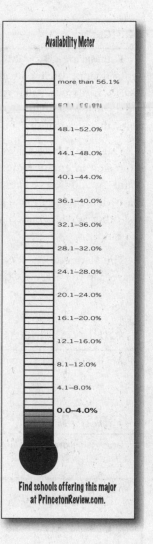

Availability Meter

more than 56.1%

52.1–56.0%

48.1–52.0%

44.1–48.0%

40.1–44.0%

36.1–40.0%

32.1–36.0%

28.1–32.0%

24.1–28.0%

20.1–24.0%

16.1–20.0%

12.1–16.0%

8.1–12.0%

4.1–8.0%

0.0–4.0%

Find schools offering this major at PrincetonReview.com.

CAREER OPTIONS

Biochemist

Biologist

Ecologist

Environmentalist/
Environmental Scientist

Geneticist

Zoologist

MARINE CORPS R.O.T.C.

Basics

The Marine Corps R.O.T.C. (Reserve Officer Training Corps) is a program designed to help college students finance their education and prepare for careers in the Marine Corps. If you are accepted into an R.O.T.C. program, you'll receive a scholarship that usually includes full tuition, money for books and fees, and a small stipend. In return, you agree to serve on active duty in the Marine Corps Reserve for at least four years after graduation. You will enter the corps as a second lieutenant.

You'll be able to select your own major in college, even as a Marine Corps R.O.T.C. participant. If you're interested in engineering, mathematics, or science, you can still take full advantage of your college's programs. In addition to the course work for your chosen major, you'll take several required R.O.T.C. courses that will include physical training. You'll also be required to participate in drill instruction, summer training, and other service-related activities. Summer training can include stints on helicopters, submarines, aircraft, and ships.

The Marine Corps R.O.T.C. is usually linked with the Navy R.O.T.C. in many colleges. If you're considering a career in the Marine Corps, the R.O.T.C. program might make sense for you.

If You Like Marine Corps R.O.T.C., You May Also Like . . .

Air Force R.O.T.C., Army R.O.T.C., military science, naval architecture, Navy R.O.T.C.

Suggested High School Prep for Marine Corps R.O.T.C.

Because you'll be taking the same general education classes as the rest of your classmates, your best preparation will be a broad range of courses in English, science, and math—at as advanced a level as possible. You might also want to take a few extra physical fitness courses to toughen up for the training ahead. Also, the Marine Corps awards R.O.T.C. scholarships to candidates who display leadership qualities, so get involved.

> **SAMPLE COLLEGE CURRICULUM FOR MARINE CORPS R.O.T.C.**
>
> Amphibious Warfare
>
> Courses in your chosen field of concentration
>
> Evolution of Warfare
>
> Leadership and Ethics
>
> Leadership and Management
>
> Naval Engineering
>
> Naval Weapons
>
> Navigation
>
> Seapower and Maritime Affairs

Fun Facts

My Rifle: The Creed of a U.S. Marine

by Major General William H. Rupertus, USMC, Ret.

This is my rifle. There are many like it, but this one is mine.

My rifle is my best friend. It is my life. I must master it as I must master my life.

My rifle, without me, is useless. Without my rifle, I am useless. I must fire my rifle true. I must shoot straighter than my enemy who is trying to kill me. I must shoot him before he shoots me. I will . . .

My rifle and myself know that what counts in this war is not the rounds we fire, the noise of our burst, nor the smoke we make. We know that it is the hits that count. We will hit . . .

My rifle is human, even as I, because it is my life. Thus, I will learn it as a brother. I will learn its weaknesses, its strength, its parts, its accessories, its sights, and its barrel. I will ever guard it against the ravages of weather and damage as I will ever guard my legs, my arms, my eyes, and my heart against damage. I will keep my rifle clean and ready. We will become part of each other. We will . . .

Before God, I swear this creed. My rifle and myself are defenders of my country. We are the masters of our enemy. We are the saviors of my life.

So be it, until victory is America's and there is no enemy, but peace!

Core Values

There are three core values that the Marines adhere to. These core values are honor, courage, and commitment. These values bond the Marines together and give them strength.

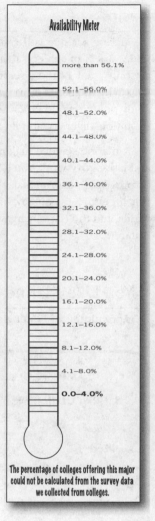

Availability Meter

more than 56.1%

52.1–56.0%

48.1–52.0%

44.1–48.0%

40.1–44.0%

36.1–40.0%

32.1–36.0%

28.1–32.0%

24.1–28.0%

20.1–24.0%

16.1–20.0%

12.1–16.0%

8.1–12.0%

4.1–8.0%

0.0–4.0%

The percentage of colleges offering this major could not be calculated from the survey data we collected from colleges.

Careers and Salary

Starting salaries for Marine Corps R.O.T.C. participants can range from $28,000 to $36,000 but depend on where participants are stationed and how they use their skills.

CAREER OPTIONS

FBI Agent	Marines (Officer)	Pilot
Human Resources Manager	Military Officer	

MARINE SCIENCE

Basics

Marine science is the study of the sea and its inhabitants. As a marine science major, you'll take on a wide variety of subjects to augment your understanding of this field: Biology, chemistry, geology, and physics are only a few of the disciplines that will be incorporated into your studies. You'll learn about the many reasons why the sea is important to us, how it affects us, and what we can and should do to preserve it. You'll study pollution and other health issues. You'll learn about the many living things that inhabit the sea and the evolution, diversity, and importance of these inhabitants.

A marine science major, like most science or engineering majors, will involve some degree of research and laboratory work. You'll learn how to gather and analyze data and how to present your results in papers or presentations. You'll also learn how to interpret others' research results and how to critically read scientific literature. Eventually, your research may take you to such exotic locations as the Sargasso Sea, Antarctica, Africa, and the Caribbean, where you might, just might, get to swim with the dolphins (in the Caribbean, not Antarctica).

If You Like Marine Science, You May Also Like . . .

Agricultural and biological engineering, animal science, biochemistry, biology, biopsychology, botany and plant biology, cell biology, ecology, environmental and environmental health engineering, environmental science, forestry, microbiology, ocean engineering

SAMPLE COLLEGE CURRICULUM FOR MARINE SCIENCE

Atoll Ecosystems

Chemical Oceanography

Coastal Processes

Conservation Biology

Development of Aquaculture

Global Environmental Change

Limnology

Long Island Marine Habitats

Marine Biodiversity

Marine Ecology

Marine Invertebrates

Marine Monitoring Techniques

Marine Plants

Physical Oceanography

Plankton Ecology

Suggested High School Prep for Marine Science

As with any science major, courses in computers, biology, chemistry, and physics are of paramount importance. Also, you'll benefit from high-level math courses such as calculus or trigonometry. English classes will give you the reading and writing skills necessary for a field involving research.

Fun Facts

A Watery Menagerie

Did you know that a coral reef is actually an accumulation of many tiny organisms? A coral is a tiny marine polyp, and when many corals join together, it is called a reef.

A coral reef may consist of 1,500 kinds of fish, 400 kinds of coral, 4,000 types of mollusks, 500 species of seaweed, 215 kinds of birds, 16 species of sea snake, six species of sea turtle, and the occasional whale.

Ask the Shark for Directions

Sharks are able to determine compass directions by using a system of sensors called the ampullae of Lorenzini. These sensors, located on a shark's forehead, can detect electrical currents as small as .01 microvolts. Electromagnetic fields become stronger or weaker depending on whether you are going north, south, east, or west, which is why the shark is able to orient itself so well.

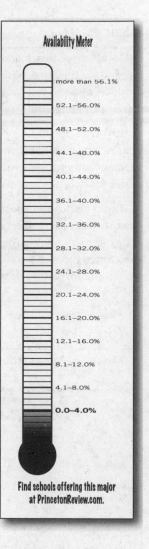

Availability Meter

more than 56.1%

52.1–56.0%

48.1–52.0%

44.1–48.0%

40.1–44.0%

36.1–40.0%

32.1–36.0%

28.1–32.0%

24.1–28.0%

20.1–24.0%

16.1–20.0%

12.1–16.0%

8.1–12.0%

4.1–8.0%

0.0–4.0%

Find schools offering this major
at PrincetonReview.com.

Careers and Salary

Marine scientists' starting salary might range anywhere from $25,000 to $35,000, but will depend heavily on their research experience, location, and area of employment. Their salary will rise as they obtain higher degrees of education.

CAREER OPTIONS

Biologist

Coast Guard (Officer)

Ecologist

Environmentalist/
Environmental Scientist

Geneticist

Researcher

Zoologist

MARKETING

Basics

Just between us, marketing is the art and the science of getting people to buy stuff. More formally, it is the study of how to determine consumer needs, translate those needs into products and services, and sell those products and services locally, nationally, and globally. Either way, marketing is a practical, career-oriented, and solidly pre-professional major that requires analytical skills, logic, and creativity.

If you decide to major in marketing, you'll learn about the distribution of goods and services, consumer behavior, pricing policies, channels of retail and wholesale distribution, advertising, sales, research, and management. Other topics you are likely to encounter include market segmentation and targeting, effective customer service, new product development, and logistics.

Upon graduation, most marketing majors find jobs in consulting, market research, and advertising. If you want to work in the marketing department though, you should expect to start in sales, where you can really get to know a company's products and its customers. In fact, starting in sales is frequently the best (and sometimes the only) way to ultimately get one of those coveted (not to mention high-paying, low stress) jobs in the marketing department.

If You Like Marketing, You May Also Like . . .

Business administration and management, computer and information science, economics, English, mass communication, political science, psychology, radio and television, sociology, technical writing

SAMPLE COLLEGE CURRICULUM FOR MARKETING

Accounting Principles

Case Studies in Marketing

Consumer Behavior

Finance

International Business

Legal Environment of Business

Macroeconomics

Managerial Marketing

Marketing Research

Microeconomics

Organizational Behavior

Principles of Human Resources

Principles of Management

Sales Management

Statistics

Suggested High School Prep for Marketing

A basic college preparatory background should be fine. If you think you might major in marketing, focus on your writing and math skills (you'll almost certainly be required to complete college algebra, statistics, and perhaps even calculus). Experience with computers and various business software programs will be helpful as well.

BUSINESS, MARKETING, AND RELATED FIELDS

Fun Facts

Top Ten Research Organizations in the World

According to the American Marketing Association

1. AC Nielsen Corp (Stamford, Connecticut)
2. GFK Group (Nuremberg, Germany)
3. IMS Health Inc. (Westport, Connecticut)
4. Ipsos Group (Paris, France)
5. Information Resources Inc. (Chicago, Illinois)
6. The Kantar Group Ltd. (Fairfield, Connecticut)
7. NFO Worldwide Inc. (Greenwich, Connecticut)
8. Nielsen Media Research (Haarlem, Netherlands)
9. Taylor Nelson Sofres (London, United Kingdom)
10. United Information Group Ltd. (London, United Kingdom)

A Joke

Q: How many marketing directors does it take to change a lightbulb?

A: Let's make a giant, red and yellow, flashing, neon billboard sign instead.

Careers and Salary

Starting salaries for marketing majors are on average $32,000 annually. The range of starting salaries is between $28,000 and $40,000.

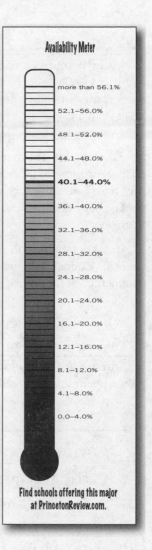

Availability Meter

more than 56.1%
52.1–56.0%
48.1–52.0%
44.1–48.0%
40.1–44.0%
36.1–40.0%
32.1–36.0%
28.1–32.0%
24.1–28.0%
20.1–24.0%
16.1–20.0%
12.1–16.0%
8.1–12.0%
4.1–8.0%
0.0–4.0%

Find schools offering this major at PrincetonReview.com.

CAREER OPTIONS

Advertising Executive	Market Researcher	Public Relations Professional
Agent	Marketing Executive	Publicist
Bar/Club Manager	Media Specialist	Retail Salesperson
Book Publishing Professional	Music Executive	Service Sales Representative
Buyer	Pharmaceutical Sales Representative	Writer
Management Consultant	Promoter	

MASS COMMUNICATION

Basics

We are bombarded with images and messages every day of our lives, from billboards towering over the highway to television commercials, newspaper ads, leaflets, brochures, and radio advertising. These messages shape our culture and define our perceptions, influencing the way we think and look at almost everything from a candy bar to geopolitics.

Mass communication majors investigate the role mass media has played, and continues to play, in American culture. They are analysts and historians, examining everything from nineteenth-century *Harper's* political cartoons to the newest McDonald's commercial. Given the enormous effect of the media on our daily lives, mass communication majors seek out how and why they reflect our social values. They also describe how public policy draws boundaries for mass communication, such as the near-prohibition of nudity on broadcast television.

Mass communication majors are sometimes located within a broader communication major that more generally examines the ways in which information is created and distributed, whether through a television commercial or a personal e-mail.

If You Like Mass Communication, You May Also Like . . .

Advertising, American studies, anthropology, business communications, English, film, journalism, marketing, public policy analysis, radio and television, sociology, urban studies

---

SAMPLE COLLEGE CURRICULUM FOR MASS COMMUNICATION

Cultural History of Advertising

Effects of the Mass Media

International Media

Mass Communication Research and Methods

Propaganda and the Mass Media

Quantitative Methods in Anthropology

Structure of Mass Communication

The First Amendment and the Press

Topics in American Television

Various electives in journalism, sociology, psychology, linguistics, anthropology, and business

---

Suggested High School Prep for Mass Communication

Strong reading and analytical skills will come in handy in mass communication, so AP courses in English and advanced math (such as statistics) are a must. Watch the news, movies, and the commercials in between them. Listen to what your friends have to say when the conversation turns to the media. They are members of the masses, after all.

Fun Facts

Did You Know?

In 2002, tobacco companies spent a total of $12.47 billion—or more than $34 million a day—to promote and advertise their products. (And they can't even advertise on TV.)

(Source: www.lungusa.org)

Did You Know?

Five times as many people read the headline of an article as read the article itself.

Careers and Salary

Starting salaries for mass communication and communication majors range from $21,000 to $30,000.

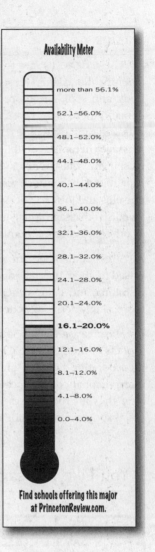

Availability Meter

more than 56.1%

52.1–56.0%

48.1–52.0%

44.1–48.0%

40.1–44.0%

36.1–40.0%

32.1–36.0%

28.1–32.0%

24.1–28.0%

20.1–24.0%

16.1–20.0%

12.1–16.0%

8.1–12.0%

4.1–8.0%

0.0–4.0%

Find schools offering this major
at PrincetonReview.com.

CAREER OPTIONS

Advertising Executive	Journalist	Telecommunications Specialist
Agent	Lobbyist	Television Producer
Attorney	Market Researcher	Television Reporter
Auctioneer	Marketing Executive	Web Editor
Consultant	Media Planner	Web Master
Editor	Radio Producer	Writer

MASSAGE THERAPY

Basics

These days, it's rare to find a top-notch resort or spa around the globe that doesn't offer the luxurious amenity of massage. Guests are clamoring for appointments, lining up to be oiled, rubbed, and soothed mind, body, and soul. The more people who reap the benefits of massage and come back for more, the more demand there is for those in this hands-on profession. If you're a touchy-feely type to begin with, a major in massage therapy will teach you how to give professional massages that are both relaxing and healing. As a massage therapist, you'll first learn about the body's structure and function—how the body moves and how its skin, muscles, bones, and connective tissues interact. Once you understand the body and what can cause it pain and discomfort, you'll begin learning how massage can aid flexibility and ease aches and tension in muscles and joints. Your new skill set will include soft tissue manipulation, deep tissue massage, Western (or Swedish) massage, Shiatsu, and reflexology. You'll also learn about acupressure and sports massage as well as other specific techniques.

Stress and anxiety are common reasons for people to seek out massage therapists, but you might be surprised to know that massage is often used to help people with allergies, depression, chronic headaches, asthma, insomnia, and many other problems. Some cancer and AIDS patients find relief with massage too. It's an increasingly active practice that many claim to be incredibly therapeutic.

Massage isn't just about the body, and most programs emphasize the emotional, creative, and intuitive aspects of the field. You'll learn how to be receptive to your clients and how to be sensitive to their needs—incorporating lighting, music, and/or aromatherapy to enhance the experience. You'll become skilled in interpersonal communication and even learn the basics of business practice. (And you'll be eagerly sought after by your roommates and friends for your killer back rubs.) By the looks on the faces of your clients, you'll soon see this is not a thankless job. Most often, they can't thank you enough!

If You Like Massage Therapy, You May Also Like . . .

Chiropractic, counseling, dance, dietetics, entrepreneurship, mental health services, physical therapy, psychology, respiratory therapy

SAMPLE COLLEGE CURRICULUM FOR MASSAGE THERAPY

Anatomy and Physiology

Business Development

Business Ethics

Cellular Biology

Kinesiology

Pathology

Principles of Acupressure

Therapeutic Massage

Suggested High School Prep for Massage Therapy

The best preparation for a major in massage therapy is a strong variety of courses in the humanities, such as philosophy, English, religion, and languages. Courses in anatomy and health will be useful as well. A solid background in math and sciences will round out your foundation and give you a good head start in your massage therapy studies. (Giving massages to your friends and family is also a good way to prepare—and you'll be popular, too.)

Fun Facts

Old Hand

How old is massage? Pretty old: Pictures of people receiving massages are even painted on Egyptian tombs!

(Source: www.massagehealththerapy.com)

Body Work

"Massage is to the human body what a tune-up is to a car."

—*Chicago Tribune*, April 6, 1995

Careers and Salary

The starting salary for a massage therapist usually depends on how you choose to use your skills. Massage therapists in private practice are generally paid by the hour, and depending on what sort of massage you do and what part of the country you live in, fees can range from $15 to more than $32 per hour. You may also be employed by sports facilities, luxury resorts, and other groups, in which case your salary will depend on your experience and qualifications.

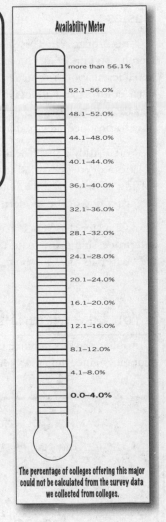

Availability Meter

more than 56.1%

52.1–56.0%

48.1–52.0%

44.1–48.0%

40.1–44.0%

36.1–40.0%

32.1–36.0%

28.1–32.0%

24.1–28.0%

20.1–24.0%

16.1–20.0%

12.1–16.0%

8.1–12.0%

4.1–8.0%

0.0–4.0%

The percentage of colleges offering this major could not be calculated from the survey data we collected from colleges.

CAREER OPTIONS

Massage Therapist   **Physical Therapist**

MATERIALS SCIENCE

Basics

The Bronze Age. The Stone Age. We wouldn't have such metallic names for eras like these if materials weren't so important to our daily lives. Materials science is a major that explores these materials in depth. You'll learn about the structure and properties of materials and the relationships between them. You'll learn what controls and affects internal structures and the processes that can alter them. Why materials act the way they do will be one area of concentration; how materials are processed will be another. You'll also learn how to produce new materials and the variety of uses for existing ones.

You'll study a great deal of physics and chemistry in this major, and you'll be immersed in a great deal of laboratory work. You'll learn how to apply mathematics to your studies, and you'll do a lot of problem-solving using your newfound skills. Communications technology, the computer industry, and biotechnology are just a few of the modern fields that require the expertise of materials scientists and engineers.

As a materials science major, you'll become skilled at identifying, characterizing, manufacturing, designing, and processing many materials we use in our everyday life. Cornell University suggests that we are living in the "Materials Age," so you can be confident that your major will lead to an exciting career.

If You Like Materials Science, You May Also Like . . .

Applied physics, ceramic engineering, ceramics, chemical engineering, chemistry, metallurgical engineering, mineral engineering, petroleum engineering, physics, textile engineering

SAMPLE COLLEGE CURRICULUM FOR MATERIALS SCIENCE

Calculus

Engineering Graphics

Engineering Mechanics

Fracture and Fatigue of Engineering Materials

Imperfections in Crystalline Solids

Mechanics of Composites

Micromechanics

Physics

Statistics

Stress Analysis

Transmission Electron Microscopy

Waves and Diffraction in Solids

Suggested High School Prep for Materials Science

To prepare for a major in materials science, try to take a variety of math and science courses. Physics and chemistry courses will be especially helpful, and make sure your math is upper-level, like calculus, trigonometry, and analytic geometry. Don't forget your English classes—good engineers must also be good communicators.

Fun Facts

For More Information . . .

Interested in what different universities are researching in the field of materials science? Then check out the Materials Research Science and Engineering site (www.mrsec.wisc.edu/), which lists research highlights from universities all over the country. You might get some ideas for your own research—or at least get a glimpse of what's ahead!

What's in a Name?

Different materials have defined various periods of history. Here are just a few of these time periods and the processes or materials that helped them flourish.

300,000 B.C./B.C.E.—Flint

5500 B.C./B.C.E.—Native gold and copper

5000 B.C./B.C.E.—Introduction of fire and hammering of copper to change properties (beginning of materials processing)

4000 B.C./B.C.E.—Melting and casting of metals (materials processing and shaping)

3500 B.C./B.C.E.—Reduction of copper from its ore (metallurgy)

3000 B.C./B.C.E.—Bronze

1450 B.C./B.C.E.—Iron making

1500 C.E.—Iron made with blast furnace

1855 C.E.—Steel making

1886 C.E.—Electrochemical extraction of aluminum

1939 C.E.—Nylon, plastics

1940s C.E.—Silicon technology

1955 C.E.—New plastics

1950s C.E.—High-temperature alloy developments, nickel-based alloy developments

1960s C.E.—Smaller silicon wafers

1970s C.E.—Materials processing of recycled scrap iron

1980s C.E.—Ceramic superconductors

(Source: The Materials Science and Engineering Career Resource Center)

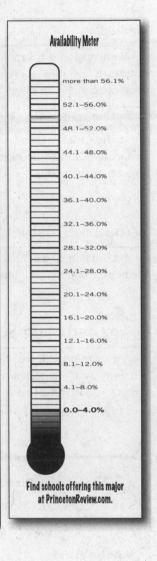

Availability Meter

more than 56.1%

52.1–56.0%

48.1–52.0%

44.1–48.0%

40.1–44.0%

36.1–40.0%

32.1–36.0%

28.1–32.0%

24.1–28.0%

20.1–24.0%

16.1–20.0%

12.1–16.0%

8.1–12.0%

4.1–8.0%

0.0–4.0%

Find schools offering this major at PrincetonReview.com.

Careers and Salary

Starting salaries for materials science majors are generally $40,000 to $50,000. The salary will greatly depend on how they use their skills, what sort of company they choose to work for, and how much experience they've had.

CAREER OPTIONS

Chemical Engineer   Structural Engineer   Textile Manufacturer

Chemist

MATHEMATICS

Basics

Mathematicians have a romance with numbers. They deal with the hard realities of statistics and the fragile beauty of complex theorems. Some become actuaries, economists, and businesspeople, working with concrete concepts. Others become professors, working with almost poetic abstractions and theories.

In short, there is lots of life beyond trig class.

Mathematics majors study exactly what you'd expect: lots and lots of math. Some math programs offer opportunities to combine a degree in mathematics with one in business, economics, physics, or computer science. As you consider schools, make sure to check the available options.

If You Like Mathematics, You May Also Like . . .

Accounting, actuarial science, applied mathematics, applied physics, business administration and management, computer and information science, computer systems analysis, physics, statistics

Suggested High School Prep for Mathematics

Are you sitting down? Because this is a shocker. . . try to get as many advanced math courses under your belt as you can. Experience with computers and programming languages is also good. Classes in logic and physics will help you understand some of the more practical applications of complex math.

SAMPLE COLLEGE CURRICULUM FOR MATHEMATICS

Abstract Algebra

Calculus I–IV

Complex Variables

Differential Equations

Geometry

History of Mathematics

Linear Algebra

Mathematical Analysis

Mathematical Statistics

Number Theory

Vector Analysis

Fun Facts

Math Humor

A physicist, a biologist, and a mathematician sat at a table at a street café looking at the house on the other side of the street. They watched two people go into the house. They ordered some coffee and waited. An hour later, they saw three people emerge from the house. This observation set the table abuzz.

The physicist shook her head and said, "Our original measurement wasn't accurate. There are three of them."

"No," said the biologist, "we weren't wrong. Obviously, they reproduced."

The mathematician smiled at his friends. "Don't be ridiculous," he laughed. "You aren't thinking clearly. Now, if exactly one person enters the house, it will be empty again."

The Perfect Science

"If all the arts aspire to the condition of music, all the sciences aspire to the condition of mathematics."

—George Santayana

Famous People Who Majored in Mathematics

John Maynard Keynes (economist, Cambridge University), J. Pierpont Morgan (tycoon, University of Gottingen), Alexander Solzhenitsyn (novelist, University of Rostov-na-Donu), Art Garfunkel (musician, Columbia University), Harry Blackmun (Associate Justice of the U.S. Supreme Court, Harvard University), David Dinkins (former mayor of New York City, Howard University), Tom Lehrer (musician/comedian, Harvard University), Bram Stoker (author of *Dracula*; Trinity College, Dublin)

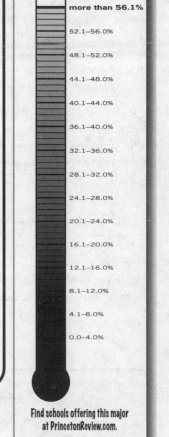

Availability Meter

more than 56.1%

52.1–56.0%

48.1–52.0%

44.1–48.0%

40.1–44.0%

36.1–40.0%

32.1–36.0%

28.1–32.0%

24.1–28.0%

20.1–24.0%

16.1–20.0%

12.1–16.0%

8.1–12.0%

4.1–8.0%

0.0–4.0%

Find schools offering this major at PrincetonReview.com.

Careers and Salary

The starting salary for a newly minted mathematics major can range from $37,000 to $45,000.

CAREER OPTIONS

Actuary	Avionics Technician	Mathematician
Astronomer	Bank Officer	Physicist
Attorney	Bookkeeper	Statistician
Auditor	Computer Operator/Programmer	

MECHANICAL ENGINEERING

Basics

"Diversity" is the key word when it comes to mechanical engineering. There are many fields in which mechanical engineering plays a role: automated manufacturing, environmental control, transportation, biomedical fields, computer fields, fossil fuel and nuclear power . . . the list goes on and on. Mechanical engineers are concerned with imagining and implementing programs and devices that improve our world and our movement in it. A mechanical engineering major's designing endeavors are diverse, from tiny measuring instruments to huge aircraft carriers or power plants. They are also involved in testing, evaluating, distributing, and marketing the devices they and their colleagues create.

If all of these challenges appeal to you, mechanical engineering might be a major to consider. As with other engineering programs, your course of study may include one or more semesters of a cooperative education program, in which you will be employed full-time with an appropriate company. A cooperative is a great way to put your knowledge to use, and often times your co-op job leads to post-graduation employment.

If You Like Mechanical Engineering, You May Also Like . . .

Aerospace engineering, agricultural and biological engineering, applied mathematics, applied physics, architectural engineering, aviation, ceramic engineering, chemical engineering, chemistry, engineering design, engineering mechanics, environmental and environmental health engineering, industrial engineering, metallurgical engineering, mineral engineering, nuclear engineering, ocean engineering, petroleum engineering

Suggested High School Prep for Mechanical Engineering

Science and math courses will be most helpful if you're looking toward a mechanical engineering major. Try to take higher-level courses if they're offered, such as calculus and any AP classes. No matter how much you get teased, go to science fairs and other scientific competitions—be that geek whose entries always win. Nothing prepares you for a mechanical engineering major better than taking the things you learn in your chemistry and physics classes and putting them to practical use.

SAMPLE COLLEGE CURRICULUM FOR MECHANICAL ENGINEERING

Electronic Devices

Engineering Graphics and Programming

Kinematics

Materials Science

Math courses such as calculus and analytic geometry

Mechanical Design

Science courses such as chemistry and physics

Statistics and Strength of Materials

Thermodynamics

Fun Facts

The Marvelous Copy Machine . . .

Ever been an intern? If so, you know a helluva lot about making copies. You can thank mechanical engineers for the technology that enables you to do so. The dry-copying process was invented in 1937. This process, according to the American Society of Mechanical Engineers, involved "applying an electrostatic charge on a plate coated with a photoconductive material." Chester Carlson, a patent attorney, created the process, and in the next year he managed to transfer an image to paper. With the foundations laid, mechanical engineers from the Battelle Memorial Institute and the Haloid Company stepped in and improved the process. The first Xerox machine, the Model A, appeared in 1949.

(Source: The American Society of Mechanical Engineers)

. . . and the Marvelous Player Piano

Mechanical engineers have their musical side—they were responsible for much of the technology that gave us the music rolls for player pianos. The master rolls used in player pianos were often recordings of performances by famous musicians—Stravinsky, Gershwin, and Ellington, for example. Recording their playing was the job of the Q-R-S Marking Piano, which was developed in 1912. This piano recorded actual piano playing by using a stylus, a carbon cylinder, and a roll of paper to record the notes; the carbon marks were later punched out. The machine was created by Melville Clark, from Chicago, and the Q-R-S piano's popularity lasted from 1912 to 1931, with a brief resurgence in 1972.

(Source: The American Society of Mechanical Engineers)

Careers and Salary

Although starting salaries depend a great deal on where you live and how you use your degree, you can expect to earn an average salary in the low-fifties. Salaries can be higher and lower depending on experience and level of education.

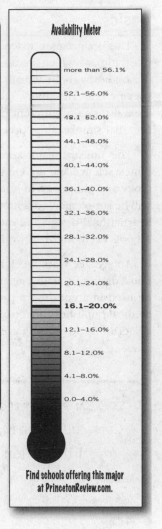

Availability Meter

more than 56.1%

52.1–56.0%

48.1–52.0%

44.1–48.0%

40.1–44.0%

36.1–40.0%

32.1–36.0%

28.1–32.0%

24.1–28.0%

20.1–24.0%

16.1–20.0%

12.1–16.0%

8.1–12.0%

4.1–8.0%

0.0–4.0%

Find schools offering this major at PrincetonReview.com.

CAREER OPTIONS

Aerospace Engineer

Air Force National Guard

Air Force (Officer)

Army National Guard

Army (Officer)

Coast Guard (Officer)

Environmentalist/
    Environmental Scientist

Machinist

Marines (Officer)

Professor

Quality Assurance Engineer

Robotics Engineer

Structural Engineer

MEDICAL ILLUSTRATION

Basics

This is a program where art meets organs. It may seem like an unusual combination at first, but medical illustrations—which are used in a variety of contexts and fields—help us understand what's going on inside our bodies without actually having to open them up. Medical illustrators are professional artists with a very specific skill: The ability to convey scientific information in their work. This could entail anything from crafting a diagram of different parts of the brain and their unique functions to creating a multimedia presentation that simulates the process of how a cancerous tumor affects the body over time.

This unusual major attracts students with an amazing aptitude and interest in two very specific disciplines: science and art. On the scientific side, you'll learn human anatomy, histology, neuroanatomy, embryology, and pathology. To hone your artistic and visual communication skills, classes in drawing and painting will be supplemented with those in computer imaging and animation, medical photography, graphic design, instructional design and multimedia, medical sculpture, surgical orientation, and business practices. Some schools even offer real-world experience programs at area hospitals and museums.

An average work week for a medical illustrator might entail creating illustrations for a med school textbook, drafting a magazine advertisement for a new drug or treatment, and constructing a moving model to be used in a courtroom presentation. Graduates often start their own consulting businesses or work for medical publishers of consumer books and textbooks, medical colleges, research centers, hospitals, medical associations, advertising agencies, law firms, or scientific museums.

SAMPLE COLLEGE CURRICULUM FOR MEDICAL ILLUSTRATION

Anatomy and Physiology

Anatomy for the Artist

Biology

Chemistry

Computer Illustration

Digital Imaging

Electronic Media Production

Graphic Design

Illustration as Communication and Interpretive Expression

Life Drawing

Open studio classes

Scientific Illustration

Vertebrate Anatomy

If You Like Medical Illustration, You May Also Like . . .

Anatomy, art, art therapy, biochemistry, biology, biomedical science, chemistry, diagnostic medical sonography, drawing, graphic design, illustration, nursing, painting, photography, pre-medicine, sculpture

Suggested High School Prep for Medical Illustration

Because this unique field requires skills in both art and science, you should take all of the classes that your school offers in these disciplines. Colleges are going to assume you have a strong science background, so don't shy away from advanced science and math classes. Work experience or community service involving art, graphic design, communications, research, hospital work, or other medical or health-related jobs could work to your advantage as well.

Fun Facts

Meet Others Like You

The Association of Medical Illustrators (www.medical-illustrators.org) has a membership category for students. Joining will give you access to the AMI's online newsletter, a subscription to the *Journal of Biocommunication*, a job hotline, and a network of professionals in the field.

Like Frog Legs?

Get the inside story on the anatomy of a frog from several websites and home programs that have entire virtual dissections. One site, Foguts.com, has a virtual dissection service subscription that lets you interact with the dissection tools and process for a frog, squid, and owl pellet. The service costs $75 for a personal home use subscription. If nothing else, the free demos are illustrative and informative—a feat that any medical illustrator would appreciate.

Careers and Salary

The average starting salary for a medical illustration graduate is about $35,000 to $45,000 a year. Experienced salaried illustrators usually earn between $45,000 and $75,000 a year. Many medical illustrators supplement their income with freelance work.

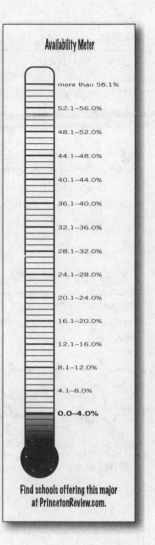

Availability Meter

more than 56.1%

52.1–56.0%

48.1–52.0%

44.1–48.0%

40.1–44.0%

36.1–40.0%

32.1–36.0%

28.1–32.0%

24.1–28.0%

20.1–24.0%

16.1–20.0%

12.1–16.0%

8.1–12.0%

4.1–8.0%

0.0–4.0%

Find schools offering this major at PrincetonReview.com.

CAREER OPTIONS

Artist	Graphic Designer	Photographer
Digital Artist	Illustrator	

MEDICAL TECHNOLOGY

Basics

If you like bodily fluids, we've got just the major for you. Medical technology, or clinical laboratory science as it is frequently called, is the study and analysis of bodily fluids and tissues. It encompasses a number of different medical specialties, including hematology, microbiology, immunology, immunohematology, and clinical chemistry. It's a fairly rigorous major that will almost assuredly lead to a secure professional career. It's a career that will require you to be quick, careful, and thorough.

Upon graduating into the real world, most medical technicians work in hospitals and laboratories, primarily in five specialty areas: blood banking, chemistry, hematology, immunology, and microbiology. They use precision electronic instruments and high-powered microscopes, and they assist doctors in diagnosing and treating diseases by performing a range of tests and laboratory procedures on blood and other such bodily fluids in order to find chemicals, microorganisms, proteins, and other substances.

If You Like Medical Technology, You May Also Like . . .

Biochemistry, biology, cell biology, chemistry, circulation technology, genetics, gerontology, mental health services, microbiology, neurobiology, neuroscience, nursing, occupational therapy, pharmacology, pharmacy, physical therapy, physiological psychology, premedicine, pre-optometry, pre-veterinary medicine, public health, radiologic technology, rehabilitation services, respiratory therapy

---

SAMPLE COLLEGE CURRICULUM FOR MEDICAL TECHNOLOGY

Biochemistry

Biology

Chemistry

Computer Applications

Hematology

Immunohematology

Internship

Lab Skills

Medical Terminology

Microbiology

Organic Chemistry

Pathology

Physiology

Statistics

Virology

Suggested High School Prep for Medical Technology

If you are thinking about majoring in medical technology, take as many chemistry and biology courses as you can. Also, because math pervades the physical sciences, you should definitely take several math courses. You also want to know your way around a lab as well as possible. If you think you might want to major in medical technology, try to get a job or a volunteer position at a local hospital or clinic. Finally, get used to the sight of blood.

Fun Facts

Nice Work If You Can Get It

According to the Jobs Rated Almanac by Les Krantz, medical technology is a great career path. Medical technologists ranked sixteenth out of 250 jobs based on factors including salary, stress levels, work environment, outlook, employment security, and physical demands.

Blood 101

Here is an interactive website where all of your blood-related curiosities can be fulfilled: www.Biology.arizona.edu/human_bio/problem_sets/blood_types/Intro.html.

Careers and Salary

Starting salaries for medical technology majors just out of college range from $21,000 to about $35,000 per year. The national average salary for newly minted medical technologists is $27,000 or so. Experienced medical technicians earn salaries ranging from $40,000 to $56,000 annually.

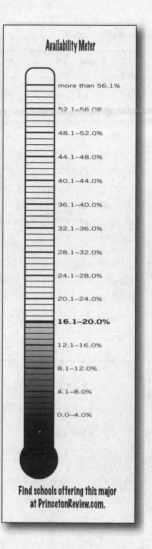

Availability Meter

more than 56.1%

52.1–56.0%

48.1–52.0%

44.1–48.0%

40.1–44.0%

36.1–40.0%

32.1–36.0%

28.1–32.0%

24.1–28.0%

20.1–24.0%

16.1–20.0%

12.1–16.0%

8.1–12.0%

4.1–8.0%

0.0–4.0%

Find schools offering this major at PrincetonReview.com.

CAREER OPTIONS

Hospice Nurse	Pharmaceutical Sales Representative	Physician Assistant
Nurse	Physician	

MEDIEVAL AND RENAISSANCE STUDIES

Basics

Medieval and Renaissance studies is an interdisciplinary major that encompasses study in (but is certainly not limited to) history, art history, philosophy, literature, music, and languages. It's a perfect major if you're interested in gaining a broad base of knowledge of two periods of time that still profoundly affect the way we interpret society and culture.

The Middle Ages and Renaissance span a period from about the fifth century to about the sixteenth century, and most of the action involved (including the invention of the printing press, the building of the Duomo in Florence, and the Protestant Reformation) took place in Europe. Interdependence of subjects and general knowledge—in contrast to the specialization of professions today—were the hallmarks of these times, so that poets might be priests, theologians might be scientists, and so forth. It's not surprising then, that this major will expose you to so many different fields; it is their connection to each other that most characterized this time period.

Many colleges offer Medieval and Renaissance studies as a major; many others offer it as a minor, certificate, or concentration. Whatever the case, if you're interested in learning about the origins of our modern world, you'll love Medieval and Renaissance studies.

SAMPLE COLLEGE CURRICULUM FOR MEDIEVAL AND RENAISSANCE STUDIES

Art History

Chaucer's *The Canterbury Tales*

Court of Charlemagne

Early Christian and Byzantine Art

Elizabethan Shakespeare: Text and Performance

French Literature

Golden Age Drama

Gothic Paris

History of Medieval Europe

Literature from the Middle Ages

Manuscript Studies

Medieval and Renaissance Prose Fiction

Rome and the Papacy since the Schism

The Italian Renaissance and the Reformation

If You Like Medieval and Renaissance Studies, You May Also Like . . .

African American studies, African studies, American studies, ancient studies, art history, Asian American studies, Biblical studies, church music, East Asian studies, East European studies, English, English literature, French, German, history, Italian, Jewish studies, Latin American studies, Middle Eastern studies, philosophy, religious studies, South Asian studies, Southeast Asian studies, theology, women's studies

Suggested High School Prep for Medieval and Renaissance Studies

English, history, religion, and philosophy courses will give you a strong foundation for this multidisciplinary major. Art and language courses—especially Latin—will be very valuable as well.

Fun Facts

Did You Know?

Many people enjoy hosting Medieval weddings complete with Medieval dress, food, and customs. But some don't realize that many marriage customs actually have their roots in ancient traditions. For example, wedding cakes trace their origin to the breaking of wheat or barley cakes over the bride's head, which was symbolic of fertility. The tradition evolved into stacking many small cakes into a tall tower that the newly married couple was required to kiss above. If they could do it without knocking the tower down, it was a sign of good luck. This stack of cakes eventually began to be iced with white sugar, and it's easy to see how today's wedding cake sprang from there.

(Source: *A Natural History of Love* by Diane Ackerman)

Careers and Salary

Starting salaries for Medieval and Renaissance studies majors vary too widely to estimate. Most students choose this major as a second major or concentration; there are really no jobs specifically for Medieval and Renaissance studies graduates. Liberal arts majors in general can expect to earn $20,000 to $30,000, but again, the career possibilities are wide open.

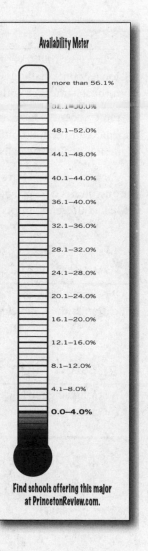

Availability Meter

more than 56.1%

52.1–56.0%

48.1–52.0%

44.1–48.0%

40.1–44.0%

36.1–40.0%

32.1–36.0%

28.1–32.0%

24.1–28.0%

20.1–24.0%

16.1–20.0%

12.1–16.0%

8.1–12.0%

4.1–8.0%

0.0–4.0%

Find schools offering this major at PrincetonReview.com.

CAREER OPTIONS

Actor	Curator	Teacher
Antiques Dealer	Philosopher	Theologian
Archaeologist	Professor	

MENTAL HEALTH SERVICES

Basics

Every year millions of Americans find themselves in need of mental health support. Mental health professionals continually develop new and innovative means to address the needs of mental health patients, from those suffering with depression to those with bipolar personality disorders.

Only recently have we begun to treat mental health problems as medical cases that demand well-informed and trained individuals. As a mental health services major you can be part of a growing network of mental health specialists who respond to the needs of patients with mental disorders.

Part science and part social work, a major in mental health services outfits you with the skills and education you need to provide a very necessary and important service to those who require it. It's a major that makes a difference in people's lives.

If You Like Mental Health Services, You May Also Like . . .

Biopsychology, child care, child development, clinical psychology, communication disorders, counseling, education, human development, nursing, psychology, social psychology, social work, sociology

Suggested High School Prep for Mental Health Services

A strong science background and the ability to effectively communicate with others are necessary skills for success in mental health services. You should try to master as much biology, chemistry, physics, and psychology as you can.

> **SAMPLE COLLEGE CURRICULUM FOR MENTAL HEALTH SERVICES**
>
> Aging and Mental Health
>
> Case Management
>
> Clinical Reasoning
>
> Community Contexts and Policy Directions
>
> Evaluation and Research Methods
>
> Health Research Methods
>
> Management Issues for Therapists
>
> Mental Health in Childhood and Adolescence
>
> Neuroscience
>
> Wellness and Community Development

Fun Facts

Did You Know?

More than 51 million Americans have a mental disorder in a single year, although only about 8 million (16 percent) seek treatment.

(Source: National Institute of Mental Health & Center for Mental Health Services)

And It's No Easier on the Kids

Less than one-third of the children under age 18 with a serious emotional disturbance receive mental health services. Often, the services are inappropriate.

(Source: Children's Defense Fund; Center for Mental Health Services-Mental Health, United States, 1994)

Careers and Salary

The starting salary for mental health counselors usually ranges between $22,000 and $30,000.

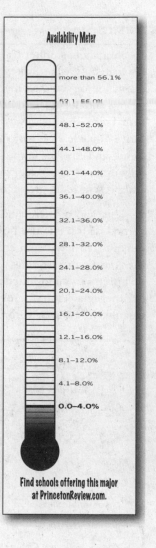

Availability Meter

more than 56.1%

52.1–56.0%

48.1–52.0%

44.1–48.0%

40.1–44.0%

36.1–40.0%

32.1–36.0%

28.1–32.0%

24.1–28.0%

20.1–24.0%

16.1–20.0%

12.1–16.0%

8.1–12.0%

4.1–8.0%

0.0–4.0%

Find schools offering this major at PrincetonReview.com.

CAREER OPTIONS

Career Counselor

Child Care Worker

Consultant

Criminologist

Guidance Counselor

Hospital Administrator

Social Worker

Teacher

MERCHANDISING AND BUYING OPERATIONS

Basics

Shopaholics unite! If the mall could be your second home—not for the sale racks, but because you're fascinated by what makes people buy what they do and how their decisions are influenced—have we got the major for you. As a merchandising and buying operations major, you'll explore the customers' innermost desires and needs—and how best to meet them. You'll keep up with the latest trends, examine how the fickle market responds to various factors, and discover what it takes for retailers and wholesalers to survive and thrive. You'll learn how to analyze merchandising data and be able to crunch numbers to determine possible trends and changes in the market. You'll learn how to plan sales, how to manage inventory, and how to skillfully evaluate and select merchandise. You'll gain the skills necessary to artfully (and wisely) develop, buy, and present retail products, from fashion to home furnishings.

The field of merchandising and buying operations (often listed individually at some colleges) is concerned with the entire buying experience. That includes all the decisions and elements that go into a customer's journey—from entering the store to examining the merchandise to making a decision to making the actual purchase. Plus, you'll be set to build an entire career out of shopping if that's your wish. This major will prepare you to function as a professional buyer of resale products and product lines for stores, chains, or other retail empires. You'll be primed for any number of careers in the merchandising world—a sales representative, a buyer, a store manager, or a boutique owner. You might go the route of business analysis or find yourself involved in catalog retail. The possibilities are far-ranging and exciting, and your newly developed eye for smart merchandising strategies will put you on the path to success.

SAMPLE COLLEGE CURRICULUM FOR MERCHANDISING AND BUYING OPERATIONS

Accounting

Buyer Behavior

Consumer Studies

Customer Service

Dress, Society, and Culture

Macroeconomics

Mathematics

Microeconomics

Nonstore Retailing

Principles of Marketing

Private Label Merchandising

Retail Buying

Retail Promotion

Textile Analysis

Visual Merchandising

If You Like Merchandising and Buying Operations, You May Also Like . . .

Accounting, advertising, business administration and management, entrepreneurship, finance, graphic design, human resources management, international business, marketing, mass communication, operations management, visual communication

Suggested High School Prep for Merchandising and Buying Operations

To prepare for a major in merchandising and buying operations, you should build a foundation of knowledge in math, science, languages, and the humanities. Communication skills are vital to this major, so take English courses to strengthen your writing and speaking skills. Math courses will prepare you for the business side of this major, and art courses will prepare you for the creative side. Take courses that challenge and interest you.

Fun Facts

Did You Know?

The songs chosen for Muzak sound systems aren't chosen randomly. In fact, Muzak practices its own form of psychology on the principle that the songs people hear as they shop can greatly influence their moods and, as a result, what they buy. A study done in a British wine shop showed that when French music was playing, people bought far more French wine. When German music was playing, they purchased more German wine. The bottles were similar in character and price—only the music had changed.

(Source originally from: www.litmuszine.com)

Good Read

Consider checking out *Why We Buy: The Science of Shopping* by Paco Underhill. The author and his consulting firm, Envirosell, have observed more than 900 aspects of interaction between shopper and store, applying anthropological techniques to the way people experience the retail environment.

Careers and Salary

The starting salary for merchandising and buying operations majors varies widely and depends on how you choose to apply your skills. Students entering their first jobs, with little experience, can expect to earn from $20,000 to just more than $30,000.

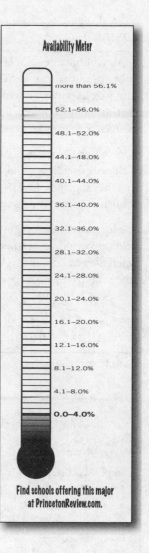

Availability Meter

more than 56.1%

52.1–56.0%

48.1–52.0%

44.1–48.0%

40.1–44.0%

36.1–40.0%

32.1–36.0%

28.1–32.0%

24.1–28.0%

20.1–24.0%

16.1–20.0%

12.1–16.0%

8.1–12.0%

4.1–8.0%

0.0–4.0%

Find schools offering this major
at PrincetonReview.com.

CAREER OPTIONS

Business Analyst	Department Sales Manager	Store Manager
Buyer	Product Developer	Supplier
Catalog Retailer	Sales Representative	Teacher
Consultant	Small Business Owner	Visual Merchandiser

METALLURGICAL ENGINEERING

Basics

Metallurgical engineering is a broad field that deals with all sorts of metal-related areas. The three main branches of this major are physical metallurgy, extractive metallurgy, and mineral processing. Physical metallurgy deals with problem-solving: You'll develop the sorts of metallic alloys needed for different types of manufacturing and construction. Extractive metallurgy involves extracting metal from ore. Mineral processing involves gathering mineral products from the earth's crust.

As a metallurgical engineering major, you'll learn the fundamentals of all three fields, as well as the basics of engineering in general. We need metals to make our society function; metals make up important parts of cars, bikes, planes, buildings, even toothpaste tubes. Your knowledge of the production, design, and manufacturing of these metals and mineral products can be rewarding and exciting.

Most metallurgical engineering programs will offer the opportunity to participate in a cooperative education program, an arrangement in which students spend a semester or more doing engineering work with a metallurgical company. Many of these co-op jobs can become actual jobs after graduation, and the experience will make you a more valuable prospective employee.

If You Like Metallurgical Engineering, You May Also Like . . .

Aerospace engineering, agricultural and biological engineering, applied mathematics, applied physics, architectural engineering, ceramic engineering, chemical engineering, civil engineering, computer engineering, engineering design, engineering mechanics, environmental and environmental health engineering, geological engineering, industrial engineering, mechanical engineering, mineral engineering, nuclear engineering, ocean engineering, petroleum engineering, welding engineering

Suggested High School Prep for Metallurgical Engineering

As with most engineering majors, you'll be taking a heavy load of math and science courses. Your best preparation will be advanced courses in calculus, analytic geometry, trigonometry, physics, chemistry, and biology.

SAMPLE COLLEGE CURRICULUM FOR METALLURGICAL ENGINEERING

Chemistry

Corrosion Engineering

Energy Resources

Engineering Mechanics

Experimental Techniques in Metallurgy

High-Temperature Chemical Processing

Hydrometallurgy

Materials Science and Engineering

Mineral Industries and the Environment

Mineral Processing

Physical Metallurgy

Physics

Statistics

Fun Facts

Did You Know?

Two facts about silver from the Silver Institute:

- Twenty-five percent of the world's production of silver is used for photography.
- Ninety-five percent of silver is used for industry, photography, and jewelry/silverware.

Remember to Recycle

Aluminum is a fascinating metal. In a polished state it is even more reflective than a mirror, and it is an excellent conductor of heat and electricity. Aluminum ore is mined in Africa, South America, Australia, and the West Indies. It can be recycled an infinite number of times without any adverse effects to its quality.

(Source: The International Aluminum Institute)

Careers and Salary

Starting salaries for metallurgical engineers fall mostly in the upper forties. Salaries depend greatly on where you live, how you choose to use your degree, and how much experience you've had through internships or cooperative education programs.

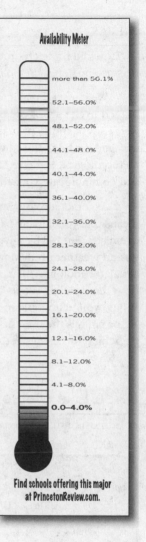

Availability Meter

more than 56.1%

52.1–56.0%

48.1–52.0%

44.1–48.0%

40.1–44.0%

36.1–40.0%

32.1–36.0%

28.1–32.0%

24.1–28.0%

20.1–24.0%

16.1–20.0%

12.1–16.0%

8.1–12.0%

4.1–8.0%

0.0–4.0%

Find schools offering this major at PrincetonReview.com.

CAREER OPTIONS

Civil Engineer	Robotics Engineer	Structural Engineer
Quality Assurance Engineer		

METEOROLOGY

Basics

How did the meteorologist on Channel 4 know that it was going to rain like cats and dogs on Tuesday? Because he's an incredible magician, that's how.

Well, maybe magic doesn't have that much to do with it. But you could say meteorologists are well trained in the art of predicting the future. Combining studies in math and a range of sciences, meteorologists use "scientific principles to explain, understand, observe, or forecast the earth's atmospheric phenomena and/or how the atmosphere affects the Earth and life on the planet," according to the American Meteorological Society. After four (or, um, five) years, you too could be in a position to "read" the weather and communicate your findings to an eager and devoted public.

As a meteorology major, you'll be working under the broader umbrella of atmospheric science. This means that you'll likely have access to a spectrum of electives including climatology, oceanography, and geochemistry. But it'll be in your core classes that you get down and dirty with the techniques of climate analysis and weather prediction. You'll become an expert at working with the computer, satellite, radar, and other aerial technologies that are the heart of modern meteorology. You'll also learn about the connections between weather events and human activities; in other words, if it looks like a nasty storm is brewing, what should you tell people to do? Training in broadcast meteorology is certainly available for people who think TV or radio is the direction they want to go. That being said, remember that most meteorological work goes on behind the scenes at the National Weather Service, media outlets, governmental bodies, and private firms.

If You Like Meteorology, You May Also Like...

Atmospheric science, ecology, environmental science, geology, geophysics, natural resources conservation, oceanography, physics, planetary science, sustainable resource management

SAMPLE COLLEGE CURRICULUM

Atmospheric Dynamics

Broadcast Meteorology

Climatology

Dynamic Meteorology

Introduction to Atmospheric Science

Meteorological Technology

Physical Meteorology

Precipitation Physics

Severe Weather

Weather Analysis

Weather Observation

Weather and Climate Processes

Suggested High School Curriculum for Meteorology

The more science and math classes you take the better. Computer science and technology-based courses are good ideas too, since a lot of a meteorologist's work involves tinkering with techno-gadgets. If you think you might want to be a broadcast meteorologist, then it's a good idea to take courses like English or speech communications that will help improve your way with words.

Fun Facts

The Dayton Daily News in Ohio published a list of severe-weather-related myths compiled by meteorologist Jamie Simpson. Here are a few of the misconceptions that he cleared up:

Myth: Mobile homes attract tornadoes.

Truth: Mobile homes are not more likely to be hit, they are just more vulnerable to wind damage because of their weaker construction.

Myth: Tornadoes can suck things up from the ground as they [did] at the beginning of the movie Twister.

Truth: This is not true. That is why if you are stuck outside in the path of a tornado, you should lie in a ditch. But always cover your head to protect yourself from flying debris.

Myth: Lightning never strikes the same place twice.

Truth: Lightning can and does strike the same place numerous times. The following strike will not be immediate, but once electrical charges build up again, a second strike is possible.

Myth: It is the rubber tires on a car that keeps you safe from lightning.

Truth: It is the metal frame of the vehicle that provides safety. The electrical current will remain on the outside of the car if lightning strikes it, because the metal offers the path of least resistance for the current to travel into the ground.

(Source: www.daytondailynews.com)

Careers and Salary

The average starting salary for a meteorologist is between $25,000 and $30,000, though some positions can begin as low as $18,000. According to the American Meteorological Society, of broadcast meteorologists at all levels, the average salary is $46,000. This said, about 10 percent are earning less than $20,000, and another 10 percent are pulling in more than $100,000.

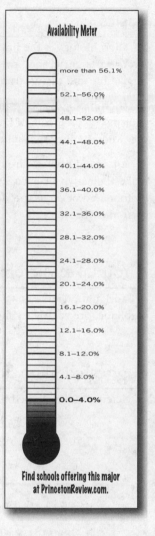

Availability Meter

more than 56.1%
52.1–56.0%
48.1–52.0%
44.1–48.0%
40.1–44.0%
36.1–40.0%
32.1–36.0%
28.1–32.0%
24.1–28.0%
20.1–24.0%
16.1–20.0%
12.1–16.0%
8.1–12.0%
4.1–8.0%
0.0–4.0%

Find schools offering this major at PrincetonReview.com.

CAREER OPTIONS

Environmental Writer

Broadcast (TV or Radio) Meteorologist

Research Meteorologist

Teacher

MICROBIOLOGY

Basics

Microbiology is the branch of biology that deals with the smallest organisms in the world, such as bacteria, yeasts, algae, and protozoa. These organisms rank among the most helpful—and the most harmful—to human life and the environment. Microbiologists work to swing the balance in our favor.

Microbiologists perform extensive medical research, investigating pathogenic (disease-causing) microorganisms. If you dream of finding the cure for cancer, AIDS, or the common cold, this could be the major for you. Microbiologists also help protect crops and purify our drinking water.

An added bonus: Through their work with bacteria and yeasts, microbiology majors can learn how to make their own beer, cheese, yogurt, wine, bread, and pickles. Many microbiologists are, in fact, employed by food and beverage producers to make these very products. Upon graduation, you could even open your own microbrewery.

If You Like Microbiology, You May Also Like . . .

Agricultural and biological engineering, biochemistry, biology, genetics, neurobiology, pharmacology, pre-medicine, pre-veterinary medicine

Suggested High School Prep for Microbiology

Science! Take all the biology and chemistry you can. Advanced mathematics is also recommended.

SAMPLE COLLEGE CURRICULUM FOR MICROBIOLOGY

Biology I–II

Calculus I–II

General Physics I–II

General Chemistry

Organic Chemistry

Microbiology

Microbial Physiology

Genetics

Virology

Fun Facts

For More Information . . .

Find out more about microbiology at the American Society for Microbiology website (www.asm.org).

And You Get Bonus Points for Pronouncing It Correctly

Know your forefathers! Find out more about the father of microbiology, Antony van Leeuwenhoek, at www.Ucmp.berkeley.edu/history/leeuwenhoek.html.

Careers and Salary

The starting salary for a microbiology major fresh out of college ranges from $25,000 to $40,000.

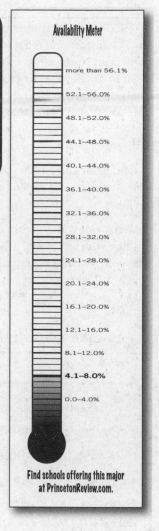

Availability Meter

more than 56.1%

52.1–56.0%

48.1–52.0%

44.1–48.0%

40.1–44.0%

36.1–40.0%

32.1–36.0%

28.1–32.0%

24.1–28.0%

20.1–24.0%

16.1–20.0%

12.1–16.0%

8.1–12.0%

4.1–8.0%

0.0–4.0%

Find schools offering this major at PrincetonReview.com.

CAREER OPTIONS

| Biochemist | Biologist | Geneticist |

MIDDLE EASTERN STUDIES

Basics

Middle Eastern studies is a comparative and interdisciplinary major that focuses on the culture, geography, law, history, and religion of the vast, diverse, and politically pivotal region of the world that extends generally from North Africa to Central Asia and from the Mediterranean to the Indian Ocean. If you choose to major in Middle Eastern studies, you'll learn about the ancient history of this area and, especially, about the emergence of Islam and what has happened since. You'll study and compare the texts of Judaism, Christianity, and Islam, and you'll see how they are very different yet closely intertwined with one another. You'll also be required to undertake an intensive study of one of the many regional languages of the Middle East, usually Arabic, Persian, Turkish, Hindi/Urdu, or ancient Egyptian.

Middle Eastern studies is an interdisciplinary field. Translation: If it's your major, you are likely to end up taking courses in a variety of disciplines including (but certainly not limited to) art, philosophy, literature, and history.

What can you do with a major in Middle Eastern studies? You can be in the foreign service, of course. Just like with any liberal arts major, though, you can do virtually anything. A major in Middle Eastern studies will mold you into a cultural critic, and it will enhance your abilities to think, write, speak, and do research, which will take you far.

If You Like Middle Eastern Studies, You May Also Like . . .

> ### SAMPLE COLLEGE CURRICULUM FOR MIDDLE EASTERN STUDIES
>
> Ancient Israel
>
> Architecture of the Mosque
>
> Culture of the Modern Arab World
>
> Elementary Arabic I–II
>
> History of Islam
>
> History of the Arab World
>
> History of the Ottoman Empire
>
> Intermediate Arabic I–II
>
> Islamic Law
>
> Islamic Philosophy and Theology
>
> Middle East: 1800 to Present
>
> Modern Arabic Literature
>
> Religion and Politics in Islam
>
> The *Qur'an*

African American studies, ancient studies, anthropology, Arabic, art history, Asian American studies, classics, economics, English, geography, Hebrew, historic preservation, history, international relations, Jewish studies, linguistics, Modern Greek, philosophy, political science, religious studies, sociology, theology, urban studies, women's studies

Suggested High School Prep for Microbiology

Middle Eastern Studies is a field that incorporates almost all areas of the humanities, therefore, a diverse course load will prove beneficial to any prospective major. Enrolling in a number of literature and history courses should expose you to some social, political, and cultural facets of the region. They will also improve your analytical and writing skills, abilities this major requires. Additionally, political science courses (if your school offers them) can introduce you to global politics and the international perspectives behind them. Furthermore, the Middle East is an area steeped in religious ties and convictions, so any religion classes offered will also be valuable.

Fun Facts

Pack Your Bags

If you major in Middle Eastern studies, it's a really good idea to take a semester (or two or three) abroad. You can study abroad in a number of exciting and fairly exotic places, including Jerusalem, Cairo, and Amman.

Did You Know?

The Arabic term *Islam* means, literally, *surrender*. The essential religious principle of Islam is that the believer (called a Muslim, from the active particle of Islam) accepts surrender to the will of *Allah*, the Arabic term for God.

Careers and Salary

It varies, but the average starting salary for a Middle Eastern studies major is about $24,000 to $30,000 per year.

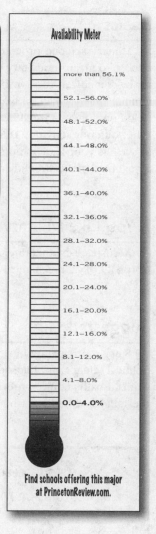

Availability Meter

more than 56.1%

52.1–56.0%

48.1–52.0%

44.1–48.0%

40.1–44.0%

36.1–40.0%

32.1–36.0%

28.1–32.0%

24.1–28.0%

20.1–24.0%

16.1–20.0%

12.1–16.0%

8.1–12.0%

4.1–8.0%

0.0–4.0%

Find schools offering this major
at PrincetonReview.com.

CAREER OPTIONS		
Anthropologist	Archaeologist	Officer
Antiques Dealer	Diplomat/Attaché/Foreign Service	

MILITARY SCIENCE

Basics

Military science programs aim to prepare students for careers in the United States Army. Should you choose to major in military science, you'll be taking traditional university courses while learning how to foster soldier-citizen relationships in an academic setting. Your training in a military science program includes familiarizing yourself with leadership roles, American history, ethics, and military law. There are also several field components; you'll be participating in rifle shooting, running obstacle courses, rappelling, and many other outdoor activities. During your college experience you'll be working to improve your physical fitness as well as your leadership skills. Generally, many activities are held outside the university, such as visiting actual battlefields or studying in other army-run programs such as airborne and air assault training.

If You Like Military Science, You May Also Like . . .

Aerospace engineering, Air Force R.O.T.C., Army R.O.T.C., aviation, cell biology, civil engineering, Marine Corps R.O.T.C., mechanical engineering, naval architecture, Navy R.O.T.C.

Suggested High School Prep for Military Science

Since participating in a military science program most often includes taking traditional courses, English, political science, or philosophy will give you a good foundation on which to build. Also, military science programs usually require proficiency in writing, American history, and computer skills, so any courses related to these fields will be valuable.

> ### SAMPLE COLLEGE CURRICULUM FOR MILITARY SCIENCE
>
> Applied Leadership
>
> Ethics and Military Law
>
> Field Training Exercises
>
> Leadership Skills
>
> Logistics
>
> Management Skills
>
> Military Management
>
> Military Roles and National Objectives
>
> Physical Fitness
>
> Staff Operations
>
> Writing Memoranda

Fun Facts

How to Fold the United States Flag

Showing respect for our country's symbols is a major part of any military training. Here, the *U.S. Military Guide* provides instructions for folding the U.S. flag:

1. Hold the flag waist high.
2. Fold the flag in half, from bottom to top, folding the lower (striped section) of the flag over the blue field.
3. Fold the flag in half again, from bottom to top (the section with the fold up, to the open edged section).
4. Starting at the end away from the stars, fold the bottom part of the flag (folded section) toward the top, forming a triangle.
5. Fold the outer point of the triangle inward toward the stars, forming another folded triangle.
6. Continue the triangular folding for the entire flag.
7. After folding, tuck the loose end of the flag into the fold on the bottom side.

Tips:

1. Once the flag is completely folded, only the blue field should be visible and it should be folded in the triangular shape of a cocked hat.
2. Flag folding is best accomplished by two people.

Army Officer Appointment Acceptance and Oath of Office

"I (insert name), having been appointed a (insert rank) in the U.S. Army under the conditions indicated in this document, do accept such appointment and do solemnly swear (or affirm) that I will support and defend the Constitution of the United States against all enemies, foreign and domestic, that I will bear true faith and allegiance to the same; that I take this obligation freely, without any mental reservation or purpose of evasion; and that I will well and faithfully discharge the duties of the office on which I am about to enter, so help me God."

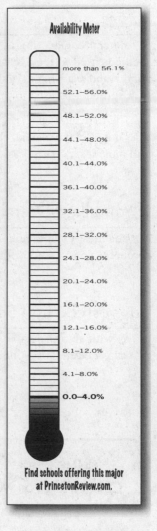

Availability Meter

more than 56.1%

52.1–56.0%

48.1–52.0%

44.1–48.0%

40.1–44.0%

36.1–40.0%

32.1–36.0%

28.1–32.0%

24.1–28.0%

20.1–24.0%

16.1–20.0%

12.1–16.0%

8.1–12.0%

4.1–8.0%

0.0–4.0%

Find schools offering this major at PrincetonReview.com.

Careers and Salary

Depending on location and military ranking, salaries can range anywhere from $19,000 to $29,000.

CAREER OPTIONS

Aerospace Engineer	Army (Officer)	Marines (Officer)
Air Force National Guard	Avionics Technician	Navy (Officer)
Air Force (Officer)	Coast Guard (Officer)	Police Officer/Manager
Army National Guard	FBI Agent	Private Investigator

MINERAL ENGINEERING

Basics

Mineral engineering is the science of mining. Minerals have many important industrial uses, and the methods used to remove them from the earth must be safe and environmentally sound. Mineral engineers survey and plan mines, including systems of ventilation, and participate in their management. They also design the blasts used to open mines. Dy-no-mite!

The mineral engineering major sometimes falls under geological engineering. If your prospective college does not offer the mineral engineering major, ask which of the school's programs covers the science of mining and minerals.

If You Like Mineral Engineering, You May Also Like . . .

Chemical engineering, civil engineering, geology, materials science, metallurgical engineering, natural resources conservation, petroleum engineering

Suggested High School Prep for Mineral Engineering

As with all prospective engineering majors, you'll want to take all the mathematics and science classes you can squeeze into your schedule. Calculus, physics, and chemistry will all be required subjects.

SAMPLE COLLEGE CURRICULUM FOR MINERAL ENGINEERING

Calculus I–II

General Chemistry

Geology

Metallurgy

Mineral Extraction

Mineral Processing

Mining

Physics I–II

Site Investigation

Soil and Rock Mechanics

Surveying

Fun Facts

For More Information . . .

Find out more about the mining industry at www.Mininglife.com.

Careers and Salary

The starting salary for a mineral engineering major fresh out of college is about $45,000.

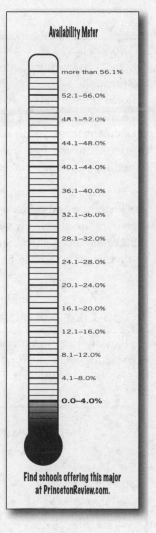

Availability Meter

more than 56.1%

52.1–56.0%

48.1–52.0%

44.1–48.0%

40.1–44.0%

36.1–40.0%

32.1–36.0%

28.1–32.0%

24.1–28.0%

20.1–24.0%

16.1–20.0%

12.1–16.0%

8.1–12.0%

4.1–8.0%

0.0–4.0%

Find schools offering this major at PrincetonReview.com.

CAREER OPTIONS

Petroleum Engineer

MISSIONS

Basics

Do you have a strong faith? Are you committed to spreading the tenets of your religion and to converting others? Then consider a life in missions. Missionaries believe that one of their most important tasks in life is to spread the word of God and bring people into their church, whichever church it may be. Missions as a major is offered mostly at religious universities, and it deals with the fundamentals of evangelism and the ways missionaries work. You'll learn about the biblical basis for mission work and why missionaries do what they do. You'll study your faith and learn how to evangelize effectively. You'll learn about the history of world missions, and the role missions play in contemporary society. You'll learn the skills of church planning, preaching in urban settings, and discipleship.

The main goal of most people who major in missions is to pursue overseas missionary work. To this end, you'll study world religions and see how Christianity affects and is affected by them. You'll learn how to communicate effectively with people of other cultures in order to spread your faith. You'll learn how to deal with economic, political, and spiritual crises that might arise during mission work. Throughout your studies you'll gain an understanding of and a devotion to the importance of worldwide evangelism.

If You Like Missions, You May Also Like . . .

Biblical studies, counseling, international relations, international studies, pastoral studies, peace studies, pre-seminary, religious studies, social work, teaching English as a second language, youth ministries

SAMPLE COLLEGE CURRICULUM FOR MISSIONS

Bible Exegesis

The Christian Life

Christian Thought

Christianity and the World's Religions

Contemporary World Missions

Cultural Anthropology

Discipleship

Expository Preaching

Global Issues on Missions

God and Church

God and History

The Missionary Process

Personal Evangelism

Sociology of Religion

Suggested High School Prep for Missions

Besides getting a solid background in math, science, and the humanities, you can prepare for a missions major by getting involved in faith-based groups in your church, school, or community. The experiences you'll gain will give you an idea of what missions entails. If you attend a religious school, religion courses will be good as well.

Fun Facts

It's a Vocation

The missionary life isn't easy, but it's what many people feel they are called to do. The Church of Jesus Christ of Latter-day Saints is especially devoted to missionary work, and they adhere to this general schedule when they are on a mission.

6:30 A.M. Arise

7:00 A.M. Study with companion

8:00 A.M. Breakfast

8:30 A.M. Personal study

9:30 A.M. Teaching and contacting

12:00 P.M. Lunch

1:00 P.M. Teaching and contacting

5:00 P.M. Dinner

6:00 P.M. Teaching and contacting

9:30 P.M. Plan next day's activities

10:30 P.M. Retire

Read more about missionary life at www.Mormons.org.

Did You Know?

St. Patrick—of St. Patrick's Day fame—was a missionary. For 30 years he preached Christianity to pagans in hopes of converting them. He also built churches, schools, and monasteries. The shamrock, usually linked with his name and his holiday, was actually something he used in his preaching; he used the three leaves to explain the concept of the Holy Trinity.

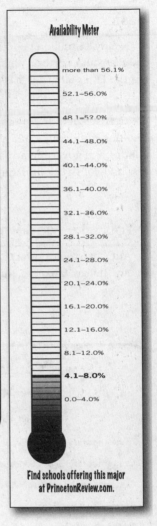

Availability Meter

more than 56.1%

52.1–56.0%

48.1–52.0%

44.1–48.0%

40.1–44.0%

36.1–40.0%

32.1–36.0%

28.1–32.0%

24.1–28.0%

20.1–24.0%

16.1–20.0%

12.1–16.0%

8.1–12.0%

4.1–8.0%

0.0–4.0%

Find schools offering this major at PrincetonReview.com.

Careers and Salary

Mission work is generally unpaid, and most missionaries live from the generosity of their church's missionary funds or donations.

CAREER OPTIONS

Clergy—Priest, Rabbi, Minister	Social Worker	Theologian
Philosopher	Teacher	

MODERN GREEK

Basics

Nearly 11 million people speak Modern Greek, a descendant of the language in which Homer composed and Plato and Aristotle philosophized. There are 24 letters in both the Ancient and Modern Greek alphabets, but the latter language has changed a bit in grammar, syntax, and pronunciation.

Modern Greek is a multidisciplinary major encompassing courses in literature, art, history, language, political science, and philosophy. You'll take language courses on an increasingly difficult level, hopefully resulting in fluency, both written and oral, by graduation. You'll learn about Modern Greek culture, society, politics, and government. You'll be able to speak, read, and write in Greek and will be able to appreciate the vast body of Greek literature and writings.

If You Like Modern Greek, You May Also Like . . .

Ancient studies, Arabic, Chinese, comparative literature, French, international relations, international studies, Italian, Japanese, Russian, Spanish

Suggested High School Prep for Modern Greek

Mastering a language is the best preparation for a major in Modern Greek. So take as many classes as you can of one language in high school. You shouldn't slack in history, religion, English, and philosophy, either. Math courses will be useful as well, since many mathematical symbols and concepts are Greek in origin.

SAMPLE COLLEGE CURRICULUM FOR MODERN GREEK

Contemporary Greek Poetry

Contemporary Greek Prose

Culture of Contemporary Greece

Formal Modern Greek

Informal and Colloquial Modern Greek

Issues in Greek-American Society and Culture

The Modern Greek Language Controversy

Modern Greek Folk Literature

Modern Greek Literary Translation

Modern Greek Literature

Philhellenism and Greek Nationalism

Reading the Past: Katharevousa

Successive classes in language and grammar

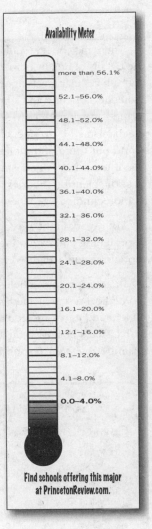

Availability Meter

more than 56.1%

52.1–56.0%

48.1–52.0%

44.1–48.0%

40.1–44.0%

36.1–40.0%

32.1 36.0%

28.1–32.0%

24.1–28.0%

20.1–24.0%

16.1–20.0%

12.1–16.0%

8.1–12.0%

4.1–8.0%

0.0–4.0%

Find schools offering this major
at PrincetonReview.com.

Fun Facts

What's for Dinner?

Try this recipe for a traditional Greek dish called Gemista.

6 medium tomatoes

1 cup rice

2 chopped onions

1 cup olive oil

diced parsley

bread crumbs

2 cups tomato juice

salt and pepper

Slice off the top of the tomatoes and carve out the insides. Save the carvings, mash them and mix them with the rice, onion, parsley, salt and pepper, and half the oil. Stuff the tomatoes with the rice mixture, lid them with their previously sliced-off tops, and place them in a pan. Top with the tomato juice, bread crumbs, and the rest of the olive oil, and bake in a medium oven for about 1 to 2 hours. You can also substitute peppers for tomatoes.

(Source: www.eatgreektonight.com)

Did You Know?

The Greek alphabet consists of 24 symbols. The symbols are called (you'll probably recognize some from math class): alpha, beta, gamma, delta, epsilon, zeta, eta, theta, iota, kappa, lambda, mu, nu, xi, omicron, pi, rho, sigma, tau, upsilon, phi, chi, psi, omega.

Careers and Salary

Salaries for Modern Greek majors are typically in the $24,000 to $30,000 range, but vary widely depending on the chosen career and level of education.

CAREER OPTIONS

Archaeologist	Professor	Translator
Diplomat/Attaché/Foreign Service Officer	Teacher	Writer

MOLECULAR BIOLOGY

Basics

There may be few subcultures of folks on Earth more detail-minded than molecular biologists. We're talking the details of details here; we're talking macromolecules. A major in molecular biology explores the cellular and sub-cellular levels of organisms, how these levels are structured, and how they function. You'll learn how molecules operate and some of the chemical changes they encounter. Genetics is covered, too—how it has shaped and continues to shape us and how molecules control our life processes. Regulation of cell growth, mechanisms of enzyme action, and DNA-protein interaction are all of interest. There's a whole molecular world out there, and molecular biologists are bent on understanding it and using it for the forces of good. You'll learn how organisms fight diseases and how they react to the environment. And after examining a host of scientific theories and questions, you'll be ready to apply your molecular know-how to fields such as biotechnology, genetics, cell biology, and physiology.

Your work in the classroom will be supplemented by extensive laboratory work, so you'll get experience in designing and executing experiments and interpreting the data obtained from them. Your course work, though heavily weighted toward biology, will also consist of courses in chemistry, physics, and math.

In addition to the fields mentioned above, a molecular biology major might lead you into the realm of biomedical research, medicine, or even something like technology law or technology business analysis. Your understanding of molecular structures and molecular skills will be a strong foundation for any of these paths. That's because you'll take away a wealth of knowledge and way of thinking that will enable you to examine, question, respond, and communicate intelligently in the world of biology and all it entails.

SAMPLE COLLEGE CURRICULUM FOR MOLECULAR BIOLOGY

Biomolecular Structure

Biophysical Chemistry

Cell Biology

Developmental Biology

Evolution

Functional Genomics

Genetics

Macromolecular Structure and Function

Metabolic Pathways

Molecular Aspects of Cell Biology

Molecular Genetics

Population Biology

Protein and Gene Technology

Protein Structure

If You Like Molecular Biology, You May Also Like . . .

Biology, biomedical engineering, biomedical science, botany and plant biology, cell biology, chemistry, epidemiology, experimental pathology, genetics, molecular genetics, neurobiology, neuroscience, pharmacology, pharmacy, premedicine, toxicology

Suggested High School Prep for Molecular Biology

Your best preparation for a major in molecular biology is a wide range of courses in math, science, and the humanities. Upper-level math and science classes like calculus and biology or chemistry with lab components will be most valuable—the more you can learn about these fields before college, the better head start you'll have. And biologists must be good communicators, so strengthen your writing, reading, and speaking skills with English, history, and a foreign language.

Fun Facts

Did You Know?

Aspirin is a molecule! It is an aromatic acetate, and its scientific name is acetylsalicylic acid. As you most likely know, aspirin is a pain reliever, an anti-inflammatory agent, and an antipyretic compound (a fever reducer). Ever wonder how much aspirin we take in this country every year? About 40 million pounds of it—in other words, about 300 tablets for every person.

(Source: http://encarta.msn.com/encnet/refpages/)

Quote from the Field

And you thought your homework was tough: "Trying to determine the structure of a protein by UV spectroscopy was like trying to determine the structure of a piano by listening to the sound it made while being dropped down a flight of stairs."

—Francis Crick, molecular biologist

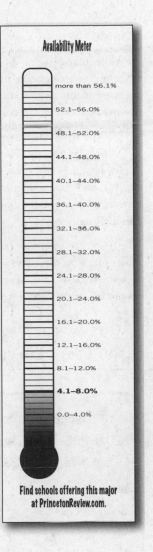

Availability Meter

more than 56.1%

52.1–56.0%

48.1–52.0%

44.1–48.0%

40.1–44.0%

36.1–40.0%

32.1–36.0%

28.1–32.0%

24.1–28.0%

20.1–24.0%

16.1–20.0%

12.1–16.0%

8.1–12.0%

4.1–8.0%

0.0–4.0%

Find schools offering this major at PrincetonReview.com.

Careers and Salary

The starting salary for biologists with an undergraduate degree is in the $21,000 to $35,000 zone. The more experience you gain through lab work and research and the further you pursue your education, the higher this figure will be.

CAREER OPTIONS		
Biologist	Professor	Scientist
Physician	Researcher	

MOLECULAR GENETICS

Basics

Molecular genetics is a field that is becoming more important every day. Advances in technology and research have opened countless doors in the fields of disease prevention and diagnosis—and there are endless opportunities and advancements yet to come. If you're inspired by the possibilities presented by the discoveries of the Human Genome Project, cancer research, or genetic engineering, consider molecular genetics as a major.

Molecular genetics is concerned with the molecules that make up genes. You'll study the ways these molecules function and how they themselves control the functioning of cells. You'll learn how molecules have evolved and changed and what has brought about these changes. By studying so closely the molecular structure of a gene, you'll be able to discover ways to control, alter, and replicate the gene—the foundations of genetic engineering.

Molecular genetics has numerous practical applications. Biomedical research is one field in which molecular genetics plays a vital role. You might study human gene therapy and investigate such things as the molecular basis of cancer, cell growth and development, and diseases such as AIDS. Expect a great deal of research—and a future full of exciting new discoveries.

If You Like Molecular Genetics, You May Also Like . . .

Biology, cell biology, chemistry, genetics, neurobiology, neuroscience, pharmacology, pharmacy, premedicine, public health, zoology

SAMPLE COLLEGE CURRICULUM FOR MOLECULAR GENETICS

Biochemical Genetics

Biological Chemistry

Classical Human Genetics

Energy Transfer and Development

Genes and Cancer

Genes, Race, and Evolution

Genes: Clinical and Social Issues

Genetics of Common Disorders

Medicine in the New Millennium

Modern Physics

New Molecular Techniques in Cytogenetics

Organic Chemistry

Red Cell Membranes

Suggested High School Prep for Molecular Genetics

Since the field of molecular genetics involves a great deal of science, try to take courses in biology, chemistry, physics, and any other science your high school offers. Also important are complex math courses such as calculus and analytic geometry, and computer science courses. And don't forget English—as a scientist you'll need good reading and writing skills.

Fun Facts

Before You Swat That Fly . . .

You've probably heard a lot about the Human Genome Project, but do you really know what a genome is? A genome is the entire set of DNA and genes in an organism, whether that organism is a human or a fly. Genes carry proteins that are especially important because they determine all the details about an organism, such as its looks and behavior.

"Bases" are the building blocks of DNA. There are only four, and they are called adenine, thymine, cytosine, and guanine. The order of the pairing of these bases is what determines what sort of an organism is created. Humans and fruit flies, for instance, both have the same bases but in very different orders. The genome of a human has 3 billion pairs of bases.

(Source: Human Genome Project Information, www.ornl.gov/hgmis/project/about.html)

Where'd You Put My DNA?

The DNA of a human being is organized in threads. If you stretched out these threads end to end, they'd be 5 feet long and 50 trillionths of an inch wide.

(Source: Johns Hopkins Medical Institutions)

Careers and Salary

Your starting salary will depend mainly on how you choose to use your degree, but you can expect compensation between $25,000 to $35,000. Engineering fields generally have salaries in the $40,000 to $50,000 range. Your salary will increase substantially as you continue your studies in graduate or medical school.

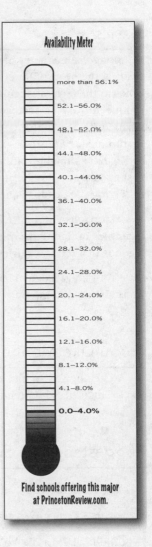

Availability Meter

more than 56.1%
52.1–56.0%
48.1–52.0%
44.1–48.0%
40.1–44.0%
36.1–40.0%
32.1–36.0%
28.1–32.0%
24.1–28.0%
20.1–24.0%
16.1–20.0%
12.1–16.0%
8.1–12.0%
4.1–8.0%
0.0–4.0%

Find schools offering this major at PrincetonReview.com.

CAREER OPTIONS

Biochemist	Geneticist	Physician
Biologist	Pharmacist	Professor
Chemist		

MONGOLIAN LANGUAGE AND LITERATURE

Basics

Mongolia, a country of more than 2.5 million people, sits smack in the middle of Siberia and China, effectively at the heart of Inner Asia. This location has exposed Mongolia to heavy international influence—sometimes in the form of occupation—for nearly two millennia. All the while, Mongolia has chiseled out its own unique history—a history that includes Genghis Kahn, Kublai Kahn, Chinese imperialism, and Russian alliance. It's also a history that's seen languages mingle and dialects evolve. As a Mongolian language and literature major, the stories, histories, and languages of Mongolia will become your subjects of study. Courses in Khalkha Mongol—often simply called Mongolian—will lend fluency in the language used orally by the vast majority of Mongolians. However, when written, the language employed by most Mongolians is Cyrillic, reflecting the heavy historical influence of nearby Russia.

Mongolian literature has traditionally been an oral, rather than written, form of expression. Among the examples of traditional Mongolian literature that you'll explore in the major are üligers, which are oral folk legends that tell the stories of tremendous heroes battling great evils.

Your knowledge of Mongolian language, literature, and history will allow you to address complex questions about contemporary Mongolia's national identity, geopolitical position, economic potential, and more.

If You Like Mongolian Language and Literature, You May Also Like...

Archeology, Asian history, Chinese, East Asian studies, history, political science, religious studies, Russian, Slavic languages and literatures, South Asian studies, Southeast Asian studies, Urdu language and literature

Suggested High School Prep for Mongolian Language and Literature

Learn one language and all the rest will come easier. With this maxim in mind, study a language—any language—during your high school years. Courses in world history and literature will provide a strong contextual framework for the topics covered in the major.

SAMPLE COLLEGE CURRICULUM FOR MONGOLIAN LANGUAGE AND LITERATURE

Beginning–Advanced Mongolian

Buddhism

Cyrillic

Inner Asian Civilizations

Intermediate Mongolian

Introduction to Mongolian Philology

Life in Ulan Bator

Mongolian History after 1921

Oral Literatures

Fun Facts

Dollars and Cents . . . sort of

The tugrug became Mongolia's official currency in 1925. In the past, 100 hundred mongos equaled 1 tugrug, but don't expect to find a mongo in your pocket these days; the low value of Mongolian coins has driven them from circulation.

Lay of the Land

Mongolia is a land of diverse natural features. It's home to the Gobi Desert, snow-capped mountains, glaciers, moist meadows, steppe grasslands, and more than two thousand lakes.

(Source: www.discover.mn/mongolia/)

Careers and Salary

Expect a starting salary between $25,000 and $30,000 a year.

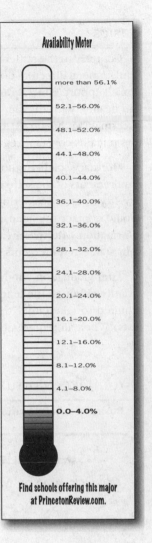

Availability Meter

more than 56.1%

52.1–56.0%

48.1–52.0%

44.1–48.0%

40.1–44.0%

36.1–40.0%

32.1–36.0%

28.1–32.0%

24.1–28.0%

20.1–24.0%

16.1–20.0%

12.1–16.0%

8.1–12.0%

4.1–8.0%

0.0–4.0%

Find schools offering this major at PrincetonReview.com.

CAREER OPTIONS

Consultant	Journalist	Translator
Diplomat/Attaché/Foreign Service Officer	Lobbyist	Travel Guide
Editor	Politician	Tutor
Historian	Teacher	Writer

MORTUARY SCIENCE

Basics

Contrary to the rather severe-sounding name, mortuary science is primarily a human service occupation. While funeral directors do work with bodies, they spend much of their time helping families in need of emotional support. Funeral directors guide families through a difficult process, advising them on their options and dealing with the clinical details of death. They bring order to an otherwise emotionally jarring experience, making the job extremely rewarding. It is also a very stable profession, as the demand for funeral directors remains constant regardless of the economic climate.

Mortuary science students must fulfill the requirements of their academic institution and the licensure requirements of the state in which they intend to practice. This program is very much dependent upon state law. If you are considering mortuary science and you plan on attending a school in a different state, you should contact the licensing board or a funeral director in the state in which you want to work for more information. Alternately, a school should be able to provide information on how its program works with your state's requirements.

After graduation, a mortuary science major is usually required to complete an internship of about twelve months, although the length of the requirement varies from state to state. After the internship, the intern is required to take either the state examination or a national board examination (some states require both tests). When all requirements are met, the state awards a license to practice.

If You Like Mortuary Science, You May Also Like . . .

Business administration and management, business communications, clinical psychology, counseling, experimental psychology, health administration, medical technology, social psychology, social work

SAMPLE COLLEGE CURRICULUM FOR MORTUARY SCIENCE

Accounting

Anatomy

Embalming

Funeral Service Directing

Funeral Service Equipment

General Chemistry

General Psychology

Introduction to Business Law

Introduction to Funeral Service

Microbiology

Pathology

Restorative Art

Suggested High School Prep for Mortuary Science

Mortuary science, as the name implies, requires a good deal of science. Classes in biology, chemistry, and physics are useful. In addition, any classes your school offers in psychology and business will certainly be helpful.

Fun Facts

For More Information . . .

The American Board of Funeral Service Education (ABFSE) has an informative site about mortuary science. Go to www.abfse.org to learn about state requirements, careers, and academics.

Careers and Salary

The starting salary for a mortuary science major fresh out of college is about $28,000.

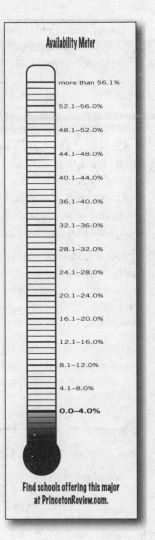

Availability Meter

more than 56.1%

52.1–56.0%

48.1–52.0%

44.1–48.0%

40.1–44.0%

36.1–40.0%

32.1–36.0%

28.1–32.0%

24.1–28.0%

20.1–24.0%

16.1–20.0%

12.1–16.0%

8.1–12.0%

4.1–8.0%

0.0–4.0%

Find schools offering this major at PrincetonReview.com.

CAREER OPTIONS

| Coroner | Funeral Director | Hospital Administrator |

MUSEUM STUDIES

Basics

Imagine running a renowned museum that has the size and grandeur of a palace. Your days are spent gazing upon masterful paintings, curating brilliant new works of genius, and, on occasion, getting to decide exactly where that larger-than-life Matisse should go. To top it off, you wine and dine at art openings, you can speak for hours on just one of Jackson Pollock's paint splatters, and you've come to see the world as one great expanse of white exhibit space. All right, snap out of it. As a museum studies major, you'll get an insider's view of how a museum works and who really runs the show. You'll learn about the roles curators, directors, conservators, collection managers, and exhibit designers play in creating exhibitions and presenting artwork to the public. There are various types of museums, from natural history to photography to history to art, and you'll take a look at how their operations differ. Technology is playing a larger and larger role in the museum world, and you'll examine how best to use this element to reach audiences and expedite museum processes. And you'll gain an understanding of the history of museums—how they began, where they're going, and why. This major may not feel quite as luxurious as spending a long, rainy Saturday wandering the great halls of a museum, but you may someday be a crucial factor in helping other people do just that.

There's a lot of nitty-gritty that goes into managing a museum, including cataloging, research, and fundraising. You'll be primed on all of it, plus you'll study the role museums play in education, how various educational goals are set and achieved, and how museums can best reach their audiences. Preservation is integral to the survival of museums worldwide, and you'll learn how to evaluate the condition of works of art, how to properly store and care for them, and how to transport them (beyond carefully!).

This course of study is highly interdisciplinary, and your course work will be drawn from the departments of art, history, education, and philosophy, to name a few. In fact, some colleges offer museum studies as a certificate or concentration instead of a major.

SAMPLE COLLEGE CURRICULUM FOR MUSEUM STUDIES

Collecting in History

Collections and Curation

Fund-raising and Human Resources

History of Museums

Information Technology

Museology

Museum Education

Museum Environment

Museum Exhibition

Museum Planning and Management

Preservation

Public Programs

If You Like Museum Studies, You May Also Like . . .

Art, art education, art history, ceramics, drawing, graphic design, historic preservation, painting, printmaking, visual communication

Suggested High School Prep for Museum Studies

You can prepare for a major in museum studies by getting a very strong foundation in humanities courses such as history, English, art, and music. Language courses often include sections on art and culture, making them a great way to learn about art outside the United States. A career in the museum world requires excellent communication skills, so take courses that will strengthen your writing, reading, and speaking abilities. And one of the best ways to prepare for this major is to visit as many museums as you can. Then spend an afternoon at your favorite one to study how the exhibitions are put together, which artworks were chosen, and how you feel based on the created environment.

Fun Facts

First of the Bunch

The first museum in the United States was founded in 1773, in Charleston, North Carolina. It is called, appropriately, the Charleston Museum.

(Source: www.charlestonmuseum.org)

Met Life

Some facts about the Metropolitan Museum of Art: The Met, a landmark museum in New York City, has a gigantic collection of artwork—around 2 million pieces—from all over the world and from throughout history. A sampling of their holdings:

- About 2,200 Old Master and European paintings
- About 2,500 pieces of American drawings
- More than 1,000 American paintings
- More than 600 American sculptures

(Source: www.metmuseum.org)

Careers and Salary

The starting salary for museum studies majors is in the $20,000 to $28,000 range. This is a field where you must gain experience over a long period of time, and your salary will reflect how much experience and learning you've obtained.

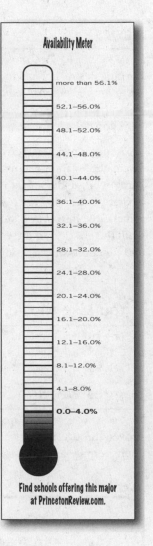

Availability Meter

more than 56.1%

52.1–56.0%

48.1–52.0%

44.1–48.0%

40.1–44.0%

36.1–40.0%

32.1–36.0%

28.1–32.0%

24.1–28.0%

20.1–24.0%

16.1–20.0%

12.1–16.0%

8.1–12.0%

4.1–8.0%

0.0–4.0%

Find schools offering this major at PrincetonReview.com.

CAREER OPTIONS		
Anthropologist	Curator	Public Relations Professional
Archaeologist	Librarian	Registrar
Art Educator	Museum Director	Teacher
Artist	Professor	Writer
Collections Manager		

MUSIC

Basics

Whether it's Beethoven or Louis Armstrong, the Beatles or Bach, a major in music is sure to satisfy that burning desire of yours to create, analyze, and study the history of music in all of its varied shapes and forms. From music composition to history, education, and theory, those with a love of music can develop the skills to prepare them for a career as the conductor of the National Symphony Orchestra or the next Duke Ellington.

A music major can cover a broad range of concentrations depending on your areas of interest. For those fascinated by the structural composition of a piece of music, whether it's Schubert's "Ave Maria" or an avant-garde work understandable only to a trained ear, focusing on music theory and composition is a great way to start. You'll also learn how to arrange and compose your own works. Music, like all of the arts, has a remarkable history. A concentration in music history means you'll explore the historical evolution of music from the classical to the contemporary. In the process you'll gain a greater appreciation for the varied forms and functions of music in society.

If You Like Music, You May Also Like . . .

Jazz studies, music history, music therapy, piano, voice

Suggested High School Prep for Music

Yes, if you want to major in music you will have to have an exceptionally strong background in it, as proven through mastery of one or more instruments. Though it depends upon your concentration, most programs require auditions, so practice, practice, practice. . . .

SAMPLE COLLEGE CURRICULUM FOR MUSIC

Advanced Composition and
  Orchestration

Conducting

Ensembles

Form and Analysis

Lessons on Minor Instruments

Lessons on Principal Instruments

Music Aural Training

Music History

Music Theory I–III

Fun Facts

Actual Program Notes from an Unidentified Piano Recital

Tonight's page turner, Ruth Spelke, studied under Ivan Schmertnick at the Boris Nitsky School of Page Turning in Philadelphia. She has been turning pages here and abroad for many years for some of the world's leading pianists.

Ouch!

Q: What's the difference between a musician and a pizza pie?

A: The pizza can feed a family of four.

Famous People Who Majored in Music

Yo-Yo Ma, Leonard Slatkin, George Fenton, Pandit Ravi Shankar

Careers and Salary

The starting salary for a music major with an advanced degree is $28,000 to $35,000. Other salaries depend on the field you chose to enter.

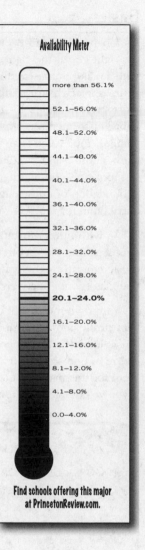

Availability Meter

more than 56.1%

52.1–56.0%

48.1–52.0%

44.1–48.0%

40.1–44.0%

36.1–40.0%

32.1–36.0%

28.1–32.0%

24.1–28.0%

20.1–24.0%

16.1–20.0%

12.1–16.0%

8.1–12.0%

4.1–8.0%

0.0–4.0%

Find schools offering this major at PrincetonReview.com.

CAREER OPTIONS		
Artist	Music Executive	Musician

MUSIC EDUCATION

Basics

Johann Sebastian Bach once said, "It's easy to play any musical instrument: All you have to do is touch the right key at the right time and the instrument will play itself." You'll be teaching people to do just that with a major in music education. Despite its title, music education is a multidisciplinary major encompassing courses in art, history, English, languages, psychology, philosophy, and, of course, music. You'll first and foremost study music itself—its history, its theories, the very philosophies of music. You'll experiment with individual instruments as you learn the best way to teach children how to play the string, brass, and woodwind families. Your voice is an instrument, too, so get ready to sing and encourage others to sing as well. You'll learn about sight reading and ear training, and how to build those skills in your future students. Composition, conducting, orchestration, and improvisation will all be part of your course work. You'll build a foundation of knowledge in instrumental and chorale repertoire and get a head start designing a sample curriculum for the classroom.

As with other education-related majors, you'll get classroom experience through observation and student teaching. This is often a semester-long endeavor, and you'll get to see firsthand what goes into being a music educator—the ways music comes alive for students in the classroom and what goes into managing that classroom effectively.

Your own music will be part of your studies as well, and most programs require you to concentrate and gain proficiency in an instrument of your choice. Often, music education majors go on to teach private music lessons; others become teachers in elementary or high schools. Most programs will ask you to specialize in one area, such as instrumental music, vocal music, or general music. The most important requirement for this major is a love of music and a desire to bring that music—and that passion for it—to others. If you've got talent to boot, you should really enjoy the ride.

SAMPLE COLLEGE CURRICULUM FOR MUSIC EDUCATION

Aural Skills

Chorale Repertoire

Curriculum Building

Educational Psychology

Instrumental and Classroom

Instrumental Conducting

Music History

Music Methods

Music Theory

Sight Singing and Ear Training

Student Teaching

Vocal and Classroom

Vocal Pedagogy

World Music

If You Like Music Education, You May Also Like . . .

Art education, art history, child care, child development, church music, counseling, dance, education, education administration, educational psychology, jazz studies, music history, music management, music therapy, physical education, religious education, special education, teacher education, voice

Suggested High School Prep for Music Education

The best preparation for a major in music education is a variety of humanities courses including English, history, art, and languages. Obviously, music courses will be valuable as well. You should get involved in music groups in your school or community, such as bands or orchestras. Most music education programs require some degree of proficiency in a musical instrument or voice, so explore the option of private lessons if you haven't already. The stronger your own music skills are when you get to college, the better.

Fun Facts

They Said That?!?

Kids have some funny ideas about music. Here are some of their test answers, submitted by Missouri music teachers from 1989.

- "Agnus Dei was a woman composer famous for her church music."
- "John Sebastian Bach died from 1750 to the present."
- "Music sung by two people at the same time is called a duel."
- "Most authorities agree that music of antiquity was written long ago."
- "Instruments come in many sizes, shapes, and orchestras."
- "Henry Purcell is a well-known composer few people have ever heard of."
- "Refrain means don't do it. A refrain in music is the part you better not try to sing."
- "A virtuoso is a musician with real high morals."

(Source: http://privateschool.about.com/blmsub_humor12.htm)

Careers and Salary

The starting salary for music education majors is about $30,000, but this number depends on what sort of school you teach in and where your school district is located. Also, music teachers are usually paid additional sums for their involvement in school music groups like bands and orchestras.

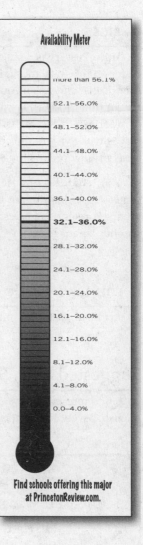

Availability Meter

more than 56.1%
52.1–56.0%
48.1–52.0%
44.1–48.0%
40.1–44.0%
36.1–40.0%
32.1–36.0%
28.1–32.0%
24.1–28.0%
20.1–24.0%
16.1–20.0%
12.1–16.0%
8.1–12.0%
4.1–8.0%
0.0–4.0%

Find schools offering this major at PrincetonReview.com.

CAREER OPTIONS		
Educational Administrator	Musician	Teacher
Music Librarian	Performing Arts Administrator	Writer
Music Teacher	Professor	

MUSIC HISTORY

Basics

Music history is a major that deals with music of all types and from all times and places. You'll learn the history of classical music from all parts of the world. You'll study ethnic music from African Americans, Latin Americans, and Asian Americans. You'll study Medieval and Renaissance music, as well as Baroque and Romantic forms. You'll study orchestral and chamber music from various time periods and the many forms of American music, including the stuff you hear on the radio today. Studying music from different times and places will give you the ability to compare various forms and trends, and you'll be able to develop your own ideas of how today's music has been informed and influenced by music from the past.

Your studies in music history will include music training; most programs require you to take several semesters of instrument or voice lessons, as well as involve yourself in band, choir, orchestra, or another group. Foreign languages are also part of music history, so expect to take courses in French, German, or another language.

If You Like Music History, You May Also Like . . .

Art history, church music, dance, education, English, film, history, jazz studies, music, theater, voice

Suggested High School Prep for Music History

Since music history is an interdisciplinary major, a broad foundation of courses in languages, history, English, psychology, art, math, and science will be most valuable. Music and fine arts courses will also offer you opportunities to widen your horizons. Most universities require an audition, so you should get involved in music lessons, band, orchestra, choir, or another group in your school or community. You can also listen to a variety of music on your own and read about famous composers and musicians on the Internet or at your library.

> **SAMPLE COLLEGE CURRICULUM FOR MUSIC HISTORY**
>
> American Folk Music
>
> American Jazz
>
> Music Criticism
>
> Music from the European Baroque
>
> Music History Survey
>
> Music Theory
>
> Popular Music from Brazil
>
> Russian Folk Music
>
> Twentieth-Century Music
>
> Western Art Music
>
> World Music

Fun Facts

Do You Know the History of the Blues?

The first blues recording was in 1895—"Laughing Song" by George W. Johnson. This paved the way for blues music to be produced in music rolls. In 1920, blues became more mainstream when Mamie Smith recorded "Crazy Blues" and "It's Right Here for You." This record cost $1 and sold 75,000 copies in the first month. In the 1920s and 1930s, the blues market was almost exclusively African American—the records were even known as "race records."

Careers and Salary

Starting salaries for music history majors generally range from $20,000 to $30,000. As with most liberal arts majors, however, music history gives you a range of career options, so salaries are difficult to accurately pinpoint.

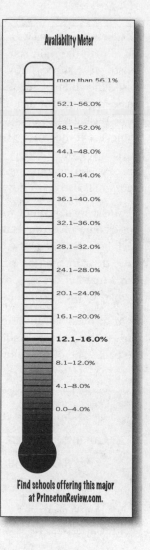

Availability Meter

more than 56.1%

52.1–56.0%

48.1–52.0%

44.1–48.0%

40.1–44.0%

36.1–40.0%

32.1–36.0%

28.1–32.0%

24.1–28.0%

20.1–24.0%

16.1–20.0%

12.1–16.0%

8.1–12.0%

4.1–8.0%

0.0–4.0%

Find schools offering this major
at PrincetonReview.com.

CAREER OPTIONS

Agent	Musician	Radio Producer
Music Executive	Performing Arts Administrator	

MUSIC MANAGEMENT

Basics

Celebrities may swap managers like kids swap baseball cards, but that doesn't mean it's a bad gig. If you're with the right star, you travel the world, live the good life, take at least some of the credit for wildly boosting the success of your client, and get the star-studded insider scoop the tabloids would kill for. Plus, no singing abilities necessary! So what's the catch? Dealing with divas. But if you can live with that. . . . As a music management major, you'll learn about every aspect of the music world as seen through the eyes of a music business professional. You'll examine the ethical dilemmas, legal matters, and the juggling of all things financial. On the artistic side, you'll look at the challenges musicians face and how to best overcome them. Music history and theory—as well as performance—are included to provide insight and expertise. On the business end, accounting, marketing, copyright laws, unions, arts patronage, and advertising will all be covered. You'll also learn how to fund-raise effectively and how to write a professional grant.

Music management majors go beyond the music itself to understand the entire industry that makes music come alive. You'll take courses in both music and business, and by becoming well versed in both fields, you'll be able to see how they affect and are affected by each other, and you'll be on your way to helping to make their interaction smooth and profitable for all. (As for knowing how to respond when your client insists that her dressing room, hotel room, and car interior be decorated only and entirely in white—that's not part of the curriculum. You're on your own!)

Your major in music management can take you many exciting places, and many colleges offer internships with recording studios, orchestras, music publishers, and other arts organizations. Music management, the backstage of the industry, is vital to the life of music. And your efforts as a music manager will play a unique and crucial role in spreading the latest sounds around the world.

SAMPLE COLLEGE CURRICULUM FOR MUSIC MANAGEMENT

Accounting

Arts Management

Arts Organization Management

Arts Patronage

Business Organization and Management

Ethics in the Music Industry

Financial Management

Human Resource Management

Macroeconomics

Marketing

Music History

Music Literature and Appreciation

Music Performance

If You Like Music Management, You May Also Like . . .

Accounting, business administration and management, business communications, entrepreneurship, finance, human resources management, jazz studies, managerial economics, marketing, music education, music history, music therapy

Suggested High School Prep for Music Management

The best preparation for a major in music management is a solid background in math, science, and humanities courses. Music classes will be especially helpful. All managers must be excellent communicators, so take courses that will strengthen your reading, writing, and speaking skills, such as English courses. Knowledge of a foreign language is an asset to any job, so explore courses in languages as well.

Fun Facts

Some Words on Music

"Music is spiritual. The music business is not."

—Van Morrison, musician

"Music is a beautiful opiate, if you don't take it too seriously."

—Henry Miller, writer

"Music, of all the arts, stands in a special region, unlit by any star but its own, and utterly without meaning . . . except its own."

—Leonard Bernstein, composer

(Source: www.bartleby.com)

Music Notes

Interested in learning more about the commercial aspects of music management? Check out the *Music Business Journal*, an online publication that, according to its website, aims to "spread knowledge and understanding about music and its relation to commerce." Go to www.musicjournal.org for more information.

Careers and Salary

The starting salary for music managers is usually in the $30,000 range. Your salary depends on where you live and how you use your skills, and the number will rise as you gain more experience and knowledge in your field.

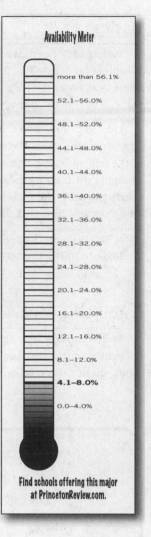

Availability Meter

more than 56.1%

52.1–56.0%

48.1–52.0%

44.1–48.0%

40.1–44.0%

36.1–40.0%

32.1–36.0%

28.1–32.0%

24.1–28.0%

20.1–24.0%

16.1–20.0%

12.1–16.0%

8.1–12.0%

4.1–8.0%

0.0–4.0%

Find schools offering this major at PrincetonReview.com.

CAREER OPTIONS

Arts Administrator	Music Manager	Musician
Booking Agent	Music Teacher	

MUSIC THERAPY

Basics

Perhaps it's Beethoven that gets your blood pumping, or maybe it's a little Andrew W.K. Whatever the case may be, music has the ability to smooth over that troubled soul of yours—get you excited, happy, or depressed. From the idea that music can express something through notes and sounds that plain old words just can't grew the music therapy major.

Our emotions aren't always the easiest thing to get in touch with, and sometimes we need more than just a soothing voice. We've got physical, psychological, social, emotional, and cognitive needs that your run-of-the-mill therapist can't address. Sometimes what we really need to do is sit down and compose our thoughts through tones and melodies, symphonic harmonies and dissonance, and this is where the music therapist enters the picture. Part psychoanalyst and part conductor, the music therapist helps us to play our emotions and thoughts through music.

With a solid background in music theory and performance, and of course some serious training as a psychologist, a music therapy major pulls both hemispheres of the brain into harmony.

If You Like Music Therapy, You May Also Like . . .

Biopsychology, clinical psychology, counseling, developmental psychology, educational psychology, experimental psychology, human development, industrial psychology, music, music history, neurobiology, neuroscience, occupational therapy, physiological psychology, piano, psychology, social psychology

Suggested High School Prep for Music Therapy

In addition to taking introductory psychology courses at your high school, students should also prepare themselves by having a strong background in science, math, English, and computer courses. Spending your time volunteering at a local hospital or mental health clinic is also a great opportunity to gain firsthand experience in the field. There is also a wealth of information out there for those who have an interest in psychology, from scholarly journals to newspapers and magazines.

SAMPLE COLLEGE CURRICULUM FOR MUSIC THERAPY

Abnormal Psychology

Applied Instrument I–II

Child Development

Clinical Applications in Music Therapy

Counseling

Imagery and Metaphor

Introduction to Music History

Lessons on principal instruments

Music History

Music Theory I–III

Psychology of Personality

Quantitative Reasoning

Fun Facts

How to Deal with Your Therapist
- Try to talk him into sitting on the floor.
- Tell him you think his secretary is really a man.
- Take random objects in his office and glue them to the floor.
- Bring pots and pans and bang them together when he asks a question you don't like.
- Complain that his chair looks more comfortable.
- Sit underneath your chair.

Shine on You Crazy Diamond
The epic, nine-part song "Shine on You Crazy Diamond"—from their best-selling *Wish You Were Here* album—is Pink Floyd's tribute to their founder and past leader Syd Barrett, who, shortly after the success of their first album, became severely mentally unstable and retired to his home in Cambridgeshire, England, from which he rarely ventured.

Careers and Salary

The average starting salary for a psychology major ranges from $27,000 to $28,000 a year in jobs like those of a mental health specialist, consultant, and program director. These salaries increase with education and experience, though, as entry positions for those holding master's and doctoral degrees range from $25,000 to $45,000 annually.

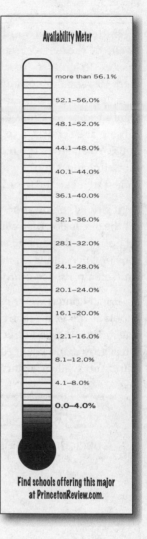

Availability Meter

more than 56.1%

52.1–56.0%

48.1–52.0%

44.1–48.0%

40.1–44.0%

36.1–40.0%

32.1–36.0%

28.1–32.0%

24.1–28.0%

20.1–24.0%

16.1–20.0%

12.1–16.0%

8.1–12.0%

4.1–8.0%

0.0–4.0%

Find schools offering this major at PrincetonReview.com.

CAREER OPTIONS

Career Counselor	Occupational Therapist	Psychologist

MUSICAL THEATER

Basics

In the immortal words of Gus the Theater Cat from T. S. Eliot's *Old Possum's Book of Practical Cats*, "Well, the theater is certainly not what it was!" You can say that again. *Cats* has closed on Broadway and so has *Les Misérables*. Now, in addition to the few classics like *42nd Street* that have managed to survive, there's a new crop of musicals like *Spamalot* and *The Producers*. With all the change, it's an exciting time to major in musical theater—whether your talents lean more toward sweet Christine in *Phantom* or sultry Mimi in *Rent*. As a musical theater major, you'll learn about every aspect of putting on a show—from the lighting and set design to costumes and makeup to the acting, singing, and dancing that brings those scores to life. You'll study the technical aspects of the theater, like how to make a production run smoothly from the set changes to the curtain call. After blocking scenes and choreographing lively dances, you'll be challenged to make those old songs seem new again—and to make the new songs part of our cultural history.

If strengthening your own acting, singing, and dancing skills is what you're after, you're in luck. As a musical theater major, that will be your primary concern. You'll get plenty of practice in musical performances on both small and large scales, and you may even have the opportunity to direct your own. You'll take lessons in voice and learn the fundamentals of movement for the stage. You'll also learn what it takes to make yourself a presence on the stage, a valued addition to any cast.

Prima donnas won't escape a bit of backstage grunt work, as musical theater majors are required to take a look at the gears that turn behind the scenes to make musicals such a success—including production, stage managing, and directing. You'll learn about the history of musical theater—where it got its start, how it has grown and changed, and the struggles it faces today. You'll study musical theater repertoire and literature. And while a major in musical theater is no guarantee that you'll see your name in Broadway lights, you'll learn a great deal about this art form and you'll definitely have a very good time.

SAMPLE COLLEGE CURRICULUM FOR MUSICAL THEATER

- Acting Fundamentals
- Dance
- Diction
- Dramatic Literature
- Ear Training
- History of Musical Theater
- Musical Performance
- Script Analysis
- Speech and Voice
- Stage Directing
- Stage Movement
- Stagecraft and Lighting
- Technical Production
- Theater Repertory
- Vocal Ensemble

If You Like Musical Theater, You May Also Like . . .

Art, creative writing, dance, English, fashion design, film, music, music management, radio and television, theater

Suggested High School Prep for Musical Theater

The best preparation for a major in musical theater is a broad selection of courses, with a focus on those in the humanities. Courses in English, religion, philosophy, psychology, and history will be especially valuable in giving you perspective on the world—necessary for any skilled actor or actress. Math will help, too; music and math go hand in hand. Studying a foreign language is always a good idea and might be valuable to your career in theater. And we'll bet you're already involved with the drama club at your school or theater groups in your community— there's no better way to prepare for a major in theater than by actually doing it.

Fun Facts

Rodgers and Who?

Two names any fan of musical theater will recognize are Rodgers and Hammerstein. But it wasn't always Hammerstein. Did you know that Rodgers originally worked with a man named Lorenz Hart? Richard Rodgers began writing songs in high school, and while a student at Columbia University he met Hart. The two worked together for nearly 25 years and created such famous shows as *On Your Toes* and *Babes in Arms*. Hart died in 1943, but by then Rodgers had already begun to work with Oscar Hammerstein, and their first show together was *Oklahoma!* Needless to say, the collaboration was a long and fruitful one, transforming the field of musical theater forever.

(Source: www.rnh.com/org)

How Fantastick!

The longest-running musical of all time was *The Fantasticks*. It opened on May 3, 1960, and closed on January 13, 2002. Total number of performances: 17,162.

(Source: www.thefantasticks.com/webpages/home.html)

Careers and Salary

The starting salary for musical theater majors is impossible to predict. A true career in theater is very difficult to establish, and there are too many "actor/waiters" out there to count. Almost all aspiring actors have day jobs to pay the bills while they audition and learn their craft. When you're lucky enough to win a role, your salary will depend on what sort of theater group you're involved with and where in the country you live.

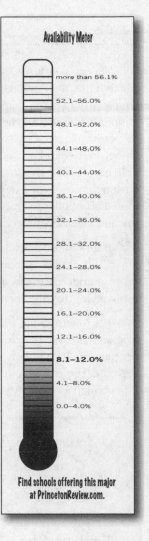

Availability Meter

more than 56.1%

52.1–56.0%

48.1–52.0%

44.1–48.0%

40.1–44.0%

36.1–40.0%

32.1–36.0%

28.1–32.0%

24.1–28.0%

20.1–24.0%

16.1–20.0%

12.1–16.0%

8.1–12.0%

4.1–8.0%

0.0–4.0%

Find schools offering this major at PrincetonReview.com.

CAREER OPTIONS

Actor	General Manager	Teacher
Box Office Manager	Musician	Technical Director
Choreographer	Performing Arts Administrator	Theme Park Performer
Dancer	Producer	Vocal Coach
Director	Stage Manager	Writer

MUSICOLOGY AND ETHNOMUSICOLOGY

Basics

The University of Illinois at Urbana-Champaign defines musicology as "a study of music in all its dimensions." Seem a little broad? Good—that's the point. While all majors will get a thorough training in the research practices of musicology, the history of music, and the basics of musical method and form, there are many possible paths that a student can follow. To a large degree, it depends on individual interests. After completing your core classes, you might focus on the nuts and bolts of nineteenth century German ensemble performance, or you might decide to hone in on the life and works of Leonard Bernstein. As you might expect, musicology and ethnomusicology is an incredibly interdisciplinary major. Just how interdisciplinary? Well, have a look at this list of complementary subjects for ethnomusicology students at the University of Washington: anthropology, comparative religions, approaches computer applications, cultural ecology, ethnomedicine, folklore, history, library science, linguistics, literary studies, musicological approaches, philosophy, and video documentation.

Ethnomusicology is a branch of musicology with a specific emphasis on the connection between music and culture. Because of this, ethnomusicologists often train their eyes on movements in foreign music—modern African music, say, or the homespun sounds of Bulgaria. They might also look at American music styles that are deeply embedded in cultural identity and influence, such as jazz or folk music.

It's worth noting that not all majors are the same. At some schools, musicology and ethnomusicology programs will expect you to enroll in instrument performance courses, while others will require you to take a certain number of courses outside of the program, and yet others will expect foreign language training. Look at each program closely to see which ones match your goals. Choosing the right school is the first step in becoming a major player in the world of music.

SAMPLE COLLEGE CURRICULUM FOR MUSICOLOGY AND ETHNOMUSICOLOGY

Anthropology of Music

Baroque and Classical Music

European Folk Music

Forms of Music

History of Western Music

Introductory–Intermediate German

Medieval and Renaissance Notation

Methods of Musicological Research

Music and Culture

National Identity and Music

World Music

If You Like Musicology and Ethnomusicology, You May Also Like...

History, general studies and humanities, music, music education, music therapy, music theater, voice

Suggested High School Prep for Musicology and Ethnomusicology

Aside from the obvious music classes, you'll want to sample widely from your high school's arts and humanities curricula. Since musicology and ethnomusicology will ask you to make sense of information from the arts, anthropology, history, and range of other disciplines, be sure to take courses that ask you to read, research, and write often.

Fun Facts

Rockin' It

If chipping away at the relationship between religion and musical expressions of love in the seventeenth century music of the Counter-Reformation is your thing, by all means charge ahead. But there are plenty of modern options as well. Case in point: Seattle's Experience Music Project, a musicological Mecca for anyone who loves American popular music. The exhibits at EMP range from the history of the guitar in American music to the punk rock explosion to the beginnings of hip hop. Check out www.emplive.org. What they've done may you give you some ideas for your own studies in the future.

The Artist Formerly Known As . . .

Though Prince was not a musicology major in college—in fact, he didn't even attend college—he did name his 2004 album *Musicology*. Coincidence? We think not.

Careers and Salary

If you plan to stick with musicology as a career, you're probably going to have to go on to graduate school. This said, the major prepares you for a wide range of music- and humanities-related professions. For these jobs, expect a starting salary between $24,000 and $30,000.

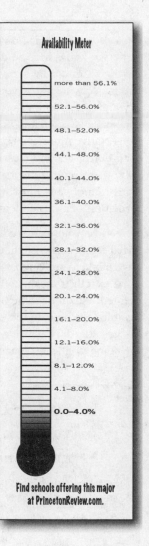

Availability Meter

more than 56.1%

52.1–56.0%

48.1–52.0%

44.1–48.0%

40.1–44.0%

36.1–40.0%

32.1–36.0%

28.1–32.0%

24.1–28.0%

20.1–24.0%

16.1–20.0%

12.1–16.0%

8.1–12.0%

4.1–8.0%

0.0–4.0%

Find schools offering this major at PrincetonReview.com.

CAREER OPTIONS		
Agent	Curator	Musicologist
Archivist	Editor	Producer
Arts Consultant	Fundraiser	Teacher
Composer	Historian	Writer

NATIVE AMERICAN STUDIES

Basics

Most Americans know shockingly little about the native people of our country. And what we do know, or think we know, may be derived from simplified explanations we were given in grade school or misguided portrayals in old TV shows or films. Native Americans have a rich and troubled history in this country, and this major will expose you to the unique situations this group has faced with respect to independence, identity, and recognition. During your studies, you'll gain vast knowledge of Native American cultures and how they have affected and been affected by American culture. You'll learn about the difficulties and discriminations Native Americans have faced in the past and the challenges they still face today—their victories and their defeats. Economics and politics pose special problems to Native Americans, and you'll learn about the tribes' sovereign powers within the United States. You'll also learn about the persistent stereotypes that Native Americans must work against in popular culture and how these affect, inform, and complicate the formation of a racial identity.

Native American studies is a multidisciplinary major that encompasses courses in the humanities and social sciences. Throughout your studies you'll gain exposure to the valuable contributions Native Americans have made to art, language, music, politics, psychology, spirituality, and literature. You'll begin to form ideas of what exactly it means to be a Native American and how identity, gender, and race have been challenged and defined. As you become better acquainted with the Native American people, you'll come to understand and be able to articulate the sacrifices they've made, the history and culture they've preserved, and what possibly lies ahead. This major will give you the opportunity to become knowledgeable in many different fields, including political science, English, women's studies, psychology, sociology, history, and others.

SAMPLE COLLEGE CURRICULUM FOR NATIVE AMERICAN STUDIES

The American Indian, 1870–Present

American Indian Art History

American Indian Literature

Contemporary Indian Problems

Ethnology of the Greater Southwest

The Indian in American Popular Culture

Native American Health

Native American Philosophy

Native American Sovereignty

Oral Literature and Oral Tradition

Plains Indian Peoples

Tribal Economic Development

Tribal Justice Systems

Tribal Water Rights

If You Like Native American Studies, You May Also Like . . .

African American studies, African studies, American history, american literature, American studies, Asian American studies, art history, Caribbean studies, comparative literature, East Asian studies, East European studies, French, German, Hispanic American/Puerto Rican/Chicano studies, history, international business, international relations, international studies, Middle Eastern studies, peace studies, philosophy, Russian, South Asian studies, Southeast Asian studies, Spanish

Suggested High School Prep for Native American Studies

History is key to your understanding of Native American studies, so take advantage of whatever history courses your high school offers. Other humanities courses such as English, philosophy, religion, and languages will be valuable as well. Since this is an interdisciplinary major, a well-rounded background in a variety of courses in all disciplines will be your best preparation.

Fun Facts

Who Was Sacagawea?

She was a Native American woman who accompanied Lewis and Clark as they set out to explore the territory west of the Mississippi in 1804, after the Louisiana Purchase was made. Sacagawea's husband, Charbonneau, a Canadian trapper, was slated to accompany the duo, and Sacagawea went along as well. Though there are conflicting reports, legend has it that Sacagawea was relied on as a guide and translator and that she was instrumental in helping Lewis and Clark eventually reach the Pacific. Sacagawea and her son now appear on the face of the golden dollar coin.

Native Wordsmiths

The Native Writers' Circle of the Americas (NWCA) was established in 1992, and each year it recognizes Native American writers with prizes: the Lifetime Achievement Award, the First Book Award, and the Theresa Palmer Award. In 2000, Louise Erdrich was given the Lifetime Achievement Award.

Careers and Salary

The starting salary for most liberal arts majors is in the $20,000 to $30,000 range, though this varies widely depending on where you live and how you use your skills. Your major might take you in any number of directions. Advanced degrees will also make a big difference in liberal arts disciplines.

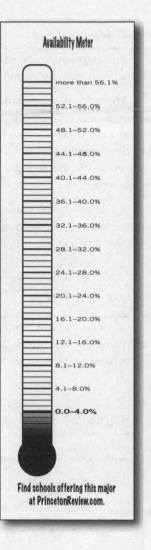

Availability Meter

more than 56.1%

52.1–56.0%

48.1–52.0%

44.1–48.0%

40.1–44.0%

36.1–40.0%

32.1–36.0%

28.1–32.0%

24.1–28.0%

20.1–24.0%

16.1–20.0%

12.1–16.0%

8.1–12.0%

4.1–8.0%

0.0–4.0%

Find schools offering this major at PrincetonReview.com.

CAREER OPTIONS

Archaeologist

Diplomat/Attaché/Foreign Service Officer

FBI Agent

Journalist

Professor

Sociologist

Teacher

Translator

Writer

NATURAL RESOURCES CONSERVATION

Basics

From drilling for oil in the Alaskan Wildlife Refuge to decreasing levels of pollution in our nation's cities, the importance and significance of preserving our natural environment has never before seemed so urgent.

From dreadlock-wearing, tree-hugging activists to serious scientists, environmental conservationists have changed the way we look at our natural resources. Standing at the forefront of the fight to protect our delicate environment are natural resources conservation majors. Scientists by training and tree lovers by conviction, natural resources conservation majors study the delicate balance between consumption and conservation that humankind must strike in order to preserve the availability of natural resources like coal, oil, and trees.

As we all should know by now, we can't consume our resources interminably. Natural resources conservation majors help us determine what we need and what the environment can support. They are the vanguards of nature, ensuring that we leave something for the next generation.

If You Like Natural Resources Conservation, You May Also Like . . .

Agricultural and biological engineering, biology, botany and plant biology, ecology, environmental and environmental health engineering, environmental science, forestry, geological engineering, geology, horticulture, plant pathology, sustainable resource management, wildlife management

Suggested High School Prep for Natural Resources Conservation

It's never too early to get involved with a local conservation movement, whether it's the Sierra Club or you're local recycling program. Activism is just one part though, so to make sure you're really prepared focus on the sciences, particularly biology, chemistry, physics, and environmental science.

> **SAMPLE COLLEGE CURRICULUM FOR NATURAL RESOURCES CONSERVATION**
>
> Forest Ecology
>
> Forests, Conservation, and People
>
> Integrated Natural Resource Management
>
> Integrated Principles of Biology
>
> Microeconomics
>
> Natural Resource Communication
>
> Natural Resource Policy and Administration
>
> Natural Resource Sampling
>
> Statistics

Fun Facts

Did You Know?

Hugh Hammond Bennett, the father of soil conservation, made his early discoveries of the effects of sheet erosion in 1905 when he was a young soil scientist mapping soils in Louisa County, Virginia.

Did You Know?

The Wildforest Protection Plan preserves more than 60 million acres of unspoiled national forests.

Careers and Salary

The starting salary for a natural resources conservation major can range from $24,000 to $30,000.

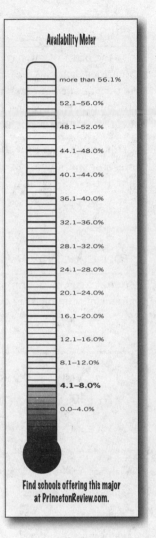

Availability Meter

more than 56.1%

52.1–56.0%

48.1–52.0%

44.1–48.0%

40.1–44.0%

36.1–40.0%

32.1–36.0%

28.1–32.0%

24.1–28.0%

20.1–24.0%

16.1–20.0%

12.1–16.0%

8.1–12.0%

4.1–8.0%

0.0–4.0%

Find schools offering this major at PrincetonReview.com.

CAREER OPTIONS

Biologist

Ecologist

Environmentalist/
Environmental Scientist

Geologist

Lobbyist

NAVAL ARCHITECTURE

Basics

At the heart of the naval architecture major are ships. Very, very large ships. Battleships, aircraft carriers, submarines, sailboats, destroyers—the types of ships that take your breath away and that form the physical structure of our country's naval defense system. Building these colossal floating forts involves cutting-edge mathematics, engineering brilliance, and a creative soul. After all, military superiority is the product of not only great scientists, but also creative minds.

This isn't a major for the faint of heart. It involves not only some intense science, mathematics, and real hands-on experience, but also, perhaps, even serving in the navy itself. If you pursue the naval architecture major at the U.S. Naval Academy, you will earn both a Bachelor of Science and a commission as an officer in the U.S. Navy.

If You Like Naval Architecture, You May Also Like . . .

Aerospace engineering, architectural and biological engineering, architectural history, architecture, civil engineering, engineering design, engineering mechanics, Navy R.O.T.C.

SAMPLE COLLEGE CURRICULUM FOR NAVAL ARCHITECTURE

Advanced Marine Vehicles

Analytical Applications in Ship Design

Applied Fluid Dynamics

Dynamics

Engineering of Thermodynamics

Naval Materials and Engineering

Principles of Ocean Systems
  Engineering

Resistance and Propulsion

Sea-Keeping and Maneuvers

Ship Design I–II

Ship Hydrostatics and Stability

Ship Structures

Statistics

Strength of Materials

Submarine Design Analysis

Suggested High School Prep for Naval Architecture

As you probably won't have any ship-building courses in your high school curriculum, focus on enhancing those advanced math and physics skills. Calculus will be especially helpful in preparing you for the rigorous math courses that lie ahead. Getting experience in mechanics, such as taking automotive shop, could come in handy, too. Don't forget those humanities courses like history and English—courses that will be essential to your learning how to think outside of the box and solve problems.

Fun Facts

They Do More Before 9 A.M. . . .

The United States Navy has 371,229 people on active duty who maintain a fleet of 316 ships and 4,108 aircraft.

Did You Know?

The Nimitz class aircraft carriers, the largest warships in the world, are more than 1,000 feet long, 252 feet wide, can carry 85 airplanes, and cost $4.5 billion apiece.

Careers and Salary

The starting salary for a naval architecture major ranges from $25,000 to $40,000 and could be much more depending on your level of education and whether you enter the public or private sector.

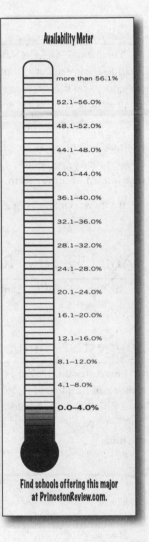

Availability Meter

more than 56.1%

52.1–56.0%

48.1–52.0%

44.1–48.0%

40.1–44.0%

36.1–40.0%

32.1–36.0%

28.1–32.0%

24.1–28.0%

20.1–24.0%

16.1–20.0%

12.1–16.0%

8.1–12.0%

4.1–8.0%

0.0–4.0%

Find schools offering this major at PrincetonReview.com.

CAREER OPTIONS	
Consultant	Navy (Officer)

NAVY R.O.T.C.

Basics

The Navy R.O.T.C. (Naval Reserve Officer Training Corps) is a program designed to help college students finance their education and prepare for careers as U.S. naval officers. If you are accepted into an R.O.T.C. program, you'll receive a scholarship that sometimes includes full tuition, money for books and fees, and a small stipend. In return, you agree to serve on active duty in the navy for at least four years after graduation.

As a participant in the Navy R.O.T.C., you'll be able to select your own major—so if you're interested in political science, say, or philosophy, you're still able to major in it. In addition to the course work for your chosen major, you'll also take several required naval science courses and be required to participate in drill instruction, summer training, and other service-related activities.

If you're considering a career in the Navy, the R.O.T.C. program might make sense for you.

If You Like Navy R.O.T.C., You May Also Like . . .

Air Force R.O.T.C., Army R.O.T.C., Marine Corps R.O.T.C., military science, naval architecture

Suggested High School Prep for Navy R.O.T.C.

Since you'll be taking the same general education classes as the rest of your classmates, your best preparation will be a broad range of courses in English, the physical sciences, and mathematics at the most advanced level possible. You should also take a few extra physical fitness courses to toughen up for the training ahead. And get involved; R.O.T.C scholarships are awarded to those young men and women who display leadership qualities.

SAMPLE COLLEGE CURRICULUM FOR NAVY R.O.T.C.

Amphibious Warfare

Courses in your chosen field of concentration

Evolution of Warfare

Leadership and Ethics

Leadership and Management

Naval Engineering

Naval Weapons

Navigation

Seapower and Maritime Affairs

Fun Facts

When Did It All Begin?

The United States Navy was founded on October 13, 1775.

The Department of the Navy was founded on April 30, 1798.

Perfection Is the Standard

Navy officers don't just wear their rank insignias (pins, etc.) wherever they want to—there are specific spots for them depending on an officer's rank, rate, and type of uniform. Here is a brief description of where to wear insignias on the three major types of uniforms:

Khakis: Pins on the collar

Whites: Stripes on shoulder boards

Blues: Stripes sewn on the lower sleeve

(Source: www.chinfo.navy.mil)

Careers and Salary

Starting salaries for Navy R.O.T.C. participants can range from $28,000 to $36,000, but depend greatly on where they are stationed and how they use their skills.

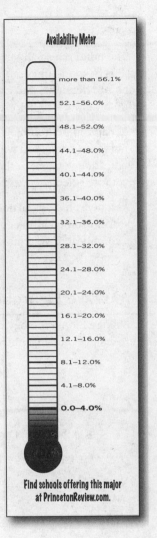

Availability Meter

more than 56.1%

52.1–56.0%

48.1–52.0%

44.1–48.0%

40.1–44.0%

36.1–40.0%

32.1–36.0%

28.1–32.0%

24.1–28.0%

20.1–24.0%

16.1–20.0%

12.1–16.0%

8.1–12.0%

4.1–8.0%

0.0–4.0%

Find schools offering this major at PrincetonReview.com.

CAREER OPTIONS
Navy (Officer)

NEUROBIOLOGY

Basics

The mind is a small but complicated thing. In addition to being a terrible thing to waste, much of it also remains beyond our comprehension, even though it provides our comprehension. All of those synapses and axons and dendrites and chemical reactions take someone with a thorough understanding of biology—and a little bit more—to help reveal the secrets of the brain and nervous system.

A major in neurobiology submerges you in the science of the brain. It's biology with one specific focus, the nervous system. You will go through all of the rigorous training of a biology major, with the added bonus of dedicating yourself to the study of the mind and its control over the body. Perhaps if Descartes had taken a few more science courses, we would have remembered him as the first neurobiologist.

As a neurobiology major you'll have excellent preparation for a career in medicine. You will not only get to perform some cutting-edge research, you will also have the opportunity to explore one of the most delicate, complicated systems of the body.

If You Like Neurobiology, You May Also Like . . .

Biology, biopsychology, cell biology, chemistry, clinical psychology, ecology, genetics, medical technology, neuroscience, nursing, nutrition, occupational therapy, pharmacology, premedicine, psychology

SAMPLE COLLEGE CURRICULUM FOR NEUROBIOLOGY

Biochemistry

Biology

Cell Biology

Chemistry

Developmental Biology

Immunology

Microbiology

Molecular Biology

Molecular Mechanisms of
   Carcinogenesis

Neurobiology

Physics

Physiology

Suggested High School Prep for Neurobiology

Get in all of the high school science classes that you can, including AP biology, chemistry, and physics. In addition you'll need strong math and writing skills as you prepare to publish that dissertation.

Fun Facts

Did You Know?
There are between 100 and 200 billion neurons in the brain.

In Some People, You Can Practically Hear It Sloshing
About 85 percent of the brain is water.

Careers and Salary

Similar to professionals in other science-related fields, a neurobiologist can expect to earn between $28,000 and $35,000 with a bachelor's degree. Advanced degrees, including a PhD or MD, will raise that income substantially.

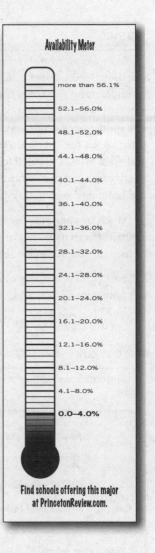

Availability Meter

more than 56.1%

52.1–56.0%

48.1–52.0%

44.1–48.0%

40.1–44.0%

36.1–40.0%

32.1–36.0%

28.1–32.0%

24.1–28.0%

20.1–24.0%

16.1–20.0%

12.1–16.0%

8.1–12.0%

4.1–8.0%

0.0–4.0%

Find schools offering this major at PrincetonReview.com.

CAREER OPTIONS

Biochemist	Geneticist	Physician
Biologist	Health Care Administrator	Psychologist
Ecologist		

NEUROSCIENCE

Basics

Ever wonder how our minds work? A major in neuroscience might put you on a path to answering that question. Neuroscience, according to Kenyon College, is "the study of brain-behavior relationships in order to understand the roles they play in regulating both animal and human behavior." A relatively new field of study, neuroscience combines the fields of biology, psychology, chemistry, engineering, and others to come to a more specific understanding of how brain structures influence behavior. As a neuroscience major, you'll learn about the evolution of the brain, cellular neuroscience, and genetics. You'll learn about consciousness and what affects it. You'll learn about the nervous system and what factors might enhance or destroy it. You'll study various types of both normal and abnormal behavior. And then you'll put them together and see how the brain and nervous system are themselves factors in why we act the way we do.

Much of your neuroscience course work will require research and laboratory work. You might study the electrical activity of nerve cells or evaluate the effects of drugs on behavior; there are any number of directions your research may lead you.

You can apply your neuroscience major to any number of fields—medicine, research, and psychology are only a few of the options. Let your own vision and passion for the brain lead you.

If You Like Neuroscience, You May Also Like . . .

Agricultural and biological engineering, biochemistry, biology, biopsychology, cell biology, chemistry, child development, clinical psychology, developmental psychology, experimental psychology, microbiology, neurobiology, nursing, premedicine, pre-veterinary medicine, psychology

SAMPLE COLLEGE CURRICULUM FOR NEUROSCIENCE

Cells, Metabolism, and Heredity

Cognitive Neuroscience

Comparative Animal Physiology

Developmental Biology

Drugs and Behavior

Electrophysiology

Evolution and Human Evolution

Neurobiology

Neuropsychology

Neuropsychopharmacology

Physiological Psychology

Sensation and Perception

Sensory Biology

Suggested High School Prep for Neuroscience

Advanced classes in math and science are a must if you're considering a major in neuroscience. Not only will many schools accept only students who already have a strong math and science background, but you'll also be glad you have a strong foundation of knowledge in these areas once your college courses begin. A good knowledge of computers is also necessary for your success.

Fun Facts

My Brain Is Bigger Than Your Brain . . .

How big, exactly, is the brain? The human brain weighs about 1,400 grams. Here are some more Fun Facts about brain weight.

- Elephant brain: 6,000 grams
- Rhesus monkey brain: 95 grams
- Cat brain: 30 grams
- Rat brain: 2 grams
- Beagle dog brain: 72 grams
- Chimpanzee brain: 420 grams

(Source: Neuroscience for Kids, http://faculty.washington.edu/chudler/what.html)

More of the Finer Points About the Brain

- There are about 100 billion neurons in the brain. These neurons connect to form almost 1 quadrillion synapses.
- The brain takes up about 2 percent of our body weight.
- According to a PubMed search, 34,734 papers dealing in some way with the brain were published in 2000.
- One neuron is about 10 micrometers wide. A micrometer is 1 millionth of a meter.

(Source: Neuroscience for Kids)

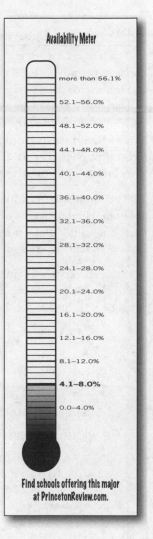

Availability Meter

more than 56.1%

52.1–56.0%

48.1–52.0%

44.1–48.0%

40.1–44.0%

36.1–40.0%

32.1–36.0%

28.1–32.0%

24.1–28.0%

20.1–24.0%

16.1–20.0%

12.1–16.0%

8.1–12.0%

4.1–8.0%

0.0–4.0%

Find schools offering this major at PrincetonReview.com.

Careers and Salary

The starting salary for neuroscience majors is close to $30,000, but this can vary depending on experience and the field chosen. Level of education also makes a world of difference, and most neuroscience majors continue their studies in graduate or medical school.

CAREER OPTIONS		
Biochemist	Geneticist	Physician
Biologist	Nurse	

NUCLEAR ENGINEERING

Basics

Nuclear engineering is a relatively new field of study; only in the past 50 years have the applications of the field been realized. Nuclear engineering deals with the production and application of nuclear energy and the use of radioactive materials. As a nuclear engineering major, you'll be building a strong foundation of math and science that will enable you to pursue a career in one of many exciting fields. You'll learn about nuclear reactors and how to ensure their safety, the behavior of heat and fluids, and how to measure radiation and decrease its harmful effect on people and the environment. Eventually, you may choose to focus on medical physics, thermal hydraulics, nuclear materials, nuclear waste management, radiation technology, or any number of medical and scientific fields.

The applications of nuclear technology form a huge, multibillion-dollar business in the United States. Environmental concerns mandate that new and cleaner energy sources be explored, and the medical industry is constantly seeking advancements. Your nuclear engineering major may lead you to make discoveries that could truly alter the world.

Be prepared for a lifetime of learning. As with any scientific field, nuclear engineering is subject to new discoveries that are being made daily and new technologies that are constantly being developed. Eventually, you'll be part of this constantly evolving and growing community of engineers, researchers, and teachers.

SAMPLE COLLEGE CURRICULUM FOR NUCLEAR ENGINEERING

Chemistry

Computer Programming

Elements of Nuclear Engineering

Fusion Reactor Technologies

Nuclear Engineering Ethics

Nuclear Engineering Materials

Nuclear Fuels

Physics

Radiation and Environment

Radiation Measurement

Reactor Engineering

Reactor Safety Analysis

Reactor Theory

Thermodynamics

If You Like Nuclear Engineering, You May Also Like . . .

Biology, chemical engineering, chemistry, computer and information science, electrical engineering, mathematics, physics, pre-med

Suggested High School Prep for Nuclear Engineering

Take as many math and science courses as you can handle—chemistry, biology, physics, physical science, calculus, geometry, and algebra. Advanced courses will certainly help get you into competitive engineering programs. And since part of your nuclear engineering training will be learning how nuclear engineering affects our world, classes in politics and international affairs might be useful as well.

Fun Facts

Did You Know?

One unit of radiation, equal to the quantity of a radioactive material that will have one transformation (or decay) per second, is called a Becquerel.

A Little Light Makes All the Difference

In 1896, Antoine Henri Becquerel observed that uranium, when exposed to light, actually changed into another element—the phenomenon that today has applications in nuclear energy and radiological science. Becquerel received the 1903 Nobel Prize for his discovery.

According to the Nuclear Energy Institute

If the United States closed all 103 nuclear plants and replaced them with fossil fuel-fired plants, we would have to remove 90 million cars from America's highways just to maintain air quality.

Careers and Salary

Depending on where you live and exactly what your job entails, an estimated starting salary for a nuclear engineering major with a bachelor's degree is about $57,000.

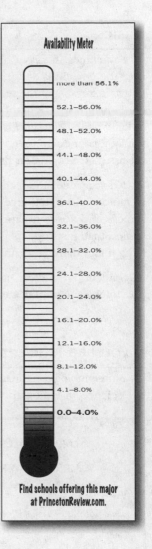

Availability Meter

more than 56.1%

52.1–56.0%

48.1–52.0%

44.1–48.0%

40.1–44.0%

36.1–40.0%

32.1–36.0%

28.1–32.0%

24.1–28.0%

20.1–24.0%

16.1–20.0%

12.1–16.0%

8.1–12.0%

4.1–8.0%

0.0–4.0%

Find schools offering this major at PrincetonReview.com.

CAREER OPTIONS

| Aerospace Engineer | Navy (Officer) | Nuclear Engineer |

NUCLEAR MEDICINE TECHNOLOGY

Basics

Sometimes an x-ray isn't enough, and when that happens, a nuclear medicine technician will help administer the chemicals and imaging that your doctor needs to diagnose certain ailments. The major difference between x-rays and the tests that utilize nuclear medicine is that an x-ray can only see the static anatomy of the human body; it cannot see the dynamic physiology of an ailment. Here's an example: if your doctor needs to know whether a bone is broken or not, and x-ray will be able to reveal it because your bones function structurally. If your doctor needs to know for instance which gland is over or under stimulated, he or she will need the assistance of nuclear medicine because that is a question of how your body is functioning as a system.

Nuclear medicine technicians are responsible for conducting medical imaging tests that require the aid of radionuclides that give off gamma rays. Technicians will be required to administer the radioactive substances and position patients so that the correct images are taken by what are called gamma cameras. In some situations students with degrees in nuclear medicine technology will work with the equipment, servicing it and training technicians for proper use.

Students of nuclear medicine technology can expect training in imaging, biology, radiology, anatomy, physiology and patient care.

If you like Nuclear Medicine Technology, you may also like...

Biotechnology, medical imaging technology, radiation therapy, nursing, biology, forensics and investigative science, or radiography

SAMPLE COLLEGE CURRICULUM FOR

Anatomy

Basic Computer Visual Programming

Calculus

Computer Applications

Gamma Cameras

Mathematical Evaluation of Clinical Data

Organic Chemistry

Physics

Physiology

Radiation Biology

Radiation Protection

Radionuclides in Medicine

Records and Administrative Procedures

Suggested High School Prep for

Since nuclear medicine technology requires an understanding of the technology and the science the technology is striving to image, a combination of biology, chemistry, calculus and anatomy as well as computer training will prepare students for coursework and careers.

ALLIED MEDICAL AND HEALTH PROFESSIONS

Fun Facts

Nuclear medicine technology uses healthy does of radiation to diagnose various diseases and physical problems to fit patients with the right treatment. In the 1940s and 1950s radiation was used in unhealthy doses to help consumers fit into their shoes. The fluoroscope was an x-ray machine that projected and image of your foot inside of the shoe into a viewfinder so you could judge how well the shoe fit. By the 1970s 33 states had banned their use because of their radiation contamination.

(Source: www.MuseumofQuackery.com)

Careers and Salary

Graduates may work in hospitals, doctors' offices, imaging centers or clinics, or in commercial capacities servicing equipment. Because the type of employment ranges so greatly the starting salary for nuclear medicine technicians ranges from $35,000 to $70,000 with a median salary of $50,000.

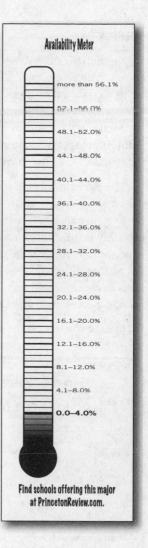

Availability Meter

more than 56.1%

52.1–56.0%

48.1–52.0%

44.1–48.0%

40.1–44.0%

36.1–40.0%

32.1–36.0%

28.1–32.0%

24.1–28.0%

20.1–24.0%

16.1–20.0%

12.1–16.0%

8.1–12.0%

4.1–8.0%

0.0–4.0%

Find schools offering this major at PrincetonReview.com.

CAREER OPTIONS

Forensic Scientist   Nuclear Medical Technician   X-Ray Technician

NURSING

Basics

Nursing is a diverse and rewarding discipline that combines compassion with sophisticated health technology. Nurses evaluate, diagnose, and treat health problems. They help people meet basic health needs, adapt to physical changes, recover from illness, and die with dignity. But you knew all that. The profession offers a variety of employment and career opportunities. Nurses are employed in clinics, hospitals, schools, corporations, the military, and in private practice. Of course, you probably knew that, too. You may not know that job prospects in nursing are, in a word, awesome. "Bursting at the seams" doesn't adequately describe the magnitude of the current need for nurses.

The Bachelor of Science in Nursing is the basic professional degree in nursing and it provides the foundation for graduate study (which you can pursue if you want to, but is by no means required for job security). If you major in nursing, you'll take traditional science and liberal arts courses as a first-year student and probably begin clinical rotations at hospitals and other health care facilities during the second semester of your sophomore year. In practice, what that means is you'll start working at a hospital doing the kinds of things that nurses do. You'll receive patient reports, treat patients, and administer everything from medications to endotracheal suction procedures—the whole nine yards. In the course of your college career, you'll receive a substantial amount of practical, hands-on training.

One of the important things to know about the field of nursing is that there is a national standardized test involved. All would-be nurses are required by law to take the National Certification Licensure Examination for Registered Nurses (NCLEX) after graduating from an accredited nursing program before they can be officially registered.

SAMPLE COLLEGE CURRICULUM FOR NURSING

Abnormal Psychology

Biochemistry

Biology

Chemistry

Clinical Rotations

Foundations of Nursing

Human Anatomy

Mental Health Nursing

Microbiology

Nursing Care of Adults

Nursing Care of Children

Nursing Care of Older Adults

Nursing Care of the Childbearing
Family

Nutrition

Sociology

Statistics

If You Like Nursing, You May Also Like . . .

Agricultural and biological engineering, biochemistry, biology, biopsychology, botany and plant biology, cell biology, chemistry, chiropractic, circulation technology, dietetics, health administration, human development, medical technology, occupational therapy, pharmacology, pharmacy, physical therapy, premedicine, pre-optometry, pre-veterinary medicine, radiologic technology, rehabilitation services, respiratory therapy

Suggested High School Prep for Nursing

Admission to many nursing programs is competitive, to say the least. If you want to get an edge, you should take as many high school science and math courses as possible. Advanced Placement biology, chemistry, and physics classes will prove especially helpful.

ALLIED MEDICAL AND HEALTH PROFESSIONS

Fun Facts

Did You Know?

Nursing is the largest health care profession in the United States. There are more than 2.5 million registered nurses nationwide.

Nursing Has Become a Highly Specialized Field

If you major in nursing, you can specialize in a number of fields, including

- Geriatrics
- Pediatrics
- Neurology
- Recovery Room
- Operating Room
- Pulmonary
- Critical Care
- Oncology
- Medical
- Emergency Room and Trauma
- Surgical
- Obstetrics
- Home Health Care
- Mental Health

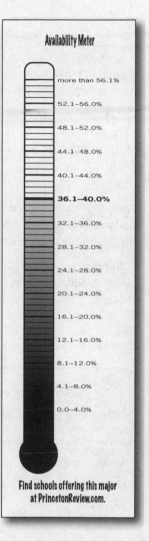

Availability Meter

more than 56.1%

52.1–56.0%

48.1–52.0%

44.1–48.0%

40.1–44.0%

36.1–40.0%

32.1–36.0%

28.1–32.0%

24.1–28.0%

20.1–24.0%

16.1–20.0%

12.1–16.0%

8.1–12.0%

4.1–8.0%

0.0–4.0%

Find schools offering this major
at PrincetonReview.com.

Careers and Salary

The average starting salary for a newly registered nurse ranges from about $26,000 to $37,000 per year. The median salary nationwide for nurses is about $52,000. The highest paid nurses can earn more than $74,000.

CAREER OPTIONS

Dentist	Occupational Therapist	Physician
Health Care Administrator	Paramedic	Public Health Administrator
Hospice Nurse	Pharmaceutical Sales Representative	Substance Abuse Counselor
Nurse		

NUTRITION

Basics

Ever read the side of a box of cereal and wonder what the heck niacin is and why you need it? If you majored in nutrition, you'd know that it's a part of the vitamin B complex, which helps prevent pellagra, just one of many diet-linked diseases whose butts you'll learn how to kick.

As a science, nutrition is concerned with the ways in which the food we eat affects our physical well-being. Nutritionists are not only our fitness guides, reminding us of how much or how little we should be eating, but they're also interested in helping us understand the relationship between our diets and our health.

A blend of several of the sciences—including chemistry, biology, and anatomy—nutrition involves identifying the nutrients that are necessary for growth and sustaining life. Nutrition majors work to understand how nutrients interact with one another and precisely how much of any given nutrient is needed under various environmental conditions.

Interlinked with the other sciences, nutrition majors fulfill all of the requirements of a premedicine program, providing a broad background in each of the disciplines necessary to entering a career in health or medicine.

SAMPLE COLLEGE CURRICULUM FOR NUTRITION

Advanced Human Nutrition

Animal Cell Physiology

Biochemistry

Biology

Chemistry

Data Analysis

Fundamentals of Human Nutrition

Introductory Physiology

Math

Molecular Genetics

Nutrition: The Life Cycle

Nutritional Therapy

Organic Chemistry

Physics

Physiological Basis for Food

Quantitative Analysis

If You Like Nutrition, You May Also Like . . .

Chemistry, child care, food science, genetics, gerontology, home economics, human development, medical technology, microbiology, neurobiology, neuroscience, nursing, occupational therapy, pharmacology, pharmacy, physical therapy, physiological psychology, premedicine, pre-optometry, pre-veterinary medicine, public health

Suggested High School Prep for Nutrition

If you are interested in studying nutrition, take as many courses as possible in chemistry, biology, and math as well as home economics and health classes.

NUTRITION, HOME ECONOMICS, AND RELATED FIELDS

Fun Facts

Did You Know?

According to a study reported by the National Center for Health Statistics, 49 percent of American women and 59 percent of American men are overweight.

Fact or Fiction

Fiction: Sugar, white bread, and pasta are fattening.

Fact: No single food causes weight gain. Cutting extra calories or portions by first reducing fat, not carbohydrates, will help you manage your weight in a healthier way.

Careers and Salary

Starting salaries range from $25,000 to $32,000, depending on the level of practical experience. Those holding advanced degrees can earn significantly more.

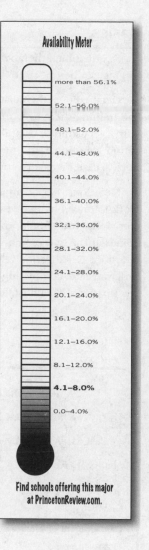

Availability Meter

more than 56.1%

52.1–56.0%

48.1–52.0%

44.1–48.0%

40.1–44.0%

36.1–40.0%

32.1–36.0%

28.1–32.0%

24.1–28.0%

20.1–24.0%

16.1–20.0%

12.1–16.0%

8.1–12.0%

4.1–8.0%

0.0–4.0%

Find schools offering this major at PrincetonReview.com.

CAREER OPTIONS

Caterer	Child Care Worker	Public Health Administrator
Chef	Nutritionist	Teacher

OCCUPATIONAL THERAPY

Basics

Occupational therapy is a relatively new and a definitely expanding specialty in the health care field. Its origins can be traced to increasing industrialization and the disastrous effects of modern warfare.

Occupational therapists help people of all ages prevent, reduce, and overcome disabilities by encouraging and training them to work, draw, dance, and express themselves in social settings. They work with patients with every kind of disability: heart problems, cerebral palsy, arthritis, serious physical injuries, mental retardation, emotional and neurological disorders—you name it, really. They also work with families, doctors, nurses, case managers, social workers, and other therapists.

Most four-year occupational therapy programs consist of two years of science-heavy classroom course work followed by two years of professional, hands-on fieldwork, particularly during senior year. One important thing you should know about occupational therapy is that an important, national standardized test comes at the end of your undergraduate years. To be an occupational therapist, you must take the National Board for Certification in Occupational Therapy (NBCOT) examination after graduating from an accredited program and completing all your fieldwork. It is only then that you will officially earn the designation Occupational Therapist, Registered (OTR).

If You Like Occupational Therapy, You May Also Like . . .

Agricultural and biological engineering, biochemistry, biology, biopsychology, botany and plant biology, cell biology, chemistry, chiropractic, circulation technology, dietetics, health administration, human development, medical technology, pharmacology, pharmacy, physical therapy, premedicine, pre-optometry, pre-veterinary medicine, radiologic technology, rehabilitation services, respiratory therapy

Suggested High School Prep for Occupational Therapy

Occupational therapy programs can be somewhat competitive. If you want to get an edge, you should take as many high school science and math courses as possible. Advanced Placement biology, chemistry, and physics classes will prove especially helpful. Also, take psychology if your school offers it.

SAMPLE COLLEGE CURRICULUM FOR OCCUPATIONAL THERAPY

Abnormal Psychology

Biology

Chemistry

Development of Children and Adolescents

Developmental Psychology

Ergonomics

Fieldwork

Human Anatomy

Human Development

Human Physiology

Neurodevelopment

Principles of Disease

Research Methods

Sociology

Fun Facts

Quantity and Quality

Occupational therapy is one of the fastest growing professions in the country, and occupational therapists consistently rate their field as having high job satisfaction and low stress. (Source: United States Bureau of Labor Statistics)

When Money's a Little Tight

The American Occupational Therapy Foundation offers nearly 100 scholarships each year to students enrolled in all manner of occupational therapy programs. Each award has some of its own requirements, but all recipients must:

- be full-time, currently enrolled occupational therapy majors
- be members of the American Occupational Therapy Foundation
- need financial assistance
- have a record of outstanding academic achievement
- provide two personal references, a statement about themselves from their school's occupational therapy department, and official transcripts.

For more information, check out the American Occupational Therapy Foundation's website at www.Aota.org.

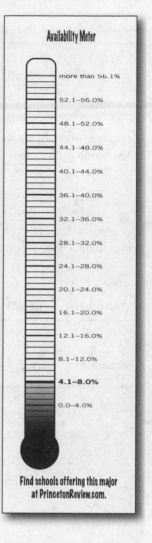

Availability Meter

- more than 56.1%
- 52.1–56.0%
- 48.1–52.0%
- 44.1–48.0%
- 40.1–44.0%
- 36.1–40.0%
- 32.1–36.0%
- 28.1–32.0%
- 24.1–28.0%
- 20.1–24.0%
- 16.1–20.0%
- 12.1–16.0%
- 8.1–12.0%
- **4.1–8.0%**
- 0.0–4.0%

Find schools offering this major at PrincetonReview.com.

Careers and Salary

Typical starting salaries for occupational therapists range from $32,000 to almost $45,000 per year.

CAREER OPTIONS

Mediator   Occupational Therapist

OCEAN ENGINEERING

Basics

It's big and it's blue and you can bet that we haven't even begun to understand its depth. The ocean is one of the richest and most complicated bodies in the world, providing us with everything from oil to oxygen. Someone out there has to help us understand its potential and resources, and you can bet that we're not looking to Eugenie Clark (a.k.a. the Shark Lady) to answer our questions (or at least not all of them). No, for this we depend on the ocean engineer, the scientist who has brought the math and the analytical tools of engineering to bear on the largest physical mass on the face of the earth. We turn to the ocean engineers of the world to help us understand such complex things as ocean thermal dynamics or the best way to preserve the balance of delicate resources that we can find only in the ocean.

The career options with an ocean engineering major are varied because not only will you have the skills of an engineer (the ability to figure out differential math equations while leaping a tall building), but you'll also have the entire ocean as your specialty. So whether you want to help design the next battleship or help preserve the Great Barrier Reef, the world is your oyster.

If You Like Ocean Engineering, You May Also Like . . .

Applied mathematics, applied physics, atmospheric science, biology, chemical engineering, chemistry, ecology, engineering design, engineering mechanics, environmental and environmental health engineering, environmental science, marine science, petroleum engineering, zoology

SAMPLE COLLEGE CURRICULUM FOR OCEAN ENGINEERING

Differential Equations

Dynamics

Engineering Graphics

Engineering Math

Fluid Mechanics

Network Analysis

Ocean and Environmental Data Analysis

Ocean Engineering Laboratory

Ocean System Control and Design

Oceanography

Programming in Computer Science

Statistics and Buoyancy

Vibrations

Suggested High School Prep for Ocean Engineering

A lot of deep sea diving is a good way to begin preparing for a major in ocean engineering. If your diving suit happens to be at the cleaners, consider very strong math and science skills, particularly advanced mathematics like trigonometry and calculus, as solid preparation for what lies ahead. On the science side, advanced physics is probably the subject your school offers that is most pertinent to this major.

Fun Facts

Did You Know?

The oceans and marginal seas of the world cover 71 percent of Earth's surface.

The Upstart Ocean

The Indian Ocean is the youngest and smallest of the world's oceans, and yet it's also considered the most complex, stretching for more than 6,200 miles, with its deepest point at 24,442 feet.

Careers and Salary

This major gives you a wide reach. Starting salaries, depending on where you focus your work, can range from $27,000 to $53,000.

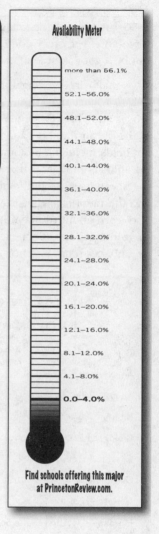

Availability Meter

more than 56.1%

52.1–56.0%

48.1–52.0%

44.1–48.0%

40.1–44.0%

36.1–40.0%

32.1–36.0%

28.1–32.0%

24.1–28.0%

20.1–24.0%

16.1–20.0%

12.1–16.0%

8.1–12.0%

4.1–8.0%

0.0–4.0%

Find schools offering this major at PrincetonReview.com.

CAREER OPTIONS

Ecologist

Environmentalist/
Environmental Scientist

OCEANOGRAPHY

Basics

Great white sharks can go up to three months without eating. If the ocean's total salt content were dried, it would cover every continent to a depth of five feet. Dolphins can whistle, coral can sting, and seaweed can be a good source of calcium, zinc, and even protein. Want more?

A major in oceanography focuses—obviously—on oceans. Not just the deep, dark, mysterious waters, but also what they're made of, what lives in them, how they create and use resources, and how the sea moves and changes. Oregon State describes oceanography as "the application of the sciences to the study of the oceans," and oceanography is truly an interdisciplinary major. You'll study elements from many different fields, including biology, chemistry, physics, geology, math, and geography. You'll learn about the captivating animals and plants that make the sea their home—what they eat, and how they live, and how they affect the ocean itself. From the nutrients and gases in ocean waters to tides, currents, shoreline formation, waves, and the motion of the sea, you'll become an expert on every aspect of the world's greatest feature. You'll also learn about the complex relationship between the ocean and the rest of the environment, and how their interactions affect each other—and us. Finally, you'll examine some of the challenges and threats the ocean faces today and how we might best address them.

Many oceanography programs give students the opportunity to work directly with the ocean through on-site laboratories, internships, and research projects. The field of oceanography—like the oceans themselves—is extraordinarily rich, and some programs may ask you to focus on one specific area. Specializations might include biological oceanography, chemical oceanography, marine geology, and physical oceanography. Through your studies, you'll gain a deep (so to speak) understanding of oceans and their ever-changing role in our world.

If You Like Oceanography, You May Also Like . . .

Animal sciences, biochemistry, biology, cell biology, ecology, environmental and environmental health engineering, environmental science, marine science, ocean engineering

Suggested High School Prep for Oceanography

To prepare for a major in oceanography, you should take a variety of courses in biology, chemistry, physics, and math. Science courses with laboratory components will be especially valuable. Reading, writing, and speaking skills are important to this major as well, so take courses in English, languages, and other humanities.

SAMPLE COLLEGE CURRICULUM FOR OCEANOGRAPHY

Aquaculture Production

Aquatic Pollution

Biological Oceanography

Biological Pollution Control

Chemical Oceanography

Coastal Law

Geography of the Pacific

Human Adaptation to the Sea

International Ocean Law

Living Resources of the Sea

Marine Geology

Marine Geophysics

Mineral and Energy Resources of the Sea

Ocean Mapping

Ocean Minerals

Paleooceanography

Sea and Society

Sedimentology

Fun Facts

That's Deep, Man, Deep

How deep is the ocean? The depth of the ocean changes from spot to spot, but here are the average depths of the four major oceans.

- Pacific Ocean: 14,050 feet
- Atlantic Ocean: 10,930 feet
- Indian Ocean: 12,760 feet
- Arctic Ocean: 3,250 feet
- The largest ocean is the Pacific; the smallest is the Arctic.

(Source: www.oceanlink.island.net/ask/oceanography.html)

Challenge This!

Ever hear of the Challenger Deep? This is the deepest part of any of the oceans. It is in the Mariana Trench, between Japan and New Guinea. Get ready for this: The Challenger Deep is 36,204 feet deep, or 6.89 miles. Mount Everest, 5.53 miles high, could fit inside with room to spare.

(Source: www.oceanlink.island.net/ask/oceanography.html)

Careers and Salary

Oceanographers usually earn a salary near $50,000. Your level of education and the amount of experience you've had will make a big difference, and salaries often go much higher as you progress in your field.

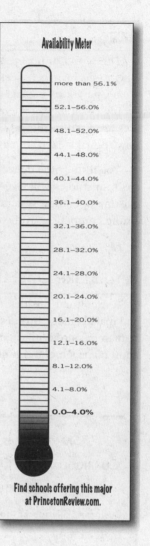

Availability Meter

more than 56.1%

52.1–56.0%

48.1–52.0%

44.1–48.0%

40.1–44.0%

36.1–40.0%

32.1–36.0%

28.1–32.0%

24.1–28.0%

20.1–24.0%

16.1–20.0%

12.1–16.0%

8.1–12.0%

4.1–8.0%

0.0–4.0%

Find schools offering this major at PrincetonReview.com.

CAREER OPTIONS

Aquarium Manager	Ocean Resources Manager	Researcher
Biologist	Oceanographer	Scientist
Environmental Consultant	Professor	Teacher
Marine Scientist		

OPERATIONS MANAGEMENT

Basics

The world of business involves many intricate workings, and operations management covers them all. Operations managers seek to control the processes that determine outputs from businesses. In other words, as an operations management major you'll study operating systems, quality management, product design, supply chain management, and inventory control. You'll study how equipment, information, labor, and facilities are used in the production process. You'll learn what steps go into making a product or service and how to make each step as efficient and beneficial to the company as possible.

You'll study the delivery systems that serve customers and the ways to administer helpful customer service. Your studies will give you the knowledge you'll need to identify and evaluate problems with a business's existing operating system and the skills you'll need to improve the system to help turn the business into a strong competitor in the marketplace.

If You Like Operations Management, You May Also Like . . .

Agricultural business and management, agricultural technology management, business administration and management, business communications, computer and information science, computer systems analysis, human resources management, industrial management, logistics management, managerial economics, recreation management, risk management

Suggested High School Prep for Operations Management

Your best preparation for any management major is to become familiar with math and humanities courses. Computer skills and a foreign language are assets. And English classes will give you the writing, reading, and speaking skills you'll need to become a successful manager.

SAMPLE COLLEGE CURRICULUM FOR OPERATIONS MANAGEMENT

Business Skills and Environment

Decision Theory

Designing, Managing, and Improving Operations

Finite Math

Legal Environment of Business

Managing Product Development

Managing Technology Ventures

Operations Planning and Control

Operations Strategy

Organizational Behavior

Principles of Economics

Principles of Finance

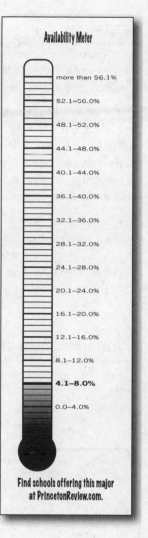

Fun Facts

What Is Benchmarking?

Every manager wants his or her business to be the best producer of whatever product(s) or service(s) it provides, and an important part of operations management is figuring out what being the "best" means and what standards there are to measure it. Once managers understand the concept of the "best" and determine who in the industry holds that title, they can formulate goals for their own business and make appropriate changes. This process of determination is benchmarking.

A Few Good Words for Effective Operations Managers

"Everything should be made as simple as possible, but not simpler."

—Albert Einstein

"If a man will begin with certainties, he shall end in doubts; but if he will be content to begin with doubts, he shall end in certainties."

—Francis Bacon

"The secret of good direction does not consist of solving problems, but in identifying them."

—Lawrence A. Appley

"Genius is one percent inspiration and 99 percent perspiration."

—Thomas Alva Edison

Careers and Salary

Starting salaries for operations management majors are usually in the mid-thirties, but they depend greatly on your level of education, amount of experience, place of employment, and type of work you do.

CAREER OPTIONS

Human Resources Manager	Management Consultant	Quality Control Manager
Information Manager	Office Manager	Small Business Owner
Internet/Intranet Technologies Manager	Production Manager	

OPHTHALMIC MEDICAL TECHNOLOGY

Basics

When you go for and eye exam you spend time being diagnosed and checked by and ophthalmologist, but also you are cared for by an ophthalmic medical technologist who assists the ophthalmologist in the same way that nurses assist general practitioners.

The main role of an ophthalmic tech is to help an ophthalmologist see more patients in a day. As an ophthalmic tech, you may be asked to perform any number of tasks including first aid, pre- and post-operative cleansing and preparation, changing dressings, conducting diagnosis tests, taking ophthalmologic photographs and instructing patients about how to care for glasses or contact lenses. Other duties such as verifying prescriptions for lenses, fitting patients for glasses and frames, or dispensing prescriptions may be included as duties depending on the size of the office or hospital.

Receiving a degree or certification as an ophthalmic technician can be done through several colleges, two-year institutions or in online courses. While most positions will be found in eye-care offices and hospitals, there is a growing need for trained technicians who can work proficiently in wholesale capacities with labs, or selling equipment and lenses. Depending on the level of certification, an ophthalmic technician has, he or she may be asked to assist in surgeries or coordinate other technicians in a larger office.

If you like Opthalmic Medical Technology, you may also like

Ophthalmology, optics, optical surgery

Suggested High School Prep for Ophthalmic Medical Technology

To streamline work in a hectic office setting an ophthalmic technologist will need to have good communication skills and be highly organized in addition to the technical training of the ophthalmology field. Coursework that will lead to these skills are writing, reading and basic anatomy and physiology.

SAMPLE COLLEGE CURRICULUM FOR OPHTHALMIC MEDICAL TECHNOLOGY

Anatomy

Biology

Computer Literacy

Health Sciences

Medical Office Insurance

Medical Office Procedures

Medical Terminology

Professional Development Skills

Vision Care

Writing

Fun Facts

The earliest corrective lenses date back to early Roman and Egyptian times. Emperor Nero was known for watching the gladiatorial games through an emerald as far back as the 1st century. Modern lenses as we know them stem from Abbas Ibn Firnas who devised a way to fix sand into glass that could be polished into usable lenses known as reading stones in the 9th century.

(Source: www.wikipedia.com)

Careers and Salary

For most starting ophthalmic medical technologists, the starting salary ranges from $28,500 to $42,600 with most beginning salaries being $34,400.

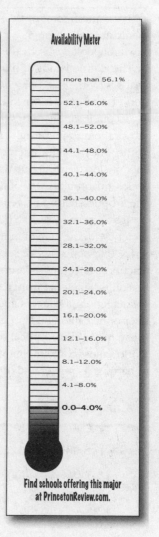

Availability Meter

more than 56.1%

52.1–56.0%

48.1–52.0%

44.1–48.0%

40.1–44.0%

36.1–40.0%

32.1–36.0%

28.1–32.0%

24.1–28.0%

20.1–24.0%

16.1–20.0%

12.1–16.0%

8.1–12.0%

4.1–8.0%

0.0–4.0%

Find schools offering this major
at PrincetonReview.com.

CAREER OPTIONS	
Ophthalmologist	Physician

OPTICS/OPTICAL SCIENCES

Basics

It's a question of optics, really. When light from the sun enters the atmosphere, most of the colors of the spectrum pass through without incident. But blue light, due to its high frequency and small wave length, inevitably collides with the innumerable particles of oxygen and nitrogen we more commonly refer to as air. These little bands of blue light bounce here, there, and everywhere above our heads, and . . . wait for it: That's why the sky's blue! Or, why it looks blue anyway. (So what if you didn't ask? You were wondering. Don't try to deny it. We know these things. We're very perceptive.)

To put it simply, optics (or optical science) majors find their primary point of focus on the very thing that allows them to focus: light. From the Greek word meaning "to look," optics is the branch of physics devoted to the study of light energy—its structure, properties, and behavior under different conditions. Optical science majors learn about wave theory, wave mechanics, electromagnetic theory, physical optics, geometric optics, quantum theory of light, photon detecting, laser theory, wall and beam properties, chaotic light, nonlinear optics, harmonic generation, optical systems theory, and applications to engineering problems.

It's all very technical, but the study of light has led to lots of applicable technologies for contemporary society. With the help of more advanced lenses—from the ones in our glasses to the ones powering the Hubble Space Telescope—we're seeing the world and universe with greater detail than ever before. Doctors and manufacturers alike utilize lasers to perform delicate surgeries or to make precise cuts in metal. The medical profession is benefiting from CAT scans, MRI technology, digital monitoring of life support systems, and the optical detection of cancers and tumors. Information bounces all over the world at light speed with the help of fiber optic cable, and laser-guiding technology has helped to make our military's weaponry the most reliable. If you major in the optical sciences you're not only going to be let in on the explanations behind some of the world's most confounding visual phenomena, you'll also be learning how to manipulate light—of all things—to harness its power and further the goals of human progression. Doesn't that sound like a bright idea?

If You Like Optics/Optical Sciences, You Might Also Like...

Actuarial science, aerospace engineering, applied mathematics, applied physics, astrophysics, atmospheric science, biochemistry, biology, ceramic engineering, chemical engineering, chemistry, civil engineering, computer and information science, computer engineering, computer systems analysis, economics, electrical engineering, engineering design, engineering mechanics, environmental and environmental health engineering, geology, geological engineering, industrial engineering, mathematics, mechanical engineering, metallurgical engineering, mineral engineering, nuclear engineering, ocean engineering, petroleum engineering, physics, statistics, textile engineering

Suggested High School Prep for Optics/Optical Sciences

Without a doubt, take all the math and science classes you can. Optics is not the kind of major that starts slow. If you're not ready for college-level coursework in calculus and physics the first semester, you'll be asking for trouble. Take advanced placement classes in all of that stuff.

SAMPLE COLLEGE CURRICULUM FOR OPTICS/OPTICAL SCIENCES

Advanced Optics

Calculus

Classical Mechanics

Differential Equations and Linear Algebra

Electricity and Magnetism

Electromagnetism

Introduction to Quantum Physics

Matter, Space, and Energy

Mechanics and Gravity

Multivariate Calculus

Optics Lab

Quantum Mechanics

Relativistic Electrodynamics

Waves, Optics, and Optical Technology

Fun Facts

Roy G. Biv

Our ability to see color is simply the way our eyes differentiate between light at different wavelengths. Red: 780 nm, orange: 620 nm, yellow: 585 nm, green: 570 nm, blue: 490 nm, indigo: 440 nm, violet: 420 nm. Their varying wavelengths and frequencies are specifically responsible for the perceived color of, well . . . everything.

Did You Know?

Don't tell Superman, but the sun is white. The reason we see the sun as being yellow is the same reason we see the sky as blue. The atmosphere deflects and redirects much of the blue and violet light from the sun, and because the light that takes the straight shot from the sun to our eyes has an apparent blue/violet deficiency, the sun looks more yellow as a result. At dawn and dusk, the sun's light has much more of the atmosphere to cross, so even more of the remaining blue and violet light is deflected before reaching our eyes. As it gets closer to the horizon, and as there are more opportunities for its blue and violet light to be sidetracked, the sun appears to shift in color from yellow, to orange, to red. When there are a lot of foreign particles in the air (e.g., dust, pollen, pollutants), the sunset can become spectacularly saturated.

(Source: http://acept.la.asu.edu)

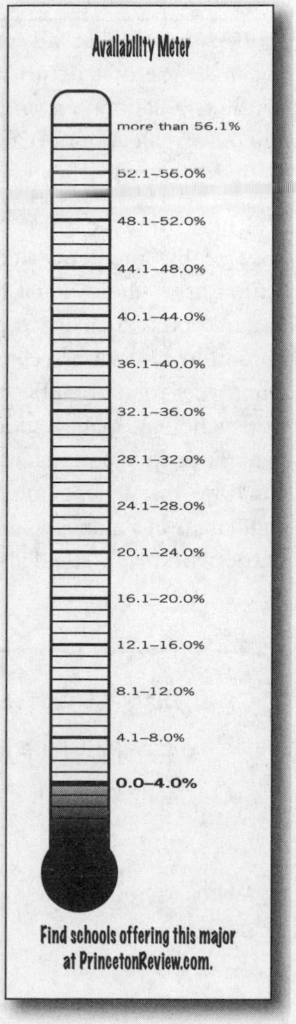
Availability Meter
more than 56.1%
52.1–56.0%
48.1–52.0%
44.1–48.0%
40.1–44.0%
36.1–40.0%
32.1–36.0%
28.1–32.0%
24.1–28.0%
20.1–24.0%
16.1–20.0%
12.1–16.0%
8.1–12.0%
4.1–8.0%
0.0–4.0%
Find schools offering this major at PrincetonReview.com.

Careers and Salary

Starting salaries for optics majors vary, but it is not uncommon for them to make between $30,000 and $40,000 per year with a bachelor's degree.

CAREER OPTIONS

Laser Technician	Optical Engineer	Professor
Optical Physicist		

ORGANIZATIONAL BEHAVIOR STUDIES

Basics

If you were that kid who always brought an ant farm to show-and-tell because you were fascinated by the ants' orderly structure and seamless group efforts, you may have found your calling. The essence of group conflict, collaboration, and cooperation form the basis of a major in organizational behavior studies. Here, you'll learn all about organizations: how they work, who's involved, and why things sometimes fall apart—or, better yet, why they don't.

The workplace is one of the best examples of organizational behavior, so the major will focus largely on how people interact with one another on the job and how their behavior has a crucial impact on the organization as a whole. You'll learn about why people behave the way they do and how their actions can be understood and analyzed psychologically. In addition to taking a look at human resources, employee compensation, and labor relations, you'll also examine the more emotional aspects, such as what motivates employees to do their best and what happens when the quality of their work weakens. You'll study elements of psychology, management, sociology, political science, government, education, and industry in order to reach a deeper understanding of organizational behavior. By understanding the fundamentals of the field, you'll be able to not only predict behavior but also control it. Also important are the responsibilities and challenges of a manager and such principles as reinforcement and punishment and how they come into play in the workplace. You'll also touch on employment law.

Your studies in organizational behavior will take you from the individual level to the group level, and you'll see that the effects of individual behavior are truly profound. (Just like back in that ant farm . . . a workplace in and of itself.) No matter where your major takes you, you'll have the knowledge you need to observe, analyze, and manage individuals and groups with intelligence, compassion, and dignity.

If You Like Organizational Behavior Studies, You May Also Like . . .

Accounting, business administration and management, business communications, entrepreneurship, human resources management, industrial management, international business, logistics management, marketing, operations management, risk management

Suggested High School Prep for Organizational Behavior Studies

The best preparation for a major in organizational behavior studies is a good selection of courses in the humanities, math, and sciences. This field requires excellent communication skills, so take courses in English and languages that will strengthen your reading, writing, and speaking abilities. History courses might give you some new perspectives on the role of work in the world. Understanding the larger world will give you a strong foundation on which to build your knowledge in this field.

SAMPLE COLLEGE CURRICULUM FOR ORGANIZATIONAL BEHAVIOR STUDIES

Arbitration

Business Ethics

Career Development

Compensation

E-Commerce

Employee Benefits

Employment Law

Ethnocultural Issues in the Workplace

Gender and Management

Human Resource Management

Labor Relations

Models of Organizational Change

Negotiating Strategies

Organizational Consulting and Development

Power and Politics in Organization Behavior

Fun Facts

One Man's Thoughts

"The organizations of men, like men themselves, seem subject to deafness, nearsightedness, lameness, and involuntary cruelty. We seem tragically unable to help one another to understand one another."

—John Cheever, writer

(Source: www.bartleby.com)

Work Ethics

Has anyone ever told you that you have a "Protestant work ethic"? Chances are, they meant you are self-disciplined and work very diligently and carefully. This phrase comes from the Protestant Reformation, when work began to take on a new moral significance. This "Protestant ethic" put emphasis on this world instead of the next world, and work became a profound moral duty. Martin Luther said, "All men possess a calling in the world and the fulfillment of its obligation is a divinely imposed duty," and people began working under the spell of his words. Work was—and, in some respects, is—seen as a path to salvation.

(Source: http://web.cba.neu.edu/~ewertheim/introd/history.htm)

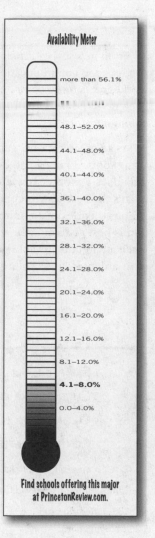

Availability Meter

more than 56.1%

48.1–52.0%

44.1–48.0%

40.1–44.0%

36.1–40.0%

32.1–36.0%

28.1–32.0%

24.1–28.0%

20.1–24.0%

16.1–20.0%

12.1–16.0%

8.1–12.0%

4.1–8.0%

0.0–4.0%

Find schools offering this major at PrincetonReview.com.

Careers and Salary

Starting salaries for organizational behavior studies majors are difficult to predict since there is a wide array of careers you might choose to pursue. If you choose to follow a management path, for instance, your starting salary could be from $30,000 to $50,000, depending on what sort of business you work for and how much experience you've had in your field.

CAREER OPTIONS

Benefits Administrator	Labor Relations Specialist	Researcher
Business Consultant	Management Consultant	Teacher
Business Valuator	Office Manager	Writer
Human Resources Manager	Quality Control Manager	

ORGANIZATIONAL COMMUNICATION

Basics

From newspaper articles and advertisements on television to Fortune 500 companies and political campaigns, good communication is essential. How else do we build relationships or pass on information? As the world grows more complicated and evolving technology moves to unite us, effective communication skills become more important than ever. The best leaders in most any career field also happen to be superstar communicators.

As an organizational communications major you will acquire a mastery of language and communication. Using tools of media and design, you'll study how individuals learn and engage new material. For example, why does a mother buy a certain brand of toothpaste or cereal for her children over another brand? Or, what's the best way to conduct a company-wide meeting with key stockholders? By analyzing and applying various theories of communication, you'll gain an understanding of corporate interaction and how information is best disseminated within an office environment. Most importantly, by pursuing this course of study, you'll attain unbelievable powers of persuasion and will most likely be able to change the mind of even the most ardent skeptic. Your career calling could come from the business sector, law, media, or education.

SAMPLE COLLEGE CURRICULUM FOR ORGANIZATIONAL COMMUNICATION

Case Studies in Public Relations

Communication and Pop Culture

Communication in Bargaining and Negotiation

Corporate Communication: Strategy and Design

Essentials of Argumentation

Freedom of Expression and Communications Ethics

Human Resources Coordinator

Interpersonal Communication

Language and Behavior

Organizational Writing and Interactive Multimedia

Public Speaking

If You Like Organizational Communication, You May Also Like . . .

American studies, comparative literature, English, journalism, linguistics, mass communication, philosophy, psychology, public relations, radio/television/film studies, sociology, speech pathology, visual communication

Suggested High School Prep for Organizational Communication

As an organizational communications major, you will need exceptional writing and analytical skills. Sign up for loads of English courses as well as any statistics classes available. Introductory psychology and business courses may also prove beneficial. Outside the classroom, you might want to check out the debate club. Of course, you can always provoke an argument at the dinner table, in the name of your continuing education (wink, wink).

Fun Facts

Listen to This!

It is now known that rhinos use their nostrils, ears, posture, and, above all, a complex system of exhalations (like Morse code) for communication and expression.

(Source: www.bluerhino.com/eprise/main/BlueRhino/RhinoPreservation/funFacts)

Feeling Emotional

Is it okay to yell at your boss if he or she deserves it? According to a study by two University of Missouri professors, it might not be a good idea. Although positive emotions can sometimes be shown inappropriately (such as the case of a person who loudly praised his friend for a promotion, while in the presence of the person who was passed over for that same promotion), it is more often the display of negative emotions that gets people into hot water. In general, in organizational or business settings, people prefer that we control our negative emotions. People often equate "masking" (hiding) our negative feelings with proper emotion management.

Careers and Salary

Starting salaries for communications majors vary widely as there are a vast number of fields they typically enter. Entry level salaries usually range from $27,000 to $38,000.

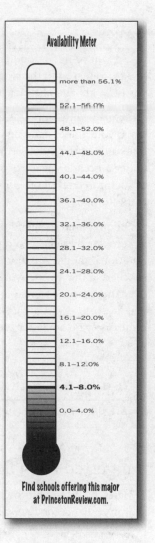

Availability Meter

more than 56.1%

52.1–56.0%

48.1–52.0%

44.1–48.0%

40.1–44.0%

36.1–40.0%

32.1–36.0%

28.1–32.0%

24.1–28.0%

20.1–24.0%

16.1–20.0%

12.1–16.0%

8.1–12.0%

4.1–8.0%

0.0–4.0%

Find schools offering this major at PrincetonReview.com.

CAREER OPTIONS

Advertising Manager	Lawyer	Professor
Creative Director	Lobbyist	Public Relations Consultant
Event Planner	Marketing Executive	Sales Executive
Fund Raiser	Media Planner	Teacher
Journalist	Media Specialist	Writer

PAINTING

Basics

So you've been doodling in your notebooks for years and filling your room with prints by avant-garde artists from around the world. Maybe you've converted the family basement into your own studio, complete with still life and abstract paintings. You have a feeling that deep inside of you lies a great painter.

A major in painting is an opportunity to develop your creativity, refine your technical skills, and challenge your understanding of art. As a major, you will have the chance to give focus to your artistic inclinations under the tutelage of accomplished and practicing painters. Because painting is sometimes listed under a broader major of art, fine arts, or studio art, majors try their hands with other artistic media, such as sculpture and photography, as well as study the history of art, from the Caves of Lascaux to the works of Mark Rothko.

Be prepared to spend the majority of your time in the studio and in critiques. You will learn how to use watercolor, oil, acrylic, and possibly egg tempera to create engaging images on wood panels, canvas, and less traditional media. A major in painting also equips you with the intellectual and critical tools necessary to succeed in the artistic world, whether it's as an artist, museum curator, or art dealer. The development of art over the centuries, including the social and political conditions behind the work and lives of some of the major artists, is just a part of some of the courses you will take as you expand your understanding of what it means to be a painter today.

If You Like Painting, You May Also Like . . .

Art, drawing, graphic design, photography, printmaking

Suggested High School Prep for Painting

First, paint on your own. Classes in art history and fine arts—including drawing, painting, photography, sculpture, dance, and ceramics—are a great way to begin to develop your ability to think critically about art. In addition, a continuous personal engagement with art through frequent museum visits, reading art history books, and studying your favorite artists and their works will help prepare you for the major. Since most schools value strong observational skills, draw from life as often as you can. For feedback on your portfolio, or for a review of your portfolio from several schools in one day, visit a National Portfolio Day (www.npda.org).

SAMPLE COLLEGE CURRICULUM FOR PAINTING

Art Concepts/Issues

Art History I–II

Art Studio Elective

Drawing I–II

Painting I–IV

Senior Exhibition

Three-Dimensional Design

Two-Dimensional Design

Fun Facts

Thus Spake Cezanne

"One cannot be too scrupulous, too sincere, too submissive before nature . . . but one ought to be more or less master of one's model."

—Paul Cezanne

Jack of All Trades

Gauguin had completely separate careers before becoming a full-time painter at the age of 35. He was first a merchant marine and then a stockbroker, finally settling down in Tahiti to become an artist.

Famous People Who Majored in Painting

Francis Barth, Richard Lytle, Sylvia Plimack Mangold, Frank Stella, Cy Twombly

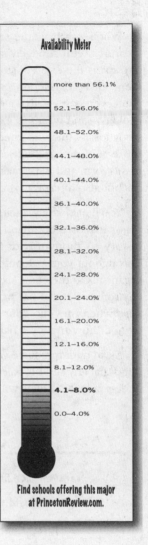

Availability Meter

more than 56.1%

52.1–56.0%

48.1–52.0%

44.1–48.0%

40.1–44.0%

36.1–40.0%

32.1–36.0%

28.1–32.0%

24.1–28.0%

20.1–24.0%

16.1–20.0%

12.1–16.0%

8.1–12.0%

4.1–8.0%

0.0–4.0%

Find schools offering this major at PrincetonReview.com.

Careers and Salary

Starting salaries for artists vary dramatically depending on the career and success of the artist. Introductory salaries for artists entering art administration range from $30,000 to $35,000. An independent artist could make less than $20,000 a year.

CAREER OPTIONS

Animator	Auctioneer	Product Designer
Art Dealer	Curator	Teacher
Artist		

PALEONTOLOGY

Basics

When you hear the term paleontology, you probably think of dinosaurs. Plant-tearing, earth-stomping creatures with strangely shaped heads and spiky plates down their backs. And you're right. But paleontology spans the entire history of life on this planet. As a paleontology major, epic phrases like "glacial movement," "mass extinction," "tundra ecosystem," and "evolutionary theory" will all become a nonchalant part of your everyday vocab. Paleontology draws elements from physics, botany, ecology, chemistry, biology, and geology—and works to explain how all of these fields are intertwined in our planet's geological past. You'll study fossils, first and foremost, in order to learn what sorts of organisms used to live on Earth. That includes those of both vertebrates and invertebrates of every size, in addition to the fossils of plants. You'll learn how fossils form and what makes up their chemistry, and you'll gain the skills necessary to not only identify fossils but also interpret what they mean for your field.

You'll also study ancient ecosystems and how they formed, evolved, and sometimes disappeared. This major explores both land and sea, from all sorts of layered rocks holding the clues to our planet's ancient history to thousands of feet under the ocean, where underwater fossils hold their own telling clues. Throughout your paleontology major, you'll be focusing on how life has evolved from the tiniest single-cell organisms to the complex life forms we are today. You'll learn how plants and animals have adapted to their environment, what has happened when adaptation was unsuccessful, and what becomes of plants and animals when they die. Your added paleontological bonus: Every time someone throws out a sentence like, "I wonder how that ever happened," you'll be the one to step up with a planet-savvy explanation.

As an undergraduate you'll gain a great deal of basic knowledge of the field of paleontology. But keep in mind that any serious paleontological career usually requires at least a master's degree and often a PhD. Your undergraduate studies will be just the beginning if this is a field to which you plan to devote your life.

If You Like Paleontology, You May Also Like . . .

American history, anthropology, archaeology, biology, chemistry, ecology, environmental science, forestry, geography, geological engineering, geology, history, marine science, oceanography, surveying

Suggested High School Prep for Paleontology

The best preparation for a major in paleontology is a solid selection of courses in sciences and math such as biology, chemistry, and calculus, and a selection of humanities courses, especially history and English. Paleontologists must have good communication skills, so take classes that will make you a better writer, speaker, and reader. And any reading you do on your own on dinosaurs and the earth's history will only help you in the college courses ahead!

SAMPLE COLLEGE CURRICULUM FOR PALEONTOLOGY

Carbonate Rocks

Clay Mineralogy

Evolutionary Biology

Functional Morphology

Micropaleontology

Paleoecology

Paleooceanography

Plate Tectonics

Sedimentary Petrology

Sedimentology

Stratigraphy

Fun Facts

Indiana Andrews?

Did you know that the movie character Indiana Jones was based, in part, on a paleontologist? Roy Chapman Andrews (1884–1960) is rumored to have been the inspiration for the creation of this character. Andrews is most famous for his treks through the Gobi Desert and Mongolia in the early part of the twentieth century, journeys on which he discovered fossilized dinosaur eggs—the first of their kind that were ever found. He brought these eggs back home to the American Museum of Natural History, where he was the director. Andrews graduated from Beloit College.

(Source: http://en.wikipedia.org)

Dino-Myte

Here are some Fun Facts about dinosaurs.

- Tyrannosaurus rex was 20 feet tall and 40 feet long.
- The brontosaurus is actually the apatosaurus.
- Inganodon was one of the first dinosaurs ever identified. It weighed about 7 tons and had humanlike hands.
- Pterodactyls traveled and lived in flocks.
- The stegosaurus's brain was only as large as a walnut.

(Source: www.abcteach.com)

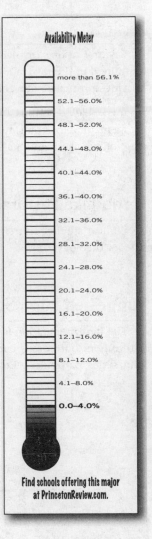

Availability Meter

more than 56.1%
52.1–56.0%
48.1–52.0%
44.1–48.0%
40.1–44.0%
36.1–40.0%
32.1–36.0%
28.1–32.0%
24.1–28.0%
20.1–24.0%
16.1–20.0%
12.1–16.0%
8.1–12.0%
4.1–8.0%
0.0–4.0%

Find schools offering this major at PrincetonReview.com.

Careers and Salary

The starting salary for paleontologists is in the $20,000 to $30,000 range. Most paleontological careers require advanced degrees, and your salary will rise once you pursue your education and gain experience in your field.

CAREER OPTIONS

Archaeologist	Mineralogist	Scientist
Geologist	Paleontologist	Seismologist
Geophysicist	Professor	Teacher
Laboratory Supervisor	Researcher	Writer

PASTORAL STUDIES

Basics

Pastoral studies involves the ministering of religious faith. As a pastoral studies major you will not only be trained in the intricate details and workings of your church and denomination, but also be prepared to provide spiritual advice and counseling to those seeking it.

If you have a serious and committed interest in the ministry, or even if you are already a practicing minister, a major in pastoral studies can be an invaluable experience. It will help you expand and develop knowledge of your faith and make you a better servant of it.

If You Like Pastoral Studies, You May Also Like . . .

Biblical studies, church music, great books, Hebrew, Islamic studies, Jewish studies, missions, religious studies, theology

Suggested High School Prep for Pastoral Studies

The best preparation for a pastoral studies major is a strong faith. Being able to effectively communicate with others, both orally and in writing, is also essential, so make sure you have a strong background in the humanities, particularly English and speech.

SAMPLE COLLEGE CURRICULUM FOR PASTORAL STUDIES

Fundamentals in Moral Theology

Introduction to Pastoral Care

Lay Preaching

New Directions in Ministry

The Pastoral Use of Scripture

Pauline Literature

Sacramental Theology

Seminar in Social Justice

Women Theologians

Fun Facts

Give Me the Good News First

Good News: You baptized seven people today in the river.

Bad News: You lost two of them in the swift current.

Good News: The Women's Guild voted to send you a get-well card.

Bad News: The vote passed by 31 to 30.

Good News: The Elder Board accepted your job description the way you wrote it.

Bad News: They were so inspired by it, they also formed a search committee to find somebody capable of filling the position.

Set Free on a Technicality

A pastor had had a bad week. On Sunday he was very frustrated and began his sermon, "Everyone in this parish is going to hell if they don't change their ways." One man in the back began to laugh. So the pastor said it again louder. The man continued to laugh. The pastor walked back to him and asked him why he was laughing. He answered, "Because I don't belong to this parish!"

Careers and Salary

The average salary for someone working as a member of the clergy is approximately $30,000.

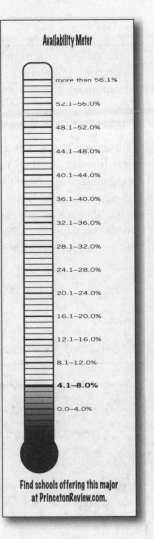

Availability Meter

more than 56.1%

52.1–56.0%

48.1–52.0%

44.1–48.0%

40.1–44.0%

36.1–40.0%

32.1–36.0%

28.1–32.0%

24.1–28.0%

20.1–24.0%

16.1–20.0%

12.1–16.0%

8.1–12.0%

4.1–8.0%

0.0–4.0%

Find schools offering this major at PrincetonReview.com.

CAREER OPTIONS
Clergy—Priest, Rabbi, Minister

PEACE STUDIES

Basics

The field of peace studies is alternatively known as peace and conflict studies, conflict analysis and resolution, and peace and justice studies. It is concerned with the roots of conflict, the conditions for peace, and ultimately, the daunting challenge of realizing peace on our little planet. To that end, if you major in peace studies, you'll read about and (hopefully) add to the large body of scholarship on the causes and prevention of war and ways to create a more just and peaceful world.

Peace studies is interdisciplinary (which means that most of the courses you take will be in other departments like history and international relations). The major began to develop in the 1960s and early 1970s, during and shortly after the Vietnam War and at the height of the Cold War, and it encompasses a mishmash of concepts. Among other things, peace studies includes the analysis of peace movements, arms control and nuclear disarmament, peace activism, and conflict resolution. Courses in peace studies are likely to cover topics such as civil disobedience, international economic development, international security in the post-Cold War world, and conflict management at every level of society, from family violence to warfare between nations.

At many colleges and universities, peace studies is offered only as a minor or a certificate program.

If You Like Peace Studies, You May Also Like . . .

African American studies, American studies, anthropology, biblical studies, English, history, human resources management, international relations, Islamic studies, Middle Eastern studies, philosophy, political science, psychology, religious studies, social work, sociology, Southeast Asian studies, theology, women's studies

SAMPLE COLLEGE CURRICULUM FOR PEACE STUDIES

Colonial Literature

Comparative Economic Systems

Conflict Resolution

Group Dynamics

International Relations

Introduction to Peace Studies

The Literature of Peace

Mediation and Negotiation

Mediation Practice

Middle East Culture and Society

Philosophies of War and Peace

Regional International Affairs

Strategic Planning

United States Foreign Policy

Suggested High School Prep for Peace Studies

What? Peace studies courses aren't offered at your high school? Don't sweat it. Peace studies involves lots of writing, reading, analysis, and criticism. If you think you might want to major in peace studies, history and English composition courses are important, as are any other courses you can take in which you will be required to read a lot and write essays.

Fun Facts

Recommended Reading

Here are a few good books on the subject of peace, according to the Peace Studies Association.

- *Getting to Yes* by Roger Fisher and William Ury
- *What Uncle Sam Really Wants* by Noam Chomsky
- *My Experiments with Truth* by Mohatma K. Gandhi
- *The Art of the Impossible: Politics as Morality in Practice* by Vaclav Havel
- *The Perennial Philosophy* by Aldous Huxley
- *A Testament of Hope* by Dr. Martin Luther King, Jr.
- *Culture and Imperialism* by Edward Said
- *Walden & The Duties of Civil Disobedience* by Henry David Thoreau

Did You Know?

In 1948, Manchester College in North Manchester, Indiana, became the first school to offer an undergraduate program and major in peace studies in the United States. The second school to catch the peace train was Manhattan College in Riverdale, New York, which began offering courses in peace studies in 1966 and established a full-fledged program in 1971. Today, more than 200 colleges and universities in the United States offer peace studies majors, minors, or certificate programs.

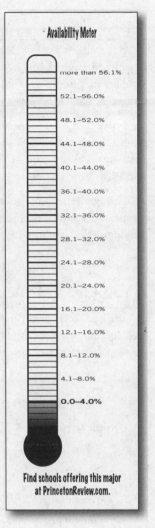

Availability Meter

more than 56.1%

52.1–56.0%

48.1–52.0%

44.1–48.0%

40.1–44.0%

36.1–40.0%

32.1–36.0%

28.1–32.0%

24.1–28.0%

20.1–24.0%

16.1–20.0%

12.1–16.0%

8.1–12.0%

4.1–8.0%

0.0–4.0%

Find schools offering this major at PrincetonReview.com.

Careers and Salary

Though we can't give you specific figures for peace studies majors, we can tell you that peace studies falls, broadly speaking, into the category of social science. Annual salaries for social science graduates range from $18,000 to about $31,000. The average annual starting salary for social science grads is about $23,000.

CAREER OPTIONS

Anthropologist

Attorney

Clergy—Priest, Rabbi, Minister

Diplomat/Attaché/Foreign Service Officer

Ecologist

Environmentalist/ Environmental Scientist

Journalist

Mediator

Philosopher

Political Aide

Political Campaign Worker

Politician

Public Relations Professional

Theologian

PETROLEUM ENGINEERING

Basics

Not quite what Jed Clampett or J. R. Ewing studied in order to make their millions, but if you major in petroleum engineering you might get to know some oil barons. After all, petroleum engineers are responsible for helping to find and drill new oil reserves so that we can continue driving our cars and heating our homes.

Petroleum engineers are the scientists behind the oil industry. They're the ones who help determine where those big oil rigs should go and where we should and should not drill for more of that black gold, Texas tea. Using some of the most sophisticated technology and complicated math, petroleum engineers also learn how to determine the cost efficiency of any drilling project.

Though increasing pollution and global warming has worried lawmakers and environmentalists looking for cleaner sources of energy, the oil industry isn't going away anytime soon. Jobs will be awaiting petroleum engineering graduates for the foreseeable future.

If You Like Petroleum Engineering, You May Also Like . . .

Aerospace engineering, agricultural and biological engineering, applied mathematics, applied physics, architectural engineering, biochemistry, ceramic engineering, chemical engineering, chemistry, civil engineering, computer engineering, electrical engineering, engineering design, engineering mechanics, geological engineering, mechanical engineering, mineral engineering, ocean engineering

SAMPLE COLLEGE CURRICULUM FOR PETROLEUM ENGINEERING

Advanced Drilling Technology

Drilling Practices and Well Completions

Environmental Petroleum Applications

Fundamental Digital Applications in Petroleum Engineering

Natural Gas Engineering

Offshore Petroleum Technology

Petroleum Engineering Design

Petroleum Production Laboratory

Petroleum Reservoir Engineering

Petroleum Valuation and Economics

Properties of Hyrdocarbon Fluids

Well Logging

Well Test Analysis

Suggested High School Prep for Petroleum Engineering

Short of beginning your own drilling company, a strong background in mathematics is great preparation for any career in engineering. The higher the level of math you can take the better, particularly calculus and beyond. You'll be happy you took those AP-level physics and chemistry courses—perhaps two of high school's most difficult classes—when you really start digging into the major curriculum.

Fun Facts

OPEC

The 11 countries that make up OPEC produce 24.2 million barrels of oil a day, 40 percent of the world's crude oil supply.

Gas Guzzlers

According to the U.S. Department of Energy, the United States consumes 19.9 million barrels of oil a day.

Careers and Salary

The average starting salary of petroleum engineering majors is between $42,000 and $50,000. Not too shabby. These salaries increase with experience and level of education.

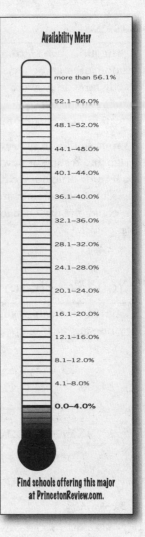

Availability Meter

more than 56.1%

52.1–56.0%

48.1–52.0%

44.1–48.0%

40.1–44.0%

36.1–40.0%

32.1–36.0%

28.1–32.0%

24.1–28.0%

20.1–24.0%

16.1–20.0%

12.1–16.0%

8.1–12.0%

4.1–8.0%

0.0–4.0%

Find schools offering this major at PrincetonReview.com.

CAREER OPTIONS

Chemical Engineer

Environmentalist/
Environmental Scientist

Geologist

Petroleum Engineer

PHARMACOLOGY

Basics

The *American Heritage Dictionary* defines pharmacology as "the science of drugs, including their composition, uses, and effects." Falling within the realm of pharmaceutical sciences, pharmacology focuses on exactly how drugs work and what kinds of reactions certain drugs cause in our bodies. As a pharmacology major you'll gain a solid foundation in biology and chemistry. Most students then choose to pursue further education in graduate or medical school.

Your studies in pharmacology should expose you to the molecular mechanics of a medication and the design and testing of new drugs. You might choose to focus on the clinical side of pharmacology, in which you'll study drug dosage regimens and ways to improve treatment and minimize risk. You'll learn about how different drugs interact and which drugs treat certain diseases most effectively. With all of this knowledge, you could one day change the way medicine is practiced by inventing the drug that cures AIDS or the common cold.

If You Like Pharmacology, You May Also Like . . .

Agricultural and biological engineering, biochemisty, biology, cell biology, chemical engineering, chemistry, nursing, pharmacy, premedicine, public health, rehabilitation services

Suggested High School Prep for Pharmacology

The field of pharmacology involves a great deal of science, especially chemistry—but explore also biology, physics, and others. Complex math (such as analytic geometry and calculus) and computer courses will lay a strong foundation for your college studies.

SAMPLE COLLEGE CURRICULUM FOR PHARMACOLOGY

Biopharmacy

Fundamentals of Oncology

Insecticides and Herbicides

Medicinal Chemistry

Metabolism of Drugs and Toxins

Organic Chemistry

Pathophysiology of Blood

Pharmaceutical Administration

Pharmacokinetics

Physiology

Principles and Methods of Toxicology

Receptorology

Risk Assessment Methodologies

Fun Facts

When in Need of Guidance

The patron saints of pharmacy and medicine are the brothers Damian and Cosmas, who are buried in Cyprus. They practiced together and performed many miracles, and used both religion and medicine to heal their patients. They were martyred in the year 303 A.D./C.E.

Strong Constitution

If you'd been alive around 100 B.C.E., Mithridates VI, King of Pontus, would have been a good man to know. Besides becoming an expert on the art of poisons, he was also an expert on the art of counteracting poisons. He built a tolerance by taking gradually increased doses of them. He used himself and people he imprisoned as the test subjects for his formulas. Mithridatum was his famous creation; the formula allegedly had pan-antidotal powers.

Careers and Salary

Starting salaries for pharmaceutical fields are, on average, in the $40,000 area but are greatly influenced by your field of expertise and your location of employment.

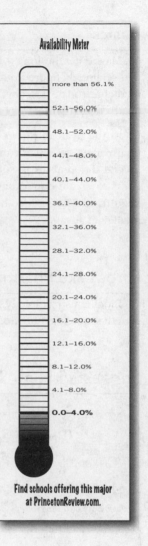

Availability Meter

more than 56.1%

52.1–56.0%

48.1–52.0%

44.1–48.0%

40.1–44.0%

36.1–40.0%

32.1–36.0%

28.1–32.0%

24.1–28.0%

20.1–24.0%

16.1–20.0%

12.1–16.0%

8.1–12.0%

4.1–8.0%

0.0–4.0%

Find schools offering this major at PrincetonReview.com.

CAREER OPTIONS

Biochemist	Hospital Administrator	Pharmacist
Biologist	Nurse	Physician
Chemist	Nutritionist	Veterinarian
Health Care Administrator	Pharmaceutical Sales Representative	

PHARMACY

Basics

Maybe it's the long white coats or the curiosity of what goes on behind that big counter. Or perhaps you've already figured out that the pharmaceutical industry is one of the most rapidly developing fields in medicine today. It seems as if we're able to go to our local pharmacist for just about everything, from headaches to foot pains to cures for high blood pressure.

At the heart of pharmaceuticals is the pharmacy major. Pharmacy is sometimes listed within a broader pharmaceutical science major, which provides its students with the opportunity to pick a concentration in several different areas, such as medicinal chemistry or pharmacology. A major in pharmacy prepares students to create new drugs that can fight cancer as well as to administer prescription drugs to those who need them. The science behind pharmaceuticals is expanding at an incredible rate, ushering in numerous medicinal advances.

If You Like Pharmacy, You May Also Like . . .

Biochemistry, biology, botany and plant biology, chemistry, dietetics, economics, environmental science, genetics, nursing, nutrition, pharmacology, premedicine

Suggested High School Prep for Pharmacy

> **SAMPLE COLLEGE CURRICULUM FOR PHARMACY**
>
> Analytical Chemistry
>
> Anatomy and Physiology
>
> Biological Chemistry
>
> Calculus
>
> Chemistry
>
> General Biology
>
> Medicinal Chemistry
>
> Microbiology
>
> Organic Chemistry
>
> Pharmaceutics
>
> Pharmacology
>
> Physical Chemistry
>
> Physics
>
> Statistics

In a word: chemistry. Pharmacists create and dispense chemicals—both combined with others and in pure form—that prevent or cure diseases. You should take the toughest chemistry courses your school offers and master the subject. Biology and complex math are also essential to the pharmacy major.

Fun Facts

Big Money

Research-based pharmaceutical companies reached sales of more than $149 billion in 2000. The pharmaceutical industry had more than $300 billion in sales in 1998.

R&D

Pharmaceutical companies spent more than $24 billion dollars on research and development in 1999 alone.

Careers and Salary

The average starting salary for a pharmacy major ranges from $40,000 to $60,000.

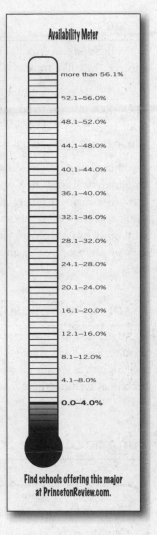

Availability Meter

more than 56.1%

52.1–56.0%

48.1–52.0%

44.1–48.0%

40.1–44.0%

36.1–40.0%

32.1–36.0%

28.1–32.0%

24.1–28.0%

20.1–24.0%

16.1–20.0%

12.1–16.0%

8.1–12.0%

4.1–8.0%

0.0–4.0%

Find schools offering this major at PrincetonReview.com.

CAREER OPTIONS

Pharmaceutical Sales Representative   Pharmacist

PHILOSOPHY

Basics

Philosophy majors like the big questions. Why are we here? How should one act? What is man's true nature? They like to read difficult books by writers like Plato, Kant, Nietzsche, Hegel, and Kierkegaard.

Seriously, philosophy majors are critical thinkers who leave no stone unturned, no thought unexplored. They pick up where Socrates left off, trying to figure out what it means to be human by asking hard questions (e.g., Why believe in God? And for that matter, why not?) and doing their best to answer them clearly and logically. Everything, and we do mean everything, falls into their realm of inquiry.

Philosophy involves more than just thinking in abstract terms. Underlying the major is a set of critical and analytical tools that will help you intellectually engage the world around you. Philosophy majors learn how to construct nearly airtight rational and logical arguments, present their thoughts convincingly, and think and respond to difficult questions and situations from various perspectives. As a philosophy major you will study philosophy in all its different forms, from logic to ethics, metaphysics, epistemology, and the history of philosophy. Oh, and by the time you graduate you'll be able to argue circles around your friends.

If You Like Philosophy, You May Also Like . . .

African studies, American studies, anthropology, art, art history, classics, comparative literature, creative writing, East Asian studies, East European studies, English, French, German, Hebrew, history, international studies, linguistics, Medieval and Renaissance studies, Modern Greek, peace studies, political science, sociology, technical writing, theater, theology, women's studies

Suggested High School Prep for Philosophy

SAMPLE COLLEGE CURRICULUM FOR PHILOSOPHY

Ancient Philosophy

Eighteenth-Century Philosophy

Ethical Theory

Metaphysics

Philosophy of Language

Philosophy of Law

Philosophy of Mind

Political and Social Philosophy

Seventeenth-Century Philosophy

Symbolic Logic

Since few high schools offer their students the opportunity to study philosophy, it's important to have a strong background in the humanities, including English, history, and social studies. Math classes are also extremely helpful for those who have an interest in studying the logical aspects of philosophy. Taking introductory philosophy courses at a local college or university is also a great way to see if this is the right major for you.

Fun Facts

Quotable

"The point of philosophy is to start with something so simple as to seem not worth stating, and to end with something so paradoxical that no one will believe it."

—Bertrand Russell, Science and Religion

A Joke

Dean, to the physics department:

"Why do I always have to give you guys so much money for laboratories and expensive equipment and stuff? Why couldn't you be more like the math department; all they need is money for pencils, paper, and wastepaper baskets. Or even better, like the philosophy department; all they need are pencils and paper."

Careers and Salary

The average starting salary for a philosophy major is between $25,000 and $35,000 depending on the field.

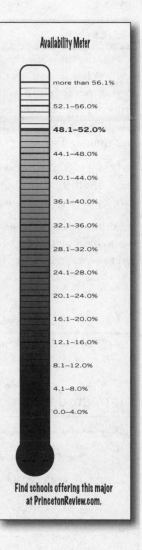

Availability Meter

more than 56.1%

52.1–56.0%

48.1–52.0%

44.1–48.0%

40.1–44.0%

36.1–40.0%

32.1–36.0%

28.1–32.0%

24.1–28.0%

20.1–24.0%

16.1–20.0%

12.1–16.0%

8.1–12.0%

4.1–8.0%

0.0–4.0%

Find schools offering this major
at PrincetonReview.com.

CAREER OPTIONS

Attorney	Mediator	Public Relations Professional
Book Publishing Professional	Philosopher	Teacher
Editor	Political Scientist	Writer
Journalist	Professor	

PHOTOGRAPHY

Basics

Photography involves much more than just pointing and clicking a camera. If you major in it, you'll learn how to choose a subject and compose it effectively, how to orchestrate color and light, and how to develop your photographs. You'll also explore the possibilities of digital and computer-enhanced images. Other forms of visual art will be part of your major as well, such as painting, drawing, and sculpture. You'll learn how to create photographs that capture your vision and make the statement you want—pictures that say your thousand words.

Besides learning how to create your own meaningful photographs, you'll be studying other photographers—both historical and contemporary—who have made important advancements in the field. You'll learn by seeing what other students are creating and by receiving critiques of your own projects.

Although universities with photography majors have darkrooms and facilities for students' use, expect to purchase quite a bit of equipment, such as cameras, tripods, lenses, film, developing chemicals, and computer software. In other words, be prepared for some extra expenses.

If You Like Photography, You May Also Like . . .

Art history, drawing, journalism, printmaking, radio and television, visual communication

Suggested High School Prep for Photography

> ### SAMPLE COLLEGE CURRICULUM FOR PHOTOGRAPHY
>
> Art History
> Color Theory and Printing
> Digital Imaging
> Digital Tools
> Documentary Photography
> Drawing
> Fundamentals of Visual Thinking
> Large Format Photography
> Multimedia Projects
> Photographic Lighting
> Photography Installation
> Two-Dimensional Design

Any and all art classes are great preparation for a photography major. English and history will give you a good background in culture and society, and foreign languages might give you an edge in this highly multicultural field. You probably wouldn't consider chemistry a relevant class, but it is; as a photographer you'll be working with a variety of chemicals to develop your images.

Since photography majors at most schools are required to take the same core curriculum as fine arts majors, brush up on your drawing skills. You'll have to submit a portfolio for admission to a fine arts program; it should include some drawings.

Fun Facts

Did You Know?

The word photography comes from the Greek words for *light* and *writing*. Johann von Maedler, a Berlin astronomer, first used the word in 1839.

A Little History

The first camera was called the *camera obscura*, which means *dark chamber*. In a dark room, a small hole in the wall allowed an outside image to be projected into the room, upside down. Eventually, smaller-sized cameras were developed and mirrors were added to right the image.

Famous People Who Majored in Photography

Sally Gall, Emmet Gowin, Ben Larrabee, and Starr Ockenge (all of the Rhode Island School of Design); Paul Aresu (School of Visual Arts); Sally Apfelbaum (Tyler School of Art)

Careers and Salary

Salaries in this field are almost impossible to estimate, since photography majors go on to pursue an eclectic variety of projects and careers, but a reasonable estimate would be in the $20,000 to $30,000 range.

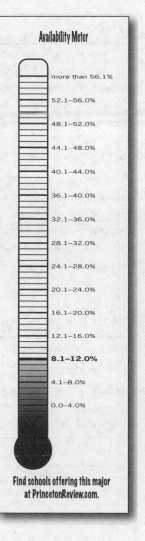

Availability Meter

more than 56.1%
52.1–56.0%
48.1–52.0%
44.1–48.0%
40.1–44.0%
36.1–40.0%
32.1–36.0%
28.1–32.0%
24.1–28.0%
20.1–24.0%
16.1–20.0%
12.1–16.0%
8.1–12.0%
4.1–8.0%
0.0–4.0%

Find schools offering this major at PrincetonReview.com.

CAREER OPTIONS

Art Dealer	Fashion Designer	Photographer
Artist	Journalist	Web Art Director
Digital Artist		

PHOTOJOURNALISM

Basics

A photograph can tell a powerful story; no one knows this better than a photojournalist. Media images of dramatic events become burned into our collective memory, acting as visual shorthand for emotions long after specific details have faded. From Dorothea Lange's photographs of the Depression, to images of police brutality during the civil rights movement of the 1960s to recent television coverage of the falling Twin Towers, still and motion photography has played an important role in delivering the news and influencing public opinion. Photojournalists cover a wide range of subjects in addition to national and international news, including human interest stories, sports, and prominent people, like celebrities and politicians.

As a photojournalism major, you'll learn photography basics, including camera and equipment operation and technique, subject surveillance, and digital editing. You'll also learn the fundamentals of journalism, from news editing and layout to news team field operations to professional standards and ethics. Many schools offer internship programs, where you'll be able to get firsthand experience by working at a local paper or news broadcasting station. By the time you graduate, you'll know how to shoot and lay out photo stories and produce and edit your own features.

If You Like Photojournalism, You May Also Like . . .

Digital communications and media/multimedia, English, film, journalism, mass communication, photography, radio and television, visual communication

Suggested High School Prep for Photojournalism

> ### SAMPLE COLLEGE CURRICULUM FOR PHOTOJOURNALISM
>
> Advanced Editing and Design
>
> Advanced Journalism Practicum:
>
> Latin America in Words and Pictures
>
> Delivering the News Online
>
> Graphics of Journalism
>
> Introduction to Advertising Design and Graphics
>
> Magazine Management and Publication
>
> Newspaper Editing
>
> Specialized Journalistic Photography

Take as many English and history classes as you can, in addition to photography classes offered at your school or in the community. A great way to get some practical experience and enjoy editorial freedom is to work on your school newspaper and/or yearbook. It's also a good idea to stay on top of local, national, and international current events, so read a wide variety of papers and magazines, in addition to watching the news on TV.

Fun Facts

Did You Know?

Before she was married, Jackie Kennedy worked as a photojournalist for the *Washington-Times Herald*.

(Source: http://en.wikipedia.org)

The word *paparazzi*, surprisingly, is not Italian for "aggressive photographers who take pictures of celebrities." The word originates from Federico Fellini's 1959 film *La Dolce Vita*. The film's protagonist is a freelance photographer named Paparazzo.

(Source: www.word-detective.com/122002.html)

Careers and Salary

Photojournalism majors just starting out can expect to make somewhere between $24,000 and $32,000 a year.

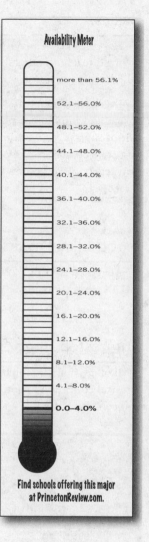

Availability Meter

more than 56.1%

52.1–56.0%

48.1–52.0%

44.1–48.0%

40.1–44.0%

36.1–40.0%

32.1–36.0%

28.1–32.0%

24.1–28.0%

20.1–24.0%

16.1–20.0%

12.1–16.0%

8.1–12.0%

4.1–8.0%

0.0–4.0%

Find schools offering this major at PrincetonReview.com.

CAREER OPTIONS

Digital Artist	Journalist	Professor
Editor	Photographer	Web Art Director
Filmmaker	Photojournalist	

PHYSICAL EDUCATION

Basics

Do you like to play? Are you happiest out on the field? Could you imagine yourself in a career that involved teaching others how to get active and take good care of their bodies? It could be the inner physical education major in you.

Every elementary, middle, and high school needs qualified teachers and coaches to run sports programs, design and implement plans for healthy living, and teach physical education. You don't need an ultratight pair of shorts or a weird moustache to teach P.E. What you do need, however, is a degree in physical education. Phys ed majors work as coaches, team managers, recreational managers, personal trainers, and health and gym teachers. Some end up working in one sport; others teach a wide range of sports and fitness-related subjects.

If You Like Physical Education, You May Also Like . . .

Air Force R.O.T.C., child development, education, health administration, Marine Corps R.O.T.C., Navy R.O.T.C., nutrition, physical therapy, public health, recreation management, sport and leisure studies

Suggested High School Prep for Physical Education

Biology, nutrition, anatomy and physiology, statistics, and general chemistry will all come into play in the physical education major. All sporting activities are useful, so try to get involved with and learn them as best you can.

> ### SAMPLE COLLEGE CURRICULUM FOR PHYSICAL EDUCATION
>
> Community Health
>
> First Aid
>
> Fundamental Sports Skills
>
> General Biology
>
> General Psychology
>
> Motor Learning and Control
>
> Physiology of Exercise
>
> Principles of Human Anatomy
>
> Principles of Human Physiology
>
> Sports Nutrition
>
> Tests and Measurements in Physical Education

Fun Facts

For More Information . . .

The American Alliance for Health, Physical Education, Recreation, and Dance (AAHPERD) is the national organization for physical education professionals. It offers many services and programs. You can find out more by calling 800-213-7193 or visiting www.aahperd.org.

Shape Up America!

Former Surgeon General Dr. C. Everett Koop has started a comprehensive health and fitness website (www.shapeup.org) for professionals and nonprofessionals alike. Check it out.

Careers and Salary

The starting salary for a physical education major with a four-year degree is about $30,000.

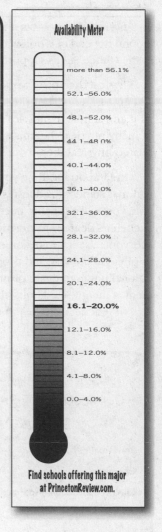

Availability Meter

more than 56.1%

52.1–56.0%

48.1–52.0%

44.1–48.0%

40.1–44.0%

36.1–40.0%

32.1–36.0%

28.1–32.0%

24.1–28.0%

20.1–24.0%

16.1–20.0%

12.1–16.0%

8.1–12.0%

4.1–8.0%

0.0–4.0%

Find schools offering this major
at PrincetonReview.com.

CAREER OPTIONS		
Baseball Player	Referee	Teacher
Coach		

PHYSICAL THERAPY

Basics

Physical therapy—as a major and as a profession—has grown by leaps and bounds since its inception around the end of World War I. In fact, these days it's considered to be among the fastest growing professions in the United States. Opportunities for employment are abundant and starting salaries are relatively lucrative.

Physical therapists work with doctors and other therapists to rehabilitate people with injuries, diseases, and impairments. They prescribe exercise schedules and use heat, cold, electricity, sound, and water to relieve pain and stimulate muscles and motor functions. Though rehabilitation following injury is the primary focus of many physical therapists, board-certified specialization is available in a number of areas including sports-related physical therapy, orthopedics, and pediatrics.

One important thing you should know about majoring in physical therapy is that passing an important, national, standardized test is necessary before you can practice as a therapist. Also, and possibly more important, you will probably need a master's degree or some other advanced degree (i.e., something beyond a bachelor's degree) to practice. Consequently, you should expect to stay in college a little longer than most everyone else if you major in physical therapy. It takes a minimum of six years to complete a master's degree in physical therapy, and programs are often split into two required parts. The first part is a more or less traditional undergraduate program that takes three years to complete (four if you dilly-dally). The second segment is the nuts-and-bolts, three-year physical therapy graduate program during which you'll receive a great deal of practical, on-the-job type training.

Sample College Curriculum for Physical Therapy

Abnormal Psychology

Chemistry

Clinical Instruction and Practice

Human Anatomy

Kinesiology

Medical Ethics

Musculoskeletal Evaluation

Neuroanatomy

Neurophysiology

Orthopedics

Physics

Physiology

Psychology of Disability

Rehabilitation

Statistics

If You Like Physical Therapy, You May Also Like . . .

Agricultural and biological engineering, biochemistry, biology, biopsychology, botany and plant biology, cell biology, chemistry, chiropractic, circulation technology, dietetics, health administration, human development, medical technology, nursing, occupational therapy, pharmacology, pharmacy, premedicine, pre-optometry, pre-veterinary medicine, radiologic technology, rehabilitation services, respiratory therapy

Suggested High School Prep for Physical Therapy

Mark our words: It's not easy to get into physical therapy programs. Not easy at all. To begin with, you need a very strong background in the physical sciences. Take Advanced Placement biology, chemistry, and physics courses. Take lots of math, too. It's a really good idea to try to gain some experience (by volunteering or working) with real, live physical therapists. Such experience will look great on your resume. Finally, you need to be in good physical shape yourself.

Fun Facts

Does Your Backpack Make the Grade?

Come on, every real college student has a backpack, right? The American Physical Therapy Association (APTA) warns, however, that an incorrectly worn backpack can harm your joints and muscles. Here are a couple backpacking pointers.

Wear both straps. Yeah, you'll look a little nerdy, but it beats a curved spine, eventual upper back pain, strained neck, and even scoliosis. Teenage girls are especially susceptible to scoliosis.

Get a backpack with wide straps. Narrow straps dig into shoulders (you may have noticed this phenomenon if you own a crappy backpack). They also impede circulation, which is no good for all kinds of reasons, causing numbness or tingling in the arms, which over time may cause weakness in the hands.

Did You Know?

Time and again, *Money* magazine and the U.S. Department of Labor (citing a variety of factors) have ranked physical therapy among the top ten professional fields. The Department of Labor projects that it will remain a top field well into the twenty-first century.

Careers and Salary

The starting salary for a physical therapy major fresh out of school ranges between $37,000 and $48,000 per year.

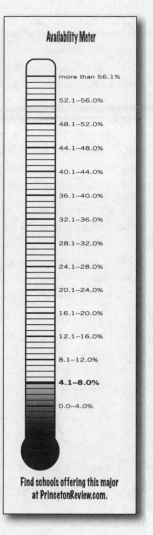

Availability Meter

more than 56.1%

52.1–56.0%

48.1–52.0%

44.1–48.0%

40.1–44.0%

36.1–40.0%

32.1–36.0%

28.1–32.0%

24.1–28.0%

20.1–24.0%

16.1–20.0%

12.1–16.0%

8.1–12.0%

4.1–8.0%

0.0–4.0%

Find schools offering this major at PrincetonReview.com.

CAREER OPTIONS

Physical Therapist

PHYSICIAN ASSISTANT

Basics

Here's an option if you're interested in a health profession but feel faint at the idea of the 7 to 13 years and probably hundreds of thousands of dollars involved in going to med school and becoming a doctor. Physician assistants perform many of the same tasks doctors do but go through a much more reasonable period of training. Physician assistants (PAs) receive their certification by attending a PA program accredited by the Accreditation Review Commission on Education for the Physician Assistant. And they don't do exactly the same things doctors do—they, well, assist. In some cases, you might enter a PA program after you graduate from college; in other cases, you'll take general college courses for two years and then transfer into a PA program. (Some schools even offer a major in pre-physician assistant studies that includes this 2-2 split.) Programs are generally competitive, and you must pass the NCCPA (National Commission on Certification of Physician Assistants) exam to become certified after your course work has been completed.

Even though you won't bear the burdens of med school, PA programs are rigorous too, and demand focus, dedication, and a lot of time. As a PA major, you'll learn how to take patient histories, request and perform laboratory tests, and read and analyze the results. You'll learn about preventive medicine and how to counsel patients on their health and wellness. By the time you graduate, you'll be able to give a physical exam, diagnose illnesses, and develop treatment plans. Some PAs even write prescriptions. However, since you are an "assistant" you'll always practice under a doctor's supervision.

There are specialties within the field of physician assisting, such as surgery and emergency room care. (A surgical PA, for example, is the one who responds when the surgeon commands, "Scalpel!") In all cases, you'll provide assistance to the doctors you work for in addition to caring for patients to a certain extent on your own. And while your paycheck won't look quite the same as those of the doctors you're assisting, it's a rewarding way to combine your love of medicine with a true desire to help people.

SAMPLE COLLEGE CURRICULUM FOR PHYSICIAN ASSISTANTS

Cardiology

Clinical Decision Making

Clinical Procedures

Clinically Oriented Anatomy

Health Systems

History Taking

Medical Ethics

Pathophysiology

Pharmacology

Physical Assessment

Physical Examination

Physiology

Preventive Medicine

If You Like Physician Assisting, You May Also Like . . .

Child care, chiropractic, dentistry, health administration, medical technology, nursing, physical therapy, pre-dentistry, premedicine, public health

Suggested High School Prep for Physician Assistants . . .

A strong background in math and science will be to your benefit as you begin your major in physician assisting, so load up your schedule with upper-level courses such as physics, calculus, and chemistry. Physician assistants must also be good communicators, so be sure to hone your reading and writing skills in humanities courses such as English and languages. Some hospitals, nursing homes, or social services organizations accept volunteers, which may give you some good hands-on experience.

Fun Facts

Get With the Group

Interested in physician assisting? You might be interested in the American Academy of Physician Assistants, which is the only national organization representing PAs in all medical fields. Check out their website at aapa.org to find out what they do and how they might help you in the future.

Truth in Numbers

As of 2001, there were 52,716 licensed physician assistants in the United States. (Source: www.aapa.org)

Careers and Salary

The starting salary for physician assistants is about $50,000, though this number varies depending on where you are employed, what sort of practice you're assisting, and what experience you've had.

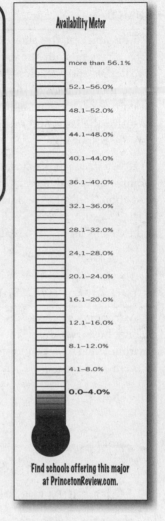

Availability Meter

more than 56.1%

52.1–56.0%

48.1–52.0%

44.1–48.0%

40.1–44.0%

36.1–40.0%

32.1–36.0%

28.1–32.0%

24.1–28.0%

20.1–24.0%

16.1–20.0%

12.1–16.0%

8.1–12.0%

4.1–8.0%

0.0–4.0%

Find schools offering this major at PrincetonReview.com.

CAREER OPTIONS

Physician Assistant for family practice, surgery, pediatrics, gynecology, and many other medical fields

PHYSICS

Basics

In a nutshell, the sum of physics is a continually evolving mathematical model of the natural world. Physics majors study the exact, fundamental laws of nature. They study the structure of all sizes and kinds of materials and particles—the very universe itself. They also seek to understand and define the properties of energy, temperature, distance, and time, and they try to describe all of these things through mathematical equations. It's mind-blowing stuff, and what emerges from physics labs is cutting-edge technology. The transistor, the laser, MRI medical systems, and superconductors are just a few of the things for which physicists are responsible.

If you major in physics, you'll study a remarkably broad range of natural phenomena—everything from submicroscopic elementary matter to black holes to the endless reaches of the galaxy. You'll carry out and read about tons of experiments, and you'll do more complicated math than most mortals would ever want to shake a stick at. Yours will be the quest for the underlying logic and the theoretical structure that unifies and explains all the different phenomena of the universe. It's a dirty job, but somebody's got to do it.

If You Like Physics, You May Also Like . . .

Astronomy, astrophysics, atmospheric science, biochemistry, biology, biopsychology, botany and plant biology, business administration and management, cell biology, chemistry, dietetics, economics, entomology, environmental science, forestry, genetics, geology, marine science, mathematics, microbiology, molecular genetics, neurobiology, neuroscience, nutrition, pharmacology, pharmacy, plant pathology, public health, statistics

Suggested High School Prep for Physics

Physics requires a solid footing in mathematics. Take all the math and physics that your high school offers. It's a really good idea to take calculus. It's essential that you are ready to jump right into college-level calculus your first semester if you think you might major in physics. Experience with computers and computer programming will also prove very valuable. Contact a local university for information about programs in physics, so you can choose courses that satisfy admission requirements and prepare you for the workload ahead.

SAMPLE COLLEGE CURRICULUM FOR PHYSICS

Calculus and Analytic Geometry

Chemistry

Computer Science

Differential Equations

Dynamics of Particles and Waves

Electromagnetic Theory

Linear Algebra

Physics I–II

Quantum Physics

Thermodynamics and Statistical Mechanics

Vector Analysis

Fun Facts

Words to the Wise

We found this excellent advice from Daniel F. Styer, professor of physics at Oberlin College, at Oberlin College's website. Check it out. It's good stuff.

Don't rush into solving physics problems. Formulate a strategy first. Usually, all this means is classifying the problem according to its method of solution. Does it involve constant acceleration? Work-energy? Gauss's law?

Physics is not algebra. If you find yourself working reams of algebra, then you are off on the wrong track. Stop, reread the problem, reformulate your strategy, and start over from the beginning.

Don't search through your book for the right equation. Again, it's physics, not algebra. You won't be able to solve your problem by finding an appropriate equation and plugging in numbers. No self-respecting college-level teacher would ever assign such a problem.

Problems won't always be cut and dry. Sometimes, problems will give you more information than you need. Sometimes, you won't get enough, and you'll be asked not for an answer but for a list of the unknown information required to find an answer. These problems can be exasperating, but they are the kind you'll see in the real world. The ability to spot relevant information is an important skill.

Learn from your mistakes. You'll definitely make them. Review problem solutions. Figure out why you made the mistakes you did. How could you have avoided them? Five or ten minutes spent in this review can save hours by preventing similar mistakes in the future.

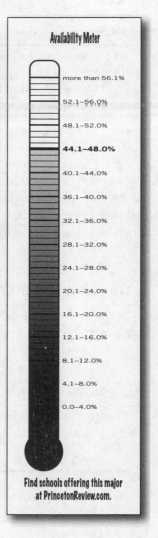

Availability Meter

more than 56.1%

52.1–56.0%

48.1–52.0%

44.1–48.0%

40.1–44.0%

36.1–40.0%

32.1–36.0%

28.1–32.0%

24.1–28.0%

20.1–24.0%

16.1–20.0%

12.1–16.0%

8.1–12.0%

4.1–8.0%

0.0–4.0%

Find schools offering this major at PrincetonReview.com.

Careers and Salary

The median starting annual salaries for physics majors with bachelor's degrees vary. They range from $39,000 to $49,000 in private industry, to $30,000 for government and high school teaching positions.

CAREER OPTIONS

Aerospace Engineer	Demolition Expert	Physicist
Architect	Electrical Engineer	Robotics Engineer
Astronaut	Inventor	Structural Engineer
Astronomer	Nuclear Engineer	Teacher

PHYSIOLOGICAL PSYCHOLOGY

Basics

When Descartes first said, "I think, therefore I am," he was opening up what would eventually become one of the biggest questions about human nature. How is the mind related to the body? Where do they intersect, and how do they interact? The mind/body divide has been pestering philosophers for centuries now, and yet here it is, mind and body joined together in one large and complicated major.

Similar to a biopsychology major, a physiological psychology major (try saying that three times fast) is interested in the relationship between the brain and our behavior. This is some complicated material, and it should be, since what you will be dealing with could offer mankind insight into the essence of humanity. You will have all of the skills and training of a psychologist, along with unique insights into the structure and function of the human brain normally left to neuroscientists. There are also, of course, some extra benefits here because the next time your parents ask you why you took the car and broke curfew, you can tell them that it had nothing to do with you, and everything to do with your superior colliculus.

If You Like Physiological Psychology, You May Also Like . . .

Biology, biopsychology, chemistry, child care, child development, clinical psychology, counseling, criminology, developmental psychology, educational psychology, human development

Suggested High School Prep for Physiological Psychology

Take psychology if your school offers it. Biological sciences are essential to this major, so load up on them. Quantitative skills, especially those taught in calculus and statistics, will also prove very useful.

SAMPLE COLLEGE CURRICULUM FOR PHYSIOLOGICAL PSYCHOLOGY

Advanced Writing in Psychology

Biological Psychology

Biology I–II

Cognitive Psychology

Developmental Psychology

General Psychology

History of Psychology

The Human Animal

Psychopathology

Statistics

Fun Facts

It's All Downhill from Here

According to the American Physiological Society, our resting metabolic rate (the rate at which our bodies burn calories doing nothing at all, including sleeping) decreases with age.

Welcome to the Psychiatric Hotline

- If you are obsessive-compulsive, please press 1 repeatedly.
- If you are codependent, please ask someone to press 2.
- If you have multiple personalities, please press 3, 4, 5, and 6.
- If you are paranoid-delusional, we know who are and what you want. Just stay on the line so we can trace the call.
- If you are schizophrenic, listen carefully and a little voice will tell you which number to press.
- If you are depressed, it doesn't matter which number you press. No one will answer.
- If you are delusional and occasionally hallucinate, please be aware that the thing you are holding on the side of your head is alive and about to bite off your ear.

Careers and Salary

The average starting salary for physiological psychology majors is similar to that of biology and psychology majors, $25,000 to $35,000.

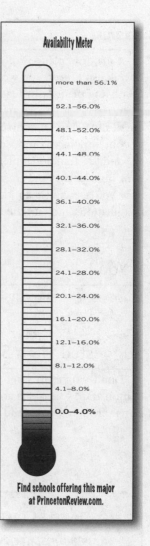

Availability Meter

more than 56.1%
52.1–56.0%
48.1–52.0%
44.1–48.0%
40.1–44.0%
36.1–40.0%
32.1–36.0%
28.1–32.0%
24.1–28.0%
20.1–24.0%
16.1–20.0%
12.1–16.0%
8.1–12.0%
4.1–8.0%
0.0–4.0%

Find schools offering this major at PrincetonReview.com.

CAREER OPTIONS

Biologist	Guidance Counselor	Social Worker
Career Counselor	Physician	Substance Abuse Counselor
Child Care Worker	Psychologist	Teacher
Criminologist		

PIANO

Basics

A major in piano is often listed as a concentration within a broader music or music performance major. This doesn't mean you won't have the opportunity to play your heart out as well as study with some of the best living pianists. Instead, it means that you'll be able to supplement all of those piano lessons with some intensive music theory and history courses that will develop and expand your appreciation and understanding of the piano. Of course, all of the great pieces will be here, from Mozart, to Beethoven, to Rachmaninoff, to contemporary composers. This combination of both practice and study will provide you with something beyond the traditional piano lessons you may have taken, because as a piano major you will not only learn your instrument (and learn it well), but you will also develop your understanding of music as a whole and how you as a musician just might have something to contribute to the body of work that has shaped our imaginations and enriched our lives.

If You Like Piano, You May Also Like . . .

Jazz studies, music, music history

Suggested High School Prep for Piano

Don't expect to walk in just on your music teacher's laurels. You will have to do some auditioning to demonstrate your skills and talent, so make sure you have taken the time to develop those musical inclinations through lessons and practice, practice, practice.

SAMPLE COLLEGE CURRICULUM FOR PIANO

Conducting

Large Ensembles

Music Aural Training I–IV

Music Form and Analysis

Music History

Music Theory I–IV

Piano Lessons

Piano Literature

Piano Pedagogy

Small Ensembles

Fun Facts

A Joke

What do you get when you drop a piano on an army base?

A flat major.

Did You Know?

The average number of pounds of pressure on a piano string: 165.

Famous People Who Majored in Piano

Sergei Rachmaninoff (Saint Petersburg Conservatory)

Careers and Salary

The music industry is a fickle business so starting salaries can vary dramatically depending on your success as a musician or whether you intend to enter a specific career, such as teaching. For those considering teaching, starting salaries range from $19,000 to $30,000.

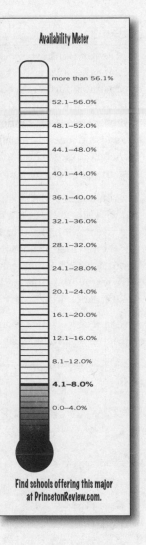

Availability Meter

more than 56.1%

52.1–56.0%

48.1–52.0%

44.1–48.0%

40.1–44.0%

36.1–40.0%

32.1–36.0%

28.1–32.0%

24.1–28.0%

20.1–24.0%

16.1–20.0%

12.1–16.0%

8.1–12.0%

4.1–8.0%

0.0–4.0%

Find schools offering this major at PrincetonReview.com.

CAREER OPTIONS

Music Executive	Performing Arts Administrator	Teacher
Musician	Professor	

PLANETARY SCIENCE

Basics

Do you think we'll ever live—or even vacation—on the moon? Do you believe in that "face" on Mars or life on other planets? A major in planetary science will touch on these issues—and then take your studies much, much further. Needless to say, you'll distinguish the planets by their properties, sizes, and unique characteristics. You'll learn how each was formed—from its surface to its interior to its inner core—and you'll study the processes that continue to change them. You'll compare and contrast the planets and study how the changes on one planet affect the others. And you'll explore the universe's physics, chemistry, and geology. Planetary atmospheres, satellites, orbital mechanics, asteroids and comets, and the very evolution of the solar system will give you and your colleagues a fair amount to ponder.

You'll also address some pretty big questions throughout your planetary science major, such as: Where did we come from and where are we going? What has happened to our planet over the past billions of years, and what will happen to it in the future? What will the effects be of our actions today? You'll examine how our own planet fits into the solar system and how changes in the universe affect us. (Sort of bizarre to think about, isn't it?) You'll learn about the ways in which we've explored the solar system in the past and the advancements being made for further—and more elaborate—exploration. And when someone calls you a "space cadet," you'll start to lift your chin and stand proud.

Planetary science is an interdisciplinary major, and your studies will involve geology, physics, chemistry, astronomy, biology, oceanography, and many other sciences.

SAMPLE COLLEGE CURRICULUM FOR PLANETARY SCIENCE

Astronomy

Differential Calculus

Earth Materials

Earth Physics

Earth System History

Evolution of a Habitable World

Fluid Earth Processes

Geochemistry

Geophysics

Oceans and Atmospheres

Origin of the Universe

Physics

Planetary Physics

Science of Life Beyond Earth

Solar System Physics

If You Like Planetary Science, You May Also Like . . .

Aerospace engineering, applied mathematics, applied physics, astronomy, atmospheric science, chemistry, geography, geology, molecular biology

Suggested High School Prep for Planetary Science

To prepare for a major in planetary science, take courses in physics, chemistry, biology, calculus, and any other challenging science and math courses your school offers. Be sure to take a selection of humanities courses, including English, history, and languages. A math and science background will be a big help once you begin your major.

Fun Facts

Did You Know?

- There are only two days in a year on Mercury.
- A day on Jupiter is only 9 hours and 55 minutes long.
- One Neptune year lasts 165 Earth years.
- Saturn is the lightest planet.
- The largest volcano in the solar system is the Olympic Mons, on Mars.

(Source: www.kidzone.ws/planets)

One Far-Out Poem

Here's a brief verse about the planets.

"Whether we wake or we sleep,
Whether we carol or weep,
The Sun with his Planets in chime,
Marketh the going of Time."

—Edward FitzGerald, *Chronomoros*

(Source: www.bartleby.com)

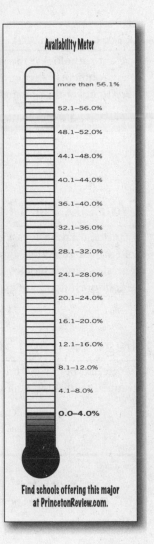

Availability Meter

more than 56.1%

52.1–56.0%

48.1–52.0%

44.1–48.0%

40.1–44.0%

36.1–40.0%

32.1–36.0%

28.1–32.0%

24.1–28.0%

20.1–24.0%

16.1–20.0%

12.1–16.0%

8.1–12.0%

4.1–8.0%

0.0–4.0%

Find schools offering this major at PrincetonReview.com.

Careers and Salary

The starting salary for most scientists is in the area of $30,000 and up. Pursuing advanced education will make a marked difference in your salary, and your pay will increase as you gain more experience in your field.

CAREER OPTIONS

Aerospace Engineer	Meteorologist	Scientist
Astronaut	Professor	Teacher
Astronomer	Researcher	

PLANT PATHOLOGY

Basics

Plant pathology is the study of diseases in plants. It's an agricultural discipline and its applications extend to environments ranging from the cornfields of Iowa to the tropical rain forests of Brazil. That's a lot of territory to cover for one major, but somehow its teachers and students manage to do just that.

Plant pathologists study the physical makeup of plants and the diseases that affect them. If you don't have a love for fungi, bacteria, viruses, and carnivorous plants then expect to develop one, because as a plant pathology major you'll cover them extensively.

If You Like Plant Pathology, You May Also Like . . .

Agricultural business and management, agricultural economics, agricultural education, agricultural and biological engineering, agricultural journalism, agricultural mechanization, agricultural technology management, agriculture, biology, botany and plant biology, environmental science, forestry, genetics, grain science, horticulture, microbiology

Suggested High School Prep for Plant Pathology

You had better get on those science courses, particularly biology and chemistry, not to mention some advanced math, including geometry and calculus.

SAMPLE COLLEGE CURRICULUM FOR PLANT PATHOLOGY

Applied Ecology

Bacterial Epidemiology

Biology

Chemistry

Diagnostic Plant Pathology

Disease Physiology

Economic Entomology

Introductory Plant Pathology

Microbiology

Plant Anatomy and Physiology

Soil Science

Fun Facts

Did You Know?

There are approximately 250,000 different types of flowering plants in the world.

They've Saved You Some

Scientists estimate that anywhere between 10 and 15 percent of the world's flowering plants haven't been written about yet, so there's still time to make yourself immortal with florid phrases.

Careers and Salary

Depending on where you choose to apply that degree, you can expect starting salaries to range from $20,000 to $30,000.

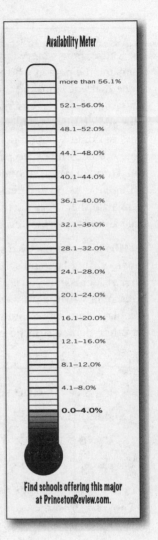

Availability Meter

more than 56.1%

52.1–56.0%

48.1–52.0%

44.1–48.0%

40.1–44.0%

36.1–40.0%

32.1–36.0%

28.1–32.0%

24.1–28.0%

20.1–24.0%

16.1–20.0%

12.1–16.0%

8.1–12.0%

4.1–8.0%

0.0–4.0%

Find schools offering this major at PrincetonReview.com.

CAREER OPTIONS

Biologist

Ecologist

Environmentalist/
Environmental Scientist

Farmer

PLAYWRITING AND SCREENWRITING

Basics

Who can forget, "Leave the gun. Take the cannoli." Or, "You can't expect to wield supreme executive power just 'cause some watery tart threw a sword at you!" Or, "I am serious. And don't call me Shirley." Whether you can name the person who actually penned those lines or not, they're etched in your mind forever. A lot of the magic that goes into the theater and the cinema is due to the tireless imaginations and undeniable talent of playwrights and screenwriters. A major in playwriting and screenwriting will have you honing your writing skills and crafting your art to create original plays and scripts that ideally will live in your public's mind for years to come. Working on one-act farces, full-length musical productions, short films, and long films, you'll take your cue on how to pace and plot a story through each so that it attracts and holds an audience's attention. Through words and ideas alone you'll sculpt believable characters and learn how to make them move through the world and deal with affecting problems and challenges. You'll practice making the audience love them, hate them, fear for them, and cry with them. Once you've studied the technicalities of writing for the stage and screen, you'll eventually be set to join the ranks of the professionals.

This is not a strictly tests-and-papers major. Much of your learning will come in the doing; you'll learn how to write plays and screenplays by actually writing them and then discussing them with professors and other students. But you'll also learn how to write well by studying the work of established writers as well as learning why the classics have endured. Here's one major where you'll sit back and watch a movie or go to a play—but only to study the work in action in order to see how the writing affects and is affected by the other elements of the production.

Keep in mind that not all colleges pair these two fields, and not all colleges offer them as majors. Often, they are offered as concentrations within broader disciplines, such as theater, film, or creative writing.

If You Like Playwriting and Screenwriting, You May Also Like . . .

Advertising, choreography, cinematography and film/video production, creative writing, dance, English, film, journalism, musical theater, technical writing, theater, visual communication

Suggested High School Prep for Playwriting and Screenwriting

The best preparation for a major in playwriting and screenwriting is a solid selection of courses in English, history, languages, and other humanities to polish up those writing skills. You should also take some courses in math and science. Then grab a notebook and get your great ideas on paper. It's never too soon to start. Reading plays and scripts is also great preparation for your major in this field.

Fun Facts

Bookish Types

Want to hear what some experts say about screenwriting? Check out one of these books, then get busy on your own script.

- *You Can Write a Movie* by Pamela Wallace
- *Making a Good Script Great* by Linda Seger
- *Writing Screenplays That Sell* by Michael Hauge
- *Screenwriting Tricks of the Trade* by William Froug
- *The Art of Dramatic Writing* by Lajos Egri
- *How Not to Write a Screenplay: 101 Common Mistakes Most Screenwriters Make* by Denny Martin Flinn

The Oscars: A Selection of Best Screenplays

1941—*Citizen Kane*; 1947—*Miracle on 34th Street*; 1953—*Roman Holiday*; 1961—*Splendor in the Grass*; 1975—*One Flew Over the Cuckoo's Nest*; 1986—*Hannah and Her Sisters*; 1988—*Rain Man*; 1990—*Ghost*; 1992—*The Crying Game*; 1994—*Pulp Fiction*; 1996—*Fargo*; 1997—*Good Will Hunting*; 1998—*Shakespeare in Love*; 1999—*American Beauty; 2000*

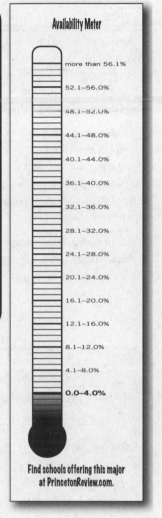

Availability Meter

more than 56.1%

52.1–56.0%

48.1–52.0%

44.1–48.0%

40.1–44.0%

36.1–40.0%

32.1–36.0%

28.1–32.0%

24.1–28.0%

20.1–24.0%

16.1–20.0%

12.1–16.0%

8.1–12.0%

4.1–8.0%

0.0–4.0%

Find schools offering this major at PrincetonReview.com.

Careers and Salary

The starting salary for playwriting and screenwriting majors is difficult to predict. In most cases it takes a lot of time and hard work to get your big break, and until then, writers take all sorts of jobs to make ends meet. Once you do sell a script, the rates vary—from $10,000 for an optioned script to $85,000 or more for a purchased one. Plays that are produced on Broadway earn the playwright royalties, which are based on weekly box office receipts. The Dramatists Guild and the League of American Theatres and Producers, Inc., have established the following royalty system for the playwright's earnings: 5 percent of the gross weekly box office receipts pre-recoupment, 10 percent of the same post-recoupment.

CAREER OPTIONS

Director	Producer	Script Doctor
Editor	Professor	Teacher
Filmmaker	Screenwriter	Writer
Playwright		

POLITICAL COMMUNICATION

Basics

You memorized the names of all the U.S. presidents when you were five. Your idea of TV is limited to CNN, and you check the Drudge Report at least twice a day. You are destined to become a political communication major. But what is political communication, exactly? According to George Washington University, political communication is "the study of the flow of information through political processes: the study of who knows what, when, where and how; and how people use their information to further political goals."

In this program, you'll receive instruction in the practice and theory of contemporary political communication. On the practical side, you'll learn skills like social science research techniques, journalistic methods, electronic media production, and political speaking and debating, as well as do political fieldwork to acquire hands-on experience. Abstract thinking, however, is also a component; the political communication major, like political science, involves heady political analysis through historical, psychological, and philosophical perspectives.

An undergraduate degree in political communication is very marketable; students pursue jobs in political consulting, public affairs, political journalism, public diplomacy, speechwriting, and political advertising. Other students choose to continue on to law or graduate school.

SAMPLE COLLEGE CURRICULUM FOR POLITICAL COMMUNICATION

Campaign Reporting

Information, Media, and National Security

Introduction to Political Communication

Media and Foreign Policy

Media, Politics, and Government

Principles of Public Relations

The Psychology of Attitudes and Public Opinion

Public Affairs and Government Information

Public Diplomacy

Public Opinion, Media, and Democracy

Strategic Political Communication

Television and Politics

If You Like Political Communication, You May Also Like . . .

Political science, government, advertising, digital communications and media/multimedia, English, government, history, international relations, journalism, marketing, mass communication, photojournalism, public policy analysis, radio and television, public relations, psychology

Suggested High School Prep for Political Communication

English and history classes are an essential prep for this major. If your school offers courses in government, journalism, or public speaking, take them. If not, another great way to get a background (and stay on top of current events) is through extracurricular activities like debate club, Model UN, and the school newspaper.

Fun Facts

Interested in interning in Washington, DC? Check out these websites for more information:

- The Fund for American Studies (www.dcinternships.org/index.asp)
- Institute for Experiential Learning (www.ielnet.org)
- The Washington Center (www.twc.edu)

Careers and Salary

Political communication majors fresh out of school make between $25,000 and $35,000 a year, depending on the career path chosen.

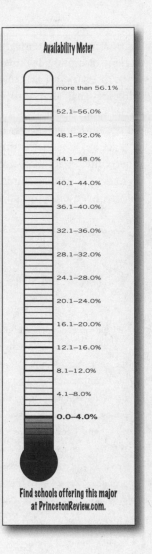

Availability Meter

more than 56.1%

52.1–56.0%

48.1–52.0%

44.1–48.0%

40.1–44.0%

36.1–40.0%

32.1–36.0%

28.1–32.0%

24.1–28.0%

20.1–24.0%

16.1–20.0%

12.1–16.0%

8.1–12.0%

4.1–8.0%

0.0–4.0%

Find schools offering this major at PrincetonReview.com.

CAREER OPTIONS

Consultant	Market Researcher	Professor
Diplomat/Attaché/Foreign Service Officer	Media Specialist	Public Relations
Journalist	Political Aide	Speech Writer
Lawyer	Political Campaign Worker	Television/Radio Producer
Lobbyist	Political Scientist	Television/Radio Reporter
	Politician	

POLITICAL SCIENCE

Basics

In a nutshell, political science is the academic study of politics and government. In one sense, it is an ancient discipline. It remains central to any classical study of the liberal arts, firmly grounded as it is in the work of Plato and Aristotle. In another sense, because it often deals with current events and sophisticated statistical analysis, political science is a cutting-edge area of study. Whether you're analyzing the Israeli parliament, the voting patterns in a presidential campaign, or the pros and cons of different systems of government, political science is timely, fascinating, and perpetually changing.

Like any liberal arts major, political science makes no claims to be a pre-professional program. However, it certainly doesn't exist to teach disconnected facts about politics. Instead, political science majors develop excellent critical thinking and communication skills and, more broadly, an understanding of history and culture. Even more broadly, political science tackles those big, serious, heavy, eternal questions. What is the best way to reconcile individual desires and community needs? Is it possible to have both freedom and equality? Authority and justice? And so on.

If you major in political science, you'll study everything from revolutions to political parties to voting behavior to public policy. You are also likely to explore the political issues inherent to different regions of the world, such as the Middle East, East Asia, Latin America, and Eastern Europe.

If You Like Political Science, You May Also Like . . .

Anthropology, archaeology, architectural history, Asian American studies, Biblical studies, East Asian studies, East European studies, geography, great books, international relations, Islamic studies, Jewish studies, Medieval and Renaissance studies, Middle Eastern studies, philosophy, public policy analysis, religious studies, Slavic languages and literatures, sociology, South Asian studies, Southeast Asian studies, theology, urban studies, women's studies

Suggested High School Prep for Political Science

Political science involves heavy doses of reading, writing, and often—if you can believe it—rigorous statistical analysis. Translation: math. We're not suggesting anything nearly as challenging as AP calculus, but you should stay in practice. In addition, if you think you might major in political science, concentrate primarily on honing your reading and writing skills. Take courses in American history, civics, world history, and English composition so you can get good at writing essays. Mastery of a foreign language is a big plus too, because you will probably be required to take several foreign language classes as a political science major.

SAMPLE COLLEGE CURRICULUM FOR POLITICAL SCIENCE

Political science is a pretty broad subject, and most departments offer a handful of concentrations for you to choose from. Some of the common concentrations are American government, public policy, foreign affairs, political philosophy, and comparative government. Whatever concentration you choose (or even if you don't choose one), you'll probably take a few of these courses:

American Political Thought

The American Presidency

Asian Politics

Comparative Government

Data Analysis

Gender and Politics

International Political Economy

Internship in state or local government

Latin American Politics

Legislative Process

Philosophy of Law

Political Philosophy

Politics and Religion

Statistics

U.S. Foreign Policy

Fun Facts

The Legend of Cincinnatus

According to Roman legend, the popularly elected Senate of the early fledgling Republic found itself staring down a pressing military threat. A worried Senate delegation traveled to the farm of one Lucius Quinctius Cincinnatus, a venerable retired general who was busy plowing his fields at the time, and asked him to become the dictator of the Roman Republic during the crisis. Cincinnatus accepted and headed to Rome immediately, leaving his plow right there in his field. The new dictator quickly attacked the enemy, and a few days later, Rome was victorious. The elated Senate declared that Cincinnatus should remain the dictator of Rome. Wanting no part of absolute power, however, Cincinnatus graciously declined. He went back to his field, picked up his plow where he had left it, and resumed his normal life. What a guy!

Quotable

"Politics ain't beanbag."

—Tip O'Neill, Speaker of the United States House of Representatives (1977–1987)

Famous People Who Majored in Political Science

Jerry Springer (trashy talk show host and one-time mayor of Cincinnati, Tulane University), Mia Hamm (world champion soccer player, University of North Carolina), Earl Warren (former Chief Justice of the United States Supreme Court, University of California—Berkeley), Jane Pauley (television journalist, Indiana University)

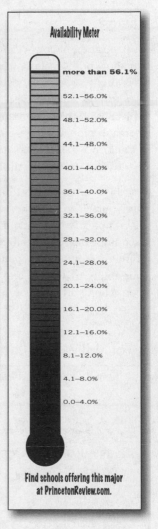

Availability Meter

more than 56.1%

52.1–56.0%

48.1–52.0%

44.1–48.0%

40.1–44.0%

36.1–40.0%

32.1–36.0%

28.1–32.0%

24.1–28.0%

20.1–24.0%

16.1–20.0%

12.1–16.0%

8.1–12.0%

4.1–8.0%

0.0–4.0%

Find schools offering this major at PrincetonReview.com.

Careers and Salary

Salaries vary greatly for political science majors because the possible career paths are so diverse. A high percentage of political science majors go to professional school or graduate school after college. First-year attorneys who graduate at the top of their law school classes command salaries of $125,000 or more. Those who get a PhD and enter academia can expect to start out at about $40,000. Those who go to work straight out of college can expect to earn a yearly salary of about $27,000 to $30,000 (a little less if they go to work for the government).

CAREER OPTIONS

Attorney	Lobbyist	Political Scientist
Corporate Lawyer	Management Consultant	Politician
Diplomat/Attaché/Foreign Service Officer	Market Researcher	Professor
	Marketing Executive	Public Relations Professional
Investment Banker	Political Aide	Publicist
Journalist	Political Campaign Worker	Trial Lawyer
Labor Relations Specialist		

POPULATION BIOLOGY

Basics

Population biology (PB) is a branch of science that investigates the ecological and evolutionary processes that allow biological populations to exist and persist. In other words, it's a discipline that wrestles with some pretty hefty issues—the evolution of life on Earth, extinction, migration, cohabitation, and the ways in which living things interact with, affect, and are affected by their environments. As a PB major, you're likely to explore everything from mites to hummingbirds to human beings, examining these populations "at all levels of organization ranging from molecules to ecosystems," as the Center for Population Biology at the University of California—Davis puts it. Your studies will range from the foundational theories of Thomas Malthus and Charles Darwin to the cutting-edge technologies and techniques used by population biologists today.

PB is often closely linked to ecology, evolutionary biology, and environmental science majors—so prepare yourself to draw heavily on work done in these fields. But this is just the beginning. To grapple with the complex issues at hand, PB majors employ a highly interdisciplinary approach. Here's just a selection of disciplines that contribute to PB pursuits: agriculture, biology, botany, chemistry, entomology, environmental philosophy, forestry, genetics, geology, microbiology, ornithology, paleontology, physiology, and zoology. Your ability to analyze and synthesize information from such a broad academic palette will prove a great boon when you move on to graduate school or the workforce.

If You Like Population Biology, You May Also Like...

Animal behavior and ethology, animal science, aquatic biology, biology, botany and plant biology, chemistry, conservation biology, ecology, entomology, environmental science, forestry, marine biology, marine science, natural resources conservation, paleontology, range science and management, wildlife management, zoology

SAMPLE COLLEGE CURRICULUM FOR POPULATION BIOLOGY

Animal Behavior

Conservation Biology

Entomology

Evolution

Field Ornithology

Genetics

Introduction to Ecology

Introduction to Population Systems

Molecular Biology

Organic Chemsitry

Terrestrial Ecosystems

Theories and Ethics in Population Science

Suggested High School Prep for Population Biology

A science class or two—or four, or eight, maybe ten—couldn't hurt. Math will come in handy as well. Courses in literature and history will give you practice in the art of bringing together a lot of different ideas, just as you'll be doing as a PB major.

Fun Facts

No Limits

Take a quick a look at the resume of prominent population biologist Paul Ralph Ehrlich and you'll see that there are few limits to what a PB major can do. He's a longtime professor at Stanford University, the founder of the activist organization Zero Population Growth, a correspondent for NBC news programs, the author of a handful of books, and the proud holder of plenty of honors and awards.

(Source: www.bookrags.com)

The Population Biologist Speaks

Ehrlich, who is primarily interested in human population biology, said this in a 1974 interview: "If you want to know the truth, I'd say that the biggest mistake mankind ever made was the agricultural revolution. We were a great hunting and gathering animal. If you look—and I have, I've lived with Eskimos and seen bushmen and aborigines and so on—you may be struck, as I have, by the fact that each individual in that kind of society was—at least before they had contact with us—almost a carrier of a full culture. Every individual knew exactly where he or she fit into the picture, had more personal worth and was less alienated than any member of our modern civilization. There are a lot of aspects of our civilization I like, you understand, but I refuse to accept—at least automatically—that what we have today has been worth destroying wide areas of the world for."

(Source: www.motherearthnews.com)

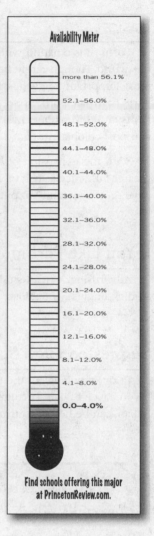

Availability Meter

more than 56.1%

52.1–56.0%

48.1–52.0%

44.1–48.0%

40.1–44.0%

36.1–40.0%

32.1–36.0%

28.1–32.0%

24.1–28.0%

20.1–24.0%

16.1–20.0%

12.1–16.0%

8.1–12.0%

4.1–8.0%

0.0–4.0%

Find schools offering this major at PrincetonReview.com.

Careers and Salary

The starting salary for a population biologist is between $20,000 and $25,000, though sometimes lower and sometimes higher. Tack on a graduate degree and you'll see your salary and job prospects increase.

CAREER OPTIONS

Ecologist	Conservationist	Ranger
Environmental Assessor	Consultant	Researcher
Environmentalist/ Environmental Scientist	Lobbyist	

PORTUGUESE

Basics

Portugal is a nation with a history, language, and culture that has had sweeping influences throughout the world. Though rarely heard in the United States, Portuguese maintains its status as one of the world's most important languages. Spoken in Portugal (obviously), Brazil (South America's largest economy), and parts of Africa, Portuguese is a bridge to a rich and diverse cultural history that spans across three continents and dozens of centuries, from the exploration of the New World in the fifteenth century to colonial and post-colonial Africa.

With the expansion of American investment interests in Latin America, Portuguese has taken on even greater influence as half of all U.S. businesses in South America have offices in Brazil. Portuguese majors will have the opportunity to put their language skills into use in a wide array of fields in a number of countries.

If You Like Portuguese, You May Also Like . . .

Advertising, African studies, French, international relations, international studies, Italian, Latin American studies, linguistics, Spanish

Suggested High School Prep for Portuguese

Prior knowledge of the language isn't necessary to major in it in college, but it certainly won't hurt you. If you haven't taken Portuguese in high school, then other Romance languages, such as French, Spanish, and Italian, can be helpful starting points.

SAMPLE COLLEGE CURRICULUM FOR PORTUGUESE

Brazilian Culture and Civilization

Elementary Portuguese

Grammar and Composition Review

Intermediate Portuguese

Portuguese Conversation and Composition

Portuguese Culture and Civilization

Portuguese Translation

Survey of Portuguese and Brazilian Literature I–II

Topics in Literature of the Portuguese Speaking World

Fun Facts

Did You Know?

The statue of Christ in Rio de Janeiro, Brazil, exactly faces the statue of Christ in Lisbon, Portugal.

Their Claim to Fame

The westernmost point in continental Europe is Cabo de Rocha, Portugal.

Careers and Salary

With the globalization of business, knowledge of any foreign language, including Portuguese, will help make you an attractive candidate for any number of jobs. If it's any indication, starting salaries for Spanish majors range from $25,000 to $33,000.

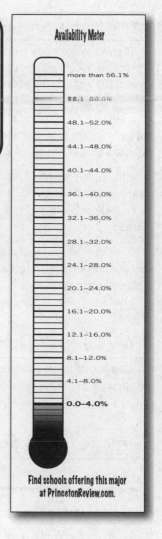

Availability Meter

more than 56.1%

52.1—56.0%

48.1—52.0%

44.1—48.0%

40.1—44.0%

36.1—40.0%

32.1—36.0%

28.1—32.0%

24.1—28.0%

20.1—24.0%

16.1—20.0%

12.1—16.0%

8.1—12.0%

4.1—8.0%

0.0—4.0%

Find schools offering this major at PrincetonReview.com.

CAREER OPTIONS

Diplomat/Attaché/Foreign Service Officer

Editor

Foreign Exchange Trader

Journalist

Lobbyist

Translator

Writer

PRE-DENTISTRY

Basics

If you have your eye on a career as a dentist, a pre-dentistry program might be what you're looking for. Pre-dentistry, like all pre-professional programs, offers focused course work in both general education and areas more specific to your intended field. You'll take courses in the natural sciences like biology and chemistry. You'll take science laboratories to get hands-on experience with research and documentation. You'll take courses in communication, social sciences, and humanities. Ohio State University suggests volunteering or working in a dental office during your undergraduate years—a great way to make sure you want to pursue a dentistry career after graduation.

Although you won't specialize until you're on your way to becoming a dentist, it doesn't hurt to be aware of what's out there. Dentistry includes many areas of expertise, including orthodontics, pediatric dentistry, and oral surgery. Your own interests and concerns will help you to choose a specialty when the time comes.

You should know that most dentistry programs don't require a pre-dentistry major, just as medical schools don't always require premed. Keep in mind that good grades and dedication in all your courses are the best preparation.

If You Like Pre-Dentistry, You May Also Like . . .

Dietetics, health administration, medical technology, nursing, nutrition, pharmacology, pharmacy, physical therapy, pre-law, premedicine, pre-optometry, pre-seminary, pre-veterinary medicine, public health

Suggested High School Prep for Pre-Dentistry

Pre-dentistry involves a great deal of math and science courses, so take as many as possible—biology, chemistry, and advanced-level math such as calculus. Health courses, such as anatomy, will broaden your foundation. And English courses will give you the chance to become a better reader, writer, and communicator.

SAMPLE COLLEGE CURRICULUM FOR PRE-DENTISTRY

Anatomy

Biochemistry

Biology

Oral Biology

Oral Rehabilitation

Organic Chemistry

Physics

Physiology

Qualitative Analysis

Fun Facts

A Dentistry Joke (Like There Aren't Enough of Those)

Dentist to patient: "Could you help me? Could you give out a few of your loudest, most painful screams?"

Patient: "Why? Doc, it isn't all that bad this time."

Dentist: "There are so many people in the waiting room right now, and I don't want to miss my seven o'clock tennis game."

(Source: Dental World, www.dentalw.com)

Important Dates in the History of Toothpaste and Toothbrushes

1850s—Chalk is added to toothpaste.

1873—Colgate produces toothpaste in a jar.

1885—Companies begin mass production of toothbrushes.

1892—Dr. Washington Sheffield puts toothpaste in a tube.

1896—Soap in toothpaste is replaced with sodium lauryl sulphate and sodium ricinoleate.

1938—The first nylon bristle brushes are developed.

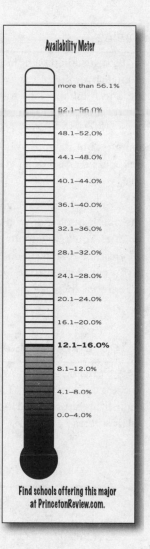

Availability Meter

more than 56.1%

52.1–56.0%

48.1–52.0%

44.1–48.0%

40.1–44.0%

36.1–40.0%

32.1–36.0%

28.1–32.0%

24.1–28.0%

20.1–24.0%

16.1–20.0%

12.1–16.0%

8.1–12.0%

4.1–8.0%

0.0–4.0%

Find schools offering this major at PrincetonReview.com.

Careers and Salary

Starting salaries for new dentists—that means after they've graduated from dental school—begin about $40,000. If you choose to specialize, your salary will be higher. Median earnings for salaried dentists are roughly $130,000.

CAREER OPTIONS

Biologist	Dental Lab Technician	Dentist
Chemist		

PRE-LAW

Basics

First, it should be pointed out that most law schools do not require that you major in pre-law. If you major in English, or say, history, you'll still be on the right track. Crucial to a pre-law major are critical reading, writing, and thinking skills. After all, as a lawyer, your job will require drafting cogent arguments and solutions to problems, then communicating those arguments and solutions effectively to persuade and convince a judge or jury. With a pre-law major, you'll be taking courses dealing with crime, government, and international issues, but most of your study will consist of courses in the humanities and social sciences. Your education will give you perspectives on human nature, skills in oral and written communication, and the knowledge you'll need to be a careful and creative thinker.

A pre-law major will give you the opportunity to take courses in many different disciplines. Political science, anthropology, psychology, government, English, logic, philosophy, and history are only a few of the possibilities. You'll be encouraged to take math and science courses as well. You'll have to unravel quantitative mysteries as a lawyer, too. Your chances of being accepted into a good law school will be greatly improved if you can demonstrate knowledge in many areas. Knowledge of a foreign language will also give you an edge in our increasingly international culture.

If You Like Pre-Law, You May Also Like . . .

Advertising, African American studies, African studies, American history, American literature, American studies, anthropology, Asian American studies, biblical studies, economics, English, English composition, English literature, great books, history, journalism, Latin American studies, South Asian studies, Southeast Asian studies

Suggested High School Prep for Pre-Law

Pre-law majors are immersed in reading and writing, so now's the time to polish your skills. Read as much as you can. Get engaged in your English courses and strive to write well. History, political science, and language courses will also be valuable. Remember, the key is to build knowledge in a wide variety of subjects.

SAMPLE COLLEGE CURRICULUM FOR PRE-LAW

Advanced Constitutional Law

American National Government

Courses in English, political science, philosophy, history and other humanities

Courses in psychology, sociology and other social sciences

Foreign Languages

Introduction to Logic

Math and science courses

Writing courses

Fun Facts

Legalese

Ever heard of legalese? Take a look at an excerpt from *The Night Before Christmas, Legally Speaking*:

Whereas, on or about the night prior to Christmas, there did occur at a certain improved piece of real property (hereinafter "the House") a general lack of stirring by all creatures therein, including, but not limited to, a mouse.

A variety of foot apparel, e.g., stockings, socks, etc., had been affixed by and around the chimney in said House in the hope and/or belief that St. Nick (a.k.a. St. Nicholas; a.k.a. Santa Claus; hereinafter "Claus") would arrive at sometime thereafter.

The minor residents, i.e., the children, of the aforementioned House were located in their individual beds and were engaged in nocturnal hallucinations, i.e., dreams, wherein visions of confectionery treats, including, but not limited to, candies, nuts and/or sugar plums, did dance, cavort, and otherwise appear in said dreams.

The Constitution of the United States of America

Fifty-five delegates drafted the Constitution in 1787 at a convention in Philadelphia. The purpose of this convention was to amend the Articles of Confederation, our country's first attempt at a constitution. The Constitution of the United States of America is the oldest written national constitution still honored.

Famous People Who Majored in Pre-Law

Jamie Lee Curtis (actress, University of the Pacific)

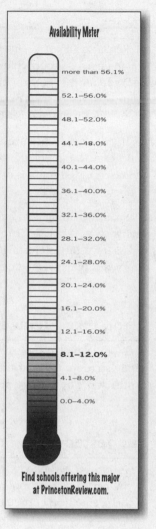

Availability Meter

more than 56.1%

52.1–56.0%

48.1–52.0%

44.1–48.0%

40.1–44.0%

36.1–40.0%

32.1–36.0%

28.1–32.0%

24.1–28.0%

20.1–24.0%

16.1–20.0%

12.1–16.0%

8.1–12.0%

4.1–8.0%

0.0–4.0%

Find schools offering this major at PrincetonReview.com.

Careers and Salary

If you're a pre-law major, your studies will continue in law school. The starting salary for young lawyers is usually between $50,000 and $70,000.

CAREER OPTIONS		
Agent	Editor	Politician
Attorney	Mediator	Private Investigator
Corporate Lawyer	Paralegal	Trial Lawyer
Detective/Private Investigator		

PRE-MEDICINE

Basics

Reality check: A premedical degree does not guarantee that you will be accepted into medical school. Premedicine is a curriculum designed to best prepare you for the MCAT (the Medical College Admission Test) and for the rigors of medical school. Rich in biology and chemistry, this major dovetails neatly into several other related areas of study (such as chemistry, biology, and biochemistry). It also provides a solid background in physics and mathematics.

If you declare premedicine as your major, be prepared to forget about a social life from time to time. Colleges design premed programs to weed out prospective applicants to medical school (two words: organic chemistry). Med schools can accept only a certain number of students each year because a limited number of doctors may be licensed in the United States each year.

So, if the thought of hundreds of hours spent poring over organic chemistry notes appeals to you in a strange way, if you refer to *ER* as one of your "stories," if you think that the unabridged *Gray's Anatomy* makes for some interesting reading, or if you think you can really study harder than most of your friends for four years, then premedicine just might be the major for you.

If You Like Premedicine, You May Also Like . . .

Biology, biopsychology, cell biology, chemistry, chiropractic, circulation technology, genetics, health administration, medical technology, neurobiology, neuroscience, nutrition, pharmacology, pharmacy, pre-dentistry, pre-optometry, pre-veterinary medicine, public health, radiologic technology, respiratory therapy

Suggested High School Prep for Premedicine

A firm background in science will serve you well. Take as many courses in chemistry, biology, and physics as you can. If your school offers anatomy and physiology, sign up for those. Advanced math is usually a part of the premedical curriculum as well, so courses in calculus and trigonometry are also useful.

**SAMPLE COLLEGE
CURRICULUM FOR
PREMEDICINE**

Calculus I–II

General Anatomy and Physiology

General Biology I–II

General Chemistry I–II

Organic Chemistry I–II

Physics I–II

Fun Facts

The 411 on the MCAT

For more information on the MCAT, try the Association of American Medical Colleges website (www.aamc.org/students/mcat). You should also check your local library or bookstore for books about the test. The Princeton Review publishes the *Cracking the MCAT* and offers classroom courses. Visit PrincetonReview.com to find out more.

Sparknotes

Is senior-itis starting to affect your brain? Need a little help to push you through those exams and papers? Try Sparknotes.com. This site is the brainchild of a group of Harvard undergrads, alumni, and graduate students, each writing on his or her field of expertise. It offers comprehensive notes and guides arranged by subject—everything from quick-click tables of physical constants, the periodic table, and unit conversions to literature notes and an entire section devoted to Shakespeare. Might just come in handy on some long night. . . .

Famous People Who Majored in Premedicine

Denzel Washington (actor, Fordham University), Jerry Greenfield (Jerry of Ben & Jerry's, Oberlin College), Bob Dole (politician, University of Kansas), Robin Cook (author, Wesleyan University), Neil Diamond (singer/songwriter, New York University), Bill Murray (actor, Regis College), James Earl Jones (actor, University of Michigan)

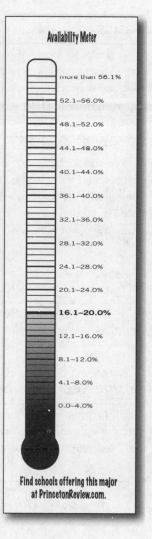

Availability Meter

more than 56.1%

52.1–56.0%

48.1–52.0%

44.1–48.0%

40.1–44.0%

36.1–40.0%

32.1–36.0%

28.1–32.0%

24.1–28.0%

20.1–24.0%

16.1–20.0%

12.1–16.0%

8.1–12.0%

4.1–8.0%

0.0–4.0%

Find schools offering this major at PrincetonReview.com.

Careers and Salary

Premedicine majors generally go directly into medical school or another type of related professional training. A premedical student can expect to make about $36,000 in the first year of residency after medical school. This figure increases substantially once internships and fellowships are complete.

CAREER OPTIONS

Biochemist	Health Care Administrator	Optometrist
Biologist	Hospital Administrator	Pharmacist
Dentist	Nurse	Physician
Dermatologist	Nutritionist	Public Health Administrator
Geneticist		

PRE-OPTOMETRY

Basics

If you're looking ahead to a future as an optometrist, you might want to consider a major in pre-optometry. Optometrists are concerned with all aspects of the eye—the promotion of eye health and safety, vision care, and basic examinations of the internal and external parts of the eye. They write prescriptions for glasses and contact lenses. There are many options for optometrists; for example, you might become involved with sports vision or geriatrics. Expanding technology is creating new and exciting opportunities for optometrists, so if the eye is your interest, consider this path.

Pre-optometry is not a major at most universities. It is, rather, a concentration—a focused selection of courses that will give you the necessary foundation for admission to optometry school. Keep in mind that admission to optometry school depends largely on your scores on the Optometry Admission Test, as well as your background in math and science. Although most students complete an undergraduate degree before attending optometry school, many optometry schools do not require it for admission.

If You Like Pre-Optometry, You May Also Like . . .

Biology, chemistry, health administration, pre-dentistry, premedicine, pre-veterinary medicine, public health

Suggested High School Prep for Pre-Optometry

Since pre-optometry programs involve a great deal of math and science, take advanced courses such as calculus and analytic geometry, as well as courses in biology, chemistry, and physics. Become familiar with the eye in health or anatomy classes.

SAMPLE COLLEGE CURRICULUM FOR PRE-OPTOMETRY

Anatomy and Physiology

Biochemistry

Histology

Microbiology

Optics

Organic Chemistry

Pathology

Pharmacology

Statistics

Fun Facts

So You Want to Be a Doctor?

If you're interested in the eye but really want that MD on the end of your name, consider a career in *ophthalmology*. This field also deals with the eye, but you'll attend medical school and you'll have the ability to treat eye diseases, perform surgery, and prescribe medication, as well as prescribe glasses and contact lenses.

Eye Humor

Q: What happened to the eye-clinician who fell into his lens-grinding machine?

A: He made a spectacle of himself.

(What did you expect? It's eye humor.)

Careers and Salary

The starting salary for most optometrists is usually between $45,000 and $55,000. Your level of experience and the type of practice you run will influence your salary greatly.

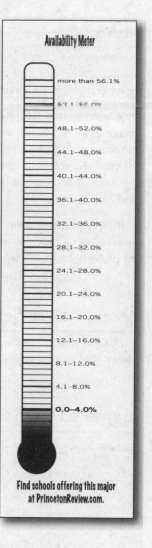

Availability Meter

more than 56.1%

52.1–56.0%

48.1–52.0%

44.1–48.0%

40.1–44.0%

36.1–40.0%

32.1–36.0%

28.1–32.0%

24.1–28.0%

20.1–24.0%

16.1–20.0%

12.1–16.0%

8.1–12.0%

4.1–8.0%

0.0–4.0%

Find schools offering this major at PrincetonReview.com.

CAREER OPTIONS
Optometrist

PRE-SEMINARY

Basics

Contrary to what this may sound like, you're not making any vows of poverty or chastity. You won't get to hear confessions, and the closest you'll come to wearing a long white robe in front of a crowd is if you get locked out of your dorm room on your way to the shower.

While you may not quite be ready for the pulpit, a major in pre-seminary affords you the opportunity to engage in all of the intense theological and moral debates of your dreams, and better yet, by the time you graduate, you will have received such a thorough education in philosophical reasoning and biblical thought that you'll be able to make a much stronger argument than "because you're just wrong." Pre-seminary majors are theological and philosophical heavyweights. They study everything from Aristotle to contemporary Christian thought.

If a religious vocation is your calling, consider this excellent preparation for a life of the cloth. But even if you're not already planning your first sermon, a pre-seminary major is an excellent way to bridge theology and philosophy, to learn how to think and write critically.

If You Like Pre-Seminary, You May Also Like . . .

Biblical studies, classics, comparative literature, English, Hebrew, history, Jewish studies, missions, peace studies, philosophy, religious studies, theology

Suggested High School Prep for Pre-Seminary

> **SAMPLE COLLEGE CURRICULUM FOR PRE-SEMINARY**
>
> The Christian Faith
>
> Church Vocations Practicum
>
> Contemporary Philosophical Issues
>
> Introduction to Philosophy
>
> Introduction to *The Bible*
>
> Modern Christian Thought
>
> New Testament Theology
>
> Old Testament Theology
>
> Religion in America
>
> Sociology
>
> World Religions

You will need some strong critical reading and writing skills developed through a genuine interest in the humanities. Beef up your intake of history, English, and philosophy (if possible). If you go to a school that offers them, take some religion classes, always playing the role of the healthy skeptic. And remember, it's never too early to begin working your way through Aristotle's *Ethics*.

Fun Facts

Nature of God (submitted by Father Pius)

A man trying to understand the nature of God asked him some questions:

"God, how long is a million years to you?"

And God said, "A million years is like a minute."

Then the man asked, "God, how much is a million dollars to you?"

And God said, "A million dollars is like a penny."

The man thought for a moment and asked, "God, will you give me a penny?"

And God said, "In a minute."

Theology Final Exam

1. Summarize Thomas Aquinas' *Summa Theologiae* in three succinct sentences. You may use your *Bible*.
2. St. Martin of Tours, Pope Clement VII, and Karl Barth were not contemporaries. Had the known each other, how might the history of the Reformation have turned out differently?
3. Define a moral system that satisfies liberals, conservatives, moderates, and the entire population of Ancient Rome, ca. 3 B.C./B.C.E.
4. Memorize *The Bible*. Recite it in tongues.

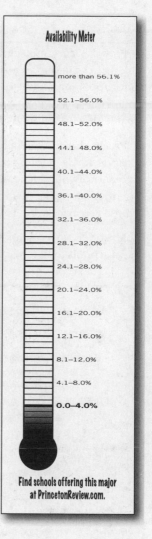

Availability Meter

more than 56.1%

52.1–56.0%

48.1–52.0%

44.1 48.0%

40.1–44.0%

36.1–40.0%

32.1–36.0%

28.1–32.0%

24.1–28.0%

20.1–24.0%

16.1–20.0%

12.1–16.0%

8.1–12.0%

4.1–8.0%

0.0–4.0%

Find schools offering this major
at PrincetonReview.com.

Careers and Salary

Starting salaries for a pre-seminary major are similar to those of other humanities majors, currently between $20,000 and $30,000.

CAREER OPTIONS

Clergy—Priest, Rabbi, Minister	Philosopher	Teacher
Editor	Professor	Writer
Journalist	Social Worker	

PRE-VETERINARY MEDICINE

Basics

Pre-veterinary medicine is for those students who have an eye on veterinary school. Veterinarians are skilled at caring for animals—diagnosing and treating their health problems, preventing further problems from happening, and basically ensuring these critters' well-being. Vets often choose between working with small animals and working with larger ones (such as farm animals), but there are plenty of vets who are capable of working with all sizes.

Pre-veterinary medicine programs at most colleges encompass science and math courses that most veterinary schools require for admittance. Biology, chemistry, organic chemistry, and other courses will form a large part of your curriculum, as will classes in animal sciences and zoology. Getting involved in an internship or volunteering in a vet's office are both great ways to augment your studies and get a little experience before veterinary school.

Most veterinary schools don't require you to major in pre-veterinary medicine. The most important things schools look for is a strong background in science and math and, if possible, actual veterinary observation or experience.

SAMPLE COLLEGE CURRICULUM FOR PRE-VETERINARY MEDICINE

Undergraduate:

Animal Sciences

Biology

General Chemistry

Genetics

Math

Organic Chemistry

Physics

Veterinary School:

Anatomy of Companion Animals

Equine Surgery

Infectious Diseases and Preventive Medicine

Microscopic Anatomy

Pathogenic Microbiology

Pathology and Immunology

Principles of Morphology

Small Animal Soft Tissue Surgery

Veterinary Immunology

If You Like Pre-Veterinary Medicine, You May Also Like . . .

Animal science, biology, entomology, environmental science, forestry, wildlife management, zoology

Suggested High School Prep for Pre-Veterinary Medicine

Pre-veterinary medicine will require a great deal of math and science, so now's your chance to get prepared. Biology, chemistry, calculus, and other advanced courses will be your best bets. Courses dealing with animals—such as husbandry courses, if you live in a rural area—will be of obvious help to your getting a head start on your college curriculum.

Fun Facts

Save My Dog!

In a natural disaster, pets are often forgotten—or else their owners protect them at all costs, risking their own safety and the safety of others. To aid animals and their owners in times of crisis, the Veterinary Medical Assistance Teams come to the rescue. The first of these teams was formed in Massachusetts in 1994, and since then it and many others have assisted in disasters such as Hurricane Katrina. All VMAT groups rescue both large and small animals, providing medical care, food, water, and other necessities. Read more about these incredible rescuers at the official website for the American Veterinary Medicine Association (www.avma.org).

A Few Dog Quotes for Pet Lovers

"Whoever said you can't buy happiness forgot about puppies."

—Gene Hill

"To his dog, every man is Napoleon; hence the constant popularity of dogs."

—Aldous Huxley

"If I have any beliefs about immortality, it is that certain dogs I have known will go to heaven, and very, very few persons."

—James Thurber

"The average dog is a nicer person than the average person."

—Andrew A. Rooney

"I've seen a look in dogs' eyes, a quickly vanishing look of amazed contempt, and I am convinced that basically dogs think humans are nuts."

—John Steinbeck

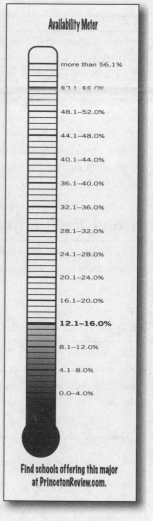

Availability Meter

more than 56.1%

52.1–56.0%

48.1–52.0%

44.1–48.0%

40.1–44.0%

36.1–40.0%

32.1–36.0%

28.1–32.0%

24.1–28.0%

20.1–24.0%

16.1–20.0%

12.1–16.0%

8.1–12.0%

4.1–8.0%

0.0–4.0%

Find schools offering this major at PrincetonReview.com.

Careers and Salary

Vets who start in private practice after graduating from veterinary school generally earn between $35,000 and $45,000. Salaries will increase as you get more experience and your practice expands.

CAREER OPTIONS

Animal Control Officer	Biologist	Zoologist
Animal Trainer	Veterinarian	

PRINTMAKING

Basics

Printmaking originally arose from a demand for multiple copies of a written or artistic work. Since then, printmaking has developed into a fine art in itself. Printmaking is the production of original images on a separate medium, usually in multiples. Depending on the printmaking process, an artist will draw on a surface such as a metal plate, stone, or sheet of silk, which is then treated, inked, and run with paper by hand through a press to print the desired number of original pieces.

Printmaking students study intaglio (etching and engraving), monotype lithography, serigraphy (silk screen), and relief printmaking (woodcut and linocut). Most programs, after introducing all the basic techniques, require the printmaking major to choose one area of concentration.

If You Like Printmaking, You May Also Like . . .

Advertising, art, art education, art history, drawing, fashion design, graphic art, interior design, painting, photography

Suggested High School Prep for Printmaking

If you want to major in printmaking, you will (in most cases) need to have a portfolio of artwork in order to be admitted to a program. So, draw, draw, draw! Schools look for strong observational drawing skills, so draw from life as often as you can. For feedback or reviews form several schools at once, visit a National Portfolio Day (www.npda.org). Check out local museums, community colleges, and universities for pre-college programs or seminars. Sometimes museums also offer volunteer opportunities for students.

> **SAMPLE COLLEGE CURRICULUM FOR PRINTMAKING**
>
> Advanced Printmaking I–II
>
> Art History I–II
>
> Design I–II
>
> Drawing I–IV
>
> Introductory Intaglio
>
> Introductory Lithography
>
> Introductory Relief
>
> Introductory Serigraphy
>
> Painting
>
> Sculpture
>
> Studio I–IV

Fun Facts

Useful Resources—Printmaking Links

This site, sponsored by Middle Tennessee State University, is exactly what it says it is—a huge directory of helpful printmaking links. www.Mtsu.edu/~art/printmaking/print_links.html.

Careers and Salary

A printmaking major who begins a career in a print shop straight out of college can expect to make about $23,000 to $30,000. Freelance illustration could bring in some additional funds.

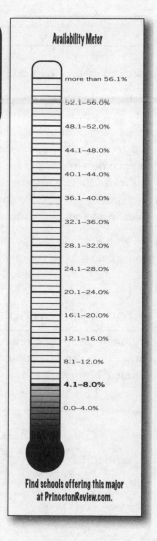

Availability Meter

more than 56.1%

52.1–56.0%

48.1–52.0%

44.1–48.0%

40.1–44.0%

36.1–40.0%

32.1–36.0%

28.1–32.0%

24.1–28.0%

20.1–24.0%

16.1–20.0%

12.1–16.0%

8.1–12.0%

4.1–8.0%

0.0–4.0%

Find schools offering this major at PrincetonReview.com.

CAREER OPTIONS

Art Dealer	Digital Artist	Web Art Director
Artist	Fashion Designer	Website Designer
Curator	Printer	

PSYCHOLOGY

Basics

Psychology is the study of the way humans and animals interact and respond to their environment. The manner in which they do is called behavior.

Psychology combines humanities and science. Psychologists try to discover why certain people react to certain aspects of society and the world at large in a certain way, and from those reactions, they try to deduce something about the biology of our brains and the way the environment influences us. Sound complicated? It is, but it's also a profoundly fascinating major. If you major in psychology, you'll look for the essence of why people are the way they are, from their personality type to their sexual orientation. Within this broad framework, psychology majors focus on such features of the human mind as learning, cognition, intelligence, motivation, emotion, perception, personality, mental disorders, and the ways in which our individual preferences are inherited from our parents or shaped by our environment.

With a strong background in research and the scientific method, a psychology major pursues a field of study that seeks to educate, communicate, and resolve many of the problems surrounding human behavior.

If You Like Psychology, You May Also Like . . .

American studies, anthropology, biology, business administration and management, chemistry, communication disorders, computer and information science, criminology, East Asian studies, education, English, German, history, human development, linguistics, mathematics, philosophy, religious studies, sociology

SAMPLE COLLEGE CURRICULUM FOR PSYCHOLOGY

Adolescence

Counseling Psychology

Experimental Psychology

General Psychology

Introduction to Psychobiology

Learning Memory and Cognition

Organizational Psychology

Psychology of Childhood

Psychology of Personalities

Psychopathology and Psychotherapy

Quantitative and Statistical Methods

Research in Psychology

Social Psychology

Statistics

Suggested High School Prep for Psychology

In addition to taking introductory psychology courses at your high school, you should also prepare yourself by having a strong background in science, math, English, and computer courses. Spending your time volunteering at a local hospital or mental health clinic is also a great opportunity to gain practical experience in the field. There is also a wealth of reading material available to those who have an interest in psychology, from scholarly journals to newspapers and magazines.

Fun Facts

Did You Know?

Sigmund Freud barely escaped persecution by the Nazis in his native Austria, fleeing to England just a few days before the Gestapo entered his home.

Did You Know?

Thanks to Carl Jung, the eminent Swiss psychologist and collaborator of Freud, we have the terms *introverted* and *extroverted*.

Famous People Who Majored in Psychology

William James and Jacques Lacan

Careers and Salary

For someone with a baccalaureate degree, the average starting salary for a psychology major ranges from $25,000 to $35,000 a year. This increases with education and experience, though, as entry-level positions for those holding master's and doctoral degrees are in the $40,000 to $55,000 range.

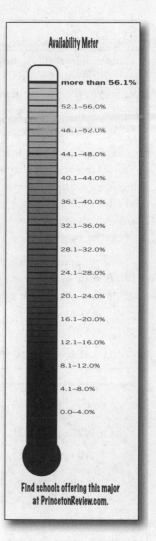

Availability Meter

more than 56.1%

52.1–56.0%

48.1–52.0%

44.1–48.0%

40.1–44.0%

36.1–40.0%

32.1–36.0%

28.1–32.0%

24.1–28.0%

20.1–24.0%

16.1–20.0%

12.1–16.0%

8.1–12.0%

4.1–8.0%

0.0–4.0%

Find schools offering this major at PrincetonReview.com.

CAREER OPTIONS

Advertising Executive	Crisis Negotiator	Psychologist
Career Counselor	Guidance Counselor	Social Worker
Child Care Worker	Marketing Executive	Substance Abuse Counselor
Criminologist	Professor	

PUBLIC ADMINISTRATION

Basics

This major applies the principles of good business—management, problem-solving, decision-making, organization, and leadership—to the public sector. Public administration careers can exist on a state or local level and in federal agencies (such as housing, law enforcement, and labor relations) and nonprofit organizations (such as health care and social services).

Public administration is a hybrid field that arose from the close relationship between government and business. Politics and public policy are equally important in this field. As a public administration major you'll see how laws and regulations have affected society, how those laws are either problematic or beneficial, and sometimes a combination of both. You'll learn about current problems with the law and the ways those laws might be changed. You'll gain an understanding of social problems and see the ways people respond to changes. You might choose to work as a city planner, a tax administrator, an insurance regulator, or one of many other options.

Your program might offer areas of special interest in public administration such as urban studies, criminal justice, or public opinion. No matter where your interests lie, you'll be expected to have a good knowledge of government, an interest in business, and a passion for serving others effectively.

If You Like Public Administration, You May Also Like . . .

Accounting, business administration and management, education administration, health administration, public health

---

SAMPLE COLLEGE CURRICULUM FOR PUBLIC ADMINISTRATION

Accounting for Governmental
   Organizations

Administrative Law

Applied Research Methods

Contemporary Government and
   Business Relations

Federalism and Intergovernmental
   Relations

Human Resource Management

Mathematics for Decision-Making

Public Budgeting

Public Finance

Public Policy Analysis

State and Local Government

Urban and Regional Economic Analysis

Suggested High School Prep for Public Administration

Communication skills are vital to any administration major, so make an effort to take classes in English, languages, writing, and other humanities subjects. Computer skills are also important, so take classes in computer science if they're offered at your school. Math courses will also help in making you an effective administrator. And learn how to type—you'll be glad you did.

Fun Facts

Words on Public Service

"Work the object of which is merely to serve one's self is the lowest. Work the object of which is merely to serve one's family is the next lowest. Work the object of which is to serve more and more people, in widening range   is social service in the fullest sense, and the highest form of service we can reach."

—Charlotte Perkins Gilman

Careers and Salary

Starting salaries for public administrators fall somewhere between $20,000 and $40,000—a fairly wide range—and depend greatly on how you use your degree and for what type of organization you choose to work.

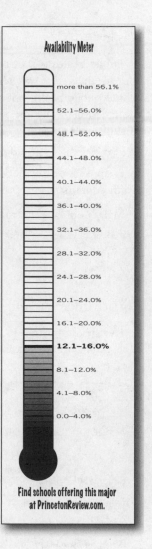

Availability Meter

more than 56.1%

52.1–56.0%

48.1–52.0%

44.1–48.0%

40.1–44.0%

36.1–40.0%

32.1–36.0%

28.1–32.0%

24.1–28.0%

20.1–24.0%

16.1–20.0%

12.1–16.0%

8.1–12.0%

4.1–8.0%

0.0–4.0%

Find schools offering this major at PrincetonReview.com.

CAREER OPTIONS

Accountant/Auditor	College Administrator	Hospital Administrator
Attorney	Consultant	Office Manager
Bank Officer	Financial Aid Officer	Political Campaign Worker
Benefits Administrator	Health Care Administrator	Public Health Administrator

PUBLIC HEALTH

Basics

Public health is the study of how health issues affect populations and the development of methods to improve the general well-being of the public at large. Public health majors study the science and the politics behind public health policies. Whether investigating communicable diseases, working with the mentally ill, implementing nutrition programs, or studying policy, public health majors strive to fulfill the mission of the World Health Organization, as given in its definition of health: "Health is a state of complete physical, mental, and social well-being and not merely the absence of disease or infirmity."

Some schools further divide this major into separate concentrations, such as nutrition, biostatistics, and health administration. Other schools require classes in each of these areas.

Many public health programs begin at the graduate level, but some schools do offer this major to undergraduates. Graduate study is not necessarily required to work in public health, but it is definitely something to consider.

If You Like Public Health, You May Also Like . . .

Health administration, mental health services, microbiology, nursing, nutrition, physical therapy, premedicine, public administration, public policy analysis

SAMPLE COLLEGE CURRICULUM FOR PUBLIC HEALTH

Biology I–II

Epidemiology

General Chemistry

General Psychology

Health and Public Policy

Introduction to Health Administration

Introduction to Public Health

Introduction to the U.S. Health Care System

Microbiology

Organic Chemistry

Principles of Statistical Interference

Social and Behavioral Sciences in Public Health

Statistics

Suggested High School Prep for Public Health

Classes in biology, chemistry, and advanced math will be useful, if not required. A second language (especially Spanish) couldn't hurt, either.

ALLIED MEDICAL AND HEALTH PROFESSIONS/
SCIENCE AND TECHNOLOGY

Fun Facts

For More Information . . .

Harvard University's School of Public Health publishes an online magazine called *World Health News*. You can find it at www.Worldhealthnews.harvard.edu.

The school also has a very informative website about the twelve most common types of cancer (www.yourcancerrisk.harvard.edu/index.htm). The site allows you to determine your risk factor for each type and gives information on how to prevent the disease.

To find out more about the World Health Organization, visit www.Who.int.

Careers and Salary

The starting salary for a public health major fresh out of college ranges from $30,000 to $40,000.

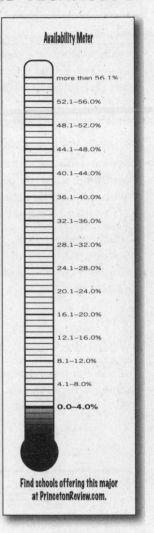

Availability Meter

more than 56.1%

52.1–56.0%

48.1–52.0%

44.1–48.0%

40.1–44.0%

36.1–40.0%

32.1–36.0%

28.1–32.0%

24.1–28.0%

20.1–24.0%

16.1–20.0%

12.1–16.0%

8.1–12.0%

4.1–8.0%

0.0–4.0%

Find schools offering this major at PrincetonReview.com.

CAREER OPTIONS

| Health Care Administrator | Nutritionist | Public Health Administrator |

PUBLIC POLICY ANALYSIS

Basics

Ever wonder why governments do things that no one seems to understand? Ever want to know why your hometown has six stoplights on four blocks, or what exactly goes on inside of a "think tank"? Perhaps you've always wanted to be behind the political scene, helping to shape and inform the decisions that affect policy.

A major in public policy analysis will place you right at the heart of some of the most important economic and social decisions made by businesses and governments. Using statistical information, theories, and economic tools such as cost-benefit analyses and case studies, a public policy analysis major will provide you with the skills you need to evaluate policy decisions. Whether you are working in the corporate world or with the federal and local government, you will be ready to formulate and critique policies that have a direct bearing on our society and environment.

Public policy analysis majors can play a number of roles given their strong background in mathematics and economics. You will improve your critical thinking skills as well as strengthen your organizational and decision-making abilities. When it's all over, you will be ready to enter one of the fastest growing fields in the job market.

If You Like Public Policy Analysis, You May Also Like . . .

Economics, political science, public administration, public health, social psychology, statistics, urban planning, urban studies

Suggested High School Prep for Public Policy Analysis

A strong background in the liberal arts and the sciences, especially math, is good preparation if you're considering a major in public policy analysis. The major also includes advanced calculus and statistics, so prepare well in these areas.

SAMPLE COLLEGE CURRICULUM FOR PUBLIC POLICY ANALYSIS

Calculus

Data Analysis I

International Political Economy

Introduction to Policy Analysis

Normative Theories of Policy Analysis

Policy Process

Public Ethics

Quantitative Methods

Statistics

Theory of Public Finance

Fun Facts

For More Information . . .

To find out more about some of the most recent policy debates and issues in the United States, visit www.Public-policy.org, a website dedicated to public policy issues.

Did You Know?

The statistician George Gallup, founder of the now famous Gallup poll, began collecting information in 1935 for what would be the first public opinion poll on social and economic issues throughout the United States.

Careers and Salary

Starting salaries for public policy analysis majors range from $24,000 to $36,000.

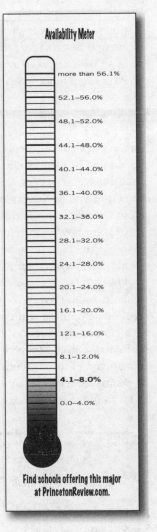

Availability Meter

more than 56.1%

52.1–56.0%

48.1–52.0%

44.1–48.0%

40.1–44.0%

36.1–40.0%

32.1–36.0%

28.1–32.0%

24.1–28.0%

20.1–24.0%

16.1–20.0%

12.1–16.0%

8.1–12.0%

4.1–8.0%

0.0–4.0%

Find schools offering this major at PrincetonReview.com.

CAREER OPTIONS

Labor Relations Specialist	Political Campaign Worker	Sociologist
Lobbyist	Political Scientist	Statistician
Political Aide	Politician	

PUBLIC RELATIONS

Basics

You're always into what's new and now, you've got a knack for organization and a catchy flair for writing, and people always listen to what you have to say. If you're all that, with a soft spot for glitz and glamour, welcome to the fast-paced, results-driven, done-yesterday world of PR.

According to Kent State University, public relations is "the strategic management of communication and relationships between organizations and their key publics." In other words, public relations specialists control how organizations and their products or services are perceived by the public—and, in turn, what image their paying clients (the organizations) portray. As a public relations major, you'll learn about all the written, verbal, and visual elements that go into effective public relations. You'll be prepped on how to write a press release and how to handle media attention on your client's behalf. Your studies may also include forays into publishing newsletters, designing effective promotional ads, newswriting, broadcast media, and videography. Once you have a grasp on these basics, you'll learn how to use them effectively to drive sales for your client and earn favor in the public eye. Knowing when to communicate what is essential in public relations. You'll learn how to develop your information and messages and how to make sure that information is portrayed in the best possible way to your targeted audience. The best PR pros will also know a little about event planning, product launches, public speaking, and damage control.

Public relations is in many ways an interdisciplinary major, and you'll study elements from many other fields, including psychology, philosophy, languages, business, art, and many others. You'll learn how to analyze public opinion and various research studies in order to determine what the public relations needs are for a certain organization. Problem solving and strategic planning abilities go a long way in the field, so hone them now. Oh, and there are ethical issues, too, when it comes to "influencing" public opinion—you'll want to maintain ethical business practices for the sake of your PR firm and your firm's loyal clients.

Many programs require students to participate in an internship, which is a great way to see the world of PR from the inside. Some programs also require students to choose a concentration, often in the business field. Be sure to research exactly what's required as you determine what program is best for you.

SAMPLE COLLEGE CURRICULUM FOR PUBLIC RELATIONS

Advertising and Society
Business Writing
Communication Theory
Media Management
Newsletter Publication
Photojournalism
Public Broadcast and Culture
Public Relations Campaigns
Public Relations Ethics
Publication Design
Reporting
Strategic Planning
Videography
Writing for Public Relations

If You Like Public Relations, You May Also Like . . .

Accounting, advertising, business administration and management, business communications, entrepreneurship, finance, human resources management, marketing, merchandising and buying operations, music management, recreation management

Suggested High School Prep for Public Relations

Although you probably won't have any actual public relations courses in your high school, you can prepare for this major by taking classes that strengthen your communication skills, such as English, languages, history, and art. Great interpersonal skills are also vital to a career in PR, so get involved in extracurricular activities to get used to interacting with all different kinds of people.

Fun Facts

Did You Know?

There is an actual Museum of Public Relations. It's located at 26 Broadway in New York City, and its exhibits show how PR has developed over the years for industry, government, and education. Learn more about the museum at www.Prmuseum.com.

The Father of Public Relations

This so-called Father of Public Relations was Edward Bernays, who died at age 103 in 1995. Bernays took the fundamentals of attempting to change government policy and expanded them into a brand-new realm: influencing and changing the opinions and behaviors of the general public. It was Bernays who came up with the idea of "endorsements"—using celebrities or other famous people to lend their weight to arguments and ad campaigns. And it was Bernays who changed public opinion about the appropriateness of women smoking in public; under his auspices, a Lucky Strike campaign had women demonstrators smoking on street corners. The cigarettes were, for a time, known as "torches of freedom."

(Source: "Edward Bernays, 'Father of Public Relations' and Leader in Opinion Making, Dies at 103," *The New York Times*, March, 10 1995, B7)

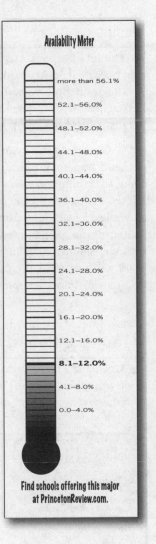

Availability Meter

more than 56.1%

52.1–56.0%

48.1–52.0%

44.1–48.0%

40.1–44.0%

36.1–40.0%

32.1–36.0%

28.1–32.0%

24.1–28.0%

20.1–24.0%

16.1–20.0%

12.1–16.0%

8.1–12.0%

4.1–8.0%

0.0–4.0%

Find schools offering this major at PrincetonReview.com.

Careers and Salary

Salaries for public relations majors range from approximately $20,000 to $42,000, but this number depends on what sort of company you work for and where in the country you live. Salaries will increase as you gain experience in your field.

CAREER OPTIONS

Advertising Executive

Agent

Bar/Club Manager

Human Resources Manager

Manager

Public Relations Consultant

Publicist

Various careers in advertising, marketing, or product development

Writer

PUBLISHING

Basics

Though this book may have seemed to magically appear on the shelf at your local bookstore, we beg to differ, dear friend. Many months—nay, years—of work went into getting this book ready for the public eye. And many people were involved. Authors, editors, publishers, marketers, printers, distributors, and now booksellers. With a degree in publishing, you'll understand the ins and outs of what each of these jobs entails—and, if desired, you'll likely be able to step into one of these roles yourself.

Consider a degree in publishing a no-holds-barred immersion into the publishing industry—past, present, and hopefully future. Your studies will span the centuries, from the groundbreaking ninth century Chinese printing practices to the fifteenth century Gutenberg press to today's rapid innovations in publishing technologies and electronic media. It's in the here-and-now that you'll spend most of your time, getting a handle on marketing principles, contracting practices, editing styles, editor/author relations, desktop publishing, printing equipment, paper stocks, electronic publications, multimedia platforms, copyright laws, professional standards, industry trends, business, finance—there's a lot of material to cover. But all the hard work will pay off. As the publishing industry continues to grow and innovate, it's always on the lookout for bright, well-trained people who are primed to carry it into the future.

If You Like Publishing, You May Also Like...

Arts management, creative writing, digital communications and media/multimedia, English, English composition, graphic design, great books, journalism, marketing, printmaking, public relations, technical writing, web design

SAMPLE COLLEGE CURRICULUM FOR PUBLISHING

Business and Finance

Desktop Publishing

Editors and Authors

Electronic Publishing

History of Publishing

Marketing and Branding

New Media

Periodical Publications

Principles of Composition

Professional Standards and Publishing Laws

Publications: The Raw Materials

Styles of Editing

Suggested High School Prep for Publishing

There's no doubt that courses in the humanities—particularly English—will help you hammer out any of the kinks in your grammar and composition skills (and good grammarians and good writers tend to be great editors). That being said, the best way to prepare is to get yourself on the staff of any and all publications that your school puts out. That means the newspaper, the yearbook, the literary magazine, whatever. Hands-on experience is the best kind of experience.

Fun Facts

The Insider Track

If you want to get the scoop on the latest news in the publishing industry—and get a taste of what sorts of issues you'll be wrestling with as a publishing major—check out www.PublishersWeekly.com, the website of the industry's cornerstone publication.

The Good News

According to the Association of American Publishers, Inc., between 2002 and 2005, 10 of the 12 major categories of book publishing saw net growth. Those categories are adult hardbound, adult paperbound, juvenile hardbound, juvenile paperbound, audio books, religious, e-books, professional, K–12 education, and higher education.

The Not-so-good News

On the other hand, it was rough going for book clubs/mail order and mass market paperbacks between 2002 and 2005. They saw a combined decrease in net sales of almost 12 percent during that time.

Careers and Salary

Starting salaries vary according to location and title, but generally a rookie in the field can expect between $22,000 and $28,000.

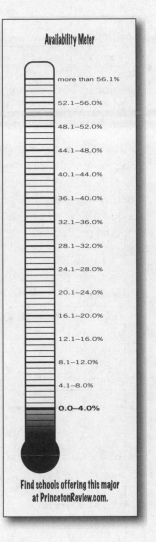

Availability Meter

more than 56.1%

52.1–56.0%

48.1–52.0%

44.1–48.0%

40.1–44.0%

36.1–40.0%

32.1–36.0%

28.1–32.0%

24.1–28.0%

20.1–24.0%

16.1–20.0%

12.1–16.0%

8.1–12.0%

4.1–8.0%

0.0–4.0%

Find schools offering this major at PrincetonReview.com.

CAREER OPTIONS

Agent	Editor	Printer
Bookseller	Journalist	Product Manager
Business Manager	Graphic Designer	Publisher
Distribution Representative	Marketing Manager	Writer

RADIO AND TELEVISION

Basics

The very hands-on, creative, and professionally oriented radio and television major goes by a variety of names, including broadcasting, among many others. It's usually offered as a specialty within a university's department of communications or department of journalism. If you choose to make radio and television your major, you'll study the history, theory, criticism, and nuts-and-bolts production practices of radio, television, and film. In short, you'll learn how to create all manner of electronic media from scratch.

The goal of any radio and television program is to prepare you for an entry-level position and, ultimately, a successful career in media. Upon graduation, you'll be qualified to work for radio and television stations as well as in government, public relations, and a number of other fields. To make sure you are extra-polished when you get your diploma, many schools that offer degree programs in radio and television maintain their very own, student-run radio and television stations at which you can practice and gain expertise in all facets of media production.

If You Like Radio and Television, You May Also Like . . .

American studies, English, film, mass communication, psychology, visual communication

Suggested High School Prep for Radio and Television

SAMPLE COLLEGE CURRICULUM FOR RADIO AND TELEVISION
Audience Research
Audio Production
Broadcast Management
Directing
Ethics of Mass Media
Graphics for Video Production
Introduction to Broadcasting
Introduction to Mass Media
Law and Mass Media
Media Criticism
News Writing, Editing, and Reporting
Statistics
Television and Video Production

Prior experiences with high school newspapers or broadcast stations will obviously give you an edge. You might take several English courses and join the yearbook staff so as to polish your writing skills, too. Beyond that—believe it or not—you'll probably be required to take a course in statistics. Consequently, you shouldn't ignore math completely.

Fun Facts

Must-See TV

Here is a list of the most-watched television programs of all time (excluding Superbowls, Olympics coverage, and episodes of the epic miniseries *Roots*).

1. *M*A*A*S*H*, final episode. February 1983 (CBS)
2. *Dallas*, "Who Shot J. R.?" November 1980 (CBS)
3. *Gone with the Wind (Part 1)*. November 1976 (NBC)
4. *Gone with the Wind (Part 2)*. November 1976 (NBC)
5. *Bob Hope Special Christmas*. January 1970 (NBC)
6. *The Day After*. November 1983 (ABC)
7. *The Fugitive*, final episode. August 1967 (ABC)
8. *Cheers*, final episode. June 1993 (NBC)
9. *The Ed Sullivan Show*, first appearance by the Beatles. February 1964 (CBS)
10. *Bob Hope Special Christmas*. January 1971 (NBC)
11. *Beverly Hillbillies*, "Granny Mistakes a Kangaroo for a Giant Jackrabbit." January 1964 (CBS)

Funny and Philanthropic

Ball State University, alma mater of David Letterman, offers three scholarships endowed by the *Late Night* stalwart himself. The scholarships are for $10,000, $5,000, and $3,333, respectively. To be eligible, you must be a junior or senior who is a full-time telecommunications major at Ball State, and you must submit a creative project. Recipients of the scholarships are chosen based on the quality of their projects.

Famous People Who Majored in Radio and Television

David Letterman (*Late Night* comedy czar, Ball State University); Al Michaels (sports commentator, Arizona State University)

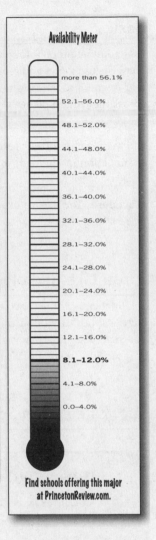

Availability Meter

Find schools offering this major at PrincetonReview.com.

Careers and Salary

Starting salaries in radio and television aren't very high. They range from about $16,000 to $25,000, and it's not uncommon to start as low as $15,000. On the other hand, if you can claw your way to the top of the heap, there's definitely room for salary increases: Howard Stern makes a little less than $20 million per year.

CAREER OPTIONS

Advertising Executive	Film Editor	Stage Technician
Agent	Graphic Designer	Telecommunications Specialist
Animator	Journalist	Television Producer
Disc Jockey	Media Specialist	Television Reporter
Editor	Music Executive	Web Master
Film Director	Photographer	Website Designer

RADIOLOGIC TECHNOLOGY

Basics

Radiologic technology is a very professionally oriented major in the health care field. Radiologic technologists use x-rays and radioactive substances to diagnose and treat diseases and injuries. Two-year and four-year degree programs in radiologic technology and radiography are available at colleges and universities all across the fruited plain.

One of the important things to know about the field of radiologic technology is that there is a big, national standardized test involved. Would-be practitioners must sit for the National Certification Examination in Radiography.

If you major in radiologic technology, what you'll learn is how to perform sophisticated diagnostic x-ray procedures. You'll learn exactly what an x-ray is and how to operate radiography equipment, and you'll learn more than you ever wanted to know about radiation safety.

If You Like Radiologic Technology, You May Also Like . . .

Biochemistry, biology, botany and plant biology, cell biology, chemistry, chiropractic, circulation technology, dietetics, health administration, human development, medical technology, nursing, occupational therapy, pharmacology, pharmacy, physical therapy, premedicine, pre-optometry, pre-veterinary medicine, rehabilitation services, respiratory therapy

Suggested High School Prep for Radiologic Technology

You'll need a strong foundation in the basic sciences. If you are planning to major in radiologic technology in college, you should take courses in biology, chemistry, and physics. You'll need a decent background in math as well.

SAMPLE COLLEGE CURRICULUM FOR RADIOLOGIC TECHNOLOGY

Biology

Biomedical Instrumentation

Chemistry

Clinical Fieldwork (several courses)

Digital Imaging

Human Anatomy

Introduction to Radiologic Technology

Physics

Physiology

Principles of Disease

Radiologic Pathophysiology

Fun Facts

A Brief History of X-rays

Wilhelm Conrad Roentgen (who majored in mechanical engineering and physics) was doing some experimentation that involved light phenomena, cathode rays, electrical current, and glass tubes.

One day, while working in his darkened laboratory, he noted—much to his surprise—that an object across the room began to glow when his cardboard-shrouded tube was charged. What was it? It was a screen coated with barium platinocyanide. He continued to work, telling a friend simply, "I have discovered something interesting, but I do not know whether or not my observations are correct."

From his observations, modern x-ray technology was (rather quickly) born.

Did You Know?

An established radiologic technologist working in Jacksonville, Florida, earns a base salary of about $31,500.

Careers and Salary

Average starting salaries for radiologic technologists with a bachelor's degree range from $22,000 to about $30,000 annually. If you get an associate's degree in radiography, you will probably make about $12 per hour ($24,000 per year).

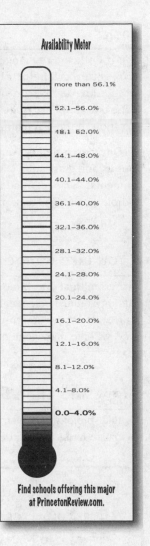

Availability Meter

more than 56.1%

52.1–56.0%

48.1–52.0%

44.1–48.0%

40.1–44.0%

36.1–40.0%

32.1–36.0%

28.1–32.0%

24.1–28.0%

20.1–24.0%

16.1–20.0%

12.1–16.0%

8.1–12.0%

4.1–8.0%

0.0–4.0%

Find schools offering this major at PrincetonReview.com.

CAREER OPTIONS

Radiologic technology is such a specific and newly developed field of study that the only career directly associated with it is that of the radiologic technologist.

RANGE SCIENCE AND MANAGEMENT

Basics

Ah, home on the range. But what exactly is a range, anyway? Rangelands are the grassy areas where livestock graze. Back in their heyday, cowhands used to work and camp across the west on forage lands, raising and herding animals on plentiful wild grasses and plants. Unfortunately, the contemporary American landscape does not have quite the space and resources for livestock and wildlife it once did. Protection and conservation of these remaining pastures falls to students of range science and management.

One part scientist, one part cowhand, range science and management majors study rangelands, arid regions, and grasslands, learning how to manage these areas for maximum efficiency, animal health, and environmental balance. In addition, you'll take classes in wildlife biology, plant sciences, ecology, soil science, hydrology, and livestock management.

If You Like Range Science and Management, You May Also Like . . .

Agricultural and biological engineering, agriculture, agronomy and crop science, animal behavior and ethology, animal science, botany and plant biology, ecology, environmental science, feed science, forestry, grain science, horticulture, plant pathology, soil science, sustainable resource management, turf grass science, wildlife management, zoology

Suggested High School Prep for Range Science and Management

Take biology, chemistry and any other physical science courses your school offers. Some high schools specialize in agricultural education; others offer vocational agricultural programs that cater to students in nearby towns, so investigate the possibilities in your area. In your free time, get involved in an agricultural organization, such as the 4-H Club.

SAMPLE COLLEGE CURRICULUM FOR RANGE SCIENCE AND MANAGEMENT

Arid Land Plants

Farm and Ranch Management

Fire Ecology

Grassland Ecosystems

Grazing Cattle and Sheep

Introduction to Animal Sciences

Plant Species and Physiology

Range and Animal Nutrition

Resource Measurements

Wildland Restoration and Ecology

Fun Facts

"Home on the Range"

Oh, give me a home,

Where the buffalo roam,

And the deer and the antelope play,

Where never is heard a discouraging word,

And the sky is not clouded all day.

"Home on the Range," the state song of Kansas, was written in 1872 by a settler named Dr. Brewster Higley. Inspired by the blue skies and abundant wildlife of the prairie where he lived, Higley wrote the song as a poem, "My Western Home," without intending it for an audience. When a friend found the poem and encouraged him to turn it into a song, Higley agreed and enlisted a fiddler to help set the poem to music. The result proved to be a hit with fellow home-steaders, and soon found its way across the country on the lips of cowboys, settlers, and other travelers. Over the years, the song has morphed into countless versions, each praising the glory of the vast and verdant American landscape.

(Source: www.npr.org/programs/morning/features/patc/homeontherange)

Careers and Salary

Range science and management majors can expect a starting salary of about $25,000 to $32,000.

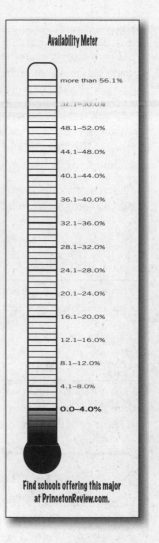

Availability Meter

more than 56.1%

52.1–56.0%

48.1–52.0%

44.1–48.0%

40.1–44.0%

36.1–40.0%

32.1–36.0%

28.1–32.0%

24.1–28.0%

20.1–24.0%

16.1–20.0%

12.1–16.0%

8.1–12.0%

4.1–8.0%

0.0–4.0%

Find schools offering this major at PrincetonReview.com.

CAREER OPTIONS

Agricultural Scientist

Animal Scientist

Biologist

Conservation Scientist

Ecologist

Environmentalist/
   Environmental Scientist

Farmer

Natural Sciences Manager

Park Ranger

Science Technician

REAL ESTATE

Basics

Linked closely with the fields of finance and business, real estate is a major that leads directly to a specialized career. Although most states require specific licenses to practice real estate, a major will give you all the basics you need to get on your way.

As a real estate major you'll learn the difference between residential and commercial real estate. You'll learn about brokerage and financial management. You'll study construction management and property management. You'll learn about land development, real estate valuation, and marketing. Finance, accounting, and economics will be part of your studies as well.

There are many different career options for real estate majors—consulting firms, insurance companies, and banks are just a few of the organizations that need real estate experts on their teams.

If You Like Real Estate, You May Also Like . . .

Accounting, advertising, business administration and management, entrepreneurship, finance, interior design, landscape architecture

Suggested High School Prep for Real Estate

For a major in real estate, your best preparation will be courses in business, math, English, and communications. Most of your course work will be on material that high schools don't offer, so the ability to organize and learn new information—as well as good reading and writing skills—will be the best tools to help you out. And it wouldn't hurt to familiarize yourself with real estate brochures, ads (and all that slick marketing jargon they include), and the industry in general.

SAMPLE COLLEGE CURRICULUM FOR REAL ESTATE

Accounting

Computer Problem-Solving

International Business

Legal Environment of Business

Marketing

Mathematics

Operations Management

Principles of Economics

Real Estate Finance

Real Estate Investment Analysis

Statistics

Urban Studies

Fun Facts

Some Real Estate Humor

Realtor sign: We have "lots" to be thankful for.

Did you hear about Robin Hood's house? It has a little john.

If you want to know exactly where the property line is, just watch the neighbor cut the grass.

The trouble with owning a home is that no matter where you sit, you're looking at something you should be doing.

Oh, Frank

"A lot of homes have been spoiled by inferior desecrators."

—Frank Lloyd Wright

Recommended Reading

If you're interested in real estate, take a look at a story called "Janus" by Ann Beattie. It's about a real estate agent who becomes obsessed with a bowl she considers good luck—and gives a nice image of an agent who has her own ideas of what makes a place feel like home.

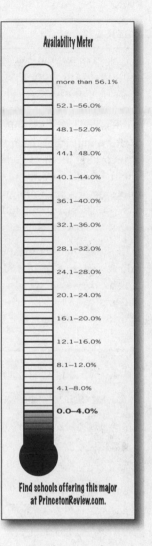

Availability Meter

more than 56.1%

52.1–56.0%

48.1–52.0%

44.1 48.0%

40.1–44.0%

36.1–40.0%

32.1–36.0%

28.1–32.0%

24.1–28.0%

20.1–24.0%

16.1–20.0%

12.1–16.0%

8.1–12.0%

4.1–8.0%

0.0–4.0%

Find schools offering this major at PrincetonReview.com.

Careers and Salary

Starting salaries for real estate majors are almost impossible to predict because there are so many different ways to apply your degree. A job in corporate real estate in a large city, for example, will yield a vastly different salary than a position in real estate in a small residential community. As with any field, the more experience you have, the more your salary will increase.

CAREER OPTIONS		
Buyer	Property Manager	Real Estate Agent/Broker
Entrepreneur		

RECORDING ARTS TECHNOLOGY

Basics

If you're not cut out to be a rock star, you can still be the driving force behind one. Picture yourself as the boss in the booth who sits there shouting, "Cut!" "Again, from the top!" and finally, "Brilliant! That's a wrap!" A major in recording arts technology is just what its title suggests—you'll be learning about the art of recording and all that goes along with it. Industry jargon; how to use basic equipment such as microphones, speakers, amplifiers, and equalizers; and the principles of acoustics, sound, and hearing—such as pitch, volume, timbre, and dynamics—will all be covered loud and clear. You'll learn about analog and digital recording methods, when to use each, and how to make effective multitrack recordings. After you're proficient in editing and mixing, you'll learn how to make unique recordings that are truly your own. In a recording arts technology major, you'll learn how to record and mix both music and audio for video projects. You'll learn about audio for the Internet and other multimedia ventures and how to reinforce live audio so that the sound is as effective as possible.

Besides the technical aspects of recording arts technology, you'll also learn the basics of the recording industry in general, including studio maintenance, copyright laws, and sales strategies. Hands-on learning is vital, as there's a wide variety of equipment used in this field. Many programs offer opportunities for students to do an internship in a recording studio. Students may also have the chance to practice their recording skills with live musicians. By the end of your college studies, you'll be well on your way to making professional audio recordings in the field of your choice.

SAMPLE COLLEGE CURRICULUM FOR RECORDING ARTS TECHNOLOGY

Acoustics

Analog Tape Machines

Audio for TV and Film

Audio Signal Processing

Basic Audio Electronics

Critical Listening

Digital Audio Mixing

Independent Recordings

Live Sound Reinforcement

Location Recording

Microphones

Mixing Consoles

Music Business

Recording Theory

Small Business Management

Studio Operations

If You Like Recording Arts Technology, You May Also Like . . .

Advertising, computer and information science, computer systems analysis, dance, digital communications and media/multimedia, engineering design, entrepreneurship, graphic design, music, music management, radio and television, visual communication

Suggested High School Prep for Recording Arts Technology

Any technical experience you can get in the field of recording arts technology will give you a great head start with your major. You might see what opportunities are available for recording experience through your school's band, orchestra, or drama club or even in your local community. Experimenting with recording on your own can only help you when you begin your actual college studies. And, of course, you should take a well-rounded selection of math, science, and humanities courses to prepare you for the college-level work ahead.

Fun Facts

Join the Academy

Once you begin your career in recording arts technology, you might seek out the National Academy of Recording Arts & Sciences, Inc. Known as the Recording Academy, this organization is committed to "improving the quality of life and cultural conditions for music and its makers," according to its website. There are more than 11,000 recording professionals involved in the Recording Academy, and it is known mostly for the Grammy Awards it gives out. Find out more at www.grammy.com.

The Invention of the Microphone

The microphone was invented by David Edward Hughes, who was born in London in 1831. He was originally responsible for creating the telegraph machine in 1855. In 1878, he put the finishing touches on his carbon microphone, which he'd developed after discovering that "a loose contact in a circuit containing a battery and a telephone receiver would give rise to sounds in the receiver corresponding to the vibrations impinged upon the diaphragm of the mouthpiece or transmitter." In other words, a microphone.

(Source: http://web.mit.edu/invent/iow/hughes.html)

Careers and Salary

Starting salaries for recording arts technology majors vary widely and depend on where you live and in what capacity you use your skills. Recording technicians usually make from $19,000 to $35,000 annually.

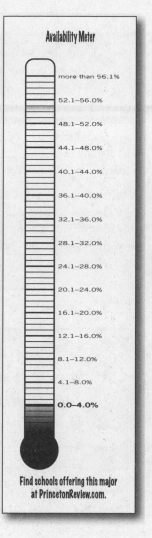

Availability Meter

more than 56.1%

52.1–56.0%

48.1–52.0%

44.1–48.0%

40.1–44.0%

36.1–40.0%

32.1–36.0%

28.1–32.0%

24.1–28.0%

20.1–24.0%

16.1–20.0%

12.1–16.0%

8.1–12.0%

4.1–8.0%

0.0–4.0%

Find schools offering this major at PrincetonReview.com.

CAREER OPTIONS

Media Specialist

Musician

Professional Recording Artist

Recording Arts Technician

Sound Designer

Sound Technician

Special Effects Artist

RECREATION MANAGEMENT

Basics

Sounds simple enough, right? Your pleasure is someone else's leisure. You provide diversion for other people, maybe by leading a game of volleyball or officiating at a soccer game.

Oh, if only life, and this major, were that simple.

Recreation management, while it of course involves the study of recreation, also trains you to look at the business and structure of the recreation industry, from national parks to amusement parks, from forests to sport fishing. It is a combination of business and social science, where you have the opportunity to take courses such as The Psychology of Sports alongside Microeconomics and Accounting.

With the continuous demand for a break from hectic lives, recreation management majors could find it relatively easy to land a job in this lucrative industry. As more people explore national parks or vacation at posh resorts, you will find yourself poised not only to provide top-notch recreational options, but also to use your business and managerial skills to make whatever activity you're selling a financially worthwhile endeavor.

SAMPLE COLLEGE CURRICULUM FOR RECREATION MANAGEMENT

Business Law

Business Organization

Developmental Psychology

Financial Accounting

History and Philosophy of Recreation

Information Process

Leisure Activities

Marketing

Outdoor Recreation I–II

Park and Recreation Facilities Operations

Recreation and Leisure Exploration

Recreation Safety and First Aid

Recreation Services for Special Populations

Recreational Programs and Leadership

Recreational Sports Methods

If You Like Recreation Management, You May Also Like . . .

Advertising, agricultural business and management, business administration and management, business communications, entrepreneurship, hospitality, international business, logistics management, sport and leisure studies

Suggested High School Prep for Recreation Management

Experience playing sports might be helpful, but don't forget that you will also need strong math skills as well as solid footing in the humanities. Take statistics, calculus, and any business courses your school might offer. Take some challenging English classes as well.

BUSINESS, MARKETING, AND RELATED FIELDS

Fun Facts

Did You Know?

Yellowstone National Park is the first and oldest national park in the United States. It was established on March 1, 1872, with 2,219,789.13 acres of federal land and more than 10,000 hot springs and geysers.

Did You Know?

The Grand Canyon National Park has more than 4 million visitors each year.

Careers and Salary

Recreation management is one of the hottest growing fields today, with an average starting salary of $25,000 to $30,000.

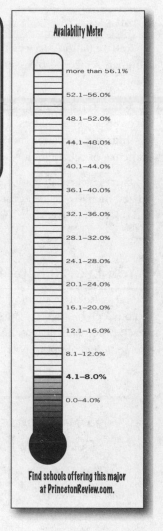

Availability Meter

more than 56.1%

52.1–56.0%

48.1–52.0%

44.1–48.0%

40.1–44.0%

36.1–40.0%

32.1–36.0%

28.1–32.0%

24.1–28.0%

20.1–24.0%

16.1–20.0%

12.1–16.0%

8.1–12.0%

4.1–8.0%

0.0–4.0%

Find schools offering this major at PrincetonReview.com.

CAREER OPTIONS

Entrepreneur	Small Business Owner	Travel Agent
Hotel Manager	Sports Manager	

REHABILITATION SERVICES

Basics

Rehabilitation services is a very professionally oriented major. If you decide to major in it, you'll become a human services professional who vocationally rehabilitates adults with developmental and physical disabilities.

While rehabilitation services has traditionally focused on restoring the well-being of individuals who have physical disabilities, the field is growing to encompass a wider array of disabilities. Emotional disabilities, mental retardation, substance abuse, and continued patterns of criminal behavior are a few of the newer branches of rehabilitation services.

Entry-level rehabilitation services graduates can pursue careers in a variety of private and government-subsidized human service agencies. Many students who major in rehabilitation services eventually seek master's and doctoral degrees.

If You Like Rehabilitation Services, You May Also Like . . .

Agricultural and biological engineering, applied physics, biochemistry, biopsychology, botany and plant biology, cell biology, chemistry, chiropractic, circulation technology, dietetics, health administration, human development, medical technology, nursing, occupational therapy, pharmacology, pharmacy, physical therapy, premedicine, pre-optometry, pre-veterinary medicine, radiologic technology, respiratory therapy

---

SAMPLE COLLEGE CURRICULUM FOR REHABILITATION SERVICES

Abnormal Psychology

Alcoholism and Drug Abuse

Behavior Analysis and Therapy

Case Management

Field Experience

Human Anatomy

Internship

Medical Aspects of Disability

Physiology

Principles of Counseling

Psychosocial Rehabilitation

Research Methods

Vocational Rehabilitation

Suggested High School Prep for Rehabilitation Services

If you are thinking about majoring in rehabilitation services, concentrate your course work in the basic sciences. Take biology, chemistry, and physics courses. Take lots of math, too. It's a really good idea to try to gain some experience (by volunteering or working) at real live rehabilitation services centers. It's good experience and they'll appreciate having you. Such experience will also look great on your resume.

Fun Facts

Did You Know?

An estimated 34 million to 43 million people in the United States have chronic disabilities.
(Source: Methodist Hospital of Houston, Texas)

The Most Dangerous Profession in the United States Is . . .

Logging. The accident rate in the logging industry has been estimated to be 142 per 100,000 workers. Taxi drivers and chauffeurs are a distant second.
(Source: National Forest Protection Alliance)

Careers and Salary

Annual starting salaries for those with a four-year degree range from $22,000 to about $33,000.

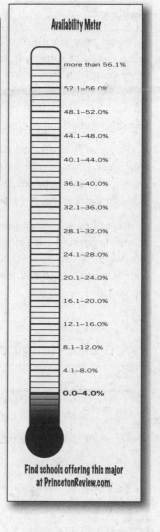

Availability Meter

more than 56.1%

52.1–56.0%

48.1–52.0%

44.1–48.0%

40.1–44.0%

36.1–40.0%

32.1–36.0%

28.1–32.0%

24.1–28.0%

20.1–24.0%

16.1–20.0%

12.1–16.0%

8.1–12.0%

4.1–8.0%

0.0–4.0%

Find schools offering this major at PrincetonReview.com.

CAREER OPTIONS

Hospital Administrator

Physical Therapist

Social Worker

Substance Abuse Counselor

RELIGIOUS STUDIES

Basics

Some people mistakenly think the only reason you'd want to major in religious studies (or just religion, as it's called at some schools) is to have a career as a priest, minister, or rabbi. We hope you aren't one of those people. It's true that religious studies is a very good major for students who want to go on to seminaries for further training as religious professionals. Religious studies is also, however, an excellent way to prepare for other professions, not least because most departments offer a low student-faculty ratio and a breadth of curriculum that few majors can equal.

Religion is central to all aspects of human life, and it profoundly shapes the thought and values of its adherents. If you major in religious studies, you'll study the diverse myths, rituals, original texts, and moral systems of the world's many different religious traditions. Religious studies, like other liberal arts majors, provides an extraordinary opportunity to think about the core beliefs of civilizations past and present.

Regarding the more practical problem of finding work after college, a religious studies major will significantly improve your critical thinking and writing skills. And it makes for an interesting topic during job interviews. Trust us on this one. Employers will invariably find the major fascinating when they see it on your resume, and they'll ask about it, and you'll get to impress them with your knowledge and insight about the world.

If You Like Religious Studies, You May Also Like . . .

Anthropology, Arabic, archaeology, art history, biblical studies, church music, classics, English, great books, Hebrew, history, Islamic studies, Jewish studies, Medieval and Renaissance studies, Modern Greek, pastoral studies, peace studies, philosophy, social work, sociology, theology, youth ministries

> ### SAMPLE COLLEGE CURRICULUM FOR RELIGIOUS STUDIES
>
> Black Religion in America
>
> Buddhism
>
> Comparative Religions
>
> Early Islamic Institutions
>
> The Epistles of Paul
>
> Introduction to Judaism
>
> Introduction to the *Qur'an*
>
> Japanese Religious Traditions
>
> Myth, Ritual, and Symbol
>
> Native American Religions
>
> The New Testament
>
> The Old Testament
>
> Women and Religion

Suggested High School Prep for Religious Studies

There is no special additional high school preparation required for the major in religious studies. Try to take courses in literature, foreign languages, history, and anything else that will challenge you to develop your critical reading and writing skills.

Fun Facts

So What Are the Major Religions of the World, Anyway?

Here is a very Western civilization-centered list.

Baha'i	Episcopal Church	Presbyterianism
Baptist	Hinduism	Religious Society of
Buddhism	Islam	Friends (Quakers)
Catholicism	Jehovah's Witnesses	Seventh-Day Adventist
Church of England	Judaism	Shinto
Church of Jesus Christ of	Lutheranism	Sikhism
Latter-day Saints	Methodist	Taoism
(Mormons)	Orthodox Eastern	Unitarian Universalist
Confucianism	Pentecostalism	United Church of Christ

A Few Interesting Books on the Subject of Religion

- *The Power of Myth* by Joseph Campbell with Bill Moyers. This book presents a fascinating cross-cultural analysis of the world's myths and religions.
- *The Golden Bough* by Sir James Fraser. This must-read classic about magic and realism describes the methods of worship, sex practices, strange rituals, and festivals of yore.
- *Chinese Religion* by Laurence G. Thompson. Thompson's book is a good overview of the complex religious history of China.
- *The Tao of Pooh* by Benjamin Hoff. Pooh just is in this Taoist revision of the classic children's book character.
- *Back to the Sources* edited by Barry W. Holz. This is a good introduction to many original Jewish texts.

Famous People Who Majored in Religious Studies

Shane Battier (basketball star, Duke University), Willard Scott (wiseguy weather forecaster on NBC's *Today Show*, American University)

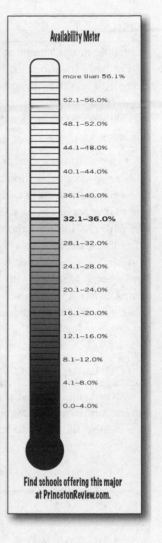

Availability Meter

more than 56.1%

52.1–56.0%

48.1–52.0%

44.1–48.0%

40.1–44.0%

36.1–40.0%

32.1–36.0%

28.1–32.0%

24.1–28.0%

20.1–24.0%

16.1–20.0%

12.1–16.0%

8.1–12.0%

4.1–8.0%

0.0–4.0%

Find schools offering this major at PrincetonReview.com.

Careers and Salary

Some religious studies majors head straight to graduate or professional school. In the various other career fields that you might enter after graduating with a religious studies major, you can expect starting salaries to range from $21,000 to $30,000 or so.

CAREER OPTIONS

Anthropologist	Journalist	Teacher
Childcare Worker	Philosopher	Theologian
Clergy—Priest, Rabbi, Minister	Professor	Writer

RESORT MANAGEMENT

Basics

Pebble Beach, Pinehurst, Vail, Grand Geneva Resort and Spa—most people dream about spending merely a week or (if they're really lucky or imaginative) two at one those destinations. For someone thinking about going into resort management however, this litany of locations offers only a smattering of possibilities for exquisite locales in which they can reside. While working in this field provides for beautiful backdrops, it also allows you to meet a diverse group of people from across the globe and can challenge you in numerous ways.

As a resort management major, you'll be expected to have an understanding of a variety of areas. Courses will range from marketing and finance to food and beverage management. You'll also learn about property maintenance as well as consumer behavior. (For instance: How much will someone pay for a hot-stone massage? How far in advance do most people book hotel rooms? How likely are they to return to your resort and why?) Additionally, most programs have a focus on human resources as well as crisis management—critical skills for interacting with an array of employees and patrons. Chances are, your program will also help you gain hands-on experience working at a resort and will assist you in finding a summer internship. Some colleges have special alliances with big-name hotel companies, allowing you to get practical experience during the semester and apply lessons from the classroom. Few people in the world have as beautiful a workplace as those who find a career in resort management.

If You Like Resort Management, You May Also Like . . .

Advertising, business administration and management, business communications, entrepreneurship, hospitality, international business, logistics management, marketing, merchandising and buying operations, public administration, public relations, real estate, recreation management, sports and leisure studies, tourism

SAMPLE COLLEGE CURRICULUM FOR RESORT MANAGEMENT

Crisis Management

Finance and Budget

Food and Beverage Management

Hospitality and Resort Law

Introduction to Marketing

Leisure and Society

Retail and Consumer Behavior

Social Responsibility in Business

Theories and Techniques of Leadership

Suggested High School Prep for Resort Management

A career in resort management requires a multitude of talents. Therefore, a diverse course load will be beneficial. Since this industry entails dealing with a wide assortment of people, strong communication skills are essential. Enrolling in a number of English courses will help to strengthen both your writing and speaking abilities. Secondly, people from all over the world travel to resorts, so taking foreign language courses will facilitate those interactions, as well as expose you to different cultural norms and expectations. Both math and economics courses will allow you to start building a foundation for the business side of this profession. Overachievers also tend to convince their parents of the need to travel to places like Aspen or the Caribbean for spring break. There, you'll obtain first-hand observation of the industry while simultaneously working on your tan; everyone loves a multi-tasker.

Fun Facts

Who Would Have Thought?

There are more than thirty Mickey Mouse costumes alone at each Disney Resort. All the people employed as Mickey Mouse have to be exactly 5 ft. 2 in. tall. And FYI, men can play Minnie Mouse and women can play Mickey Mouse.

Currently Not a Candidate for Most Popular Tourist Destination . . .

Maldives, a nation located south west of Sri Lanka along the equator, consists of a series of 1,190 islands. A mere 200 of those islands are inhabited and 88 have been set aside for exclusive tourist resort development. If you've got a wad of cash sitting around, try getting in on the action now. It's warm and sunny year-round, and you probably won't have to worry about hosting an abundance of house guests since most people don't even know where it is.

Careers and Salary

There are a variety of factors which effect salaries within the resort management and hospitality industry, chief among them are resort size and location. However, entry level positions typically yield between $28,000 and $32,000.

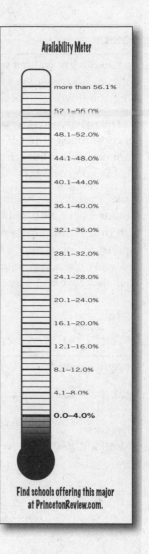

Availability Meter

more than 56.1%

52.1–56.0%

48.1–52.0%

44.1–48.0%

40.1–44.0%

36.1–40.0%

32.1–36.0%

28.1–32.0%

24.1–28.0%

20.1–24.0%

16.1–20.0%

12.1–16.0%

8.1–12.0%

4.1–8.0%

0.0–4.0%

Find schools offering this major at PrincetonReview.com.

CAREER OPTIONS

Convention Center Manager	Hotel Manager	Real Estate Developer
Food and Beverage Management	Human Resources	Reservation Agent
Front Desk Manager	Marketing Director	Resort Manager
Guest Services Manager	Publicist	Tourism Manager
Hospitality Manager		

RESPIRATORY THERAPY

Basics

You can live without water for a few days and without food for a few weeks. Without air, though, you'll suffer brain damage within a few minutes and die after about ten minutes. Breathing, then, would be a pretty good thing about which to become an expert.

The practice of respiratory care requires comprehensive knowledge of many technical and physiological concepts. Among a ton of other things, respiratory therapy programs will teach you about the therapeutic use of medical gases, oxygen-administering apparatuses, drugs and medications, ventilatory control, pulmonary rehabilitation, and home care.

As a respiratory therapist, you'll probably treat people with breathing disorders (and, by the way, you shouldn't have any trouble finding a job). Respiratory therapists work in hospitals and intensive care units with (often critically ill) patients who have asthma, cystic fibrosis, emphysema, and AIDS. They provide life-support for premature infants; perform cardiopulmonary resuscitation and maintain life-support systems; and assist physicians with bronchoscopies, arterial cannula insertions, and heart catheterizations. In a nutshell, they save and perpetuate human lives on a daily basis.

If You Like Respiratory Therapy, You May Also Like . . .

Agricultural and biological engineering, biochemistry, biology, biopsychology, botany and plant biology, cell biology, chemistry, chiropractic, circulation technology, dietctics, health administration, human development, medical technology, nursing, occupational therapy, pharmacology, pharmacy, physical therapy, premedicine, pre-optometry, pre-veterinary medicine, radiologic technology, rehabilitation services

SAMPLE COLLEGE CURRICULUM FOR RESPIRATORY THERAPY

Biology

Cardiopulmonary Critical Care

Chemistry

Ethics for Health Professionals

Health Care Management

Human Anatomy

Introduction to Respiratory Care

Medical Terminology

Pediatric Respiratory Care

Pharmacology

Respiratory Care Procedures

Respiratory Clinical Experience

Seminar in Respiratory Care

Statistics

Suggested High School Prep for Respiratory Therapy

Take courses in biology, chemistry, physics, and math. Lots of them. Pay particular attention in math, as respiratory therapy involves a significant amount of basic mathematical problem-solving.

Fun Facts

Did You Know?

The average human being breathes about 6.5 quarts of air in and out every minute. (Source: www.infoplease.com)

How to Get There

To become a respiratory therapist, you must complete either a two-year associate's degree or a four-year bachelor's degree program. Then you must pass a standardized test to officially become a Certified Respiratory Therapist (CRT). Upon passing not one but two more examinations, you can become a Registered Respiratory Therapist (RRT).

Careers and Salary

Licensed respiratory therapists who are fresh out of college earn starting salaries ranging from $29,000 to $35,000. Experienced respiratory therapists make $50,000 to $70,000.

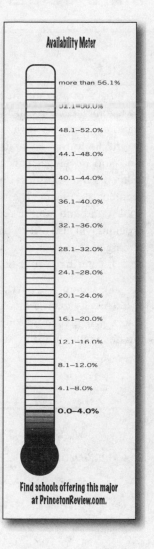

Availability Meter

more than 56.1%

52.1–56.0%

48.1–52.0%

44.1–48.0%

40.1–44.0%

36.1–40.0%

32.1–36.0%

28.1–32.0%

24.1–28.0%

20.1–24.0%

16.1–20.0%

12.1–16.0%

8.1–12.0%

4.1–8.0%

0.0–4.0%

Find schools offering this major at PrincetonReview.com.

CAREER OPTIONS

Respiratory Therapist

RESTAURANT, CULINARY, AND CATERING MANAGEMENT

Basics

What's in a name? In this case, everything. As its name suggests, the restaurant, culinary, and catering management major will allow you to examine the food service industry from every angle, combining training in culinary arts with an education in the business and management of hospitality services. The emphasis will lie in the day-to-day operations of a restaurant or catering establishment, including issues such as food and beverage management, menu planning, purchasing practices, storage techniques, and sanitary upkeep. Larger business concerns will be examined as well; among them finance and human resources management, staffing decisions, insurance options, and a whole mess of laws and regulations that you'll need to understand and adhere to out in the professional world. A restaurant, culinary, and catering management program will also offer a host of electives tailored to the different career paths a major might follow. If you're hoping to start your own restaurant, for instance, you'll want to take a course or two in entrepreneurial business. If catering is your thing, you should set your sights on event planning courses.

Restaurant, culinary, and catering management courses are sometimes housed under the larger umbrella of hospitality management. This means that you might also decide to take a few electives in related fields like resort management or lodging operations—courses that will give you a more well-rounded understanding of the hospitality industry and may well be useful in one of your endeavors down the road.

SAMPLE COLLEGE CURRICULUM FOR RESTAURANT, CULINARY, AND CATERING MANAGEMENT

Catering

Culinary Arts I

Event Planning

Financial Management

Food and Beverage Operations

Human Resources Management

Inside the Hospitality Industry

Insurance, Regulations, and Laws

Logistics of Entrepreneurialism

Menu Management

Purchasing and Storage

Sanitation and Safety

If You Like Restaurant, Culinary, and Catering Management, You May Also Like...

Accounting, bakery science, business administration and management, culinary arts, entrepreneurship, food science, hospitality, nutrition, operations management, recreation management, resort management

Suggested High School Prep for Restaurant, Culinary, and Catering Management

Get yourself into a solid college prep curriculum and you should be good to go. This is a major that will draw heavily on organizational skills, so courses in business, statistics, and mathematics will help sharpen the right parts of your brain.

Fun Facts

Add It Up

According to the National Restaurant Association's 2006 Restaurant Industry Forecast, America is host to some 925,000 restaurants. That's a lot of managing—and a lot of eating.

The National Restaurant Association also points out that the restaurant industry, which employs about 12.5 million people, is second only to the government as America's largest employer.

One more interesting fact from the National Restaurant Association: In 2004, the average American spent $974 on food eaten outside of the home. Which side of the average do you fall on?

Careers and Salary

The location and type of establishment have a lot to do with the numbers you'll see on those early paychecks. You can expect to start anywhere between $20,000 and $40,000 a year.

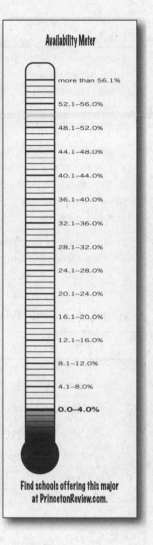

Availability Meter

more than 56.1%

52.1–56.0%

48.1–52.0%

44.1–48.0%

40.1–44.0%

36.1–40.0%

32.1–36.0%

28.1–32.0%

24.1–28.0%

20.1–24.0%

16.1–20.0%

12.1–16.0%

8.1–12.0%

4.1–8.0%

0.0–4.0%

Find schools offering this major at PrincetonReview.com.

CAREER OPTIONS

Bar/Club Manager

Casino Food and Beverage Manager

Caterer/Catering Service Manager

Food/Beverage Distributions Manager

Food Preparations Manager

Host/Hostess

Operations Manager

Restaurateur

RISK MANAGEMENT

Basics

This is sort of what your mother used to do when she wouldn't let you swing upside down over a pile of rocks, or when she refused to let you go on a date with that guy who had the pierced lip and a tattoo that read "Heartbreaker." Though she was ruining your social life, she was, in her own way, also managing your risk.

Unfortunately, risk management isn't a sixth sense you're born with. It's a science that helps businesses and individuals determine the potential outcomes of their actions. Should you invest in that undeveloped real estate in central Florida? Or what about that new dot-com? In these situations, and similar ones, risk management specialists help people understand the consequences of their endeavors. They are the personal trainers of the business world, helping their clients map out strategies that take into account their aspirations and liabilities.

Risk management majors are in demand in just about every industry. From Fortune 500 corporations to a three-man skydiving company, almost any business will find a major in risk management a valuable asset.

If You Like Risk Management, You May Also Like . . .

Actuarial science, agricultural business and management, agricultural economics, applied mathematics, economics, entrepreneurship, international business, logistics management, managerial economics, mathematics, statistics

Suggested High School Prep for Risk Management

The best preparation for a major in risk management is to not do anything of which your parents wouldn't approve. In addition to this, become a lover of statistics. You'll be studying a lot of them in college and even generating them yourself. Solid understanding of calculus helps in predicting trends as well. To learn to turn numbers into argument, take writing-intensive courses like AP English.

SAMPLE COLLEGE CURRICULUM FOR RISK MANAGEMENT

Business Skills and Environment

College Algebra

Decision Theory

Elements of Statistics

Finite Math and Calculus

Insurance and Risk

Introduction to International Business

Legal Environment of Business

Life and Health Risk Management

Operations Management

Principles of Accounting

Principles of Economics

Principles of Finance

Principles of Marketing

Property and Liability Risk Management

Fun Facts

Did You Know?

According to the U.S. Department of Health and Human Services, the federal government's Medicaid program covers approximately 41.4 million low-income individuals, including 20.2 million children.

Car Insurance Excuses

"The other car collided with mine without giving warning of its intention."

"The accident occurred when I was attempting to bring my car out of a skid by steering it into the other vehicle."

"I was driving my car out of the driveway in the usual manner when it was struck by the other car in the same place it had been struck several times before."

"Coming home, I drove into the wrong house and collided with a tree I don't have."

"The indirect cause of this accident was a little guy in a small car with a big mouth."

"As I approached the intersection, a stop sign suddenly appeared in a place where no stop sign had ever appeared before. I was unable to stop in time to avoid the accident."

"The telephone pole was approaching fast. I was attempting to swerve out of its path when it struck my front end."

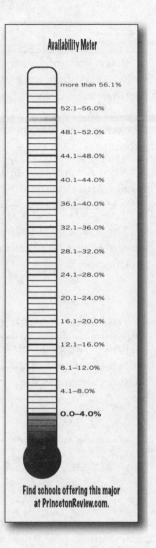

Availability Meter

more than 56.1%

52.1–56.0%

48.1–52.0%

44.1–48.0%

40.1–44.0%

36.1–40.0%

32.1–36.0%

28.1–32.0%

24.1–28.0%

20.1–24.0%

16.1–20.0%

12.1–16.0%

8.1–12.0%

4.1–8.0%

0.0–4.0%

Find schools offering this major at PrincetonReview.com.

Careers and Salary

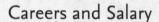

The average starting salary for a risk management major is $40,000 to $45,000. Expect that number to increase depending on location and level of experience.

CAREER OPTIONS

Actuary	Consultant	Entrepreneur
Attorney	Corporate Lawyer	Investment Banker
Bank Officer		

ROMANCE LANGUAGES

Basics

Relax. Romance language majors don't spend four years steeped in grammar, incessantly conjugating verbs in the future tense. While students clearly encounter the more mundane facets of learning a foreign language, most departments take an exciting, interdisciplinary approach to the field. You'll be exposed to a range of literary, historical, and cultural topics which in turn will help you develop a broader world view. Of course, you'll also graduate with a proficiency in reading, writing, and speaking a second language (if not a third!).

Need another reason? Learning another language is also a great motive to study abroad. And honestly, reading Baudelaire on the banks of the Seine is a little more exhilarating than reading anything on the steps of your college library.

The wide career path of the romance language major, like those of other liberal arts majors, will not be clearly defined. Your journey will be what you make of it, but this major will open your eyes to plenty of romantic possibilities.

If You Like Romance Languages, You May Also Like . . .

Anthropology, art history, comparative literature, Chinese, Eastern European studies, European history, French, German, international relations, Italian, Latin American Studies, linguistics, Medieval and Renaissance studies, Portuguese, Russian, Scandinavian studies, Slavic languages and literatures, Spanish

SAMPLE COLLEGE CURRICULUM FOR ROMANCE LANGUAGES

Advanced Spanish: Texts and Contexts

Borders and Disorders

Dante's *Divine Comedy*

Elementary French I and II

Elementary Italian Conversation I

Hybrid Cultures: Latin American Intersection

Italian in Film Comedy

Paris: Myths and Stereotypes

Social Justice in Hispanic Literature

Spanish Theater of the Golden Age

Translation: Theory and Practice

Suggested High School Prep for Romance Languages

If you're feeling academically adventurous (and we hope you are), taking any French, Spanish, Italian, Portuguese, etc. courses will help immensely. Outside of the obvious, enrolling in Latin classes would also be helpful, as most romance languages are based on Latin. English classes and any linguistics classes available will help you gain an understanding of language and grammatical structure. Additionally, a variety of sociology and history classes will expose you to the many of the social, political, and economic aspects of these various cultures.

Fun Facts

How Do You Insult a Chef in French?

Ce restaurant n'est pas aussi bon que le McDonald's.

(This restaurant isn't as good as McDonald's.)

(Source: http://yoyo.cc.monash.edu.au/~mongoose/french/phrases.html)

Everybody's Doing It

If you include the number of people who are fluent in Spanish as a second language, the total number of Spanish speakers in the world is well over 400 million people.

There Was A Little Bird...

The shortest French word with all five vowels is "oiseau" meaning bird.

Some Italian Wisdom

As the proverb goes, "*A tutto c'è rimedio, fuorchè alla morte.*" Meaning, there is a cure for everything except death.

Did You Know?

Venice is built on 117 islands and features 150 canals.

Careers and Salary

Starting salaries for foreign language majors range from $25,000 to $33,000.

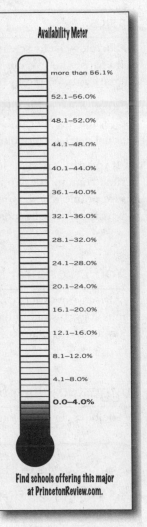

Availability Meter

more than 56.1%

52.1–56.0%

48.1–52.0%

44.1–48.0%

40.1–44.0%

36.1–40.0%

32.1–36.0%

28.1–32.0%

24.1–28.0%

20.1–24.0%

16.1–20.0%

12.1–16.0%

8.1–12.0%

4.1–8.0%

0.0–4.0%

Find schools offering this major
at PrincetonReview.com.

CAREER OPTIONS

Diplomat/Attaché/Foreign Service Officer

Foreign Exchange Trader

Journalist

Professor

Teacher

Translator

Writer

RURAL SOCIOLOGY

Basics

Sociology is the scientific study of groups of humans. So, rural sociology is the scientific study of groups of humans who live out in the country. At some schools, rural sociology is offered as a minor only, and at others, it is offered only to graduate students.

Rural sociologists analyze the problems of rural people and their communities all over the world. It's a good thing, too, because rural areas are pivotal in providing for national and international energy needs, national defense, agricultural production, and outdoor recreation.

If you major in rural sociology, you'll learn about how groups, organizations, and societies are structured in rural communities. You'll study crime and violence, sex and gender, families, health and illness, work and leisure, ethnic relations, religions and cultures, and social classes. You'll also study the very fascinating ways in which perpetually increasing technology affects and transforms rural life.

If You Like Rural Sociology, You May Also Like . . .

African American studies, American studies, anthropology, art history, Asian American studies, counseling, criminology, history, international relations, linguistics, philosophy, political science, psychology, public policy analysis, religious studies, sociology, urban studies, women's studies

Suggested High School Prep for Rural Sociology

Sociology involves lots of writing, reading, analysis, and criticism. American history and English composition courses are probably the most similar subjects in high school. You'll probably be required to take a college-level statistics course, so some math isn't a bad idea, either. Knowledge of a foreign language is a big plus, too, because you will probably be required to take several foreign language classes as a sociology major.

SAMPLE COLLEGE CURRICULUM FOR RURAL SOCIOLOGY

Gender Relations and Social Change

Introduction to Rural Sociology

Latin American Society

Local Impacts of Global Commodity Systems

Population Dynamics

Principles of Community Development

Research Design and Analysis

Rural Areas in Metropolitan Society

Technology and Society

Topics in Rural Sociology

Fun Facts

Did You Know?

About 1800, approximately 95 percent of the people in the United States lived in rural areas. Today, though, only about 25 percent live in rural areas.

Careers and Salary

The average starting salary offered to freshly minted sociologists is approximately $25,000 to $32,000 annually. It's somewhat less for rural sociologists, though, because rural sociologists are more likely to work in rural areas where salaries are lower and goods and services cost less.

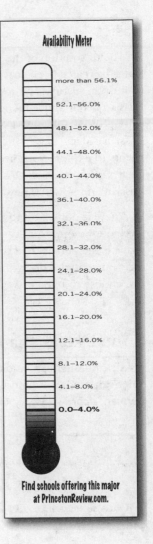

Availability Meter

more than 56.1%

52.1–56.0%

48.1–52.0%

44.1–48.0%

40.1–44.0%

36.1–40.0%

32.1–36.0%

28.1–32.0%

24.1–28.0%

20.1–24.0%

16.1–20.0%

12.1–16.0%

8.1–12.0%

4.1–8.0%

0.0–4.0%

Find schools offering this major at PrincetonReview.com.

CAREER OPTIONS

Anthropologist	Criminologist	Social Worker
Archaeologist	Lobbyist	Sociologist
Attorney	Professor	Teacher

RUSSIAN

Basics

The dissolution of the Soviet Union in 1991 created many newly independent republics, and the United States has since been striving to strike or maintain political and economic bonds with them all. Knowledge of Russian history, culture, economics, and language is fundamental to the success of this endeavor. As a Russian major you'll spend most of your time becoming skilled in the Russian language, which will mean, among other things, learning a completely different alphabet (unless you already have experience with Russian). Many universities offer multimedia instruction for languages classes, so you'll have a variety of means to explore your use and understanding of Russian. You'll learn about Russian literature by studying great writers such as Dostoevsky. You'll study politics and economics. You'll learn what it means to be a Russian and how the new republics define their places in the world.

There is quite a bit to learn about the Russian culture, and the interdisciplinary nature of the major will give you the opportunity to explore many different fields. One of the benefits of majoring in a foreign language is the perspective you'll gain on your own language and culture. Since our world is becoming increasingly integrated, a deep knowledge of another language and culture will be an asset no matter what career you choose to pursue.

If You Like Russian, You May Also Like . . .

African American studies, African studies, American studies, ancient studies, anthropology, Arabic, Asian American studies, Chinese, East Asian studies, East European studies, English, English literature, French, German, Hebrew, history, international business, international relations, international studies, Islamic studies, Italian, Japanese, Jewish studies, Latin American studies, linguistics, Middle Eastern studies, Modern Greek, peace studies, Portuguese, sociology, South Asian studies, Southeast Asian studies, Spanish

SAMPLE COLLEGE CURRICULUM FOR RUSSIAN

A Russian Master: Dostoevsky

Business Russian

Current Events

Masterpieces of Russian Literature

Political Russian

Practical Russian Pronunciation

Russian Composition

Russian Conversation

Russian in Cultural Contexts

Russian Women Writers

Russian Writers: Pushkin to Turgenev

Structure of the Russian Language

Survey of Russian Literature

Suggested High School Prep for Russian

When you're planning to major in a foreign language, the most valuable courses you can take are . . . drum roll, please . . . courses in other languages! See what your high school offers in French, Italian, Spanish, Latin, or others. Take a lot of courses in history, art, music, English, and political science; foreign language programs usually include a great deal about the culture of the mother country.

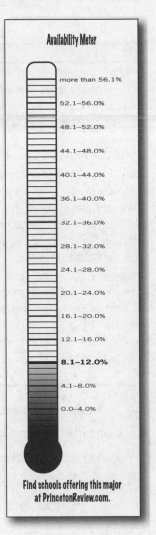

Fun Facts

The Russian ABCs

There are 33 letters in the Russian alphabet: 21 consonants, 10 vowels, and 2 that do not represent sounds.

Careers and Salary

As a Russian major you can expect your starting salary to depend on where and how you apply your skills. Ohio State University suggests a range of $24,000 to $30,000, stressing the fact that possibilities for upward mobility are plentiful.

Availability Meter

more than 56.1%

52.1–56.0%

48.1–52.0%

44.1–48.0%

40.1–44.0%

36.1–40.0%

32.1–36.0%

28.1–32.0%

24.1–28.0%

20.1–24.0%

16.1–20.0%

12.1–16.0%

8.1–12.0%

4.1–8.0%

0.0–4.0%

Find schools offering this major at PrincetonReview.com.

CAREER OPTIONS

Anthropologist	Foreign Exchange Trader	Professor
Consultant	Journalist	Sociologist
Diplomat/Attaché/Foreign Service Officer	Political Scientist	Television Reporter
		Translator

SANSKRIT AND CLASSICAL INDIAN LANGUAGES, LITERATURES, AND LINGUISTICS

Basics

Question: How many of the *Vedas* are there in ancient Indian culture? Answer: Four.

So anyway what in the heck are the *Vedas*? They're a large and culturally significant collection of spiritual texts composed in Vedic Sanskrit. Okay, but what's Vedic Sanskrit? Vedic Sanskrit was the language's first incarnation. The use of Vedic Sanskrit began to wane around 500 B.C./B.C.E., when Classical Sanskrit started to take hold.

Do you find this sort of Q & A interesting? If so, then there's a good chance you're cut out for the Sanskrit and classical Indian languages, literatures, and linguistics major. The major will provide you with language training in Vedic Sanskrit and Classical Sanskrit, as well as offer you a chance to try out other ancient Indian languages like Pali and the Prakrits. As scholars have been doing for more than two hundred years now, you'll investigate the linguistic connections between Sanskrit, Greek, and Latin—as well as the links between Sanskrit and the languages spoken in India today. (Just as Greek and Latin have formed the basis for most Western languages, the majority of India's modern languages have been derived from Sanskrit.) The language is no longer spoken on a daily basis—that ended about a thousand years ago—but it still features prominently in forums ranging from celebrated poetry to Hindu ritual.

Your skills in Sanskrit will allow you to dive into the wealth of texts produced in Vedic and Classical Sanskrit. These texts include—you guessed it!—the four *Vedas*, as well a wide range of drama, poetry, philosophy, and treatises on social, artistic, and scientific issues. And by then end of your tenure as a Sanskrit and classical Indian languages, literatures, and linguistics major, you'll be able to give us the answers to these questions: What are the *Vedas* trying to say? And how have these texts influenced contemporary India?

SAMPLE COLLEGE CURRICULUM FOR SANSKRIT AND CLASSICAL INDIAN LANGUAGES, LITERATURES, AND LINGUISTICS

Advanced Classical Sanskrit

Advanced Readings in Sanskrit

Ancient Indian Philosophy and Religion

Classical Indian Linguistics

Hindu Studies

History of Southeast Asia

Intermediate Classical Sanskrit

Introduction to Classical Sanskrit

Introduction to Pali

Languages in Contemporary India

The Prakrits and Middle Indic Languages

Vedic Sanskrit

If You Like Sanskrit and Classical Indian Languages, Literatures, and Linguistics, You May Also Like...

Ancient Near Eastern and biblical languages, literatures, and linguistics, Asian studies, comparative literature, Hindi, Hindu studies, linguistics, religious studies, Southeast Asian studies, Urdu language and literature

Suggested High School Prep for Sanskrit and Classical Indian Languages, Literatures, and Linguistics

Ancient Indian languages aren't too common in American high schools, so you'll probably have to sharpen your language-learning skills by studying something like Spanish or French. History and literature courses will equip you with the analytic and communications tools you'll find useful as well.

Fun Facts

Coming Back?

Spend a little time checking out Sanskrit resources on the Internet and you'll start to notice that there's a notable movement that wants to see Sanskrit once again used in everyday conversation. As one website, www.samskrutam.com, says, "Let us bring Sanskrit back to our daily life." To learn more, check out the website. You'll find information about Sanskrit literature, grammar, organizations, and more.

Words from the Past

"Yesterday is but a dream, tomorrow but a vision. But today well lived makes every yesterday a dream of happiness, and every tomorrow a vision of hope. Look well, therefore, to this day."

—Sanskrit proverb

Careers and Salary

Matriculating to grad school is the best way to secure a spot in the field. But if grad school isn't in the cards for you, expect to earn between $20,000 and $25,000 your first year of work.

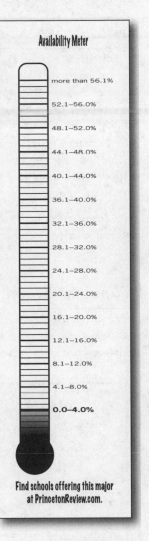

Availability Meter

more than 56.1%

52.1–56.0%

48.1–52.0%

44.1–48.0%

40.1–44.0%

36.1–40.0%

32.1–36.0%

28.1–32.0%

24.1–28.0%

20.1–24.0%

16.1–20.0%

12.1–16.0%

8.1–12.0%

4.1–8.0%

0.0–4.0%

Find schools offering this major at PrincetonReview.com.

CAREER OPTIONS		
Anthropologist	Curator	Translator
Archaeologist	Teacher	Writer

SCANDINAVIAN STUDIES

Basics

You already know about Vikings, Ikea, and Ingmar Bergman, but if you delve a bit deeper into the rich cultural history of Northern Europe as a Scandinavian studies major, you'll learn about the cultures of Denmark, Sweden, Norway, and their neighboring countries. You'll explore Scandinavian history, folklore, literature, theater, film, politics, economics and government from the medieval to modern eras, and take classes in Danish, Swedish, or Norwegian, reading novels, plays, and poetry in their original language. Some schools offer exchange programs, and spending a semester abroad is a great opportunity to experience Scandinavian people, language, and culture firsthand. By senior year, most majors undertake an independent study project; possible topics vary from Norse mythology, to the design of the "Welfare State," to twentieth-century Finnish architecture.

A Scandinavian studies major can be applied to many fields, including arts, business, economics, filmmaking, political science, social science, tourism, and translation.

If You Like Scandinavian Studies, You May Also Like . . .

Anthropology, archaeology, classics, comparative literature, economics, East European studies, English, European history, film, history, international relations, international studies, linguistics, Medieval and Renaissance studies, peace studies, political studies, public policy analysis, Russian, Slavic languages and literatures, sociology

SAMPLE COLLEGE CURRICULUM FOR SCANDINAVIAN STUDIES

Danish Novel

Introduction to Folklore

Introduction to Scandinavian Linguistics

Old Norse Paleography and Philology

Scandinavian Mythology

Strindberg and Europe

Studies in Drama and Film: Ingmar Bergman

Swedish Literature and Culture

Topics in Finnish Literature and Culture

Viking and Medieval Scandinavia

War and Occupation in Northern Europe

Women in Scandinavian Society

Suggested High School Prep for Scandinavian Studies

English and history classes are essential preparation for this major; European history and world literature will come in particularly handy. In addition, take three or four years of a foreign language to round out a solid humanities background and make learning subsequent languages easier.

Fun Facts

Sampling Scandinavian Languages

Icelandic, Norwegian, Swedish, and Danish are Germanic languages, like English. Finnish is a Finno-Ugrian language, like Hungarian.

(Source: www.bbc.co.uk)

	Icelandic	Swedish	Finnish
Yes.	Já.	Ja.	Joo.
No.	Nei.	Nej.	Ei.
Welcome!	Velkomin!	Välkommen!	Tervetuloa!
Pleased to meet you.	Gaman.	Trevligt att träffas.	Hauska tavata.
Hello.	Hallo.	Hej.	Hei.
Goodbye.	Bless.	Hej då.	Näkemiin.
Thank you.	Takk fyrir.	Tack.	Kiitos.

(Source: www.bbc.co.uk)

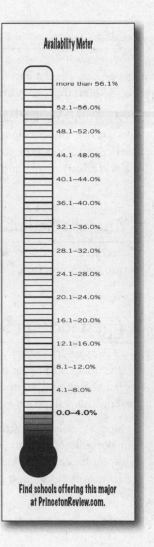

Availability Meter

- more than 56.1%
- 52.1–56.0%
- 48.1–52.0%
- 44.1 48.0%
- 40.1–44.0%
- 36.1–40.0%
- 32.1–36.0%
- 28.1–32.0%
- 24.1–28.0%
- 20.1–24.0%
- 16.1–20.0%
- 12.1–16.0%
- 8.1–12.0%
- 4.1–8.0%
- **0.0–4.0%**

Find schools offering this major at PrincetonReview.com.

Careers and Salary

Career options are varied, but starting salary for liberal arts majors range from $20,000 to $30,000.

CAREER OPTIONS

Anthropologist	Economist	Professor
Archivist	Foreign Exchange Trader	Sociologist
Consultant	Historian	Translator
Curator	Journalist	Writer
Diplomat/Attaché/Foreign Service Officer	Political Scientist	

SCULPTURE

Basics

Whether it's the elegant, smooth line of Michelangelo or the abstract forms of Henry Moore, sculpture has been an integral part of the fine arts throughout history. Artists have used and continue to use sculpture as a medium through which they can represent their own perceptions and understanding of the world.

Majors in sculpture learn a variety of skills that often include welding, glassblowing, ceramics, and woodworking. Beginning sculptors experiment with materials and techniques; as the artist's goals and skills develop, independent long-term projects will most likely dominate the curriculum. Students will also gain exposure to a wide array of arts and humanities courses to develop critical thinking skills.

If You Like Sculpture, You May Also Like . . .

Architectural history, architecture, art, art education, art history, drawing, fashion design, interior architecture, interior design, painting, photography

Suggested High School Prep for Sculpture

Classes in art history and fine arts—including painting, photography, sculpture, dance, and ceramics—are a great way to begin to develop your ability to think critically about art and actually create it yourself. Keep a sketchbook to document your ideas, especially those that are too grand in scope to accomplish at present. This will prove especially important at admissions interviews and portfolio reviews.

Most schools value strong observational skills, so draw from life as often as you can. To get feedback on your portfolio or to get your portfolio reviewed by several schools in one day, visit a National Portfolio Day (www.npda.org). In addition, a continued personal engagement with art through frequent museum visits, reading art history books, and studying your favorite artists and their works will help prepare you for sculpture.

SAMPLE COLLEGE CURRICULUM FOR SCULPTURE

Art Concepts/Issues

Art History I–II

Art Studio Elective

Drawing I–II

Sculpture I–IV

Senior Exhibition

Two-Dimensional Design

Fun Facts

Effective Recycling

Michelangelo began work on his famous sculpture of *David* at the age of 26 using a marble block on which another sculptor had already started work.

Careers and Salary

Starting salaries for artists vary dramatically depending upon the career and success of the artist. An independent artist could make less than $20,000 a year. Introductory salaries for artists entering art administration range from $30,000 to $35,000.

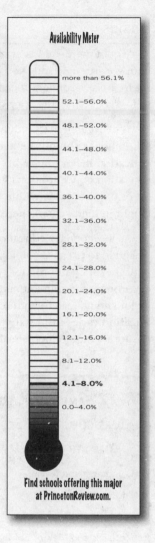

Availability Meter

more than 56.1%

52.1–56.0%

48.1–52.0%

44.1–48.0%

40.1–44.0%

36.1–40.0%

32.1–36.0%

28.1–32.0%

24.1–28.0%

20.1–24.0%

16.1–20.0%

12.1–16.0%

8.1–12.0%

4.1–8.0%

0.0–4.0%

Find schools offering this major at PrincetonReview.com.

CAREER OPTIONS

Art Dealer	Artist	Curator

SECONDARY EDUCATION AND TEACHING

Basics

We know it sounds crazy: You're trying to figure out what to do when you get out of high school, and here we are suggesting you devote the next four years to getting back there! Seriously though, if you've ever sat in a classroom and been inspired by one of your teachers—and if you're an inspiring individual yourself—secondary education and teaching may be just the major for you.

While elementary education majors (endowed with the basic tools necessary to lead a single-room schoolhouse should the need arise) are learning to become general practitioners of a sort, as a secondary education major you're becoming more of a specialist. At the very least, your school will offer secondary education concentrations in English, history, foreign languages, math, and science; but most schools offer a lot of other options within the education program or in the form of interdisciplinary majors. All told, if it's taught in high school, there's probably a corresponding secondary education major to be found—or made.

As a secondary education major, you'll be exposed to a number of teaching methods and philosophies designed to prepare you for leading a class of as many as 30 students from different backgrounds and learning types. As you progress, you'll spend time at local schools to test what you've learned in a "real world" classroom environment and do some teaching of your own. Essentially, the path of a secondary education major should lead to high school certification and, eventually, to the classroom. Since criteria for teacher certification varies from state to state, make sure you check with the education department at your college to ensure its requirements match those of the state in which you hope to reside and work later on.

SAMPLE COLLEGE CURRICULUM FOR SECONDARY EDUCATION AND TEACHING

Computers and Teaching

Educational Psychology

Foundations of Education

Materials and Methods of Teaching Middle

Grades and Secondary English/ Mathematics/Science/Social Studies

Meeting Special Learning Needs of Children

Reading in the Content Areas

School and Society

Student Teaching Seminar

Supervised Observation and Student Teaching

Various classes within your concentration

If You Like Secondary Education and Teaching, You May Also Like . . .

Agricultural education, art education, education, education administration, education of the deaf, educational psychology, elementary education, special education, teacher education, technology education

Suggested High School Prep for Secondary Education and Teaching

As you might expect, education majors should have a strong foundation in the fields required of every student: English, math, science, and social studies. As the demand for bilingual teachers increases, foreign language classes—especially Spanish—are a must. It's also a good idea to take psychology classes where available. If you know what you want your teaching specialization to be, take classes in that, too.

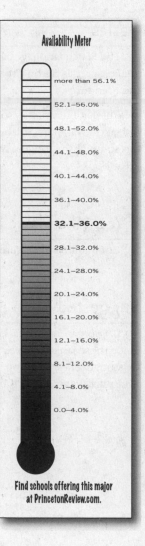

Availability Meter

more than 56.1%

52.1–56.0%

48.1–52.0%

44.1–48.0%

40.1–44.0%

36.1–40.0%

32.1–36.0%

28.1–32.0%

24.1–28.0%

20.1–24.0%

16.1–20.0%

12.1–16.0%

8.1–12.0%

4.1–8.0%

0.0–4.0%

Find schools offering this major at PrincetonReview.com.

Fun Facts

The Long Haul

While it's true that keeping qualified teachers in the classroom remains a major challenge to public schools, the National Education Association (NEA) says things could be much worse. In fact, private school teachers are 64 percent more likely than teachers at public schools to leave the profession over the course of their tenure.

On Good Teaching

"Good teaching rests neither in accumulating a shelfful of knowledge nor in developing a repertoire of skills. In the end, good teaching lies in a willingness to attend and care for what happens in our students, ourselves, and the space between us. Good teaching is a certain kind of stance, I think. It is a stance of receptivity, of attunement, of listening."

—Laurent A. Daloz

Careers and Salary

Teacher salaries usually depend on the area in which they work. A secondary education major could expect to make from $26,000 to $35,000 a year right out of school.

CAREER OPTIONS		
Guidance Counselor	Professor	Teacher
Librarian	School Administrator	

SLAVIC LANGUAGES AND LITERATURES

Basics

The Slavic languages and literatures major is the study of Russian, along with work in another Slavic language, such as Serbo-Croatian, Polish, or Czech. The study of the languages is combined with the study of the literatures.

Russian literature is some of the greatest in the world. You're entering the realm of Pushkin, Mayakovksy, Bulgakov, Nabokov, Solzhenitsyn, Tolstoy, Turgenev, Chekhov, and Dostoevsky. These writers have also written some of the longest works ever committed to paper, so you'll have great doorstops after you read these great books.

If You Like Slavic Languages and Literatures, You May Also Like . . .

Comparative literature, East European studies, great books, Russian

Suggested High School Prep for Slavic Languages and Literatures

If you can take Russian or Polish (or by some chance, Serbo-Croatian or Czech) at your school, do it. Since these languages are not often offered, you can start getting experience in mastering a foreign language by studying one that your school does offer. Classes in European history and world literature will be useful. And start digging into those Russian novels.

SAMPLE COLLEGE CURRICULUM FOR SLAVIC LANGUAGES AND LITERATURES

Dostoevsky and Tolstoy

Russian I–IV

Serbo-Croatian I–III

Survey of Russian Literature

Survey of Serbo-Croatian Literature

Twentieth-Century Russian Literature

Fun Facts

Recommended Reading

One of the best ways to prepare for this major is to begin reading some of the great works of Russian literature. Some recommendations: *War and Peace* by Leo Tolstoy; *Eugene Onegin* by Aleksandr Pushkin; *Crime and Punishment* or *The Brothers Karamazov* by Fyodor Dostoevsky; *The Sea Gull*, *The Cherry Orchard*, or *The Collected Stories of Anton Chekhov*; and *The Master and Margarita* by Mikhail Bulgakov. These books are all easy to get at any bookstore, library, or online.

Russian Grammar on the Web

Check out one Bucknell University professor's interactive online reference grammar for Russian at www.bucknell.edu.

Careers and Salary

The starting salary for a Slavic languages and literatures major fresh out of college is about $20,000 to $30,000.

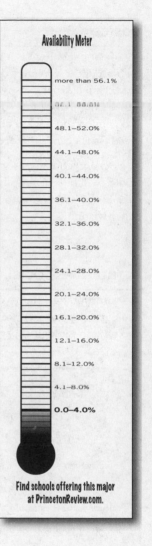

Availability Meter

more than 56.1%

52.1–56.0%

48.1–52.0%

44.1–48.0%

40.1–44.0%

36.1–40.0%

32.1–36.0%

28.1–32.0%

24.1–28.0%

20.1–24.0%

16.1–20.0%

12.1–16.0%

8.1–12.0%

4.1–8.0%

0.0–4.0%

Find schools offering this major at PrincetonReview.com.

CAREER OPTIONS

Book Publishing Professional	Editor	Translator
Diplomat/Attaché/Foreign Service Officer	Journalist	Writer

SOCIAL PSYCHOLOGY

Basics

Social pychology is a branch of the social sciences that deals with how and why people interact with each other the way they do. As a social psychology major you'll learn about how our attitudes form and why they change; what causes social conflict, aggression, and violence; and what influences judgment. You'll dig into arcane theories of conformity, emotion, motivation, personality, negotiation, persuasion, social identity, and gender. You'll learn about interpersonal dynamics in different types of relationships and discover how social issues can influence physical health.

Social pychology, as with most of the social sciences, is a research-oriented discipline. Integral to your studies will be learning about past research and its influences on the field. You'll do your own research, perhaps in conjunction with faculty or other students. Be prepared for a load of laboratory work, statistics, and paper-writing.

If You Like Social Psychology, You May Also Like . . .

Anthropology, biopsychology, child development, clinical psychology, counseling, developmental psychology, education, educational psychology, experimental psychology, human development, industrial psychology, physiological psychology, psychology, rural sociology, social work, sociology

SAMPLE COLLEGE CURRICULUM FOR SOCIAL PSYCHOLOGY

Adolescence

Aggression and Violence

Attitudes and Persuasion

Biological Foundations of Behavior

Interpersonal Relations

Motivational Theories for Informal Learning Settings

Organizational Psychology

Psychological Testing

Psychology of Childhood

Psychology of Gender

Psychology of Personality

Social Development

Social Psychology of Health

Stereotyping and Prejudice

Suggested High School Prep for Social Psychology

As psychology often involves science courses, try to get a good foundation in biology and chemistry. English classes are imperative because much of psychology involves writing up your experiments and giving close readings to others' research. Math courses, statistics especially, will give you a great head start. Social sciences, such as history and economics, will obviously come into play with social psychology. And of course, if your school offers psychology courses, you should take them.

Fun Facts

Some Psychologist Jokes

Q: What do psychologists say to each other when they meet?

A: "You're fine, how am I?"

Q: How many psychologists does it take to change a light bulb?

A: Just one, but the bulb has to be ready to change.

An Anecdote for Psychology Majors

When I first started college, the dean came in and said "Good morning" to all of us. When we echoed back to him, he responded, "Ah, you're freshmen."

He explained, "When you walk in and say 'Good morning,' and they say 'Good morning' back, it's freshmen. When they put their newspapers down and open their books, it's sophomores. When they look up so they can see the instructor over the tops of the newspapers, it's juniors. When they put their feet up on the desks and keep reading, it's seniors.

"When you walk in and say 'Good morning,' and they write it down, it's graduate students."

Careers and Salary

Starting salaries for psychology majors are generally in the $25,000 to $35,000 range and depend mainly on how the psychology majors choose to use their degree. Many social psychology students (and psychology students in general) opt to continue their studies in graduate school.

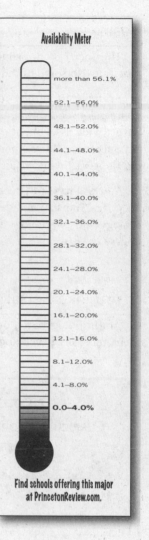

Availability Meter

more than 56.1%

52.1–56.0%

48.1–52.0%

44.1–48.0%

40.1–44.0%

36.1–40.0%

32.1–36.0%

28.1–32.0%

24.1–28.0%

20.1–24.0%

16.1–20.0%

12.1–16.0%

8.1–12.0%

4.1–8.0%

0.0–4.0%

Find schools offering this major at PrincetonReview.com.

CAREER OPTIONS

Anthropologist	Political Campaign Worker	Psychologist
Labor Relations Specialist	Political Scientist	Social Worker
Management Consultant	Politician	Sociologist
Organizational Developer	Professor	

SOCIAL WORK

Basics

The social work major is definitely not for the faint of heart. It leads to some of the most demanding jobs, but also some of the most fulfilling.

At the heart of the social work major is a desire and willingness to respond to people in need. It means compassion, dedication, and a genuine desire to improve someone else's life. As a social work major you will have a wide assortment of problems on which to focus your talents. Whether it is inner-city poverty, illiteracy, substance abuse, homelessness, racial inequalities, or any of the hundreds of other ills affecting our society, the social work major prepares you to counsel and aid people as they struggle to better their lives.

You will have the freedom to study the problems and crises in today's society from several different perspectives. Translation: lots of exposure to the humanities and social sciences. Your courses will range from biology and psychology to direct fieldwork with clients who, in the end, may teach you more than any course or textbook.

If You Like Social Work, You May Also Like . . .

Anthropology, child development, counseling, criminology, developmental psychology, human development, missions, psychology

---

SAMPLE COLLEGE CURRICULUM FOR SOCIAL WORK

Determinations of Social Functioning

Field Practice

Human, Natural, and Economic Resources

Individual Needs and Societal Response

Minority Perspectives: Race, Ethnicity, and Gender

Philosophy

Political Science

Problems, Policies, and Programs in Social Work

Psychology

Quantitative Analysis of Social Date

Social Work Practice

Sociology

Suggested High School Prep for Social Work

It's never too early to begin practicing what you preach. There are always organizations looking for volunteers to spend a few hours a week teaching, reading, or just talking to people. It's a great way not only to explore the field firsthand, but also to start making a difference. As far as course work goes, take psychology if your school offers it and all the history and economics classes available.

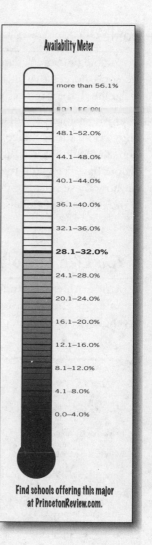

Availability Meter

more than 56.1%

52.1-56.0%

48.1-52.0%

44.1-48.0%

40.1-44.0%

36.1-40.0%

32.1-36.0%

28.1-32.0%

24.1-28.0%

20.1-24.0%

16.1-20.0%

12.1-16.0%

8.1-12.0%

4.1-8.0%

0.0-4.0%

Find schools offering this major at PrincetonReview.com.

Fun Facts

Did You Know?

According to the U.S. Census Bureau, a family of four—two of them children—earning $18,000 per year or less, is below the poverty line.

Did You Know?

The United States's poverty rate dropped to its lowest level in 20 years in 1999 at 11.8 percent, or 32.3 million people.

(Source: U.S. Department of Commerce)

Careers and Salary

The starting salary for a social work major is between $20,000 and $27,000. Those with an advanced degree can expect to earn more.

CAREER OPTIONS

Anthropologist	Labor Relations Specialist	Social Worker
Attorney	Lobbyist	Sociologist
Crisis Negotiator	Relief Worker	Substance Abuse Counselor

SOCIOLOGY

Basics

Sociology is the scientific study of groups of humans. It is the study of collective human behavior and the social forces that influence it. Sociologists also seek to discover the broad patterns of interaction of social life that influence individual behaviors.

If you major in sociology, you'll learn about how groups, organizations, and societies are structured. You'll study crime and violence, sex and gender, families, health and illness, work and leisure, ethnic relations, religions and cultures, social classes, and communities and cities. You'll study the rules that different groups of people have for living together and the principles upon which groups of people are organized. You'll find out how these rules are created, how they are sustained, how they are broken, and how they give meaning to the lives of individuals.

If You Like Sociology, You May Also Like . . .

African American studies, American studies, anthropology, art history, Asian American studies, counseling, criminology, English, history, international relations, Jewish studies, linguistics, philosophy, political science, psychology, public policy analysis, religious studies, urban studies, women's studies

SAMPLE COLLEGE CURRICULUM FOR SOCIOLOGY

Introduction to Sociology

Medical Sociology

Quantitative Research Methods in Sociology

Rural Sociology

Social Stratifications

Social Thought

Sociology of Aging

Sociology and Crime

Sociology of the Family

Sociology of Gender

Sociology of Sports

Sociology of Women

Theories of Social Change

Urban Sociology

Work and Occupations

World Population

Suggested High School Prep for Sociology

Sociology involves lots of writing, reading, analysis, and criticism. American history and English composition courses are important. You'll probably be required to take a college-level statistics course, so some math isn't a bad idea, either. And familiarity with computers won't hurt. Foreign language is a big plus, too, because you will probably be required to take several foreign language classes as a sociology major.

Fun Facts

A Few Projects

By Students in the Sociology Program at Hamilton College

- New England Towns Up Against the Wall: A Study of Coalitions to Oppose Wal-Mart Expansion
- Dominican Migration into the United States
- Factors Favoring Contraceptive Use Among Hispanic American Women in Utica, NY
- Teacher Expectations in Urban and Suburban Schools

Recommended Reading

If you are thinking about majoring sociology, here are a few good introductory books.

- Invitation to Sociology by Peter Berger (1972)
- Introduction to Sociology by Anthony Giddens (1996)
- Down to Earth Sociology by James Henslin (1999)
- Social Construction of Reality by Peter Berger (1972)
- Classical Social Theory by Ian Craib (1997)

Famous People Who Majored in Sociology

Jesse Jackson (American civil rights leader, North Carolina A&T State University), C. Wright Mills (Marxist sociologist, University of Texas)

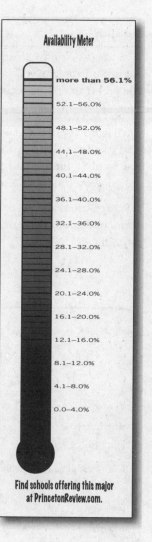

Availability Meter

more than 56.1%
52.1–56.0%
48.1–52.0%
44.1–48.0%
40.1–44.0%
36.1–40.0%
32.1–36.0%
28.1–32.0%
24.1–28.0%
20.1–24.0%
16.1–20.0%
12.1–16.0%
8.1–12.0%
4.1–8.0%
0.0–4.0%

Find schools offering this major at PrincetonReview.com.

Careers and Salary

Beginning salaries range from $19,000 to about $38,000 The average starting salary offered to freshly minted sociologists is approximately $27,500 annually.

CAREER OPTIONS		
Anthropologist	Lobbyist	Professor
Career Counselor	Marketing Executive	Social Worker
Criminologist	Political Scientist	Sociologist
Labor Relations Specialist	Politician	Teacher

SOIL SCIENCE

Basics

Soil is, to say the least, an incredibly valuable natural resource. Don't think so? Try growing crops without it. No problem, you say, we'll all eat meat. Okay, but where is the food for animals going to come from? The fact is that 75 percent of the planet's food and almost all of its fiber come from soil.

Soil science is the study of the soil as a component of natural and artificial systems. If you major in it, you'll learn about the classification, physical properties, chemistry, and fertility of all kinds of soils. Along the way, you'll develop a working knowledge of ecology, microbiology, chemistry, and physics. You'll have to if you want to understand issues that are central to soil science, including water and air quality, landscape design, crop production, and waste management.

Once you graduate, you should find a wealth of career opportunities. Many soil science majors take management positions at farms and ranches, at soil and water conservation agencies, and in the area of land-use planning.

SAMPLE COLLEGE CURRICULUM FOR SOIL SCIENCE

Biology

Chemistry

Crop Production

Crop Production in Developing Countries

Geology

Internship

Irrigation

Pesticide Chemistry

Plant Physiology

Seed Science

Soil Chemistry

Soil Classification

Soil Conservation

Soil Management

Soil Microbiology

Statistical Methods

Weed Science

If You Like Soil Science, You May Also Like . . .

Agricultural economics, agricultural and biological engineering, agricultural technology management, agriculture, agronomy and crop science, animal science, atmospheric science, biochemistry, biology, botany and plant biology, cell biology, chemistry, ecology, entomology, environmental science, feed science, forestry, genetics, geology, grain science, horticulture, microbiology, natural resources conservation, plant pathology, sustainable resource management

Suggested High School Prep for Soil Science

You don't need to know anything about soil science to major in it, but having an endearing love of biology and the physical sciences will help you immensely. Take all the biology and chemistry courses that your high school offers. Don't slack on math, either. Everything that you can learn about genetics, water, and plants will be helpful. Obviously, you should also learn as much as you can about the properties of different kinds of soil. Get out there. Get your hands dirty. If your high school offers agriculture courses, take a few.

Fun Facts

Earthworms 101

- The most common garden earthworm is the nightcrawler (*lumbricus terristris*). Though it has thrived in North America, the species initially arrived here in the potted plants of transported Europeans.
- Earthworms are known to have lived for as long as six years, but the average life span of an earthworm is about 20 months.
- Earthworms do not have lungs. They breathe through their skin.
- The largest earthworms in the world are found in Australia. They have been known to grow to nearly 10 feet in length.

Careers and Salary

Starting salaries for soil science majors range from $20,000 to about $35,000 per year.

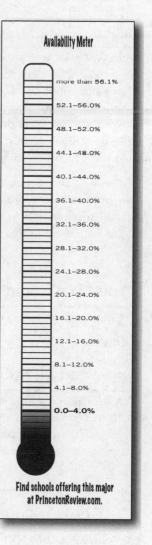

Availability Meter

more than 56.1%

52.1–56.0%

48.1–52.0%

44.1–48.0%

40.1–44.0%

36.1–40.0%

32.1–36.0%

28.1–32.0%

24.1–28.0%

20.1–24.0%

16.1–20.0%

12.1–16.0%

8.1–12.0%

4.1–8.0%

0.0–4.0%

Find schools offering this major at PrincetonReview.com.

CAREER OPTIONS

Biochemist	Environmentalist/	Farmer
Ecologist	Environmental Scientist	Lobbyist

SOUND ENGINEERING

Basics

So, you want to learn how to lay down phat beats or make music the way only Cher seems to make music these days? Well, there is one option (dressing up and becoming a Cher impersonator doesn't really count as an option), and that's to become a sound engineering (a.k.a. sound recording, or sound recording technology) major, by which you will learn how to engineer sound. Still not clear? Then think of this major as the meeting point of the conductor and the DJ, a symphonic blend where you will learn how the theory and history of music, from the classical to the contemporary, can be joined together in the recording studio or on the stage to create a whole new sound.

This isn't DJ training, though. Sure, you'll learn how to spin and mix and do anything else a decent DJ does, but you'll do a lot more than merely change CDs. Sound engineers are essential for everything from making an album to helping stage a concert. They are the technicians behind the musicians, allowing musical innovations and sounds to explore new areas and grow in depth.

If You Like Sound Engineering, You May Also Like . . .

Church music, music, music history, music therapy, piano, voice

Suggested High School Prep for Sound Engineering

A strong background in music, including knowledge of an instrument, is, of course, going to be very helpful. However, what you might be missing you can make up for once you get to college. Strong writing and reading skills are also going to be essential in helping you communicate in a business based on communication. So take some reading- and writing-intensive courses such as English and history.

SAMPLE COLLEGE CURRICULUM FOR SOUND ENGINEERING

Advanced Communication Skills

Basic Audio Wiring Lab

MIDI Electronic Music

Multitrack Production Techniques

Music Business I

Music History I–II

Music Theory

Sound Recording I–II

Sound Reinforcement Fundamentals

Fun Facts

Most of the earliest blues recordings available are those that John Lomax made in the 1930s. He recorded blues legends such as Leadbelly, and his son, Alan Lomax, followed in his footsteps. (The recordings he made were heavily sampled years later by Moby for his hit album *Play*.)

Careers and Salary

The starting salary for a sound engineer is about $28,000 to $30,000, although that can vary with experience and of course, who you know (we are, after all, talking about the music business).

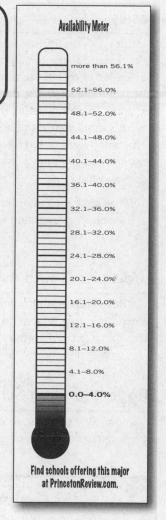

Availability Meter

more than 56.1%

52.1–56.0%

48.1–52.0%

44.1–48.0%

40.1–44.0%

36.1–40.0%

32.1–36.0%

28.1–32.0%

24.1–28.0%

20.1–24.0%

16.1–20.0%

12.1–16.0%

8.1–12.0%

4.1–8.0%

0.0–4.0%

Find schools offering this major at PrincetonReview.com.

CAREER OPTIONS		
Music Executive	Musician	Television Producer

SOUTH ASIAN STUDIES

Basics

South Asia comprises some of the most geographically diverse and populous countries in the world. Afghanistan, Bangladesh, Bhutan, India, Nepal, Pakistan, Sri Lanka, and Tibet are all South Asian countries. That's a lot of real estate to cover, not to mention history, which in some cases stretches back for several millennia—almost to the dawn of civilization itself. There are hundreds of languages and several religions (including Hinduism, Islam, Buddhism, and Christianity) that converge in the South Asian studies major. Part of what's important about a South Asian studies major is that you don't try to learn everything in detail. In combination with an interdisciplinary approach that includes related fields such as history, political science, literature, and economics, you will have the opportunity to pick a region or country that interests you most and focus on it.

Not all colleges and universities offer a major specifically in South Asian studies. In some cases it is listed as a possible concentration within a larger major such as international studies or Asian studies.

If You Like South Asian Studies, You May Also Like . . .

African studies, anthropology, archaeology, architectural history, art history, Asian American studies, comparative literature, East Asian studies, history, international agriculture, international business, international relations, international studies, Islamic studies, Japanese, Jewish studies, Southeast Asian studies

Suggested High School Prep for South Asian Studies

Knowledge of a language spoken in South Asia (besides English) is, of course, a great skill to have, but such language courses are not easy to come across in most high schools. In lieu of speaking fluent Urdu, you can always do your own research about the region, as well as keep up on current events. *The Economist* is an excellent, albeit dense, resource for keeping up on world politics and business from week to week. Keep those critical reading and writing skills finely honed because you will definitely need them.

> ### SAMPLE COLLEGE CURRICULUM FOR SOUTH ASIAN STUDIES
>
> Civilization of South Asia
>
> Electives in International Studies
>
> Electives in South Asian Philosophies
>
> Hindu Mythology
>
> History of India
>
> History of Indian Art
>
> Indian Demographics
>
> Readings in South Asian Islam
>
> Religion in Modern South Asia

Fun Facts

Did You Know?

India, with a population close to 1 billion, has 2 official national languages, 18 major languages, and 418 "listed languages" spoken by 10,000 or more people.

Did You Know?

The Dalai Lama governed Tibet from 1642 to 1959.

Careers and Salary

The starting salary for a South Asian studies major can vary dramatically depending on the field he or she chooses to enter. Average starting salaries range from $24,000 to $30,000.

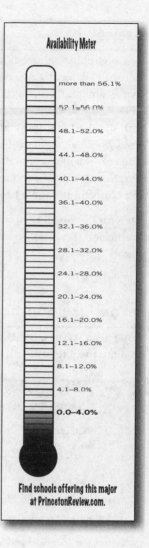

Availability Meter

more than 56.1%

52.1–56.0%

48.1–52.0%

44.1–48.0%

40.1–44.0%

36.1–40.0%

32.1–36.0%

28.1–32.0%

24.1–28.0%

20.1–24.0%

16.1–20.0%

12.1–16.0%

8.1–12.0%

4.1–8.0%

0.0–4.0%

Find schools offering this major at PrincetonReview.com.

CAREER OPTIONS

Anthropologist

Archaeologist

Curator

Diplomat/Attaché/Foreign Service Officer

Lobbyist

Sociologist

SOUTHEAST ASIAN STUDIES

Basics

Geographically speaking, Southeast Asia encompasses the countries of Indonesia, the Philippines, Vietnam, Thailand, Laos, Burma, and the immediate vicinity. It's a lot of territory and home to diverse languages and cultures, but don't be overwhelmed, because this major is more about depth than breadth. You will, of course, develop a knowledge of the whole region, including its geography, history, and relationship with the West, but you'll also get the opportunity to focus your study on the single country (or religion or philosophy) that interests you most. That could mean anything from learning how to speak one of the indigenous languages of the Philippines to tracking the development of Vietnam through the twentieth century. Not all colleges and universities offer a major specifically in Southeast Asian studies. Often you'll find it as a concentration in a broader major program, such as international studies or Asian studies.

With the opening of trade relations between Southeast Asian countries and the United States, a major in Southeast Asian studies prepares you to enter the job market in a number of different fields. The interdisciplinary approach of the major provides you with solid skills in economics, history, and anthropology.

If You Like Southeast Asian Studies, You May Also Like . . .

African studies, ancient studies, anthropology, archaeology, architectural history, Asian American studies, comparative literature, East Asian studies, East European studies, geography, international agriculture, international business, international relations, international studies, Islamic studies, Jewish studies, Latin American studies, Middle Eastern studies, South Asian studies

SAMPLE COLLEGE CURRICULUM FOR SOUTHEAST ASIAN STUDIES

Art of the Silk Route

Asian Archaeology

Buddhism and Asian Culture

Cultures of Mainland and Island Southeast Asia

Eastern Philosophy

History of the Philippines

Issues in Southeast Asian History

Pacific Island Archaeology

Requirements in a Southeast Asian Language

Southeast Asia in Modern Times

Southeast Asian Political Novels and Films

Vietnam and the United States

Suggested High School Prep for Southeast Asian Studies

Knowledge of a language spoken in Southeast Asia (besides English) is a great start, but most high schools don't have courses in any of them. In lieu of speaking fluent Vietnamese, you can always do your own research about the region, as well as keep up on current events. *The Economist* is an excellent, albeit dense, resource for keeping up on world politics and business from week to week. Keep those critical reading and writing skills finely honed because you will definitely need them.

Fun Facts

Did You Know?

Southeast Asia technically extends for about 4,000 miles. It contains approximately 5 million square miles of land and sea.

Careers and Salary

The starting salary for a Southeast Asian studies major can vary dramatically depending on the field one enters. Average starting salaries range from $24,000 to $30,000.

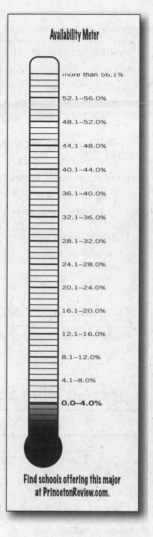

Availability Meter

more than 56.1%

52.1–56.0%

48.1–52.0%

44.1 48.0%

40.1–44.0%

36.1–40.0%

32.1–36.0%

28.1–32.0%

24.1–28.0%

20.1–24.0%

16.1–20.0%

12.1–16.0%

8.1–12.0%

4.1–8.0%

0.0–4.0%

Find schools offering this major at PrincetonReview.com.

CAREER OPTIONS

Anthropologist

Archaeologist

Curator

Diplomat/Attaché/Foreign Service Officer

Lobbyist

Sociologist

SPANISH

Basics

Perhaps you've already fallen in love with the poems of Pablo Neruda and the novels of Gabriel García Márquez and have realized that you want a deeper look into the culture and language in which these writers have flourished. Or maybe you've got a businesslike mind and see a lot of potential in the developing economies of South America. Regardless of what your interest may be, a Spanish major will provide you a unique insight into the second most widely spoken language in the world.

Spoken throughout Central and South America, Spain, and many parts of the United States, knowledge of Spanish is a bridge into varied cultures that span several continents and dozens of centuries. In addition to becoming fluent in the language, a Spanish major also obtains a broad knowledge of the history of the Spanish-speaking world. From Aztec ruins to Argentine fascism, you'll delve into the social, political, and economic elements that have made Spanish one of the most important languages in the world.

Many colleges recommend or require that you spend at least a semester studying in a Spanish-speaking country of your choice.

If You Like Spanish, You May Also Like . . .

Comparative literature, French, German, history, Italian, Latin American studies, linguistics, Portuguese

Suggested High School Prep for Spanish

Most high schools offer Spanish as an elective, and even if you don't decide to major in it, getting as deeply as you can into the language will help you pass the general education requirements in a foreign language that many colleges now have. So take it from your freshman year until you graduate. Geography and history are also useful, as Spanish has been spoken all over the world for many centuries. If you're lucky enough to find a linguistics class, take that too.

SAMPLE COLLEGE CURRICULUM FOR SPANISH

Advanced Spanish Composition

Intermediate Spanish

Intermediate Spanish Composition

Introduction to Spanish American Culture

Introduction to Spanish Literature

Masterpieces of Modern Spanish Literature

Modern Hispanic American Literature

Modern Spanish Syntax

Seminar in Hispanic Culture

Spanish Grammar Review

Spanish Pronunciation

Fun Facts

The Changing Face of America

According to the most recent U.S. Census Bureau statistics, 13 percent of the United States population is of Hispanic origin, making it the fastest growing minority in the country.

Did You Know?

Venezuela was given its name by Spaniards visiting the country who, upon seeing Maracaibo Lake, were reminded of the island city of Venice and named the country Venezuela, which means "little Venice."

Careers and Salary

Knowledge of any foreign language, Spanish in particular, will help make you an attractive candidate for any number of jobs. Starting salaries for Spanish majors range from $24,000 to $30,000.

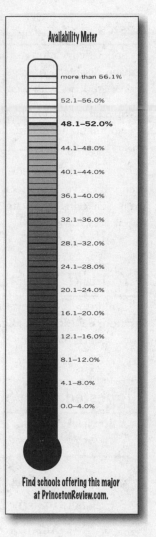

Availability Meter

more than 56.1%

52.1–56.0%

48.1–52.0%

44.1–48.0%

40.1–44.0%

36.1–40.0%

32.1–36.0%

28.1–32.0%

24.1–28.0%

20.1–24.0%

16.1–20.0%

12.1–16.0%

8.1–12.0%

4.1–8.0%

0.0–4.0%

Find schools offering this major at PrincetonReview.com.

CAREER OPTIONS

Consultant	Editor	Teacher
Diplomat/Attaché/Foreign Service Officer	Foreign Exchange Trader	Translator
	Professor	

SPECIAL EDUCATION

Basics

Special education majors learn how to teach children with specific needs, such as visually impaired or hearing disabled students, students with learning or behavior disorders, mentally handicapped students, and/or students with a combination of moderate or severe disabilities.

Special education majors take highly specialized classes on disability and disorder assessment, child development, and classroom management. They incorporate standard educational practice into a specialized program to meet the needs of their students.

The special education major requires exceptional patience and a tremendous desire to work with children who have very special needs. They must manage all of the activities in the classroom while still effectively delivering their curriculum. With its many challenges, majors who go on to teach special education find it very rewarding.

If You Like Special Education, You May Also Like . . .

Child care, child development, communication disorders, developmental psychology, education administration, education of the deaf, educational psychology, elementary education, social psychology, social work, speech pathology

Suggested High School Prep for Special Education

A firm background in English, math, and science is required for all education majors. If your school offers classes in psychology or sign language, try to take them. Volunteer work with exceptional students is probably the most valuable background you can acquire. Ask around at local schools and hospitals to see what opportunities might be available.

SAMPLE COLLEGE CURRICULUM FOR SPECIAL EDUCATION

Behavior Management

Child Growth and Development

Classroom Management

Cognitive Psychology

Evaluating Exceptional Children

Foundations of Education

Fundamentals of Teaching Special Education

Introduction to Behavior Disorders

Introduction to Learning Disabilities

Reading Methods

Fun Facts

Words of Wisdom

"To stimulate life, leaving it then free to develop, to unfold, herein lies the first task of the teacher."

—Maria Montessori

For More Information . . .

The University of Virginia maintains a large database of websites of special education programs around the country (http://curry.edschool.virginia.edu/sped).

Careers and Salary

Teacher salaries usually depend on where one works. A special education major could make from $25,000 to $35,000 a year to start, depending on location.

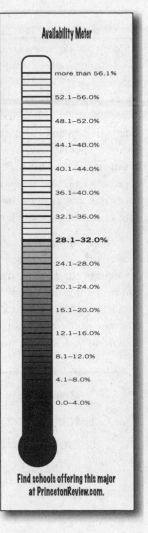

Availability Meter

more than 56.1%

52.1–56.0%

48.1–52.0%

44.1–48.0%

40.1–44.0%

36.1–40.0%

32.1–36.0%

28.1–32.0%

24.1–28.0%

20.1–24.0%

16.1–20.0%

12.1–16.0%

8.1–12.0%

4.1–8.0%

0.0–4.0%

Find schools offering this major at PrincetonReview.com.

CAREER OPTIONS		
Librarian	Speech Therapist	Teacher

SPECIAL PRODUCTS MARKETING OPERATIONS

Basics

Why is vitamin-enhanced water suddenly selling like hotcakes? How can the floral industry add new life to its autumn sales numbers? How can the inventors of a fancy new cheese grater market their product for optimal sales? These are the sorts of questions that occupy the mind of a special products marketing operations major (SPMO). SPMO programs tend to focus on several key industries: floral, food and beverage, home products, and office supplies. (Some programs are devoted exclusively to only one or two fields.) This means that as an SPMO major you'll receive very specialized training that's geared toward your progression into the "special products" corner of the marketing trade. As you might expect, courses in business and marketing make up the bulk of an SPMO curriculum. You'll study everything from accounting to marketing strategies to brand development. You'll learn how to find and interpret market research, as well as how to apply that research to the marketing of specific products or entire industries. Regional, national, and global marketing strategies will be examined as well.

So imagine that a national organic fruit growers organization comes to you with a healthy expense account and desire to see the industry's sales increase. You'll have some questions to answer. What is the target market for organic fruit? Who are the producers? The possible sellers? The likely consumers? How do you best communicate with sellers and consumers? What sorts of advertising mediums should you use? TV? Radio? Internet? Billboards? Some combination? How do you distribute the product? Display it? Basically, what are you going to do to help your clients achieve their goals? After completing the SPMO major, you'll be able to tackle these questions with confidence and panache.

SAMPLE COLLEGE CURRICULUM FOR SPECIAL PRODUCTS MARKETING OPERATIONS

Advertising Media

Basic Accounting

Brand Development

Customer and Consumer Behavior

Food and Beverage Marketing

Geographical Markets

History of Food and Beverage Service Industry

Introduction to Economics

Principles of Marketing

Product Distribution and Logistics

Sales Communications

Special Product Marketing Research

If You Like Special Products Marketing Operations, You May Also Like...

Accounting, advertising, business communications, industrial management, marketing, merchandising and buying operations, organizational communications, public relations

Suggested High School Prep for Special Products Marketing Operations

Success in the SPMO field will come from your analytic and creative abilities. After all, you'll need to process market research carefully and then think outside of the box to come up with exciting and innovative ways to market your products. With this in mind, a standard college prep curriculum should serve you well. Just remember that everything from art classes to English classes to math classes will have something to offer you.

Fun Facts

It Does a Body Good

One of the most successful marketing campaigns in recent decades was "Got Milk?"—you know, the campaign that spawned photos of high-profile people proudly donning milk mustaches. It began in California in 1993, and within a year had turned around the industry's revenues. The campaign extended nationally, and has since resulted in books, contests, websites, and—most important from a marketing standpoint—strong milk sales.

For a detailed history of the "Got Milk?" campaign, check out an essay by Douglas B. Holt, a University of Oxford marketing professor, at www.Aef.com/on_campus/classroom/case_histories/3000.

Careers and Salary

Starting salaries in the marketing field often range between $28,000 and $40,000.

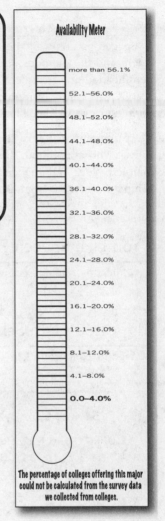

Availability Meter

more than 56.1%

52.1–56.0%

48.1–52.0%

44.1–48.0%

40.1–44.0%

36.1–40.0%

32.1–36.0%

28.1–32.0%

24.1–28.0%

20.1–24.0%

16.1–20.0%

12.1–16.0%

8.1–12.0%

4.1–8.0%

0.0–4.0%

The percentage of colleges offering this major could not be calculated from the survey data we collected from colleges.

CAREER OPTIONS

Advertising Executive	Lobbyist	Researcher
Consultant	Marketing Strategist	Salesperson
Distributor	Public Relations Professional	

SPEECH PATHOLOGY

Basics

Speech pathology is the study of speech, language, communication, voice, swallowing, and fluency disorders, and the methods of their treatment. It is usually connected to the field of audiology, which is the identification and treatment of hearing disorders. Speech pathologists work with a wide range of people, treating everything from minor speech problems to the total loss of speaking ability. Speech pathologists work in hospitals, rehabilitation centers, schools, and private practice.

At a minimum, you will need a master's degree in order to practice as a speech pathologist; in some states, a PhD is required. The undergraduate program will prepare you for that course of study. When you complete your training and meet all requirements, you will be awarded the Certificate of Clinical Competence (CCC) from the American Speech-Language-Hearing Association.

If You Like Speech Pathology, You May Also Like . . .

Clinical psychology, communication disorders, developmental psychology, educational psychology

Suggested High School Prep for Speech Pathology

A good background in the arts and sciences will serve you well. Classes in biology, anatomy, and psychology will also come in handy.

SAMPLE COLLEGE CURRICULUM FOR SPEECH PATHOLOGY

Acoustics and Perception

Anatomy and Physiology of Speech Production

Audiology I–II

Biology

General Psychology

Introduction to Aural Rehabilitation

Introduction to Speech and Hearing Processes and Disorders

Normal Language Acquisition and Usage

Organic and Fluency Disorders

Phonetics

Speech and Language Development

Fun Facts

For More Information . . .

- The American Speech-Language-Hearing Association is the professional organization of speech pathologists and audiologists. Check out their site at www.Asha.org.
- Find out more about speech pathology in schools at www.Speakingofspeech.com.

Careers and Salary

You will probably go right on to graduate school after getting your baccalaureate degree if you are considering speech pathology as a major. Starting salaries for a speech pathologist with a master's degree are about $34,000 to $42,000.

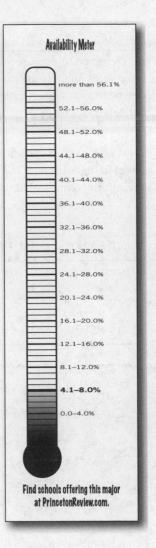

Availability Meter

more than 56.1%

52.1–56.0%

48.1–52.0%

44.1–48.0%

40.1–44.0%

36.1–40.0%

32.1–36.0%

28.1–32.0%

24.1–28.0%

20.1–24.0%

16.1–20.0%

12.1–16.0%

8.1–12.0%

4.1–8.0%

0.0–4.0%

Find schools offering this major at PrincetonReview.com.

CAREER OPTIONS

Speech Therapist

SPORT AND LEISURE STUDIES

Basics

Designed to prepare you for graduate work in education or a career in the sports and recreation industry, a sport and leisure studies major arms you with the skills you will need to render informed and accurate advice on almost every aspect of the sports world. Whether you're coaching a baseball team or advising Nike on how to develop a better basketball shoe, the skills you learn here will have real, practical applications.

With a gym in almost every neighborhood in America, sport and leisure studies majors can find themselves in high demand. The more health conscious our society becomes, the more we will need well-trained and informed individuals to guide us through the litany of workout programs available to us.

If You Like Sport and Leisure Studies, You May Also Like . . .

Anthropology, hospitality, nutrition, recreation management, sociology, wildlife management

Suggested High School Prep for Sport and Leisure Studies

Athletic experience is beneficial, but hardly enough. You will definitely need strong math skills, as well as a solid background in the social sciences, such as history or sociology courses. Psychology, if your school offers classes in it, could come in handy. Volunteer as a coach for younger athletes in your spare time.

> ### SAMPLE COLLEGE CURRICULUM FOR SPORT AND LEISURE STUDIES
>
> Advanced Skill Techniques
>
> Coaching Disabled Athletes
>
> Coaching Effectiveness
>
> Coaching the Young Athlete
>
> Health and Well-Being in American Society
>
> History of Sport and Leisure
>
> Human Nutrition
>
> Introduction to Sport and Leisure Studies
>
> Introductory Physiology
>
> Legal Aspects of Sport and Physical Activity
>
> Mathematics
>
> Sports Officiating
>
> Statistics

Fun Facts

Did You Know?

The human body has fewer muscles than a caterpillar's.

How Muscles Grow Stronger

To gain strength, you have to rupture your muscle fiber. Nerves connected to your muscles register the pain brought on by this tearing, and your body overcompensates to heal them. Within 48 hours, the muscle fiber is made stronger.

Careers and Salary

The average starting salary for a sport and leisure studies major is $18,000 to $30,000. Starting salaries in the private sector can vary widely, depending on the field entered.

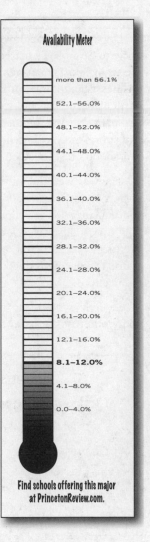

Availability Meter

more than 56.1%

52.1–56.0%

48.1–52.0%

44.1–48.0%

40.1–44.0%

36.1–40.0%

32.1–36.0%

28.1–32.0%

24.1–28.0%

20.1–24.0%

16.1–20.0%

12.1–16.0%

8.1–12.0%

4.1–8.0%

0.0–4.0%

Find schools offering this major at PrincetonReview.com.

CAREER OPTIONS

Advertising Executive	Coach	Referee
Agent	Consultant	Sports Manager
Anthropologist	Hotel Manager	Talent Scout

SPORTS MANAGEMENT

Basics

Do you like to be down in front—courtside, ringside, or on the sidelines at the 50-yard line? If you're not game to be a player, mascot, or coach, you can still catch all the action up close and personal as manager of the team. Sports management lets you participate in—and cash in on—the exciting world of sports from a business standpoint. In this major, you'll learn about sports themselves (perhaps focusing on one or two in particular), the psychological principles at work behind them, and how sports fit into our society. But you'll also gain a strong foundation of knowledge in the field of business, examining how the worlds of business and sports interact and how you can make those interactions more profitable and beneficial for every person and interest involved.

The way we think of sports has drastically changed over the years; these days few people would say that a sport is "just a game." Indeed, sports provide serious entertainment and big business in this country, and sports managers are crucial to ensuring that the players, fans, coaches, and financial backers coexist peacefully (or as close to peacefully as possible). You'll learn how to market sports effectively and how to plan events, diving into the areas of sports publicity, coaching, and administration. An interdisciplinary field, sports management encompasses elements of economics, accounting, marketing, psychology, law, and communications.

Students who major in sports management go on to pursue careers as agents, managers, publicists, and many other positions in the sports industry. Sports management is a broad field, and the knowledge you acquire about both business and sports makes for a whole arena of action-packed possibilities.

SAMPLE COLLEGE CURRICULUM FOR SPORTS MANAGEMENT

- Administration of Sport
- Coaching Skills
- Exercise Physiology
- Facilities Planning and Management
- Health and Fitness
- History of Sports
- Macroeconomics
- Managerial Accounting
- Microeconomics
- Organization and Administration of Physical Education
- Sport Marketing
- Sports and the Law
- Sports Officiating
- Sports Psychology
- Theory of Leisure and Recreation

If You Like Sports Management, You May Also Like . . .

Accounting, advertising, business administration and management, business communications, entrepreneurship, finance, human resources management, journalism, marketing, merchandising and buying operations, music management, public relations, recreation management

Suggested High School Prep for Sports Management

Sports managers must be fantastic communicators, so take courses such as English and languages that will strengthen your writing, reading, and speaking skills. Any business courses your school offers will be helpful, but it's more important to build up a strong foundation in a variety of disciplines, including math and science. Of course, any experience you can get with your school's sports teams—as team manager, statistician, fan, or player—will give you more insight into this exciting field and give you a head start on your studies.

Fun Facts

What Was the First Sporting Event?

The first sporting event was a foot race, and it was held—of course—at Olympia, in the western part of Peloponnese. It took place in 776 B.C./B.C.E. and was held to honor Zeus. The list of winners from this and other early sporting events was compiled by Hippias of Elis, who lived in the fifth century B.C./B.C.E.

(Source: www.olympics.org.uk)

Wild World of Sports:

"We can't win at home. We can't win on the road. As general manager, I just can't figure out where else to play."

—Pat Williams, general manager of Orlando Magic, 1992

"One player was lost because he broke his nose. How do you go about getting a nose in condition for football?"

—Darrell Royal, Texas football coach, 1966, in response to a question of whether injuries to his team could have been prevented by better conditioning

"I'm not allowed to comment on lousy officiating."

—Jim Finks, general manager of the New Orleans Saints, 1986

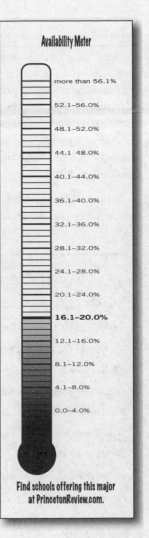

Availability Meter

more than 56.1%

52.1–56.0%

48.1–52.0%

44.1 48.0%

40.1–44.0%

36.1–40.0%

32.1–36.0%

28.1–32.0%

24.1–28.0%

20.1–24.0%

16.1–20.0%

12.1–16.0%

8.1–12.0%

4.1–8.0%

0.0–4.0%

Find schools offering this major at PrincetonReview.com.

Careers and Salary

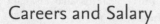

The starting salary for sports management majors is difficult to estimate, and the number depends greatly on what sort of career you pursue. In general, managers earn from $30,000 to $50,000 to start, and your salary will rise as you gain more experience.

CAREER OPTIONS

Coach	Sports Agent	Team Manager
Public Relations Manager	Sports Manager	Various careers in advertising and marketing
Referee	Sportswriter	

STATISTICS

Basics

According to the University of Tennessee—Knoxville, statistics is "the science of learning from data"—a simple way to describe a complex field of study. As a statistics major, you'll use mathematics to reach logical conclusions about probability, you'll learn how to analyze and interpret empirical data from surveys and experiments, and by the time you graduate you'll know how to design your own experiments and other research methodologies. Statistics is aimed at problem-solving. By analyzing trends and patterns in data you'll be able to hypothesize about probable and possible (and you'll know the difference between these two words better than almost anyone) future developments and create solutions that anticipate probable (and possible) problems.

As a statistics major, you should have a strong background in math and computers because most statistical analysis is done by sophisticated computer programs designed especially for that purpose. Eventually, you'll be using statistics in countless ways to improve our society; you might help our economy, protect the environment, develop new marketing strategies, or evaluate a drug's effectiveness. The possibilities are endless.

Sample College Curriculum for Statistics

Analysis of Categorical Data

Analysis of Qualitative Data

Applied Linear Statistical Methods

Applied Regression Analysis

Biostatistical Methods

Design and Analysis of Experiments

Distribution Theory

Generalized Linear Models

History of Statistics

Introduction to Mathematical Probability

Linear Regression Models

Nonparametric Statistics

Numerical Computation

Probability and Statistics in the Natural Sciences

Probability Models

Statistical Inference

Statistical Methods and Their Applications

Statistics for the Social Sciences

Time Series Analysis

If You Like Statistics, You May Also Like . . .

Accounting, applied mathematics, computer and information science, computer engineering, computer systems analysis, data processing, economics, finance, mathematics

Suggested High School Prep for Statistics

Math, math, math! Take as many math courses as you can handle, especially higher-level ones like calculus. Also, if your high school offers any psychology classes, you might want to look into those—psychology is one field that uses quite a bit of statistics.

Fun Facts

A Little Statistics Humor from Jokes.com

Forty-seven percent of all statistics are made up on the spot.

Quotable

"Statistical thinking will one day be as necessary for efficient citizenship as the ability to read and write."

—H. G. Wells, who wrote, among other things,
The War of the Worlds and *The Time Machine*

Careers and Salary

The $40,000 to $50,000 range would be a reasonable estimate for a starting salary, but salaries for statistics majors vary widely and depend mostly on where and how they apply their skills.

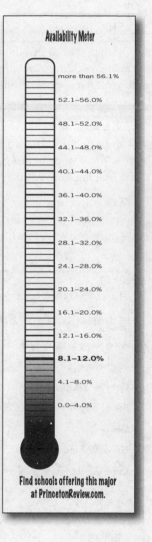

Availability Meter

more than 56.1%

52.1–56.0%

48.1–52.0%

44.1–48.0%

40.1–44.0%

36.1–40.0%

32.1–36.0%

28.1–32.0%

24.1–28.0%

20.1–24.0%

16.1–20.0%

12.1–16.0%

8.1–12.0%

4.1–8.0%

0.0–4.0%

Find schools offering this major
at PrincetonReview.com.

CAREER OPTIONS

Accountant/Auditor	Bookkeeper	Investment Banker
Actuary	Financial Analyst	Psychologist
Bank Officer	Financial Planner	Statistician

SURVEYING

Basics

It's like this: You sit down in the back seat of your grandparents' car and immediately spy the jumbo road atlas. You pick it up and are enraptured by each map, thankfully blocking out your grandfather's thirty-sixth telling of his appendectomy story.

Surveying, a field of study often listed under a civil engineering program, is concerned with all aspects of the land around us. As a surveying major you'll study data collection techniques such as photogrammetry and satellite positioning. You'll learn about geographic information systems and other computer programs. You'll study drafting and site planning, and you'll be exposed to astronomy, geography, and other fields involving measurement.

As a surveying major, your primary concern will be the physical environment—its beauties, problems, resources, and effects. You'll study how natural resources should and can be preserved and protected. You'll investigate the ways in which different aspects of the land affect each other and tackle issues such as hazardous waste, deforestation, wildlife endangerment, and border disputes.

Eventually, your major in surveying might lead you into a career with railroads, urban planning, architecture, land development, or public utilities. Your knowledge of the land—and the skills you develop to study it—can lead to endless opportunities.

If You Like Surveying, You May Also Like . . .

Applied mathematics, architectural engineering, architecture, civil engineering, computer engineering, drawing

Suggested High School Prep for Surveying

To prepare for a major in surveying, make an effort to take courses in geography, geology (you study some of this in physical science), and computer science, as well as a lot of math. These will give you a good foundation for your college courses.

SAMPLE COLLEGE CURRICULUM FOR SURVEYING

Astronomy for Surveyors

Cartography

Construction Surveying

Ethics and Professionalism

Geodesy

Geodetic Models

Land Development Design

Land Information Systems

Legal Principles of Boundary Surveying

Map Projections and Coordinate Systems

Photogrammetry

Plane Surveying

Practical Field Problems

Public Land Survey System Boundaries

Remote Sensing

Route Surveying

Stormwater Design

Surveying Data Adjustment and Analysis

Surveying Drafting

Fun Facts

What's That Mean?

There's quite a bit of slang that surveyors use on the job. Here are a few examples, with their meanings.

Beep it: Use a metal detector to find a corner

Beer thirty: Quitting time

Break chain: Shortening the chain going up or down hills

Can't see it from my house: Good enough—let's get out of here

Cartoon: Construction plan

Crick: Creek in Pittsburgh

Desk jockey: Office worker

Careers and Salary

The average starting salary for surveyors is in the mid twenties, but that might be higher or lower depending on what sort of company they work for and what experience they've had.

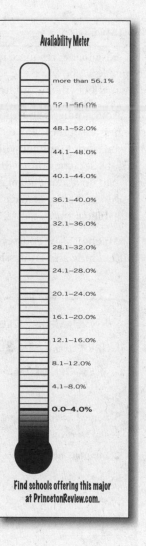

Availability Meter

more than 56.1%

52.1–56.0%

48.1–52.0%

44.1–48.0%

40.1–44.0%

36.1–40.0%

32.1–36.0%

28.1–32.0%

24.1–28.0%

20.1–24.0%

16.1–20.0%

12.1–16.0%

8.1–12.0%

4.1–8.0%

0.0–4.0%

Find schools offering this major at PrincetonReview.com.

CAREER OPTIONS

Civil Engineer	Landscape Architect	Surveyor
Construction Manager	Structural Engineer	

SUSTAINABLE RESOURCE MANAGEMENT

Basics

Sustainable resource management deals with the protection of all natural resources. If you major in this, you'll learn how we use said resources, how we should use them (which isn't always how we do use them), what affects them, and how they can be best protected and preserved.

Your studies will expose you to all the different sectors that play a role in the abuse and preservation of natural resources. For example, you'll learn how social systems affect the environment, how people and organizations interact with natural resources, how values affect people's views of the environment, and how various societies differ in their treatment of it. You'll learn about the importance of biodiversity and what we can do about endangered species of animals and plants. Ultimately, you'll investigate ideas for what you can do to better manage the environment and utilize resources in a way that will ensure their long-term availability.

Much of your course work will be based on research and field study, giving you firsthand experience in this exciting and endlessly important field.

SAMPLE COLLEGE CURRICULUM FOR SUSTAINABLE RESOURCE MANAGEMENT

Biodiversity

Biological Sciences: Energy Transfer and Development

Community Resource Management

Conservation Science

Ecosystem Management

Environmental and Resource Economics

Evaluation of Environmental Impact

Natural Resources Data Analysis

Natural Systems

Planning for Sustainability

Resource Assessment and Monitoring

Silviculture

Social Systems

Values and Sustainability

Water Resources Institutions and Policies

Wildlife Management

If You Like Sustainable Resource Management, You May Also Like . . .

Agricultural business and management, biology, business administration and management, chemistry, civil engineering, ecology, environmental and environmental health engineering, environmental science, forestry, industrial management, natural resources conservation, wildlife management

Suggested High School Prep for Sustainable Resource Management

Prepare for a major in sustainable resource management with AP courses in biology, chemistry, math, and computer science. Business courses would be useful if your high school offers them. And groups or clubs with environmental concerns could provide you with valuable perspectives.

Fun Facts

For More Information . . .

Did you know there is a Law of the Sea? The United Nations created the Law of the Sea to regulate all aspects of the ocean, such as environmental control, economic and commercial activities, and marine scientific research. The Law of the Sea has 320 articles and 9 annexes, and you can learn all about it by visiting the United Nations website (www.un.org/Depts/los/index.htm).

Keep in Mind

"In nature there are neither rewards nor punishments—there are consequences."

—Robert G. Ingersoll

Careers and Salary

According to Ohio State University, the starting salary for most sustainable resource management majors ranges from $20,000 to $30,000.

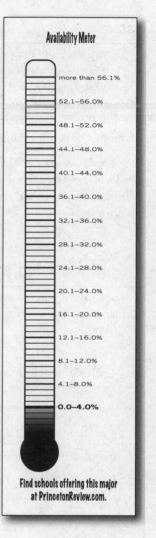

Availability Meter

more than 56.1%

52.1–56.0%

48.1–52.0%

44.1–48.0%

40.1–44.0%

36.1–40.0%

32.1–36.0%

28.1–32.0%

24.1–28.0%

20.1–24.0%

16.1–20.0%

12.1–16.0%

8.1–12.0%

4.1–8.0%

0.0–4.0%

Find schools offering this major at PrincetonReview.com.

CAREER OPTIONS

City Planner

Civil Engineer

Ecologist

Environmentalist/
Environmental Scientist

Geologist

Hazardous Waste Manager

Park Ranger

SWEDISH LANGUAGE AND LITERATURE

Basics

More than 9 million people worldwide speak Swedish, and before long, you may be one of them. The Swedish language and literature major offers the ideal training grounds for someone interested in learning the Swedish language and exploring a rich artistic legacy that includes the plays of August Strindberg and the films of Ingmar Bergman. Because many Swedish language and literature majors are associated with larger Scandinavian studies departments, you'll be able to use your studies in Swedish as a platform for wider considerations of regional languages, dialects, literatures, and cultural developments.

Ideally, you'll be able to put your knowledge of the language and culture to the test when you study abroad in, say, Stockholm or Göteborg. Spending some time on Swedish turf will add new dimensions to your education. As a well-rounded student, you'll be prepared to continue in graduate school or move into the professional world.

If You Like Swedish Language and Literature, You May Also Like...

Comparative literature, European history, Finnish and related languages, literatures, and linguistics, German, great books, Russian, Scandinavian studies, Slavic languages and literatures

Suggested High School Prep for Swedish Language and Literature

The Swedish language rarely makes its way into the high school curriculum, so choose a language that your high school does offer and get to work. It'll be good practice. History, literature, and art appreciation classes will give you a strong background as well.

SAMPLE COLLEGE CURRICULUM FOR SWEDISH LANGUAGE AND LITERATURE

Advanced Swedish

Conversation and Composition

Elementary Swedish

Films of Ingmar Bergman

History of Sweden

Intermediate Swedish

Introduction to Scandinavian Literature

Scandinavian Linguistics

Strindberg

Swedish Poetry of the Eighteenth and Nineteenth Centuries

The Swedish Short Story

Twentieth Century Swedish Literature

Fun Facts

Runs in the Family

Iconic Swedish film director Ingmar Bergman is not the only creative member of the family. He has "at least" nine children (as the Internet Movie Database puts it), a number of whom have notable artistic feathers in their caps. They include:

- daughter Anna Bergman, actress
- son Daniel Bergman, director
- daughter Eva Bergman, director
- son Mats Bergman, actor
- daughter Linn Ullman, child actress, literary critic, and novelist

(Source: www.imdb.com)

The New Page

Interested in checking out the writers making waves in Sweden today? You might look at the works of Kerstin Ekman, Torbjörn Flygt, Elsie Johansson, Jonas Hassen Khemiri, Kristina Lugn, Mikael Niemi, and Alejandro Leiva Wenger.

Careers and Salary

Average starting salaries will range from $25,000 to $30,000. You may also opt to step into a graduate degree.

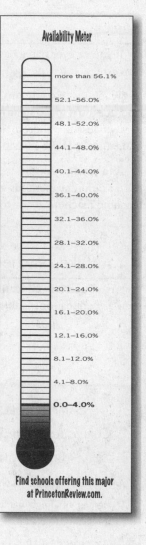

Availability Meter

more than 56.1%

52.1–56.0%

48.1–52.0%

44.1–48.0%

40.1–44.0%

36.1–40.0%

32.1–36.0%

28.1–32.0%

24.1–28.0%

20.1–24.0%

16.1–20.0%

12.1–16.0%

8.1–12.0%

4.1–8.0%

0.0–4.0%

Find schools offering this major at PrincetonReview.com.

CAREER OPTIONS

Diplomat/Attaché/Foreign Service Officer	Journalist	Travel Agent/Guide
Editor	Lobbyist	Tutor
Historian	Teacher	Writer
	Translator	

TEACHER EDUCATION

Basics

If you've ever had a bad teacher, I'm sure you can understand why it makes perfect sense to teach people how to teach teachers so that they can teach better.

Teaching, like any profession, has its own body of knowledge, including research, methods, and theory. And contrary to popular belief, the ability to speak English doesn't mean you're ready to go out and teach it, much less to children. Teaching is hard work, and that work is made more efficacious by a major in teacher education. It is the invisible muscle behind the strength of any great teacher.

As a teacher education major you will explore several fields, including psychology, as well as immerse yourself in different methods and styles of teaching. And at the end of the day you will learn to be a lean, mean teaching machine, ready to take on those students who may be more like you than you would care to admit.

If You Like Teacher Education, You May Also Like . . .

Art education, education, education administration, education of the deaf, educational psychology, elementary education, Spanish, special education, teaching English as a second language

Suggested High School Prep for Teacher Education

The best preparation for a teacher education major and a career as a teacher is a strong background in the liberal arts, particularly in English and history, because you will need strong critical reading and writing skills at your disposal.

SAMPLE COLLEGE CURRICULUM FOR TEACHER EDUCATION

Analysis of Subject Difficulties

Designing and Implementing a Thinking Curriculum

Education of the Culturally Different

Educational Psychology

Foundations of Reading Instruction

Fundamentals of Teaching with Audio-Visual Technology

History of Education

Philosophy of Education

Principles and Practices of Guidance and Pupil Personnel

Selected Topics in Teacher Education

Teaching Reading in the Secondary School

Fun Facts

A Joke

A professor was administering a big test one day to his students. He handed out all of the tests and went back to his desk to wait. Once the test was over, the students all handed the tests back in.

The professor noticed that one of the students had attached a $100 bill to his test with a note saying, "A dollar per point." The next class the professor handed the tests back out. The student got back his test with $64 in change.

Careers and Salary

The average starting salaries for teacher education majors range from $23,000 to $34,000, depending on experience and level of education.

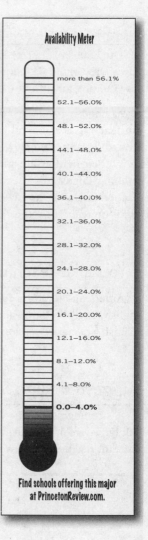

Availability Meter

more than 56.1%

52.1–56.0%

48.1–52.0%

44.1–48.0%

40.1–44.0%

36.1–40.0%

32.1–36.0%

28.1–32.0%

24.1–28.0%

20.1–24.0%

16.1–20.0%

12.1–16.0%

8.1–12.0%

4.1–8.0%

0.0–4.0%

Find schools offering this major at PrincetonReview.com.

CAREER OPTIONS

Career Counselor	Guidance Counselor	Teacher
College Administrator	Librarian	

TEACHING ENGLISH AS A SECOND LANGUAGE

Basics

The English language is one of the most widely used in the world. For immigrants arriving in the United States, the United Kingdom, Ireland, Australia, and Canada, it's an aspect of assimilation and adaptation to a new culture; for others, it's a necessary skill for entering the global business world.

As English continues to be the lingua franca of the world, the demand for well-trained professionals who can teach it as a second language will continue to increase. As any teacher can tell you, though, knowing how to do something does not mean knowing how to teach it. Teaching requires trained professionals who know their field inside and out, including the different theoretical approaches to its instruction. A major in teaching English as a second language will equip you with the tools you'll need to become a successful teacher, including knowledge of different cultures, training in different teaching methods, and of course, hands-on teaching experience.

If You Like Teaching English as a Second Language, You May Also Like . . .

American literature, education, education administration, educational psychology, elementary education, English, English composition, English literature, French, Hebrew, Italian, journalism, Modern Greek, Russian, Spanish, special education, speech pathology, technical writing

Suggested High School Prep for Teaching English as a Second Language

A strong grasp of the English language is essential for anyone who wants to teach it, so make sure you indulge yourself in as many humanities courses as you can. In addition, you can start volunteering as an ESL assistant teacher, where you will get hands-on experience teaching to foreign students.

SAMPLE COLLEGE CURRICULUM FOR TEACHING ENGLISH AS A SECOND LANGUAGE

Advanced Grammar for TESL

Cultural Anthropology

History of the English Language

Instructional Technology

Structure of Modern English

Teaching English as a Second Language Practicum

Teaching Reading in the Secondary School

Fun Facts

Did You Know?

According to the U.S. Department of Labor, more than one out of three adult and vocational education teachers works part time.

Did You Know?

The writer Samuel Johnson published his famous English dictionary in 1755, surpassing every other English language dictionary before it and setting a new standard for English lexicography.

Careers and Salary

The average salary for a teacher of English as a second language ranges from $24,000 to $33,000 depending on where you teach.

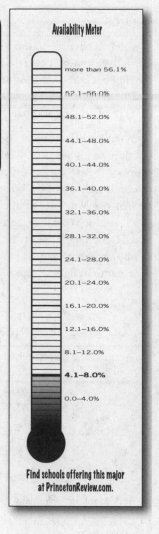

Availability Meter

more than 56.1%

52.1–56.0%

48.1–52.0%

44.1–48.0%

40.1–44.0%

36.1–40.0%

32.1–36.0%

28.1–32.0%

24.1–28.0%

20.1–24.0%

16.1–20.0%

12.1–16.0%

8.1–12.0%

4.1–8.0%

0.0–4.0%

Find schools offering this major at PrincetonReview.com.

CAREER OPTIONS		
Editor	Journalist	Teacher

TECHNICAL THEATER

Basics

Do you have a passion for theater but dislike getting in front of an audience? Are you excited by the physical movement of a curtain rising? Do you find yourself enamored with the people you see in the shadows, moving backdrops during scene changes? And most importantly, are you fascinated by how an evocative set or a bold lighting choice can really enhance a production? If the answer is yes to any or all of these questions then technical theater might be the major for you.

A major in technical theater will delve into the collaborative process behind any performance or production. In addition to a schedule that includes courses in theater history, script analysis, and acting, your primary focus will be on technical and design aspects of the stage. You'll acquire artistic, analytical, and research skills necessary to develop set, sound, light, and costume designs for both period and contemporary pieces. You'll learn about drafting, acoustics, and scenic carpentry. As you're getting schooled in class, you'll also be working hands-on with the backstage aspects of your school's main stage and student productions. Generally, students begin as crew hands, board operators, and prop assistants then work their way up to master electrician, lighting/scene/costume designer, and prop master. Upon graduation, we may not see your name in lights—but we'll know who's responsible for all the spot-on special effects.

If You Like Technical Theater, You May Also Like . . .

Acoustic, art, architecture, cinematography and film/video production, construction management, fashion design, furniture design, historic preservation, industrial design, radio and television, recording arts technology, sound engineering, theater

---

SAMPLE COLLEGE CURRICULUM FOR TECHNICAL THEATER

Acting for Non-Majors

Basic Lighting Technology

Color Basics: Scene and Lighting Technology Lab

Costume Construction

Creative Sound

Drafting for the Theater

Figure Drawing

Introduction to Set Construction

Scenic Carpentry

Scenic Painting

Script Analysis

Stage Management

Theater History

Suggested High School Prep for Technical Theater

Becoming involved in your school's drama club is excellent preparation for a technical theater major. Make sure to volunteer with the stage crew, assisting with set construction and lighting design/installation. Literature classes will expose you to a variety of plays, both classical and contemporary. This is vital knowledge for any theater insider, regardless of whether they are on stage or behind the curtain. Art and shop classes will give you practical, hands-on experience applicable to the design and building of sets. Now go see some live theater!

Fun Facts

Did Gypsy *Get Gypped?*

The original Broadway production of *Gypsy* was nominated for six 1960 Tony Awards, including Best Musical, Best Actress, Best Featured Actor and Actress, and Director—but surprisingly won none! The Best Musical prize that year went to *The Sound of Music*.

Light My Fire

During the first 1,000 performances of *Beauty and the Beast* on Broadway, 3,000 ounces of liquid butane were used in the flaming hands of Lumiere—the equivalent of 6 million flicks of a BIC lighter.

(Source: www.hiddenmickeys.org)

The Big Bucks of Broadway

Broadway shows generate approximately 25 million paid admissions each year, half in New York and half in 140 cities across North America.

Careers and Salary

As we all know, theater is a very competitive field whether you're pursuing acting or stage management. Starting salaries for recent graduates can be difficult to predict as they vary greatly depending on the size and caliber of the theater. Entry level jobs range from unpaid internships to production jobs that can pay $30,000.

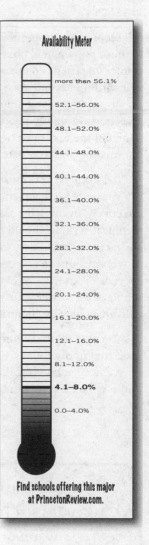

Availability Meter

more than 56.1%

52.1—56.0%

48.1—52.0%

44.1—48.0%

40.1—44.0%

36.1—40.0%

32.1—36.0%

28.1—32.0%

24.1—28.0%

20.1—24.0%

16.1—20.0%

12.1—16.0%

8.1—12.0%

4.1—8.0%

0.0—4.0%

Find schools offering this major at PrincetonReview.com.

CAREER OPTIONS

Director	Property Artist	Theater/Arts Administration
Costume Designer	Scenic/Set Designer	Theater Historian
Lighting/Sound Designer	Stage Manager	Theater Technician

TECHNICAL WRITING

Basics

Technical writing surrounds you every day, from the instructions for putting together that new furniture to those pop-up help boxes on your computer. Tech writers may be anonymous—nary a byline on that color-printer manual or company-policy booklet—but they author some of the most useful, informative, and important writing around. As a technical writing major, you'll review the fundamentals of writing well: clarity, brevity, and correct grammar and syntax. But technical writing differs from other types of writing in that it goes beyond simply good writing. It is intended to inform in a very specific way, so the information contained in the text must be organized, clear, and concise. Basically, tech writers take potentially complicated information and "translate" it into user-friendly layman's terms that most everyone can understand.

Technical writers must strike a fine balance between expertise and accessibility. You'll learn how to identify your intended audience and figure out what sort of communication will reach and speak to them most effectively. By studying how people use technical documents, you'll better understand how your work in technical writing should be shaped and focused. Put your skills to the test with writing assignments like abstracts, instructions, technical reports, and Internet text. You'll examine how visual and written elements of websites interact to convey the intended message. It may sound funny, but you don't need to have any specialized knowledge of the field for which you'll be writing. However, the more you know about your chosen field, the better your writing will be, so some programs require students to take a few courses in a specific area (such as computers) to broaden their knowledge base.

You may think technical writers write only in computer-related fields, but their work seeps into a wide spectrum of disciplines. Clear, concise writing is vital to all types of business, and you'll learn how to write for science, technology, the computer industry, and many other fields. Plus, even if you've got a novel or two in the works, a career in technical writing can keep you nicely afloat until you make your millions.

SAMPLE COLLEGE CURRICULUM FOR TECHNICAL WRITING

Expository Writing

Grammar Basics

Internet Publishing

Rhetoric for Technical Writers

Science Writing

Technical Editing

Technical Writing Style

Website Design and Copywriting

Writing for Computer Professions

Writing for the Professions

If You Like Technical Writing, You May Also Like . . .

Business administration and management, computer and information science, computer systems analysis, creative writing, entrepreneurship, marketing, mass communication, playwriting and screenwriting, public relations, visual communication

Suggested High School Prep for Technical Writing

Technical writers practice in any number of fields, so your best preparation for this major is to take a broad spectrum of courses including math, science, and the humanities. Load up on any courses that will improve your writing skills—even if that means term papers for history or biology. Many technical writers write for scientific or high-tech companies, so the more you know about computers and technology, the better.

Fun Facts

These Are "Professional" Writers?

Here are some actual lines from newspaper articles and ads.

- At least half their customers who fly to New York come by plane.
- The conviction carries a penalty of 1 to 10 years in Alabama.
- If your eye falls on a bargain, pick it up!
- Include your children when baking cookies.
- The bride was wearing an old lace gown that fell to the floor as she walked down the aisle.

(Source: www.writejustified.com)

Technically Speaking

Once you've become established in your career as a technical writer, you might want to check out the Society for Technical Communication. All sorts of technical communicators belong to STC, and the organization helps its members with continuing education, networking, and finding employment. Find out more at www.Stc.org.

Careers and Salary

Starting salaries for technical writers are usually in the area of $30,000 to $40,000, but can go much higher as you gain more experience. The field you choose to work in will also make a difference in your salary.

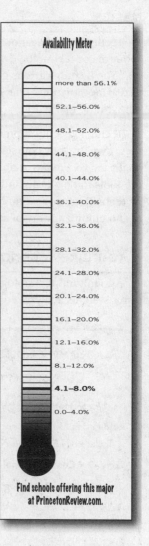

Availability Meter

more than 56.1%

52.1–56.0%

48.1–52.0%

44.1–48.0%

40.1–44.0%

36.1–40.0%

32.1–36.0%

28.1–32.0%

24.1–28.0%

20.1–24.0%

16.1–20.0%

12.1–16.0%

8.1–12.0%

4.1–8.0%

0.0–4.0%

Find schools offering this major at PrincetonReview.com.

CAREER OPTIONS

Computer Systems Analyst	Media Specialist	Technical Writer
Copy Editor	Proofreader	Writer
Editor		

TECHNOLOGY EDUCATION

Basics

Technology education isn't very mysterious; the major delivers just what its name promises. You'll learn about major technological systems, such as those dealing with production, communication, and transportation. You'll study various computer programs, like computer-aided design (CAD), and apply those programs to real-life situations. One of the most satisfying parts of a technology education major is its instant applicability to the real world.

Technology education majors spend their time both studying existing technological systems and designing their own. In your courses you might plan and build a computer-controlled device or design a website. You might try your hand at digital electronics or create a new transportation vehicle. Your studies will give you the tools to do all this and more. Besides the obvious rewards of becoming knowledgeable about technology, technology education majors have the added benefit of learning to work well in teams, think innovatively, and enjoy a variety of satisfying careers in education and business.

If You Like Technology Education, You May Also Like . . .

Agricultural technology management, computer and information science, computer engineering, computer systems analysis, education, engineering design, engineering mechanics, mechanical engineering

---

SAMPLE COLLEGE CURRICULUM FOR TECHNOLOGY EDUCATION

Automation of Production Systems for Technology Education

Computer Control Technology

Construction in Technology Education

Design of Constructed and Manufactured Goods

Electrical Systems and Servicing

Graphic Reproduction Practices

Materials and Processes

Mechanical Systems and Servicing

Printing and Publishing Practices

Technical Drawing

Technology Education Electronics

Technology Education Practices in Schools

Transmitting and Using Mechanical Power

Values, Science, and Technology

Suggested High School Prep for Technology Education

Computer courses of all kinds will be your best preparation for a major in technology education. Becoming acquainted with various computer programs, software packages, and the like will give you a good foundation for the new information you'll gather from your college courses.

Fun Facts

Tune In

Possible "New Cable TV Shows" of interest to technology education majors, from www.minot.com.

- *This Old Mainframe*: Host Bob Villa revamps a Univac and shows you how you can turn an old PC into a functional doorstop or other decorative object.
- *Mad About UNIX*: Urban comedy about a cute couple of system administrators and their home www server.
- *Name That Software*: Contestants attempt to identify well-known business programs by looking at the least number of lines of code.
- *Mr. Rom's Neighborhood*: Mr. Rom puts young ones to sleep by reading selections from various IBM documents.
- *WordPerfect Strangers*: Larry decides that using groupware would be a good way to meet women, but Balki's laser printer explodes, ruining any chances of connectivity.

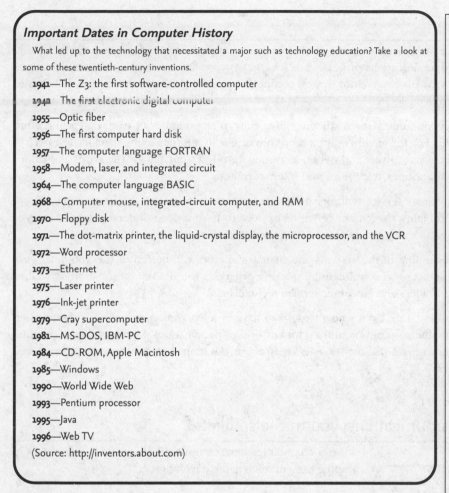

Important Dates in Computer History

What led up to the technology that necessitated a major such as technology education? Take a look at some of these twentieth-century inventions.

1941—The Z3: the first software-controlled computer

1942—The first electronic digital computer

1955—Optic fiber

1956—The first computer hard disk

1957—The computer language FORTRAN

1958—Modem, laser, and integrated circuit

1964—The computer language BASIC

1968—Computer mouse, integrated-circuit computer, and RAM

1970—Floppy disk

1971—The dot-matrix printer, the liquid-crystal display, the microprocessor, and the VCR

1972—Word processor

1973—Ethernet

1975—Laser printer

1976—Ink-jet printer

1979—Cray supercomputer

1981—MS-DOS, IBM-PC

1984—CD-ROM, Apple Macintosh

1985—Windows

1990—World Wide Web

1993—Pentium processor

1995—Java

1996—Web TV

(Source: http://inventors.about.com)

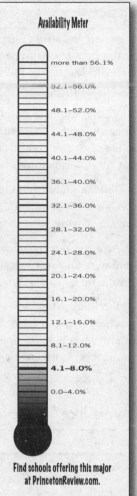

Availability Meter

more than 56.1%

52.1–56.0%

48.1–52.0%

44.1–48.0%

40.1–44.0%

36.1–40.0%

32.1–36.0%

28.1–32.0%

24.1–28.0%

20.1–24.0%

16.1–20.0%

12.1–16.0%

8.1–12.0%

4.1–8.0%

0.0–4.0%

Find schools offering this major at PrincetonReview.com.

Careers and Salary

The starting salary for most technology education majors is in the $30,000 to $40,000 range. Salaries are difficult to estimate, however, because there are so many capacities in which you can use your degree.

CAREER OPTIONS

Computer Engineer/Systems Analyst

Computer Operator/Programmer

Information Manager

Internet/Intranet Technologies Manager

Network Engineer

Professor

Software Developer

Teacher

Telecommunications Specialist

TELECOMMUNICATIONS

Basics

When you answer the phone, send an e-mail, or relax in front of your favorite sitcom, you are being supported by a team of telecommunications professionals whether you realize it or not. Telecommunications professionals are the folks who make all of our newest technology possible because they either deliver it to our fingertips or cook it up from scratch.

Within the field of telecommunications, a student can specify in any number of roles that will require different levels of education. For those who want a more physical role, a job as a line installer is a perfect fit. Line installers construct poles, towers and networks of underground trenches for the wires and cables that run information through phones, televisions and Internet routers.

Telecommunication customer service technicians set up new accounts and act as the first line of support for customers with problems. Customer service techs need to have a deep understanding of the systems they work with to troubleshoot and request on-site service for outages.

An even deeper understanding of the systems and their parameters is required of the computer programmers and software engineers who write and apply the programs the deliver information as well as those who supervise line installers and customer service technicians.

Deciding which level of involvement a student wants to have in telecommunications is up him or her, but the varying degrees of education can be utilized for any of the specifications. Students can be certified for entry-level jobs in online courses that may take less than a year, but longer course work will be required for managers and engineers.

If you like Telecommunications, you may also like...

Mass communications, computer sciences, video production, graphic design, video game development

---

SAMPLE COLLEGE CURRICULUM FOR TELECOMMUNICATIONS

Business Communication

Calculus

Computer Networking

Database Systems

English Composition

Management

Network Management

Systems Architecture

Technical Writing

Telecommunication Systems

Suggested High School prep for Telecommunications

Students looking for an edge in the telecommunications realm should familiarize themselves with basic math, science, computer and communication or social sciences. Additionally, it may be advantageous to work with professionals in telecommunications to see the day-to-day activities involved with the various roles a telecommunications specialist includes. Some co-op programs may offer shadowing or work-study programs.

Fun Facts

The U.S. Bureau of Labor and Statistics expects careers in telecommunications to grow by approximately 7 percent through the year 2012. This growth is based mainly on additional demand for upgrading to improved services such as fiber optic lines, wireless technology and advance equipment.

Careers and Salary

Data from the Bureau of Labor Statistics in 2002 cites several different salary ranges for each of the careers within Telecommunications. Customer service representatives reported a median salary of $39,000, line installers reported an average of $45,000 a year, and telecommunications managers reported a median salary of $70,000.

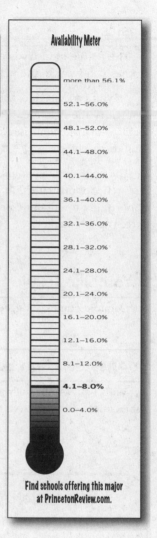

Availability Meter

more than 56.1%
52.1–56.0%
48.1–52.0%
44.1–48.0%
40.1–44.0%
36.1–40.0%
32.1–36.0%
28.1–32.0%
24.1–28.0%
20.1–24.0%
16.1–20.0%
12.1–16.0%
8.1–12.0%
4.1–8.0%
0.0–4.0%

Find schools offering this major at PrincetonReview.com.

CAREER OPTIONS

Advertising Executive	Marketing Executive	Telecommunications Specialist
Computer Programmer	Media Specialist	Video Game Designer/Developer
Customer Service Technician	Network Manager	Web Master/Manager
Digital Artist	Phone Line Installer	Website Designer
Graphic Designer	Publicist	Writer

TEXTILE ENGINEERING

Basics

The textile industry is one of the largest in America, producing everything from the fabric used in the clothes you wear to the plastic in IV tubes.

As you can imagine, an industry so vital and important to our society needs well-trained engineers to help carry the field forward. As a textile engineer, you could help fill that role. From research and development to management issues, textile engineering majors have a wide array of options into which they can plug themselves.

The engineering behind the textile industry is cutting-edge, so be prepared for some intense and exciting research opportunities. In addition to research, many schools also offer textile engineering majors the opportunity to combine engineering and business courses, giving them an added edge as they prepare to enter the job market.

If You Like Textile Engineering, You May Also Like . . .

Ceramic engineering, ceramics, industrial design

Suggested High School Prep for Textile Engineering

Math, baby—especially algebra, trigonometry, and calculus. Physics and chemistry are important secondary subjects you should strive to master.

SAMPLE COLLEGE CURRICULUM FOR TEXTILE ENGINEERING

Applied Statistics for Textiles

Calculus

Dynamics I

Fabric Design and Engineering

Fiber to Yarn Engineering

Introduction to Dye and Finish

Linear Differential Equations

Statistics

Textile Engineering Design

Textile Test Instruction

Fun Facts

Did You Know?

The U.S. textile industry is the most efficient and productive manufacturer of textiles in the world. It's an $8a billion a year industry.

Careers and Salary

The average starting salary for textile engineering majors is $30,000.

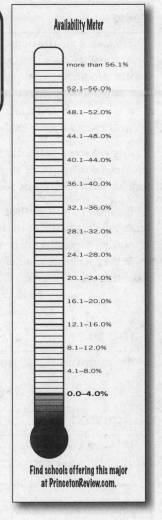

Availability Meter

more than 56.1%

52.1–56.0%

48.1–52.0%

44.1–48.0%

40.1–44.0%

36.1–40.0%

32.1–36.0%

28.1–32.0%

24.1–28.0%

20.1–24.0%

16.1–20.0%

12.1–16.0%

8.1–12.0%

4.1–8.0%

0.0–4.0%

Find schools offering this major at PrincetonReview.com.

CAREER OPTIONS

Plastics Manufacturer	Product Designer	Textile Manufacturer

THEATER

Basics

Theater is an artistic expression in which actors and actresses perform in front of a live audience. But theater majors do more than just act on stage. As a theater major, your college experience will of course involve productions, but your role in those productions will vary widely. Theater majors get experience in stage management, directing, stage lighting, costuming, set design, and scriptwriting. As an actor you'll study movement, voice, and dance. And as with any art form, you'll learn how it got where it is today by exploring the history and theory of theater as well as a great deal of literature.

In most schools' theater programs, in the course of four years you'll be asked to choose a concentration. Choices usually include musical theater, production, stage management, and scriptwriting, but concentrations vary by school—be sure your area of interest is offered.

It's important to realize that a theater major is not an automatic ticket to Broadway. Theater is a competitive field; the image of the actor/waiter is both a cliché and a reality. Only a very few people will end up supporting themselves from theater alone, and many choose to work at jobs such as waiting tables or temping while they seek out auditions and opportunities. However, those with a true passion for theater are willing to make these sacrifices.

If You Like Theater, You May Also Like . . .

Art, creative writing, dance, English, fashion design, industrial design, music

Suggested High School Prep for Theater

If you're considering a theater major, by all means get involved with your high school drama club. Usually, high school productions are managed mainly by students, giving you the opportunity to explore various musical and dramatic productions both on stage and off. Music and English courses will be useful. And read as much as you can. Get to know Shakespeare, Tennessee Williams, and Arthur Miller, for example, to name just a few of the great writers for the stage.

> ### SAMPLE COLLEGE CURRICULUM FOR THEATER
>
> Acting Fundamentals
>
> Dance and Movement
>
> Directing
>
> Dramatic Literature
>
> History of Theater
>
> Oral Interpretation
>
> Script Analysis
>
> Set Design
>
> Stage Lighting
>
> Technical Production Fundamentals

Fun Facts

Quotable

"All the world's a stage."

—William Shakespeare

Star Light, Star Bright . . .

Best Play: *The History Boys*

Best Musical: *Jersey Boys*

Best Revival—Play: *Awake and Sing!*

Best Revival—Musical: *The Pajama Game*

Best Actor—Play: Richard Griffiths, *The History Boys*

Best Actress—Play: Cynthia Nixon, *Rabbit Hole*

Best Actor—Musical: John Lloyd Young, *Jersey Boys*

Best Actress—Musical: LaChanze, *The Color Purple*

Best Featured Actor—Play: Ian McDiarmid, *The History Boys*

Best Featured Actress—Play: Frances de la Tour, *The History Boys*

Best Featured Actor—Musical: Christian Hoff, *Jersey Boys*

Best Featured Actress—Musical: Beth Leavel, *The Drowsy Chaperone*

Best Director—Play: Nicholas Hytner, *The History Boys*

Best Director—Musical: John Doyle, *Sweeney Todd*

(Source: www.tonyawards.com/en_US/nominees/winners.html)

Famous People Who Majored in Theater

From the New York University drama program: Alec Baldwin, Keith Cobb, Andrew McCarthy, David Petrarca, Adam Sandler, Chandra Wilson

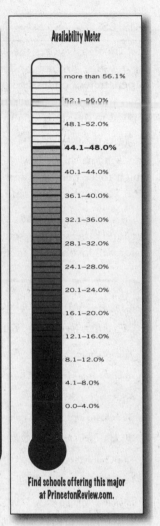

Availability Meter

more than 56.1%

52.1–56.0%

48.1–52.0%

44.1–48.0%

40.1–44.0%

36.1–40.0%

32.1–36.0%

28.1–32.0%

24.1–28.0%

20.1–24.0%

16.1–20.0%

12.1–16.0%

8.1–12.0%

4.1–8.0%

0.0–4.0%

Find schools offering this major at PrincetonReview.com.

Careers and Salary

Starting salaries for theater majors are difficult to predict; they depend on your level of commitment, the opportunities in your area, and who is employing you. Salaries can range from $6,500 to $41,600. Many theater opportunities are seasonal.

CAREER OPTIONS

Actor	Comedian	Stage Technician
Agent	Film Director	Talent Scout
Artist	Performing Arts Administrator	Writer

THEOLOGY

Basics

"Theology," writes theologian Patrick Granfield in the introduction to his book, *Theologians at Work*, "is the questing, probing, and searching of the Word of God; it is a rational effort, guided by faith, that attempts to penetrate the message of God." You might think that theology is the study of the Christian faith alone. Not so. Although linguistically theology is Western-rooted (the Greek theos means god), the term can be applied to the study of all world religions.

As a theology major, you'll explore how, according to the *Encyclopedia Britannica*, "the believer understands his faith" or how "a religion's practitioners understand their religion." You'll examine the ways in which these believers and practitioners define, defend, and verify various elements of their religious doctrine. You'll attempt to find a place for religious beliefs among the realms of science, history, and logic.

"Theology deals with great words," writes Granfield, words like "love," "fatherhood," "motherhood," "justice," and others that describe issues of universal importance no matter what one's religion is. Your theology major will involve you in an array of other disciplines, including history, philosophy, literature, international studies, anthropology, cosmology, ethics, science, and languages. This field of study is so variegated, in fact, that the *Encyclopedia Britannica* considers it "a microcosmic image of the university."

SAMPLE COLLEGE CURRICULUM FOR THEOLOGY

Afro-Atlantic Religions

Ancient and Medieval Church History

Apocalyptic Literature

Buddhism and Social Change

Buddhism in America

The Character of God

Early Christian Monasticism

Hispanic Ministry

Introduction to Hinduism

Introduction to Liturgy

Introduction to Mesopotamian Religion

Liturgical Theology

Modern Spirituality

New Testament Ethics

The Spiritual Senses

Spirituality in the Scientific Age

The Synoptic Gospels

Theology and Science

Theology of St. Bonaventure

Three Covenants of Israel

If You Like Theology, You May Also Like . . .

Ancient studies, biblical studies, classics, Hebrew, history, Islamic studies, Jewish studies, Medieval and Renaissance studies, Middle Eastern studies, peace studies, philosophy, religious studies, youth ministries

Suggested High School Prep for Theology

If you go to a parochial high school, you're in luck—chances are some sort of theology or religion courses will be part of the curriculum. But because theology involves such a wide variety of disciplines, you'd be wise to explore courses in history, philosophy, literature, ethics, science, and languages.

Fun Facts

Potential Theologians, Beware

Theologian Robert McAfee Brown points out that a study of theology can occur only after some event takes place that can then become the subject of that study. He points out a potential danger in overzealous theology endeavors: "It is the perennial temptation of theology to seek to replace that about which it is reporting, as though (to borrow an image from Kierkegaard) one could expect a love letter to be intrinsically more important to its possessor than the actual presence of the beloved."

(Source: quoted in *Theology and Church in Times of Change*, edited by Edward LeRoy Long and Robert Handy)

Quotable

"The true meaning of religion is thus not simply morality, but morality touched by emotion."
—Matthew Arnold (1822–1888)

Careers and Salary

Your starting salary will depend mostly on where you choose to live and how you use your degree, but an estimated average for religious clergy is in the $30,000 to $40,000 range.

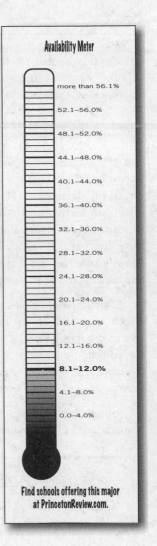

Availability Meter

more than 56.1%

52.1–56.0%

48.1–52.0%

44.1–48.0%

40.1–44.0%

36.1–40.0%

32.1–36.0%

28.1–32.0%

24.1–28.0%

20.1–24.0%

16.1–20.0%

12.1–16.0%

8.1–12.0%

4.1–8.0%

0.0–4.0%

Find schools offering this major
at PrincetonReview.com.

CAREER OPTIONS		
Clergy—Priest, Rabbi, Minister	Professor	Writer
Philosopher	Theologian	

TOURISM

Basics

World events, the economy, tastes and trends, and the technology of travel—all of these and more have an effect on global tourism. Despite a decline in American travel in recent years, Peopleandplanet.net reports, "By some measure, tourism may already be the world's largest industry, with annual revenue approaching $500 billion." A major in tourism will get you a foot in the door to this ever-booming industry. And the sky's the limit—quite literally—on where you go from there. Tourism majors aim to discover the world's top destinations and how to best encourage people to visit them. From the dreamy, steamy islands of the South Pacific to Sweden's Icehotel, you'll learn how to make guests feel welcome and enjoy a safe and memorable stay. A tourism major covers the whole spectrum of travel—you'll study everything from the booking of flights to facilitating operations at a resort hotel. You'll use the tourism industry's most prevalent electronic databases and discover how to navigate other travel-related computer programs and systems. Count on learning how to market and sell travel destinations and products, including how to promote tourism in new places and how to sustain interest in classic tourist destinations. In addition, you'll examine how Internet technology is affecting the tourism industry and how to use this technology most advantageously. Your tourism major should also touch on the effect tourism has on the environment—and how certain aspects of the industry are working to minimize those effects.

Tourism is more global than ever, and this major will explore the role it plays in the world—how it affects cities and countries both economically and culturally. You'll learn where the industry has been and where it might go in the future. (Is a moon resort really viable? You'll be able to tell us.) Before you graduate, you should be a pro at giving knowledgeable and friendly customer service and managing all aspects of the travel experience. After college, you'll have the skills you need to pursue a career for an airline, a travel agency, or many other sorts of travel service organization.

Tourism is an interdisciplinary major, and your course work will draw from accounting, marketing, communication, and other business courses, as well as courses in geography and specific elements of tourism.

SAMPLE COLLEGE CURRICULUM FOR TOURISM

Airline Computer Reservations

Business Travel

Computerized Reservation Systems

Customer Service

Economics of Tourism

Geography

Hospitality Operations

Tour Guiding and Management

Tour Organization

Tourism Marketing

Tourism Products

World Tourism

If You Like Tourism, You May Also Like . . .

Advertising, business administration and management, economics, entrepreneurship, international business, international relations, international studies, managerial economics

Suggested High School Prep for Tourism

Since you'll be taking courses in a wide variety of fields for your tourism major, the best way to prepare is to take classes in many different areas in high school. Math, sciences, and the humanities are all important. People who work in tourism must be excellent communicators, so any classes that improve your writing, public speaking, and reading skills will be especially valuable. Try to become familiar with the world we live in. Take a course in geography, or pore over maps. Tourism is a major economic force in even the smallest towns, so you might investigate how tourism is at work in your own community.

Fun Facts

The World's Top Tourism Destinations

1. France
2. United States
3. Spain
4. Italy
5. China
6. United Kingdom
7. Russian Federation
8. Mexico
9. Canada
10. Germany
11. Austria
12. Poland
13. Hungary
14. Hong Kong
15. Greece

(Source: www.infoplease.com)

Top International Destinations for American Tourists

1. Mexico
2. Canada
3. United Kingdom
4. France
5. Germany
6. Italy
7. Japan
8. Spain
9. Netherlands
10. Switzerland
11. Bahamas
12. Jamaica
13. Hong Kong
14. Republic of Korea
15. Ireland

(Source: www.infoplease.com)

Careers and Salary

Since tourism majors pursue a wide variety of careers, determining an average starting salary is difficult. Travel agents, to choose just one field, make approximately $26,000 to start.

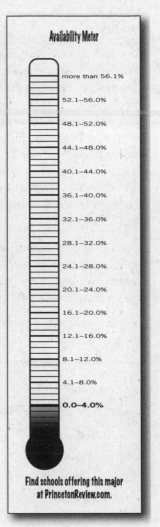

Availability Meter

more than 56.1%
52.1–56.0%
48.1–52.0%
44.1–48.0%
40.1–44.0%
36.1–40.0%
32.1–36.0%
28.1–32.0%
24.1–28.0%
20.1–24.0%
16.1–20.0%
12.1–16.0%
8.1–12.0%
4.1–8.0%
0.0–4.0%

Find schools offering this major at PrincetonReview.com.

CAREER OPTIONS

Brochure Writer	Journalist	Tourism Manager
Entrepreneur	Publicist	Travel Agent
Hospitality Manager	Tour Guide	Writer
Hotel Manager		

TOXICOLOGY

Basics

A skull and crossbones might be a suitable symbol for this major. (That's one way to explain that tattoo. . .) Toxicology basically tackles issues involved with various types of poisons. According to the University of Arizona, toxicology is "the study of how chemical and physical agents adversely affect living organisms." If you choose to major in toxicology, you'll learn about these chemical and physical agents—where they lurk in the environment, how humans are exposed to them, and the problems they create in different arenas, like the clinical, industrial, and legal fields. This includes the study of how these agents enter the body, what happens to them once they're inside, and how they can damage cells, tissues, and organs. You'll also learn how toxicants pose a threat to our animal friends, along with examining poisons found in plants and foods, such as pesticides, food additives, and waste from industry. You'll learn how to test food and water for unhealthy or dangerous levels of toxicants, and you'll gain the skills necessary to counteract their effects or eliminate them altogether.

Toxicology is an important field for obvious reasons, and advancements can be rapid. Your course work might involve studying what sorts of environmental agents lead to cancer or the effects these agents have on the neurosystem. You might engage in a study of chemical genomics and examine how toxicants affect gene expression—a hot topic these days. Or you might immerse yourself in drug research and development.

Of course, your studies will go beyond the toxic agents themselves. You'll study safety procedures necessary to implement and adhere to during research, and you'll learn how to collect and analyze data from the experiments you perform. Legal aspects of chemical use by industries and individuals will also be hashed out. And you'll gain experience with research through laboratory work and, perhaps, an internship.

SAMPLE COLLEGE CURRICULUM FOR TOXICOLOGY

Analytical Chemistry

Aquatic Toxicology

Bioorganic Chemistry

Biostatistics

Chemical Speciation

Ecological Toxicology

Ecology

Environmental Geoscience

Food Toxicology

Mathematical Modeling

Molecular Biology

Neurobehavioral Toxicology

Paleobiology

Pesticides in the Environment

Pharmacology

Veterinary Toxicology

If You Like Toxicology, You May Also Like . . .

Biology, biomedical engineering, biomedical science, chemical engineering, chemistry, epidemiology, experimental pathology, molecular biology, nursing, occupational therapy, pharmacology, pharmacy, physical therapy, premedicine, pre-pharmacy, public health, rehabilitation services

Suggested High School Prep for Toxicology

Toxicology is a science-intensive field, so your focus in high school should be on taking as many challenging science courses as possible. Biology, chemistry, and physics are all invaluable, especially if they have laboratory components. And since all scientists must be able to pass their ideas along to others clearly and effectively, you should take humanities courses that will improve your communication skills.

Fun Facts

Toxicology Fights Cancer

Have you ever heard of the National Toxicology Program? The purpose of this program is to identify chemicals in the environment that contribute to cancer. The NTP and the National Institute of Environmental Health Sciences are connected either directly or indirectly with about one-third of the toxicology studies around the world. Because of their efforts, many cancer-causing substances have been banned, such as methylene chloride, which was once used to decaffeinate coffee, and dichlorvos, once used in pets' flea collars.

(Source: http://ntp-server.niehs.nih.gov/)

Insider's Journal

For more on toxicology, check out jatox.com, the website for the *Journal of Analytical Toxicology*, which claims to be "the international source for practical clinical and forensic applications for isolating, identifying, and quantitating potentially toxic substances." Read abstracts of articles and peruse the contents of current and past issues.

Careers and Salary

Although the starting salary for toxicology majors varies depending on where you live, how much experience you've had, and how you use your skills, you can most likely expect a starting salary of about $30,000 or more for most toxicology jobs.

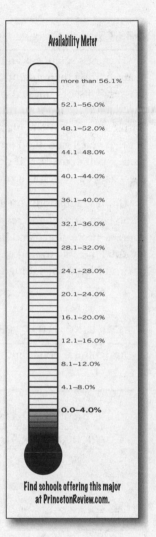

Availability Meter

more than 56.1%
52.1–56.0%
48.1–52.0%
44.1 48.0%
40.1–44.0%
36.1–40.0%
32.1–36.0%
28.1–32.0%
24.1–28.0%
20.1–24.0%
16.1–20.0%
12.1–16.0%
8.1–12.0%
4.1–8.0%
0.0–4.0%

Find schools offering this major at PrincetonReview.com.

CAREER OPTIONS

Chemist	Pharmacologist	Scientist
Drug Developer	Professor	Teacher
Drug Researcher	Researcher	Toxicologist
Pharmacist		

TURFGRASS SCIENCE

Basics

Turfgrass science is an interdisciplinary major that involves the use of grasses and plants to improve and beautify the environment. It combines business and management theory with the down-to-earth study of grasses, soils, ornamental plants, and all those pesky critters that affect lawns and fairways far and wide. If you decide to major in turfgrass science, you'll take courses in—among other things—biology, chemistry, business management, plant pathology, entomology, and soil and water science. During summers, it's a good bet that you'll gain good on-the-job experience in mandatory internships with landscape and lawn care companies, golf courses, and departments of parks and recreation. You'll probably make tall cash over the summers as well, which is a pretty nice perk.

Upon graduation, you'll be prepared for careers in the landscape industry, producing and maintaining plants and grasses for recreational, aesthetic, and environmental uses. You'll know your way around golf courses, professional and big-time college athletic fields, sod farms, and every other landscape-related industry. You'll be able to find employment with lawn care companies, parks, agri-chemical firms, cemeteries, and environmental consulting firms.

If You Like Turfgrass Science, You May Also Like . . .

Agricultural economics, agricultural and biological engineering, agricultural technology management, agriculture, agronomy and crop science, animal science, art, biochemistry, biology, botany and plant biology, cell biology, chemistry, ecology, entomology, environmental science, feed science, forestry, genetics, geology, grain science, landscape architecture, microbiology, natural resources conservation, plant pathology, sculpture, soil science, sustainable resource management

> ### SAMPLE COLLEGE CURRICULUM FOR TURFGRASS SCIENCE
>
> Chemistry
> Crop Science
> Soil Science
> Entomology
> Internship
> Plant Pathology
> Plant Physiology
> Plant Propagation
> Plant Taxonomy
> Turfgrass Diseases
> Turfgrass Management
> Turfgrass Selection
> Urban and Sports Turf
> Weed Science

Suggested High School Prep for Turfgrass Science

You'll need a strong foundation in the basic sciences. If you are planning to major in turfgrass science in college, you should take courses in biology, chemistry, algebra, and trigonometry. And don't forget about art. You want to develop an adequate understanding of design elements. Everything that you can learn about climate, soil, water, and plants will be helpful as well.

AGRICULTURE AND RELATED FIELDS/SCIENCE AND TECHNOLOGY

Fun Facts

Name That Legend . . .

"What an incredible Cinderella story, this unknown comes outta nowhere to lead the pack, at Augusta. He's on his final hole, he's about 455 yards away—he's gonna hit about a two-iron, I think. Oh, he got all 'a that one! The crowd is standing on its feet here, the normally reserved Augusta crowd—going wild—for this young Cinderella, he's come outta nowhere, he's got about 350 yards left, he's gonna hit about a five-iron, don't you think? He's got a beautiful back swing—that's—Oh, he got all 'a that one! He's gotta be pleased with that . . . The crowd is just on its feet here, uh—He's the Cinderella boy, uh—tears in his eyes I guess as he lines up this last shot, he's got about 195 yards left, he's got about a—it looks like he's got about an eight-iron. This crowd has gone deathly silent—Cinderella story—outta nowhere, a former greens keeper now . . . about to become the Masters champion. It looks like a mirac—It's in the Hole!"

—Bill Murray as Carl Spackler, assistant greens keeper, in *Caddyshack* (1980)

What Makes a Good Quality Turfgrass?

According to the folks at *Digmagazine*:

- Dark green color
- Good density
- Fine leaf texture
- Carpet-like feel and appearance
- Resistance to damage from disease or insects
- Adaptability to a wide range of temperatures, soils, and mowing heights

Careers and Salary

Starting salaries for turfgrass science majors range from about $22,000 to $32,000 annually.

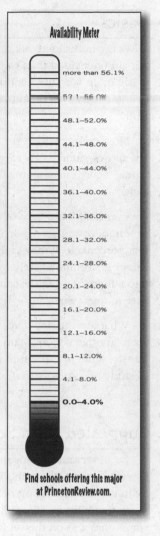

Availability Meter

more than 56.1%

52.1–56.0%

48.1–52.0%

44.1–48.0%

40.1–44.0%

36.1–40.0%

32.1–36.0%

28.1–32.0%

24.1–28.0%

20.1–24.0%

16.1–20.0%

12.1–16.0%

8.1–12.0%

4.1–8.0%

0.0–4.0%

Find schools offering this major at PrincetonReview.com.

CAREER OPTIONS

Ecologist	Environmentalist/	Environmental Scientist

UNDECIDED

Basics

Being undecided (a.k.a. undeclared) in your major is a decidedly good thing. Why? Because it's better to remain undecided than to jump into a major, or multiple majors, for no other reason than "everyone else is doing it." In fact, the majority of college students remain undecided through their freshman year, and academic advisors warn students against declaring a major without a wholehearted commitment to a field of study.

Most colleges don't require students to declare a major until the end of their sophomore year. This policy allows students to explore their interests during their first couple of semesters in a college setting, where a core curriculum and required survey classes can help students assess their passion for different subjects.

Ever heard of a "rate of attrition"? That's the percentage of students that colleges don't expect to return to school over a set academic period. Students who rush prematurely to declare a major sometimes add to that percentage. If they end up not liking what they're studying or find that it won't help them achieve their career goals immediately out of college, they panic. They feel desperate, as though they've dug themselves into a hole they can't escape. They think they've progressed too far into the course work to be able to graduate in four years.

What are the drawbacks to being undecided? You could run into some red tape if you decide to transfer to another school. Many colleges require a declaration of major on prospective transfers' applications, as transfer students are often well into their college careers and have reached the point where having a focus of study becomes crucial to successful completion of a degree in four years.

Suggested High School Prep for Undecided

Be observant of your interests. Do not, however, confuse interests with aptitude. You may be excellent at a subject but don't find it thrilling. With college still ahead of you, any field of study can be mastered, no matter how challenging or intimidating it seems. One tool that empowers incoming college students with more flexibility is AP credit. If you complete an Advanced Placement course and receive a 4 or a 5 (and sometimes a 3) on the subject test, you can earn college credits toward graduating early or fulfill some core requirements. This frees you up to explore more electives and niche subjects.

SAMPLE COLLEGE CURRICULUM FOR UNDECIDED

Undecided majors should focus on completing the core curriculum of the school they're attending. A core curriculum usually covers a wide array of subjects, so as you complete it, you'll get a better idea of what it is you want to study. Plus, you'll be earning credit toward graduation. A core curriculum traditionally consists of one or two philosophy or theology courses, one or two English or literature courses, one or two math or science courses, one or two history courses, and one or two language courses.

Fun Facts

Don't Panic

Harvard University urges undecided students to pay attention to their tastes—the articles they read in the newspaper, the sections of the bookstore in which they browse, the issues about which they are passionate, and the people in the news whom they admire the most—as they consider possible majors. "Remember," Harvard's website reads, "just looking at something does not in any way commit you to it. You could decide right away that it bores you or you could pursue it a little deeper."

To encourage students to take the proper time and consideration into the declaration of a major, many schools have designed departments to support their students' process of self-discovery. State University of New York—Farmingdale, for example, offers an Undeclared Major Program as well as a course called Holistic Education and Career Planning, a 100-level course through which students gain course credit as well as insight into possible majors.

The main thing is to feel secure about your indecision, which seems to be something of a paradox. As the University of North Texas's website explains, "Indeed, you may help yourself in the long run by not declaring [a major] right away. Most first-year students are unsure about their educational direction. Studies show that two-thirds of the students who declare their major on admission to college change it two or three times before they graduate [and as many as 75 percent change it at least once]. Many high-achieving high school students come to college as undeclared because they have multiple fields of interest and are not ready to select only one. It makes you no less serious about your education." Some schools count their undeclared major "department" as their largest on campus. So you won't be alone.

Savor It

Recent grads on how to choose a major:

"Treat your first four years of college like a second high school without parents and have fun learning who you want to be. Save your specializing for grad school."

—C. S. Mann, University of Florida alumnus. C. S. had six majors.

"I enjoyed college, enjoyed engineering, made good friends . . . however, with the knowledge I have now, I would have sucked more out of college than I did. I would have taken any elective I was curious about, regardless of whether or not I considered it part of my 'career path'—whatever that may be. I would have been involved in theater earlier, and probably studied it in school (at least as a minor)."

—J. P. Lopez, Rice University alumnus. J. P. earned an engineering degree and worked in that industry for four years before turning to acting.

"I just felt so much pressure [to choose a major], like if I made the wrong decision now, the rest of my life would turn out wrong. . . . I actually feel bad for people who pick a major based on what they think they want to do later. As a sophomore in college, you don't even know about a quarter of the different jobs that are out there, so it's kind of a crime that in this country we're encouraged to get so specialized so soon."

—Magda Pecsenye, Bryn Mawr College alumna. Magda was a comparative literature major and now works in the culinary arts.

"Seven years of college down the drain."

—Faber College's John "Bluto" Blutarsky, played by the late John Belushi in the movie *Animal House*. Bluto had just learned that he would be expelled. He was premed.

Careers and Salary

All careers are possible, and the sky's the limit on salary. (It should be noted that salary could also be in the cellar.)

URBAN PLANNING

Basics

In New York it's knowing how to cram yourself and two roommates into a one-bedroom apartment that costs $2,500 a month and still be able to tell yourself, "It's worth it." In Chicago it's knowing how to actually get from your house to your car in the winter without the loss of any extremities to frostbite.

Every city in America has its own feel, style, and culture. The point of the urban planning major is to get beyond all that by looking at the way our cities are designed, constructed, and planned. Urban planning majors study the socioeconomic factors and conditions behind housing projects while also studying the effect of public transportation in suburban areas. It's both an analytical and quantitative approach, one that combines policy, statistics, a sense of history, and a lot more.

Urban planners help us look at the ways we can improve our neighborhoods, preserving some of the past while keeping an eye open for future improvements. So whether you want to help plan the next Central Park in Peoria, Illinois, or design a way to unclog freeway congestion in Los Angeles, the urban planning major will give you the tools you need to literally change the face of the American landscape.

If You Like Urban Planning, You May Also Like . . .

American studies, archaeology, architectural history, architecture, civil engineering, economics, environmental science, political science, public administration, public policy analysis, sociology, statistics, surveying, urban studies

Sample College Curriculum for Urban Planning

Analytical Methods and Graphic Design Techniques

Community Planning Workshop

Economics

Issues in Planning

Issues in Urban and Environmental Planning

Physical and Environmental Planning

Planning Administration and Law

Planning Methods

Quantitative Reasoning

Theory and Ethics

Theory and Ethics in Planning

Urban and Regional Planning Analysis

Suggested High School Prep for Urban Planning

Although years of playing *Sim City* may be helpful, the best possible preparation you can have is a strong background in math (trigonometry could come into play here) and the humanities. After all, before you can plan an entire city, you'll have to make your ideas understood.

Fun Facts

Did You Know?

Nationally, 70 percent of all state and local law enforcement activities are spent on traffic-related issues.

Careers and Salary

The average starting salary for an urban planning major is between $24,000 and $36,000.

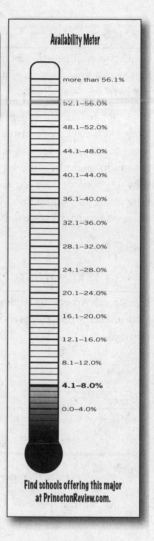

Availability Meter

more than 56.1%

52.1–56.0%

48.1–52.0%

44.1–48.0%

40.1–44.0%

36.1–40.0%

32.1–36.0%

28.1–32.0%

24.1–28.0%

20.1–24.0%

16.1–20.0%

12.1–16.0%

8.1–12.0%

4.1–8.0%

0.0–4.0%

Find schools offering this major
at PrincetonReview.com.

CAREER OPTIONS

City Planner

Ecologist

Economist

Environmentalist/

Environmental Scientist

URBAN STUDIES

Basics

Urban studies is an interdisciplinary major borrowing from history, public policy, government, economics, and sociology. Cities have a lot going on in them, and the study of them requires a working knowledge of many related fields.

Why are cities arranged the way they are? What are the economic and social factors that physically shape a city? What's a city's history, and what role does that history play in the city's continuing development or regression? These are just some of the difficult questions that urban studies majors try to answer. Their goal is to help us understand how and why our cities function the way they do. From the operation of local politics to problems of race and class, everything is closely scrutinized to improve municipal physical layout, education, and commerce. With the help of urban studies majors, we can address and resolve some of the most complicated issues affecting our cities.

If You Like Urban Studies, You May Also Like . . .

African American studies, American history, American studies, Asian American studies, business administration and management, economics, public administration, public policy analysis, sociology, statistics, urban planning

Suggested High School Prep for Urban Studies

Much of what you will encounter as an urban studies major will be unique to your college education. The best preparation you can have is a strong background in history and economics. That civics class you thought was silly might come in handy with urban studies.

> ### SAMPLE COLLEGE CURRICULUM FOR URBAN STUDIES
>
> Homelessness
>
> The Industrial City
>
> Origins and Cultures of Cities
>
> Philanthropy and the City
>
> Planning Urban Spaces
>
> Race and Ethnic Relations
>
> Religion and Public Life
>
> Social Justice and Urban Development
>
> U.S. Urban History Since the Civil War
>
> Urban Education
>
> Urban Redevelopment

Fun Facts

Some of the Most Important Books on Urban Studies

- *Exploring the City* by Ulf Hannerz (1980)
- *Urban Anthropology* by Richard G. Fox (1977)
- *Anthropology of the City* by Edwin Eames and Judith Granich Goode (1977)
- *Cities in Transformation: Class, Capital, and the State* by Michael Peter Smith (ed.) (1984)
- *Marxism and the Metropolis*, 2nd ed. by William K. Tabb and Larry Sawers (eds.) (1984)
- *The Grand Domestic Revolution: A History of Feminist Designs for American Homes, Neighborhoods, and Cities* by Dolores Hayden (1981).

Expected Population of the World's Five Largest Cities in 2015

1. Tokyo, Japan: 28.7 million
2. Bombay, India: 27.4 million
3. Lagos, Nigeria: 24.4 million
4. Shanghai, China: 23.4 million
5. Jakarta, Indonesia: 21.2 million

Careers and Salary

Urban studies starting salaries are dependent on the career path you choose; the average range is $24,000 to $30,000.

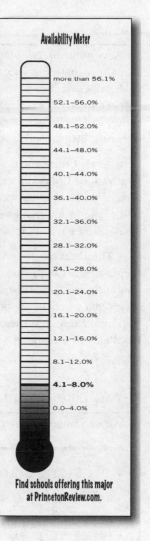

Availability Meter

more than 56.1%

52.1–56.0%

48.1–52.0%

44.1–48.0%

40.1–44.0%

36.1–40.0%

32.1–36.0%

28.1–32.0%

24.1–28.0%

20.1–24.0%

16.1–20.0%

12.1–16.0%

8.1–12.0%

4.1–8.0%

0.0–4.0%

Find schools offering this major at PrincetonReview.com.

CAREER OPTIONS

Attorney	Political Aide	Politician
City Planner	Political Campaign Worker	Professor
Labor Relations Specialist	Political Scientist	Sociologist
Lobbyist		

URDU LANGUAGE AND LITERATURE

Basics

According to *Ethnologue*, a world languages reference project, Urdu can be found in Afghanistan, Bahrain, Bangladesh, Botswana, Fiji, Germany, Guyana, India, Malawi, Mauritius, Nepal, Norway, Oman, Pakistan, Qatar, Saudi Arabia, South Africa, Thailand, the United Arab Emirates, the United Kingdom, and Zambia. In fact, it's the official language of Pakistan, one of the numerous official languages of India, and a prominent language in portions of Afghanistan. And let's not forget the United States. The *2006 Time Almanac* estimates that more than 260,000 Americans over the age of five speak Urdu in their homes.

As an Urdu language and literature major, you'll tap into this vibrant language, progressing from basic to advanced Urdu courses, delving into linguistics and dialects along the way. As Pakistan and its neighbors assume an increasingly prominent position on the global stage, your Urdu training will prepare you to play a key role in international relations, business ventures, and academic studies associated with South Asia. You'll also be poised to work with Urdu-speaking immigrant communities in America and abroad.

The Urdu language will also serve as your portal into a long literary legacy. You'll start back in the thirteenth-century with Muhammad Urfi and stretch all the way to the contemporary accomplishments of wide-ranging poets, dramatists, novelists, short-story writers, and critics. The literature will help you discover incredible works of art and uncover the evolution of ideas—religious, social, political, and so on—over the period of many centuries. In this sense, the timeline of literature will inform your knowledge of present-day Pakistan and the region.

If You Like Urdu Language and Literature, You May Also Like...

African languages, literatures, and linguistics, Australian/Oceanic/Pacific languages, literatures, and linguistics, African studies, anthropology, archeology, Asian American studies, Asian history, Chinese, East Asian studies, Egyptology, Hindi, Hindu Studies, Islamic studies, Middle Eastern studies, Mongolian language and literature, religious studies, South Asian studies, Southeast Asian studies

> ### SAMPLE COLLEGE CURRICULUM FOR URDU LANGUAGE AND LITERATURE
>
> Advanced Urdu
>
> Contemporary Pakistan
>
> Conversation and Composition
>
> Intermediate Urdu
>
> Introduction to Urdu
>
> Modern Islam
>
> Postmodernism and Pakistani Literature
>
> Selections in Hindi-Urdu Poetry
>
> South Asian History
>
> Urdu Script: Nastaliq

Suggested High School Prep for Urdu Language and Literature

While many aspects of a college prep curriculum will serve your needs, you'll find literature, world history, and foreign language classes particularly helpful. We realize Urdu probably isn't offered at your high school, but training in any foreign language will get you moving in the right direction.

Fun Facts

Did You Know?

Urdu and Hindi are very similar languages—when spoken, at least. The grammar and much of the vocabulary you memorize for Urdu translates noun for noun into Hindi. (Considering that Hindi and Urdu are the two most common languages on the Indian subcontinent, this is pretty good bang for your buck.) Though, the primary difference comes in the script. Urdu script is called *Nastaliq*, while Hindi script is *Nagari*.

Did You Know?

Writing in Urdu goes from the right side of the page to the left—the opposite of English.

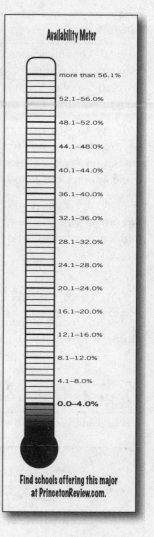

Availability Meter

more than 56.1%

52.1–56.0%

48.1–52.0%

44.1–48.0%

40.1–44.0%

36.1–40.0%

32.1–36.0%

28.1–32.0%

24.1–28.0%

20.1–24.0%

16.1–20.0%

12.1–16.0%

8.1–12.0%

4.1–8.0%

0.0–4.0%

Find schools offering this major at PrincetonReview.com.

CAREER OPTIONS

Anthropologist

Archaeologist

Archivist

Curator

Diplomat/Attaché/Foreign Service
   Officer

Documentary Filmmaker

Fundraiser/Institutional Solicitor

Journalist

Lobbyist

Professor

Sociologist

Translator

Writer

VISUAL COMMUNICATION

Basics

Visual communication is a multidisciplinary field encompassing graphic design, illustration, fine arts (like drawing and painting), multimedia, and photography. Visual communication, according to Towson University, applies the fundamentals of major art forms to "professional problem-solving." In other words, you'll be using art to convey specific ideas and messages.

There are many practical applications for visual communication. Advertising is one of many fields that rely heavily on images to convey ideas. Other fields include interior design, industrial design, and publication design. Visual communication, whether it be print-based (such as for books or magazines) or based on new computer technology is growing increasingly important in our fast-paced, image-reliant society.

Many programs require you to choose a concentration such as graphic design, illustration, or photography; others will give you a taste of many different fields. Whatever the case, an eye for detail, the ability to think creatively, and good problem-solving skills will be integral to your success.

If You Like Visual Communication, You May Also Like . . .

Advertising, art, art education, art history, drawing, fashion design, film, graphic art, interior design, painting, photography, printmaking, radio and television, sculpture, theater

Suggested High School Prep for Visual Communication

Exposing yourself to various art courses will be your best preparation for a major in visual communication. Art history, history, English, religion, and philosophy courses will start you thinking about the really big ideas that inspire people to action. And explore the world of art in your area; go to museums and galleries, look at art books, and delve into your own artistic experiments.

SAMPLE COLLEGE CURRICULUM FOR VISUAL COMMUNICATION

Advertising Design

Basic Typography

Communication and Social Behavior

Desktop Publishing

Graphics Systems Management

Multimedia Authoring

Photo Graphics

Technical Drawing

3D Animation

Typography for Industrial Design

Visual Thinking and Problem-Solving

Fun Facts

The Real Reason to Watch the Superbowl

Are you fascinated by television advertisements? If so, you might enjoy www.adcritic.com. You can watch advertisements both old and new and see which ads AdCritic considers the best.

Careers and Salary

The starting salaries for visual communication majors vary widely because visual artists often choose to work as freelancers. A reasonable estimate is in the $25,000 to $35,000 range, but that can vary depending on how you use your skills.

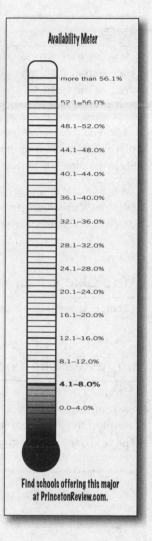

Availability Meter

more than 56.1%

52.1–56.0%

48.1–52.0%

44.1–48.0%

40.1–44.0%

36.1–40.0%

32.1–36.0%

28.1–32.0%

24.1–28.0%

20.1–24.0%

16.1–20.0%

12.1–16.0%

8.1–12.0%

4.1–8.0%

0.0–4.0%

Find schools offering this major
at PrincetonReview.com.

CAREER OPTIONS

Advertising Executive	Artist	Interior Designer
Animator	Digital Artist	Web Art Director
Art Dealer	Graphic Designer	Website Designer

VOICE

Basics

Singing your favorite parts of *Carmen* in the shower before school each morning doesn't quite count as preparation for a major in voice, but hey, it's a start. The same thing holds true for that garage band you started, or the a capella group you're in. Each of them sort of prepares you for the rigorous training and education you will receive in college as a voice major.

The voice major, as you may have already guessed, is exactly what it sounds like (no pun intended). Sometimes a concentration within a broader music major, voice is designed to develop and enhance your skills as a singer. Voice helps you to sing longer, louder, and better than ever before.

A major in voice, especially if it's a part of a broader music major, offers you more than just vocal training. Alongside your singing lessons will be classes in music theory, history, performance, and conducting, helping to make you an all-around better musician.

If You Like Voice, You May Also Like . . .

Dance, jazz studies, music, music history, piano, theater

Suggested High School Prep for Voice

Don't expect to walk in just on your music teacher's laurels. You will probably have to complete several rounds of intense auditioning to demonstrate your talent and skills, so make sure you have taken the time to develop those musical inclinations through lessons and practice. Take choir, and if your school produces them, act in the school musical for as many years as you can.

SAMPLE COLLEGE CURRICULUM FOR VOICE

Conducting

Large Ensembles

More Voice Lessons

Music Aural Training I–III

Music Form and Analysis

Music History

Music Technology

Music Theory I–V

Vocal Literature

Vocal Pedagogy

Voice Lessons

Fun Facts

Did You Know?

Jacopo Peri wrote the first opera, *Dafne*, based on the Greek myth of Daphne.

Did You Know?

During the "golden age" of opera in the late nineteenth and early twentieth century, there were more than 3,000 theaters in Italy where one could go to hear the opera. By 1992, that number had fallen to 840.

Famous People Who Majored in Voice

Kathleen Battle, Placido Domingo, Leontyne Price

Careers and Salary

The music industry is a fickle business, so starting salaries can vary dramatically and depend on your success as a musician and whether you intend to enter a specific career, such as teaching. For those considering teaching, starting salaries range from $19,000 to $30,000.

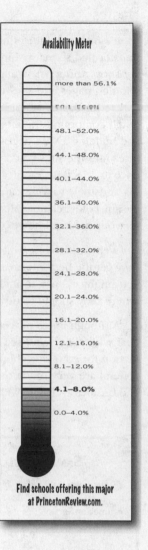

Availability Meter

more than 56.1%

50.1–56.0%

48.1–52.0%

44.1–48.0%

40.1–44.0%

36.1–40.0%

32.1–36.0%

28.1–32.0%

24.1–28.0%

20.1–24.0%

16.1–20.0%

12.1–16.0%

8.1–12.0%

4.1–8.0%

0.0–4.0%

Find schools offering this major at PrincetonReview.com.

CAREER OPTIONS

Actor	Musician	Performing Arts Administrator
Music Executive		

WEB DESIGN

Basics

It's not unusual to find a fifth-grade kid who can design his own website these days. The Internet has transformed so many things about our world: how we conduct business, how we communicate, even how we shop. And what would the Internet be without its web pages? Not the fifth-grade kind, but the award-winning pages and sites that rethink the medium and exploit its features to the fullest extent. If you have an eye for design and a knack for computers, you might be a prime candidate for a major in web design. You'll compound the interest and knowledge you already have by starting from the beginning—designing and building a Web page—and working your way up to incorporating the latest ideas, technology, and features into the sites you create. Your course work will go over everything from identifying an intended audience to selecting graphics that best portray your message. You'll learn about different web browsers and plug-ins and their varying capabilities. And since the Web has an artistic element, too, you'll explore aesthetic design, color relationships, and the application of font styles. You'll learn how to create animated elements for your sites and how to incorporate a range of motions.

Websites are often interactive, and you'll learn how to engage and guide the visitors to your site so that they get the best information possible. You'll learn how to build chat rooms and discussion boards, and why you might choose to include them in your site's design. You'll learn all about links—when to use them, where they should lead your audience, and how to determine what other sites will best supplement yours.

Although much of web design lies in learning the basics of Internet technology, you'll also learn how to deal with clients and see a project through from beginning to end. And you'll be equipped to gather information for your site, choose an appropriate style, and test your site's effectiveness. Though Internet jobs in general are very much on the wane, more and more companies and individuals are taking their products and businesses to the Web and will need your expertise and creative vision to bring their own ideas to life.

> **SAMPLE COLLEGE CURRICULUM FOR WEB DESIGN**
>
> Animation Techniques
> Browser and Plug-in Basics
> Color Theory
> Conflict Management
> Designing Interactivity
> Fonts
> The Intended Audience
> Interactive Sites
> Interface Design
> Navigation
> Production Scheduling
> Technical Writing
> Workflow and Proofing

If You Like Web Design, You May Also Like . . .

Advertising, animation and special effects, art, art education, computer and information science, computer graphics, computer systems analysis, digital communication and media/multimedia, drawing, engineering design, entrepreneurship, fashion design, graphic design, interior design, photography, radio and television, visual communication

Suggested High School Prep for Web Design

It goes without saying that the more you know about computers and the Web, the more prepared you'll be for your major in web design. Take any computer courses your school offers, as well as courses in art, English, and other humanities. However, some of the best preparation is probably what you do at home, experimenting with your own computer and learning design and programming skills. A basic familiarity with web design and some of the language and skills that go along with it will give you a great head start on your major.

Fun Facts

To Err Is Human

Web designers must constantly juggle many different elements to make their websites better than the competition's. Here are a few common mistakes that web designers make that weaken their sites and obscure their messages:

- Slow download times
- Nonstandard link colors
- Long scrolling navigation pages
- Scrolling text or looping animation
- Frames
- Orphan pages
- Complex URLs
- Lack of navigation support
- Outdated information

(Source: www.useit.com/alertbox/990516.html)

Did You Know?

Though the Internet was developed as early as the 1960s, the World Wide Web as we know it was born in 1989. Originally, it was meant as a tool for physicists to exchange information, but it quickly grew in popularity and spread to universities, libraries, schools, and businesses. In the early 1990s, its popularity soared. Now it's difficult to imagine life without it.

(Source: http://encarta.msn.com)

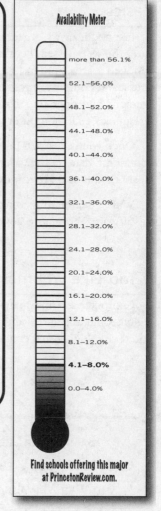

Availability Meter

- more than 56.1%
- 52.1–56.0%
- 48.1–52.0%
- 44.1–48.0%
- 40.1–44.0%
- 36.1–40.0%
- 32.1–36.0%
- 28.1–32.0%
- 24.1–28.0%
- 20.1–24.0%
- 16.1–20.0%
- 12.1–16.0%
- 8.1–12.0%
- **4.1–8.0%**
- 0.0–4.0%

Find schools offering this major at PrincetonReview.com.

Careers and Salary

Although careers for web designers have tapered off in recent years (unfortunately, you've probably missed your chance to earn a million dollars just by building websites), websites are still becoming more important for many sales and professional organizations, and web design majors can expect to earn a salary in the $30,000 to $40,000 range for full-time work. But many web designers work on a freelance basis, where salaries are unpredictable.

CAREER OPTIONS

Animator

Artist

Computer Programmer

Entrepreneur

Graphic Designer

Internet/Intranet Technologies Manager

Media Specialist

Software Developer

Web Master

Website Builder

Website Designer

Website Editor

WEBMASTER AND WEB MANAGEMENT

Basics

Just about every organization has a website these days, and someone has to create and manage them; enter the webmaster. The webmaster and web management major prepares individuals to develop and maintain web servers, and to function as webmasters. To learn how to develop and design web pages, you'll take courses in computer programming languages such as Java and C++, as well as networking, database management, and operating systems. Of course, websites should be user-friendly and aesthetically-pleasing, so design classes in computer graphics, color theory, and animation are also part of the program.

Once you've learned how to put up a website, you'll learn housekeeping details, like systems security, e-commerce, data transfer, user interfacing, and other relevant management skills. You'll also learn how to troubleshoot and to fix hardware and software issues.

With a degree in web management, you can work for all kinds of organizations, from small businesses, to software start-ups, to government agencies.

If You Like Webmaster and Web Management, You May Also Like . . .

Computer and information science, computer engineering, computer graphics, computer systems analysis, digital communications and media/multimedia, graphic design, information resources management, information technology, visual communication

Suggested High School Prep for Webmaster and Web Management

You probably know what we're going to say here—math and computer courses! Take whatever your school has to offer in these areas. In your spare time, learn html and practice being a webmaster by creating your own site.

SAMPLE COLLEGE CURRICULUM FOR WEBMASTER AND WEB MANAGEMENT

Artificial Intelligence

Computer Architecture

Computer Networks

Concepts of Problem Solving and Programming

Data Structures and Algorithm Analysis

Database Systems

Operating Systems

Programming Languages

Simulation of Discrete and Continuous Systems

Website Design

Fun Facts

Who Invented the World Wide Web?

Believe it or not, the World Wide Web, unlike so many revolutionary inventions, was created by one man. Twenty years ago, a software consultant named Tim Berners-Lee devised a program that could, as he put it, keep "track of all the random associations one comes across in real life," since "brains are supposed to be so good at remembering but sometimes mine wouldn't." The World Wide Web-prototype fitting this unwieldy description was called "Enquire Within Upon Everything," or "Enquire" for short, named after a Victorian-era encyclopedia he had as a child.

(Source: www.w3.org/People/Berners-Lee/ShortHistory)

Careers and Salary

The starting salary for a webmaster is between $40,000 and $50,000 a year.

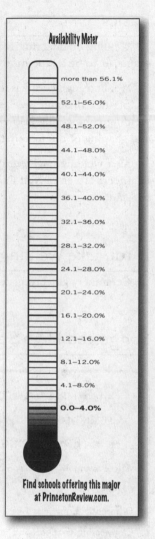

Availability Meter

more than 56.1%

52.1–56.0%

48.1–52.0%

44.1–48.0%

40.1–44.0%

36.1–40.0%

32.1–36.0%

28.1–32.0%

24.1–28.0%

20.1–24.0%

16.1–20.0%

12.1–16.0%

8.1–12.0%

4.1–8.0%

0.0–4.0%

Find schools offering this major
at PrincetonReview.com.

CAREER OPTIONS

Computer Engineer	Information Manager	Technical Support Specialist
Computer Programmer	Network Administrator	Web Programmer
Computer Security Specialist	Systems Administrator	Web Master/Manager
Consultant	Systems Analyst	

WELDING ENGINEERING

Basics

Welding engineering is a bond that holds this country together. Without it, we'd be falling apart at the seams, or to be a little more accurate, at the joints.

Welding engineering is the science of holding things together. Instead of crazy glue you have ceramics, metals, plastics, titanium, steel, and dozens of other different materials. Beyond just holding materials together, welding engineering also encompasses almost every aspect of construction, from the actual development and shaping of the material to the creation of new welding methods.

As a welding engineering major you will find yourself in constant and high demand, because welding engineers are employed in a wide array of fields. You can help develop the newest space shuttle or a dent-resistant car.

If You Like Welding Engineering, You May Also Like . . .

Ceramic engineering, ceramics, civil engineering, engineering design, engineering mechanics

Suggested High School Prep for Welding Engineering

In addition to your superior blowtorch skills, you should have very strong math and science skills, particularly advanced mathematics (calculus, trigonometry) and physics as solid preparation for the intense differential math you'll be doing later.

SAMPLE COLLEGE CURRICULUM FOR WELDING ENGINEERING

Calculus and Analytic Geometry

Chemistry

Differential Equations

Engineering Graphics and Programming

Introduction to Materials Science

Physical Principles in Welding Engineering

Physics

Strength of Materials

Survey of Welding Engineering and Labs

Welding Applications

Welding Design

Welding Production

Fun Facts

Did You Know?

The first known engineer was Imhotep, who lived around 2550 B.C./B.C.E. and was responsible for building the Step Pyramid at Saqqarah, Egypt.

Did You Know?

More than half of the United States gross domestic product is related in one way or another to welded products.

Careers and Salary

Welding engineering is one of the most highly paid engineering subfields. Recent grads can expect starting salaries between $45,000 and $55,000.

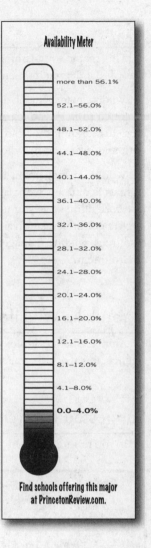

Availability Meter

more than 56.1%

52.1–56.0%

48.1–52.0%

44.1–48.0%

40.1–44.0%

36.1–40.0%

32.1–36.0%

28.1–32.0%

24.1–28.0%

20.1–24.0%

16.1–20.0%

12.1–16.0%

8.1–12.0%

4.1–8.0%

0.0–4.0%

Find schools offering this major at PrincetonReview.com.

CAREER OPTIONS

Civil Engineer	Plastics Manufacturer	Structural Engineer
Construction Manager	Quality Assurance Engineer	

WILDLIFE MANAGEMENT

Basics

This major sounds more dangerous than it actually is. There are no whips or cages, no herding of animals, and a degree in it isn't a guarantee you'll appear on *Animal Kingdom*.

Wildlife management, despite what it sounds like, is a science program, full of biology and ecology courses designed to help you learn how to find and address problems concerning animal life. Questions and troubles surrounding the scarcity of resources, endangerment, and preservation of natural habitats are all dealt with and overseen by wildlife management specialists.

Wildlife management involves a lot of direct, hands-on experience in the field. Protecting endangered animals is difficult work, and as a wildlife management major you will have the opportunity to experience just *how* difficult as you tackle the job with both an academic and hands-on approach. Whether it's ensuring the continued survival of the bald eagle or working with corporations to better manage environmental resources, wildlife management majors can play an essential role in preserving and protecting our natural environment.

If You Like Wildlife Management, You May Also Like . . .

Animal science, biology, ecology, environmental and environmental health engineering, environmental science, forestry, pastoral studies, zoology

Suggested High School Prep for Wildlife Management

If you're interested in majoring in wildlife management, it's important to have a strong background in the sciences, particularly physics, chemistry, and biology, as well as strong written and oral communications skills.

> **SAMPLE COLLEGE CURRICULUM FOR WILDLIFE MANAGEMENT**
>
> Biological Sciences
>
> Calculus and Analytical Geometry
>
> General Chemistry
>
> Introduction to Ecology
>
> Introduction to Environmental Science
>
> Natural Resource Management
>
> Natural Resource Policy
>
> Principles of Wildlife Management
>
> Society and Natural Resources
>
> Soil Science

Fun Facts

Gone Like the Dodo

More than 100 species and subspecies of animals have become extinct over the past 2,000 years, two-thirds of which disappeared since the mid-nineteenth century.

Did You Know?

The Endangered Species Act in the United States, passed in 1973, makes it illegal to hunt, trap, or collect endangered animals and plants.

Careers and Salary

The starting salary for wildlife management majors ranges from $20,000 to $30,000.

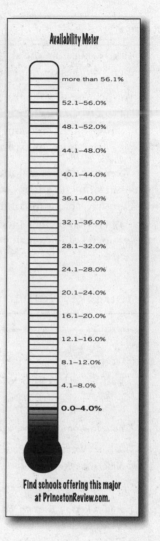

Availability Meter

more than 56.1%

52.1–56.0%

48.1–52.0%

44.1–48.0%

40.1–44.0%

36.1–40.0%

32.1–36.0%

28.1–32.0%

24.1–28.0%

20.1–24.0%

16.1–20.0%

12.1–16.0%

8.1–12.0%

4.1–8.0%

0.0–4.0%

Find schools offering this major
at PrincetonReview.com.

CAREER OPTIONS

Ecologist	Park Ranger	Veterinarian
Environmentalist/ Environmental Scientist	Professor	Zoologist

WOMEN'S STUDIES

Basics

Borrowing from the skills and information found in related fields such as English, history, and sociology, women's studies examines the ways in which women have helped to shape and define the world.

At the core of women's studies are the contributions women have made to politics, culture, history, arts and sciences, and society. These contributions are combined with a set of critical and theoretical approaches that allow you the freedom to examine how race, gender, sexuality, and nationality have influenced the way women have lived and worked in both the past and present.

Women's studies majors explore some of the most difficult and troubling questions of our society. If you major in women's studies, you will have the opportunity to think and write critically about the experiences women have had throughout history and how these experiences have shaped our understanding of our society (which includes men). By considering various controversial issues through multiple perspectives, the women's studies major develops your critical thinking skills and ability to argue effectively.

If You Like Women's Studies, You May Also Like . . .

> ### SAMPLE COLLEGE CURRICULUM FOR WOMEN'S STUDIES
>
> American Women's Movement
>
> The Black Woman: Her Role in the Liberation Struggle
>
> Communication, Gender, and Society
>
> Feminist Perspectives on Women and Violence
>
> Introduction to Women's History
>
> Issues in Women's Health
>
> Psychology of Women
>
> Sociology of Women
>
> Women and Addiction
>
> Women of Color and Social Activism
>
> Women and Film
>
> Women and Literature
>
> Women and Politics
>
> Women and Religion
>
> Women, Culture, and Society

African American studies, African studies, American history, American studies, anthropology, art, art history, Asian American studies, child development, clinical psychology, comparative literature, developmental psychology, East Asian studies, economics, English, international relations, Jewish studies, Latin American studies, peace studies, political science, psychology, public policy analysis, religious studies, social work, sociology, urban studies

Suggested High School Prep for Women's Studies

A major in women's studies requires that you know how to read, think, and write critically. To this end, a strong background in the liberal arts will help prepare you for the degree of intellectual engagement you will encounter at the college level. A lot of English and history and a psychology class or two will serve you well. Community service experiences that deal with issues related to women are great opportunities to see how this major can be applied.

Fun Facts

Know Your History

The right of citizens of the United States to vote shall not be denied or abridged by the United States or by any State on account of sex . . . Congress shall have power to enforce this article by appropriate legislation

—Nineteenth Amendment to the Constitution of the United States of America, granting women the right to vote

Did You Know?

Susan B. Anthony registered and voted in 1872, prior to the Nineteenth Amendment. She was later arrested and fined $100, of which she insisted she would never pay a penny.

Careers and Salary

The average starting salary for a women's studies major generally ranges from $20,000 to $30,000.

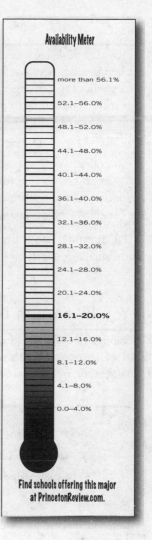

Availability Meter

more than 56.1%

52.1–56.0%

48.1–52.0%

44.1–48.0%

40.1–44.0%

36.1–40.0%

32.1–36.0%

28.1–32.0%

24.1–28.0%

20.1–24.0%

16.1–20.0%

12.1–16.0%

8.1–12.0%

4.1–8.0%

0.0–4.0%

Find schools offering this major at PrincetonReview.com.

CAREER OPTIONS

Actor	Professor	Social Worker
Anthropologist	Public Relations Professional	Writer

YOUTH MINISTRIES

Basics

You'd better have some faith if you're interested in a youth ministries major because you're going to need it when dealing with some of the most hard-headed people on the planet (the young) and trying to convince them of something about which they might be skeptical (God). Youth ministries involves studying religion and learning how to pass it on to youth. In this uniquely Christian major, you'll study the Old and New Testaments while learning evangelistic strategies and the basics of preaching. You'll learn theology, church history, and Christian philosophy.

Of course, you'll also study adolescents—their psychology, problems, beliefs, and needs. You'll learn the best way to convey the teachings of a doctrine to teenagers, and you'll investigate how adolescent issues are portrayed and dealt with in the *Bible*. You'll learn how adolescents develop and how to deal with problems such as teen pregnancy, suicide, and substance abuse.

Finally, you'll also learn the practicalities of being a youth minister—how to structure meetings, how to utilize small groups, how to conduct successful wilderness retreats, and how to work with volunteers.

If You Like Youth Ministries, You May Also Like . . .

Biblical studies, child care, child development, church music, counseling, developmental psychology, education, mental health services, missions, nursing, pastoral studies, pre-seminary, psychology, recreation management, religious studies, social work, special education

SAMPLE COLLEGE CURRICULUM FOR YOUTH MINISTRIES

Adolescent Psychology

Christian Education of Youth

Church History

Disciplining Youth

Doctrine of Holiness

Evangelistic Strategy

The Gospel and Adolescent Culture

Introduction to Preaching

The Minister as Counselor

Ministry and the Local Church

Religions of the World

Systematic Theology

Youth Ministry in an Urban Setting

Suggested High School Prep for Youth Ministries

Since youth ministries will involve using a variety of skills and life experiences, your best preparation will be a broad foundation of college preparatory course work, including math and science. A foreign language is always a good idea. If your church or high school offers any service clubs or youth groups, getting involved might give you some great experiences.

Fun Facts

World Youth Day

Pope John Paul II began World Youth Day in 1984 when he invited the Catholic youth of the world come to the Vatican on Palm Sunday in honor of the 1,950th anniversary of the death and resurrection of Christ. Over 250,000 youths responded to the invitation. Soon after, Pope John Paul II established World Youth Day as an annual event for Catholic youth to embrace their faith, community, morality, and place in the world. The next World Youth Day will take place in Sydney, Australia in 2008.

Careers and Salary

The starting salary for youth ministries graduates is typically in the $20,000 to $30,000 area. A youth ministries coordinator might earn as much as $37,000. Many youth ministers also choose to volunteer.

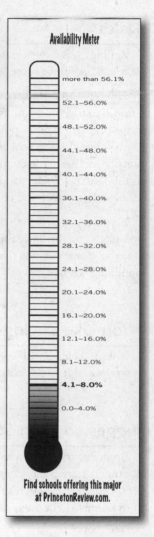

Availability Meter

more than 56.1%

52.1–56.0%

48.1–52.0%

44.1–48.0%

40.1–44.0%

36.1–40.0%

32.1–36.0%

28.1–32.0%

24.1–28.0%

20.1–24.0%

16.1–20.0%

12.1–16.0%

8.1–12.0%

4.1–8.0%

0.0–4.0%

Find schools offering this major at PrincetonReview.com.

CAREER OPTIONS

Career Counselor	Clergy—Priest, Rabbi, Minister	Substance Abuse Counselor
Child Care Worker	College Administrator	Theologian

ZOOLOGY

Basics

Zoology has almost nothing to do with zoos, so put away your ideas of lion cages and monkey houses. We're talking about some hard-core science here.

Zoology is the study of animals—that is, every animal you can think of from the sponge to the elephant. It doesn't stop there, though, because not only do zoologists study everything from the single cell to the entire organism and population of any given animal, they also take into consideration the larger environmental conditions in which animals live. From the desert to the rainforest to the ocean, zoologists study the interplay between life elements. It's everything you've ever wanted to know about animals but couldn't find on the Discovery Channel. Here you can study the genetic evolution of the chimpanzee or the conditions necessary to sustain the cheetah in its natural environment.

Prepare yourself for a lot science, because—just like biology or chemistry—zoology is dependent on understanding the basic nuts and bolts of how life functions. The usual science courses are all here, so when you're all done, you will find yourself prepared to enter a number of scientific fields, from medicine to environmental science.

If You Like Zoology, You May Also Like . . .

Animal science, biology, biopsychology, botany and plant biology, cell biology, chemistry, ecology, forestry, genetics, molecular genetics, neurobiology, wildlife management

Suggested High School Prep for Zoology

Frequent trips to the zoo, while fun and the source of some great trivia, probably aren't going to help too much here. Take chemistry, biology, and advanced math courses. If your high school offers more advanced courses (such as Biology II and Chemistry II), take these as well. Volunteer at a veterinary hospital or animal shelter, and of course, love animals.

SAMPLE COLLEGE CURRICULUM FOR ZOOLOGY

Biology

Calculus

Inorganic Chemistry

Molecular Genetics

Organic Chemistry

Physics

Zoology I–III

Fun Facts

Bugs

About 80 percent of all known animal species belong to the *phylum arthropoda*. About 800,000 species have been described, and recent estimates put the total number of species in the phylum at about 6 million.

Your Grandaddy Was Swamp Thing

The development of vertebrates living on land started in the Devonian period (about 350 million years ago). At about this time, fish started crawling out of the water, walking on land, and breathing air.

Careers and Salary

Entry-level positions for zoology majors range from $24,000 to $30,000. With an advanced degree, salaries increase dramatically.

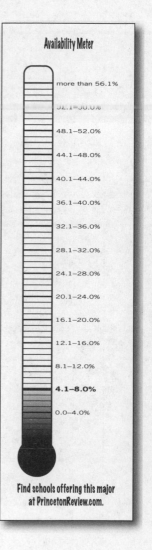

Availability Meter

more than 56.1%

52.1–56.0%

48.1–52.0%

44.1–48.0%

40.1–44.0%

36.1–40.0%

32.1–36.0%

28.1–32.0%

24.1–28.0%

20.1–24.0%

16.1–20.0%

12.1–16.0%

8.1–12.0%

4.1–8.0%

0.0–4.0%

Find schools offering this major at PrincetonReview.com.

CAREER OPTIONS

Biologist	Environmentalist/	Park Ranger
Ecologist	Environmental Scientist	Zoologist

FAST TRACK TO A CAREER

Maybe you don't want to wait four years or more before you can start your career. Maybe you want to keep your current job while you go to school part-time—and you don't want to spend the next eight years of your life going part-time. Maybe you want to make sure you're in the right field before you transfer into a four-year college. Maybe you just simply don't have the funds for a four-year college.

There are lots of reasons why students go to or start out at a community college or a technical college working toward certification, an associate's degree, or even a bachelor's degree.

If you are graduating from high school with a clear vision of your career path and a desire to hit the workforce running, then you might be considering continuing your education at a technical college. Technical colleges, sometimes referred to as "vocational" or "trade" schools, can be a good choice since they offer focused curricula and job training in a specific field in a short amount of time. Typically, they grant two-year associate degrees, technical diplomas, apprenticeships, and certificates—some even have bachelor's and master's programs.

Most people associate technical colleges with fields like HVAC, automotive repair, cosmetology, and electrical technology. While these are still offered, it's anachronistic to think that's all technical colleges have to offer; nowadays, you can enroll in such diverse curricula as fashion design, culinary arts, web design, business administration, criminal justice, or engineering, and the list goes on. Many schools have state-of-the-art facilities; most offer night courses and job-placement assistance after completion of the program.

Another reason to consider technical college: Time is money, and a technical college won't cost you a lot of either. For more programs, two years is the maximum amount of time you'll be enrolled—some programs require more time; others, less—and some certification programs can be completed in as little as five months. Class schedules are designed to accommodate full-time workers and are more flexible than at a traditional four-year undergraduate school. Tuition at a trade school is generally less than what you'd pay at a private four-year college. Students are eligible for federal loans and grants, and some schools have their own scholarship and loan programs.

> **IS THE SCHOOL ACCREDITED OR LICENSED?**
>
> - **Accreditation**
>
>   Accreditation is a good indicator of quality, although not every school chooses to be accredited. If a school is accredited by a nationally recognized agency, it means it has met certain quality standards established by the accrediting agency.
>
> - **Licensure**
>
>   Most states have laws requiring that career colleges and technical schools be licensed or certified to offer instructional courses and programs. If a school has a license or certificate to operate, it means it has gone through a process to make sure that it meets certain standards. Some states do not require certain schools to be licensed or certified to operate legally in the state.
>
> (Source: www.collegeanswer.com)

Specialized career training is one of the biggest advantages of a technical college. Your program will teach you employable skills and everything you need to know to break into, say, graphic design, real estate, or information technology. Not only that, but technical schools usually keep close ties with area employers, so they have solid connections and job leads. But focused job training can also be a disadvantage. While your program will prepare you to be an awesome dental hygienist, it won't offer you the kind of well-rounded education needed to transition into another career (in case you get sick of sticking your fingers in other people's mouths).

Another potential drawback: While a technical college will put you on a direct career path, it might not earn you more in the end. For example, if you complete a nursing technical program, you'll have more applicable skills to land a nursing job than a biology major from a four-year undergraduate school will have; however, the bio major has the option of going on to medical school and becoming a doctor. You won't have that option, unless you go back to school and complete a bachelor's degree first. This doesn't mean that you can't earn a good salary and get promoted to a supervisory position—it just limits your options a little. Keep in mind, too, that the lifetime earnings of graduates from four-year college are nearly twice as much as those holding high-school degrees—and those holding associate's degrees earn somewhere between these two extremes. Over the long term, earning a four-year bachelor's degree is more lucrative on average than earning a two-year associates degree or technical degree.

The upshot: If you've known that you've wanted to be a paralegal ever since you were two, then a technical college is probably the perfect choice for you. If you kind of think you maybe want to be a paralegal because you like Law and Order—but you also like writing and drawing and animals—then you may benefit more from a traditional four-year undergraduate school. There, you'll be able to take pre-law, writing, art, and zoology classes and decide from there. At a four-year college, you'll also be exposed to lots of new things. Maybe you'll discover that you love theater and want to be a director. A four-year undergraduate school gives you the freedom to explore, discover, and decide your career path, albeit at a higher price tag. At a technical school, your goal is to get trained and in the workforce as quickly as possible.

Another option is attending a community college.

Community colleges can serve as a fast track to a career, but they can also serve as an excellent stepping-stone to a four-year university. Studies show that students who transfer to four-year schools end up doing as well as those who started there as freshmen. The following are a few reasons you might consider beginning your higher education at a two-year college.

COMMUNITY COLLEGES AT THE FOREFRONT

- **Health care:** 50 percent of new nurses and the majority of other new health care workers are educated at community colleges.

- **International programs:** Close to 100,000 international students attend community colleges—about 39 percent of all international undergraduate students in the United States.

- **Workforce training:** 95 percent of businesses and organizations that employ community college graduates recommend community college workforce education and training programs.

- **Homeland security:** Close to 80 percent of firefighters, law enforcement officers, and EMTs are credentialed at community colleges.

- **Five hottest community college programs:** registered nursing, law enforcement, licensed practical nursing, radiology, and computer technologies.

- **Earnings:** The average expected lifetime earnings for a graduate with an associate degree are $1.6 million—about $0.4 million more than a high school graduate earns.

(Source: www.aacc.nche.edu/Content/NavigationMenu/ AboutCommunityColleges/Fast_Facts1/Fast_Facts.htm)

You Want to Save Money

According to one report, the average annual tuition at a community college is $1,905, compared to $4,694 for a four-year public university and $19,710 for a four-year private university. Add in room and board and those figures jump up to $10,636 total for a year at a public school and $26,854 for a private school. Even with the relatively low rates at community colleges, nearly a third of students receive financial aid. It's no wonder then that these colleges are an attractive option for cutting costs, especially in a struggling economy. Spending two years in a junior college (and living at home) can give you time to work and save up for the four-year college of your choice. You might even find that you qualify for a scholarship from the school you're transferring to or from an outside organization like Phi Theta Kappa, the honor society for two-year colleges.

You're Looking for Additional Academic Support

For some, community college is a chance to make up for a poor high school record. For others, it is an opportunity to get the extra academic guidance that a four-year school may be unable to offer. "At many four-year colleges, it's sink or swim," says Norma Kent, vice president for communications at the American Association of Community Colleges. "Community colleges have smaller class sizes and the priority of the faculty is on teaching. Plus there are lots of support services, like mentoring programs and organized study groups."

This support can give students the boost they need to get admitted to and succeed at a four-year school. Many community colleges have articulation agreements with universities outlining coursework and GPA requirements that, if met, guarantee admission.

You Need or Want to Live at Home

There is a community college within commuter distance of 90 percent of the U.S. population, so convenience is a big selling point. If you have family obligations or just don't feel emotionally ready to strike out on your own, a community college can enable you to continue your education without changing your whole life.

ACCORDING TO THE AMERICAN ASSOCIATION OF COMMUNITY COLLEGES:

Number and Type of Colleges

Public institutions	.991
Independent institutions	.180
Tribal institutions	.31
Total	.1,202

Enrollment

11.6 million students

Enrolled full time	.40%
Enrolled part time	.60%

Employment Status

Full-time students employed full-time	.27%
Full-time students employed part-time	.50%
Part-time students employed full-time	.50%
Part-time students employed part-time	.33%

Percentage of Students Receiving Financial Aid

Any aid	.47%
Federal grants	.23%
Federal loans	.11%
State aid	.12%

Percentage of Federal Aid Received by Community Colleges

Pell Grants	.32%
Campus-based aid	.9%

Average Annual Tuition and Fees

Community colleges (public)	.$2,272
4-year colleges (public)	.$5,836

Data are derived from the most current information available as of January 2007.

(Source: www.aacc.nche.edu/Content/NavigationMenu/ AboutCommunityColleges/Fast_Facts1/Fast_Facts.htm)

Unlike the schedules at the majority of four-year schools, most community college students take classes part-time, leaving more time to maintain a job. A number of two-year colleges have multiple locations and offer courses online for added flexibility. Because of their convenience, open admissions policies, and low cost, community colleges draw a more varied population than the typical four-year school in terms of race, age, and socioeconomic background. This diversity is, in itself, a draw, particularly to international and older students.

As with all college decisions, it's personal, so make sure you do your research and get tons of information so you can make an informed decision.

ADMINISTRATIVE SUPPORT TECHNOLOGY

Basics

An associate's degree in administrative support technology will best suit those who want to find employment in an office setting. Day-to-day tasks will include correspondence, transcription, coordinating office services, printing, e-mailing, and other office duties such as answering phone calls, distributing mail, or taking messages.

In most office settings those who have been trained in administrative support technology will be the first line of contact with customers or clients and will thus need to conduct themselves in a professional manner. Often, contact with executives and decision makers within a company will be a daily occurrence. As you become more experienced in an office, it may be possible to offer support in a wider range that includes roles of payroll or data compilation.

Fun Facts

The "QWERTY" type of keyboard, the type used today gets its name from the first row of letter on a keyboard. The non-alphabetical arrangement was patented in 1860 by Christopher Sholes, who separated common letter sequences to reduce the amount of times the key arms on his typewriter jammed into each other.

If you like Administrative Support Technology, you may also like . . .

Administrative assistant, medical transcription, editing/proofreading

Suggested High School prep for Administrative Support Technology

Word processing, computer applications, writing composition, typing.

Careers and Salary

Salaries start at about $28,000 and can go as high as $54,000 for administrative supporters with high experience.

SAMPLE COLLEGE CURRICULUM FOR TYPING

Business Communication

Desktop Publishing

Editing/Proofreading

Keyboarding for Computer Usage

Keyboarding for Information Processing

Office Administration

Word Processing

CAREER OPTIONS

Administrative Assistant

Medical Transcriptionist

Proofreader

Transcriptionist

CERTIFIED NURSING ASSISTANT

Basics

For students who want to work in a patient care environment as quickly as possible or who are working on becoming a registered nurse or LPN, becoming a certified nursing assistant is a great way to work in a healthcare environment.

Certified nursing assistants are board certified, and have to complete at least 120 hours of preparation education 16 of which are supervised clinical hours. In addition to formal training, a certified nursing assistant must take and pass a standardized test administered by their state's board of nursing.

Working as a certified nursing assistant will mean performing basic care duties such as grooming, bathing and feeding patients, working closely with nurses to allow them to see a larger population of patients, sterilizing rooms, changing sheets and recording basic patient statistics like temperature and respiration.

If you like Certified Nursing Assistant, you may also like . . .

Patient care technician, registered nurse, nurse's aide

Suggested High School prep for Certified Nursing Assistant

Students would benefit from exposure to courses that will familiarize them with terminology used in certified nursing assistance such as biology, anatomy, physiology and mathematics.

SAMPLE COLLEGE CURRICULUM FOR CERTIFIED NURSING ASSISTANT

Caring for Children and Infants

Clinical training

Communicating with Patients

Confidentiality

CPR

End of Life Care

Lifting Safety

Medical Record Documentation

Medical Terminology

Patient Care

Careers and Salary

As nursing shortages continue, roles like certified nursing assistant that support nurses will be in high demand. Starting salaries range from $22,000 to $37,000.

CAREER OPTIONS

Emergency Medical Technician

Nurse

Occupational Therapist

Paramedic

Physician

Physician Assistant

Researcher

CORRECTIONS SCIENCE

Basics

The goal of formal correction science training is to produce individuals who can be mindful of the logistics behind correcting and rehabilitating people who have been convicted of various crimes. Degrees at the associates and bachelors level in correction science prepare a graduate for a career working in city, county, juvenile, state or federal correctional facilities.

Career opportunities from guarding, remotely monitoring or directly monitoring the inmate population to running the operations of a facility will await students with correction science degrees. Students should expect to couple physical ability with knowledge of correctional theory surrounding the way an inmate population is treated and managed.

If you like Corrections Science, you may also like . . .

Criminal justice, police training, investigative studies, forensics

Suggested High School prep for Corrections Science

Local and sate government, social studies, psychology, physical education.

SAMPLE COLLEGE CURRICULUM FOR CORRECTIONS SCIENCE

Communication

Corrections & the Community

Corrections Law

Criminal Justice

Criminal Law

Evidence Gathering

Juvenile Justice System

Management of Correctional Facilities

Narcotics and Dangerous Drugs

Careers and Salary

Salary rage for a job in corrections science will pay from $27,000 to $48,000.

CAREER OPTIONS

Correctional Counselor

Corrections Officer

Inmate Records

Interviewer

Parole Officer

Police Officer/Manager

Warden

ELECTRICAL WIRING

Basics

One of the remaining professions that require lengthy apprenticeships and journeymen tenures is that of an electrician. Becoming a master electrician can take up to a decade of field work to achieve. Because working with electricity can be deadly in even if the smallest mistake is made, direct supervision of a new apprentice lasts for three to five years.

Once an electrical apprentice passes a state administered exam detailing codes and regulation, he or she will work directly with a Journeyman who is under the direction of a master electrician. Work can range from interior wiring to outside line running from power stations and power poles. Electricians install and repair wiring, circuit breakers, fixtures and control switches.

Fun Facts

Most people think that Thomas Edison invented the light bulb, but Edison is simply the first person produce a useful incandescent bulb. The first bulb dates back to 1802 when Humphry Davy used a platinum filament to create the first incandescent light using a battery.

If you like Electrician, you may also like . . .

Electrical engineering, general contracting, building science, fire inspection

Suggested High School prep for Electrician

Applied science classes that deal with circuitry and flow of electricity and energy will help students gain a basic knowledge of the medium in which they will work.

Careers and Salary

Hourly wages will vary before an electrician has more experience, but salaries for journeymen range from $37,000 to $62,000.

SAMPLE COLLEGE CURRICULUM FOR ELECTRICIANS

Circuits and Circuit Boards

Electrical Code

Intro to Electricity

Wiring Principals

CAREER OPTIONS

Building Inspector

Construction Manager

Electrician

HOLISTIC/WHOLISTIC HEALTH

Basics

Students who want to integrate physical health with spiritual health as a way to achieve overall well being are leading themselves down the path of holistic health. Characterized by the attempt to treat the "whole person" and not just their physical symptoms, holistic health practice a form of medicine that is increasingly becoming more main stream.

As a holistic health professional you will be asked to draw upon knowledge of the body's organ systems and how they are affected by physical and emotional distress. Patients who seek out holistic medicine are often looking for a way to treat chronic illnesses without venturing down the channels of narcotics or surgery that would often be called for by traditional medical philosophy.

If you like Holistic Health, you may also like . . .

Massage therapy, aroma therapy, naturopathy, nutrition, integrative medicine

Suggested High School prep for Holistic Health

Classes that predispose students to holistic health will include sciences from a variety of aspects like health, biology, anatomy, stress management and Eastern medicines.

SAMPLE COLLEGE CURRICULUM FOR HOLISTIC HEALTH

Applications of Alternative Healing Modalities

Clinical Case Studies

Eastern Medicine

Healing States

Health Care Practicum

Holistic Techniques

Mind/Body/Spirit Connection

Nutrition

Careers and Salary

Holistic health practioners are in higher demand in different areas across the country, making salary dependant on demand for holistic health services. Most graduates will go into business for themselves, thus determining their own salary.

CAREER OPTIONS

Aromatherapist

Holistic Health Professional

Massage Therapist

Nutritionist

HYPNOTHERAPY

Basics

Hypnotherapy has moved into more mainstream circles lately in conjunction with its assertions of behavior modification like helping someone quit smoking or relieving stress associated with phobias like dentistry. Hypnotherapy has also found its way into pain management regimens. Battling the social stigma of hypnotherapy as a mystic practice is one of the industry's biggest challenges.

Careers in hypnotherapy will be mostly self-start businesses unless hypnotherapy is being used in conjunction with another service such as professional counseling or nutrition. Certification for hypnotherapists can be obtained online or in some new age training facilities where skills like indirect suggestion, awakening techniques and hypnotic theory are introductory course work.

Fun Facts

Hypnosis relies on leading subjects into a state of hyper-suggestibility and was first studied by James Braid in 1843 who called it neuro-hypnotism, which he intended to mean sleep of the nervous system.

If you like Hypnotherapy, you may also like . . .

Nutrition, psychology, psychiatry, human behavior, massage therapy

Suggested High School prep for Hypnotherapy

Classes that may expose student to the goals and practices of hypnotherapy include psychology, meditation practices, stress management courses, nutrition, and biology.

SAMPLE COLLEGE CURRICULUM FOR HYPNOTHERAPY

Discovering Underlying Issues

Directive vs. Permissive Styles

Ericksonian Techniques

Hypnotic Metaphors

Indirect Suggestion

Shamanism

Transforming Resistance

Careers and Salary

Starting salaries for hypnotherapy will be base on the demand for services in any given area. Some markets bear higher hourly wages than others, falling from $9 to $50 an hour.

CAREER OPTIONS

Hypnotherapist

Psychiatrist

Psychologist

MAMMOGRAPHY TECHNOLOGY

Basics

Mammography uses sophisticated x-ray equipment to conduct mammograms or breast checks in women. These tests are used to spot lumps and other abnormalities in breast tissue. Mammography technologists are not exposed to radiation during the exams.

Mammography technologists will be required to use the radiology equipment and position patients properly so that accurate results can be used sent to the radiologists who reads the tests. They will also speak with the patients to find out any material facts about their breast health that may have bearing on the test results. Mammography techs must have proper certification for the state in which they wish to practice. Certification programs require several hours of on-site training.

> ### Fun Facts
> Mammograms can be used to detect pre-cancerous cells as early as two years before a lump can be felt by touch.

If you like Mammography Technology, you may also like . . .

Radiology, medicinal imaging, x-ray technology, ultrasound technology

Suggested High School prep for Mammography Technology

Students will benefit from classes in anatomy, science, and chemistry.

Careers and Salary

The salary range for mammography is between $35,000 and $58,000.

> ### SAMPLE COLLEGE CURRICULUM FOR MAMMOGRAPHY TECHNOLOGY
> Achieving Quality Imaging
> Anatomy
> Clinical Training (250 hours)
> Didactic Training (40 hours)
> Equipment protocol
> Mammography
> Patient Positioning
> Radiation Safety

> ### CAREER OPTIONS
> Mammography Technician
> Nuclear Medical Technician
> X-Ray Technician

MEDICAL TRANSCRIPTION

Basics

A Medical Transcriptionist is the person who transcribes a doctor's notes on his or her patients from dictations, correspondence or medical records into one collusive document. It is important to have an understanding of medical terminology, dictation hardware, computer processing software and excellent typing skills.

Work in this field is performed either in an office setting within hospitals, doctor's offices, or laboratories, or it can be done from home. The demands of each position will vary depending on the case load and requirements of each employer. In highly qualified individuals, transcription of surgical procedures or diagnostic tests may be part of a job description. Medical Transcriptionists must be detail oriented because any errors can lead to serious medical discrepancies.

> ### Fun Facts
> Medical transcriptionists now compete with voice recognition software that can write up to 200 words per minute with better than 98 percent accuracy.

If you like Medical Transcription, you may also like . . .

Medical Billing and Coding, Medical Office Assistant, Administrative Assistant

Suggested High School prep for Medical Transcription

Students should focus on writing and computer application skills as precursors to their work in medical transcription. Also, beneficial is basic knowledge of medical terminology from biology or anatomy classes.

Careers and Salary

Salaries range from $24,000 to $44,000, and work may be done from office or home.

SAMPLE COLLEGE CURRICULUM FOR MEDICAL TERMINOLOGY

Computer Applications

Medical Abbreviations

Medical Billing and Coding

Medical Office Charting

Transcripting

Typing

CAREER OPTIONS

Admin Assistant

Medical Billing Specialist

Medical Office Assistant

Medical Office Manager

Medical Transcriptionist

PARALEGAL STUDIES

Basics

Do you object to three years' worth of expensive law school to be able to work in the legal profession? If so, paralegal studies may be a perfect fit.

Paralegals work directly under lawyers researching cases, contracts, precedent and torts. Paralegals prepare and often submit filings with the court officers, and manage daily tasks for cases. Paralegals are strictly forbidden from working directly with court proceedings, but serve an important role in the preparation and research leading up to court cases.

Education level for paralegals varies depending upon the needs of a legal office. There are no requirements to work as a paralegal—some paralegals even learn on the job—but highly technical cases and offices will require formal training ranging from a two-year associate's degree to post graduate work.

Fun Facts

Erin Brockovitch, despite no formal legal training, was an integral force behind a lawsuit against Pacific Gas & Electric in 1993. The movie that bears her name details the case that surrounded unsafe level of hexavalent chromium in water in the city of Hinkley, California. The case settled for $333 million and is the largest settlement to date from direct action lawsuit in the United States.

If you like Paralegal Studies, you may also like . . .

Court reporting, legal studies, criminal justice

Suggested High School prep for Paralegal Studies

Professional paralegals work closely with lawyers and legal counselors in administrative and logistic capacities. Classes in typing, law, word processing, social studies and ethics will prepare students for college courses in paralegal studies.

SAMPLE COLLEGE CURRICULUM FOR PARALEGAL STUDIES

Constitutional Law

Contracts

Criminal Law

Legal Research and Writing

Legal Theories

Partnerships and Corporations

Real Properties

Torts

Wills and Trusts

Careers and Salary

Paralegals can expect salary ranges between $30,000 and $35,000 for entry-level positions with highly skilled Paralegals in large firms earning up to $80,000.

CAREER OPTIONS

Attorney

Mediator

Paralegal

PHLEBOTOMY/VENIPUNCTURE

Basics

There are people in this world who have absolutely no fear of needles. Those people would fit in perfectly with phlebotomy or venipuncture, as it is also called. Graduates of phlebotomy training will work in doctors' offices, hospitals, donation centers, or labs collecting, processing, and testing blood samples.

These tests may be conducted for any number of reasons ranging from blood typing to disease detection. Because phlebotomy will rely on both patient contact and use of very technical diagnosis equipment training will involve a wide range of topics. Programs are offered in one- and two-year segments and include internships or direct lab work.

If you like Phlebotomy, you may also like . . .

Biology, genetics, lab assistance, lab technician, lab equipment technology

Fun Facts

New technology in blood donation allows donors to give only part of their blood. Known as aphaeresis, donors' whole blood is run from their arms into a centrifuge machine that separates out platelets and plasma, then returns the remaining blood components to the donor's other arm. While it takes longer than donating whole blood, aphaeresis donation can be done more often than whole blood donation.

Suggested High School prep for Phlebotomy

Biology, anatomy, algebra, chemistry.

Careers and Salary

Salary can range from $30,000 to $60,000 depending on levels of expertise.

SAMPLE COLLEGE CURRICULUM FOR PHLEBOTOMY

Biology

Centrifuge Machinery

Hemitropic Studies

Medical Terminology

On-Site Training

Storing and Packaging Biological Materials

Venipuncture

CAREER OPTIONS

Phlebotomist

Lab Assistant

Lab Technician

PLUMBING

Basics

Every modern building with running water or public sewer connections will need to be serviced by a plumber at some point. One of water's inescapable powers is its power to erode making pipe replacement inevitable. Because modern materials require advanced equipment and water damage can be very devastating, a large portion of plumbing work can not be performed by untrained professionals.

Work as a certified plumber will consist of assembly, installation and repair to pipes, fitting and fixtures that bring water to and from buildings. More technical plumbing will require the ability to read blueprints and city grids. A Plumber will use a variety of machinery including pipe cutters, cutting torches, and pipe-threading machines in addition to hand tools.

Certification depends upon the state in which plumbing work is to be completed. Prep courses are available at technical colleges and community colleges.

> ## Fun Facts
> The word plumbing comes from the Latin word plumbum which means lead. Before the harmful effects of leaden water were evident, most pipes in the United States were made of lead right up until the 20th century.

If you like Plumbing, you may also like . . .

Building science, land surveyor, water treatment, general contracting

Suggested High School prep for Plumbing

Shop classes that teach students the proper safety and use of hand tools and heavy machinery would be excellent exposure for those interested in plumbing.

Careers and Salary

Certified plumbers can garner wages ranging from $26,000 to $52,000 depending upon the quantity and difficulty of work. Higher pay is available for odd-hour work late at night.

> ### SAMPLE COLLEGE CURRICULUM FOR PLUMBING
> Joint Bending
> Pipe Threading
> Plumbing Code
> Plumbing Safety
> Sweating Pipes
> Valve Replacement

> ### CAREER OPTIONS
> Building Inspector
> Construction Manager
> Plumber
> Welder

SIGN LANGUAGE INTERPRETER

Basics

Have you always wanted to learn a new language, but have had trouble training your tongue to roll the 'r' or conjugating verbs? If so, perhaps becoming a sign language interpreter is a fit for you. American Sign Language (ASL) uses gestures to convey words, thoughts without using sounds.

More technical than simply winding your finger round and round to tell someone to keep going, ASL translation requires someone to be proficient in both languages as well as to have an understanding of public speaking, professional aptitude, and a strong code of ethics.

Careers in sign language interpretation can be found in schools, businesses with deaf employees and television networks.

Fun Facts

American Sign Language is based on gesture communication. Other professions rely on gesture communication that is not a sanctioned language. Those professions include baseball, football, television production, stock exchange floor traders, and factory work that may require employees to wear ear plugs around loud machinery.

If you like Sign Language Interpretation, you may also like . . .

Mass communication, foreign languages, business ethics

Suggested High School prep for Sign Language Interpretation

Students will need a proficiency in written and oral communication. Some high schools offer rudimentary training in American Sign Language.

Careers and Salary

Professional Sign language Interpreters can expect to earn from $22,000 to $40,000.

SAMPLE COLLEGE CURRICULUM FOR SIGN LANGUAGE INTERPRETATION

Advanced ASL

Basic ASL

Business Communication

Conversational ASL

General Liberal Arts courses

Public Speaking

Interpretation Ethics

CAREER OPTIONS

Public Speaker

Teacher

Translator

INDEX BY FIELD

Items marked with an asterisk * are listed in multiple fields

COMMUNICATIONS

EDUCATION

ENGINEERING

FINE ARTS

LIBERAL ARTS

NUTRITION, HOME ECONOMICS, AND RELATED FIELDS

PRE-PROFESSIONAL FIELDS

SCIENCE AND TECHNOLOGY

INDEX BY CAREER

Guest Services Manager—300

Guidance Counselor—160, 250, 302, 306, 334, 336, 428, 534, 642, 674, 722, 756, 760

Hair Stylist—174

Hazardous Waste Manager—184, 212, 228

Health Care Administrator—90, 128, 172, 228, 274, 280, 344, 398, 410, 586, 594, 624, 664, 676, 678,

Health Care Manager—180

Health Care Worker—286

Historian—280, 308, 340, 346, 362, 382, 416, 430, 432, 464, 484, 494, 558, 576, 718, 758

Holistic Health Professional—398

Homeopathic Medicine Practitioner—530

Horse Trainer—594

Horticulturist—174

Hospice Nurse—228, 302, 410, 438

Hospital Administrator—174, 266, 534, 560, 624, 664, 676, 698, 702, 706, 778,

Hospital/Laboratory Cytotechnologist—264

Hospitality Manager—434, 696

Host/Hostess—702

Hotel Manager—58, 110, 198, 302, 702, 748, 778

Human Resources—410

Human Resources Manager—88, 352, 438, 446, 482, 484, 504, 508, 512, 528, 604, 610, 682

Hypnotherapist—444

Illustrator—88

Image Consultant—110

Immigration Administrator—174

Import Specialist—234

Industrial Engineer—240

Industry Journalist—450

Information Manager—242, 244, 258, 496, 502, 504, 506, 604, 768, 798

Information Systems Manager—20

Inmate Records—298, 360

Inspector—104

Instrumental Conductor—106

Insurance Agent/Broker—108, 114, 284

Interior Designer—84, 232, 234, 238, 282, 378, 452, 454, 792

Internet/Intranet Technologies Manager—66, 122, 192, 258, 604, 768, 796

Interpreter—214

Interviewer—234, 640

Inventor—20, 24, 176, 298, 360

Investment Banker—34, 36, 48, 254, 272, 446, 458, 474, 504, 508, 654, 708, 752,

Jewelry Designer—64, 68

Journalist—82, 100, 126, 128, 138, 150, 172, 176, 180, 182, 210, 216, 226, 230, 244, 256, 286, 292, 298, 326, 342, 344, 346, 362, 382, 396, 400, 408, 414, 416, 418, 424, 426, 438, 460, 464, 472, 478, 482, 484, 500, 502, 518, 558, 578, 612, 620, 628, 630, 632, 652, 654, 658, 668, 684, 686, 700, 710, 714, 718, 724, 758, 762, 778, 790,

Lab Assistant—448

Lab Technician—610

Labor Relations Specialist—108, 332, 486, 488, 616, 654, 680, 726, 728, 730, 788

Laboratory Supervisor—490

Land Use Planner—754

Landscape Architect—154, 344, 346, 400, 608

Laser Technician—482

Lawyer—68, 72, 74, 118, 216, 484, 612, 652

Lexicographer—312

Librarian—74, 80, 124, 326, 408, 482, 494, 496, 562, 722, 742, 760, 764,

Lighting/Sound Designer—36

Linguist—42, 44

Literary Agent—48

Livestock/Facility Inspector—54

Lobbyist—26, 50, 56, 68, 80, 82, 110, 140, 126, 138, 216, 292, 294, 334, 344, 408, 414, 416, 424, 426, 462, 464, 478, 484, 492, 500, 502, 518, 558, 580, 612, 652, 654, 656, 658, 680, 712, 728, 730, 732, 736, 738, 744, 758, 788, 790

Long-term Care Administrator—526

Machinist—20, 68, 110, 506

Mammography Technician—174

Management Analyst—176

Management Consultant—42, 174, 226, 234, 248, 250, 298, 438, 446, 448, 504, 508, 516, 604, 610, 654, 682, 726

Manager—360, 446

Manicurist—84

Manufacturing Executive—232, 234, 238, 602

Map Maker—310, 512

Marine Scientist—526

Marines (Officer)—28, 42, 174,180, 298, 546

Market Research Analyst—354

Market Researcher—28, 42, 174, 176, 360, 516, 518, 652, 654, 702

Marketing Director—298

Marketing Executive—88, 112, 288, 354, 396, 404, 516, 518, 612, 654, 674, 684, 730, 744, 770

Marketing Manager—520

Marketing Service Manager—179

Marketing Specialist—92

Marketing Strategist—524

Massage Therapist—28, 122, 176

Mathematician—518, 612

Mechanical Engineer—28

Media Planner—48, 84, 176, 226

Media Specialist—62, 68, 174, 226, 238, 252, 282, 478, 516, 612, 652, 686, 694, 766, 770, 796

Mediator—154, 342, 422, 438, 502, 598, 620, 628, 662

Medical Office Assistant—474

Medical Office Manager—646

Medical Scientist—58

Medical Transcriptionist—110, 214

Metalsmith—422

Meteorologist—512

Military Officer—74, 138, 148, 226, 616

Mineralogist—124

Missionary—244, 562

Motivational Speaker—176

NOTES

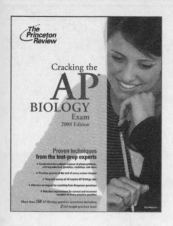

AP Exams

Cracking the AP Biology Exam,
2008 Edition
978-0-375-76640-4 • $18.00/C$22.00

Cracking the AP Calculus AB & BC Exams,
2008 Edition
978-0-375-76641-1 • $19.00/C$23.00

Cracking the AP Chemistry Exam,
2008 Edition
978-0-375-76642-8 • $18.00/C$22.00

**Cracking the AP Computer Science
A & AB Exams,** 2006–2007 Edition
978-0-375-76528-5 • $19.00/C$27.00

**Cracking the AP Economics (Macro &
Micro) Exams,** 2008 Edition
978-0-375-42841-8 • $18.00/C$22.00

**Cracking the AP English Language and
Composition Exam,** 2008 Edition
978-0-375-42842-5 • $18.00/C$22.00

Cracking the AP English Literature Exam,
2008 Edition
978-0-375-42843-2 • $18.00/C$22.00

**Cracking the AP Environmental
Science Exam,** 2008 Edition
978-0-375-42844-9 • $18.00/C$22.00

Cracking the AP European History Exam,
2008 Edition
978-0-375-42845-6 • $18.00/C$22.00

Cracking the AP Physics B Exam,
2008 Edition
978-0-375-42846-3 • $18.00/C$22.00

Cracking the AP Physics C Exam,
2008 Edition
978-0-375-42854-8 • $18.00/C$22.00

Cracking the AP Psychology Exam,
2008 Edition
978-0-375-42847-0 • $18.00/C$22.00

**Cracking the AP Spanish Exam,
with Audio CD,** 2008 Edition
978-0-375-42848-7 • $24.95/$29.95

Cracking the AP Statistics Exam,
2008 Edition
978-0-375-42849-4 • $19.00/C$23.00

**Cracking the AP U.S. Government
and Politics Exam,** 2008 Edition
978-0-375-42850-0 • $18.00/C$22.00

Cracking the AP U.S. History Exam,
2008 Edition
978-0-375-42851-7 • $18.00/C$22.00

Cracking the AP World History Exam,
2008 Edition
978-0-375-42852-4 • $18.00/C$22.00

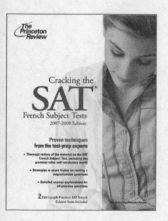

SAT Subject Tests

**Cracking the SAT Biology E/M
Subject Test,** 2007–2008 Edition
978-0-375-76588-9 • $19.00/C$25.00

Cracking the SAT Chemistry Subject Test,
2007–2008 Edition
978-0-375-76589-6 • $18.00/C$22.00

Cracking the SAT French Subject Test,
2007–2008 Edition
978-0-375-76590-2 • $18.00/C$22.00

Cracking the SAT Literature Subject Test,
2007–2008 Edition
978-0-375-76592-6 • $18.00/C$22.00

**Cracking the SAT Math 1 and 2
Subject Tests,** 2007–2008 Edition
978-0-375-76593-3 • $19.00/C$25.00

Cracking the SAT Physics Subject Test,
2007–2008 Edition
978-0-375-76594-0 • $19.00/C$25.00

Cracking the SAT Spanish Subject Test,
2007–2008 Edition
978-0-375-76595-7 • $18.00/C$22.00

**Cracking the SAT U.S. & World History
Subject Tests,** 2007–2008 Edition
978-0-375-76591-9 • $19.00/C$25.00